Please remember that this is a library book,
and that it belongs only temporarily to each
person who uses it. Be considerate. Do
not write in this, or any, library book.

Social Work

*"Give me your tired, your poor, your
huddled masses yearning to breathe free."*
—*Lazarus, 1883*

Social Work

A Profession of Many Faces

ARMANDO T. MORALES ◆ BRADFORD W. SHEAFOR
University of California *Colorado State University*
at Los Angeles

MALCOLM E. SCOTT
Colorado State University

PEARSON

Boston   New York   San Francisco
Mexico City   Montreal   Toronto   London   Madrid   Munich   Paris
Hong Kong   Singapore   Tokyo   Cape Town   Sydney

Senior Series Editor: Patricia Quinlin
Series Editorial Assistant: Sara Holliday
Marketing Manager: Laura Lee Manley
Production Editor: Claudine Bellanton
Editorial Production Service: Elm Street Publishing Services, Inc.
Composition Buyer: Linda Cox
Manufacturing Buyer: JoAnne Sweeney
Electronic Composition: Elm Street Publishing Services, Inc.
Interior Design: Elm Street Publishing Services, Inc.
Photo Researcher: Naomi Rudov
Cover Administrator: Kristina Mose-Libon

For related titles and support materials, visit our online catalog at www.ablongman.com.

Between the time website information is gathered and then published, it is not unusual for some sites to have closed. Also, the transcription of URLs can result in typographical errors. The publisher would appreciate notification where these errors occur so that they may be corrected in subsequent editions.

Library of Congress Cataloging-in-Publication Data

Morales, Armando.
    Social work : a profession of many faces / Armando T. Morales, Bradford W. Sheafor.— 11th ed.
        p.   cm
    Includes bibliographical references and index.
    ISBN 0-205-47772-0
    1. Social service—United States.   2. Social work education—United States.   3. Social service—Vocational guidance—United States.   4. Social work with minorities—United States.
I. Sheafor, Bradford W.   II. Title

HV91.M67 2007
361.973—dc21

Printed in the United States of America

10   9   8   7   6   5   4   3   2   1   RRD-VA   10   09   08   07   06

Photo Credits: Photo credits can be found on page 620, which should be considered an extension of the copyright page.

I dedicate this Eleventh Edition to my dear wife, Cynthia,
my children, Roland, Gary, and Christina Mia, my daughter-in-law,
Soo, my grandchildren, Rocco and Vincent, my co-author, Brad Sheafor,
and over 150,000 students who have expanded their knowledge
in social work using our text over the last thirty years.
—ATM

To my beloved wife, Nadine, and my children: Christopher,
Perry, Brandon, and Laura, and the many social work educators who
have found our approach to introducing students to social work
useful and encouraged us to continue updating this text to support
their teaching about the dynamic profession of social work.
—BWS

To my loving mother, Barbara, and to my brother, Jessie III.
—MES

Table of Contents

chapter 14   Social Work with U.S. Casualties
of the Middle East Wars   273

part five
Social Work Practice with Special Populations   288

chapter 15   Social Work Practice with Women   295

part six
Social Workers in Action   578

Preface

The title of this book, *Social Work: A Profession of Many Faces*, reflects the several themes that have guided the book's development. We chose this title because it focuses our attention on social work and the common features that characterize this profession. Only then do we examine the different ways social work practice plays out in serving the many different people who become the clients of social workers. When we first started writing this textbook the available texts focused primarily on the differences among the various social work practice settings or practice approaches. A title for those books might have been something like "The Many Faces of Social Work: How They Differ," emphasizing divergence rather than similarity. As you will discover when reading the following pages, we focus on the unifying features that make social work a single profession—albeit one that appears in quite varied forms.

What, then, are the threads that tie together the differing forms of social work practice? Its very name, social work, suggests two features that are present in all expressions of this profession. The term *social* emphasizes that the practice is concerned with enhancing the interactions among individuals and groups of people, as well as between people and the broader institutions of the society. The term *work* was initially used to distinguish paid employment from volunteer work aimed at helping people address social issues. This book title, too, captures a third critical element of social work—the evolution of social work from work that is just a job, to work that is "professional," meaning that social workers are required to draw on the best available knowledge to address complex issues and then skillfully and ethically provide services to people in need of assistance. Finally, by describing social work as a profession of "many faces," our intent is to (1) identify the multiple ways in which this profession reveals itself in delivering human services; (2) reflect the varied population groups that social workers are most likely to serve; and (3) highlight the strength social work has gained by embracing people reflecting racial, cultural, and social diversity as members of the profession.

Most people beginning to examine social work are aware of only a few forms that social work practice might take. In fact, social workers simultaneously use two approaches to helping people: helping individuals, families, and groups deal with a problem or issue in their lives and, at the same time, attempting to change aspects of the society that create or contribute to people's problems. For example, social workers are on the frontlines of delivering services and developing programs that respond to such human needs as homelessness, poverty, family breakup, mental illness, physical and mental disabilities, alcohol and substance abuse, domestic violence, and many other problems. In addition, social workers are regularly engaged in more long-range activities aimed at keeping those problems from occurring in the first place. This might be done by helping people become contributing members of their neighborhood, school, church, synagogue, mosque, or other community groups in an effort to make larger social institutions more responsive to the needs of all people. Indeed, social work is an umbrella term that covers a diverse set of practice activities.

The clients of social workers might be anyone, ranging from individuals to families to corporations and even to whole communities. Another thread central to the fabric of social work, however, is an emphasis on achieving social justice and giving priority to the most "vulnerable" members of the society, i.e., those most likely to experience a problem in their social interactions due to age, gender, race or ethnicity, sexual orientation, or other characteristics. Thus, social workers tend to focus their efforts more on the poor than the rich, on the ill and disabled over the healthy, on those that experience discrimination over those that enjoy the full opportunities offered by the society, and so on. Social work clients, therefore, portray the faces of these vulnerable people to a greater extent than is true for most professions.

Social workers, themselves, reflect many different faces. The authors of this text, for example, reflect some of the many faces of social workers. Armando Morales is of Mexican American descent and has spent most of his life living on the West Coast and practicing as a clinical social worker and educator. He is a professor of psychiatry and biobehavorial sciences in the School of Medicine at the University of California at Los Angeles (UCLA). Brad Sheafor is of white non-Hispanic origin, growing up in the Midwest and practicing social work through community change efforts and social work education in the Rocky Mountain region. He is a professor in the School of Social Work at Colorado State University. Malcolm Scott, our new co-author for this eleventh edition, is of African American heritage and grew up in the Deep South. His practice experience has been in corrections and child welfare, and he now is an assistant professor in the School of Social Work at Colorado State University. The authors have played prominent leadership roles in the National Association of Social Workers, the Council on Social Work Education, and the Association of Baccalaureate Program Directors, bringing an informed national perspective regarding social work to this book. We believe that these diverse experiences have enriched the quality of our work—just as diversity among social workers has enriched the profession.

In order to assist our readers in critically analyzing the contents of this book, we believe it is important to confess to some biases we hold that no doubt affect the manner in which we present our description of social work. We are not apologizing for these biases, only admitting to them.

▶ *We are proud to be social workers.* We believe that the social work profession brings an important perspective to the human services by simultaneously performing the role of providing direct services to people in need and, at the same time, advocating for social change. We also believe that the basic values and ethical guidelines that social workers hold in common represent a sound approach to protecting the interests of clients while maximizing the well-being of all people.

▶ *We recognize that the United States has made progress in creating social programs that respond to the needs of vulnerable people, but we also believe that much more is needed.* According to the U.S. Census Bureau, for example, the poverty rate for individuals was 12.6 percent in 1970 and had worsened to 12.7 percent in 2004.[1] On the positive side, for older people (who have become a political force), the poverty rate improved from 24.6 percent in 1970 to 9.8 percent in 2004. On the negative side, the percent of older African Americans (23.9 percent) and Hispanics (18.7 percent) living below the poverty level has not improved proportionally.[2] Also, we have seen phenomenal improvements in the treatment of illnesses and diseases, yet many of these benefits that accrue from living in U.S. society are simply too expensive for many of our citizens. In addition, we have improved our mental health and family counseling services to levels not available elsewhere in the world, but have not found ways to provide them in culturally sensitive ways to attract persons of minority background or older people. In other areas of special concern to social workers (e.g., corrections, child protection, prevention of substance abuse), we regret that the United States has made very little progress.

▶ *We believe that trends in the United States favoring those who already have resources, rather than to those in need of resources, are heading us in the wrong direction.* To illustrate what we view as moving in the wrong direction, consider the distribution of wealth in the United States. Although the overall economy improved substantially in the past three decades, we have made little progress in low-income people earning enough to achieve a decent quality of life. In 1974, for example, the income (in money) of the poorest 20 percent of the people was only 4.1 percent of the total income, while the richest 20 percent had 42.9 percent of that total. By 2004, the proportion of the U.S. income held by the lowest 20 percent had declined to 3.4 percent and the richest 20 percent of the people had increased their share to 50.1 percent.[3] The poor are getting poorer and the rich are getting richer! Another example is found in the area of educational advancement where the average earning power of a person with a college education is almost twice that of a person with a high school education (i.e., $51,206 per year compared to $27,915 per year).[4] Yet, the 2000 U.S. Census found that if a job requires more than a high school education, 54 percent of the white population would be eligible as compared to only 42.5 percent of the black population and 30.4 percent of the Hispanics. Further, if a job requires a bachelor's degree or higher, 26 percent of the white population is qualified compared to only 14.3 percent of the African Americans and 10.5 percent of the Hispanics.[5] For a variety of reasons, the distribution of our educational resources substantially disadvantages the black and Hispanic members in this society where education is the prerequisite for the more adequate paying jobs. Similarly, 11.3 percent of the white population is uninsured (a problem in itself), but 19.7 percent of the black population and 32.7 percent of the Hispanic population do not have the protection of health insurance against the spiraling costs of health care.[6] Our bias is that these and other factors are evidence that many social issues are not necessarily the fault of the affected individuals. When persistent patterns reveal that whole classes of people are disadvantaged, we must conclude that policies and practices that are part of the structure of the society contribute to those problems and should be changed.

▶ *We are pleased that social work has evolved as an established profession that has the discipline and capacity to address both individual and societal social issues.* Social work has successfully expanded its knowledge base, increasingly assesses the effectiveness of its interventions, and plays a role in policing its membership to help protect vulnerable clients from the errors and misrepresentations of those that are ill-prepared, incompetent, or unethical in providing these important services. One feature of becoming a full-fledged profession is job protection (often provided through state licensing of social work practice) for those who are qualified for this work, thus helping to attract an increasingly competent group of social workers to the profession. In addition, we are proud that social work has become a recognized profession throughout the world, adding to the ability to apply social work knowledge and skills to issues of global importance.

Although our view of social work and social issues is shaped by the biases confessed above, please be aware that we have attempted to present an analysis of social work that is best described as "mainline social work." We have avoided both the radical and conservative orientations found among social workers, have rooted our information in the best data we could locate, and, we believe, reveal the current state-of-the-art for social work.

 ## A Note to Our Readers

We began writing parts of this book in 1972, long before most of our readers were born. We like to think that rather than being too distant from the budding social workers of today, we bring the experience of carefully tracking changes in the profession for each new edition. In addition, adding the "youthful" Malcolm Scott as a new author helps to remind us of the perceptions and experiences our readers bring to this book.

In reading this book, it may be useful to be clear about two guiding principles that have shaped how we present the material. First, as social work educators we know from experience that most students who study social work are action oriented—they want to know how what they learn applies to helping people achieve a better quality of life. Thus as we have presented conceptual or descriptive material, we have included case examples in an effort to provide a basis for understanding its relevance. In addition, we have started this edition with "Part One: A Social Worker Makes a Difference," a short introductory chapter that features a beginning-level social worker on her first case. This case serves as a reference point for materials in the beginning chapters of the book. We conclude the book with "Chapter 26: Social Workers in Action," a comprehensive case illustrating two social workers providing services at an advanced level of practice. Second, we believe that a text that is intended to introduce students to social work must include the underpinnings of the profession, and thus must include a certain amount of historical and theoretical information. To avoid a single chapter that is likely to become a "sleep aid" for students, we have disbursed this important, but maybe not "edge-of-your-seat," information throughout the appropriate chapters.

The four parts of the book between the cases follow a pattern of unfolding our description of social work. Part Two begins with the identification of a selected few large social issues (e.g., poverty, discrimination, industrialization, urbanization, technological advancements) that have created the need for human services beyond what can be provided by families and friends, and thus has created the need for a profession such as social work. We then follow the emergence of social work and its eventual maturity as a profession. Part Three examines the current educational requirements for preparation as a social worker, along with descriptions of the career patterns and options available to social workers in the different fields of practice and practice settings. Next, in Part Four, we turn to the values and ethical prescriptions that guide social work practice and the competencies expected of the social worker, how social workers might more aggressively work at preventing social issues from developing, and an overview of the differing expressions of social work throughout the world. Further, as a new feature in this edition, we have included in Part Four three short chapters intended to highlight social work's need to adapt to some critical issues facing social work now and in the future: adapting to a changing rural environment, addressing international and domestic terrorism, and working with U.S. casualties (both soldiers and their families) from the wars in Iraq and Afghanistan. Finally, in Part Five we turn our attention to some of the most vulnerable population groups in the United States and either have written ourselves, or have commissioned other experts to write, chapters highlighting key issues that affect eleven of the most vulnerable groups—along with providing guidelines for social workers when serving them. We view these chapters as a starting point for social workers in building their cultural competence.

In order to assist students in preparing for examinations over this material, Allyn and Bacon maintains a website with summaries of chapter objectives, practice essay and multiple-choice questions, and links to sources of information on key topics. This material can be found at http://www.ablongman.com/morales11e.

A Note to Instructors

We want to be sure that those who teach from this book are aware of the *Instructor's Manual and Test Bank* that accompanies it. In the manual we share teaching techniques developed over many years. For each chapter, the manual gives a synopsis of the most important content; lists key concepts and terms that the student should master; offers sample exercises for teaching the materials; and provides sample discussion, essay, and multiple-choice questions. A computerized version of the test bank is available from Allyn and Bacon, formatted for both Macintosh and IBM personal computers.

Also, please visit our website (www.ablongman.com/morales11e) for other useful information.

Through the years, many people directly or indirectly influenced our ideas and helped us prepare this material for publication. We want to acknowledge our universities, the University of California at Los Angeles and Colorado State University, as well as our colleagues and students who have in countless ways helped by sharing ideas and offering critical reviews of these materials. Their critiques have often led to revisions that improved the quality and readability of this material.

We want to thank the reviewers of this eleventh edition for their kind remarks and helpful suggestions: Patricia Burke, *University of Texas at Arlington*; Catherine N. Dulmus, *University of Tennessee, Knoxville*; Tina Hancock, *Campbell University*; Gay S. Jordan, *University of North Carolina, Charlotte*; Carla Mueller, *Lindenwood University*; Janelle Peeler, *Western Kentucky University*.

Special thanks are particularly in order for Karen Hanson, Patricia Quinlin, Janice Wiggins, and others at Allyn and Bacon who have nurtured this book through our many years of publication. We appreciate their combination of professional competence and personal warmth, and we regret that we have not yet succeeded in recruiting them to social work.

Finally, thanks to our families and friends for sacrificing some of our precious time together so that the activity of preparing this edition could be included in our already busy lives. Their love, support, and encouragement provide meaning to our work and enhance the quality of our lives.

Useful Websites for Social Workers

PROFESSIONAL ORGANIZATIONS

Association of Social Work Boards (information on licensing requirements in all states and schedule of licensing examinations) http://aswb.org

Canadian Association of Social Workers (CASW programs, Code of Ethics) http://www.caswacts.ca

Council on Social Work Education (lists of accredited BSW and MSW programs, publications) http://www.cswe.org

International Federation of Social Workers (IFSW position papers, Code of Ethics) http://www.ifsw.org

National Association of Social Workers (NASW activities, Code of Ethics, and publications) http://www.naswdc.org

SEARCH ENGINES FOR SOCIAL WORK RELATED TOPICS

Library of Congress (search for all books with U.S. copyrights) http://catalog.loc.gov

Statistical Information (centralized data source from most government agencies) http://www.fedstats.gov

Social Work Access Network (links to relevant information sources, social work chatroom, message board, etc.) http://cosw.sc.edu/swan

Google Scholar (search for peer-reviewed papers, theses, books, abstracts from many academic disciplines) http://scholar.google.com

Government Printing Office Access (link to policy databases including federal budget, economic indicators, federal register, legislative reports, presidential papers, judicial decisions) http://www.gpoaccess.gov/index.html

ENDNOTES

1. Carmen, DeNavas-Walt, Bernadette D. Proctor, and Cheryl Hill Lee. U.S. Census Bureau, Current Population Reports, P60-229, *Income, Poverty, and Health Insurance Coverage in the United States: 2004.* Washington, DC, U.S. Government Printing Office, 2005, Table 3. http://www.census.gov/prod/2005pubs/p60-229.pdf
2. Ibid. Table B-2.
3. Ibid. Table A-3.
4. The Chronicle on Higher Education. "Data Show Value of College Degree." *The Chronicle* (4/8/2005), p. A22. Also, http://www.census.gov/Press-Release/www/releases/archives/education/004214.html
5. *U.S. Census Bureau News.* "College Degree Nearly Doubles Annual Earnings, Census Bureau Reports." http://www.census.gov/Press-Release/www/releases/archives/education/004214.html
6. DeNavas-Walt, Table 7.

part one

A Social Worker Makes a Difference

If the world were a perfect place, it would provide for everyone warm and safe housing, an adequate supply of nutritious food, challenging jobs, good health care, and love and caring from friends and family. It would be a world with minimal stress, crime, and suffering. All people would find their lives satisfying and fulfilling. Social work exists because the world is less than perfect. Social workers serve people and the institutions of society as they confront this imperfection.

The social worker is not satisfied with this imperfect world that sends too many children to bed hungry at night, has effectively declared too many older people useless, restricts too many physically disabled people from productive living, allows too many women and children to be physically and sexually abused, deprives too many members of minority groups of the full opportunity to share in the benefits of this affluent society, has too many single parents trying to raise children in substandard housing without enough money for proper nutrition and food, and deprives too many emotionally and intellectually impaired people of satisfying lives because they behave or learn differently from the majority in the society. In fact, when even

one person suffers from loneliness, hunger, discrimination, poor housing, domestic violence, or emotional upset, there is a need for social work.

Although social work practice is built on a strong base of *knowledge*—knowledge about the people or social institutions being served, knowledge of the most appropriate practice approach(s) in a specific situation—social workers and other helping professionals use knowledge as the underpinning for *doing*. As opposed to many academic disciplines that develop and synthesize information to expand our knowledge, social workers are primarily concerned with applying knowledge to do a better job of serving clients. Because social work is an applied profession, this book begins (Chapter 1) with a case example of a social worker in action. The case depicts the work of a beginning-level social worker employed in a child welfare agency. As the information provided in Parts Two, Three, and Four of this book will indicate, it would have been just as accurate to portray this social worker as employed in a probation office, nursing home, family center, hospital, mental health center, youth agency, or any of many other settings.

The purpose of beginning with this case is two-fold. First, for many people beginning to examine the profession of social work it is useful to observe (at least as well as the case description allows) what a social worker does. Second, this case example will serve as a basis for connecting at least some of the material presented in the following chapters to the activities in which a social worker engages.

A Child Welfare Case: The Social Worker in Action

Prefatory Comment

Social workers are action oriented. They do things to make the lives of people better. Certainly social workers' actions are backed up by a set of human services programs that are designed to meet the social needs experienced by people in a community, and social workers depend on a sizeable body of knowledge about social functioning and the problems that diminish the quality of people's lives. However, because social workers are action oriented they also need to have considerable skill in working with people to bring about change to improve their conditions. Much of what makes it possible for the social worker to successfully help clients deal with their issues is not readily apparent to either the clients or the general public.

This book is designed to help people studying social work begin to understand the underlying factors that make it possible for professional social workers to effectively serve their clients. But first, in the spirit of observing some of the work typically performed by a social worker, it is useful to examine the following case, which reflects the activities of a social worker dealing with a case of suspected child abuse or neglect.

Demetria's First Case

The school year was well under way as the somewhat cooler fall air was beginning to turn the once deep-green leaves of the oak trees to a vibrant red. As was the case most mornings for Demetria, a social worker in the county's child welfare division, hot tea and French doughnuts made for a refreshing start to the usually full day of client visits, child protection investigations, reviewing of case files, and the necessary paperwork. One particular case, however, had been consistently in her thoughts. Just before 5:00 P.M. several days prior a call had come from a local public school teacher to the office intake worker concerning the possibility that one of the teacher's students was experiencing child abuse or neglect. The office administrator assigned the investigative responsibilities to Demetria, who subsequently made an appointment to meet with school officials and the 12-year-old child who was allegedly the victim of the abuse.

Demetria was a bit on edge when preparing for this neglect or abuse investigation as it was her first "solo" case assignment as a full-time social worker. She would have been anxious if the case had been referred by anyone, but particularly since it was from a "mandated reporter" [a person required by law to report suspicions of child abuse, such as a teacher, doctor, social worker, or nurse]. Demetria had only recently completed her Bachelor of Social Work (BSW) degree and was fortunate to have been hired on at the agency where she had completed her field placement during the senior year. Having now completed her training as a social worker in the child welfare division, she was hopefully prepared for this case assignment—or at least that is what her supervisor had said. Nevertheless, it was pretty scary to have been given so much responsibility for the well-being of a child. It was one thing to talk about working with a child abuse accusation in the classroom and even working with clients under the careful monitoring of a field instructor during her internship, but quite another to be dealing with a case on her own.

When Demetria arrived at the school on the day of her initial interviews, she first spoke with the teacher and school officials about their specific concerns. The school officials reported that Joseph Miles, a 12-year-old Caucasian male, had enrolled in their school just a few months prior. They were concerned that Joseph was having some adjustment issues; he had been late to school numerous times (if he showed up at all) and had been reported of smelling of alcohol by several of his peers. When Joseph did show up for school, he appeared restless and angry, often was dirty and had offensive body odor, and frequently was ridiculed by other students for his apparent lack of personal hygiene.

On the day that the telephone call was made to the child welfare office, Joseph had shown up for school that unusually cold fall morning without a jacket and in short sleeves, which allowed some unexplained bruising to be visible on his arms. In addition, he smelled of alcohol and was acting erratically. When questioned by his teacher about the bruising and why he did not have a coat in the cool weather, he only shrugged his shoulders and said nothing. Out of concern for the child's safety the school decided to call child welfare to express their concerns over the apparent lack of parental supervision and the possibility that he had been a victim of family violence. Previous attempts by the school to contact the parents had not gone well, and there was no working number for making telephone contact with the household.

After hearing the specific concerns of the school officials, Demetria decided to meet with Joseph, as there was reason to suspect child abuse and neglect. The school principal brought Joseph to the school's counseling room to meet with Demetria. As Joseph sat down in the chair Demetria also observed the bruises on his arms and his tattered clothing, and she noted that Joseph appeared well underweight for a child his age and height. After a little small talk about his favorite games, subjects in school, and foods (they called this "building rapport" and "initiating client engagement" in school), Demetria shifted the conversation to more personal questions of how things were at home, and where his mother and father were. Joseph shut down and stopped talking, only shrugging his shoulders without saying a word. Clearly, the new discussion was making Joseph somewhat uncomfortable. Demetria, not to be shaken by this behavior, asked Joseph if his mother and father would be at home today, as she wanted to stop by for a short visit and speak to them about some concerns that both she and the school staff were having about his missing school so often. Joseph said his mother would be, but he did not know where his father was, that his father had not been home in several weeks. "He just up and left us here," Joseph stated strongly in a clearly agitated voice. Demetria thanked Joseph for talking with her and sharing his favorite things to do, as some had also been her favorites as well, and indicated to the principal that Joseph could return to class.

Demetria took several minutes to write down a few notes and thanked the school officials for their call and concern, mentioning that she would follow up on the matter with an investigation and a home visit. After returning to the office and meeting with her supervisor about the interviews with Joseph and the school officials, Demetria made a trip to Joseph's home.

As she entered Joseph's neighborhood, Demetria noticed how run-down and dilapidated the mobile homes were in this somewhat older mobile home park; the yards were not well maintained, and trash and graffiti littered the streets and vacant homes. When Demetria arrived at the address, after some difficulty because the numbers were not clearly visible at the residence, she found a woman sitting on the steps of the small wooden porch at the front entrance of the home.

Demetria approached the home and said "hello" and then indicated that she was looking for Ms. Miles. "Hello," the lady on the porch said, "I'm Mrs. Miles." Demetria then explained that she was a social worker with the Division of Child Welfare and would like to speak with her about her son, Joseph. Hesitantly, Mrs. Miles invited her inside.

Demetria noticed that the mobile home was without electricity and barely looked lived in, except for the hot plate on the kitchen counter and a small college dorm-size refrigerator with the cord draped over the front. The house had an apparent roach problem as several scurried across the counter as Mrs. Miles tried to put a few dishes in the sink before offering Demetria something to drink. While Mrs. Miles was fixing a pot of tea on the hot plate, Demetria surveyed as much as she could from the well-used sofa where she sat. She noticed a long orange extension cord running out the window and over to the neighboring mobile home connecting the hot plate and a small space heater in the front room. She also observed that there were no visible signs of a supply of food in the house.

Demetria explained the reason for her visit and began with some basic questions about the family's situation. Mrs. Miles explained that she and Mr. Miles had fallen on hard times and both she and her husband were currently out of work. They had recently moved to the area in hopes of finding jobs; Mr. Miles had worked on a few odd jobs in construction but had not been called for several months. She had been working part-time cleaning homes and offices through a temporary employment agency, but fell ill several months prior with a severe case of the flu and lost her job assignments with the agency. The medical bills had mounted and although Medicaid covered most of her expenses, the family's lack of income had made meeting basic needs very difficult.

Mr. Miles had left about two weeks earlier to find work in a larger metropolitan area and Mrs. Miles had not heard from him since, due in part to their lack of a telephone and lack of transportation. She was not sure when exactly he would be returning, though he had never been gone that long without at least some mail correspondence. Nevertheless, she was hopeful that she would be receiving a letter and maybe a check from him very soon—in fact, she had been sitting on the porch awaiting the day's mail delivery.

Mrs. Miles admitted that their struggles were taking an emotional toll on her and that sometimes she did not even want to get out of bed in the mornings to make Joseph's lunch and get him ready for school, so often he would not go at all. Since they were new to the area, she knew very little about the community and where to find resources, and neither she nor her husband had family they could turn to for assistance. Demetria also asked about the bruising on Joseph's arms. Mrs. Miles explained that Joseph had become very distant since they moved to the area and was not talking to her very much. He seemed to be increasingly angry and frustrated and had started hanging out with older teenagers from the neighborhood, teenagers she suspected were involved in a gang and, maybe, that was where he got the bruises. She had caught Joseph sneaking back into the house after 1:00 A.M. several times since his father had gone away, and she smelled alcohol on him a couple of times.

As she told the story, Mrs. Miles' eyes filled with water several times as she struggled to hold back tears. "I am at the end of my rope. I don't know what will happen now," she said, her voice shaking in fear and uncertainty. "I need help, but where do I turn?" she asked Demetria. "My only child doesn't talk to me, my husband is away, and my family and I are in disarray," she said with much agitation and disappointment in her voice.

Demetria attempted to be supportive and assured Mrs. Miles that she would work to help her access the services she might need to obtain support for the family. Demetria had grown up in the area, just over the bridge in a neighboring community, and had been very active as a young leader in her community and surrounding area. She was well aware of the many services available in the community, as she had many dealings with churchs, civic organizations, and local social service agencies in the past. Demetria had been very active as a young college student; through her work as a tutor and as a Big Sister volunteer, as well as through her involvement in student government during her college years, Demetria knew the resources in the community pretty well.

Demetria returned to the office and met with her supervisor about the Miles's family situation. They discussed which community resources would best help the family to meet their basic needs of food, clothing, electricity, etc., and what referrals Demetria might make to get the necessary emergency assistance to this family in crisis.

Where to begin? Demetria prepared an assessment of the family's presenting issues and needs and drafted a case plan for discussion at the upcoming staff meeting called to review current and new cases. During the staffing, administrators and caseworkers would have an opportunity to share expertise, knowledge, and insights about how to best approach a presenting case situation. Often, this sharing process allows for cases to be discussed at greater depth, which leads to a more comprehensive and competent assessment of the situation and how the agency might better serve clients. Demetria worried that people might think she wasn't very well prepared for her job but decided the client's well-being was more important than maintaining her own comfort level.

The action plan was both thoughtful and comprehensive. After all, this was her first case, and Demetria wanted to be as prepared as possible when presenting her plan to the more seasoned staff members and administrators. When the meeting focus turned to Demetria's case, her skills as a BSW-level professional social worker were clearly evident. She shared background information about the Miles family and highlighted some key points from her initial assessment. Her supervisor complimented her on effectively developing her case plan from a generalist and systems perspective, which Demetria had learned as a BSW student.

The members of the staff team agreed with Demetria that child neglect was present and that the undetermined source of Joseph's bruising needed to be addressed as the child's safety was of immediate concern. Demetria's investigation had not sufficiently documented evidence to open an active case of child abuse at this time, but the investigation was clearly a conduit through which the family's condition of poverty and other struggles had been exposed. In addition, Joseph's difficulties with adjustment, his possible drinking problem, truancy, and gang participation, were all areas of concern. Thus, there were points of focus at a number of levels—individual, family, group, school, and community—that should be addressed in Demetria's work with this family in need.

After the staffing, Demetria called the director of the energy assistance program to see about getting the electricity turned on at the residence. The director assured her that they could get the family's lights turned on before the close of the business day. Demetria was concerned that the family also needed some basic food items and that their lack of transportation and money would make shopping for food problematic. Because there was no telephone, Demetria made a trip back to the Miles' home but first stopped by the local food bank and picked up some basic food items that the family could use. Demetria helped Mrs. Miles complete eligibility forms for subsidized rent and energy assistance and attempted to get the family qualified for the food stamp program. Because of the family's financial problems, Demetria connected them to a child health program that would help with any medical needs that Joseph might have and through which Joseph could obtain a thorough medical checkup.

Last, Demetria wanted to help Joseph deal with his adjustment issues and confront his possible involvement in gang activities and underage drinking. She thought that the Big Brother program in the local community was an excellent way for Joseph to build positive relationships with his peers; the local Boys and Girls Club building had just been renovated and had an indoor pool, basketball court, pool tables, table tennis, and a variety of other activities. In fact, a former classmate of Demetria's was conducting a teen group that focused on development issues, sex education, substance abuse, anger management, and self-esteem building. What a fitting opportunity for Joseph to deal with his adjustment and anger issues and to meet some new people, as well. Demetria knew that getting Joseph to go to the group meeting might be a challenge, but she also knew that he would have a lot to contribute to the other group members and would learn from them. At an age where peer relationships are becoming especially important to young people, this might become a healthy alternative to gang participation for Joseph.

A few weeks later Demetria and her supervisor sat down to review this case. Working from her generalist perspective, Demetria had understood that this wasn't just a problem about Joseph. It was also the absence of Joseph's dad from the family and the issues he faced at school, both of which contributed to his need to belong and his ill-advised decision to seek that sense of belonging through association with a gang. It also had to do with a family that faced a financial crisis and didn't know how to access the existing resources in the community. Demetria had been able to assist in all of these areas. Her generalist approach to this case, however, left her aware of the lack of resources to help both Mr. and Mrs. Miles with their employment problems. Demetria's supervisor suggested that this issue might be a good discussion topic at an upcoming meeting of the local chapter of the National Association of Social Workers. If the problem was widespread, perhaps an action plan could be developed to create a more adequate job counseling service in the community.

Looking back, Demetria felt pleased with her decision to major in social work and attend an accredited social work education program that provided her with the professional recognition, knowledge, and skills she needed to be reasonably effective in working with her first case. What's more, she knew she would get better with experience. She felt she was off to a good start in her chosen profession.

Concluding Comments

In the above case, we have the opportunity to observe a new social worker dealing with her first case as a full-time child welfare worker. Demetria was apprehensive at first (and who wouldn't be?), but ultimately she was successful in helping address both the short- and long-term issues that were negatively affecting Joseph and his family. What made it possible for the Miles family to receive this assistance? The answer is "many factors," including the creation of a set of human services in the community that allowed people with professional expertise, like Demetria, to deliver helpful programs, the knowledge and skill possessed by this new social worker, and many other elements that underpin social work practice. A box at the conclusion of each of the next few chapters highlights some of the factors that contributed to Demetria's ability to make a difference in the life of this family.

part two

Social Work in U.S. Society

Social work emerged during the twentieth century as a critical profession in U.S. society. Its development paralleled a seeming roller coaster of public interest in human welfare and social services. At times, particularly during the 1960s, the political climate placed considerable emphasis on improving human welfare, and the popularity of social work soared. At other times, this emphasis yielded to a conservative orientation more concerned with economic prosperity for a few than with meeting the basic needs of all. In such times the appeal of social work to many young people declined as they sought employment in jobs where there was greater financial opportunity. Clearly, social work is closely tied to the political and economic philosophy that dominates at any time.

Although the supply of social workers may increase or decline from time to time, it is likely that there will always be a strong demand for this profession. Certain fundamental needs of the members of a society must be met if it is to survive, and any successful political philosophy must provide for these needs, even if at a very minimal level. There may be disagreement over how these needs should be met, but there will always be some mechanism for providing those services. In relation to needs regarding social functioning, social workers are established as the central providers.

Providing needed human services and contributing to improvement of the quality of life for all people are personally rewarding experiences. Each social worker can enjoy the satisfaction of knowing that he or she makes a small but important contribution to the well-being of society. Yet, social work is not easy work. It can be as emotionally draining as it is rewarding. It can be as frustrating as it is satisfying. The prerequisite to developing the knowledge, values, and skills necessary for competent social work practice must be a basic commitment to social betterment and a willingness to invest oneself in facilitating the process of change.

To understand the current status of social work in the United States, one must first understand the nation's changing social philosophy. In Chapter 2 we examine the efforts and issues that U.S. society confronts as it responds to the needs of its members. A summary of some of the important events and philosophies that have shaped the current social programs and its methods of delivering human services is presented. In addition, some of the continuing issues regarding the provision of human services are highlighted because, as it will later become evident, they affect the tools that social workers have available to serve their clients.

Within the framework of an evolving social welfare institution, a profession concerned with helping people interact more effectively with the world around them, and simultaneously change that world to make it more supportive of human welfare, has emerged. An overview of that profession, social work, is the substance of Chapter 3. While the central focus of social work is seemingly obscured when one looks at the many different expressions of social work in the wide range of human service organizations and the varied practice activities in which social workers engage, its central feature—attending to the quality of people's social functioning—makes it an important profession in fulfilling society's commitment to the welfare of its people.

Building on the concept of social work as a comprehensive helping profession concerned with enhancing social functioning, Chapter 4 charts its evolution as a profession from well-meaning volunteers to a recognized and respected helping profession.

chapter 2

Social Welfare: A Response to Human Need

Prefatory Comment

The Preamble to the Constitution of the United States asserts that this nation was formed to "insure domestic tranquility, provide for the common defense, promote the general welfare, and secure the blessings of liberty to ourselves and our posterity. . . ." In the months and years since the terrorist attacks on September 11, 2001, our tranquility has surely been broken, the commitment to providing common defense has been translated into preemptive strikes against Afghanistan and Iraq, and many of the blessings of liberty have been compromised in the name of homeland security. In this context the main focus of social work, promoting the general welfare (or well-being of the people) has been difficult to achieve. Indeed, people's perceptions of what constitutes well-being have changed, and the country's willingness to share its resources is increasingly characterized by self-interest and a response to special interests, rather than a promotion of the welfare of all of its members. The altruism that once flourished in the United States has diminished.

Human needs periodically change. Sometimes there is gradual change that occurs incrementally over time, and at other times dramatic change occurs quickly, such as in response to a local disaster or the terrorist attacks on September 11, 2001. It is within the context of these changing needs, and people's expectations that new programs and services will emerge to respond to changed conditions, that the social welfare institution has evolved. It is also in this context that several professions, including social work, have emerged to assume responsibility for helping to "promote the general welfare" of the nation's people.

Identifying Human Needs

Although each person has his or her unique constellation of needs, some needs are common to all people. Logically, efforts should be made to address the most basic needs and then, if there is sufficient commitment and resources, to deal with those of lesser priority. Maslow suggests the following priorities, or *hierarchy of human needs*, beginning with the most basic:[1]

▶ *Physiological survival needs:* nourishment, rest, and warmth
▶ *Safety needs:* preservation of life and sense of security
▶ *Belongingness needs:* to be a part of a group and to love and be loved
▶ *Esteem needs:* approval, respect, acceptance, and appreciation from others
▶ *Self-actualization needs:* opportunity to fulfill one's potential

A society must decide which of these needs it will attempt to serve and which needs individuals and families should be expected to meet themselves. The more basic the need, the more likely it is that society will make some provision for meeting that need.

Although individual philosophies vary along a continuum regarding how much responsibility the society should take for responding to human needs, two basic philosophies dominate thinking in the United States and shape political debate. A *conservative* philosophy argues for placing primary responsibility for maintaining the well-being of people with the individual and family, depends on the market system to drive the economy, and tends toward a protectionist national view of issues. In contrast, a *liberal* position favors a more substantial role for government and other social structures in meeting basic needs and in the use of social programs to redistribute income and at least partially influence the economy, and it expects the government to actively address global issues. Thus, the political climate at any time will affect the degree to which the society will take responsibility for the welfare of its members and embrace social programs to maximize the well-being of its citizens. When a more conservative orientation is dominant, the society is most likely to assume responsibility for only the most basic needs (e.g., physiological survival and safety). Social programs would typically be limited to activities such as food programs, provision for the homeless, and intervention in cases of child abuse. If a more liberal orientation dominates, the society would be viewed as needing to also address belongingness, esteem, or self-actualization needs. Thus there would likely be support for additional social programs such as family counseling, mental health, and services to persons with disabilities, and even for programs aimed at changing social structures to try to prevent social problems from emerging.

Social Welfare Programs

Society's efforts to meet some human needs are labeled *social welfare*. The term *social,* when applied to humans, addresses the interactions of individuals or groups with other people, groups, organizations, or communities. The term *welfare* implies concern for the well-being of people. Social welfare programs, then, are developed to help people function more satisfactorily in their interactions with others and thus to lead more fulfilling lives. A useful definition of *social welfare* is the translation of society's dominant social philosophies into social policies, to be carried out by a system of human services agencies and delivered by human services professionals, in order to meet the socially related needs of individuals, families and other households, groups, and/or communities through programs offering social provisions, personal services, and/or social action.

In its early years, the United States was largely rural and the economy was based on family farms and local trade. Except in the cases of widows and orphans or persons experiencing major physical disabilities or mental illnesses, the social programs were typically of limited scope. With the transition to an industrial society in the 1800s, the family, and particularly the extended family, could not meet many of the needs of its members. Family members often had to move to distant locations to find jobs, making the mutual support one might expect from family members less available. Also, the work depended more on the specialized skills in the use of machines than on an individual's manual labor, and those without suitable skills or intelligence became expendable. Life was further complicated by competition for jobs, with large numbers of skilled immigrants also seeking to enter the labor market. In this environment, social welfare programs began to expand because many individuals and families could no longer be self-sufficient.

More recently, the economy has become more global and increasingly tied to electronic technology, which again is altering the structure of the society. Families are no longer required to work as a unit to survive, although the general well-being of their members often depends on multiple breadwinners. In addition, individuals can work somewhat in isolation (often in a home office) and thus their opportunity for regular social interaction with colleagues is lessened. Further, a few people who are highly skilled in the use of technology can complete much of the necessary work (for example, through mechanized farming, robotics), leading to job displacement—especially for those experiencing educational, emotional, or mental disabilities or those who are not computer literate. These and other trends have moved social welfare programs from a relatively minor role in U.S. society to an increasingly central place.

The social welfare programs that emerged took many forms. These programs were not intended to replace individual caring but were rather to reflect the society's social concern by formalizing (or institutionalizing) needed services.

The Evolution of Social Welfare

An index of a nation's continued commitment to its people is its investment in social programs. These programs are the mechanisms by which public concerns are translated into methods of assisting individual people. They are expressed in laws and other policies that represent the society's plans to provide for an identified need. In the United States, social welfare programs have been subject to ever-changing philosophies, and consequently support for these programs has increased and decreased at various periods. Knowledge of the evolution of social welfare provides an important context for understanding the social programs today.

Colonial Times to the Great Depression

Picture life in the rural United States in the 1700s when land was plowed and families worked to tame the wilderness. Although there were many trials and tribulations in an agricultural society, the person with average intelligence and a willingness to work hard could usually succeed. Given an open frontier and liberal government policies for staking a claim to fertile land, an individual could readily acquire property and produce at least the necessities of life. Because the family was strong and each member had sharply defined roles that contributed to the family's welfare, people survived and, in time, usually prospered. The "American Dream" could become a reality for most (unless one was of African, Asian, Mexican, or Native American background) in this simple agrarian society.

The family was not usually completely independent and self-supporting. All members (i.e., grandparents, children, and other relatives) performed the required work and, perhaps as important, were needed. Even the mentally or physically disabled person could find meaningful ways to contribute. For mutual protection, social interaction, and opportunity to trade the goods they produced, families would band together into loosely knit communities. Trade centers eventually emerged as small towns; a market economy evolved; and merchants opened stores, bought and sold products, and extended credit to people until their products were ready for market.

Efforts to meet human needs in this environment can best be characterized as *mutual aid*. When special problems arose, neighbors and the community responded. The barn that burned was quickly rebuilt, widows and orphans were cared for, and the sick were tended to. People shared what they had with needy friends and neighbors, knowing that the favor would be returned some day. In this preindustrial society, the quality of life depended on the "grace of God" and hard work. Society rarely needed to respond to unmet human needs; but when it did, churches and synagogues usually provided that service.

Conditions began to change in the mid-1800s and early 1900s when industrialization and urbanization created rapid and dramatic changes in both the family and the market system. People congregated in cities where there were jobs, the individual breadwinner rather than the family unit became the key to survival, and interactions with others were increasingly characterized by impersonality. Those from the vulnerable population groups (e.g., immigrants, the aged, minorities, women, persons with disabilities) in particular experienced reduced opportunity for employment or, if employed, access to meaningful and personally rewarding jobs. Not only were social problems increased, but with the changed roles of the family and market system, society had to create new means of responding to human needs.

Early social welfare programs were heavily influenced by the *Puritan ethic,* which argued that only those people with a moral defect required assistance. According to Puritan reasoning, those who failed did so because they suffered from a moral weakness and were viewed as sinful. It is not uncommon even today for clients to feel that their troubles represent God's means of punishing them for some sin or act of immoral behavior. Following the same philosophy, grudging taxpayers often resent contributing to human services when they believe the client is at fault for needing assistance. This view, however, does not take into consideration the structural factors in the society that contribute to or even may cause an individual's problems.

The United States was not settled by wealthy people. When social needs were addressed by this developing society, small voluntary organizations were formed to provide services. Puritan judgmentalism was evident in the names of organizations such as the "Home for Intemperate Women" or the "Penitent Females Refuge." If voluntary organizations did not meet needs, town meetings were held and actions taken to provide assistance, thus creating the first public social services. Any assistance was considered charity, not a right. Requests for help were either supported or rejected, depending on the judgments made by the townsfolk.

The philosophy derived from the *French Enlightenment* of the eighteenth century contradicted the Puritan view. It argued that people are inherently good and that need for assistance is not related to morality. People needing help were considered worthy of that assistance depending on the causes of their problems. Persons with limited income, for example, were classified as worthy poor or unworthy poor. The *worthy poor* were viewed as good people who required help because they were afflicted with an ailment or were women and children left destitute by the death or desertion of the breadwinning husband and father. The *unworthy poor* were thought to have flaws of character. That one's plight may have been caused by others, by chance, or even by structural conditions in the society was only beginning to be recognized.

There were, of course, those who held a sympathetic view of persons in need and attempted to reform the punitive and uncaring approaches to providing services. One of the first great social reformers, Dorothea Dix, chronicled the deplorable conditions in prisons and almshouses (also referred to as "poor farms") and sought to establish government responsibility for meeting human needs. Her effective lobbying contributed to the passage of a bill in the U.S. Congress to grant federal land to states to help them finance care for the mentally ill. The veto of that bill in 1854 by President Franklin Pierce established a precedent that was to dominate thinking about society's responsibility for social welfare for the next three-quarters of a century—that the federal government should play no part in providing human services. As late as 1930, President Herbert Hoover relied on the precedent established by the Pierce Veto when he approved an appropriation of $45 million to feed livestock in Arkansas during a drought while opposing an additional $25 million to feed the farmers who raised that livestock.[2]

Other social reformers, too, began to advocate for programs to meet needs—mostly through voluntary associations such as the Charity Organization Societies, Settlement Houses, the Mental Hygiene Movement, and programs to assist former slaves to integrate into the dominant society. When the federal government refused to engage in providing human services, the states sporadically offered services, with several states creating state charity boards or public welfare departments. However, not until the Great Depression of the 1930s led to severe economic crisis and the ensuing New Deal programs of President Franklin D. Roosevelt was it recognized that private philanthropy, even in combination with limited state and local government support, could not adequately address the major human needs.

This picture of life in the United States is based largely on the experience of the white European immigrant. But what if one were African American, Mexican American, or Native American? Certainly life was different for these segments of the population. Consider, for example, the experience of African Americans in the 1800s. Families brought to this nation as slaves often had little control over their lives or their ability to function as a family unit. In slave families, males were often demeaned and females sexually abused, and family members were frequently sold as property to other slave owners. Even after emancipation, few social programs were available to meet even basic needs as the former slaves either remained as sharecroppers in the South or struggled to meet their basic needs in the discriminatory society in the North.

Similarly, Morales carefully documented the movement of people from Mexico into the Southwest United States in the mid-eighteenth and nineteenth centuries. Mexico was ruled by Spain until it achieved independence in 1821. But through the aggressive Anglo American conviction of Manifest Destiny, the United States had acquired by purchase and military force nearly one million square miles of Mexican territory, or half of all of Mexico. The Mexicans, who subsequently became Mexican Americans because of U.S. birth, were subjected to extensive acts of brutality at the hands of the Texas Rangers and lynchings by Anglo Americans who resented their competition for farming, grazing, and water rights.[3]

Native Americans, too, lived a different experience. As the westward movement progressed, the original Americans increasingly had their sources for meeting basic needs and maintaining their cultural identity taken away through treaties (often to be broken later) and government policies that dramatically changed the Native Americans' way of life. Policies during this period were intended to accomplish *extermination* of the Native Americans through war, lack of disease control, provision of alcohol, and slavery; to lead to their *expulsion* from their land; to *exclude* them from their community life by being sent to Indian schools and to reservations; and to *assimilate* them by destroying tribal collective action through the termination of working relations with tribal groups and allotment of Indian land to individuals, with much of that land later sold to non-Indians. Under these conditions, social programs for Native Americans were virtually nonexistent.

The Great Depression to the Present

The Great Depression was also the great equalizer. People who had previously been successful suddenly required help. These were able-bodied people of European descent who needed assistance. Could they be blamed for their condition or did other factors contribute to their troubles? In this case it was the deterioration of the worldwide economy that forced many people into poverty. U.S. society began to recognize that indeed there were structural factors in modern society responsible for many social problems. Thus began an unprecedented period of expansion in social welfare in the United States that became inclusive of all people.

World War II rallied the United States to a common cause and helped people recognize their interdependence. Each person was counted on to contribute to the common good during wartime conditions, and the nation could ill afford to create "throwaway" people by failing to provide for their basic needs. By the 1960s economic recovery was complete, and a brief period of prosperity and responsiveness to human needs followed. The Kennedy and Johnson administrations fostered the War on Poverty and Great Society programs, and the Human Rights Revolution was in its heyday. These activities focused public concern on the poor, minorities, women, the aged, the mentally and physically disabled, and other population groups that had previously been largely ignored. Legislation protecting civil rights and creating massive social programs was passed; court decisions validated the new legislation, and a vast array of new social programs emerged.

The bloom on social programs began to fade in the middle of the 1970s, and public apathy replaced public concern. Under the Carter administration, a deteriorating economy was accompanied by a growing political conservatism, and the continued commitment to human services was placed in direct competition with military buildup and the maintenance of U.S. superpower status. By the 1980s, the time was ripe for conservatives to attempt to dismantle the social programs that had developed over the past two decades. Echoing the political rhetoric based on the distrust of government that had characterized the philosophies of Presidents Franklin Pierce and Herbert Hoover, and mixed with punitive, moralistic views regarding the recipients of human services that revealed vestiges of the Puritan philosophy, President Ronald Reagan set out to limit the federal government's social programs. The Reagan administration had only moderate influence over expenditures for "mandated" social programs such as Social Security, but was able to decrease by almost 15 percent the expenditures on "discretionary" social programs.

The Reagan administration set out not only to cut federal expenditures, but also to shift responsibility to state and local governments or, where possible, to the private sector of the human services. However, the combination of a more liberal Congress and a series of Supreme Court decisions that protected the gains made in human services and civil rights during the prior two decades partially blunted the radical changes that President Reagan, and later President George H. Bush, promised. Implementation of President Clinton's moderate social agenda was blunted somewhat by a very conservative Congress, leaving little opportunity to roll-back the decreased support for human services.

With the exception of the cost of the Vietnam War and the military buildup during the Reagan and G. H. Bush administrations, examination of federal expenditures reveals a continuous decline in expenditures on national defense. At the same time, only the conservative Reagan era has countered the trend for the United States to increasingly invest in its human resources. Even the George H. Bush presidency saw a rather dramatic increase in human resource spending. At the beginning of the Kennedy administration in 1962, almost twice as much was spent on defense as on human resources. By the end of the Clinton administration, the amount of money invested in national defense was only slightly more than one-fourth of that spent on human resources (i.e., for the year 2000, $295 billion was spent on defense and $1,196 billion on human resources—including health, education, Social Security, Medicare, and veterans benefits).[4] This was to later change under the George W. Bush administration and entry into the wars in Afghanistan and Iraq.

The Clinton administration, in office throughout most of the 1990s, was blessed with a strong economy. Yet President Clinton's social agenda was of limited success. His proposal to fulfill a campaign pledge to make some form of health care available to all citizens failed, and his proposal for welfare reform was passed and signed, but seriously compromised. As opposed to the "War on Poverty," which was the hallmark of the Johnson administration in the 1960s, the political rhetoric cast the Clinton effort as a "War on Welfare," suggesting that the primary intent was not so much to reduce poverty as to change the system of income maintenance. The basic philosophies driving this legislation were that (1) at least one person in every family should be employed and a family should receive benefits for no more than five years, (2) noncitizens and felons should not receive welfare benefits, (3) more power and responsibility should shift to the individual states, and (4) illegitimacy rates should be reduced by establishing paternity, requiring fathers to pay child support, and thus reducing benefits for out-of-wedlock children.[5] The upbeat title of the act, the Personal Responsibilities and Work Opportunity Reconciliation Act, belied its mean-spirited intent, which was to remove the most basic income support program from supporting families in economic need as an unconditional guarantee of citizenship.[6]

Welfare reform has achieved mixed results. A summary of the outcomes of welfare reform after eight years of experience prepared by the Urban Institute indicates:

▶ The number of recipients dropped from 4 million to 2 million
▶ The number of eligible recipients dropped from 85 percent to 50 percent
▶ The percent of working welfare recipients increased from 22 percent to 33 percent
▶ 20 percent of the welfare recipients had two or more barriers to employment (e.g., limited education, little or no work experience, need for care of a child with disabilities, language challenges), yet employment in this group increased from 5 percent to 14 percent

▶ Only 15 percent of recipients participated in TANF (Temporary Assistance to Needy Families)-funded education and training activities

▶ 26 percent of the recipients who left welfare programs had returned and 57 percent of the former recipients who had not returned to welfare were employed

▶ Former recipients earned at about the 20th percentile of the wage scale (about $8.00 per hour) and only about 33 percent had health insurance coverage[7]

Perhaps the greatest concern today is for the eligible but nonparticipating families. These families are poor, and almost one-half are extremely poor.[8] They are families that choose not to subject themselves to the stigma of welfare, to depend on support of other family members—particularly Hispanic families (often drawing them into poverty), to risk periodic hunger, or to fear depleting their eligibility in case they should face worse conditions in the future. These families not only fail to secure income that could improve the quality of life for the adults and children, but also no longer have access to food stamps or health care assistance.

Perhaps an unintended benefit to the poor and other disenfranchised people was that the administration of George W. Bush was forced to focus on international issues. Domestic policy, other than the attempt to revamp Social Security by permitting workers to invest part of their social security funds into personal investments rather than fully maintaining the concept of social insurance as a protection for all citizens, received short shrift. During the G. W. Bush administration, the national defense budget rose to 82 percent of the health and human services budget; the budget deficit rose from a $126 billion surplus in 1999 to a $363 billion deficit in 2003 (the highest deficit since his father's administration); and the national debt increased from $2.9 trillion to a record $7.9 trillion.[9] The long-term implications of these actions are that until the United States begins reducing expenditures or increasing revenue to erase the annual deficit, it will not be possible to pay off the national debt (plus its interest) and reinstate domestic programs.

Social Welfare in the Early 2000s

Sources of Funds to Support Social Programs

The emphasis on federal programs in the areas of health and income security should not detract from appreciation of the programs provided at the state and local levels of government, or from voluntary contributions from individuals, foundations, and businesses. As Table 2.1 indicates, almost $2.1 trillion are spent each year on health, education, income security, and other human services. That amounts to over $7,200 for each of the 294 million people in the United States in 2004. The United States in many respects is a generous nation.

Our historical review of social programs indicates that in the most simple form of U.S. society the expectation was that the individual would take care of himself or herself, or, if not, that the families would ensure that their members' needs were met.

Table 2.1

Government and Private Sector Allocations to Health, Education, and Social Welfare (in billions of dollars)

	Federal Government 2004	State/Local Government 2002–2003	Private/ Nonprofit 2004	Total
Health, hospitals, Medicare	$ 479.5B	$ 154.9B	$ 22.0B	$ 656.4B
Elementary, secondary, higher education and job training	67.5	621.3	33.8	722.6
Human services (social services, recreation, housing, community planning)	98.4	67.0	19.2	184.6
Income security (cash assistance, other public welfare except Social Security)*	250.3	306.5	0	556.8
Total	$ 895.7B	$ 1149.7B	$ 75.0	$ 2120.4B
% Total Expenditures	41.2%	54.2%	3.5%	100.0%

*Note: The federal government collects and distributes an additional $495.6B, not reflected in these data, through employment taxes to fund the Social Security program. In addition, the federal government transfers $389.3B to state and local government; some of this offsets state/local expenditures reported in this table.

Sources:
Federal Government. Office of Budget Management. Fiscal Year 2006 Budget. Table 3.2. Outlays by Function and Subfunction: 1962–2010. http://www.whitehouse.gov/omb/budget/fy2006/pdf/hist.pdf; State & Local Government. U.S. Census Bureau. Summary of State & Local Government Finances by Level of Government: 2002–2003. http://www.census.gov/govs/estimate/03sl00us.html; Private/Nonprofit. American Association of Fund Raising Counsel. 2004 Contributions: $248.5 Billion by Type of Recipient Organization. http://www.aafrc.org.

Laws placed primary responsibility on the family unit for caring for its members, and, to a larger extent than in many societies, these laws have protected the sanctity of the family's decisions about how to achieve this goal. If this expectation could have been fulfilled, there may not have been the need for a social welfare institution, or perhaps society would reluctantly intervene only in cases where family members were being damaged (e.g., child abuse or neglect, domestic violence, elder maltreatment).

U.S. society evolved, however, in a way that the family became unable to meet many social needs, and voluntary social services provided by religious or voluntary human services agencies began to expand. Today, these contributions amount to only a small portion (3.5 percent) of the total expenditures on human resources, yet they are particularly important because they are relatively flexible funds that can be used to respond to changing needs. Although some of these important human services continue to be offered under the auspices of religious organizations, most are now related to secular nonprofit human service organizations, such as those typically associated with the United Way or that raise their own funds to supplement client fees. As revealed in Table 2.1, these private nonprofit organizations are more likely to contribute their resources to educational programs rather than to health or human services programs, and they simply do not have the funds to support income maintenance programs.

Local and state governments were the next line of defense. Today, city, county, and state governments supply approximately 54 percent of the funds that underwrite the health, education, and social welfare programs in the United States. These government units focus largely on education at all levels (see Table 2.1), but they also provide significant support in other human resource areas.

Finally, the federal government provides a large portion of all human resource funding. The massive social programs that evolved have made it evident that voluntary and local government resources are insufficient to provide for people's basic needs. Although controversy continues over the extent of participation and the role of the federal government in providing human resources, today over $800 billion is invested annually in health, income security, and other programs. The rationale for this extensive involvement of the federal government is that many human problems are created by national and international factors such as chronic unemployment, pervasive discrimination, inflation, the international trade deficit, and even the volatile price of goods and services on the worldwide market. Local areas have little, if any, influence over these factors, and it is necessary to create national programs to equalize the burden of responding to the needs of the victims of these largely uncontrollable events.

An outcome of the varied patterns of funding for human services has resulted in a patchwork of programs, and it is often difficult for potential clients to navigate their way through the collection of services. Social workers perform an important role in helping people find their way through the maze of human services.

Purpose and Goals for Social Programs

Social programs are created to accomplish three general purposes. First, most are designed for the *remediation* of a social problem. When a sufficient number of people experience difficulty in a particular aspect of social functioning, social programs are created to provide services intended to correct that problem—or at least to help the clients deal with it more effectively. Remediation programs include services such as income support for the poor, counseling for the mentally ill, and job training for the displaced worker. Remediation has historically been the central form of human service.

A second general purpose of human services has evolved more recently—the *enhancement* of social functioning. In this form of social program the emphasis is on the growth and development of clients in a particular area of functioning without a "problem" having necessarily been identified. Well-baby clinics, parent-effectiveness training, and various youth recreation programs are all examples of social programs designed for personal enhancement.

Finally, the purpose of some social programs is the *prevention* of social problems. As opposed to treating symptoms, prevention programs attempt to identify the basic causes of difficulties in social functioning and seek to stimulate changes that will keep problems from ever developing. Prevention programs, for example, might include helping parents learn appropriate ways to discipline children or conducting community education to make the public aware of the negative impact racism or sexism has on the growth and development of children.

Social programs have been created to serve at least four specific goals: socialization, social integration, social control, and social change. Each goal responds to different human needs—some programs are focused on the needs of individuals or families and others address the needs of the society.

One goal of social programs is to facilitate the *socialization* of people to the accepted norms and behaviors of society. Such programs are designed to help people develop the knowledge and skills to become full participating and contributing members of society and include, for example, such programs as scouting, Boys Clubs and Girls Clubs, and YMCA or YWCA activities. A goal of other social programs is to assist in *social integration* where people are helped to become more successful in interacting with the world around them. Counseling, therapy, and rehabilitation programs, for example, attempt to achieve this goal. A third goal of social programs is, at times, to provide *social control* by removing people from situations when they might place themselves or others at risk or when they require some period of isolation from their usual surroundings in order to address problems. Examples of these programs are found in mental hospitals and correctional facilities. Finally, some programs are intended to achieve *social change,* that is, to express the conscience of society by stimulating changes that will enhance the overall quality of life. For example, public education to encourage the practice of safe sex to reduce the risk of AIDS and the solicitation of employers to hire the developmentally disabled are activities that help to bring about social changes that benefit the society.

Social Program Conceptions

The design of social programs also reflects differing perceptions about who should be served and when services should be given. The most basic programs are based on a *safety net approach* and are planned as a way for society to assist people when other social institutions (e.g., family and market system) have failed to resolve specific problems. An alternative conception of social programs, the *social utilities approach,* views human services as society's frontline manner in addressing common human needs.

The Safety Net Approach.   One conception views human services as a safety net that saves people who have not had their needs met by their primary resources such as the family or employment/economic systems. This approach begins with the presumption that a predefined problem exists—for example, that a family's income is too low, that a person's behavior is deviant, that a child is at risk. Services are then provided to address the problems, and, when a satisfactory level of problem reduction is achieved, the services are terminated. One negative aspect of such programs is that to be eligible for a safety net program, a client must also take on the stigma of having failed in some aspect of social functioning. Further, at times clients must be terminated from service because they have reached a predefined level of functioning, even though the service providers recognize that the clients would benefit from additional assistance.

Safety net programs are thought of as *residual* because they are designed to deal with the residue of human problems—that is, those problems that are left after all other processes of helping are exhausted. Programs based on this approach are also *selective* in the sense that they are designed to serve a specific population experiencing a specific need. Finally, safety net programs are *time-limited* in the sense that services are terminated when a problem is solved (or at least reduced) or a predetermined level of functioning is achieved.

The Social Utilities Approach.   The social utilities conception of human services views social programs as one of society's first-line social institutions for meeting needs. Like public utilities for water and electricity, these social utilities are available to all people who wish to make use of them. They do not assume that the person who receives services is at fault or has necessarily failed if he or she requires services. Rather, this concept recognizes that society creates conditions where all people can benefit from social programs, whether the program is designed to help people solve problems or enhance already adequate functioning.

Social utility programs are *universal* in the sense that they do not have strict eligibility requirements. Such programs are also based on an *institutional* conception of human services that considers social programs a regular or institutionalized way of meeting human needs. They do not assume that the individual, family, or any other social institution has failed if, for example, parents place a child in day care, if a young person joins a scouting program, or if a senior citizen takes advantage of a senior center's lunch program.

Human Services Program Categories

It is also useful to recognize that social programs can be divided into three distinct categories: social provisions, personal services, and social action. In the broad perspective of the responsibilities of a social welfare institution in a developed nation, all of these program categories are required.

Social Provisions.   This category of social programs is designed to meet the most fundamental needs of the population, and such programs are typically viewed as part of the safety net. *Social provisions* are the tangible resources given to persons in need, either as cash or as direct benefits, such as food, clothing, or housing.

Social provisions are the most costly programs in outlay of actual dollars. As social programs have evolved, governmental agencies have assumed the primary responsibility for providing these services, and the private sector has taken the role of providing backup for those people who slip through the mesh of the public safety net. Such major social provision programs as Temporary Assistance to Needy Families (TANF), Supplemental Security Income (SSI), Food Stamps, Low-rent Public Housing, and many others are provided under governmental auspices. Meals and lodging for transients and the homeless, emergency food programs, financial aid in response to crisis situations, shelters for battered wives, and many other social provision programs, however, are offered by voluntary social agencies.

Personal Services.   The personal services category of programs includes both problem-solving and enhancement programs. Unlike social provisions, *personal services* are intangible services that help people resolve issues in their social functioning. Examples of personal service programs are marriage and family counseling, child protection services, client advocacy, family therapy, care for the disabled, job training, family planning and abortion counseling, foster care programs, human service brokering and referral activities, and many other programs aimed at helping clients strengthen their social functioning.

Social Action.   When one works with people, it quickly becomes evident that it is often inadequate just to help a person or group cope with an unjust world. Efforts must be made to create a more just and supportive environment. For example, it is not enough to help a woman understand and cope with discrimination in the workplace. Although these activities may be important for her ability to keep her job, they do not resolve the basic problem, and they place the burden of change and adjustment on the victim. *Social action* programs help change conditions that create difficulties in social functioning. They require specialized knowledge and skill to effect change in organizations and communities. These efforts involve fact finding, analysis of community needs, research and interpretation of data, and other efforts to inform and mobilize the public to action in order to achieve change.

The Successes and Failures of Human Service Programs

It is not possible to fully assess the array of human service programs in the United States in this overview chapter. The poverty rate is perhaps the most revealing single indicator of quality of life because limited income is clearly associated with many social problems that affect people's well-being, including health, disabilities, mental health, nutrition, housing conditions, and so on.

To what extent, then, have there been improvements in the rates of poverty* in the United States in recent years? Beginning with the end of the War on Poverty

---

*The experience of poverty is much more than living on a limited income; yet income is used as the single indicator of the degree of deprivation an individual or family experiences. The poverty threshold is adjusted annually by the federal government to reflect the minimum amount of money required by families of different sizes to be able to afford nutritious food, obtain adequate housing, sufficiently clothe family members for work and school, and provide needed health care. The poverty threshold in 2004, for example, was approximately $9,827 for a single-person household; $13,020 for a single parent with one child; and $19,157 for the typical two-parent family with two children. As a reference point, the median income for all families in 2004 was $43,300. Poverty thresholds for households of various sizes can be found at http://www.census.gov/hhes/poverty/threshld/thresh04.html.

(approximately in the year 1970) and ending near the conclusion of G. W. Bush's first term (2003), with the exception of older people, the black population, and to some degree households headed by single mothers, we find little change in poverty rates. The data included in Table 2.2 clearly reflect a consistent pattern of worsening economic conditions for the poor since year 2000. The socially conservative and fiscally undisciplined policies of this Bush Administration, exacerbated by the costs of the wars in the Middle East, have increased the vulnerability of the poor as jobs and other resources that could help some escape poverty are redirected elsewhere.

Table 2.2

Percent of Individuals Below the Poverty Level by Age, Gender, Family Relationship, Race and Ethnicity, and Location of Residence: 1970 to 2003.

	2003	2000	1990	1980	1970
Total Population	**12.5 %**	**11.3 %**	**13.5 %**	**13.0 %**	**12.6 %**
Children under age 18	17.6	16.2	20.6	18.3	15.1
Adults ages 18–64	10.8	9.6	11.4	10.1	9.0
Older adults ages 65 and over	10.2	9.9	12.2	15.7	24.6
Male population	11.2	9.9	11.7	11.2	11.1
Female population	13.7	12.6	15.2	14.7	14.0
White, non-Hispanic	8.2	7.4	8.8	9.1	7.3 (1973)*
Asian & Pacific Islander	11.8	10.7	12.2	**	**
Black	24.4	22.5	31.9	32.5	33.6
Hispanic	22.5	21.5	28.1	25.7	21.9 (1973)*
Married Couple	5.4	4.7	5.7	6.2	ND
Male householder (no wife present)	13.5	11.3	12.0	11.0	ND
Female householder (no husband)	28.0	25.4	33.4	32.7	32.5
Central city	17.7	16.3	19.0	17.2	14.2
Not central city (suburbs)	9.1	7.8	8.7	8.2	7.1
Nonmetropolitan area (rural)	14.2	13.4	16.3	15.4	16.9

* Classification revised in 1973.

** Data first reported in 1987.

Source: U.S. Census Bureau. Historical Poverty Tables. Tables 2, 3, 4, 7, and 8. Poverty Status of People by Age, Race and Ethnicity, Family Relationship, Gender, and Location: 1959 to 2003. http://www.census.gov/hhes/poverty/histpov/hstpov2.html. (Note: Change number, e.g., 2, in address to access each table.)

Although there are annual fluctuations in the poverty rate, examination of the rates at the end of each decade in Table 2.2 suggests that over time little progress has occurred for the total population. Several consistent patterns stand out in these data, however, that will be developed further in this book. First, in the short time from Year 2000 to Year 2003 every group in the population identified as potentially vulnerable has evidenced an increase in the rate of poverty. Second, poverty has been reduced for older people but has increased for children and youth. Third, males have consistently experienced lower rates of poverty than females, and whites have experienced less poverty than any other racial or ethnic group. Fourth, the poverty rate for married couples is considerably less than for households headed by single parents, and if the single parent is a female the rate more than doubles than if the single parent is a male. Finally, poverty is highest in the central cities of urban areas, slightly less in rural areas, and the escape of the wealthy to the suburbs is evident in these data. The picture is more complex on closer examination. A cross tabulation of these data for children under age 18, for example, reveals that young males experience less poverty than young females, white children are less likely to live in poverty than are children of color, children living with married parents are much better off than those living with a single parent, and children residing in the suburbs are much less likely to experience poverty than other children. In short, these data suggest that the person at greatest risk for experiencing poverty would be a young female of color, living with a single mother in the central city of an urban area.

These consistent patterns do not happen by chance. The data in Table 2.2 represent the culmination of laws, policies, norms, and cultural patterns that characterize life in the United States. Factors such as racism (and the opposite side of that coin, "white privilege"), sexism, and the other "isms" that separate people in this society play out in the rates of poverty and other social indicators (see Part Five of this book). Social workers are committed to helping individuals and families whose lives reflect these conditions—although some may have contributed to making their own situations more difficult. Social workers are also committed to examining these patterns and their causes in order to bring about changes that will help to prevent such unfair and disproportionate opportunities and to help people to achieve a high quality, fulfilling, and satisfying life.

Concluding Comment

More than two centuries ago the United States of America was formed with a goal of joining people to promote, among other things, the general welfare of all citizens. At times that goal has taken a backseat to individual and corporate interests, but at other times when national leadership has had support for strengthening its social programs the nation has come closer to realizing that objective. All people, however, do not equally experience that goal. If the United States is to remain strong and minimize the likelihood of attacks from internal or external terrorists—or by foreign powers—it must find ways to share the benefits of civilization with its own and other citizens.

More effective provision of social programs will require skilled professionals to help clients achieve more desirable levels of social functioning. Social workers are one of the groups of professional helpers who are central to the efforts to improve the general well-being of people. By examining Box 2.1 we can observe how the social programs that have evolved in the United States underpin the practice of a child welfare worker, Demetria, as she carried out the work in the case situation described in Chapter 1. Chapter 3 examines the profession of social work and its evolution from a group of concerned volunteers to its role today as a critical part of U.S. society.

Box 2.1

Social Welfare Programs Accessed by Demetria

In dealing with the case of Joseph Miles in Chapter 1, the social worker, Demetria, was able to make a difference in the lives of the Miles family because a number of social welfare programs were available in the community. As described in this chapter, the case involved at least three of the basic needs described by Maslow: *physiological survival needs* (the family's financial problems led to concern about adequate food and heat); *safety needs* (Joseph's bruising, whether from family violence or gang activity); and *belongingness needs* (Joseph's isolation from family and peers). Given the report that these fundamental needs may not have been met—or perhaps that the problems were caused—by Joseph's family, the society stepped in to protect a vulnerable child who may have been in danger by giving the authority and responsibility to the child welfare division to investigate.

There was no indication in the way Demetria investigated that she was influenced by the *Puritan ethic,* which would lead her to make moral judgments about why the family needed help, or even the *French Enlightenment* philosophy, which would judge the Miles family worthy or unworthy for the reasons they were poor. Rather, because a child was at risk—and indeed the whole family was at risk—several *safety net programs* were called into play. The child protection service represented by Demetria falls into the *personal services* category of social programs, while Medicaid and food stamps reflect *social provisions.* All of these programs were provided by a *government or public agency,* the county Social Welfare Department, of which the Child Welfare Division was one unit. The referral of Joseph to the teen group at the Boys and Girls Club (a *private, nonprofit agency*) was another *personal service* activity, aimed at *socialization* to more acceptable norms of behavior for a 12-year-old boy. This counseling program was open to any child in the community, with or without a defined "problem," and thus would be viewed as a *social utility program.* Finally, the recommendation by Demetria's supervisor to place the lack of resources to address employment problems on the agenda of the next local National Association of Social Workers meeting for discussion could, if the problem is determined to be widespread, lead to *social action* to correct that problem. Without these programs, Demetria would have been of limited help to this family.

KEY WORDS AND CONCEPTS

Hierarchy of needs
Social welfare
Mutual aid philosophy
Puritan philosophy
Social program goals (i.e., socialization, social integration, social control, and social action)
Social program conceptions (i.e., safety net, social utilities)

French Enlightenment philosophy
Conservative/liberal philosophies
Social program purposes (i.e., remediation, enhancement, prevention)
Human service program categories (i.e., social provisions, personal services, social action)

SUGGESTED INFORMATION SOURCES

Day, Phyllis J. *A New History of Social Welfare*, 4th Edition. Boston: Allyn and Bacon, 2002.

Ehrenreich, Barbara. *Nickel and Dimed: On (Not) Getting By in America*. New York: Henry Holt, 2001.

Herrick, John M., and Paul H. Stuart, eds. *Encyclopedia of Social Welfare History in North America*. Thousand Oaks, CA: Sage Publications, 2004.

Katz, Michael B. *The Price of Citizenship: Redefining the American Welfare State*. New York: Metropolitan Books, 2001.

Miringoff, Marc, and Marque-Lusia Miringoff. *The Social Health of the Nation: How America Is Really Doing*. New York: Oxford University Press, 1999.

Trattner, Walter I. *From Poor Law to Welfare State*, 6th Edition. New York: Free Press, 1999.

U.S. Budget. http://www.whitehouse.gov/omb/budget/fy2006/pdf/hist.pdf.

U.S. Poverty. http://www.census.gov/hhes/poverty/histpov/hstpov2.html. (Note: Change the number, e.g., htspov2, in address to access each table.)

ENDNOTES

1. Abraham H. Maslow, *Motivation and Personality* (New York: Harper & Row, 1970), pp. 25–28.

2. Harold L. Wilensky and Charles N. Lebeaux, *Industrial Society and Social Welfare* (New York: Free Press, 1965), p. 42.

3. Armando Morales, *Ando Sangrando (I Am Bleeding): A Study of Mexican American-Police Conflict* (La Puente, CA: Perspectiva Publications, 1972), p. 11.

4. Office of Budget Management. Fiscal Year 2003 Budget, Table 3.1. Outlays by Superfunction and Function: 1940–2007. http://w3.access.gpo.gov/usbudget/fy2003/sheets/hist03z1.xls.

5. Linda P. Anderson, Paul A. Sundet, and Irma Harrington, *The Social Welfare System in the United States: A Social Worker's Guide to Public Benefits Programs* (Boston: Allyn and Bacon, 2000), pp. 10–11.

6. Michael B. Katz, *The Price of Citizenship: Redefining the American Welfare State* (New York: Metropolitan Books, 2001).

7. Olivia A. Golden. "Assessing the New Federalism: Eight Years Later." *The Urban Institute*, 2005. http://www.urban.org/url.cfm?ID=311198.

8. Shelia R. Zedlewski. "Left Behind or Staying Away: Eligible Parents Who Remain Off TANF." The Urban Institute, 2002. http://urban.org/url.cfm?ID=310571.

9. National Debt Awareness Center. "How Congress Spends Your Money," July 16, 2005. http:/ /www.federalbudget.com. U.S. Department of the Treasury. "June 2004 Financial Operations Profile of the Economy," 2004. http://www.fms.treas.gov/bulletin/b24.pdf. U.S. Department of the Treasury. "The Debt to the Penny" July 28, 2005. http://www.publicdebt.treas.gov/opd/opdpenny.htm

Social Work: A Comprehensive Helping Profession

Prefatory Comment

The human services have become a central part of the fabric of U.S. society. Founded on the commitment to promote the general welfare of its people, society has gradually assumed increasing responsibility for ensuring that people have access to assistance in meeting their basic needs. This assistance takes the form of various social programs that are delivered by people who possess a variety of helping skills. The ability to help others is highly valued in all societies, whether provided to family and friends or others in one's community who are in need of assistance. In highly developed societies, including the United States, much of this helping has become so complicated that human services programs require highly trained professionals to deliver the necessary programs. It is within this context that social work was born.

What is perhaps the most basic form of helping has been termed *natural helping*. Before reaching a social worker or other professional helpers, clients often have been counseled or assisted in some way by family, friends, neighbors, or volunteers. Natural helping is based on a mutual relationship among equals, and the helper draws heavily on intuition and life experience to guide the helping process. The complexity of many social issues and the extensive knowledge and skill required to effectively provide some human services today exceed what natural helpers can typically accomplish. This has resulted in the emergence of several occupations, known as human services professions, that deliver more complicated services to people in need.

Professional helping is different from natural helping in that it is a disciplined approach focused on the needs of the client and it requires specific knowledge, values, and skills to guide the helping activity. Both natural and professional helping are valid means of assisting people in resolving issues related to their social functioning. In fact, many helping professionals first became interested in these careers because they were successful natural helpers and found the experience rewarding. Social workers often work closely with natural helping networks (i.e., both family members and friends) during the change process and as a source of support after professional service is terminated. However, natural helpers are not a substitute for competent professional help in addressing serious problems or gaining access to needed services.

Social work is the most comprehensive of human service occupations and, through time, has become recognized as the profession that centers its attention on helping people improve their social functioning. In simplest terms, social workers help people strengthen their interaction with various aspects of their world—their children, parents, spouse or other loved one, family, friends, coworkers, or even organizations and whole communities. Social work is also committed to changing factors in the society that diminish the quality of life for all people, but especially for those persons who are most vulnerable to social problems.

Social work's mission of serving both people and the social environment is ambitious. To fulfill that mission, social workers must possess a broad range of knowledge about the functioning of people and social institutions, as well as have a variety of skills for facilitating change in how individuals, organizations, and other social structures operate. This comprehensive mission has made social work an often misunderstood profession. Like the fable of the blind men examining the elephant with each believing that the whole elephant is like the leg, trunk, ear, and so on that he examined, too often people observe one example of social work and conclude that it represents the whole of professional activity. To appreciate the full scope of this profession, it is useful to examine its most fundamental characteristics—the themes that characterize social work.

The Central Themes Underpinning Social Work

Five themes reflect the character of social work. No one theme is unique to this profession, but in combination they provide a foundation on which to build one's understanding of social workers and their practice.

A Commitment to Social Betterment

Belief in the fundamental importance of improving the quality of social interaction for all people, that is, *social betterment,* is a central value of the social worker. The social work profession has taken the position that all people should have the opportunity for assistance in meeting their social needs.

Social work has maintained an idealism about the ability and responsibility of this society to provide opportunities and resources that allow each person to lead a full and rewarding life. It has been particularly concerned with the underdog—the most vulnerable people in the society. This idealism must not be confused with naivete. Social workers are often the most knowledgeable people in the community about the plight of the poor, the abused, the lonely, and others who for a variety of reasons are out of the mainstream of society or experiencing social problems. When social workers express their desire for changes that contribute to the social betterment of people, it is often viewed as a threat by those who want to protect the status quo.

A Goal to Enhance Social Functioning

The commitment to social betterment precludes a narrow focus on specific social problems. In fact, social work takes the position that social betterment involves more than addressing problems—it also involves assisting those who want to improve some aspect of their lives, even though it may not be considered as problematic. Social work, then, is concerned with helping people enhance their *social functioning*, that is, the manner in which they interact with people and social institutions.

Social workers help people and social institutions change in relation to a rapidly changing world. The technology explosion, information explosion, population explosion, and even the threat of nuclear explosion dramatically impact people's lives. Those who can readily adapt to these changes—and are not limited by discrimination due to race, cultural background, gender, age, or physical, emotional, or intellectual abilities—seldom use the services of social workers. Others who have become victims of this too rapidly changing world and its unstable social institutions, however, are likely to require professional help in dealing with this change.

An Action Orientation

Social work is a profession of doers. Social workers are not satisfied just to examine social issues. Rather, they take action to prevent problems from developing, attack problematic situations that can be changed, and help people deal with troublesome situations that cannot be changed. To do this, social workers provide services that include such activities as individual counseling, family and group therapy, linking people to the network of services in a community, fund raising, and even social action. Indeed, social work is an applied science.

An Appreciation for Human Diversity

To deal effectively with the wide range of individual and institutional change to which social work is committed, it has become a profession characterized by *diversity*—diversity of clientele, diversity of knowledge and skills, and diversity of services provided. In addition, social workers themselves come in all shapes, colors, ages, and descriptions.

Social workers view diversity as positive. They consider human difference desirable and appreciate the richness that can be offered a society through the culture, language, and traditions of various ethnic, racial, and cultural groups. They value the unique perspectives of persons of different gender, sexual orientation, or age groups, and they recognize and develop the strengths of persons who have been disadvantaged. What's more, social workers view their own diversity as an enriching quality that has created a dynamic profession that can respond to human needs in an ever-changing world.

A Versatile Practice Perspective

The wide range of human conditions with which social workers deal, the variety of settings in which they are employed, the extensive scope of services they provide, and the diverse populations they serve make it unrealistic to expect that a single practice approach could adequately support social work practice. Rather, the social worker must have a comprehensive repertoire of knowledge and techniques that can be used to meet the unique needs of individual clients and client groups.

The versatile social worker, then, must have a solid foundation of knowledge about the behavior of people and social institutions in order to understand the situations their clients bring to them. He or she also needs to understand that differing beliefs may affect the way people will interpret and react to those situations. And, finally, the social worker must have mastered a number of helping techniques from which he or she can imaginatively select and skillfully use to help individuals, families, groups, organizations, and communities improve their social functioning.

How do these themes affect social work practice? The following case example[*] is just one of many situations where a social worker might help a client:

> Karoline Truesdale, a school social worker, interviewed Kathy and Jim Swan in anticipation of the Swans' oldest son, Danny, beginning school in the fall. The Swans responded to Ms. Truesdale's invitation to the parents of all prospective kindergartners to talk over any concerns they might have about their children's schooling. When making the appointment, Kathy Swan indicated that her son, Danny, was near the cut-off age for entering school and may not be ready yet for kindergarten. When questioned further, Kathy expressed considerable ambivalence indicating that having him in school would help to relieve other burdens at home, but may be too much for Danny.

Karoline's notes from the interview contained the following information:

> Kathy Swan is 20 years old and about to deliver her third child. She indicates that they certainly did not need another mouth to feed at this time, but "accidents happen" and she will attempt to cope with this additional child when it is born (although she already appears physically and emotionally depleted). Jim is 21 years old and holds a temporary job earning minimum wage. He moved the family to the city because "money in agriculture has gone to hell" and a maintenance job was available at a manufacturing plant here. However, he was laid off after three months when the plant's workforce was reduced. Jim is angry that he moved the family for this job, yet the company felt no obligation to keep him on. He stated that "people in the country don't treat others like that." He is also worried that his temporary job will last only a few more weeks and commented that Kathy "spends money on those kids like it was going out of style." Jim said in no uncertain terms that he did not want and they could not afford another baby, but Kathy had refused to even consider an abortion.

[*]Sonia Nornes and Bradford W. Sheafor originally developed this case material for the Fort Collins (Colorado) Family Support Alliance.

The children are quite active and Danny pays little attention to Kathy's constant requests that he calm down. When Jim attempts to control Danny, Kathy accuses him of being too physical in his discipline. When questioned about this, Jim reported that his Dad "beat me plenty and that sure got results." Kathy complains that Jim does not appreciate the difficulty of being home with the children all of the time, and she objects to the increasing amount of time he is away in the evenings. Jim replied rather pointedly that "it is not much fun being at home anymore." Tension between Kathy and Jim was evident.

When questioned about their social contacts since moving to the city, both Kathy and Jim reported that it had been hard to make friends. They knew "everyone in town" before they moved, but it is different now. With his changing employment, Jim has not made any real friends at work, and Kathy feels isolated at home since Jim takes the car to work each day and the bus is her only means of transportation. She did indicate that one neighbor has been friendly, and they have met two couples they liked at church.

When asked specifically about Danny, Kathy reported that he has been ill frequently with colds and chronic ear infections. She hesitantly described his behavior as troublesome and hoped the school's structure would help him. Kathy described a Sunday school teacher who called him hyperactive and suggested that she not take him to Sunday school anymore. Kathy wondered if there was some kind of treatment that would help Danny and allowed that she was "about at the end of her rope with that child."

It was clear to Karoline that both Kathy and Jim wanted Danny to begin school. But was Danny ready for school—and would the school be ready for Danny? Would Danny's entering school be best for him? Would it resolve the family's problems? Are there other things that could be done to help this family and, perhaps, prevent other problems from emerging?

Within the strict definition of her job, Ms. Truesdale could assist the Swans in reaching a decision about school attendance and complete her service to this family. With her "social betterment" concern, however, resolution of only the question about Danny's entering school would not be sufficient. As a social worker, Karoline would hope to help the Swan family address some of the more basic issues they face in order to improve the overall quality of their lives.

Social workers are not experts on all problems clients may experience. Ms. Truesdale's experience, for example, would not prepare her to make judgments about Danny's health and the possible relationship between his chronic colds and ear infections and his behavior problems. She might refer the Swans to a low-cost medical clinic where a diagnosis of Danny's health problems can be made. She is, however, an expert in "social functioning" and can help Jim and Kathy Swan work on their parenting skills, strengthen the quality of their communication, assist them in developing social relationships in the community, and, perhaps, help Jim obtain job training and stable employment. Karoline's "action orientation" would not allow her to procrastinate. She would be anxious to engage this family in assessing the issues it faces and would support Kathy and Jim as they take action to resolve them.

The Swan family represents at least one form of "human diversity." They are a rural family attempting to adapt to an urban environment. Ms. Truesdale knows that it will take time and probably some help to make this adjustment. She will explore strengths that may have been derived from their rural background. Perhaps Jim's skills in gardening and machinery repair would prove to be an asset in some lines of employment. Also, their rural friendliness may prove beneficial in establishing new social relationships, and they might be helped to build friendships through their church or neighborhood, or to use other resources where they can find informal sources of support (i.e., natural helping).

Service to the Swan family will require considerable practice "versatility." Ms. Truesdale will need to assist the family in problem solving around whether or not to send Danny to school. She will hopefully engage them in more in-depth family counseling. She might invite them to join a parents' group she leads to discuss child-rearing practices, link them with medical and psychological testing services for Danny, and help Mr. Swan obtain job training. If Danny does attend school next year, Karoline might work closely with his teacher and Mrs. Swan to monitor Danny's progress and address any problems in his social functioning that may arise. If he does not attend school, an alternative program might be found where he can develop the socialization skills required in the classroom. Clearly, a wide range of practice activities would be needed and Karoline must be versatile in her practice to apply them.

The Mission of Social Work

While social work practice requires considerable variation in activity, at a more abstract level the profession has consistently maintained that its fundamental *mission* is directly serving people in need and, at the same time, making social institutions more responsive to people. Although this unique mission has been steadfastly held for more than a century, it has been difficult to develop public understanding of its uniqueness among the helping professions. One way to understand this profession is to examine its three primary purposes: caring, curing, and changing.

Caring

Throughout their history social workers have sought to improve the quality of life for the most vulnerable groups in the population. At times the best knowledge we can muster is inadequate to prevent or cure the many problems encountered by the disabled, elderly, terminally ill, and other persons with limited capacity for social functioning. Social workers recognize that certain conditions in life cannot be corrected. Yet, the victims of these conditions deserve not only humane but high-quality care.

Caring that makes people comfortable and helps them cope with their limitations is frequently the most valuable service a social worker can provide. Sometimes caring takes the form of arranging for meals to be delivered or for income to be supplemented, and ensuring that adequate housing is provided. At other times, the person and/or family may require caring in the form of counseling to better adjust to an unchangeable situation like a disability or terminal illness. There is also an important leadership role for social work in helping communities create the necessary services to provide such care. The fundamental intention of caring for those in need is a central purpose of social work practice.

Curing

Another thrust of social work practice has been to provide treatment for individuals and families experiencing problems in social functioning. Depending on client needs, direct services ranging from psychosocial therapy to behavioral modification, reality therapy, crisis intervention, and various group and family therapy approaches are used by social workers.[1] These approaches do not automatically cure social problems in the same way a physician might prescribe a medication to cure an infection. In fact, most social workers would argue that at best they can only help clients cure themselves. The contribution the social worker makes is the ability to engage the client in actively working toward change, to accurately assess the individual and societal factors that have created the need for change, to select appropriate techniques for a given client and situation, and to use these techniques effectively in conjunction with the clients to accomplish the desired results.

Changing the Society

Social change is the third primary purpose of social work. Social workers are committed to reforming existing laws, procedures, and attitudes until they are more responsive to human needs. Many pioneer social workers were reformers who worked to improve conditions in slums, hospitals, and poorhouses. Today, social workers actively influence social legislation in an effort to create new social programs or to change factors that contribute to damaging social conditions such as racism, sexism, and poverty.

Social workers also seek to change negative public attitudes about the more vulnerable members of society by providing public education and facilitating the empowerment of the affected members of the population to advocate for their own interests. Social workers, then, bring about change in the society by representing the interests of their clientele and/or helping clients convince decision makers at the local, state, or national levels to respond to human needs.

The mission of social work, then, is captured in the following three-part statement. Social work's mission includes:

▶ Caring for those who must live with an unchangeable social problem
▶ Curing people's social problems by helping them change and/or attempt to change the condition that causes the problem
▶ Changing conditions in the society that make some people more vulnerable to social problems

This mission, however, does not in itself clearly distinguish social work from other helping-oriented occupations. To gain further clarity, one must examine definitions of social work.

Defining Social Work

Unfortunately, social work has been hard to define. Different dictionary definitions treat social work as a set of skills, a job title, or even an activity that might be performed by volunteers. None treat this as a profession with extensive academic and practice experience required for the work. Although these definitions describe some of the tasks some social workers may perform, they fail to distinguish social workers from others who may also engage in these activities. Therefore, it is informative to examine how social workers define themselves.

Three concerted efforts by the social work profession have been made to arrive at a clear definition of social work. The first occurred in the 1920s when the American Association of Social Workers convened a series of meetings of key agency executives in Milford, Pennsylvania. These representatives from a range of practice settings identified several factors that appeared to be common to all social work practice, but they could not agree on a concise definition of social work. However, the Milford Conference encouraged further efforts at articulating a definition of social work when it concluded that social work's common features were more substantial than the differences related to practice in different settings.[2]

The 1950s brought a second surge of interest in developing a clear conception of social work. The merger of several specialized social work practice organizations and the more generic American Association of Social Workers into the National Association of Social Workers (NASW) was completed in 1955. For a time, a spirit of unity dominated the social work profession, and the effort to find a definition of social work that would reflect the commonality in diverse practice activities began in earnest. A critical step was the publication of the "Working Definition of Social Work Practice" in 1958. Although not yet providing a comprehensive definition of social work, the document established an important basis for subsequent definitions by identifying three common goals of social work practice:[3]

1. To assist individuals and groups to identify and resolve or minimize problems arising out of disequilibrium between themselves and their environment.
2. To identify potential areas of disequilibrium between individuals or groups and the environment in order to prevent the occurrence of disequilibrium.
3. To seek out, identify, and strengthen the maximum potential of individuals, groups, and communities.

Thus, the "Working Definition" established that social workers are concerned with curative or treatment goals, as well as emphasizing the importance of social change or prevention. In addition, the definition recognized the focus of social work on the interactions between people and their environments and the responsibility of social workers to provide services to people as individuals, as parts of various groups, and as members of communities.

Third, in the 1970s and 1980s, NASW published three special issues of its major journal, *Social Work,* that generated substantial debate and discussion, although not conclusions, about the nature of social work.[4] This activity enhanced understanding of the central features that characterize social work but did not lead to a definitive description of this profession.

Although NASW has never formally adopted a definition of social work, a one-sentence definition developed by one of its committees has gained widespread acceptance.

> Social work is the professional activity of helping individuals, groups, or communities enhance or restore their capacity for social functioning and creating societal conditions favorable to that goal.[5]

This statement provides a clear and concise "dictionary definition" of the profession. It draws important boundaries around social work. First, social work is considered professional activity. Professional activity requires a particular body of knowledge, values, and skills, as well as a discrete purpose that guides one's practice activities. When practice is judged professional, community sanction to perform these tasks is assumed to be present, and the profession, in turn, is expected to be accountable to the public for the quality of services provided.

Second, this definition captures a uniqueness of social work. It makes clear that social workers serve a range of client systems that include individuals, families or other household units, groups, organizations, neighborhoods, communities, and even larger units of society. For social work, the identification of one's client is tricky because a client or target of practice activity may range from an individual to a state or nation. The unique activities of the social worker are directed toward helping all of those systems interact more effectively and require professional education as preparation.

Finally, the last part of the definition concerns social work's *dual focus on person and environment.* Social workers help people enhance or restore their capacity for social functioning. At the same time, they work to change societal conditions that may help or hinder people from improving their social functioning. Herein lies another uniqueness of social work. Whereas some professions focus on change in the person and others on changing the environment, social work's attention is directed to the connections between person and environment.

When working with clients, social workers must take into consideration both the characteristics of the person and the impinging forces from the environment. In contrast, the physician is primarily prepared to treat physical aspects of the individual, and the attorney is largely concerned with the operation of the legal system in the larger environment (although both the physician and attorney should give secondary attention to other, related systems). Social work recognizes that each person brings to the helping situation a set of behaviors, needs, and beliefs that are the result of his or her unique experiences from birth. Yet it also recognizes that whatever is brought to the situation must be related to the world as that person confronts

Figure 3.1

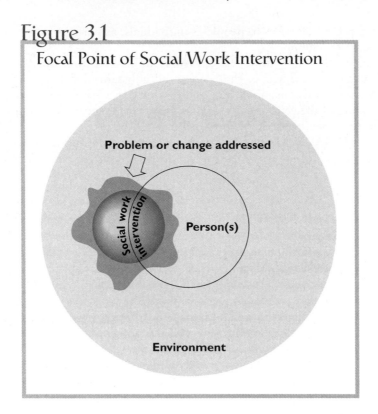

Focal Point of Social Work Intervention

Problem or change addressed

Social work intervention

Person(s)

Environment

it. By focusing on transactions between the person and his or her environment, social interaction can be improved.

Figure 3.1 depicts this unique focus of social work. Social workers operate at the boundary between people and their environment. They are not prepared to deal with all boundary matters. Rather, they address those matters that are judged problematic or have been selected as a way to contribute to the enhancement of social functioning. In sum, social workers temporarily enter the lives of their clients to help them improve their transactions with important elements of their environment. To further understand social work, it is instructive to examine the approaches social workers use when assisting their clients or advocating for social change.

Social Work Practice Approaches

Arriving at a practice approach that is sufficiently flexible and encompassing to relate to this complex profession has proven difficult. In fact, social work might be characterized during much of its history as a profession in search of a practice approach. That search began with the development of several distinct practice methods.

Traditional Practice Methods

As part of the drive to become a unique profession, social work sought to identify a distinctive method of practice that would distinguish it from other helping professions such as law, medicine, and psychology. The first practice method to develop, *social casework,* was first described in the 1917 classic social work book, *Social Diagnosis.*[6] In this book, Mary Richmond focused on the requirements for effective practice with individuals and families, regardless of the type of problem presented. The book filled an important void in social work by introducing a literature describing social work practice. The principles of social casework identified by Richmond were enthusiastically adopted by social workers, and the profession moved its primary focus to work with individuals and families. The popularity of Freudian psychology in the 1920s and 1930s also directed social work toward holding the individual primarily responsible for his or her condition, rather than to the more controversial approaches associated with changing social institutions that had previously characterized much of social work practice. Abbott noted that Richmond later expressed concern over this trend to overemphasize the person side of the person-environment mission of social work:

> The good social worker, says Miss Richmond, doesn't go on helping people out of a ditch. Pretty soon she begins to find out what ought to be done to get rid of the ditch.[7]

Social workers concerned with providing services to groups took longer to develop a set of guiding principles, partially because those social workers disagreed among themselves as to whether they should identify professionally with the emerging field of social work. This disagreement was resolved in the 1930s in favor of identifying with social work, and thus a second distinct method *social group work,* evolved.

The third practice method to develop was *community organization.* With many social agencies and social programs evolving in each community, their coordination and the evaluation of their effectiveness became important and, to meet that need, another distinct practice area emerged. Community organization became the practice method primarily concerned with coordinating the distribution of resources and building linkages among existing services.

In addition to using one of these three primary practice methods in their work, many social workers found themselves responsible for administering social agencies and conducting research on the effectiveness of social programs. Their experience and education usually left them with little preparation for these indirect service activities. By the late 1940s *administration* and *research* had evolved as practice methods in social work. Viewed as secondary methods, they were seen as a supplement to a person's ability as a caseworker, group worker, or community organizer.

Multimethod Practice Approach

Concurrent with the development of these five distinct practice approaches was the growing commitment to the evolution of social work as a single profession with a unifying practice method. A major study of social work and social work education, the Hollis–Taylor Report, was concluded in 1951. It recommended that, because the breadth of social work practice required social workers to intervene at more than one level of the client system, social work education should prepare students with a beginning level of competence in each of the five practice methods.[8]

The multimethod practice approach proved a good fit with the varied demands for social work practice, but failed to yield the unifying practice theme the profession needed. Practitioners typically identified with a dominant method and used the others sparingly.

Generalist Practice Approach

Supported by concepts drawn from social systems theory, the generalist approach to practice began to emerge in the late 1960s. As Balinsky stated, "The complexity of human problems necessitates a broadly oriented practitioner with a versatile repertoire of methods and skills capable of interacting in any one of a number of systems."[9] The generalist model provided that versatility and met the requirement for a flexible approach to social work practice demanded by the increasing complexity and interrelatedness of human problems.

Generalist practice contains two fundamental components. First, it provides a perspective from which the social worker views the practice situation. Social systems theory helps the social worker to maintain a focus on the interaction between systems—that is, the person–environment transactions—and to continually look for ways to intervene in more than one relevant system. Second, rather than attempting to make the client's situation fit the methodological orientation of the social worker, the situation is viewed as determining the practice approach to be used. Thus, the social worker is required to have a broad knowledge and skill base from which to serve clients or client systems and to have the ability to appropriately select from that base to meet the needs of the clients.

Although many social workers contend that the generalist approach has been part of social work practice since its inception, only recently have there been analysis and explication of this practice approach. With the accreditation requirement that both baccalaureate- and master's-level social workers be prepared as generalist practitioners, there has been a resurgence of activity aimed at clarifying the nature of generalist practice in recent years. In their article entitled "Milford Redefined: A Model of Initial and Advanced Generalist Social Work," Schatz, Jenkins, and Sheafor delineate the key elements of generalist social work at both the initial and advanced generalist levels.[10]

This model recognizes that there is a *generic foundation* for all social work, whether generalist or specialist, that includes such factors as knowledge about the social work profession, social work values, the purpose of social work, ethnic/diversity sensitivity, basic communication skills, understanding of human relationships, and others.

The *generalist perspective*, according to this model: (1) is informed by sociobehavioral and ecosystems knowledge; (2) incorporates ideologies that include democracy, humanism, and empowerment; (3) requires a worker to be theoretically and methodologically open when approaching a practice situation; (4) is client-centered and problem-focused; (5) considers using both direct and indirect intervention; and (6) is research-based.

At the *initial generalist* level of practice, the social worker builds on the generic foundation and, using the generalist perspective, must at least be capable of: (1) engaging effectively in interpersonal helping; (2) managing change processes; (3) appropriately selecting and utilizing multilevel intervention modes; (4) intervening in multiple-sized systems as determined by the practice situation; (5) performing varied practice roles; (6) assessing and examining one's own practice; and (7) functioning successfully within an agency.

The *advanced generalist* social worker engages in more difficult practice tasks and, therefore, operates from an expanded knowledge base about individuals, groups, organizations, and communities that is developed in master's degree programs. The advanced generalist must also develop increased skills to intervene in direct service provision with individuals, families, and groups at one end of the multiple-level practice spectrum, and, at the other end, address more complex indirect practice situations such as supervision, administration, and policy or program evaluation. Finally, the advanced generalist is expected to approach social work practice from an eclectic, but disciplined and systematic, stance and to simultaneously engage in both theoretical research and practice evaluation.

Specialist Practice Approaches

In contrast to the generalist, a number of specialized practice approaches have emerged. *Specialist* social work practice is characterized by the application of selected knowledge and skills to a narrowed area of practice based on practice setting, population served, social problems addressed, and/or practice intervention mode used. In other words, this practice approach begins with a preference about the knowledge and skills required for practice in that specialized area and serves clients whose needs fit into those more narrow, but in-depth, worker competencies.

While education for generalist practice is offered in baccalaureate programs or the early part of master's-level programs, specialist education has increasingly become the emphasis of the latter part of a master's degree. Master's social work education programs sometimes offer the advanced generalist as their area of concentration but more typically build their curricula on one or more fields of practice, problem areas, populations-at-risk, intervention methods, or specific practice contexts. Although individual schools of social work typically focus on only a small number of specialties, the following illustrates the range of specializations a school might offer.

> *Fields of Practice:* for example, services to families, children, and youth; services to the elderly; health; mental health; developmental disabilities; education; business and industry; neighborhood and community development; income maintenance; employment.

Problem Areas: for example, crime and delinquency; substance abuse; developmental disabilities; family violence; mental illness; neighborhood deterioration; poverty; racism; sexism.

Populations-at-Risk: for example, children and youth; the aged; women; single parents; ethnic populations; persons in poverty; migrants; gay and lesbian persons; the chronically mentally ill.

Intervention Methods or Roles: for example, specific practice approaches with individuals, families, and groups; consultation; community organization; social planning; administration; case management; social policy formulation; research.

Practice Contexts and Perspectives: for example, industry; hospitals; rural or urban areas.

Today social work embraces both generalist and specialist approaches to practice. The generalist viewpoint supports the commonality that unites social work into one profession; the specialist approach helps to delineate unique areas for in-depth social work practice.

Social Workers: Their Many Faces

How has the emergence of a profession concerned with helping people change conditions that affect their social functioning played out? First, a fairly specific career pattern has emerged, and, second, a substantial number of people have selected social work as a career.

Career Patterns of Social Workers

Varying career patterns have evolved as the practice of social work has changed over time. The early social workers were volunteers or paid staff who required no specific training or educational program to qualify for the work. When formal education programs were instituted at the turn of the century, they were training programs located in the larger social agencies. In fact, it was not until 1939 that accreditation standards required that all recognized social work education must be offered in institutions of higher education. There was also controversy over whether appropriate social work education could be offered at the baccalaureate level as well as at the more professionally respectable master's level. The reorganization of social work into one professional association (the National Association of Social Workers, NASW) and one professional education association (the Council on Social Work Education, CSWE) in the 1950s yielded a single-level profession. At that time, only the master's degree from an accredited school of social work was considered "legitimate" social work preparation. Today, the MSW degree still is considered the "terminal practice degree" in social work, but other professional practice levels are now recognized. In 2003, 14,482 persons received the MSW degree from one of the 159 fully accredited programs, making it the dominant qualification for social work practice.[11]

It was not until 1970 that the NASW recognized baccalaureate-level (BSW) social workers as members of the Association. The Council on Social Work Education subsequently created accreditation standards, and, by 2003, 437 schools throughout the United States graduated 11,159 persons with the BSW (at times this may be a BA or a BS degree) from an accredited social work education program.[12] Another career level had been recognized.

Increasingly, social workers are also completing doctoral degrees in social work, either the Doctor of Social Work (DSW) or the Doctor of Philosophy (Ph.D.). In 2003, for example, about 289 persons completed a doctorate in social work from sixty-six schools in the United States.[13] In addition, a number of other social workers also completed doctorates in related disciplines. Most doctoral-level social workers are employed in teaching or research positions, but an increasing number of doctoral programs aimed at preparing people for direct social work are emerging. Doctoral programs, however, are not subject to accreditation by CSWE and are not recognized as professional preparation for social work practice. Thus, the MSW continues to be viewed as the terminal practice degree.

By 1981, NASW found it necessary to develop a classification system that would help to clarify the various entry points to social work and define the educational and practice requirements at each level. This system sorts out the somewhat mixed career levels in social work:[14]

Basic Professional	Requires a baccalaureate degree from a program accredited by CSWE.
Specialized Professional	Requires a master's degree from a program accredited by CSWE.
Independent Professional	Requires an accredited MSW and at least two years of post-master's experience under appropriate professional supervision.
Advanced Professional	Requires special theoretical, practice, administrative, or policy proficiency or ability to conduct advanced research or studies in social welfare, usually demonstrated through a doctoral degree in social work or a closely related social science discipline.

NASW's classification scheme has several benefits. First, it identifies and clarifies the practice levels existing in social work and, in general terms, spells out the competencies that both clients and employers can expect from workers at each level. Second, it describes a continuum of social work practice with several entry points based on education and experience. Finally, it suggests a basis for job classification that can increasingly distinguish among the various levels of social work competence and assist agencies in selecting appropriately prepared social workers to fill their positions.

Characteristics of Today's Social Workers

Who are the people who have elected a career in social work? It is difficult to determine accurately the characteristics of today's social workers because a single source based on an agreed upon definition of social work does not exist. NASW reports a membership of approximately 153,000, but given that over 500,000 social workers graduated from CSWE accredited programs in the past 30 years, it is clear that only a fraction of the qualified social workers have elected to join NASW.[15] All social workers are not required to be licensed, but approximately 300,000[16] hold a state license to practice social work. Based on positions classified by employers as social work jobs, the Bureau of Labor Statistics (BLS) estimates there are approximately 477,000 social workers in the United States. Finally, the most current population survey in which people self-classify their occupation estimates that there are 670,000 to 730,000 social workers.[17] Each estimate is flawed, but it is likely that the BLS estimate is the most accurate representation of the number of practicing social workers in the United States today.

The data in Table 3.1 indicate that social workers (as reflected in NASW's membership) are largely white females. Less than one-fourth are males, and minority group members make up only between 11 and 14 percent. It is also clear from these data that workers at the different educational levels have established some niches regarding the settings where they are employed. Baccalaureate-level (or basic) social workers are most likely to be employed in social services agencies such as a public human services department or a small nonprofit community agency, followed by employment in a health/mental health agency, or a residential facility such as a group home or nursing home. Clearly the feature that distinguishes the basic social worker from the specialized or independent social worker is the concentration in practice positions working with older people and the relatively small proportion employed in mental health.

Master's-level workers, by contrast, are considerably more likely to work in mental health (particularly the for-profit agencies) or to maintain their own private practice in which they independently contract with their clients to provide services. The specialized- or independent-level social workers also report that they are somewhat more likely than basic workers to serve in administrative and management positions.

The doctoral-level social workers are most likely to be employed by a college or university, although about one-fourth of them are in private practice and another one-fifth are employed in health/mental health settings. Social workers at this advanced level are primarily direct service clinicians or social work faculty members and, to a lesser extent, agency administrators.

A 2004 member salary survey conducted by NASW helps to provide a picture of the earning power of social workers. The median annual income for social workers in that membership sample was $51,900 for full-time social workers during the calendar year 2003.[18] Previous membership studies indicated that social workers

Table 3.1

Characteristics of Baccalaureate-, Master's-, and Doctoral-Level Social Workers

Social Worker Characteristic	BSW	MSW	DSW
Gender: Female	89.7%	78.5%	58.5%
Minority group member	13.7	11.3	13.6
Primary employment setting			
Social services agency	33.7	20.5	10.1
Health/mental health facility (hospital and outpatient)	26.6	38.9	20.0
Residential care facility	21.1	6.4	2.2
School (preschool through grade 12)	3.8	7.1	3.2
Private practice	3.1	20.2	24.1
Courts/justice system	2.6	3.9	0.6
College/university	2.6	2.6	37.2
Other	6.3	3.0	2.5
Primary practice area			
Children-families	29.2	24.9	19.6
Mental health	18.3	39.6	40.7
Medical health	17.0	13.2	7.7
Aging	16.7	4.2	3.7
Schools	2.6	5.4	4.1
Criminal justice	2.5	1.1	1.1
Other	13.2	10.8	22.2
Primary job function			
Clinical/direct service	65.5	71.1	40.4
Administration/management	10.6	15.7	16.7
Teaching/training	5.9	2.8	32.1
Supervision	4.6	5.7	2.3
Other	13.5	4.2	8.4

Source: Margaret Gibelman and Philip H. Schervish, *Who We Are: A Second Look* (Washington, D.C.: NASW Press, 1997), 54, 59, 86, 103, and 114.

begin at a lower salary level upon completing the professional degree and then reach the median salary at around 15 years of experience. Prior data also indicate that the typical person with a BSW degree earns about $1,000 per month less than the person with a MSW degree, and a person with a doctorate earns about $ 1,000 per month more that the MSW graduate.[19]

These salary levels are not sufficient in themselves to draw top-quality professionals to this demanding work. Salaries in medicine, law, psychology, and many other helping professions exceed that of social workers.[20] While social work wages are considered "high" by the Bureau of Labor Statistics (i.e., in the second highest quartile of earnings for all occupations), social work salaries are relatively low for positions requiring professional preparation. Other rewards from the work must therefore be considered more important than earning power to maintain a competent labor force of social workers. In a substantial analysis of the labor market for social workers prepared for the John A. Hartford Foundation, economist Michael Barth concludes that the "taste" for providing social work services is exceptionally strong. Barth indicates that from an economist's perspective, a strong taste for a profession implies that the worker would seek that work even if it conveys greater risk of low pay and despite the potential of the worker to earn greater pay elsewhere.[21] In short, social workers appear to be more attracted to the opportunity to make a difference in the lives of people than to select a profession that will result in high earning power.

Concluding Comment

Since its inception more than a century ago, social work has emerged as a comprehensive helping profession. From the beginning, social workers sought that elusive common denominator that would depict this profession as clearly as possible and help social work form into a cohesive entity. Recognition of the common mission of working simultaneously with both people and their environments to improve social functioning has consistently served as social work's primary mission and thus differentiates social work from the other helping professions. In addition to helping people deal with their environments, social workers also consider it their mission to bring about social change in order to prevent problems or to make social institutions more responsive to the needs of people— especially the most vulnerable members of the society. With this person and environment focus, social workers provide a combination of caring, curing, and changing activities that help people improve the quality of their lives and, therefore, help the society accomplish its goal of promoting the general welfare. In Box 3.1 the practice activities of Demetria (see Chapter 1), functioning as a new social worker and all that her professional status implies, illustrates how her social work orientation plays out in her work with the Miles family.

Social work has evolved a career ladder that recognizes professionals at four levels: basic, specialized, independent, and advanced. This classification scheme recognizes that at each of the four levels somewhat different job activities occur. The two entry levels (i.e., basic and specialized professional levels) require that the worker complete the requisite educational preparation represented in the accreditation standards of the Council on Social Work Education. At the latter two levels, additional practice experience and expertise and/or advanced education warrant the recognition.

Box 3.1

Demetria's Social Work Orientation

The case in Chapter 1 revealed a social worker's approach to investigating and beginning service when addressing a possible child abuse or neglect complaint. Demetria, the social worker, had just completed her social work degree, and the report from the school related to Joseph Miles was her first "solo" case. Of course, she had the backup of her supervisor, but nevertheless she was understandably apprehensive about being able to do a good job. Clearly the demands for knowledge and skill were beyond that expected of a *natural helper* or *volunteer.* Complex human issues such as this require a well-equipped *professional helper,* in this case, a professional social worker.

Demetria's work clearly demonstrated a commitment to *social betterment* as she carried her assessment beyond the minimum required to establish or reject the suspected child abuse. She sought to understand and address the multiple issues that were combining to affect Joseph; was *versatile* in her practice approach by addressing individual, family, and community issues; and did something about what she found (an *action orientation*). Because none of the issues in this case were unchangeable, the work did not fall into the *caring* aspect of social work's mission. Most of the effort involved the *curing* and *changing* functions that social workers address. Fitting Demetria's work into the NASW *definition of social work,* the paraphrasing might read "Demetria's practice was the professional activity of helping Joseph and the Miles family restore their capacity for social functioning and (if strengthening the employment finding resources proves to be needed) creating a more supportive societal resource for those needing employment assistance."

In the NASW classification of levels of professional social work practice, Demetria was a *basic social worker,* having just completed her BSW preparation, and her supervisor was probably an *independent* or *advanced social worker* according to that classification system. Demetria's practice approach was that of an *initial generalist.* She did not try to fit Joseph and his mom into a specialized method or practice approach. Instead, she started by identifying their issues and drawing on multiple approaches to resolve those issues, such as individual counseling (for Joseph and his mother); involvement in a peer group (for Joseph); referral to other needed resources in the community; and a consideration of social action to improve the community resources.

KEY WORDS AND CONCEPTS

Natural and professional helping
Social betterment
Social functioning
Human diversity
Caring/Curing/Changing
"Working Definition" of social work
"NASW Definition" of social work
Dual focus on person and environment

Generalist social work practice
Specialist social work practice
Traditional practice methods
NASW classification of practice levels
   (basic, specialized, independent,
   advanced)
Professional education levels (BSW, MSW,
   DSW/Ph.D.)

SUGGESTED INFORMATION SOURCES

Canadian Association of Social Workers. http://www.casw-acts.ca

Corey, Mariane Schneider, and Gerald Corey. *Becoming a Helper,* 4th Edition. Pacific Grove, CA: Brooks/Cole, 2003.

National Association of Social Workers. http://www.naswdc.org

LeCroy, Craig W. *The Call to Social Work: Life Stories.* Washington, D.C.: NASW Press, 2002.

Specht, Harry, and Mark E. Courtney. *Unfaithful Angles: How Social Work Has Abandoned Its Mission.* New York: Free Press, 1994.

ENDNOTES

1. For a brief description of a number of practice approaches, see Bradford W. Sheafor and Charles R. Horejsi, *Techniques and Guidelines for Social Work Practice,* 7th Edition (Boston: Allyn and Bacon, 2006), Chapter 6.

2. American Association of Social Workers, *Social Casework: Generic and Specific: A Report of the Milford Conference* (New York: National Association of Social Workers, 1974), p. 11. (Original work published in 1929.)

3. Harriet M. Bartlett, "Towards Clarification and Improvement of Social Work Practice," *Social Work* 3 (April 1958): 5–7.

4. See *Social Work* 19 (September 1974); *Social Work* 22 (September 1977); and *Social Work* 26 (January 1981).

5. National Association of Social Workers, *Standards for Social Service Manpower* (Washington, D.C.: NASW, 1973), pp. 4–5.

6. Mary E. Richmond, *Social Diagnosis* (New York: Russell Sage Foundation, 1917).

7. Edith Abbott, "The Social Caseworker and the Enforcement of Industrial Legislation," in *Proceedings of the National Conference on Social Work, 1918* (Chicago: Rogers and Hall, 1919), p. 313.

8. Ernest V. Hollis and Alice L. Taylor, *Social Work Education in the United States* (New York: Columbia University Press, 1951).

9. Rosalie Balinsky, "Generic Practice in Graduate Social Work Curricula: A Study of Educators' Experiences and Attitudes," *Journal of Education for Social Work* 18 (Fall 1982): 47.

10. Mona S. Schatz, Lowell E. Jenkins, and Bradford W. Sheafor, "Milford Redefined: A Model of Initial and Advanced Generalist Social Work," *Journal of Social Work Education* 26 (Fall 1990): 217–231.

11. Todd N. Lennon, ed., *Statistics on Social Work Education in the United States: 2003* (Alexandria, VA: Council on Social Work Education, 2005), Table 57.

12. Ibid., Table 56.

13. Ibid., Table 57.

14. Reprinted with permission from *NASW Standards for the Classification of Social Work Practice,* Policy Statement 4 (Silver Spring, MD: National Association of Social Workers, 1981), p. 9.

15. Bradford W. Sheafor, "Three Decades of Baccalaureate Social Work: A Grade Card on How the Professionalization of the BSW has Played Out," *Journal of Baccalaureate Social Work* 6 (Spring 2001): 32.

16. "Licensed Social Workers in the United States." Draft Report, August 2005. Center for Health Workforce Studies. (New York: New York State University at Albany.).
17. Bureau of Labor Statistics, Occupational Employment and Wages, November 2003. ftp://ftp/bls.gov/pub/news.release/History/ocwage.11122004.news
18. "Survey Data Show Earnings Increased," *NASW News* 49 (October 2004): 1.
19. Practice Research Network Report 1–1. "Social Work Income" (Washington, D.C.: National Association of Social Workers, 2000).
20. U.S. Bureau of Labor Statistics. "May 2004 National Occupational Employment and Wage Estimates." http://stats.bls.gov/oes/current/oes_21co.htm
21. Michael C. Barth, "Social Work Labor Market: A First Look," *Social Work* 48 (January 2003): 9–19.

4

The Emergence of Social Work as a Profession

Prefatory Comment

The growth and development of social work were not planned events. They evolved from the humanitarian response to human suffering in the late-1800s that led to the creation of a workforce to address social problems and later to the profession of social work. The title of this book, *Social Work: A Profession of Many Faces,* highlights the importance social work has given to becoming a fully recognized profession. This chapter examines social work's emergence in the United States, with emphasis on how the desire to become a profession has shaped its actions. It begins with a review of the nature of professions, particularly the helping professions, and traces the emergence of social work during the past century. The result has been that several efforts at addressing social needs coalesced into a single, yet diverse, profession.

The Nature of Professions

A field of sociological inquiry is devoted to the definition and description of the nature of professions. One of the central figures in this field, Wilbert Moore, concluded that "to have one's occupational status accepted as professional or to have one's occupational conduct judged as professional is highly regarded in all post industrial societies and in at least the modernizing sectors of others."[1]

Professions are highly regarded, in part because they have been granted authority to perform essential services that ensure survival and help people enhance the quality of their lives. The benefit of being considered professional has drawn many occupational groups to claim professional status, for example, professional athletes and professional musicians. Thus the term has sometimes been used to describe persons who are paid for activities that others might perform for recreation or pleasure. Also, the term is at times applied when a person becomes highly specialized in an area of competence, for example, a real "pro" at finding bargains on the Internet. In this book, however, the term *profession* is used in its more traditional sense of identifying a set of carefully prepared and highly qualified persons who assist people in dealing with complex matters in their lives.

Three elements help to explain the unique characteristics of the occupations that are considered to be professions. First, professionals must be free of constraints that might limit their ability to select what they consider to be the best way to assist people in situations to resolve problems or improve the quality of their lives. The maintenance of this *professional autonomy* has been most successful in the private professions that typically contract directly with their clients (e.g., medicine, clinical psychology), although increasingly constraints imposed by managed care companies are eroding this flexibility. In agency-based or public professions such as social work and nursing, organizations employ the professionals and then contract with the clients to provide the needed services. In these situations, it is recognized that the agency's rules and regulations will inevitably limit the autonomy of the professionals to exercise independent judgment regarding the manner in which services are provided.

Second, society has granted *professional authority* to a few people who have acquired the necessary knowledge and skills to provide the needed services in a given area of professional practice. Society grants this authority because it has, in effect, determined that it is inefficient, if not impossible, for every person to acquire all the knowledge and skill needed to meet complex human needs. Thus, these professionals are given the exclusive right to make judgments and give advice to their clients. In granting this professional authority, society, in essence, gives up the right to judge these professionals except in extreme cases of incompetent or unethical practice. Society depends on the members of that profession to determine the requisite entrance preparation and to be sure those who are practicing as members of that profession do so competently.

Third, when the right to judge practice is relinquished by granting professional authority, the public becomes vulnerable and rightfully expects the professions to protect them from abuses that may accrue from the professional monopoly. Hughes indicates that the motto of the professions must be *credat emptor* ("buyer trust"), as opposed to the motto of the marketplace, *caveat emptor* ("buyer beware").[2] For example, where the layperson would rarely question the prescription of a physician, that same person might be very cautious when buying a used car and might have it thoroughly tested by an independent mechanic before making a purchase. To maintain this buyer trust, the professions must be accountable to the public that has granted them the sanction to perform these services. In order to establish and maintain this *professional responsibility,* professions develop codes that identify the expected ethical behavior of practitioners and establish mechanisms for policing their membership regarding unethical or incompetent practice.

In a sense, the professions and society struck a deal. In exchange for responsible service in sensitive areas of life, the professions were granted exclusive authority, that is, a *professional monopoly,* to offer these services.

How does an occupation achieve recognition as a profession? There is no established dividing line between other occupations and the professions. It is most useful to think of a continuum of occupations, from those that have few characteristics associated with the professions to those that have many such attributes. Pavalko summarizes the attributes necessary to achieve recognition as a profession.[3]

► The profession must possess a body of theory and intellectual understanding about the people to be served, the condition to be addressed, and the intervention approaches to be used.

► The services provided by the profession must relate to a need that is highly valued and for which the society is willing to take responsibility if that need is not met by other social institutions. These services are concerned with aspects of people's lives that require specialized knowledge and skill to address highly sensitive issues, such as their health, spirituality, learning, or their interpersonal and sometimes intimate interactions with others.

► The work to be done is not routine and cannot be reduced to tightly prescribed steps or procedures; thus the professional must have the autonomy to use individual discretion about how the work is performed.

► The professional must complete an extensive education in which both the general knowledge for informed citizenship is required and the specialized knowledge and skill needed to perform the work are transmitted from the experienced professional to the novice.

► The profession maintains its focus on service to the clients, as opposed to responding primarily to the worker's self-interest.

► The professionals are drawn to the work by a sense of commitment, a "calling," or a "taste" for the work to be accomplished.

► The professionals perceive the profession as a community of persons with common interests and goals with which they identify.

► The profession creates and promotes adherence to a code of ethical behavior that informs the members of appropriate worker–client relationships and is used to determine if members have abused the privilege of membership in that profession.

The following process, typically followed by professions when developing the requisite attributes, has been identified by Wilensky:

1. A substantial number of people become engaged on a full-time basis in providing the needed services.
2. Training schools or educational programs are established to prepare new practitioners with the advanced knowledge required for the work to be done.
3. A professional organization is formed to promote the interests of the members of that profession.
4. The professional organization engages in political activities to gain protection of the monopoly of the profession in its area through licensing or other forms of regulation of the profession.
5. The professional organization develops a code of ethical behavior to guide the professional's interactions with clients, other professionals, and the general public.[4]

The pattern identified by Wilensky accurately describes the process of social work's evolution as a profession. As professional organizations emerge, a conflict of interest becomes evident. The purely altruistic expectation of professions begins to be compromised because the professional associations operate primarily to promote the self-interest of the professionals, with the interests of clients or patients too often becoming secondary.

Social Work as a Profession: A Historical Perspective

Social work did not evolve in a vacuum. A series of events affected its development and will continue to shape social work in the future. Some of those events are represented by major factors in the history of the United States such as settlement patterns, wars, international conditions, economic fluctuations, the philosophy of elected political leaders, and others. These events influenced decisions about the extent to which this society would respond to its members' social needs and, subsequently, to the social programs that would be supported.

Table 4.1 identifies some of the important events that affected the evolution of U.S. society's approach to the human services and shows selected mileposts in the development of social work. In columns 1 and 2 the table lists dates and events that identify a historical event that had a direct influence on a social program or social work such as the Civil War or the Great Depression. Column 3 identifies important historical events that shaped social programs (e.g., the Pierce Veto), and column 4 lists some critical events in the development of the social work profession—for example, publication of *Social Diagnosis* in 1917.

From Volunteers to an Occupation (Prior to 1915)

The roots of social work may be found in the extensive volunteer movement during the formative years of the United States. In the colonial period, for example, it was assumed that individuals and families would care for themselves, but if further difficulties existed, one could depend on *mutual aid*. Friends, neighbors, or other representatives of the community could be counted on to help out when needed. Volunteer activities involved interaction with the poor, the ill, and those experiencing other social problems. As social agencies began to develop, they soon learned how to train volunteers in constructive ways to relate to clients and improved their ability to be helpful.

Developing out of this background came social work as an occupation. The first paid social work–type positions in the country were jobs in the Special Relief Department of the United States Sanitary Commission. Beginning as a voluntary agency and then receiving public support as the Civil War progressed, the Special Relief Department and its agents served Union soldiers and their families experiencing social and health problems due to the war. Wartime needs temporarily opened the door to providing social services, and the outstanding performance of these workers helped pave the way for other positions in social work. Several women involved in the war effort performed important leadership roles in the development of human services. For example, Dorothea Dix (Superintendent of Nurses in the U.S. Sanitary Commission) previously had provided leadership in an attempt to

Table 4.1

Timetable of Selected Events in Social Welfare and Social Work History

Approximate Date	U.S. History Event	Social Welfare Event	Social Work Event
Founding of United States	Agriculture-based society	Family responsibility	
	Open frontier	Mutual aid	
	Slavery	Puritan ethic	
	Open immigration	Town meetings	
		Orphan homes and first charitable societies	
		First general hospital (Pennsylvania Hospital)	
		Poorhouses	
		First public mental hospital	
1776	Declaration of Independence Revolutionary War	Growth of voluntary social agencies based on special needs	
	Act for the Gradual Abolition of Slavery (Pennsylvania)	Society for Alleviating the Miseries of Public Prisons	
1789	George Washington inaugurated	Merchant philanthropists	
1800	United States prohibits importation of slaves	Elizabeth Seton founds Sisters of Charity	
	War of 1812	Mass. General Hospital	
	Child labor laws	Gallaudet School for Deaf	
	Anti-Slavery Movement	Society for the Prevention of Pauperism	Dorothea Dix begins crusade for improved conditions in "insane asylums"
	Treaty of Guadalupe–Hidalgo		
	Chinese immigration began	NY House of Refuge (for juveniles)	
1850	Emergence of industrial society	Pierce Veto	
		Children's Aid Societies	
	Rise of cities and urbanization	Orphan Trains	
		YMCA movement	
1863	Civil War	Freedman's aid societies	U.S. Sanitary Commission (first paid social workers)
		Mass. Board of Charities	
		Tenement (housing) reforms	
	Reconstruction Era		National Conference on Charities and Correction
1877			
	Chinese Exclusion Act	Buffalo Charity Aid Society	Friendly visitors
	Dawes Act (Indian Land Allotment Act)		

(Continued)

Table 4.1

(Continued)

Approximate Date	U.S. History Event	Social Welfare Event	Social Work Event
1889		Hull House	Settlement workers
	Japanese immigration began		
	Spanish-American War		NY School of Philanthropy
1898	Immigration peaks	First Juvenile Court	
1910	World War I	White House Conference on Children	Introduction of medical social work
		U.S. Children's Bureau	Introduction of psychiatric social work
		Community Chest (federated fund raising)	Introduction of school social work
1915	Progressive Era		Flexner, "Is Social Work a Profession?"
		NAACP	Richmond, *Social Diagnosis*
		National Urban League	National Social Workers Exchange
			Association of Training Schools for Prof. SW
1920	Women's Suffrage (19th Amendment)	County and state relief agencies	
		Freudian influence	American Association of Social Workers
		Smith–Fess (Rehabilitation) Act	Milford Conference
1930	Stock market crash	American Public Welfare Association	American Association of Schools of Social Work
	The Great Depression	Indian Reorganization Act	
	"Great Migration" from Puerto Rico	Federal Emergency Relief Act	
		Civilian Conservation Corps (CCC)	
1935		Social Security Act	
		Works Progress Administration (WPA)	American Association of Group Workers
1941	United States enters World War II	U.S.O. organized	National Association of Schools of Social Administration
	Japanese relocation centers	National Social Welfare Assembly	
			Association for the Study of Community Organization

Table 4.1

(Continued)

Approximate Date	U.S. History Event	Social Welfare Event	Social Work Event
1949	End of WW II		Social Work Research Group
	Postwar recovery period		Council on Social Work Education (merger of AASSW and NASSA)
		U.S. Department of Health, Education, and Welfare	
1952	Korean Conflict		National Association of Social Workers (merger of six professional specialization groups and American Association of Social Workers)
1955	Civil Rights Movement	Indian Health Service	
1960	Women's Movement	Juvenile Delinquency Act	
	Kennedy administration	Herrington, *The Other America*	Greenwood, "Attributes of a Profession"
		Equal Pay Act	NASW "Working Definition of Social Work Practice"
1963	Kennedy assassination	Community Mental Health Act	NASW "Code of Ethics"
	Johnson administration	Food Stamp Act	
	Vietnam War	Civil Rights Act of 1964	
		Economic Opportunity Act	
		Appalachian Regional Development Act	
	Black Power Movement		
1965	Watts, Chicago, Detroit race riots	Older American Act	Academy of Certified Social Workers (ACSW)
	Welfare Rights Movement	Indian Civil Rights Act	
	Martin Luther King, Jr., assassination	Immigration Act of 1965	
		Medicare Act	
		Medicaid	
		Narcotic Addict Rehabilitation Act	
	Nixon administration	Supplemental Security Income (SSI) approved	NASW recognition of baccalaureate social worker as professional
1970	East LA police riots; Stonewall "Riot" and Gay Liberation Movement		
1972	*Roe* v. *Wade* decision	Child Abuse Prevention & Treatment Act	CSWE begins BSW accreditation process (generalist emphasis)

(Continued)

Table 4.1

(Continued)

Approximate Date	U.S. History Event	Social Welfare Event	Social Work Event
1974	Watergate and Nixon resignation		CSWE approves advanced standing for BSWs
	Ford administration		
1977		Education of All Handicapped Children Act	NASW "Conceptual Frameworks" series
	Carter administration	Indian Child Welfare Act	
1980		Privatization of human services expanded	
	Reagan administration	Social Security Block Grant Act (decentralize some programs to states)	Expansion of private practice
		AIDS Epidemic	Expansion of doctoral social work education (GADE)
		Tax Equity and Fiscal Responsibility Act of 1982 (cutbacks in human service provisions by federal government)	Association of Social Work (licensing) Boards formed
		Equal Rights Amendment (ratification fails)	
1988	George H. Bush administration		
		Americans with Disabilities Act	Academy of Certified Baccalaureate Social Workers (ACBSW)
	Persian Gulf War		
		Individuals with Disabilities Education Act	
1992	Clinton administration	Health care reform fails	Social workers licensed in all states, D.C., and some territories
	Los Angeles riot (in the wake of the Rodney King verdict)		
	Republican "Contract with America"	Family and Medical Leave Act	
1996	Oklahoma City federal building bombing		ACBSW terminated
	Clinton impeachment		
	Columbine High School gang massacre	Personal Responsibility and Work Opportunity Reconciliation Act	"Code of Ethics" revised
2000	George W. Bush administration		
2001	September 11 terrorist attacks		
2003	Invasion of Afghanistan		ACSW examination discontinued
2005	War on Iraq initiated		

secure federal government support for mental hospitals; Clara Barton later founded the American Red Cross; Josephine Shaw Lowell helped start the Charity Organization Society in New York City and also headed the Consumers' League, which worked to protect shopgirls from exploitation; Sojourner Truth gave leadership to the National Freedman's Relief Association; and Harriet Tubman, a central figure in the Underground Railroad, subsequently established a home for elderly African Americans. Following the war the Special Relief Department was closed.

Social work also appeared when the Massachusetts Board of Charities was established in 1863. Founded under the leadership of Samuel Gridley Howe, an advocate for the physically and mentally disabled, this agency coordinated services in almshouses, hospitals, and other institutions of the state. Although its powers were limited to inspection and advice, the Board gained wide acceptance. The concept of boards overseeing state services spread to other states in the 1870s and became the forerunners to today's state departments of human services and residential institutions.

The Massachusetts Board of Charities also introduced social research into human service delivery. An 1893 report, for example, identified the causes of poverty as "first, physical degradation and inferiority; second, moral perversity; third, mental incapacity; fourth, accidents and infirmities; fifth, unjust and unwise laws, and the customs of society."[5] Although the approach was perhaps more moralistic than would be found in social work today, the report reflected the understanding that both personal and societal factors contribute to poverty.

Another significant development leading to the emergence of social work was the establishment of the Charity Organization Society (COS) of Buffalo, New York, in 1877. Modeled after an organization in London, charity organization societies sprang up in a number of communities with the dual purposes of finding means to help the poor and preventing the poor from taking advantage of the numerous uncoordinated social agencies that provided financial assistance. Leaders in social work from the COS movement included Mary Richmond, who helped identify a theory of practice in her books *Friendly Visiting Among the Poor* (1899) and *Social Diagnosis* (1917); Edward T. Devine, a founder of the New York School of Philanthropy in 1898 and its first director; and Porter Lee, who was instrumental in founding the American Association of Schools of Social Work in 1919.

Another important development that contributed to the emergence of social work was the Settlement House Movement initiated in 1886. Patterning settlement houses after London's Toynbee Hall, settlements were established in New York and Chicago. Within fifteen years, about one hundred settlement houses were operating in the United States. The settlements helped the poor learn skills required for urban living and simultaneously provided leadership in political action efforts to improve the social environment. Bremner sums up the impact of the settlement movement:

> Where others thought of the people of the slums as miserable wretches deserving either pity or correction, settlement residents knew them as much entitled to respect as any other members of the community. Numerous young men and women who lived and worked in

the settlements during the 1890s carried this attitude with them into later careers in social work, business, government service, and the arts.[6]

The residents of Chicago's Hull House are a good example. Its founder, Jane Addams, won the Nobel Peace Prize in 1931; Julia Lathrop became the first director of the U.S. Children's Bureau and was succeeded by other Hull House alumnae Katherine Lenroot and Grace Abbott, thus contributing to the protection of children and youth for several decades.

The efforts to integrate the African American population into the mainstream of U.S. society following the Civil War also contributed to the development of social work. George Haynes, the first African American graduate of the New York School of Philanthropy, for example, helped found the National Urban League, while Mary McLeod Bethune, who gave leadership to the education of African American women, was a founder of the National Council of Negro Women and was influential in making New Deal policies more equitable for the African American population.

Social work expanded into another setting in the early 1900s when Richard Cabot and Ida Cannon opened a social work program at the Massachusetts General Hospital. These social workers provided services for patients experiencing health-related social problems and also worked to strengthen the services of related health and welfare agencies throughout the community. Lubove identifies the significance of this development for the professionalization of social work:

> The enlistment of medical social workers marked an important stage in the development of professional social work. A casework limited to the charity organization and child welfare societies provided too narrow a base for professional development, associated as it was with problems of relief and economic dependency. Medical social work added an entirely new institutional setting in which to explore the implications of casework theory and practice.[7]

Medical social workers became interested in professional education as a means of moving beyond social work's "warm heart" image and into a more disciplined understanding of psychological or social conditions as the base of patient distress. In 1912, with Ida Cannon's participation, a one-year training program in medical social work was established in the Boston School of Social Work.

Through these years, social work jobs were also springing up in other practice areas such as mental hygiene (mental health), prisons, employment and labor relations, and schools. Beginning in 1873 an organization designed to draw together members of this diverse occupation was formed, the National Conference on Charities. Later renamed the National Conference on Charities and Correction, this organization brought volunteer and professional staff members of social agencies together to exchange ideas about the provision of services, discuss social problems, and study the characteristics of effective practice. By the time World War I began social work was an established occupation clearly distinguishable from the many volunteer groups and other occupations concerned with the well-being of members of U.S. society.

Professional Emergence (1915–1950)

With social work firmly established as an occupation, attention then turned to its development as a profession. At the 1915 meeting of the National Conference on Charities and Correction, Abraham Flexner addressed the subject, "Is Social Work a Profession?" Dr. Flexner, an authority on graduate education, had previously done a penetrating study that led to major changes in medical education. The organizers of this session of the National Conference apparently hoped Flexner would assure them that social work was, or was about to become, a full-fledged profession. However, that was not in the cards. Flexner spelled out six criteria that an occupation must meet to be considered a profession:

1. Professions are essentially intellectual operations with large individual responsibility.
2. They derive their raw material from science and learning.
3. This material is worked up to a practical and clear-cut end.
4. Professions possess an educationally communicable technique.
5. They tend to self-organization.
6. They become increasingly altruistic in motivation.[8]

Based on these criteria, Flexner concluded that social work had not yet made it into the professional elite. Following Flexner's admonition to "go forth and build thyself a profession," social workers busily attended to these functions over the next thirty-five years.

One effort was to develop a code of ethics. In 1921 Mary Richmond indicated that, "we need a code; something to abide by, or else we will have low social standing."[9] One code, the "Experimental Draft of a Code of Ethics for Social Case Workers," was discussed at the 1923 meeting of the National Conference on Social Welfare. Although this proposed code was never acted on, it represented a beginning effort at formulating a statement of professional ethics.

Probably the greatest amount of effort was devoted to self-organization. The National Social Workers Exchange was opened in 1917 to provide vocational counseling and placement and later became actively involved in the identification and definition of professional standards. In 1921 its functions were taken over by the broader American Association of Social Workers, which made significant efforts to develop a comprehensive professional association. This effort was later weakened by the attempts of some specialized practice areas to develop their own professional organizations. A chronology of the development of these specialized groups follows:[10]

- 1918 American Association of Hospital Social Workers
- 1919 National Association of Visiting Teachers
- 1926 American Association of Psychiatric Social Workers
- 1936 American Association for the Study of Group Work
- 1946 Association for the Study of Community Organization
- 1949 Social Work Research Group

It was not clear whether social work was one or many professions.

Another development during this period concerned the required preparation to enter the social work profession. Social work education had begun as agency-based training, but a concerted effort was made during this period to transfer it to colleges and universities, where other professions had located their professional education. In 1919 the Association of Training Schools for Professional Social Workers was established with seventeen charter members—both agency and university affiliated schools. The purpose of that organization was to develop standards for all social work education. By 1927 considerable progress toward that purpose had been made, and the Association of Training Schools reorganized into the American Association of Schools of Social Work (AASSW). Although education programs had been offered in agencies, as well as at both undergraduate and graduate levels in colleges and universities, the AASSW determined that by 1939 only university affiliated programs with two-year graduate programs would be recognized as professional social work education.

That action led to a revolt by schools whose undergraduate programs prepared professionals to meet the staffing needs of the social agencies in their states. A second professional education organization was formed in 1942, the National Association of Schools of Social Administration, made up largely of public universities in the midwest that offered baccalaureate- and one-year graduate-level professional education programs. Ernest Harper, a leader in that organization, described this development as "a protest movement against unrealistic and premature insistence upon graduate training and overemphasis upon professional casework as the major social work technique."[11]

With leadership from governmental and voluntary practice agencies, the two organizations were later merged (1952) into the Council on Social Work Education (CSWE) following the landmark Hollis–Taylor study of social work education.[12] The outcome of that decision favored the two-year master's program as the minimum educational requirement for full professional status. Undergraduate social work education temporarily faded from the scene.

Another important area of concern that was given only limited attention during this period was strengthening the knowledge and skill base of social work practice. Richmond's rich contribution, *Social Diagnosis,* was the first effort to formalize a communicable body of techniques applicable to the diverse settings in which social caseworkers were found.[13] Momentum from this thrust, however, was lost as social work slipped into the grasp of the popular psychoanalytic approach. Cohen comments, "The search for a method occurred just at the time the impact of psychoanalysis was being felt. Did social work, in its haste for professional stature, reach out for a ready-made methodology for treating sick people, thus closing itself off from the influence of developments in the other sciences?"[14] This question must be answered in the affirmative. By adopting the helping methodology that was currently in vogue, social work embraced firmly, but perhaps inappropriately, the private model of professionalism. Writing in *Harper's Monthly* in 1957, Sanders accurately criticized social work for "floating with the ghost of Freud."[15]

Consolidating the Gains (1950–1970)

The move to consolidate the accrediting bodies for the schools of social work into the CSWE set an important precedent for the field and was part of a broad movement to treat social work as a single and unified profession. In 1950 the several specialized associations and the American Association of Social Workers agreed to form the Temporary Inter-Association Council of Social Work Membership Organizations (TIAC). The purpose behind the formation of TIAC was to bring these specialized groups into one central professional association. After considerable efforts by the specialties to maintain their identities, TIAC proposed a merger of the several groups in 1952. By 1955 this was accomplished, and the National Association of Social Workers (NASW) was formed.

NASW membership rose from 28,000 to 45,000 between 1961 and 1965, largely because of the formation of the Academy of Certified Social Workers (ACSW), which required both NASW membership and a two-year period of supervised experience. Many job descriptions were revised to require membership in the Academy, forcing social workers to join the NASW and obtain certification.

The late 1950s were a time of great introspection, and the professional journal, *Social Work,* was filled with articles such as "The Nature of Social Work,"[16] "How Social Will Social Work Be?"[17] and "A Changing Profession in a Changing World."[18] Perhaps the most significant work was Ernest Greenwood's classic article, "Attributes of a Profession," in 1957.[19] Greenwood identified five critical attributes of professions that, depending on the degree to which they have been accomplished, determine the degree of professionalism for any occupational group:

1. A systematic body of theory
2. Professional authority
3. Sanction of the community
4. A regulative code of ethics
5. A professional culture

He related the development of social work to each of these five criteria and concluded that social work was a profession. He observed:

> When we hold up social work against the model of the professions presented above, it does not take long to decide whether to classify it within the professional or nonprofessional occupations. Social work is already a profession; it has too many points of congruence with the model to be classifiable otherwise.[20]

To the credit of social workers, they were as stimulated by Greenwood's declaration that they had become a profession as they were by Flexner's conclusion that they were not yet in the select circle. In 1958 the NASW published the "Working Definition of Social Work Practice," a valuable beginning to the difficult task of identifying professional boundaries.[21] This was followed by Gordon's excellent critique, which helped strengthen and clarify some parts of the working definition, particularly in relation to knowledge, values, and practice methodology.[22] In 1960 the

NASW adopted a Code of Ethics to serve as a guide for ethical professional practice,[23] thus completing the steps to become a fully recognized profession.

Turning Away from the Elitist Professional Model (1970–Present)

From the turn of the twentieth century to the late 1960s, social work displayed a pattern typical of an emerging profession. It created a single association to guide professional growth and development; adopted a code of ethical professional behavior; provided for graduate-level university-based professional schools and acquired recognition to accredit those educational programs; successfully obtained licensing for social work practice in some states; conducted public education campaigns to educate the public about social work; achieved recognition for social work among the helping professions; and moved in the direction of other professions by increasing specialization and limiting access to the profession. Indeed, social work was on its way to carving its niche among the helping professions.

However, social work did not vigorously pursue the path that would lead to even greater professional status. Perhaps influenced by a renewed spirit of concern emanating from the Civil Rights, Welfare Rights, and Women's Rights movements, the development of social work as a profession during the 1970s and 1980s was marked by ambivalence over following the more traditional format of the established professions.

First, there was a resurgence of social change activity on the part of social workers. A legacy from Lyndon Johnson's Great Society programs was federal support, in the form of jobs and other resources, toward efforts to eliminate social problems and alleviate human suffering. Social work was already committed to those goals, and social workers were prepared to move away from their clinical orientation and onto the front lines of social action.

For social workers bent on achieving higher professional status, activist social workers were sometimes unpopular. Their somewhat controversial activities created an unwelcome public image of social workers as militant activists on the front lines of social change. This change in the balance of activities performed by social workers, however, helped to bring social work back to its roots and reestablish the "change" orientation in its purposes of caring, curing, and changing the society. The more liberal political climate that supported social work activism was short-lived. Federal support for programs encouraging social change dwindled and was nearly nonexistent under the Reagan and George H. Bush administrations.

Next, in 1970 NASW made a dramatic move by revising its membership requirements to give full membership privileges to anyone who had completed a baccalaureate degree in social work from an undergraduate program approved by CSWE. In opposition to the pattern of professions becoming more exclusive, social work opened its membership to more people, and a generalist approach to practice was embraced. Beginning in 1970, professional qualifications could be gained by obtaining professional education at the undergraduate level. However, social work has been uneasy about operating as a multilevel profession, and, although the NASW classification system is clear about the "basic social worker" being viewed as professional, the social worker at this level has never been fully accepted by many MSW social workers. Some advocates for the baccalaureate social worker contend that NASW has not devoted sufficient attention to this practice level and that its program priorities in the 1980s "centered too much on licensing, vendor payments, private practice and other issues that were not sufficiently relevant to the baccalaureate worker."[24] NASW's creation of the Academy of Certified Baccalaureate Social Workers in the early 1990s represented movement away from that overemphasis on the interests of master's-level social workers, but the discontinuance of that certification in 1996 was a retreat from that position.

With NASW's formal recognition of baccalaureate social work as fully professional, in 1974 the Council on Social Work Education began accrediting baccalaureate social work education (BSW) programs. Initially, 135 schools met the undergraduate accreditation requirements, and by 2005 that number had increased to 448 schools in the United States and Puerto Rico with another 18 schools in candidacy for accreditation.[25] Of particular importance was the accessibility of these programs to persons wishing to become social workers. Whereas most MSW programs were located in urban areas, undergraduate programs were located in both urban and rural communities. The professionalization of baccalaureate social work opened educational opportunities to people who could not attend schools in urban areas and who have subsequently enriched the provision of services in smaller communities by filling human service jobs in these areas. Similarly, the emergence of professionally sanctioned baccalaureate-level social work education increased the opportunity for members from minority and lower socioeconomic backgrounds to enter social work, as they could complete the requisite education preparation without needing both baccalaureate and master's degrees.

The return of a conservative political climate in the United States during the 1980s and 1990s created a perception that few jobs would be available in social work, especially when the Reagan administration promoted its objective of dismantling the Great Society programs. When it became evident that such mass destruction of human service programs was not going to occur, interest in careers in social work revived and social work education programs experienced a resurgence of student interest. After peaking at nearly 28,000 undergraduate social work majors in the late 1970s, that number declined by more than one-fourth in 1983, returned to the 28,000 level in 1990, and stabilized at about 35,000 in the early 2000s. For the MSW programs a similar pattern occurred. Full-time enrollment declined by one-fifth between 1978 and 1983, but has since reached about 23,000.[26]

Social Work on 9/11: The Case of a Maturing Profession

In the mid-1950s, Marion K. Sanders published a highly critical article on the social work profession entitled "Social Work: A Profession Chasing Its Tail." Although some of his criticism was no doubt accurate, Sanders essentially cast social work as an ill-defined occupation that had compromised too much of its original concern for the vulnerable members of society to achieve professional status. Illustrating the intangible nature of social work practice and the poor definition of the profession at that time, Sanders created the following story to illustrate his point.

> The day after the bomb fell, the doctor was out binding up radiation burns. The minister prayed and set up a soup kitchen in the ruined chapel. The policeman herded stray children to the rubble heap where the teacher had improvised a classroom. And the social worker wrote a report: since two had survived, they held a conference on Interpersonal Relationships in a Time of Intensified Anxiety States.
>
> Of course the bomb hasn't fallen. And the social workers have not yet abdicated all the hard and daring tasks to the other benevolent callings. But it could happen. Despite their shortcomings, the doctors, teachers, and reverend clergy at least know what is expected of them. . . . In contrast the social workers—though specialists in good deeds—seem to have lost track of what particular good needs doing by them.[27]

Contrast Sanders' depiction of social work in the 1950s with the reports of the activities social workers performed when terrorists crashed airplanes into several critical locations in the United States. On 9/11/2001, social workers were immediately on the front lines—in New York, Washington, D.C., and elsewhere. A few representative stories confirm that in 2001 social workers were prepared to perform the good deeds needed in a time of crisis.

▶ Already in place was an agreement with the American Red Cross that the National Association of Social Workers (NASW) would facilitate the delivery of mental health services to victims of disaster, rescue workers, military personnel, and their families. NASW, through its national and chapter offices, immediately coordinated efforts to make social work services available, and more than 1,000 social workers were contacted to provide services through this mechanism.

▶ In New York City, Madelyn Miller and the NASW Chapter's 85-member Disaster/ Trauma Working Group immediately made itself available to provide a variety of mental health and other services.[28]

▶ Ilia Rivera-Sanchez was on the scene at the Pentagon by 6:00 P.M. the afternoon of the attacks, comforting and counseling firefighters and military personnel engaged in the rescue work. She later worked at the morgue offering counseling to those bringing in the bodies recovered from the Pentagon.[29]

▶ Pat Blau and other social workers at Bellevue Hospital in New York City operated two support centers—one for staff members who were working around the clock with victims and another for families of victims. They also prepared lists of missing persons, handled emotional telephone calls from people searching for missing family members, coordinated with other human services agencies, provided clothing for persons unable to reach their homes, and so on.[30]

▶ In airports, train stations, and bus stations around the world, social workers provided services to people whose travel was interrupted by the attacks. Housing was often needed, funds for meals were provided, alternate transportation arrangements had to be made, and loved ones were contacted regarding the whereabouts of stranded travelers. Social workers were there to assist.

Unfortunately, the aftermath of 9/11 continues. The loss of loved ones, the loss of jobs, and the loss of a sense of security will last for many years. Fortunately, social work had matured in its understanding of what it has to contribute to the society and was prepared to respond to this emergency, and the society recognized and made use of the competencies of many social workers.

Concluding Comment

In the past century, social work has developed in a manner that meets the criteria for professions. Consensus about its unique purpose among the professions has been reached, and social work has achieved sanction as the appropriate profession to help people resolve problems in their interaction with their environments. Social workers have been granted the professional authority to provide the necessary helping services for people in need and have taken their authority to provide these professional services seriously. The National Association of Social Workers and the Council on Social Work Education have worked through the decades to clarify social work's knowledge, value, and skill base. Social work has developed educational programs that prepare new people to enter this profession and has established a process for accrediting the programs that meet qualitative educational standards at both the baccalaureate and master's levels. We can observe the subtle but important influence that professional recognition, educational preparation and practical training have had on Demetria (see Box 4.1) as she carries out her investigation and initiates services in the suspected child abuse case found in Chapter 1.

Social work has also adopted and regularly updated a Code of Ethics and has established procedures for dealing with social workers who might violate that code, which allows the profession to carry out its professional responsibility to protect clients and the general public from abuses that might arise from the monopoly it has achieved.

One might expect social workers to feel satisfied with these accomplishments. Yet, within this profession of many faces, there are inevitably varied opinions. While most social workers believe the progress made in becoming a recognized profession is desirable, some believe that it has become too elitist and is targeting its services too much to the white middle class. Others believe that it has lowered professional standards by opening its membership to those with less than graduate-level credentials. Some believe it should become more entrepreneurial like the private professions, and still others believe it should more fully embrace the agency-based model of the public professions where the most vulnerable members of the society are likely to be served.

Box 4.1

Demetria's Functioning as a Professional Social Worker

Demetria's work with the Miles family (see Chapter 1) illustrates professional social work activity. What made her work "professional"? First, Demetria had the recognized *educational preparation* (a BSW degree from an accredited social work education program) for a beginning social worker. It appears that at least partially because of that status, she was granted adequate *professional autonomy* to exercise her professional judgment about the case; she had sufficient *professional authority*, which allowed Mrs. Miles to trust her with quite a bit of information about family problems; and Demetria reflected *professional responsibility* in the discrete way she handled client information and her willingness to extend beyond the minimum job expectations to initiate consideration of needed social change.

Second, if one ticks through the criteria for being a profession, Demetria and her work exemplify a number of ways social work practice is professional. For example, she was prepared from her social work education with enough *knowledge about people and programs* to be able to immediately work constructively in this case; the child welfare *services she provided were highly valued by the society,* as the protection of children is one of the most strongly supported human services; Demetria functioned in a highly *ethical* manner throughout the interactions around this case, and so on. These factors, largely unseen by Joseph and Mrs. Miles, were instrumental in the agency hiring Demetria in the first place, the school personnel working with her to identify Joseph's issues, Mrs. Miles' openness to Demetria's offer to help, and Demetria's competence in carrying out the work. This preparation for social work practice and the sanction from the community facilitated Demetria's ability to quickly establish rapport and successfully begin the helping process.

KEY WORDS AND CONCEPTS

Profession
Attributes of professions
Professional autonomy
Professional authority
Professional responsibility
Public vs. private professions
U.S. Sanitary Commission

State boards of charities
Charity organization societies
Settlement houses
Social Diagnosis
Council on Social Work Education
National Association of
    Social Workers

SUGGESTED INFORMATION SOURCES

Greenwood, Ernest. "Attributes of a Profession," *Social Work* 2 (July 1957): 45–55.
Leighninger, Leslie. *Social Work: Search for Identity.* Westport, CT: Greenwood, 1987.
———. *Creating a New Profession: The Beginnings of Social Work Education.* Alexandria, VA: Council on Social Work Education, 2000.
Lubove, Roy. *The Professional Altruist.* Cambridge, MA: Harvard University Press, 1989.

ENDNOTES

1. Wilbert E. Moore, *The Professions: Roles and Rules* (New York: Russell Sage Foundation, 1970), p. 3.

2. Everett C. Hughes, "Professions," *Daedalus* (Fall 1963): 657.
3. Ronald M. Pavalko, *Sociology of Occupations and Professions,* 2nd edition (Itasca, IL: F. E. Peacock, 1988), pp. 19–29.
4. Harold Wilensky, "The Professionalization of Everyone?" *American Journal of Sociology* 70 (September 1964): 137–158.
5. Cited in Ralph E. Pumphrey and Muriel W. Pumphrey, eds., *The Heritage of American Social Work* (New York: Columbia University Press, 1961), p. 12.
6. Robert H. Bremner, *From the Depths* (New York: New York University Press, 1956), 66.
7. Roy Lubove, *The Professional Altruist* (Cambridge, MA: Harvard University Press, 1965), 32.
8. Abraham Flexner, "Is Social Work a Profession?" in *Proceedings of the National Conference on Charities and Correction, 1915* (Chicago: National Conference on Charities and Correction, 1916): 576–590.
9. Pumphrey and Pumphrey, *Heritage,* p. 310.
10. John C. Kidneigh, "History of American Social Work," in Harry L. Lurie, ed., *Encyclopedia of Social Work,* 15th edition (New York: National Association of Social Workers, 1965), pp. 13–14.
11. Herbert Bisno, "The Place of Undergraduate Curriculum in Social Work Education," in Werner W. Boehm, ed., *A Report of the Curriculum Study* Vol. II (New York: Council on Social Work Education, 1959), p. 8.
12. Ernest V. Hollis and Alice L. Taylor, *Social Work Education in the United States* (New York: Columbia University Press, 1951).
13. Mary E. Richmond, *Social Diagnosis* (New York: Russell Sage Foundation, 1917).
14. Nathan E. Cohen, *Social Work in the American Tradition* (New York: Holt, Rinehart, & Winston, 1958), pp. 120–121.
15. Marion K. Sanders, "Social Work: A Profession Chasing Its Tail," *Harper's Monthly* 214 (March 1957): 56–62.
16. Werner W. Boehm, "The Nature of Social Work," *Social Work* 3 (April 1958): 10–18.
17. Herbert Bisno, "How Social Will Social Work Be?" *Social Work* 1 (April 1956): 12–18.
18. Nathan E. Cohen, "A Changing Profession in a Changing World," *Social Work* 1 (October 1956): 12–19.
19. Ernest Greenwood, "Attributes of a Profession," *Social Work* 2 (July 1957): 45–55.
20. Ibid., p. 54.
21. Harriet M. Bartlett, "Towards Clarification and Improvement of Social Work Practice," *Social Work* 3 (April 1958): 5–7.
22. William E. Gordon, "Critique of the Working Definition," *Social Work* 7 (October 1962): 3–13; and "Knowledge and Values: Their Distinction and Relationship in Clarifying Social Work Practice," *Social Work* 10 (July 1965): 32–39.
23. National Association of Social Workers, *Code of Ethics* (Washington, D.C.: The Association, 1960).
24. Bradford W. Sheafor and Barbara W. Shank, *Undergraduate Social Work Education: A Survivor in a Changing Profession* (Austin: University of Texas School of Social Work, 1986), Social Work Education Monograph Series 3, p. 25.
25. "Most Recent Actions Taken by the Commission on Accreditation. http://cswe.,org.
26. Todd M. Lennon, ed., *Statistics on Social Work Education in the United States, 2003* (Alexandria, VA: Council on Social Work Education, 2005), Tables 56 and 57.
27. Sanders, p. 56.
28. John V. O'Neill, "Social Workers Heed Call After Attacks," *NASW News* 46 (November 2001), p. 8.
29. O'Neill, p. 1.
30. O'Neill, p. 8.

part three

Social Work Career Options

For the person entering social work, the job flexibility it permits is a very attractive feature. One can practice as a professional social worker at the baccalaureate, master's, or doctoral level. A social worker's potential fields of practice include working with children or older people, addressing physical or mental health problems, practicing in schools or the correctional system and so on. Although increasingly social workers engage in their own private practice, most are employed by some form of human service organization ranging from family centers to safehouses for battered women.

Each social worker must make certain decisions that will affect his or her career path in social work. One important decision concerns one's level of educational preparation. Chapter 5 summarizes a considerable amount of data about social workers at different educational levels and highlights the employment opportunities at each. In essence, the baccalaureate-level social worker works in direct services with clients and is most likely to serve either children and youth or older people.

The master's-level social worker may also hold administrative and supervisory positions, and those in direct service positions are most likely to address medical, mental health, and school-related issues with the breadwinning adult population. Some doctoral-level social workers can be found in advanced administrative and direct practice jobs, but the majority are concentrated in teaching positions.

A second decision concerns the practice area one chooses to enter. Chapter 6 surveys thirteen unique fields in which social workers apply their trade. Despite the differences in these fields of practice, a basic pattern emerges of the social workers helping people interact more effectively with the world around them.

Finally, a social worker must decide if he or she is to work in a human service organization or engage in private practice. Chapter 7 examines those public and private human service agencies where most social workers are employed. Factors affecting agency structure and functioning are discussed, along with the fact that some social workers have adopted an entrepreneurial approach to their work and have opted for private practice. Private practice presents a different set of problems than are experienced by those social workers employed in human service organizations.

By understanding the various career options in social work and the issues surrounding each, the prospective social worker can make informed decisions about important career choices.

5

Entry to the Social Work Profession

Prefatory Comment

Selecting a career is one of the most important decisions a person must make. Whether that decision is to become a homemaker, physician, salesperson, teacher, chemist, or social worker, it should be based on a thorough understanding of the physical, emotional, and intellectual demands of the field and a close look at one's own suitability for that type of work. Whatever the choice, it will dictate how a person spends a major part of each day. It will also spill over into other aspects of life, including lifestyle, general satisfaction with self, and quality of life.

The decision to enter a particular profession does not lock a person into that occupation for a lifetime, but it does represent a substantial commitment of time, energy, and resources to prepare for professional practice and obtain the requisite credentials. After entering a profession, a person's job consumes a major part of his or her daily activity, and, if that was a good career choice, one's job can be an exhilarating and stimulating experience. However, if there is a poor fit between a person and his or her chosen occupation, work can be frustrating and unrewarding. Further, the complexity of human situations requiring professional assistance and the growing knowledge about effective helping obligate the professional to a career of continued learning and skill development. Unless a person is willing to make such a commitment, a professional career should not be pursued.

For the person considering the social work profession, it is useful to have a clear perception of the career opportunities this profession affords. Social work has evolved a four-level career ladder that has two entry points (i.e., the basic and specialized social worker) and two additional levels based on more advanced experience and education. This chapter describes the educational preparation and practice experience required for each practice level and identifies factors that shaped the evolution of social work practice at those levels.

Making a career choice is difficult because of the wide range of careers to choose from but, more importantly, because of the problems an outsider experiences in gaining an adequate and accurate understanding of a career. Too often, only after a person has made substantial commitments in time, energy, and money or has cut off other opportunities by taking steps to enter a career does he or she find that it is not what was expected or wanted. Another difficulty lies in having a clear perception of one's own needs, interests, and abilities. Personal introspection, occupational preference testing, guidance counseling, and experience in activities related to the career are all resources for making this choice.

The person contemplating a career in social work must consider a number of factors. It is evident that social work is extremely broad in scope—ranging from social action to individual therapy—with a knowledge base that is far from stable or well developed. Thus, explicit guidelines for social work practice do not exist, leaving the social worker with the responsibility for exercising a great deal of individual judgment. Furthermore, the skills demanded of the social worker vary widely and require a flexible, creative, and introspective person to practice them. The pressures of a social work job create a degree of stress because the outcome of the work is critically important to the clients. In addition, social workers are regularly criticized by both clients and the general public, frequently in regard to programs over which they have little policy-making influence. If a person can tolerate the ambiguity, responsibility, pressures, and criticism that are a part of social work; if the values, skills, and interests required of social workers are compatible; and if it is rewarding to work constructively to help people improve their level of social functioning, social work offers a rich and satisfying career.

Issues in Social Work Preparation and Employment

Membership in any profession requires that the persons aspiring to enter it acquire the specified qualifications. The very act of defining professional membership inherently excludes some persons who operate with similar knowledge and values but lack the identified qualifications. In social work, for example, completion of the education and practice experience specified by the National Association of Social Workers (NASW) in its membership qualifications is necessary to gain professional recognition. However, social workers are cognizant that many other helping people with different educations and experiences make important contributions to the delivery of human services. For the person entering social work, or considering becoming a member of this profession, it is important to be aware of several issues that relate to professional qualifications.

Education and Accreditation

The social work profession contends that a person must have a formal social work education; that is, either a baccalaureate degree with a major in social work or a master's degree in social work (MSW) from an accredited social work education program, as a minimum for professional recognition. The *accreditation* process is administered by the Council on Social Work Education (CSWE) and has become a significant factor in social work because the graduate of the accredited program is assumed to be prepared to enter practice as a beginning-level professional social worker—ready to apply the appropriate knowledge, values, and skills in the service of clients. For all practical purposes, education is the gatekeeper of the profession. This does not mean that all graduates are equally prepared to enter practice, that some people who do not have all the required social work courses are unable to perform many tasks of the social worker, or even that all schools offer the same opportunity for learning the essentials of social work. Rather, accreditation attests to the fact that the public can have confidence that graduates are at least minimally prepared for beginning-level social work practice because they have completed an instructional program that is soundly designed and taught by competent faculty.

Professional Certification

The National Association of Social Workers provides confirmation to clientele and employing human services agencies that some social workers have demonstrated the requisite knowledge and competence to engage in practice, that is, *professional certification*. Where accreditation is testimony to the quality of an educational program, certification is the profession's testimony regarding the individual's knowledge, values, and skills.

Following it's formation in 1955, the NASW created two professional certification programs that were based on the social worker's practice level. In 1960, the Academy of Certified Social Workers (ACSW) was created. The ACSW was the profession's nationally accepted mechanism for designating those social workers who were qualified at the "independent social worker" level and was often a requirement for social work jobs. It required the MSW (or equivalent) degree, two years post–master's experience, a sufficient score on a national exam, and favorable evaluation of the worker's competence by peers. Recently, with exam-based licensing (see below) of social workers implemented in every state, the exam portion of the ACSW became redundant and in 2005 was discontinued as a requirement for membership in the Academy. In 1990, NASW also created the Academy of Certified Baccalaureate Social Workers (ACBSW), but this credential did not catch on as a prerequisite for employment and was discontinued in 1996.

For many years NASW has also maintained two professional recognition programs for advanced social workers engaged in clinical practice: the Qualified Clinical Social Worker (QCSW) and the Diplomate in Clinical Social Work (DCSW). More recently, the demand to recognize qualified social workers in specialty areas has led NASW to create credentialing programs in several practice areas—at both the MSW and BSW levels. Table 5.1 summarizes the requirements for each program. They all require NASW membership, graduation from a CSWE accredited educational program, practice experience after graduation, and adherence to the NASW Code of Ethics. Usually a state license to practice social work or a passing score on the appropriate social work exam offered by the Association of Social Work (licensing) Boards is required, as well as a favorable evaluation by the worker's supervisor. These credentials are designed to serve as indicators of competency by the profession of social work to clients and employers, as well as to the insurance companies that offer reimbursement for social workers' services.

Table 5.1

Professional Certifications Offered by NASW (2005)*

Master's-Level Certifications

	Additional Educational Requirements	Experience	Testing	Supervision
Academy of Certified Social Workers (ACSW)	None	2 years post–MSW (3,000 hours)	None	2 years with ACSW, QCSW, or DCSW worker
Qualified Clinical Social Worker (QCSW)	None	2 years post–MSW clinical practice (3000 hours)	ACSW or current state licensing exam at appropriate level	2 years with experienced clinical social worker
Diplomate in Clinical Social Work (DCSW)	Or doctorate in social work plus 20 hours clinical course work	5 years post–MSW clinical practice	ACSW or state clinical license	Positive evaluations from MSW-level professional colleague
Certified School Social Work Specialist (C-SSWS)	None	2 academic years of post–MSW practice as a school social worker	ACSW, DCSW state MSW or state school license exam	Evaluation by approved supervisor
Certified Social Worker in Health Care (C-SWHC)	None	2 years post–MSW practice in healthcare setting	ACSW, DCSW, or state license	Evaluation by approved supervisor
Certified Clinical Alcohol, Tobacco, and Other Drugs Social Worker (C-ATODSW)	Plus 180 contact hours of ATOD specific content	2 years clinical practice post–MSW (3000 hours) with 2 years substance abuse	ACSW, DCSW or highest-level state clinical social work exam	Evaluation by approved supervisor
Certified Advanced Social Work Case Manager (C-ASWCM)	None	1 year post–MSW case-management practice (1500 hours)	ACSW, DCSW and/or exam-based state license	Evaluation by approved supervisor
Certified Advanced Children, Youth, and Families Social Worker (C-ACYFSW)	Plus 20 contact hours of population-specific education	2 years post–MSW practice (3000 hours) with children, youth, or families	ACSW, DCSW, and/or MSW-level state license	Evaluation by approved supervisor

(Continued)

Bachelor's-Level Certifications			
Certified Social Work Case Manager (C-SWCM)	None	1 year post–BSW practice as a case manager (1500 hours)	State BSW-level license	Evaluation by approved supervisor
Certified Children, Youth, and Family Social Worker	Plus 20 contact hours of population-specific education	2 years post–BSW practice (3,000 hours) with children, youth, or families	State BSW-level license	Evaluation by approved supervisor

*Note: All certifications require a current NASW membership, graduation from a CSWE-accredited social work education program at the level required by the certificate, and agreement to adhere to the *NASW Code of Ethics*. Most certifications also require adherence to the *NASW Standards for Continuing Professional Education*, and many will accept a passing score on the appropriate Association of Social Work Boards (ASWB) examination for holding a state license.

Source:

National Association of Social Workers. "NASW Credentials and Specialty Certification." http://www.socialworkers.org/credentials/default.asp.

Licensing or State Regulation of Social Work Practice

The social work profession, through the Council on Social Work Education, has shaped its educational programs through accreditation requirements and, through NASW, has sought to identify its competent and experienced practitioners by creating its certification programs. However, over the past two decades perhaps the most dominant issue on NASW's agenda has been to encourage the licensing of social workers throughout the United States.

As described by the Association of Social Work Boards, *licensing* is:

> . . . a process by which an agency of state government or other jurisdiction acting upon legislative mandate grants permission to individuals to engage in the practice of a particular profession or vocation and prohibits all others from legally doing so. By ensuring a level of safe practice, the licensure process protects the general public. Those who are licensed are permitted by the state to use a specific title and perform activities because they have demonstrated to the state's satisfaction that they have reached an acceptable level of practice.[1]

The intent of licensing is to have, state governments identify those social workers who are properly prepared through professional education and experience to provide client services. Both consumers of service (particularly in private practice settings) and health insurance companies that reimburse for the cost of social work services have looked to licensing as a desirable way to determine a social worker's practice competence. In order to attract clients and to be eligible for payments from insurance companies, social workers have embraced state licensing for social work.

As opposed to the uniform national requirements for professional certification used by NASW, each state controls whether there will be licensing of social workers, the levels of practice it will license, and the requirements to be licensed. Thus there is the potential for substantial variability among the states. After many years of effort by NASW to achieve state-by-state legal regulation of social work, all fifty states, the District of Columbia, Puerto Rico, and the U.S. Virgin Islands license (or certify) social workers. Approximately two-thirds of the states provide for licensing or registration of social workers at the basic level and most have more than one level requiring the MSW as the educational preparation.[2] The Association of Social Work Boards serves as the coordinating agency for the state boards and offers testing at the following levels:

- ▶ **Basic:** BSW degree on graduation
- ▶ **Intermediate:** MSW with no post-degree experience
- ▶ **Advanced Genevalist:** MSW with two years' post-master's supervised experience
- ▶ **Clinical:** MSW with two years' post-master's direct clinical social work experience

The individual states then determine whether they want to use these test results for licensing of social workers and whether they want to grant *reciprocity* (i.e., accept the licenses of social workers from other states) when social workers move from state to state.

Professional Standards

A profession is required by society to protect the public from those members who abuse the professional monopoly. To conduct this self-policing, every profession must establish standards and develop procedures for evaluating complaints and imposing negative sanctions if a member engages in incompetent or unethical practice. State licensing, too, performs this client protection function by withdrawing the legal right to practice as a social worker if such violations occur.

NASW establishs appropriate standards of conduct and maintains a process to ensure the public that recognized professional social workers meet those standards. The standards for social workers are embodied in NASW's *Code of Ethics*. The Code spells out in some detail the social worker's ethical responsibilities to clients, colleagues, practice settings, other professionals, the profession of social work, and the broader society.[3] When a social worker becomes a member of NASW, he or she must profess willingness to practice within the guidelines prescribed by the Code of Ethics, and the Code, in turn, becomes the baseline for evaluating the professional behavior of social workers.

The process established for complaints begins with the local chapter of NASW. An individual or organization may lodge a formal complaint about the practice of a social worker. A committee of the chapter will then conduct an investigation of the complaint and make a determination that the complaint is or is not substantiated. Either party has the right to appeal to the NASW National Committee on Inquiry, which reviews the charges and makes a final judgment. If the Committee on Inquiry concludes that standards have been violated, a plan to correct the behavior through training or treatment may be developed or the individual's membership in NASW may be suspended. Action taken against either an individual or agency is published in the *NASW News*. The sanctions remain in effect until the terms established by the Committee on Inquiry are satisfied.

Options for Human Service Practice

Addressing complex human needs requires a range of service providers equipped with a variety of knowledge and skills. The human services, therefore, are made up of many people—from volunteers to highly trained professionals—who provide many different forms of helping. The person considering a career in a helping profession should carefully compare social work with other human service providers to determine if serving as a social worker would be the most satisfying way to spend one's work life.

Volunteers

One cannot fully examine the human services without recognizing the important role played by volunteers. For many people who have other vocations, one way to be involved with human services is to volunteer. The willingness to give of oneself, without monetary reward, in order to help others is expressed in the activity of millions of people who give their time, energy, and talents to make this a better world. It was from efforts to prepare volunteers to provide more effective human services that social work became a paid occupation and, later, a significant helping profession.

Today, social workers work closely with volunteers in many agencies. Their jobs often include the recruitment, selection, training, and supervision of volunteers. The qualifications of volunteers vary from activity to activity. At times professionals volunteer their services beyond their jobs in their own agencies or to help in other agencies. These volunteer activities may use their professional abilities but may also require skills unrelated to professional training. Like any other good citizen, the social worker has an obligation to donate his or her talents in order to improve social conditions.

Nonprofessional Service Providers

Not all human service practice requires the competencies of a social worker or someone with related professional skills. These providers have been referred to in the literature as *indigenous workers*. They may be clients, former clients, or others who have rapport with low-income or other client groups based on having similar experiences to the client population. At times indigenous workers can build relationships with clients when professionals have difficulty establishing rapport. Their life experience and knowledge of the individuals or groups being served are the most important qualifications.

Another important source of nonprofessional personnel for human service agencies are *graduates of community colleges*. These Associate of Arts (AA) degree programs vary considerably from school to school but focus on preparing for very specific human service jobs with titles such as mental health technician, community service aide, case aide, or social work technician. The AA degree programs usually include the study of human growth and behavior, social problems, the social service delivery system, personal values and self-awareness, and basic communication skills. These programs may provide field experiences so students have an opportunity to apply knowledge acquired in the classroom. The tasks the AA graduate can be expected to perform are typically very concrete and are carefully supervised by experienced workers.

Other Baccalaureate-Level Disciplines

Several disciplines offer majors in colleges and universities that are closely related to social work. Completing these degrees can serve as helpful preparation for some human service jobs and can also be good preparation for a subsequent degree in social work. However, these programs of study should not be confused with social work degree programs that, if accredited, carry professional recognition.

Social Science Disciplines.   Social work has traditionally had a close relationship with the social science disciplines for two reasons. First, social work has drawn on basic knowledge from the disciplines of psychology, sociology, anthropology, economics, and political science, while developing its theoretical base for understanding the individual, family, group, organization, community, and the impact of culture on all these. Second, in higher education, social work has had close administrative ties with these disciplines at the baccalaureate level. It is not uncommon to find a baccalaureate-level social work education program housed in a sociology department or in a multidisciplinary social science department.

Most positions for social scientists involve research or teaching, and, thus, a Ph.D. is necessary to be competitive in the job market. With the exception of specialized areas of clinical psychology and the small branch of applied sociology, social scientists do not typically engage in the provision of human services. Their purpose is to develop and test theories that will increase understanding of the people or places they study, but they do not intend to intervene to help people or social institutions change.

Related Helping Professions.   When making a career choice within the helping services, a person should examine a range of helping professions that might fit his or her individual talents and interests. The more established professions are medicine, law, nursing, teaching, and psychology. Other helping professions, such as physical therapy, music therapy, speech pathology and audiology, occupational therapy, recreation therapy, urban planning, and school counseling, also offer challenging and rewarding careers.

Each of these is an established profession and has prescribed and accredited educational programs a person must complete to be recognized as a member of that profession. Like social work, these professions identify standards for competent and ethical practice and take responsibility for policing the membership for compliance with these standards. The clientele of these professions, then, have some protection from the possible misuse of professional authority. Employment opportunities in these professions vary considerably, but most jobs are defined as requiring professional education for entry.

It is instructive to compare estimates of the demand for social workers with that of other helping professions. Table 5.2 provides a comparison of selected helping professions based on the projections of the U.S. Bureau of Labor Statistics (BLS). The BLS estimates of annual growth indicate that social work is already one of the largest and is expected to be a moderately fast growing occupation. Table 5.2 also reveals that the average annual earnings of social workers is on the low end of the helping professions. For comparison purposes, the table identifies the expected terminal professional degree for each discipline.

Emerging Human Service Occupations.   During the 1970s a new occupational group began to emerge, known generally as *human services* or *human development*. The human services occupations differ from the helping professions we have reviewed because they intend to be nonprofessional. Most people giving leadership to these occupations are professionally trained in other disciplines and have been largely involved in corrections and mental health services—although they branch into every aspect of the social services.

Table 5.2

Estimated Employment, Earnings and Training Requirements for Related Professions: 2002–2012

Profession	Total Employment 2002	Estimated Employment 2012	Est. Annual Growth (%)*	Annual Job Openings (Attrition and Job Growth)	Estimated Annual Earnings 2004	Expected Professional Degree
Registered Nurse	2,284,000	2,908,000	2.73	110,100	$54,210	Assoc. or Bachelor's
Elem./Middle School Teacher	1,093,000	1,282,000	1.73	49,700	48,420	Bachelor's + License
Lawyer	695,000	831,000	1.70	20,700	108,790	LLD
Physician	583,000	697,000	1.95	19,100	138,490	MD
Social Worker	477,000	604,000	2.67	20,700	39,130	Bachelor's or Master's
Special Ed. Teacher	433,000	563,000	3.00	23,300	48,910	Bachelor's + License
Vocational or School Counselor	228,000	262,000	1.50	8,600	47,590	Bachelor's or Master's
Psychologist	139,000	173,000	2.44	6,300	60,810	Ph.D.
Physical Therapist	137,000	185,000	3.53	6,200	62,390	Master's
Rehabilitation Counselor	122,000	164,000	3.38	6,900	30,710	Bachelor's or Master's
Mental Health Counselor	85,000	107,000	2.67	4,200	36,000	Bachelor's or Master's
Occupational Therapist	82,000	110,000	3.52	4,000	56,550	Master's
Urban Planner	32,000	36,000	1.07	1,400	55,600	Master's
Marriage/Family Therapist	23,000	29,000	2.24	1,100	42,040	Master's

*Annual Growth Rate: 3.6% or more = much faster than average; 2.1 to 3.5% = faster than average; 1.0 to 2.0% = average; 0 to 9% = more slowly than average; decrease = decline. Average growth rate for all occupations estimated to be at 1.52%

- (Employment Projections) U.S. Bureau of Labor Statistics. http://www.bls.gov.empl/emptab21.htm
- (Mean Wage Estimates) U. S. Bureau of Labor Statistics. http://www.bls.gov/oes/current/oes_21Co.htm
- (Expected Professional Degree) U. S. Bureau of Labor Statistics. http://www.bls.gov/oco/home.htm.

The development of the human services field was stimulated by dissatisfaction with the service delivery system. Fundamental to the philosophy behind this field are two viewpoints.[4] First, the human services have been fragmented into problem areas (e.g., public welfare, corrections, mental health) that create barriers to good service because many clients experience complex problems and must deal with multiple agencies, programs, and service providers. Second, the integration of services into "umbrella agencies" and the creation of a broad discipline that can provide a wide range of services is preferable to the more focused professional orientation.

Social workers would agree that the fragmented methods of delivering social services often make it difficult for clients to locate help. However, the profession does not regard service integration as a solution (division lines can exist just as rigidly within one large agency as in several smaller ones) and believe that the professional model, with all its limitations, continues to be the most valid means of identifying the people who are prepared with the knowledge, values, and skills to respond to specific human needs. Social work would argue that clients are better served through greater efforts at *interdisciplinary practice,* rather than the emergence of new human service disciplines that have no clear service focus or practice approach, no established standards for ethical conduct, no professional responsibility for quality control, and no standardized educational preparation subject to professional accreditation.

Levels of Professional Social Work Practice

Social work's evolution as a profession has been uneven, and the career paths one might follow as a social worker can be confusing. Figure 5.1 portrays the various career options available to the professional social worker. It recognizes that before a person decides to begin the educational preparation required to become a professional social worker, he or she will typically have had some positive experiences that have motivated this decision. This future social worker will typically have been a good natural helper or volunteer, the client of a social worker who received useful services, or perhaps a human services provider who did not have professional preparation. If he or she has not already completed a bachelor's degree, the most likely place to begin would be in a BSW program. However, if this is a person who has a degree in another discipline, a second entry point is available—an MSW program.

To make appropriate career development decisions, it is useful for the potential social worker to understand what is expected of a social worker at each of the four practice levels and how that practice level has emerged historically. The following materials, based on NASW's classification system,[5] briefly describe each level, identify the qualifications, and trace the manner in which its central characteristics have emerged.

The Basic Professional

Description: Practice as a basic social worker requires professional practice skills, theoretical knowledge, and values not normally obtainable in day-to-day experience but that are obtainable through formal social work education. This knowledge is

Figure 5.1

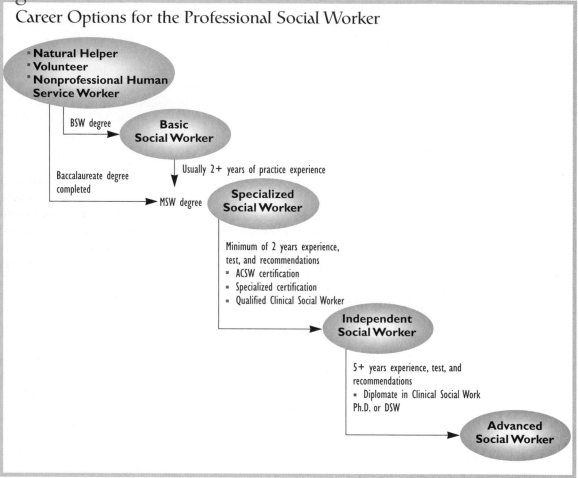

Career Options for the Professional Social Worker

distinguished from experiential learning by being based on conceptual and theoretical knowledge of personal and social interaction and by training in the disciplined use of self in relationship with clients.

Qualifications: Requires a baccalaureate degree from a social work program accredited by the Council on Social Work Education.

Characteristics: Practice at this first level has been formally recognized as professional only since 1970, when the NASW first admitted to full membership persons with a BA or BSW from a social work program approved by the Council on Social Work Education. This recognition substantially increased the quantity and quality of undergraduate social work programs.

A few schools offered baccalaureate-level social work courses as early as the 1920s.[6] However, the thrust of social work was toward graduate education. In 1932 the

American Association of Schools of Social Work (AASSW) declared that, to be recognized as professional, a social worker must graduate from a four-year college and complete at least one year of graduate education. In 1937 this position was revised to establish two years of graduate education as the minimum level for professional practice.

In response to the AASSW policy, in 1942 several schools created a competing organization, the National Association of Schools of Social Administration (NASSA), for the purpose of having undergraduate programs recognized as professional preparation. After several years of conflict over the legitimacy of undergraduate education, thirteen organizations interested in the resolution of this issue and in the overall enhancement of social work education formed the National Council on Social Work Education. In 1952 these organizations morphed into the single accrediting body for social work education: the Council on Social Work Education (CSWE).

The CSWE offered membership to both undergraduate and graduate schools and undertook a thirteen-volume curriculum study of social work education at both levels. One volume of this study recommended establishment of professional social work education at the undergraduate level with a continuum developed from undergraduate to graduate programs.[7] This recommendation was initially rejected by the CSWE. During most of the 1960s, undergraduate programs operated under CSWE guidelines that might best be described as a traditional liberal arts education oriented toward social welfare.[8] They were usually taught in departments of psychology or sociology, offered no more than three or four social work courses, and sometimes had no social workers as faculty. These programs were not professional education, and neither employers nor graduate social work education programs gave credit for this background or preference in admissions to applicants who had completed this major.

Disenchantment of students, employers, and professional social workers with undergraduate education contributed to the establishment of a joint CSWE–NASW Ad Hoc Committee on Manpower Issues in 1968. The Committee's recommendations contributed to concurrent actions in 1970 by NASW members to grant full membership to graduates of approved undergraduate programs and by the CSWE to establish standards for approval of these programs. The first standards adopted were essentially structural: they contributed to the visibility of social work programs, required that social workers be included in faculty, and demanded specification of educational objectives.[9]

CSWE "approval" was granted to 220 schools by 1973, but was at best a limited and informal type of accreditation. Its primary concern was that the schools have an adequate structure for the growth and development of a baccalaureate program. Specification of curriculum content was slower to develop because a workable division between baccalaureate- and master's-level education had not yet evolved.

In 1973 CSWE took the second step to complete legitimate accreditation: it adopted much more substantial standards for baccalaureate degree programs, placing the primary focus on preparation for professional social work practice. Some previously "approved" programs could not meet the new standards, but most were able to secure the necessary resources to upgrade their programs and achieve accredited status. The number of BSW programs gradually increased, and by 1980 a total of 261 met the accreditation requirements.[10]

In 1984 another significant step to upgrade the quality of baccalaureate social work education was taken when the CSWE operationalized a new set of accreditation standards and a much more substantive Curriculum Policy Statement. These standards spelled out the expectations for each program relative to its purpose, structure, and resources, and also required that each school's curriculum be consistent with the Curriculum Policy Statement.[11] While the standards did not dictate how a school should organize its curriculum, they were considerably more explicit than the 1974 accreditation standards about the content of the student's learning experience. Rigorous application of the accreditation standards did not deter colleges and universities of all sizes in all states from building and maintaining undergraduate social work education programs. As of 2005, 466 colleges and universities had BSW programs that were fully accredited or in candidacy status, graduating approximately 11,500 students each year.[12]

With NASW recognition came the gradual acceptance of baccalaureate-level social work, both by employers as preparation for practice and by the graduate programs as preparation for advanced education. Increasingly, jobs were defined to recognize the competence and abilities of social workers who had completed this type of educational program, and salary and work assignments were differentiated from those without this preparation. Furthermore, in 1972 CSWE granted approval for graduate schools to accept up to one year's credit for special groups of students. Approximately 85 percent of the graduate programs offer some form of *advanced standing* to graduates of accredited programs that typically amount to waiving one to two terms of graduate work.[13]

Clearly, the developments in the 1970s and 1980s enhance the conclusion that the social worker who has completed an accredited undergraduate social work program should be prepared with the competencies for that level of professional practice. Perhaps the most valid test of the acceptance of baccalaureate or basic social workers is whether they find employment as social workers. One study of 5,228 graduates of BSW programs found that 71.4 percent found their first job in social work; 86.8 percent secured employment within six months after graduation. Over time 84.3 percent of the BSW graduates were employed as social workers. These data suggest that the human service agencies found baccalaureate-level social workers attractive, especially in direct service positions, in which 90.2 percent were employed in their first social work job.[14]

The basic social worker is now well established in the United States as the first level of professional practice. The demand for social workers is increasing, and agencies readily employ these graduates. A niche has developed for BSW graduates that involves working largely with children and youth, with the aged, in the traditional nonprofit social service agencies and residential centers, and primarily on the front lines of social work practice providing services directly to clients.[15]

The Specialized Professional

Description: Practice at this level requires the specific and demonstrated mastery of therapeutic techniques in at least one knowledge and skill method, as well as general knowledge of human personality as influenced by social factors. Specialized practice also requires the disciplined use of self in treatment relationships with individuals or groups, or a broad conceptual knowledge of research, administration, or planning methods and social problems.

Qualifications: Requires a master's degree (MSW) from a social work program accredited by the CSWE.

Characteristics: Prior to the reemergence of baccalaureate-level social work education and the basic social worker, the generally accepted level of preparation for social work practice was that of the specialized social worker. It is expected that the MSW social worker, will have sufficient competence to function effectively in at least one area of specialized practice.

Historically, master's-level social work education began much like the more sophisticated in-service training programs of today. The first formal education program, known as the New York School of Philanthropy (now the Columbia University School of Social Work), was a six-week course offered under the auspices of the New York Charity Organization Society in 1898. The early curricula of the evolving schools incorporated preparation for a range of services, from individual helping approaches to economic and reform theory. They included a heavy investment in internships or field experiences as tools for learning practice skills and tended to be organized around practice settings, such as hospital social work and school social work. The MSW programs' greatest emphasis was on preparation for the services offered by private social agencies, and they tended to neglect the growing demand for social workers in the public social services.

By the 1940s the two-year MSW had become the minimum requirement for professional practice. The two-year programs were typically organized around what was known as the "Basic Eight," in reference to what at that time were considered the eight primary divisions of social work practice: public welfare, social casework, social group work, community organization, medical information, social research, psychiatry, and social welfare administration.

The period from 1950 through 1965 was one of rapid growth in the number of MSW programs and the relative standardization of these programs. By 1965 there were sixty-seven accredited graduate schools and nearly 9,000 students.[16] The schools had largely abandoned programs structured on the basis of practice setting and instead organized curricula around the practice methods of casework, group work, community organization, administration, and research.

Two factors have significantly influenced social work education at the graduate level in the past quarter-century. First, the reemergence of baccalaureate-level social work forced a reorientation of master's education; it was necessary to adapt to the student who entered the MSW program with a substantial social work education already completed. For this student, provision was made for advanced standing in the graduate-level program, which typically meant waiving or testing out of up to one year of graduate work. A continuum of education between the baccalaurcate and master's programs began to emerge.

Second, the Council on Social Work Education's Standards for Accreditation and Curriculum Policy Statement allowed individual schools increased flexibility in determining curriculum content. As the typical two-year MSW program evolved, it offered a general orientation to social work practice during the first year and then provided more specialized content based on population served, social problem addressed, practice intervention approach, or client group served during the second year. Prior to that development, students attending MSW programs could expect pretty much the same basic curriculum regardless of which school they attended. Today, because of the breadth of social work practice, the accreditation standards require that during the introductory or "foundation" part of the program the student must be educated from a generalist perspective. Thus, the first year of master's-level social work education is somewhat similar from school to school. However, after that base is developed, the final year (or its equivalent) prepares the student for a specific area of concentration, and at this level the schools differ widely. The dominant specializations increasingly have been related to the clinical aspects of social work practice. In the 2003–2004 academic year, for example, approximately 55 percent of the MSW students selected direct practice as their concentration, and more than 57 percent chose mental health, child welfare, family services, or school social work as their specialized practice area.[17]

For the 2003 academic year, approximately 23,500 full-time, 9,500 part-time, and 9,583 advanced standing applications were received by the 192 accredited and in-candidacy master's-level programs. About two-thirds of these applicants were accepted for admission and about 40 percent actually enrolled—often because students apply to several schools and end up enrolling in only one. The master's programs graduate 14,500 new MSWs each year.[18]

As opposed to the basic social worker, this specialized worker is expected to possess advanced knowledge and skill in specific areas of social work practice. The worker at this level has been awarded the highest professional social work practice degree (i.e., the terminal professional degree) in a graduate educational program that meets the accreditation requirements of the Council on Social Work Education.* Yet, he or she is not yet expected to work independently, that is, outside the structure and supervision provided in a human services agency.

The Independent Professional

Description: The independent practice level is based on appropriate specialized training beyond the MSW and continued professional development under supervision that is sufficient to ensure dependable, regular use of professional skills in independent private practice. A minimum of two years of post-master's experience is required to demonstrate this direct practice, administration, or training competence.

Qualifications: Requires an accredited MSW and at least two years of post-master's experience under appropriate professional supervision.

---

*Advanced degrees such as the DSW or the Ph.D. are not subject to accreditation standards established by the profession and are not considered to be professional practice degrees. Most doctorates in social work are academic degrees intended to prepare students for positions in teaching and research rather than in the more typical practice methods.

Characteristics: The independent social worker is expected to have developed and integrated the knowledge, values, and skills of social work in at least one practice area. From this experience, he or she should be able to develop sufficient expertise in that field to function independently and skillfully in sensitive situations and should be prepared to practice outside the auspices of a social agency. Furthermore, the independent social worker should be able to provide leadership in at least one practice arena and to supervise and consult with other social workers.

One indicator of reaching the independent professional level is membership in the *Academy of Certified Social Workers* (ACSW). The ACSW was established in 1960 to establish a more favorable public image, to obtain societal sanction, and to increase confidence and understanding in social work. Requirements for becoming a member of the Academy include maintaining membership in NASW, having a minimum of two years of full-time practice experience, and providing reference letters from professional peers.

As Table 5.1 indicates, NASW has also developed a credential to recognize the social worker with additional clinical practice experience who has demonstrated knowledge and competence above that expected of the new master's-level worker, that is, the *Qualified Clinical Social Worker* (QCSW) credential. As an additional means of recognizing practice areas where the worker has increased capability, NASW has developed three areas where specialized certification is possible—school social work, case management, and alcohol, tobacco, and other drug abuse. Although many social workers employed in human services agencies have attained greater skill and experience than required at the "specialized" social worker level, those engaged in private practice are expected by the profession to have attained this "independent" practice level. The assumption is that the social worker at this level is prepared to function independent of the monitoring typically provided by a human services agency. Therefore, credentials become an important means of verifying that the worker is prepared to perform high-quality and ethical services without the need for additional professional oversight.

The Advanced Professional

Description: Practice at the advanced level is that which carries major social and organizational responsibility for professional development, analysis, research, or policy implementation, or is achieved by personal professional growth demonstrated through advanced conceptual contributions to professional knowledge.

Qualifications: This level requires proficiency in a special theoretical, practice, administration, or policy area, or the ability to conduct advanced research studies in social welfare; usually demonstrated through a doctoral degree in social work or another discipline—in addition to the MSW.

Characteristics: This classification is reserved for the most highly experienced practitioners as well as for social workers who have obtained a doctoral in social work or a related field. In contrast to many professions, relatively few social workers seek or achieve the advanced professional level.

For direct service or clinical practitioners who aspire to the advanced level, NASW has developed the *Diplomate in Clinical Social Work* (DCSW). To be recognized as a diplomate in clinical social work, a person must have completed an accredited MSW program, possess an advanced or clinical state license, have a minimum of five years of post-master's clinical experience, perform satisfactorily on a case-based essay examination, and receive a favorable comprehensive supervisory evaluation (see Table 5.1).

Doctoral education represents the second route to the advanced social work level. The purposes for doctoral degrees (DSW or Ph.D.) in social work have not followed a consistent pattern. Most programs devote their efforts to preparing the researcher and teacher, but increasingly there has been some focus on preparation for the advanced practitioner. Since the doctorate is not viewed as an entry degree for the social work profession and it is not accredited by the profession, the doctoral programs receive their sanction only from their universities. Therefore, the schools have considerable flexibility to determine the focus of their curricula and have taken on unique identities. By 2003, sixty-six doctoral programs in social work were available throughout the United States, enrolling about 1,600 full-time and slightly fewer part-time students, yet only 289 doctoral degrees in social work were awarded.[19] These numbers do not, however, reflect the total number of social workers completing doctoral degrees because some complete doctoral work in related fields such as sociology, psychology, higher education, and public administration.

Concluding Comment

Through the years of its emergence, social work has gradually evolved four distinct practice levels. The National Association of Social Workers has codified these levels into a classification system with expectations for the practitioner at each level defined and education and experience qualifications specified. This classification system encompasses two problems in terminology—both created by the acceptance of the concept of an advanced generalist social worker. First, the MSW graduate prepared as an advanced generalist is qualified under the classification system as a "Specialized Social Worker." Can one be a specialized generalist? Also, an advanced generalist social worker is not the same as an Advanced Social Worker in NASW's classification system. Persons new to social work should be aware of this confusing terminology.

Nevertheless, the NASW classification of social work practice levels is a useful tool for both social agencies wanting to match workers with job demands and for persons considering a career in social work. For the latter, the selection of a particular practice level as a career goal requires that one assess his or her desire to provide the particular types of service and then consider the necessary preparation and the ability to arrange one's personal life to acquire the requisite professional education. In social work, in contrast to some of the other helping professions, one can change directions after entering the profession. A person might enter social work in a particular field of practice, such as providing services to the aged or developmentally disabled, and later transfer the skills used in that job to employment in mental health or corrections. Box 5.1, for example, depicts several factors our social worker, Demetria (see Chapter 1), may have considered as she thought about what her BSW degree represented and what options she might have in the future. Or the direct service worker (usually with a master's degree) might transfer into a job involving agency administration or move away from agency-based practice and into autonomous or private practice.

Box 5.1

Demetria's Career in Social Work

Demetria, the social worker investigating the report received from Joseph's school of possible child abuse or neglect (Chapter 1), was employed in her first social work job after completing her BSW degree. What did it mean for her future that she had completed the degree, had joined the National Association of Social Workers (NASW), and was now considered a professional social worker?

First, to achieve professional recognition Demetria's educational program must have met the *accreditation standards* established by the Council on Social Work Education. Her school, then, had required courses and field experiences that included the content specified in national curriculum requirements and were taught by faculty members meeting national standards, making her education comparable to the education students would receive at other accredited schools. Further, Demetria was likely to be in the process of applying for the *"Basic Social Worker"* license in her state (if her state was one that offered a license at this level) and would soon start preparing for the examination she would need to pass to become a licensed social worker. To become a NASW member Demetria signed a pledge to uphold the *"Code of Ethics"* and would be deepening her knowledge of the meaning of those guidelines to ethical practice as she periodically examines them to inform her practice decisions.

Second, Demetria was just beginning her career as a social worker. She knew that one positive feature of this profession was that the social work career ladder provided the opportunity for a social worker to make changes in the work he or she does in the future. For now it would take all Demetria could manage to perform her entry-level social work job in an effective manner, but later she might want to change to work with older people, in corrections, or in some other field of practice. For some changes, such as a move to more clinical work or agency administration, she would need a MSW degree and would transition to the next practice level, the *specialized professional*.

KEY WORDS AND CONCEPTS

Accreditation (of educational programs)
Professional certification
Academy of Certified Social Workers
Licensing (state regulation of practice)
Indigenous workers

Advanced standing
Basic social worker
Specialized social worker
Independent social worker
Advanced social worker

SUGGESTED INFORMATION SOURCES

Biggerstaff, Marilyn A. "Licensing, Regulation, and Certification." In Richard L. Edwards, ed., *Encyclopedia of Social Work,* 19th Edition. Washington, D.C.: NASW Press, 1995, pp. 1616–1624.

Gibelman, Margaret, and Phillip H. Schervish. *Who We Are: A Second Look.* Washington, D.C.: NASW Press, 1996.

National Association of Social Workers. "NASW Credentials Specialty Certification." http://www.naswdc.org.

ENDNOTES

1. Robert R. Wohlgemuth and Thomas Samph, *Summary Report: Content Validity Study in Support of the Licensure Examination Program of the American Association of State Social Work Boards* (Oak Park, IL: The Association, 1983), p. 2.

2. Association of Social Work Boards. Social Work Laws and Regulations: Online Comparison Guide. http://www.aswb.org.

3. National Association of Social Workers. *Code of Ethics.* May be downloaded from http://www.socialworkers.org/pubs/code/code.asp

4. Joseph Mehr, *Human Services: Concepts and Intervention Strategies,* 8th Edition (Boston: Allyn and Bacon, 2001), pp. 11–20.

5. National Association of Social Workers, *NASW Standards for the Classification of Social Work Practice* (Washington, D.C.: The Association, 1981).

6. A comprehensive analysis of the evolution of baccalaureate-level social work can be found in Bradford W. Sheafor and Barbara W. Shank, *Undergraduate Social Work Education: A Survivor in a Changing Profession* (Austin: University of Texas at Austin School of Social Work, 1986).
Ernest V. Hollis and Alice L. Taylor, *Social Work Education in the United States* (New York: Columbia University Press, 1951).

7. Herbert Bisno, *The Place of Undergraduate Curriculum in Social Work Education, Social Work Curriculum Study* Vol. 2 (New York: Council on Social Work Education, 1959).

8. Council on Social Work Education, *Social Welfare Content in Undergraduate Education* (New York: The Council, 1962), pp. 3–4.

9. Council on Social Work Education, *Undergraduate Programs in Social Work* (New York: The Council, 1971).

10. Allen Rubin, *Statistics on Social Work Education in the United States: 1980* (New York: Council on Social Work Education, 1981), p. 1.

11. Council on Social Work Education, *Handbook of Accreditation Standards and Procedures* (Washington, D.C.: The Council, 1984).

12. "Recent Actions Taken by Commission on Accreditation," June 2005, http://www.cswe.org.

13. Council on Social Work Education, *Summary of Information on Master of Social Work Programs: 2001–02.* (Alexandria, VA: Council on Social Work Education, 2002).

14. Bradford W. Sheafor, "Three Decades of Baccalaureate Social Work: A Grade Card on How the Professionalization of the BSW Has Played Out." *Journal of Baccalaureate Social Work* 6 (Spring 2001): 25–43.

15. Sheafor, *Ibid.*
16. Ramond DeVera, ed., *Statistics on Social Work Education in the United States: 1965–66* (New York: Council on Social Work Education, 1966), p. 6.
17. Todd M. Lennon, ed., *Statistics on Social Work Education in the United States: 2003* (Alexandria, VA: Council on Social Work Education, 2005), Tables 40 and 41.
18. Lennon, *Ibid.,* Tables 34, 35, and 57.
19. Lennon, *Ibid.,* Tables 1 and 57.

Fields of Social Work Practice

Prefatory Comment

One factor that makes social work different from many other professions is the opportunity to help people deal with a wide range of human problems without needing to obtain specialized professional credentials for each area of practice. During his or her lifetime, for example, one social worker might organize and lead self-help groups in a hospital, deal with cases of abuse and neglect, develop release plans for persons in a correctional facility, plan demonstrations protesting racist or sexist injustices, arrange for foster homes and adoptions for children, secure nursing home placements for older people, supervise new social workers, and serve as director of a human service agency. Regardless of the type of work performed, the social worker always has the same fundamental purpose—to draw on basic knowledge, values, and skills in order to help achieve desired change to improve the quality of life for the persons involved.

Although there are similarities in the tasks performed by social workers regardless of the nature of the services provided, there are also unique aspects of their practice with each population group. For example, services to children and youth differ from services to the elderly, the needs of a disabled adult differ from those of a person about to be released from a correctional facility, and the assistance required by a pregnant teenager differs from that needed by a teenager engaged in gang activity or substance abuse. Each of these fields of practice typically uses at least some specialized language, emphasizes specific helping approaches and techniques, or may be affected by different laws or social programs. Therefore, what a social worker does and needs to know will vary to some extent from field to field.

The human services system is indeed complex, and the layperson cannot be expected to negotiate this system alone. As the profession with the primary responsibility for helping people to gain access to the services in a community, the social worker must not only know what services are available, but must also be prepared to interpret them to their clients and help these clients gain access to the resources they need. To reduce the client's sense of "getting the runaround" in securing services, and perhaps reduce the chance of the client becoming discouraged and not getting the needed help, the social worker must carefully check that the referral is to an appropriate resource. In addition, the professional, at times, may need to provide a variety of supports, such as encouragement, telephone numbers, names of individuals to contact, or even transportation to facilitate the client's getting to the correct resources. Thus, the social worker must not only work within a single practice field but should also be prepared to help clients negotiate services among practice fields.

This chapter identifies some of the features of the primary fields of social work practice. *Field of social work practice* is a phrase used to describe a group of practice settings that deal with similar client problems. Each field may include a number of different agencies or other organized ways of providing services. For example, in any community, the social agencies concerned with crime and delinquency might include a juvenile court, a residential center or halfway house, a community corrections agency, a probation office for adult offenders, and/or a correctional facility where offenders are incarcerated. All of these agencies work with people who have come to the attention of the legal system and would be considered part of the practice field of corrections. Although the fields discussed in the remainder of this chapter do not exhaust the full range where social workers might practice, those identified suggest the great variety of settings in which the social worker is prepared to provide services.

Aging

Sara May is a social worker with the Senior Center, a community recreation program offering programs geared to the needs and interests of the community's older citizens. The Center's hot lunch program draws many older people daily, and Sara interacts informally with the "Lunch Crowd" as a means of building relationships and encouraging the participants to ask her for advice and counseling, if needed. Today Mrs. Jackson, a widow in her early 80s, asked if she could visit with Sara for a few minutes after lunch to talk over a difficult decision she needed to think through. Quickly Mrs. Jackson summarized her issues. It was getting much more difficult for her to manage living alone and she was considering moving to a retirement center or possibly moving to another state to be near her daughter. Some questions Sara anticipated Mrs. Jackson should be helped to consider were: If she stayed in this community, could she afford to live in such a center? What could she do with her long-time companion, her dog Sidney? Mrs. Jackson had lived in the community most of her life and in her home for 25 years. How difficult would it be to make friends somewhere else? What implications might there be for her daughter's family if she stayed here or moved to be near them?

The 2000 Census found 35 million people in the United States age 65 and over, making up 12.4 percent of the total population. This part of the population is expected to double over the next thirty years, partially as a result of the large number of "baby boomers" (those born between 1946 and 1965) reaching this age level and partially as a result of better health care that is increasing life expectancy. Of particular significance is the fact that the group aged 85 and older is expanding substantially and is becoming much more ethnically diverse. At age 85, the population is already 70 percent female, and as age increases the percentage of women living alone increases even more.[1]

The aging population is served by a substantial number of social workers. Sometimes the services are provided directly to the older persons and at other times through their families. Most of the direct work with older people is provided by basic social workers, with the specialized and independent workers more likely to work with families around the income, health, and housing problems of their older parents. Progress has been made in reducing the poverty rate for older people, although in 2003 a total of nearly 3.6 million older people (10.2 percent) had incomes at or below the poverty line.[2] Thanks to Medicare coverage, 99.3 percent of older people have health insurance, minimizing some of their financial worries over health care,[3] and the recent assistance with expensive prescriptions makes the economic position of older people less precarious. This population group is projected to be the fastest growing of all age groups at least into the mid-2000s and should represent a substantially expanding area of specialization for social workers.

A number of programs are available to help older people remain in their own homes as long as doing so is a safe and satisfying experience. Social workers help older people make links to community programs that bring health care, meals, and homemaker services into their homes; provide transportation services; and offer daycare or recreation programs. Increasingly, when older people are faced with a terminal illness, social workers help them deal with their impending death through counseling or referral to a hospice program.

For approximately 4 percent of the older people, some form of long-term care in a nursing home or other group living facility becomes a necessity. Social workers frequently help the individual and/or family select the facility and make moving arrangements; some are even staff members of the facility.

While much attention in a long-term care facility is directed toward meeting the basic physical and medical needs of the residents, social workers in these facilities contribute to the quality of life for residents by helping them maintain contact with their families and friends when possible, develop meaningful relationships with other people within the facility, and engage in a variety of activities both within and outside the facility. They also facilitate access to other social services when needed and help residents secure arrangements that protect their personal rights and ensure quality care while living in the long-term care facility.

Alcohol and Substance Abuse

Andrew Richards is a social worker in an outpatient drug and alcohol center. Each Tuesday evening Andrew facilitates a group of parents who have a high school age child experiencing a drug and/or alcohol problem. The topic of discussion tonight concerns peer influence and ways that parents might help their child deal with peers who pressure them to use drugs or alcohol. One parent argues for a get-tough, "just say no," stance, another believes getting the child to therapy is the only solution, and still another contends that giving a child room to make mistakes is the only way the child can learn to make mature judgments. Andrew knows his skills in group work will help him be sure that everyone has a chance to share his or her views and have the pros and cons of each position carefully considered. Ultimately, each parent must decide how he or she will address this matter.

Although relatively few social workers are employed in agencies that exclusively treat drug and alcohol problems, social workers in virtually every type of human services agency deal with problems that are associated with drug or alcohol use or abuse. Between 9 and 12 million individuals in the United States are alcoholics or drug abusers, and it is estimated that each individual experiencing a drug or alcohol problem affects at least four other persons in some negative, unhealthy, or destructive manner.[4] The social implications of alcohol and substance abuse are significant, since they are highly correlated with murders, suicides, accidents, health problems, and domestic violence.

Using current scientific understanding of these problems, Lawson and Lawson have identified three primary factors that should be considered in treating and preventing alcoholism and substance abuse. First, they recognize that physiological factors such as physical addiction, disease or physical disorders, medical problems, inherited risk, and/or mental disorders with physiological causes may contribute to the problem. Second, Lawson and Lawson identify several sociological factors, such as ethnic and cultural differences, family background, education, employment, and peer relationships, as also related to alcoholism and substance abuse. Finally, they note that psychological factors, including social skills, emotional level, self-image, attitude toward life, defense mechanisms, mental obsessions, judgment, and decision-making skills all can be contributors to this disease.[5] Growing understanding of these associated and interrelated factors has provided the helping professions with an opportunity to apply their knowledge and skills to helping clients prevent and resolve their problems. Social work plays a particularly important role, as the addictions inevitably have a significant effect on family, friends, coworkers, and others who are in contact with the person experiencing the addiction. Both the person and the environment must be helped to change when this disease is treated.

Child Welfare

Megan Messer, a social worker with the County Division of Child Welfare, has a difficult recommendation to make to the judge. Her job is to evaluate the conditions in the Benjamin Bradford home to determine whether Kate, the Bradford's new baby, is getting proper care. Neighbors reported that the house is always dirty, food and unwashed clothing are left around, and the baby can be heard crying at almost any time of the day or night. When Megan called Mr. Bradford to schedule an interview, he told her it was none of her damn business and to butt out of his life. Megan had to be very persistent to get an appointment scheduled. She wasn't looking forward to the interview.

The U.S. society has entrusted the family with full responsibility for the care and nurturing of children. Law and custom mandate that other social institutions must not interfere with the rights and responsibilities of the family to care for its children. Historically, it has been assumed that parents would make choices that were in the best interest of both themselves and their children. For example, if parents thought it more important for children to work in a factory or to help with farm work than to attend school or have time for play, that decision was honored. That authority, however, left children vulnerable. Legislation permitting other social institutions (e.g., child protective services, police, and courts) to intervene in family situations that were potentially harmful to children was reluctantly adopted. Today, children and youth continue to be somewhat hidden within families with only limited protection when abusive situations are present.

In most situations social workers seek to work with both the parents and the children by providing support services in order to keep children in their own homes. These services might involve one-to-one counseling with a parent, child–parent counseling to resolve a particular problem, or family counseling to resolve issues affecting some aspect of the family's functioning. Family members may also participate in group counseling with other parents of children experiencing similar problems where a social worker guides the group to address issues relevant to their problems. Finally, the social worker may assist the families to use outside resources such as day care and homemaker services.

The four primary practice activities of child welfare work involve providing protective services or arranging foster care, residential care, or adoption placements when children cannot safely be cared for in their own homes.

Protective Services

More than 825,000 cases of child maltreatment occur in the United States each year. Of these cases, 56 percent are classified as neglect, 21 percent are related to physical abuse, 11 percent involve sexual abuse, 8 percent are psychological or emotional abuse, and the remainder are unclassified or related to other forms of abuse or neglect.[6] Abuse, whether it is physical, sexual, or emotional, is an active mistreatment or exploitation of the child. Neglect is a more passive mistreatment but can be just as damaging. It can take the form of inadequate food and shelter, unwholesome conditions, failure to have the child attend school, or inadequate provision of medical care.

The social worker, as an agent of society, seeks to protect the child without infringing on the rights of the parents. When a referral is received, the social worker must determine if the child is in immediate danger, assess the ability of the parents to resolve the problem, and make a judgment about the risks of working with the family while keeping the child in the home. If the child is removed from the home (with approval of the courts), the social worker continues to work with the family in an effort to eliminate the difficulties that led to the referral. This process may involve individual, family, or group counseling; the provision of support services; or education of family members in the areas of their incompetence.

Foster Care

At times children may need to be removed from their own homes, but it is not possible, or desirable, to permanently sever their relationship with their natural parents. In these cases, temporary (and sometimes long-term) foster care is required and the social worker must work with the parents, the child, and the courts to obtain a decision to remove a child from his or her own home and make a foster home placement. The process involves a careful assessment and a plan whereby the child can return home if conditions improve. Although both federal and state laws discourage removing children from their families, a total of 588,000 children were living in foster care in 2000.[7]

The social worker is also responsible for developing a pool of good quality foster homes. He or she must recruit, select, train, and monitor those families that are entrusted with the care of foster children. The placement of a child in a foster home often creates severe stress on the child, the natural parents, and the foster parents. Considerable practice skill by the social worker is required if he or she is to help resolve these problems.

Residential Care

At times the appropriate placement for a child is a residential care facility, that is, a group home or residential treatment center. These facilities are most likely to be chosen when the child exhibits antisocial behavior or requires intensive treatment to change behaviors that may create problems for him- or herself or for others.

In these situations, one role of the social worker is to select an appropriate residential care facility, which involves working with the child, the family, and, often, the courts. In addition, other social workers are usually staff members of such a facility, providing care and treatment for the children who are placed there. They are especially involved in helping maintain positive contact between the child and the family and in making plans for the child to return home when appropriate. The fact that these residential care facilities require licensing creates another role for the social worker—evaluating facilities for the purpose of licensing.

Adoption and Services to Unmarried Parents

Child welfare work also involves assisting expectant mothers, often unmarried, address the difficult decision of whether to keep the baby or place the child for adoption. Nearly 35 percent of all children born in the United States in 2003 were born to unmarried parents, a factor that substantially increases the likelihood that the child will grow up in household with income below the poverty line.[8] A few of the factors to be considered in this decision include the mother's plans for the future, such as continuing school or securing employment and child care, the attitudes of the mother's family about the pregnancy, the feelings of the father and the mother's relationship with him, and where the mother will live while pregnant and after the baby arrives. Social workers use both individual and group counseling to help women consider the implications of their decisions. They also, at times, offer counseling to unmarried fathers to help them deal with this situation.

If the decision is made to place the child for adoption, the social worker must screen and select adoptive parents carefully. Matching parents and children is a difficult task that requires considerable knowledge and skill. To gain the best information possible on which to base these decisions, the social worker might conduct group orientation meetings and develop thorough social histories of the prospective adoptive parents. Detailed information on the child's background and even special interests of the natural mother for the child's future (religious affiliation, for example) become part of the basis for final adoptive placement. It continues to be difficult to secure satisfactory adoptive homes for older children or those who are physically or mentally disabled. An important function of the social worker is to recruit parents for these hard-to-place children.

Community/Neighborhood Work

Luis Garcia is a social worker at a storefront neighborhood center in a large city. His job is to help residents rectify substandard housing conditions in the area. Tonight Mr. Garcia is helping a group from the neighborhood plan a strategy for pressuring some of the landlords to improve the quality of housing and to demand that the city increase traffic safety in the neighborhood.

From its beginning social workers have clearly seen the need both to coordinate the multiple human services that exist in a community and to stimulate change in these communities to make them more responsive to the needs of people or change patterns of operation that have negative effects on people. When social workers provide neighborhood or community services, three forms of intervention are typically applied: community organization, community planning, and community development.

Community Organization

The primary job of some social workers is to work within the network of human services to increase their effectiveness in meeting human needs. This activity involves collecting and analyzing data related to the delivery of services, matching that information with data on population distribution, securing funds to maintain and enhance the quality of services, coordinating the efforts of existing agencies, and educating the general public about these services. The principal agencies in which social workers are employed to do this type of work are community planning councils, United Way agencies, and other federations of agencies under the auspices of religious groups, such as the Jewish Welfare Federation.

Community Planning

Social workers sometimes have the specialized training to join physical, economic, and health planners in long-range planning of communities. This work requires the ability to apply planning technology in order to project and plan the growth and development of communities. The special contribution of the social worker is to analyze the needs for human services as towns, cities, or regions undergo change. These contributions might range from anticipating the demands that follow the creating of a new ski area in rural Colorado to helping an urban ghetto plan for changes in the demand for human services when a factory shuts down, leaving the community with an eroding tax base.

Community or Neighborhood Development

Social work joins a number of disciplines in giving assistance to people in communities as they seek to improve conditions. This approach is based on a self-help philosophy that encourages members of the community to mobilize their resources in order to study their problems and seek solutions. In rural areas, the social worker contributes to this "grass roots" approach by guiding those involved toward a sound process that maximizes the participation of many concerned citizens. The social worker or other professional also serves as a resource for obtaining technical consultation in areas where there is not expertise among the community members. In urban areas this process, sometimes known as an "asphalt roots" approach, is used to help neighborhoods or special population groups (such as the poor, minorities, or older people) work together to improve the quality of their lives.

Corrections/Criminal Justice

Malinda Scott, a social worker employed as a juvenile probation officer, is preparing her testimony for a court hearing regarding one of her clients, Cheryl Graham. Following an intense argument with her mother over her increasingly frequent use of "recreational drugs" when hanging out with her friends, Cheryl impulsively decided to run away. She stole a neighbor's automobile and wrecked it when entering a nearby highway. Luckily no other vehicles were involved and Cheryl sustained no serious injuries. Since Cheryl had not been using drugs when the accident occurred, she was assigned community service and placed on probation. Cheryl presented a variety of excuses for her frequent failure to show up for community service assignments, but she and her mother had actively participated in counseling with Ms. Scott and were just beginning to deal with their conflicts more effectively. Should Ms. Scott recommend that probation be continued until more progress is made?

Another small but important part of social work practice occurs in the area of corrections and criminal justice. Correctional social workers are employed in courts, parole and probation offices, and correctional facilities. Social workers often find corrections a perplexing field of practice because the structure of services is usually based on punishment and taking custody of the lives of offenders, which conflicts with many social work values and principles. Yet, because the problems experienced by persons who come to the attention of professionals in this field are basically those of social functioning, the social worker has a valuable contribution to make.

The corrections field embraces offenders from all aspects of society—youth and adults, males and females, rich and poor, members of dominant population groups and minorities, and even well-known celebrities. In correctional settings, the poor, especially minorities, are very much overrepresented. The social worker's involvement with the criminal justice system can begin at the time of arrest and terminate at the person's release. Some social workers serve as, or work with, juvenile officers in diversionary programs, where they provide crisis intervention or referral services at the time of arrest. These programs divert people from the criminal justice system and into more appropriate community services. Social workers also prepare social histories and make psychosocial assessments of individuals charged with crimes as part of the data a judge uses in making decisions about a case. If the person is placed on probation, a social worker might be the probation officer providing individual, family, or group counseling and helping the convicted person make changes in behavior that will satisfy the terms of probation and prevent additional problems from developing.

Social workers are also found in correctional facilities. In these facilities they provide counseling and serve as a link to the outside world, which encompasses the family, potential employers, and the community service network that will provide support to that person at the time of release. If parole is granted, a social worker might serve as the parole officer or work in a halfway house where the person may live prior to a completely independent re-entry to the community.

Disabilities (Physical and Mental)

K. G. Murder is executive director of the Council on Disabled Persons. This council identifies and seeks solutions to problems experienced by persons with disabling conditions, including mental retardation, physical deformity, or hearing, visual, or speech impairments. As executive director, Mr. Murder provides leadership to the citizen board as it develops programs to meet the needs of its clientele. Tonight the board will work on designing a plan for evacuating handicapped persons throughout the community should there be a disaster that requires removing people from their homes or residential care settings.

Assisting persons with physical, mental, and developmental disabilities is a field of practice in which basic social workers are most likely to be the primary service providers. Yet helping people deal with disabling conditions affects most fields of social work. Social workers are concerned with such disabling conditions as mental retardation, visual and hearing impairment, communication disability, learning disability, and cerebral palsy, which affect not only the person's physical and intellectual functioning but also interaction with others, that is, social functioning. The special role of social work is to help these persons and their families learn to live as successfully as possible in a society structured for the more fully functioning individual.

The U.S. Center for Disease Control and Prevention estimates that in 2003 34.3 million people (12 percent of the population) experienced one or more chronic conditions that limited their activities. About one-fourth of these people (3.8 million) experienced such a severe condition that they needed help with daily living activities such as eating, dressing, or bathing. Another 7.7 million people could not do household chores or shopping without help. Health-related conditions prevented another 6 percent of the adult working-age population from employment, and another 3 percent were limited in the kind of work they could perform. Further, 6 percent of the school-age children were receiving special education services. Indeed, a substantial part of the U.S. population experiences some form of disability, and these disabilities are experienced to a greater extent among people who have the least education and the lowest income.[9] In addition to the physical disabilities many more people experience mental or emotional conditions (or both) that are disabling.

The term *developmental disability* has evolved to include a broad range of disabling conditions that affect the physical, social, and intellectual development of a person. The Developmental Disabilities Assistance and Bill of Rights Act (Public Law 95–602) includes the following definition of a developmental disability:

> . . . a severe chronic disability of a person which: a) is attributable to a mental or physical impairment or combination of mental or physical impairments; b) is manifested before the person attains age 22; c) is likely to continue indefinitely; d) results in substantial functional limitations in three or more of the following areas of major life activity, including self-care, receptive/expressive language, learning, mobility, self-direction, capacity for independent living, and economic self-sufficiency; and e) reflects the person's need for a combination and sequence of special, interdisciplinary, or generic care, treatment, or other services which are individually planned and coordinated.[10]

While the definition of a disabled person contained in PL 95-602 does not include all physically and intellectually disabled people, it does encompass a large share of the most seriously disabled. In an effort to enhance the quality of life for all people, social workers serve clients who experience both mild and severe disabilities. To accomplish this goal, social workers help people find suitable living arrangements (either with their families or in community facilities), assist in the alleviation of problems associated with the disability, contribute to public education efforts about the causes and society's responses to these disabilities, and help individuals gain access to needed services.

Family Services

Nadine Harrison is a highly specialized social worker and an expert in family casework. She has just begun working with the Machin family to help each member change his or her patterns of interacting with other family members to reduce conflict and make each a more productive member of the family. Ms. Harrison has asked that all family members come to the family counseling session and will challenge each to identify the behaviors of others that make him or her feel unsupported by the family. Then they will collectively look for ways to prevent or modify those behaviors, as well as identify ways to reinforce the improved behaviors. Ms. Harrison hopes that all members of the Machin family arrive on time as there is much to be done in the next hour.

Social workers at all levels are likely to be involved in helping families address issues in their social functioning. Why are family services such a substantial part of social work practice? Changing marital arrangements, child-rearing practices, and patterns of employment in the United States have placed considerable strain on the nuclear family. A growing number of single-parent families, reconstituted families (often involving her children, his children, and their children), duo-breadwinner families, and gay/lesbian households, for example, have dramatically affected social structures that were established for the older family pattern of a mom, a dad, and their children. Social workers have a key role in helping society address these changes and in assisting individual families and households to adapt to these newer conditions or resolve problems associated with them.

Three broad service areas capture the bulk of family services provided by social workers. First, much of the activity involves providing various forms of counseling or therapy to families. Patterns of interaction may develop that are dysfunctional for the individual members; membership may change through marriage or death, requiring new ways of relating to each other; or one member experiencing a severe social or emotional problem may create strain among the family members. Family life is often difficult and taxing for members, and issues sometimes cannot be resolved without professional help. Thus social workers working with troubled families must be skilled at providing family casework, family therapy, and other forms of family services.

Second, as opposed to working to solve family problems, social workers also work proactively to strengthen families through activities that fall under the label of *family life education*. This social work practice activity recognizes that all families face certain kinds of stress and seeks to prevent family breakdown by educating family members to cope with anticipated problems. It teaches about interpersonal, family, and sex relationships to help people to have more satisfactory and fulfilling lives.

Finally, social workers have long been sensitive to the fact that both an unwanted child and his or her parents often experience problems. Adequately carrying out the responsibilities of raising a child is difficult under the best of circumstances, and an unwanted pregnancy makes it even more difficult. Thus, helping families plan the number, spacing, and timing of the births of children to fit with the family's capacities improves the quality of life for all family members.

Income Maintenance

Dorothy Simmons, a social worker in the local public human services agency, has an appointment with Mrs. Sang Woo. She knows from a telephone call arranging the appointment that Mrs. Woo is terribly worried about her future and that of her two small children. Her husband was killed two months ago in a robbery at the neighborhood market where he worked. In addition, Mrs. Woo found that after paying funeral expenses, little money was left for raising the children. She hopes that Ms. Simmons can help her find a way to secure the financial resources to get by temporarily and to obtain job training and daycare so that she can support the family in the long run.

Once income maintenance was the primary practice activity engaged in by social workers, but today relatively few professionally prepared workers are employed in income maintenance positions. However, social workers in many fields of practice regularly deal with clients for whom financial matters are a primary factor in the situations they bring for help. Therefore, the social worker's knowledge of the various programs that can be accessed for financial assistance is a valuable resource for their clients.

On an emergency or short-term basis, there are many local agencies that provide support in the form of used clothing outlets, food banks and food kitchens, shelters for homeless individuals and families, emergency child care facilities, transportation vouchers, subsidized housing, and other resources where the poor can obtain social provisions for meeting basic needs. These resources are so unique to local areas that few people have a good understanding of what resources are available. Knowledge of these resources and how to gain access to them is therefore a special responsibility of the social worker.

In addition to locally developed services, a number of government-sponsored programs exist to meet basic needs or provide a minimum level of support in order to prevent more serious health or income problems from developing. Among the income maintenance programs are "safety net" programs that require that the recipients experience serious social or economic problems before the resource can become available to them. Examples of these programs are *Food Stamps, Temporary Assistance for Needy Families (TANF), Social Security Income (SSI),* and *Medicaid.* In addition, several social insurance programs anticipate the needs of special populations that have been designed in the "social utilities" philosophy and are available as a right for the designated client situations without the stigma of demeaning eligibility tests. These programs include *Old Age Survivors, Disability, and Health Insurance (OASDHDI), Medicare, Unemployment Insurance,* and *Worker's Compensation Insurance.* Social workers practicing in most settings need to be familiar with these programs and skilled at helping clients access them.

Medical and Health Care

Ahmed AlAwam is a social worker employed in a large community hospital. For the past two years he was assigned to the emergency room (ER), assisting individuals and families as they dealt with or adapted to the traumatic situations that brought them to the ER. Mr. AlAwam's crisis intervention skills were of primary importance in this work. Now, he has moved to the rehabilitation unit, where he is engaged in much more long-term work with patients who have experienced a substantial disabling injury. Today he is having his first session with Ted Barker, a bricklayer who sustained an injury in a construction accident that resulted in the amputation of his right arm. Mr. Barker is understandably depressed as he recognizes that he will undergo a substantial change in his life. He will no longer be able to practice his trade and therefore he has lost his source of income to support his family, his social group of fellow bricklayers will no longer be part of his life, and he believes his wife will no longer view him as the "man" she once did. Mr. AlAwam and Mr. Barker have many issues to address.

Medical social work was initiated in the early 1900s, with social workers playing a peripheral role to physicians and nurses in health and medical settings. With increased understanding that illnesses can be caused or exacerbated by social factors, social workers gained a more central role in providing medical and health care. Today, social work in hospitals, outpatient clinics, and other health-related organizations is one of the largest practice fields for both basic and specialist/independent social workers.

A primary place for social work practice in this field is in hospitals. In these settings, for example, social workers address social and psychological factors that are either contributing causes of medical ailments or are side effects of a medical condition that must be dealt with to facilitate recovery and prevent occurrences of nonfunctional dependence. Social workers help to link patients, perhaps with changed levels of functioning due to a medical problem, with their environments by providing individual, group, and family counseling; serving as patient advocates; and working with self-help groups of patients experiencing similar medical or social problems. Social workers also might be engaged in counseling terminally ill patients and their families.

In addition, social workers are involved in other health and medical care facilities besides hospitals. They work in public health clinics and private physicians' offices providing counseling and referral services to people who have sought medical treatment related to family planning, prenatal care, child growth and development, venereal disease, and physical disability, for example. They have also taken an active role in health maintenance and disease prevention programs in local communities. With the skyrocketing costs of medical care, it is even more important that these efforts be continued by the social work profession.

Mental Health and Illness

Kirsten Laurali is a social worker in the adolescent unit of a large psychiatric hospital. Although she counsels some patients individually, this afternoon she will meet with a group of adolescent girls who are expected to be released from the hospital in a few weeks. Ms. Laurali plans to facilitate the girls' expressing any concerns they feel about leaving the security of the hospital and to discuss any family, school, and peer interaction problems they anticipate experiencing when returning to home and school. She will also help to connect them and their parents with a local mental health clinic where they can receive ongoing support after their hospitalization is ended.

It has long been recognized that one's mental health and capacity for healthy social functioning are highly correlated. A person who is depressed, hyperactive, hallucinating, or experiencing any of the other symptoms of mental illness is likely at some time to become the client of the social worker. It is estimated that 15 percent of the general population experience some form of emotional disturbance at any one time, creating a high demand for social workers, who are twice as prevalent as psychologists and psychiatrists in the mental health field. In the field of mental health and illness, the specialized social worker (with a MSW degree as preparation) is the usual practice level—although social workers in other settings, at all practice levels, regularly work with clients for whom emotional illness is at least a contributing factor to their problems.

Social workers in mental health settings work with people experiencing these difficulties by treating those who have the potential to improve the quality of their lives. They help them learn to cope with problems in their social functioning and, at the same time, work to change factors in their environment to promote better mental health or eliminate social conditions that have a negative effect on their functioning.

There are three practice settings where social workers are most likely to engage in psychiatric social work: outpatient mental health clinics, inpatient psychiatric hospitals, and private practice. In an outpatient clinic, social workers provide clinical or therapeutic services to individuals and families or to small groups of clients. They may also consult or work with a variety of organizations, such as group homes or the mass media, in an effort to create an environment that is conducive to the healthy growth and development of all people. When employed in a psychiatric hospital, social workers may provide a variety of treatment activities to the patients themselves, but they also serve as a liaison to the patient's outside world and help family or friends maintain contact while the person is hospitalized. The social worker might also assess the impact of family, friends, employer, school, and so forth on the client's situation and offer assistance in helping these significant others change in ways that will benefit the client. When patients are ready to return home, social workers help to arrange appropriate living situations, ranging from housing accommodations (if needed) to on-going service from a community mental health center. Finally, the social worker in private practice is most likely to focus on treatment for individuals and families, although small group intervention approaches may be used on occasion.

Occupational or Industrial Social Work

Working for a large manufacturing firm was a new experience for Doug Perry, an experienced clinical social worker. The CEO of the company was concerned that increasingly the employees are experiencing social problems such as marital conflict, alcohol dependence, and issues related to their children that interfere with their ability to perform their work in the company's plant. Mr. Perry's first assignment was to prepare a plan to increase worker productivity by reducing these social problems. Next week a report is due to the Board of Directors, and Mr. Perry is outlining a plan that includes (1) establishing a case-finding and referral service on the premises, staffed by social workers, (2) outsourcing the most serious cases to community agencies and private practitioners; and (3) strengthening prevention efforts by creating a company foundation with sufficient funding to support research into the factors contributing to these problems.

Social work has been practiced in business and industrial settings since the late 1800s. Social workers have been employed both by management and labor unions to offer services and provide consultation through employee assistance programs. In recent years, with businesses increasingly realizing that worker productivity is closely related to the workers' general satisfaction with the quality of their lives, an investment in helping employees resolve problems in social functioning is seen as simply good business. This perspective has created a small but growing field of practice known as occupational or industrial social work. With more than 142.6 million people in the civilian labor force,[11] the workplace is an opportune setting in which to identify social problems and provide needed services. Often, early intervention at the location of one's employment can prevent more serious problems from developing later.

Shank and Jorve identify three models of social work practice in business and industry: the employee service model, the consumer service model, and the corporate social responsibility model.[12] An explanation of each follows.

The *employee service model* of occupational social work focuses on activities that provide direct service to the employees of a business or industry. The social worker using this model might develop and implement employee assistance programs and various supervisory training programs. In addition, the social worker might provide counseling to individuals or families in relation to marital, family, substance abuse, aging, health, and retirement problems, and offer referral to other community agencies or self-help groups. Typical problems the social worker might also address would be the identification of job-related factors such as boredom or stress, an employee's desire to find resources to upgrade his or her job skills, or the need for preretirement planning.

The occupational social worker following the *consumer service model* might serve as the company's representative to various consumer groups and focus on identifying consumer needs and methods of meeting them. Typically found in banks, public utilities, and government agencies, these social workers help to provide a liaison between consumer groups and social service agencies, develop outreach programs, and provide counseling to customers to meet unique needs.

The third model of practice, the *corporate social responsibility model,* places the social worker in the role of assisting corporations and businesses to make a commitment to the social and economic well-being of the communities in which they are located. The social workers consult with management on their policies concerning human resources, their donations to nonprofit organizations, and social legislation they may wish to support. In addition, social workers may administer health and welfare benefit programs for employees, represent the company in research and community development activities, and provide linkage between social service, social policy, and corporate interests.

Schools

> The death of a loved one seems to be epidemic in Cesar Chavez Elementary School this year, and Bruni Baez, the school social worker, is aware that five children in the fifth and sixth grades have experienced the deaths of grandparents or siblings in the few months since the school year began. For all of these children, performance in the classroom has deteriorated and they show little interest in extracurricular activities. With the support of their teachers, Mrs. Baez has arranged for a 30-minute group session once each week in which these children can work on their grief and loss issues. Each week they will talk about a different issue, such as normal grief reactions, healthy and unhealthy coping patterns, the effect of grief on social relationships, understanding physical and mental reactions to grief, talking about the person who died, and so on. She wonders which of these topics might be best for the first session with the students.

Just as places of employment are important locations for identifying and addressing problems of social functioning for the employed population, schools are an important place to serve children and youth. It is known that individual and family problems directly affect a child's ability to learn, and school social workers are employed to help parents, teachers, and the children themselves address these complex issues.

The traditional approach of social workers in schools has been to counsel the child and confer with the family. They have depended on the cooperation of teachers to make referrals when problems are evident and have had varying degrees of effectiveness, depending on the willingness of teachers and school systems to use them as a resource. Problems of truancy, suspected child abuse, inadequate nutrition, substance abuse, parental neglect, and inappropriate behavior are often referred to the social worker.

Social workers often serve as a link between school, family, and community. Some activities that school social workers typically perform include offering counseling to children, their families, and teachers related to factors that affect the child's performance at school; serving as an advocate for children with school administrators and community agencies when specialized services are needed; organizing parent and community groups to strengthen school and community relationships; and coordinating teams that draw on different disciplines' expertise and parents' interests to assess a child and develop a plan to assist a child's development.

Youth Services

> Diversion programs have become a hot item in human services agencies designed to work with youth. At the Michael Jordan Recreation Center, Bob Jackson draws on his social work skills to involve members of several neighborhood gangs in activities at the center. He knows that the traditional approach of attempting to engage these youths in competitive sports has not been successful, and he is seeking new forms of activities that might capture the interest of these gang members and help divert them from the more harmful activities in which they are now engaged. Mr. Jackson had decided to create an

advisory board of ex-gang members and is preparing for a focus group session in which he hopes to draw out information that will assist in his planning.

Very early in U.S. history a number of human service programs were developed to provide educational and recreational opportunities for people of all social classes. These services were aimed at character-building among youth, with organizations such as the YMCA, YWCA, Boys and Girls Clubs, and various scouting groups developing. Later, with the growth of settlement houses, programs were broadened to serve other age groups. Although other disciplines also provide staff for these organizations, this field of practice continues to be a small but important area of social work.

These services seek to enhance the growth and development of all interested participants, from the poor to the well-to-do. Through the use of such activities as crafts, sports, camping, friendship groups, drama, music, informal counseling, and other forms of group participation, the members are guided toward personal development. The role of the social worker might be to administer these agencies, to lead the group process, or to provide individual counseling.

Concluding Comment

For the person considering a career in social work, it is important to have an understanding of the many different fields of practice open to the social worker. It is evident that the attention social workers give to helping people and their environments interact more favorably makes an important contribution to resolving social problems or enhancing social functioning in many areas.

The most current data about social work practitioners indicate there are some practice areas where substantial numbers of both basic and specialist/independent social workers are employed, and this includes such areas as work with children and youth, families, and health care. BSW-level workers are much more likely than their MSW counterparts to be engaged in providing services to the aged and working in the disabilities area, while the primary practice area for the MSWs, by a substantial margin, is mental health.

A clear picture of client needs addressed by social workers emerges from data presented in this chapter. Helping clients resolve problems in family functioning stands well above all others. A second and often interrelated tier of issues are those of client functioning that have been affected by mental illness or retardation, character disorders or behavior problems, health-related matters, anxiety or depression, difficulties in interpersonal relations, and problems associated with alcohol and substance abuse.

The knowledge and skills acquired when obtaining a baccalaureate or master's degree in social work are intended to prepare one to engage in social work practice in any of these practice fields. The social work practice performed by Demetria (Chapter 1) is located in the field of child welfare practice, i.e., working with children and youth. However, the discussion presented in Box 6.1 also highlights the fact that a practicing social worker must be knowledgeable about the work performed in other fields to serve clients effectively, should he or she someday want to transition to a different field. The ability to transfer these competencies from field to field gives the social worker considerable flexibility in selecting where he or she will work and what type of client issues will be the focus of practice. This job flexibility has long been an attractive feature of social work.

Box 6.1

Demetria's Field of Practice

In the case presented in Chapter 1, the primary field of practice for our social worker, Demetria, was *child welfare*. In this case she was employed by a county social welfare department, although child welfare work is performed in virtually any type of agency setting—public, private nonprofit, private for-profit, and even in private practice. Demetria's work was related to one of several child welfare programs, *protective services*, with the mission of protecting children and youth from various forms of abuse and maltreatment.

In this field of practice Demetria might also have had responsibility for placing a child with severe emotional or behavioral problems in a *residential care* facility; placing children who can benefit from a different home environment in a *foster care* home; or arranging for the legal *adoption* of children who cannot reside with their natural parents for a variety of reasons, but who do not have such serious problems that they cannot become part of another family permanently.

Demetria's work in this case touched other fields of practice where social workers might be employed. The case was initiated from a school in which there might have been a *school social worker*, her colleague in the Boys and Girls Club was employed in a *youth services* agency, and the root of the Miles family's issues appeared to be related to unemployment and the subsequent financial problems that would be addressed by social workers in the field of *income maintenance*. Should the issues experienced by Joseph diminish and Mr. Miles return home, a helpful referral might be to a *family services* agency where in-depth counseling could occur to help this family get its life back in order. In short, although Demetria was employed in child welfare, she needed knowledge of the work that occurs in several other fields of social work practice to do her job adequately.

KEY WORDS AND CONCEPTS

Field of social work practice
Developmental disability
Occupational or industrial social work

SUGGESTED INFORMATION SOURCES

Literally hundreds of books and articles are published each year on the various fields of practice described in this chapter. The four books listed below are recommended as resources for beginning the process of acquiring additional information about the various fields of social work practice.

Edwards, Richard L., editor-in-chief, *Encyclopedia of Social Work*, 19th Edition. Washington, D.C.: NASW Press, 1995. The 2,600-page *Encyclopedia of Social Work*, is a valuable resource for investigating most topics relevant to social workers. The author(s) of each chapter is selected by the *Encyclopedia's* editorial board as a highly respected expert on the subject matter. Each author provides a "state-of-the-art" summary of the topic and a bibliography of the seminal literature on that subject.

Gibelman, Margaret, *What Social Workers Do,* 2nd Edition. Washington, D.C.: NASW Press, 2004. This book is packed with short chapters describing more than fifty different examples of social work practice. Each contains a short case vignette that helps the reader gain insight into what the social worker does while serving clients.

Grobman, Linda May, ed., *Days in the Lives of Social Workers*. Harrisburg, PA: White Hat Communications, 1996. Forty-one practitioners tell their stories about what they do in a typical day as a social worker. The sections are organized around fields of practice (for example, health care, school social work, mental health, and so on) with several examples of social work in each field.

LeCroy, Craig Winston, *The Call to Social Work: Life Stories*. Thousand Oaks, CA: Sage, 2002. Thirty-four social workers share the experiences that led them to select social work as a career and in the process they provide insight into why they selected a particular field of practice.

ENDNOTES

1. Federal Interagency Forum on Aging-Related Statistics. "Older Americans 2000: Key Indicators of Well-Being." http://www.agingstats.gov/chartbook2000/ highlights.html

2. U.S. Census Bureau. "Historical Poverty Tables Table 3. Poverty Status of People, by Age, Race, and Hispanic Origin: 1950 to 2003." http://www.census.gov/hhes/poverty/histpov/hstpov3.html

3. U.S. Department of Commerce News. "More People Have Health Insurance, Census Bureau Reports. http://www.census.gov/Press-Release/www/2001/cb01-162.html

4. Ronald E. Herrington, George R. Jacobson, and David G. Benzer, eds., *Alcohol and Drug Abuse Handbook* (St. Louis: Warren H. Green, 1987), p. xiii.

5. Gary W. Lawson and Ann W. Lawson, *Alcoholism and Substance Abuse in Special Populations* (Rockville, MD: Aspen Publishers, 1989), pp. 5–7.

6. U.S. Department of Health and Human Services, *Trends in the Well-Being of Children and Youth, 2001*. Washington, D.C.: U.S. Government Printing Office, 2001, p. 143.

7. *Ibid.*, p. 44.

8. Federal Interagency Forum on Child and Family Statistics. *America's Children in Brief: Key National Indicators of Well-Being, 2004.* http://www.childstats.gov/americas-children/tables/popfb.asp.

9. J.S. Skiller, P.F. Adams, and Nelson, Z. Coriarty. *Summary of Health Statistics for the U.S. Population: National Health Interview Survey, 2003*. National Center for Health Statistics. http://www.cdc.gov/nchs/data/series/st_10/SMO_224.pdf

10. Robert L. Schalock, *Services for Developmentally Disabled Adults* (Baltimore: University Park Press, 1982), p. 12.

11. U.S. Bureau of Labor Statistics. "Employment Situation Summary: August 2002." http://www.bls.gov/news.release/empsit.nr0.htm

12. Barbara W. Shank and Beth K. Jorve, "Industrial Social Work: A New Arena for the BSW." Paper presented at the National Symposium of Social Workers, Washington, D.C., 1983, p. 14.

chapter 7

Settings for Social Work Practice

Prefatory Comment

Our society's commitment to the welfare of its members is played out through an extensive array of social programs that are delivered by several different helping professions—including social work. For people to gain access to these programs and professionals, there must be some form of organizational structure that serves as a vehicle for delivering the services. Usually that is a formal organization that operates under the auspices of a federal, state, or local government, or it is a private organization that is structured as either a non-profit or for-profit agency. Increasingly these services are also offered by social workers who are private practitioners, that is, social workers who contract directly with their clients for services in the same manner as the private physician or attorney contracts with his or her clients.

These differing practice settings influence the nature of the problems a social worker addresses, the clients served, the amount of red tape and paperwork required, the salary earned, and many other factors that affect one's work activity and job satisfaction. This chapter examines the advantages and disadvantages for both social workers and their clients in the different practice settings.

Throughout its history, social work has been primarily an agency-based profession. Like teaching, nursing, and the clergy, social work practice emerged primarily within organizations, and today, as in the past, most social workers are employed in some form of human service organization. Accreditation standards require that all students complete a substantial learning experience in a social agency, and the profession does not consider social workers ready for the independent level of practice until they have a period of supervised work in an agency after completing the MSW.

In recent years there has been a shift in the employment patterns of social workers. Where once virtually all social workers were employed in either government or nonprofit human services agencies, a whole new sector of employment has opened for social workers today. As indicated in Table 7.1, the *voluntary sector* employs the largest percentage of today's social workers (37 percent), followed closely by the *government sector* (34 percent), with the remaining 29 percent employed in the

Table 7.1

Sector of Primary Employment for NASW Members: 2004

Employment Sector	Licensed Social Workers
Government Sector	
Local	13.0%
State	17.0
Federal	3.0
Military	1.0
Voluntary (nonprofit) Sector	37.0
Business (for-profit) Sector	
For-profit organization	12.0
Private Practice	17.0

Source: Center for Health Workforce Studies. http://workforce.socialworkers.org
"Licensed Social Workers in the United States, 2004: A Statistical Profile"
(Draft 5/16/05). Rensselear, NY: State University of New York at Albany.

business or *for-profit sector.* This chapter examines the practice conditions and issues social workers typically experience when working under the auspices of each of these three primary sectors of service delivery.

Characteristics of Practice Settings

When social programs are created, a decision must be made about how the program will be delivered. Whether it offers a direct benefit, such as food stamps, or depends on a third-party payment, such as Medicare, the program must be provided under the auspices of a human service organization or by an independent practitioner.

When programs are provided by human service organizations, the agencies establish the necessary policies and supply the administrative structure to make the program available to recipients. Clients then contract with that agency to provide the needed service and the agency employs staff to deliver the program. The organization is responsible for determining who is eligible for service and how that service will be performed, for screening and selecting its staff, assigning the work to various staff members, monitoring the quality of the work, and securing funds to pay the costs of providing the service.

When the service is delivered by a social worker in private practice, the client contracts directly with the social worker or the private practice group with which the worker is associated. The client then pays directly for the service or draws on insurance, Medicare, or other funds to pay for the service. Certification and licensing help the clients or companies paying for this service to determine if the practitioner is qualified to perform this service. One reason NASW requires two years of supervised practice experience beyond the MSW in order to be recognized as an "independent social worker" is that the person engaged in private practice does not have an agency structure to monitor the quality of service given, and, NASW has concluded, this requirement provides greater protection to clients against the possibility of contracting with an inexperienced or incompetent worker.

Government Sector Settings

Government organizations are established and funded by the general public with the intent to provide services that preserve and protect the well-being of all people in the community. These agencies reflect city, county, state, and federal governmental efforts to respond to human needs and are limited by the provisions of the laws under which they were established.

Most government sector social programs are created by lawmakers in Washington, D.C., or a state capital. These policy makers are usually geographically distant from the clients and service providers alike and, too often, are unfamiliar with the issues that arise when these laws are implemented by local agencies. For this reason social workers often find their practice in government agencies frustrating. There is inherent inflexibility in these settings because laws are difficult to change, budgeting and auditing systems are highly structured, cumbersome civil service or personnel systems are mandated, and coordination among the different governmental levels is difficult. Further, these organizations are subject to political manipulation, and financial support and program development can be significantly influenced by a changing political climate. Except through substantial political action efforts, those who must carry out these programs have limited opportunity to influence their structure and funding.

On the positive side, although sometimes client fees are required, public agencies are financed largely by taxes, and the regular flow of tax money offers some stability to the programs. Legislative bodies are authorized to levy taxes so human needs can be met, and, in times of economic difficulty when voluntary contributions may be reduced, legislators have the power to tax and, therefore, maintain the services.

It should be recognized that government sector agencies provide services that are likely to meet the most basic human needs such as food, clothing, and shelter. It simply is not possible to adequately respond to the fundamental needs of the poor, homeless, disabled, aged, and others through voluntary and for-profit human services.

Voluntary (Nonprofit) Sector Settings

Out of the history of providing assistance for persons needing help, a number of *mutual aid organizations* have been created to facilitate members of a group providing services for other members of that group. Churches and labor unions, for example, support some human service programs, yet they rarely employ professional staff.

Religious groups have created *sectarian* or *faith-based programs* that are sometimes staffed by social workers. A substantial number of human services, from counseling to social provisions, are provided to members by synagogues and various denomination groups. Until actions by the George W. Bush administration allowed federal funds to flow to faith-based programs, these programs were not eligible for public funding because they often restrict their services to their own members and thus are not considered public services. Some other organized religious groups, however, believe it is part of their mission to serve all persons in need, whether members of their faith or not, and they have a long history of providing services for the benefit of the general public. These *nonsectarian programs* include the sponsorship of hospitals, group homes, retirement centers, and family counseling agencies.

Labor unions represent another mutual aid setting where social workers might be found. Unions historically have been successful in organizing workers who are underpaid and undervalued by management and advocating for their rights. Today, the labor union setting presents an exceptional opportunity to intervene with people at the place they work and therefore improve the likelihood of resolving problems before they reach a crisis level. Social workers in these settings typically help union members with such work-related problems as finding child care, dealing with family problems related to work schedules, and addressing stress created by changed family roles when both spouses are employed.

A second type of practice setting in the voluntary sector of human services is the *private nonprofit agency*. Private agencies traditionally have depended on voluntary individual and corporate support for their operation. Their sources of funds have included gifts and bequests, door-to-door solicitations, membership dues, fees for service, and participation in federated campaigns such as a United Way or a Jewish Welfare Federation. More recently, however, private agencies have begun receiving a substantial share of their funding through contracts with government agencies to provide specific direct services, conduct research and demonstration projects, or to support their programs through block grants or revenue sharing. Government agencies have increasingly found this a desirable arrangement because it has allowed them to bypass much of the rigidity of the large bureaucratic organizations in favor of the more flexible private agency structures.

Although there has been an intermingling of taxes and donated funds in the budgets of these private agencies, they are classified as part of the voluntary sector because they operate with policies established by a governing board made up of community volunteers. In the structure of their governance, then, nonprofits differ dramatically from government agencies that have elected officials responsible for making basic policy decisions. In most instances, these agencies have the advantage of being small and primarily concerned with the provision of local services. Thus, the board members are able to become directly exposed to the agency and are more capable of responding to changing conditions and needs for services in a local community.

A board, however, does not have complete autonomy in developing policies and programs for the agency. Many nonprofit agencies receive a part of their funding from a local United Way, and that participation as part of a federation of agencies inevitably requires some loss of autonomy. Also, some agencies are affiliated with a national organization such as the Child Welfare League of America or the Family Service Association of America, which may impose some limitations on agency functioning.

The term *nonprofit* indicates that if the agency should end a year with any funds remaining, those resources are allocated to enhance the agency's operation and not paid to staff, board, or any other parties. Since no one profits financially from the operation of the agency and it serves the public good, the Internal Revenue Service has created a process to approve agencies [Section 501 (c) (3) of the Internal Revenue Code] as nonprofit organizations. With this designation, persons who donate funds to support the agency can deduct the contribution from their income taxes. In this way, the government is underwriting the voluntary sector human services.

Business Sector Settings

The most rapidly growing setting for social work practice is the for-profit or business sector. This category of practice includes both private practice and employment in large organizations that exist to earn a profit for their owners.

The term *private practice* is used to indicate a practice situation where a contract for the provision of service is made directly between the worker and the clients. Usually this term is applied in reference to social workers who provide clinical services, but sometimes private practice involves nonclinical activities such as consulting, conducting workshops or training programs, or contracting to perform research or other professional service for a fee.

With direct client–worker contracts, the practitioners have considerable autonomy in determining how the practice situation will be addressed and what intervention approaches will be used. However, without the monitoring of services that human services agencies provide, clients are more vulnerable to incompetent or unethical practitioners. It is fundamentally for client information and protection that all 50 states license or certify social workers, as well as for NASW's development of the several specialized credentials.

For some social workers, private practice is an attractive alternative to agency-based practice. Usually there is less paperwork to manage, more flexibility in scheduling, and, often, the elimination of unnecessary supervision. In addition, private practice is among the highest-paying settings for social workers. The downside of private practice is that it is a small business and, like many small businesses, is difficult to sustain. A practice must attract a sufficient number of clients who can pay high fees to support the ongoing operating costs (e.g., space, utilities, clerical staff) and also provide a wage for the social worker. For this reason, many social workers engage in private practice on a part-time basis and maintain their primary employment in a human services agency.

Another entrepreneurial setting for social work is in *for-profit organizations*. There has been a transformation in the funding of human service programs. From the 1930s through the 1970s a pattern emerged in which legislative bodies allocated substantial funds for government agencies to provide services directly to clients. Therefore, a relatively large public sector developed. Later, that pattern shifted to purchase-of-service agreements, with nonprofit agencies rather than governmental agencies providing these services themselves. A second, and perhaps even more dramatic, shift known as *privatization* is now occurring. Governmental agencies now invest a substantial amount of their funds in the purchase of service from for-profit organizations that are owned and operated as any other business. In fact, many are owned and operated by large corporations.

Several fields of practice have rapidly increased their reliance on these businesses to provide human services. For example, a national study of child welfare services found that proprietary firms were used as vendors for services for 51 percent of all residential treatment, 49 percent of institutional care, and 58 percent of the services provided in group homes.[1] To a lesser degree public agencies rely on contracts with proprietary organizations to provide daycare, day treatment services, nursing home care, correctional facilities, and health care.

Social work professionals are uneasy about the growing amount of for-profit practice. The trend toward the privatization of human services threatens to replace the profession's service orientation with the profit motive. Privatization risks making the bottom line the amount of return to the shareholder, rather than the quality of service to the client. When the shareholder is also the professional, additional ethical issues arise that can erode public trust in the professions.

One development that has affected all social workers in the business sector, whether in private practice or employed by for-profit organizations, is the evolution of *managed care*—or perhaps more accurately, managed costs. Stimulated by the escalating cost of health and mental health services, a variety of plans have been developed to provide health care consumers with needed services at controlled costs.[2] On the positive side, these plans require greater accountability for the quality of services offered, which ultimately should enhance the services clients receive. However, analysts of managed health care programs conclude that many decisions about the nature and extent of services provided are being shifted from the professionals and clients to the managers of the insurance companies. These are not typically people with the qualifications to determine an individual's need for professional services. In relation to mental health services, Stroul, Pires, Armstrong, and Meyers carefully analyzed the effects of managed care and concluded that under managed care programs children and adolescents have had greater access to outpatient services but reduced access to inpatient hospital care—particularly youths with serious emotional disorders or those who are uninsured. In addition, they note that services have become briefer, more problem-oriented, and more focused on behavioral health disorders.[3] The social worker's role with managed care also includes advocating for clients who are not receiving authorization for needed services from these health insurance companies.

Social workers have a central role to play in all three sectors of the economy—government, voluntary, and business. The ability of these professionals to perform their function depends at least partially on their ability to work effectively within a human services organization or manage a private practice. Understanding several issues typically experienced in each of these settings can help future social workers anticipate difficulties they may face and be prepared to deal with them head on.

Issues Affecting Agency-Based Practice

When considering a social work job, it is important to address issues that are likely to be experienced when working in a formal organization. Potential employing agencies should be examined in relation to their relative compatibility with professional values and standards and the autonomy workers have to exercise their professional judgment in performing the job tasks. The manner in which a human service organization deals with the following issues will affect the work of its professional staff.

Accommodating Horizontal and Vertical Influences

Social workers employed in most human service organizations, as well as those in private practice, often find they cannot successfully work in isolation from other agencies. At the local level, social workers often lead efforts to coordinate the services provided to clients by the full array of social agencies in that community. This coordination requires that interagency networks, or *horizontal affiliations,* are developed among the agencies. The form of these horizontal networks may range from informal discussions among agency representatives regarding human service programs to the formal creation of human resources planning organizations that study the local service network, encourage efforts to fill gaps in the services, and facilitate cooperation among the agencies. The ability of a social worker to effectively perform his or her professional tasks is enhanced when there is a strong interagency network in a community and the social worker's employing agency supports his or her participation in these activities.

Social agencies and social workers are also influenced by *vertical affiliations,* that is, those organizations external to the community that have the authority to at least partially shape the services or operating procedures of a local agency. Voluntary agencies, for example, might affiliate as chapters or members of a national organization, which can immediately give the agency name recognition, provide the community with some assurance that at least minimum standards acceptable in that practice field are being met, make staff development opportunities available through national meetings, and sometimes help secure financial resources. At the same time, these agencies give up some local autonomy as they are committed to operate within the guidelines of the national organization. Vertical affiliation with the American Red Cross, the Child Welfare League of America, the YWCA or YMCA, the Salvation Army, or the Family Service Association of America are typical examples of such affiliations. Further, many local voluntary agencies must meet state licensing requirements or other state standards if they are vendors of services to public agencies. This also limits their discretion.

Public agencies typically have more direct and formal vertical relationships. A local governmental agency may be implementing programs that have been created and partially funded at the federal level, further defined and partially funded at the state level, and finally modified and also funded by county government. Thus, a county human services department, for example, is constrained by requirements imposed by federal, state, and county governments. Although these vertical affiliations add to the complexity of tailoring service programs to local needs, they have the advantage of fostering greater equality in the benefits and services provided to people throughout a region and the nation. In addition, vertical affiliation creates a larger geographic area for securing funds to support the services, making it possible to more adequately meet needs in a local or regional area that lacks its own resources.

Balancing Efficiency and Effectiveness

A fundamental goal of all human service agencies, whether they are public or private, is to use the scarce resources available to provide the most and best service possible. To achieve this goal agencies must operate both efficiently and effectively. An agency that leans too far in favoring one over the other ultimately creates problems for the staff members employed in that agency.

Efficiency represents the efforts of the agency to achieve the maximum output of services with a minimum input of resources. The goal of efficiency places the emphasis on the quantity of services provided and often attracts most of the attention of lawmakers, governing boards, and local media. Yet, quantity must be related to quality if an agency is to find a balance that represents the maximum level of service. The qualitative aspects of service are represented in an agency's *effectiveness,* or the degree to which the agency achieves its goals.

The governance of most social agencies has been dominated, in both the public and voluntary sectors, by people who have given leadership to business and industrial enterprises. They often bring a strong bias toward efficiency; and, although some degree of effectiveness in producing goods was necessary for their success, low cost-per-unit production was clearly the most valued goal. That orientation is especially evident in managed care and the for-profit human service organizations. Thus, the social worker considering agency employment should carefully examine the agency's effectiveness orientation lest the quality of his or her work be seriously compromised in favor of overemphasis on efficiency.

How can efficiency be attained in human service organizations? Successful managers from business and industry have transferred one proven tool in their work to the human services—bureaucratic structure. And why not? Bureaucracy had worked to build automobiles and appliances at a fraction of the cost of handmade products. Weber created the clearest statement of bureaucratic theory. His "ideal-type" description of the characteristics of a bureaucratic organization was intended to reflect the fundamental elements of a bureaucracy. The following is a synthesis of Weber's extensive work on this topic.[4]

1. *Division of Labor.* Each person in the organization has a clearly defined and specialized assignment in the organization.
2. *Hierarchy.* Specific lines of authority exist in which every person in the administrative structure is not only responsible for his or her own assignments but is also responsible for the performance of subordinates.

3. *Consistent System of Rules.* Every task in the organization is governed by an explicit set of rules that specify the standards of performance and the relationships among tasks.
4. *Spirit of Impersonality.* Work is to be performed without favoritism or prejudice entering official decisions.
5. *Employment Constitutes a Career.* Persons are employed only on the basis of technical qualifications required by the organization, with rewards provided to encourage loyalty and offer opportunity for a career in that organization.

With some modifications, when applied to the assembly line that produces automobiles in Detroit or toasters in New Jersey, bureaucratic principles led to a high degree of organizational efficiency. This model yielded good results when the product was made from standardized parts. In fact, the greater the standardization, the more effective the bureaucratic organization becomes. A person could quickly be trained to perform a very specific function, for example, installing a fuel pump as an automobile passes on the assembly line. With a line supervisor to check for quality control and enforce the rules established for efficiency (the worker cannot be taking a break when the engine arrives for a fuel pump), the company usually produced a good-quality product. Under this system there could be no allowance for the worker's personal problems, nor could the boss play favorites. Bureaucratic theory assumes that the rewards of job security, salary increases, and retirement benefits are sufficient to keep the successful employee satisfied with the organization.

When these principles are applied to human services agencies, social workers and other professionals often find that bureaucratization has both positive and negative consequences. Indeed, the application of bureaucratic principles can ensure equity for both clients and workers, facilitate efficiency in operation, and enhance public support of the organization. Rigid application of bureaucratic principles, however, is in direct conflict with the very nature of professions. As opposed to manufacturing products, in human services the parts being worked with are people who are constantly changing, and the product (attaining maximum client well-being) differs to some degree in each situation. It is simply not realistic to provide narrow technical training, to create highly specialized assignments, or to establish an inflexible system of rules that a staff must follow regardless of the uniqueness of the client or practice situation.

Accommodating the Professional Model in Bureaucratic Organizations

When the professional model is compared to the bureaucratic model of conducting work, inherent conflicts emerge. In Table 7.2, a comparison of the two models based on the central elements of bureaucracy suggests that there are substantial areas of incompatibility that are likely to result in some level of tension for professionals employed in bureaucratic organizations. Scott suggests the following inherent conflicts between these two models:[5]

Table 7.2

Conflicts between Bureaucratic and Professional Models		
Bureaucratic Model	**Professional Model**	**Inherent Conflicts**
1. Strict division of labor determined by the organization	1. Autonomy to perform a wide range of functions within one's professional domain	1. Resistance to bureaucratic rules
2. Organizational rules regarding client eligibility and limits on employee job performance	2. Authority to use professional judgment to determine who to serve and how to perform the work	2. Rejection of bureaucratic standards
3. Hierarchy of management supervision for oversight of worker performance	3. Worker is self-managed but may use consultation from peers to gain additional insights	3. Objection to bureaucratic supervision
4. Impartiality in employee selection, evaluation, and job security	4. Ethically obligated to provide high-quality services to all clients	4. No conflict
5. Expectation that employee will view working within the organization as a long-term commitment	5. Primary commitment is to a career in the profession	5. Conditional loyalty to organization

▶ *Resistance to bureaucratic rules.* When a division of labor exists, each person provides only a narrowly defined part of the work. Procedures are then established to coordinate the activities among workers, and these procedures often make it difficult for professionals to individualize services and respond to the unique needs of each client.

▶ *Rejection of bureaucratic standards.* Standards of client eligibility for services and procedures that determine the extent of the services a worker can provide are designed to respond to the "typical client." In reality, clients represent great variability, and professionals in bureaucratic agencies often feel frustrated in their ability to fulfill their obligation to provide the best services possible to their clients.

▶ *Objection to bureaucratic supervision.* In bureaucratic organizations, authority is assigned to a position (e.g., a supervisor) that is primarily charged with responsibility to monitor the work of the supervisees for compliance with agency rules and regulations. Conversely, professional authority is generated from practice competence as judged by one's peers. Professionals, then, object to assigned supervision where the supervisor may or may not possess the desired level of practice competence.

▶ *Conditional loyalty to the organization.* Employees in bureaucratic organizations are trained in the specific job tasks needed by that organization and their success is judged by movement up the organizational ladder, that is, from line worker, to supervisor, to foreman, and so on. Thus, the workers usually have few skills that can be transferred to another organization and are therefore somewhat locked in to their companies. Professionals, however, tend to be primarily committed to careers in their professions and are prepared with competencies that are transferable from one organization to another, making it relatively easy to change their work environment.

How does a professional social worker address these areas of incompatibility? Clearly, an employee is obligated to work within the legitimate requirements of his or her employer, and a social worker cannot ethically ignore the rules and regulations of the agency. However, it is not sufficient to be merely a passive employee who unquestioningly accepts and carries out the rules and regulations of the agency. Client services can be compromised if social workers do not actively work to promote agency flexibility in service provision and, when warranted, be willing to challenge the agency's methods of operating. At times, this may mean taking some risks that may affect one's evaluations, pay increases, or even employment in the agency. Thus the successful agency-based social worker must be smart about organizational change efforts.

Many times constricting agency rules and regulations do not need to be changed. Creative interpretations that stretch the rules to fit client needs are often possible and frequently can be applied with the full support of one's supervisor. Some regulations, however, may not lend themselves to this flexibility, and it may be necessary to attempt to initiate a process to change these rules. Change, especially in large public agencies, takes considerable time and effort. With skill, patience, and perseverance, such change can be accomplished and the professional obligation of the worker to provide the best services possible fulfilled. If this effort fails, however, the worker must either learn to live with the existing regulations or make the decision to seek employment elsewhere.

Assuming that satisfactory conditions exist in an agency for performing social work practice, it becomes important for the worker to discover ways to be responsible to the agency and at the same time maximize the ability to provide services to clients. Pruger suggests four helpful tactics that a worker might employ.[6] First, it is important to understand the agency's (or supervisor's) legitimate authority. Within the guidelines of responsible behavior, the social worker seeks to discover the limits of the discretion that a worker has in providing services to clients. Second, because organizations often present demands (e.g., paperwork, staff meetings) that divert the worker's time and energy from the work of providing services, the worker should be cautious about overcommitting to these activities that are of secondary importance. Third, the worker should develop supplemental competencies that are needed by the agency. Professional work involves more than carrying out the routine job duties. It involves making a commitment to expand one's contributions by learning, for example, new practice techniques, skills in grant writing, knowledge of computer applications in practice, or methods of interpreting the agency and its services to the public. Finally, the worker should not yield unnecessarily to agency requirements established for administrative convenience. For instance, it may be convenient to have clients come to the worker's office to receive services so that back-to-back interviews can be scheduled and the worker's time used efficiently. However, for some clients the requirement of arranging transportation, leaving work, or the unfamiliarity with the agency may discourage them from keeping the appointment. In such a case, a home visit by the worker may be far more successful. Although challenging unproductive regulations may not help the social worker win popularity contests, this action can be a valuable contribution to the organization's effectiveness.

Another contribution that a social worker can make to an employing agency is to prepare to move into a supervisory role or to assume an executive or high-level administrative position in the agency. Making such a transition is difficult. As compared to direct service practitioners, the social workers who are administrators are much more involved in activities such as making staff assignments and conducting evaluations of their work, representing the agency and helping to build the service delivery system in the community, engaging in program development, and carrying various tasks (e.g., budget development, expense approval, staff coordination) that help to maintain the organization's daily operations.

Finally, a worker should be prepared to engage in teamwork and interprofessional practice. Agency practice typically draws together persons from varying professions who have their own unique areas of expertise, volunteers with their basic talents, and other staff members in an effort to respond to human needs. In theory the unique roles and capacities of each discipline appear clear and workers need only coordinate their efforts. In reality, however, there is considerable blurring of lines between the various helping disciplines. Turf problems inevitably emerge that, if not resolved, can jeopardize good client service. Thus, interprofessional collaboration and teamwork are essential.

Human services agencies continue to seek means of improving interprofessional cooperation through various administrative structures, team approaches to case situations, the development of protocols that spell out the functions to be performed by each discipline, and the use of case managers charged with coordinating the services an individual or family might require. Social workers, with their mission to facilitate the interface of clients with their environments, have a particularly important leadership role to perform in facilitating interprofessional collaboration.

Determining the Centrality of Social Work

One final factor to consider when selecting a place of employment is the centrality of social work to the mission of that particular setting. The status of social work in an agency influences the manner in which a social worker spends much of his or her time and affects the opportunity of clients to have the full benefit of the perspective that social work brings to the helping situation. When the policies and procedures of the organization are designed to maximize social work services, social workers can most effectively serve their clientele. However, in a practice setting where another discipline is dominant, social workers often spend considerable effort educating others about the contributions social work can make to the agency's clientele.

In some practice settings social work is the *primary discipline*. The primary services provided call for social work expertise, most key jobs require social work training, and social workers hold the major administrative jobs. In practice fields such as child welfare, family services, and income maintenance, social work has traditionally been the primary discipline. In these settings other disciplines may be involved to provide specialized expertise or consultation, but the services are organized to maximize the contributions of the social worker.

In other practice settings the social worker is an *equal partner* along with members of one or more other disciplines. The services are organized to maximize interdisciplinary cooperation, and a member of any of the disciplines might provide administrative leadership to the agency. The fields of aging, mental health and retardation, and community and neighborhood services are examples of practice fields that are shared by several disciplines.

In still other settings social work might provide supporting services to another profession. As the *secondary discipline* in these agencies, social work is, in one sense, a guest of the primary discipline. The agency is organized to allow the primary discipline to work as effectively as possible, and the needs of social work or other professions receive lower priority. The role of the social worker in a medical setting illustrates social work as a secondary discipline. Hospitals, a setting for medical practice, are geared to the needs of the physician. Social services are provided at the physician's referral and are organized so they do not compete with the schedule and work of the medical profession. A similar role would be assumed by the social worker in corrections, schools, and industrial settings.

Advantages of Agency-Based Practice

Given the complexities of agency practice, why does social work continue to function as an agency-based profession? Why not adopt the private practice model of other successful professions?

First, services offered through an agency are more visible and, therefore, more accessible to all persons in need. The existence of agencies in a community over time and the attendant publicity about their operations typically make both their programs and their locations familiar to all members of the community. As opposed to nonagency practice, which caters to those who can pay the cost of services, public and private human service agencies are more likely to have as clients the most vulnerable members of society. For the social worker committed to serving the part of the population experiencing the most serious social problems, agency practice is the only game in town.

Second, agencies survive because they have received the sanction, or approval, of the community for the services they provide. Clients approach the helping situation with a greater trust in the quality of services they will receive because of the agency's implied responsibility to ensure that quality services are delivered. In private practice situations the client must place full trust in the individual practitioner to perform high-quality practice.

Third, clients have the benefit of an extra layer of protection against possible misuse of professional authority in social agencies. Clients in any setting are protected by both the professional ethics of the workers and, in many cases, the legal regulation or licensing of that practice. In agencies, however, they are also protected by the agency's selection of staff and ongoing monitoring of the quality of services.

Fourth, human service agencies tend to have a broad scope and often employ persons from several different professions, which provide clients with ready access to the competencies of multiple professions and give the worker the opportunity for interdisciplinary practice activities. In addition, as opposed to the more limited service focus found in private practice, agencies typically offer a broad range of services, from direct practice to social action. Thus, they provide the social worker with the stimulation of engaging in a range of different practice activities and make it possible to change the focus of one's practice area or move into supervisory or management positions without changing employers.

Fifth, most agencies offer staff development opportunities that stimulate professional growth among workers. Characteristically, social agencies employ a large enough number of staff members that workers do not feel isolated and, in fact, typically carry out programs that contribute to the continued professional growth and development of other members. The rapidly changing knowledge and skill base of the helping professions makes continuing professional development important to the services the clients receive and adds to the intellectual stimulation of the staff.

Last, agencies have the ability to raise funds from the community, whether from taxes or voluntary contributions, and to offer a stable salary to employees. Agencies do not face as great a risk of a fluctuating income as is experienced by persons in private practice settings.

Issues in Private Practice

The principal alternative to agency-based practice for the social worker is private practice. The remarkable expansion of this setting in the past decade makes it an important feature of social work today. Why is private practice gaining such popularity among social workers? From the vantage point of the social worker, private practice is attractive partially because of the greater opportunity for financial gain, but more importantly, for the freedom to exercise professional autonomy in the conduct of social work practice. The bureaucratic constraints of many human service agencies have placed restrictions on practice activities that compromise the ability of social workers to effectively use their professional competencies for the benefit of clients. Thus, some social workers have actively sought a different practice setting that would not restrict their work.

Although private practice avoids many of the limitations that accrue from practice within a bureaucratic structure, it also places greater responsibility on the social worker to follow the ethical guidelines of the profession. There is no professional monitoring of private practice, although complaints can be filed with a state licensing board or the local NASW chapter. NASW has rightfully been concerned about establishing guidelines that will identify for the public those social workers who have the requisite preparation and experience to conduct autonomous practice.

The Organization of Private Practice

What does a social worker do in private practice? In his study of clinically oriented private practice, Wallace found that the average for these social workers was "63 percent of private practice time in individual treatment, 19 percent devoted to work with marital couples, 8 percent to group therapy, 7 percent to family treatment, and 2 percent to joint interviews with clients other than married couples."[7] For the delivery of these clinical services, three organizational approaches are used.

In the first approach, the social worker engages in multidisciplinary practice. In this arrangement the social worker participates with members of other disciplines (for example, psychiatry and psychology) to provide a *group practice* that can meet a broad range of client needs. The social worker is an equal partner with the other disciplines and, in fact, is a co-owner of the business.

In the second form of private practice, the social worker provides a *supportive practice* for a member of another profession. For example, some physicians are hiring social workers to help patients deal with social problems related to specific illnesses. The social worker might also provide more general services in the physician's office such as educating expectant parents about child development, counseling families that need help with child-rearing practices, or referring people to appropriate community resources for help with other problems.

In the third form, social workers are the *sole owners* of their private practice. Sole ownership involves securing office space, hiring staff, advertising services, making contacts to acquire referrals, overseeing the determination and collection of fees, and doing everything related to the management of a small business. Like any other business, private practice is a "sink or swim" proposition with no guarantee of income equivalent to expenses. The main problems for full-time private practitioners are generating sufficient referrals to be able to keep the business solvent, handling the business details including securing payment from third-party vendors, obtaining competent consultation, minimizing the inherent isolation, arranging for backup in managing crisis situations, and protecting practitioners against their vulnerable position if there should be malpractice charges.

It is estimated that 17 percent of all social workers are engaged in part-time private practice. Many of these social workers are employed by a social agency but maintain a small private practice as well.[8] Kelley and Alexander identify four groups of social workers who elect to engage in part-time private practice:[9]

1. Agency practitioners who welcome the independence and additional income,
2. Social workers in supervisory or administrative positions who wish to maintain client contact and clinical skills,
3. Educators who wish to have sufficient practice activity to remain sufficiently current with a practice to effectively teach clinical courses, and
4. Social workers who are parents of young children and need to control their hours of work.

Some social workers in private practice provide indirect services such as consultation. Consultation might be provided to another social worker or to a member of another helping profession concerning the handling of a case. For example, a social worker might consult with a lawyer about a divorce or child custody case. He or she might also be involved in working with a social agency, such as helping a nursing home with staff–patient relations, administrative procedures, or program development.

Concerns Related to Private Practice

The private practice approach represents a substantial departure from social work's historical agency orientation. It has not been without controversy in the profession and has experienced problems in becoming accepted and appreciated in the general community. Four issues have emerged concerning this practice mode.

First, private clients do not have an agency monitoring system to provide protection against incompetence or abuses of the professional monopoly. Therefore, social work has been careful to specify more extensive education and experience as minimum preparation for the private practitioner than for the agency-based practitioner. To be listed in NASW's *Register of Clinical Social Workers,* a social worker is required to have completed at least two years of full-time, post-master's employment as a social worker and meet the requirements for a *Qualified Clinical Social Worker* or the *Diplomate in Clinical Social Work.*

Second, because many private practitioners work on a part-time basis, some agencies are concerned that private practice will detract from agency practice. A study of twenty voluntary agencies yielded the following common concerns about private practice:[10]

1. That the worker will not do justice to his or her agency responsibilities because of the amount of time and energy that may go into private practice.
2. That the worker may take clients from the agency or gain clients in the community who may otherwise have gone to the agency.
3. That the staff person will become more his or her own agent instead of being an enabler for the agency.
4. That the staff person may not meet the minimum standards set by the National Association of Social Workers for private practice.

On the other side of this issue, it is argued that private practice offers different professional stimulation than is found in agency practice and also provides a supplemental income to agency salaries that keeps workers satisfied with their agency employment. Some agencies even encourage social workers to engage in some part-time private practice by allowing them to use their agency offices in the evenings or by arranging schedules to allow a day off each week for this purpose. Such arrangements, however, are ripe for conflict of interest issues.

Finally, some critics have accused private practitioners of diverting social work from its mission of serving the most vulnerable members of society. Barker states, "Undoubtedly, the major dilemma is that private practice services are less accessible to the very people who have historically been social work's traditional clientele—the disadvantaged."[11] Moreover, private practice has been accused of failing to perform the social action responsibilities that are central to social work's mission of person and environment change. Teare and Sheafor confirmed this accusation, but additionally found that most other direct service practitioners also failed to engage in social change activities.[12]

Advantages of Private Practice

There are also arguments in favor of social work's movement toward private practice. First, in most human service agencies clients have little opportunity to exercise individual choice in regard to which professionals will provide services. Clients typically cannot select their individual social workers nor can they fire them if unsatisfied with the services received. Clients exercise considerably more control in a private setting.

Second, from the social worker's perspective, agency rules and regulations place constraints on the worker's ability to conduct practice in the manner he or she believes would be most effective. Professional autonomy is inherently compromised. For example, agency-based social workers typically cannot choose their clients; are not completely free to determine the amount and type of service to be given; and are almost always supervised, at times by one who interferes with the professional judgment of the worker.

Third, agency salaries tend to be lower than those of the private practitioner. Further, as opposed to the market-driven income of the private practitioner that is, at least theoretically, based on competence, agency salaries are based to a greater degree on seniority and position within the agency.

Last, few agencies avoid the pitfalls that plague most bureaucratic organizations, in which workers find that a disproportionate share of their time is devoted to meetings and paperwork. The less elaborate mechanisms required for accountability in private practice free the worker from much of the less people-oriented activity found in agency practice.

Concluding Comment

Social work practice has permeated U.S. society to the extent that it occurs in every sector of society: government, voluntary, and business. Although the roots of social work are in agency-based practice, social work now is offered through both agency and private practice modes.

Most social workers continue to be employed in agency settings, and thus they must be able to work effectively within agency structures if they are to maximize their ability to serve clients. Understanding the principles on which agencies are organized and the problems social workers commonly experience in matching their professional orientation with agency requirements is, therefore, important for providing quality services. Box 7.1 identifies some of the factors related to work in a government sector agency that influenced the work of the child welfare worker, Demetria, in Chapter 1.

An increasing number of social workers have entered private practice to avoid some of the problems experienced by the agency-based practitioner and to increase potential income. However, private practice is certainly not trouble-free. Social work is beginning to address the important issues related to private practice: adequate preparation for the responsibilities of independent practice, the move away from the social work mission of focusing services on the poor and other vulnerable population groups, and client protection for this relatively new method of service delivery.

Box 7.1

The Influence of Setting on Demetria's Practice

In the case that is the substance of Chapter 1, Demetria is employed as a social worker in the child welfare division of a county social welfare department where social work would be considered the *primary discipline*. From this information we know that she works in a *local government sector setting*. Thus the programs are established through legislation and funded through taxes. At least for the child protection services, it would be likely that fees for the services performed would not be charged to the clients. Even in an agency with *sliding scale fees* based on income, the Miles family would no doubt be well below the threshold for fees.

In a government or *public* agency such as this department, it is often difficult for staff to effectively lobby for a change in the services should they become aware of ways the services could be improved. The highly *bureaucratic structure* evident in the case (e.g., presence of a supervisor, intake worker, and office administrator) indicates that Demetria would need to carefully work up the chain of command, perhaps even to the county commission or legislature, if she was to affect major change in agency functioning. Her colleague in the Boys and Girls Club, a *private nonprofit agency,* however, would have a much less cumbersome structure if she wanted to promote change.

The concept of *horizontal and vertical influences* is evident in Demetria's work. Her activity was affected by the other agencies and resources in the community (i.e., *horizontal influences*). The actions of the local school, the counseling group at the Boys and Girls Club, the limited employment counseling/finding services, and the immediate access to Medicaid, food stamps, and other social programs all supported her work with this family. However, the policies and procedures, as well as the amount of funding available to the Division of Child Welfare, are likely to be affected by *vertical influencers,* i.e., a combination of actions of county commissioners, state legislature/governor/social welfare boards, and even by federal legislation and the executive branch of the government that administers these programs—the U.S. Department of Health and Human Services.

KEY WORDS AND CONCEPTS

Government sector
Voluntary sector
Business sector
Mutual aid organization
Nonprofit agencies
For-profit organization
Private practice

Privatization
Horizontal/vertical influences
Efficiency vs. effectiveness
Bureaucratic vs. professional model
Social work as: primary discipline, equal
    partner, secondary discipline

SUGGESTED INFORMATION SOURCES

Barker, Robert L. *Social Work in Private Practice: Principles, Issues, Dilemmas,* 2nd Edition. Washington, D.C.: NASW Press, 1992.

Kamerman, Sheila, and Kahn, Alfred J., eds. *Privatization and the Welfare State.* Princeton, NJ: Princeton University Press, 1989.

"Clinical Social Workers in Practice: A Reference Guide" (brochure). Washington, D.C.: National Association of Social Workers.

http://workforce.socialworkers.org

ENDNOTES

1. Catherine E. Born, "Proprietary Firms and Child Welfare Services: Patterns and Implications," *Child Welfare* 62 (March–April 1983): 112.
2. Golda M. Edinburg and Joan M. Cotter, "Managed Care," in Richard L. Edwards, ed., *Encyclopedia of Social Work,* 19th Edition (Washington, D.C.: NASW Press, 1995).
3. B. A. Stroul, S. A. Pires, M. I. Armstrong, and J. C. Meyers. "The Impact of Managed Care on Mental Health Services for Children and Their Families." *The Future of Children* 8 (Summer–Fall 1998): pp. 119–133.
4. Peter M. Blau and Marshall W. Meyer, *Bureaucracy in Modern Society,* 2nd Edition (New York: Random House, 1973), pp. 18–23.
5. W. Richard Scott, "Professionals in Bureaucracies—Areas of Conflict," in Howard M. Vollmer and Donald L. Mills, eds., *Professionalization* (Englewood Cliffs, NJ: Prentice-Hall, 1966), pp. 264–275.
6. Robert Pruger, "The Good Bureaucrat," *Social Work* 18 (July 1973): 26–27.
7. Marquis Earl Wallace, "Private Practice: A Nationwide Study," *Social Work* 27 (May 1983): 265.
8. Center for Health Workforce Studies. http://workforce.socialworkers.org. *Licensed Social Workers in the United States, 2004: A Statistical Profile.* (Draft 5/16/05). (Rensselear, NY: State University of New York at Albany).
9. Patricia Kelly and Paul Alexander, "Part-Time Private Practice: Practical and Ethical Considerations," *Social Work* 30 (May–June 1985): 254.
10. Janice Proshaska, "Private Practice May Benefit Voluntary Agencies," *Social Casework* 59 (July 1978): 374.
11. Robert Barker, "Private Practice Primer for Social Work," *NASW News* 28 (October 1983): 13.
12. Robert J. Teare and Bradford W. Sheafor, *Practice-Sensitive Social Work Education: An Empirical Analysis of Social Work Practice and Practitioners.* (Alexandria, VA: Council on Social Work Education, 1995): p. 117.

part four

The Practice of Social Work

The payoff in social work is in the services rendered to clients and the improvements made to problematic social conditions affecting the quality of life for people. The provision of these services is commonly referred to as *social work practice*. It has long been recognized that social work practice requires attention to *values* (our beliefs about how things ought to be), *knowledge* (our perception of how things are), and *skills* (our ability to use intervention techniques in our practice). In this section of *Social Work: A Profession of Many Faces* we look at some of the fundamentals underpinning practice. In the following chapters, we examine the values/ethics and competencies that shape the practice of social work; look at ways to prevent problems from developing in the first place; examine different approaches to social work in other countries; and review three specific issues that are confronting social workers today.

Chapter 8 examines the basic values that have shaped social work's approach to practice. Examples of these values are beliefs that all people are worthy of being treated with respect; that people should be helped to have meaningful interactions with others; that people should be helped to become independent and take responsibility for themselves; and that society has a responsibility for helping people lead fulfilling lives. In addition, we examine the ethical guidelines imbedded in the NASW Code of Ethics that guide social workers in the way they conduct their work on a day-to-day basis.

Chapter 9 describes the competencies required of social workers. Based on research about the tasks social workers perform, this chapter then identifies the knowledge and skills a social worker needs to carry out those tasks. Although this is not an exhaustive list of competencies, it suggests the content that one would expect to find in a social work education program and the activities social workers will be expected to perform in working with clients.

Chapter 10 is concerned with an often neglected aspect of social work practice—prevention. Social work's mission is to facilitate change to improve social conditions for both people and the environment. Improving the environment by preventing harmful conditions for people is perhaps the most effective way to achieve the goals of social work.

Although this book is primarily concerned with how social work is practiced in the United States, an overview of this profession would be incomplete without examining some of the different expressions of this profession throughout the world. Global social work, then, is the subject of Chapter 11.

This section concludes with three short, tightly focused chapters designed to stimulate thinking and discussion about current issues facing social workers. In Chapter 12 we address changes affecting social work practice in rural America. Chapter 13 is concerned with how social workers are involved in the aftermath of terrorism, perpetrated by both domestic and international sources. Finally, Chapter 14 concerns the casualties of what appears to be the ongoing condition of the United States being at war,—where persons are killed and maimed—and families are devastated. War creates an important role for social workers in helping the casualties of war, such as the families of those in Afghanistan and Iraq, adjust their lives to these losses and deal with the trauma they have experienced.

8

Values and Ethics in Social Work

Prefatory Comment

At the heart of social work is its values. Values assist the social worker and the social work profession in setting goals related to both clients and society. Of course, like any other population group, every social worker does not have identical values. Yet, there are some common themes in social work that suggest that social workers hold some fundamental beliefs in common. As opposed to many other groups of people, for example, social workers tend to believe that society has the responsibility to assist people in meeting their needs, that people should be included in making decisions that affect their lives, that positive change in people's lives can be attained through professional help, and so on. This chapter examines these and other values that are central to social work's belief system.

The most concrete expression of social work's ethical guidelines are embodied in the NASW Code of Ethics. This Code helps social workers to make the inevitable moral choices that arise in their daily practice. If unethical practice is suspected, the Code also becomes the criteria by which the social worker's ethical behavior is evaluated.

From formulating social programs to helping clients, values affect social work practice. Social programs created to "promote the general welfare" of the people are influenced by the values held by legislators, board members, or owners of for-profit organizations who created or maintain those programs. Beliefs about who should be responsible for meeting human needs, what role government or private charity should play, and how much of the nation's wealth should be invested in meeting people's social needs are just three examples of factors that have shaped human services programs.

Also, values affect the manner in which human service organizations operate. Values, at least partially, determine the answers to important questions: Should potential clients be encouraged or discouraged from asking for help? Should clients be required to pay for services? To what extent should an agency attempt to make services readily accessible to clients and assure that the surroundings are comfortable and pleasant? Should a social worker be allowed to terminate services before a client's insurance benefits are exhausted when the agency needs the funds to meet its financial obligations? Should services be terminated just because the client can no longer pay yet continues to need help? In short, the dominant values of an agency can have a direct impact on social work practice.

The values of a social worker's clients, too, affect practice. If a client feels stigmatized, demeaned, or embarrassed to ask for assistance in addressing a social problem, the client's ability to productively use the service is affected. If the client is unnecessarily demanding of a worker's time and attention or resents being required to use social services (i.e., an involuntary client), that, too, affects the way a social worker assists the client. Further, much of practice involves helping clients identify, clarify, and resolve value issues that are almost always present in human interactions.

As members of a profession that has based many of its practice approaches and principles on certain beliefs about people and how they can best be served, social workers must be cognizant of the profession's values. Further, since social work must protect the public from potential abuses of the professional monopoly, it has adopted a code of ethical practice that prescribes certain professional behaviors related to interactions with clients, colleagues, employers, and the community. Each social worker must be prepared to adhere to the NASW Code of Ethics.

Finally, the social worker must be clear about how the profession's values and ethical standards interact with his or her own belief system. Therefore, understanding one's own values becomes critical for the social worker. Most of us do not typically contemplate our values unless they somehow create problems for us as we address the issues we confront in life. This chapter, however, asks the reader to consider the nature of values, their place in promoting people's welfare through shaping social programs, the values and ethics of social workers, and, finally, the fit between social work's values and one's own. Understanding the central place of values and ethics in social work is another important factor in making a career choice or preparing to enter the social work profession.

The Nature of Values

Unlike knowledge, which explains what is, values express what ought to be. Rokeach more precisely defines a *value* as "a type of belief, centrally located in one's total belief system, about how one ought or ought not to behave, or about some end-state of existence worth or not worth attaining."[1] This definition helps to clarify the two central functions our values perform. The first function, for example, how we should or should not behave, reflects our *instrumental values*. These values provide the moral or ethical guidelines that help determine how we conduct our lives and, as social workers, how we perform our work. The second function performed by our values, known as *terminal values*, reflects the bottom line of what we want to accomplish. Ensuring a safe environment for all people, a sufficient distribution of the world's wealth to eliminate hunger, ensuring strong families that nurture the development of children, and achieving social justice within the society are just a few examples of terminal values.

Values are much more than emotional reactions to situations or doing what feels right. Values are the fundamental criteria that lead us to thoughtful decisions. It is important to recognize, however, that people do not always behave in a manner consistent with their values. Values guide decisions but do not dictate choices. People can and do make decisions contrary to their values. Such decisions might be made when other factors are given priority ("I know that I shouldn't have done that, but when will I ever get another chance to make that kind of money?"), the person acts on emotion ("I was just so angry, I hit her without thinking"), or when one fails to adequately think through and understand the value issues in a situation ("It just didn't occur to me that my quitting school would make my parents think that they have failed").

Each person values a variety of things in life. Differences in the strength with which one holds any particular value and the priority a particular value will have among the whole constellation of that person's values, that is, the person's *value system,* is a part of what makes individuals unique. For example, for many people the most important value is feeling secure in their relationships with loved ones. For some, generating income is the driving force in their lives. For others, giving service or maintaining relationships dominates their value system.

Dealing with values is particularly difficult for several reasons. First, values are such a central part of our thought processes that we often are not consciously aware of them and therefore are unable to identify their influence on our decisions. The social worker should constantly be alert to values in practice situations as these values may subtly influence the thoughts, feelings, attitudes, and behaviors of both the client and the social worker.

Second, a person may be forced to choose among values that are in conflict with one another. Who can avoid wrestling with a *value conflict* when confronted by a person on the street asking for money to buy something to eat? We may value responding to people in need, but we may equally value encouraging people to use the organized system for receiving financial assistance that does not put the person into the degrading position of panhandling.

Third, addressing values in the abstract may be quite different from applying them in a real-life situation. The social worker must recognize, for example, that clients may not act on the basis of value choices selected in a counseling session when they are confronted with the actual people and conditions where this value must be operationalized.

Finally, values are problematic because they change over time. Various events, experiences, and even new information can lead clients to adapt their system of values to more closely fit their current situation. A person whose job is eliminated, for instance, may be much more supportive of a universal health insurance program than when he or she was employed and receiving health insurance benefits from the employer.

The Place of Values in Social Work

Helping people to be clear about their individual values, that is, *values clarification,* and facilitating their understanding of how the particular set of values they hold influences their goals and decisions is an important aspect of social work practice. At times, clients also must be assisted in recognizing and understanding the values of others. Taking into consideration the values of family members, friends, employers, teachers, or others in that person's environment may be prerequisite to making appropriate and workable decisions. The matter becomes more complicated when social work practice involves more than one person, as it is likely that each will have a somewhat different value system. In that case the social worker may need to help resolve issues that stem from differences in values.

Further, the social worker must be concerned with his or her own values and control for their inappropriate intrusion into practice situations. Value choices that may be viable personally for the social worker may not coincide with the needs, wants, priorities, or realities the client experiences. Ultimately, the client must live with the decisions that are made, and they should be consistent with his or her own value system—not the value system of the social worker. Learning to suspend one's own values (i.e., *value suspension*) to keep the focus of helping on the client or client group is an important, yet difficult task for every social worker.

With social work practice focused at the interface between person and environment, the social worker must simultaneously address several sets of values. It is no wonder that social work has perhaps devoted more attention to values than has any other helping profession. Yet it has not developed a sufficiently clear and adequately tested statement of its core values to offer a definitive description of its central beliefs. At best, there is only rather general agreement that some values are fundamental to social work practice.

Social Values in U.S. Society

Values differ from *needs.* The latter refers to people's basic biological or psychological urges, while values reflect what people hope to get out of life and how this should be accomplished. The choice of which needs a society will attempt to meet depends on what it values. The most predominant feature of Western values is the central place of the individual; that is, the society exists to help individuals lead satisfying and productive lives. Like other parts of Western culture, the values that guide choices in U.S. society focus on the individual. These values have their roots in at least four different sources, all of which are concerned with the responsibilities of the individual toward self and society and/or the society's responsibility to the individual.[2] These sources include:

1. Judaism and Christianity with their doctrine of the integral worth of humans and their responsibilities for their neighbors;

2. The democratic ideals that emphasize the equality of all people and a person's right to "life, liberty, and the pursuit of happiness";
3. The Puritan ethic, which says that character is all, circumstances nothing, that the moral person is the one who works and is independent, and that pleasure is sinful;
4. The tenets of Social Darwinism, which emphasize that the fittest survive and the weak perish in a natural evolutionary process that produces the strong individual and society.

It is evident that much of the disagreement in the United States over the provision of human services results from value conflicts inherent in the U.S. public's value system. Brill and Levine point out:

> Even the casual reader will see that a dichotomy exists within this value system. We hold that all men are equal, but he who does not work is less equal. . . . We hold that the individual life has worth, but that only the fit should survive. We believe that we are responsible for each other, but those who depend on others for their living are of lesser worth.[3]

In carrying out the commitments of the social welfare institution to respond to human needs, the social worker becomes an intermediary between people in need and society's value judgments about what needs are to be met. As one cynic phrased it, the social worker stands "between the demanding recipient and the grudging donor." Therefore, the social worker must be particularly knowledgeable about the values that are dominant in U.S. society.

What constellation of values are held by the U.S. population? In this nation of people with widely diverse backgrounds and interests, it is not surprising that there is considerable variation in belief systems. The answer to the question "Am I my brother's (or sister's) keeper?" is not a categorical "yes" or "no." Protecting a woman's "right to choose" in regard to abortion in one person's value system, for example, is viewed as a "license to kill" in another's system of beliefs. Efforts to document preferred values held by the U.S. public are the basis for considerable political debate, but rarely identify a clear consensus on issues.

Kahle's carefully constructed study of the social values held by Americans suggests that value preferences differ substantially for different segments of the population.[4] The study asked respondents to indicate which of eight fundamental social values was the most important for a person to achieve in life.* The data reveal that the more vulnerable groups consistently hold two values, security and being respected, at much higher levels than the general population. Perhaps that is not surprising. If one is poor, has a limited education, is a minority group member, or is old,

---

*The eight social values, in order of numbers of times it was selected as most important, were (1) having *self-respect* (feeling good about oneself and what has been accomplished in life); (2) attaining a *sense of security* (feeling safe and comfortable about the future); (3) having *warm personal relationships* (maintaining satisfying interpersonal relations with friends and family); (4) *feeling successful* in life's undertakings; (5) being *respected by others;* (6) *feeling fulfilled* by the quality of life experiences; (7) experiencing *a sense of belonging* to valued groups of people; and (8) finding *fun, enjoyment, and excitement* in life's activities.

he or she is likely to worry about having basic health insurance, sufficient income, and safety. It is also likely that he or she is regularly treated with some degree of disrespect by others and will suffer various forms of discrimination. Under these conditions, one values highly what he or she does not have—security and respect. From the vantage point of social work, these data reinforce the view that it is important to support the development of social programs that increase people's security and to deliver those programs in a manner that treats the recipients with dignity. With those two basic social values achieved, people are then ready to address other areas of need that can enhance their lives.

Social workers and other professionals must be particularly alert to what the clients value because those values are not likely to be held with the same strength by the professionals themselves. The data from the Kahle study indicate that attaining such basic values as security and being respected by others were not of high priority to professionals. After all, they really don't need to worry about those basics. Professionals are highly educated, usually have secure jobs with relatively high income, don't typically experience discrimination, and can feel pretty safe about their futures. Their value preferences are related to items such as achieving self-respect, having a sense of accomplishment, and experiencing fulfillment.[5] It takes discipline and commitment to avoid the trap of seeing the world only through one's own eyes and actively seeking to understand and appreciate the value preferences of others.

Values Held by Social Workers

In order to avoid imposing personal values on the client or making inappropriate judgments about a client's values, the social worker must have a clear understanding of his or her own personal values. In addition, the social worker must be fully aware of, and guided by, the fundamental values of the social work profession.

What, then, are the values commonly held by social workers? When developing its classification scheme for different levels of practice, the National Association of Social Workers identified ten basic social work values.[6] These statements express the basic values that underpin the profession of social work.

1. *Commitment to the primary importance of the individual in society.* In this value statement social work reaffirms its commitment to the individual. Social work accepts the position that the individual is the center of practice and that every person is of inherent worth because of his or her humanness. The social worker need not approve of what a person does but must treat that person as a valued member of society. Each client should be treated with dignity.

Commitment to the centrality of the individual has also led social workers to recognize that each person is unique and that practice activities must be tailored for that person's or group's uniqueness. Such individualization permits the worker to determine where and how to intervene in each helping situation, while at the same time communicating respect for the people being served.

2. *Commitment to social change to meet socially recognized needs.* Giving primacy to the individual does not minimize the commitment of the social worker to achieve societal change. Rather, it suggests that the social worker recognizes that the outcome of change activities in the larger society must ultimately benefit individuals.

Social workers, then, are committed to the belief that the society has a responsibility to provide resources and services to help people avoid such problems as hunger, insufficient education, discrimination, illness without care, and inadequate housing. Social workers serve both the person and the environment in responding to social needs.

3. *Commitment to social justice and the economic, physical, and mental well-being of all in society.* Social workers believe that social justice will be achieved if each person has the opportunity to develop his or her unique potential and, therefore, make his or her maximum contribution to society. Thus, social workers believe that each person should have the right to participate in molding the social institutions and the decision-making processes in U.S. society so that programs, policies, and procedures are responsive to the needs and conditions of all.

Of course, when resources are limited, choices must be made. Not every person can have all needs met. When they are making choices, the values held by social workers emphasize the importance of responding to the needs of the most vulnerable members of the society. Typically, these vulnerable people are children, the aged, minority group members, the disabled, women, and others who have been victims of institutionalized discrimination. Social workers are committed to ensuring that social justice is achieved for these persons, individually and as a population group.

4. *Respect and appreciation for individual and group differences.* Social workers recognize that there are common needs, goals, aspirations, and wants that are held by all people. In some ways we are all alike. However, social workers also recognize that in other ways each individual's life experience and capacities make him or her unique. Where some may fear differences or resist working with people who are not like themselves, social workers value and respect uniqueness. They believe that the quality of life is enriched by different cultural patterns, different beliefs, and different forms of activity. As opposed to efforts to assimilate persons who are in some way different from the general population, social workers value a pluralistic society that can accommodate a range of beliefs, behaviors, languages, and customs.

5. *Commitment to developing clients' ability to help themselves.* If clients are to change their social conditions, their actions that contributed to the conditions must change. Unlike medicine, where an injection or medication may solve a patient's problem, social change requires that the people affected become personally engaged in the change process and actively work to create the desired change. Underpinning social work practice, then, must be the social worker's belief that each person has an inherent capacity and drive that can result in desirable change.

Social workers do not view people as static or unchanging, nor is anyone assumed to be unable to engage in activities that may produce a more satisfying and rewarding life. Rather, social workers view people as adaptable. Although there are conditions that some people face that cannot be changed, the people themselves or the world around them can be helped to adapt to these conditions. For example, the terminally ill patient cannot be made well, the blind child cannot be made to see, and the severely retarded person cannot be made self-sustaining. Yet in each case the person involved can be helped to adjust to these conditions, and the person's environment can be adapted to more adequately accommodate special needs. Within the individual's or group's capacities, the social worker places high value on helping people take responsibility for their own decisions and actions.

6. *Willingness to transmit knowledge and skills to others.* Perhaps the most important function performed by the social worker in helping clients accomplish the change they desire is to effectively guide the change process. A significant part of this guidance involves helping clients understand the situation they experience from both a personal perspective and the perspectives of others, as well as helping them develop the skills to resolve their problems.

Effective helping avoids making clients dependent on helpers and prepares them to address other issues that arise in their lives. Thus, it is important that social workers assist clients in identifying strengths that can be mobilized for solving the immediate problem and to help them learn how to use these strengths in solving problems that may arise in the future.

A second application of this value concerns the commitment of professionals to share knowledge with colleagues. Knowledge or skills developed by a social worker are not to be kept secret or limited to clients who work only with that social worker. Rather, the social worker is obligated to transmit this information to other social workers so that they might bring the best knowledge and skill possible to their clients.

7. *Willingness to keep personal feelings and needs separate from professional relationships.* It is important for the social worker to recognize that the focus of practice must be maintained on the client—not on the social worker. Because social workers care about the people they work with, it is easy to become overidentified with clients' lives or even to develop personal relationships with them. If that happens, the client loses the benefit of an objective helper, the social worker can be placed in a compromising position, and the quality of the helping process is diminished because the relationship has changed from professional to personal.

8. *Respect for the confidentiality of relationship with clients.* Although it is rare that the social worker can guarantee "absolute confidentiality," social workers value achieving the maximum possible protection of information received in working with clients. The very nature of a helping relationship suggests that there is sensitive information that must be shared between the person being helped and the helper. For example, the social worker must learn the reasons a client has been fired from a job, why a person who is chronically mentally ill has failed in a community group home placement, what keeps a homeless person from being able to secure resources to pay rent, why an alcoholic has not been able to stop drinking, or why a couple involved in marriage counseling has not been able to solve problems without fighting. In each case, some information typically passes between client and worker

that could potentially be emotionally or economically damaging if it is inappropriately revealed to other parties. Social workers consider it of critical importance to respect the privacy of this communication.

9. *Willingness to persist in efforts on behalf of clients despite frustration.* Situations that require social work intervention typically do not develop quickly and usually cannot be resolved readily. Recognizing the frustration that they experience when change is slow to occur, social workers have come to value tenacity in addressing both individual problems and the problems that affect groups of people, organizations, communities, and society in general.

When providing direct services, a social worker may become frustrated with a client who, at a given time, is unable or unwilling to engage in activities the social worker believes would improve the situation. Or, when advocating on behalf of a client with another agency to provide needed services, the social worker may also experience frustration when the client is denied service or is placed on a waiting list. Advocacy for classes of clients or in relation to broad social issues can also prove quite frustrating. If delay tactics or the length of the change process is extended, the social worker may understandably become discouraged. Social workers must be persistent.

10. *Commitment to a high standard of personal and professional conduct.* The final value on the NASW list directs the worker to use the highest ethical standards in his or her practice. It suggests that the worker must conduct professional activities in a manner that protects the interests of the public, the agency, the clients, and the social worker. This value has been operationalized in the form of the *NASW Code of Ethics,* which is perhaps the single most unifying element among social workers.

Shortly after its founding, the NASW began to formulate a code of ethics that could serve the needs of this profession. First adopted in 1960 as a few general statements to guide ethical practice, the *Code* has undergone several major revisions and now is an elaborate document used not only as a practice guide but also as a statement on which to assess allegations against social workers of ethical misconduct.

With a clearly explicated code of ethics in place, NASW members can be clear about expectations for competent and ethical practice and the profession has a standard against which to assess complaints that the public trust has been violated. To join NASW, the social worker must sign a statement agreeing to abide by the ethical standards contained in the *Code* and to participate in the adjudication process if a complaint is made. By renewing one's membership each year, he or she reaffirms the commitment to adhere to NASW's ethical code. NASW has created an elaborate procedure for hearing grievances at the local or chapter level with appeal to the national level possible for all parties to the complaint. A member found to have violated the Code of Ethics can be asked to take corrective actions, may be listed on a published report of Code violators, or may have his or her NASW membership revoked.

Areas of Practice Addressed by the NASW Code of Ethics

The *NASW Code of Ethics* has evolved from its 1960 format of fourteen general statements to guide ethical considerations in practice to its current format that consumes twenty-seven pages of ethical prescriptions. Mastering the specifics of the *Code* and interpreting its provisions in actual practice situations is an ongoing challenge for all social workers. This process begins by recognizing the general areas of practice activity that the *Code* addresses.* The following statements summarize the main sections of NASW's *Code of Ethics*.

1. Standards related to the social worker's ethical responsibilities to clients. This section of the *Code of Ethics* is concerned with such factors and principles as the following: the worker's primary responsibility is to the client; respect for client self-determination; securing client's informed consent; the worker's competence to provide needed services; the worker's cultural competence; avoiding conflict of interest; respecting clients' rights to privacy and confidentiality; the prohibition of sexual involvement, sexual harassment, inappropriate physical contact, and abusive or derogatory language; special considerations when clients lack decision-making capacity; avoiding the interruption of services; and the planful termination of services.

2. The social worker's ethical responsibilities to colleagues. Section 2 is concerned with the social workers' responsibility to treat colleagues with respect; concern for maintaining confidentiality among professionals; appropriate collaboration and teamwork; proper handling of disputes and disagreements; developing appropriate consultation relationships; proper referral of clients to colleagues; the prohibition of sexual harassment and sexual involvement with one's supervisees or students; and the requirement for responsible action in relation to a colleague who is impaired, incompetent, or unethical in his or her practice.

3. The social worker's ethical responsibilities in practice settings. This section of the *Code of Ethics* relates to services performed that only indirectly relate to clients. The items addressed include the competence required for providing supervision, consultation, education, and training; responsible evaluation of the performance of other workers; maintaining proper client records and billing properly; carefully evaluating client needs before accepting transfers; assuring an appropriate working environment and providing ongoing education and training in human services agencies; demonstrating commitment to agency employees; and guidelines for acting responsibly in labor disputes.

---

*The full text of the *NASW Code of Ethics* can be obtained from the National Association of Social Workers, 750 First Street, NE, Washington, DC 20002-4241, or can be downloaded from NASW's web site (http://www.socialworkers.org/pubs/code/default.asp). The Canadian code of ethics (which contains similar provisions) can be downloaded by members of the Canadian Association of Social Workers at (http://www.casw-acts.ca/default.htm).

4. The social worker's ethical responsibilities as a professional. Section 4 includes items related to the social worker accepting employment and job assignments when he or she may not be competent to perform that work; prohibition from practicing, condoning, or participating in any form of discrimination; engaging in private conduct that compromises the ability to fulfill professional responsibilities; restriction from engaging in dishonesty, fraud, and deception; the responsibility to address one's own problems if impaired; the requirement to be clear in public statements regarding whether acting as a professional or a private citizen; prohibiting uninvited solicitations for business; and properly acknowledging any contributions to one's written or other work made by others.

5. The social worker's ethical responsibilities to the social work profession. The *Code of Ethics* is also concerned with issues related to the social worker promoting high standards for social work and contributing time and energy to the profession's growth and development, as well as addressing items related to social workers continuously monitoring and evaluating social policies, programs, and their own practice interventions.

6. The social worker's ethical responsibilities to the broader society. In its final section the *Code of Ethics* charges social workers with promoting the general welfare of the society and seeking to ensure social justice for all people; participating in public debate to shape social policies and institutions; providing services in public emergencies; and actively engaging in social and political action.

The maintenance of a code of ethics helps to satisfy social work's obligation to be responsible in performing its duties as a recognized profession. It provides guidance to social workers as they make ethical decisions in their day-to-day practice, spells out expected behaviors in areas where ethical compromises may arise, and provides clarity to the general public, employers, and other professionals who may feel that a social worker has violated the principles of ethical practice and wish to have NASW and/or the courts determine if a social worker has violated the public trust granted to professions.

Illustrations of Values and Ethics Operating in Social Work Practice

For most social workers, theoretical or abstract discussion of values and ethical dilemmas is not a daily event. It is usually when these issues are experienced while working with clients that they take on full significance—and they do indeed occur while working with clients. Hokenstad, for example, estimates that "half of professional decision making requires ethical rather than scientific judgment."[7] Thus examining one's values in the context of a case example helps to translate the value-related issues that regularly arise in practice from the abstract value statements to their more concrete application.

RAGAN ADAM'S VALUE DILEMMA

The interview began as most begin. The school social worker, Ragan Adams, had initiated an interview with the Warring family as a follow-up to a conference she had conducted with the Warring's oldest daughter, Sally Kay. In the conference with Sally Kay regarding her sudden change from being a model student to one who was frequently absent from school, with a sudden burst of tears Sally Kay revealed that she was pretty sure she was pregnant and was afraid to tell her parents. She was sure it would hurt her mother deeply and she was physically afraid of how her father might react.

Sally Kay indicated that her parents are deeply religious and decidedly "pro life" in their philosophy about abortion. She felt trapped in the situation as she believed that she was in no way ready to raise a child, knew her parents would not condone her having an abortion, and thought adoption was not a good option because she would need to carry the baby to term and that would ruin her future and bring shame to the family. When questioned, she indicted that "Yes, she had considered suicide as a way out," but had abandoned that thought because "it would only make things worse." She needed help in figuring out what to do and asked Ms. Adams for help.

Ms. Adams knew that an unintended pregnancy could destabilize a family, especially if the pregnant family member is an unmarried teenager. Also, Sally Kay's fear of possible violence by her father hinted that there could have been violence in the home previously. It would be important to plan helping in a way that would be supportive of Sally Kay's revealing her situation to her parents while minimizing the chances of the father's becoming violent with Sally Kay or others, and then turn the attention to making a decision that would be with Sally Kay for the rest of her life and that, hopefully, the parents would support.

Before taking any action, Ragan Adams needed to do a little soul-searching herself. What were her beliefs about these options, and could she suspend them to allow the family to make the best choice for itself? Might her own values intrude and affect her actions as a social worker? As an agent of the school, was she free to support whatever choice Sally Kay might make? What if the choice should be to help Sally Kay have an abortion and Sally Kay's parents complain to the principal that Ms. Adams had influenced Sally Kay to make that choice against their will? Who is the client and to what extent should client self-determination prevail?

Ms. Adams concluded that the safest place for the family interview would be at the school. After introducing herself to the parents, she indicated that she had called the meeting to talk over issues that were interfering with Sally Kay's success in school. As she and Sally Kay had planned and practiced before the interview began, Ms. Adams invited Sally Kay to share her thoughts on the matter. When Sally Kay indicated that she was pregnant, the father went "ballistic" wanting to know "who the hell was the father" and why had Sally Kay let him take advantage of her. The mother burst into tears, mumbling that she had failed as a mother and surely God was punishing them for something she had done wrong. Sally Kay hid her face in her hands and silently sobbed. It was clear that many different emotions and values would have to be reconciled when working with this family.

Where the above case centers around values held by both the clients and the worker, the subset of values related to the conduct of one's professional practice represents the ethical principles that should guide the social worker. Most ethical decisions, unfortunately, are not clear and require the social worker to make choices when, sometimes, none of the alternatives are desirable. The worker must weigh one choice against others and make a decision about which option is best or, too often, which is least harmful. Further, ethical issues sometimes appear relatively easy to resolve in the abstract, but are much more difficult in real-life situations. Consider the following case example.

TERRI PERRY'S ETHICAL DECISION

Terri was a good student and was pleased to have discovered social work as a career option. She had always wanted a career helping people and her friends regularly sought her out in the dormitory to ask advice about problems in relationships with parents, broken love affairs, difficulty in finding a direction in college, and getting through the freshman plague—roommate problems. Her social work professors had described these qualities as those of a good natural helper, and now she is preparing to move her talents to another level, professional helping.

To Terri, the culmination of her social work education was to be her field placement in the county probation office. There she would be able to combine her natural helping skills and the knowledge from her social work classes into her own professional helping style to start down the track of being a social worker. When the placement was planned with the school's field instruction coordinator, Terri had interviewed with the chief probation officer, Mr. DeMiranda, and Ms. Sills, the social worker who was to be her field instructor. She especially liked Ms. Sills, who indicated that she planned to regularly observe Terri working with clients, either directly or through recording, and to meet with her weekly to plan and critique her work so that Terri might improve her competence as a social worker.

At the end of the first month in placement, Terri concluded that the experience had lived up to her expectations—unlike the reports from some of her classmates in other placements. Then it happened! Mr. DeMiranda began to take a special interest in her—too special, she thought. At first he casually brushed against her at the water fountain (it might have been an accident) and then he asked her to sit next to him in a staff meeting where he pressed his leg against hers under the table (maybe he thought her leg was the table leg) making her very nervous. Terri tried to avoid Mr. DeMiranda after that and no longer looked forward to going to her placement.

Terri had learned that avoiding problems did not resolve them. What should she do? Perhaps she should not do anything? What would happen to her field placement if she makes waves? And what if she is just imagining that Mr. DeMiranda is making advances? What would happen to Mr. DeMiranda and his family? What if it is true and yet she has no "proof"? What would happen to her career as a social worker? "Maybe it is wise to just let this one go by," she thought. "After all, I'm just a student."

On the other hand, Terri pondered the implications of letting this pass. What if this happens to others who are in positions where Mr. DeMiranda possesses power over them for example, other interns, staff members, and even probationers? They are just as vulnerable, or perhaps even more vulnerable. If no one speaks up, won't this behavior continue? What policy does the Probation Office have regarding sexual harassment? Will the Department of Social Work at my university stand behind me? What guidance might I find from the NASW *Code of Ethics*?

The ethical dilemma experienced by Terri Perry, the social worker in the above case, is only one of many a social worker might encounter. The following list gives some examples of the range of decisions a social worker must address that have ethical implications. Fortunately, the *Code of Ethics* provides the worker with some guidance on each of them, but (sometimes if the worker follows one Code guideline another may be violated.)

▶ What should a social worker do if a client announces the decision to return to an abusive spouse when the worker fears for the client's safety?

▶ Is it ethical for a social worker to attempt to provide specialized therapeutic services for which he or she is not trained if the worker doubts the competence of the only credentialed person with that expertise in the area where the client lives?

▶ Should a social worker accept a personal gift from a client beyond the fee the client pays for the professional service? In lieu of a fee for professional service?

▶ Should a social worker report a colleague to NASW or the state licensing board if that colleague reveals that he or she has developed a sexual relationship with one of his or her clients?

▶ What should a social worker do if a grand jury requests a client's file that contains case notes that may be damaging to the client?

▶ Is a social worker obligated to do anything if he or she believes a colleague has developed a substance abuse problem?

▶ What should be done if a client asks a social worker in a probation setting to overlook (and not mention in the case record) a violation of a condition of parole—promising not to repeat the activity?

▶ Is it okay for a social worker not to record information given by a client in confidence in the case file when the agency's administrative procedures require recording all pertinent information to the case? If state law requires reporting that information to a central registry or a protective services agency?

▶ What should a social worker in private practice do if a local business considering a substantial service contract with the worker requests the names and addresses of current clients to contact in order to assess their satisfaction with the worker's performance?

▶ If the administrator in a nursing home directs the social work staff to transfer out of the agency all patients who do not have insurance or other benefits because the nursing home is experiencing financial difficulty, should the social workers abide by this directive?

▶ Is it ethical for a social worker who develops a successful helping technique to obtain a patent and market the technique for a profit to other social workers?

▶ Is a social worker obligated to engage in social and political action when his or her job description does not specify such activity?

Concluding Comment

One cannot understand social work without being sensitive to values. Values represent a highly individual and personal view that must be constantly examined during practice.

The social worker must be aware of the value system of the client or client group and the values held by society that impinge upon the client. These values, however, are not held equally by all people, and client groups can be expected to vary in the intensity with which they hold particular values. The social worker must also be especially cognizant of his or her personal values, lest they intrude into the helping process. Certainly it would be unrealistic to expect, or even desire, that the helping process occur in a value-free environment. Yet the social worker must attempt to avoid imposing personal beliefs inappropriately on the client or client groups. In order to practice social work, one must be prepared to accept and understand people who hold values that are different from their own.

The social worker also must be guided by the values and ethics of the social work profession. These beliefs are not held exclusively by social workers. Some overlap with the values of other professions, and there is indication that professionals hold distinctly different values from the general population.[8] Social work's constellation of core values, however, is unique. Roberts, for example, has identified five areas where the values of physicians and those of social workers are quite different, including attitudes about such factors as saving life versus quality of life, the professional's control versus patient autonomy in establishing treatment plans, and so on.[9] Further, Abbott's research identified areas of significant difference in the values held by social workers, physicians, nurses, teachers, psychologists, and business people. Of these groups, psychologists were most like social workers in their beliefs.[10] A difficulty in addressing values is that they are not usually explicitly stated and must be inferred from people's behaviors. In Box 8.1 some of the values and ethical considerations we can infer from Demetria's work with the Miles Family (see Chapter 1) are enumerated.

In many ways, values or beliefs about how things ought to be or how people ought to behave are the cornerstone of social work. Even when the knowledge available to guide practice is limited, the social worker who falls back on the values of the profession cannot go far wrong in guiding the helping process. When the worker is value-sensitive and effectively supplies the competencies of social work practice, clients receive the quality of services they should expect from a professional.

Box 8.1

Value and Ethical Considerations in Demetria's Practice

Although Demetria's values are not directly expressed in the Miles family case (Chapter 1), some values are evident in her actions. It is clear that Demetria valued creating a safe and supportive family environment for Joseph and thus elected to help the family address its issues so that Joseph would not need to be removed from the home and could get help in dealing with his problems with alcohol and gang involvement. Demetria seems to be aware that Mrs. Miles, like other vulnerable people, places a priority on attaining *security* before she could be open to addressing other issues in her life. Thus attaining food and electricity became a first order of business. Demetria also appeared to recognize that people in vulnerable situations place high priority on *being respected* and politely accepted the offer of a cup of tea (although she couldn't be sure the cup was very clean) and made herself comfortable on the worn couch that might house more of the roaches she had observed in the kitchen.

At least two of the basic social work values were evident in Demetria's performance. One was her *commitment to the primary importance of the individual*. She took Joseph seriously and honored his reluctance to provide her with much information about some of his behaviors by not prying or threatening. She also allowed Mrs. Miles to spill her heart about the issues she faced without judging her as a bad mom or incapable parent. This would be termed an *instrumental value*, or a value that guided Demetria's actions in her relationship with Mrs. Miles. In her concern about the adequacy of employment counseling for this family, Demetria reflected the basic social work value of *commitment to social change to meet socially recognized needs*. This is a *terminal value* that leads to actions regarding an outcome, better employment services, that she wanted to accomplish.

Demetria seemed not to experience any significant ethical issues in this case. One example of her practice that was in line with the *Code of Ethics* was her commitment to client *self-determination*. She pointed Joseph and Mrs. Miles to certain resources (i.e., the counseling group at the Boys and Girls Club for Joseph and the application for food stamps for Mrs. Miles), but ultimately the decision was left to them to use or not use those resources. Demetria also reflected the Code's commitment to *collegial interaction* as she risked criticism when presenting her case plan for consultation at an agency staffing meeting.

KEY WORDS AND CONCEPTS

Values	Value suspension
Ethics	U.S. society's values
Value conflict	Social workers' values
Value system	Social workers' ethics
Values clarification	NASW Code of Ethics

SUGGESTED INFORMATION SOURCES

Hultman, Ken, and Gellerman, Bill. *Balancing Individual and Organizational Values: Walking the Tightrope to Success*. San Francisco: Jossey-Bass/Pfeiffer, 2002.

Linzer, Norman. *Resolving Ethical Dilemmas in Social Work Practice*. Boston: Allyn and Bacon, 1999.

Reamer, Frederic G. *Social Work Values and Ethics*, 2nd Edition. New York: Columbia University Press, 1999.

Rothman, Julie C. *From the Front Lines: Student Cases in Social Work Ethics*. Boston: Allyn and Bacon, 2005.

ENDNOTES

1. Milton Rokeach, *Beliefs, Values, and Attitudes: A Theory of Organization and Change* (San Francisco: Jossey-Bass, 1968), p. 124.

2. Naomi I. Brill and Joanne Levine. *Working with People: The Helping Process*, 7th Edition (Boston: Allyn and Bacon, 2002), p. 29.

3. *Ibid.*, p. 12.

4. Lynn R. Kahle and Susan Groff Timmer, "A Theory and a Method for Studying Values," in Lynn R. Kahle, ed., *Social Values and Social Change: Adaptation to Life in America* (New York: Praeger Publishers, 1983), pp. 47–108.

5. *Ibid.*, p. 110.

6. National Association of Social Workers, *NASW Standards for the Classification of Social Work Practice* (Silver Spring, MD: The Association, September 1981), p. 18.

7. M. C. Hokenstad, "Teaching Practitioners Ethical Judgment," *NASW News* 32 (October 1987): 4.

8. William C. Horner and Les B. Whitebeck, "Personal versus Professional Values in Social Work: A Methodological Note," *Journal of Social Service Research* 14 (Issue 1/2 1991): 21–43.

9. Cleora S. Roberts, "Conflicting Professional Values in Social Work and Medicine," *Health and Social Work* 13 (August 1989): 211–218.

10. Ann A. Abbott, *Professional Choices: Values at Work* (Silver Spring, MD: National Association of Social Workers, 1988), pp. 74–75.

Competencies Required for Social Work Practice

Prefatory Comment

Equipped with adequate social programs to meet client needs, sanction to perform professional services, a suitable agency or private practice environment, and the requisite professional values and ethical guidelines, the social worker is prepared to deliver helping services. Little of this background for practice is usually recognized or even of interest to clients, although the absence of any one of these factors would minimize the social worker's ability to be helpful. Instead, the clients' primary concern is with the social worker and the social worker's competence to be of maximum assistance in addressing their needs and enhancing their general well-being. To understand social work, then, it is important to be familiar with the competencies needed to perform this professional activity.

The term *competence* is a particularly useful descriptor for professional practice, because it not only includes the expertise to perform a function but also suggests the capability to translate that expertise into useful actions. Synonyms for competence include skill and knowledge, art and science, as well as talent and proficiency. Competence, then, requires the worker to not only have the requisite information, but he or she must be able to use that knowledge to effectively assist clients in changing their social functioning or bringing about change in the functioning of some part of their environment.

What must a social worker be competent to do? As a profession with a mission to facilitate change in both people and the environment, a wide range of competencies are required. The requisite knowledge and abilities appear quite different depending on which part of social work one is performing.

The most complete data related to the work performed by social workers have been collected by Teare and Sheafor from 7,000 baccalaureate and master's-level social workers and, using the statistical procedure of cluster analysis, they determined that social work practice can accurately be described as involving eighteen somewhat distinct sets of activity.[1] Those clusters of tasks provide the framework for identifying the competencies required to carry out social work practice in the remainder of this chapter.

The task clusters are arranged to begin with those that are most universal, that is, those that are performed by social workers in most social work positions, and to end with those tasks that are most likely to be performed by social workers in the more specialized aspects of social work practice. In their analysis of these data, Teare and Sheafor[2] found that the most significant factor affecting the competencies required for practice were the social worker's *primary job function* (e.g., providing direct services, being a supervisor, or an administrator). The second most relevant difference was in the level of educational preparation, that is, was the worker prepared at the baccalaureate or master's level? As might be expected, the basic social workers (baccalaureate-level preparation) were mostly engaged in direct practice with their clients and in more concrete and tangible activities such as case planning and ongoing case maintenance, dispute resolution, and connecting clients with the delivery system. By contrast, the specialized and independent social workers (i.e., prepared at the master's level) were more often in supervisor and administrator roles and, when engaged in direct practice, more likely to provide therapeutic services to individuals, families, and groups.

The Universal Social Work Competencies

Two clusters of tasks, interpersonal helping and professional competence development, were consistently performed by most social workers at all levels of practice, in all job functions, and in all practice areas and settings. They represent the most clear indication of a common set of work activities that help to bind social workers into a single profession.

Interpersonal Helping.   To perform this set of activities the social worker must be prepared to use basic helping skills (e.g., interviewing, questioning, counseling) to assist individuals and/or families in understanding the problems they experience in social functioning and in helping them to examine possible options for resolving those problems. In carrying out these activities, the worker actively involves individuals and families in discussions designed to explore options for solving problems. The worker encourages people to express their points of view and share their feelings. Throughout this process the worker attempts to communicate an understanding of other people's points of view and establish a relationship of trust with clients.

What competencies are needed to carry out these interpersonal helping tasks? Interpersonal helping requires the following competencies:

1. *Self-awareness and the ability to use self in facilitating change.*   The primary tool for helping by a social worker is the social worker himself or herself. To use oneself effectively, a social worker must be sensitive to his or her own strengths and limitations, be aware of areas of knowledge and ignorance, and recognize the potential to be both helpful and harmful when serving clients.

2. *Knowledge of the psychology of giving and receiving help.*   Often a part of the motivation for entering a helping profession is the desire to give of oneself to improve the lives of others. Social workers must remember, however, that clients are often uncomfortable when receiving help—both because our society suggests that

one has somehow failed if he or she needs assistance and because we sometimes offer social programs in a manner that is demeaning to clients.

3. *Ability to establish professional helping relationships.* Prerequisite to all successful helping is the establishment of a positive helping relationship. Whether working directly with clients, co-workers, or others in the community, the social worker must establish a relationship characterized by mutual respect and trust. Personal characteristics of the worker that have been found to be critical for creating such a helping relationship include empathy, positive regard, warmth, and genuineness. Research has further indicated that the social worker whose interaction with clients is characterized by concreteness, objectivity, and the ability to introduce and maintain structure in the helping process further improves the worker's success rate.

4. *Understanding differing ethnic and cultural patterns, as well as the capacity to engage in ethnic-, gender-, and age-sensitive practice.* One's social functioning, and even perceptions of what is positive social functioning, is affected by a person's appreciation of variations in cultural background experienced by various subgroups of the population. The various ethnic and racial minority groups in the United States have had a very different experience, both in cultural background and in their experience with the dominant white culture, than have members of the majority. Similarly, women have had more limited opportunities than men, and older people often have a quite different place in society than when they were younger. To engage in effective interpersonal helping the social worker must not only be aware of these different life experiences but must also be aware of how they affect the social functioning of individual clients.

5. *Knowledge and application of the Code of Ethics as a guide to ethical practice.* Inherent in the practice of any profession is the expectation that the public trust evident in granting professional sanction is rewarded by the professional mandate to engage in ethical practice. Each social worker is expected to conduct his or her practice in a manner that attempts to bring the best services possible to clients and, at a minimum, does no damage. The NASW Code of Ethics represents social work's effort to spell out the minimum requirements for ethical social work practice. Adhering to the Code of Ethics must be part of carrying out every practice task from interpersonal helping to research and policy analysis.

6. *General understanding of individual and family behavior patterns.* Interpersonal helping must be underpinned by knowledge of people, both individually and as part of families or other households. The social worker needs a thorough grounding in expected human growth and development patterns throughout the life cycle, understanding of different family structures and their influence on family members, and sufficient knowledge of human physiology and anatomy to recognize biological factors that may affect one's social functioning. It requires synthesizing knowledge from the disciplines of biology, psychology, and sociology to understand the bio-psycho-social functioning of clients.

7. *Skill in client information gathering.* Interpersonal helping requires a set of specific skills for gathering information that will help determine the social worker's course of action in regard to the client's situation. Perhaps the most fundamental skill a social worker must have is the ability to conduct an interview that not only reveals important information but also facilitates a continuing professional relationship. Skills such as focusing an interview, listening, questioning, reflecting feeling and content, interpreting meaning, confronting, and many other techniques are necessary for the social worker to master. Information-gathering skills are used by social workers in virtually every setting, practice area, and job function and apply to work with individuals, couples, families, and even professional teams and committees.

8. *Ability to analyze client information and identify both the strengths and problems evident in a practice situation.* Once information is collected about a client situation, the social worker must interpret its meaning and arrive at an assessment about its effects on the client's situation.[3] Arriving at an accurate understanding of the problems in a case situation is central to most interpersonal helping. Yet the identification of problems does not provide a sufficient basis to resolve or overcome them. Social workers must also seek to identify client strengths as essential resources for problem resolution.

9. *Capacity to counsel, problem solve, and/or engage in conflict resolution with clients.* Interpersonal helping also includes basic skills in assisting clients to understand, accept, and come to grips with the issues in their lives that brought them to the social worker. When working with clients, social workers should avoid, where possible, actions that take over aspects of clients' lives. Instead, they should attempt to maximize a client's participation in the change process and leave final decisions in the client's hands. After all, it is the client who must live with the results of those decisions.

10. *Possession of expertise in guiding the change process.* When engaged in interpersonal helping, social workers attempt to help their clients bring about some kind of change in their lives. The social worker has a particularly important role in guiding that change process through its various phases. The worker must first *engage* the client in addressing and clarifying the situation and determine if the agency is the proper source of help. The latter is known as making an *intake* decision. Second, the worker and client cooperate in *data collection* and *assessment* of the information obtained so that both fully understand the nature of the problem or situation, as well as the various factors that may have contributed to it. Third, the worker and client must develop a *plan* for accomplishing the agreed-upon change and reach agreement (i.e., a formal or informal *contract*) about how to address the issues and choose the activities each will carry out. Fourth, the actual *intervention(s)* will occur, and the social worker will *monitor* the change activities to determine if they indeed are helping. Finally, when the helping activity has run its course, the process will be *terminated* with the expectation that the client's social functioning has been stabilized at an appropriate level. Ultimately, the social worker should *evaluate* the overall process and apply what is learned from this evaluation to future practice activities.

Professional Competence Development.   To maintain high-quality practice the social worker in every position must carefully monitor his or her own work and continually engage in activities that will improve job performance. To accomplish these goals, the social worker must regularly engage in activities that strengthen one's own practice effectiveness and expand one's professional competence. Some of the tasks involve, periodically taking stock of one's performance by evaluating actions and decisions made within the context of practice. Other tasks involve attendance at workshops, seminars, or professional meetings, as well as reading professional journals, magazines, and newspapers in order to keep abreast of new developments. The focus of the cluster is the perception of professional development as an ongoing process.

Professional development includes both learning about practice and making contributions back to the profession through sharing one's own learning. Among the competencies required for professional development are the following:

1. *Ability to be introspective and critically evaluate one's own practice.* At the heart of professional development is self-assessment. One must be willing to critically examine his or her own work and engage regularly in reflective thinking about practice events. When limitations are evident, there must be an effort to correct them. A thorough understanding of the *NASW Code of Ethics* is an important prerequisite to addressing ethical issues, while the availability of professional supervision and/or consultation provides a valuable perspective for recognizing and resolving professional issues. The social worker should also develop the capability to engage in ongoing practice evaluation wherein one's practice activities can be tracked and compared to service results.

2. *Ability to make use of consultation.* While a professional is expected to practice with considerable autonomy and has final responsibility for his or her practice decisions, the social worker is not expected to conduct these activities alone. The use of consultation from peers is a hallmark of professions. Sometimes this consultation is provided by a supervisor, while at other times consultation from persons outside the administrative structure of the agency is obtained. In either case, the purpose is to offer guidance in making practice decisions or to provide a second opinion regarding decisions that have already been made.

3. *Ability to consume and extend professional knowledge.* The social worker must be committed to participating in activities that build his or her base of practice knowledge and skills. This might include attending staff training sessions and professional workshops and conferences, and regular reading of the professional literature. In addition, as social workers gain experience and insights from their practice, they are expected to share their understanding with others in the social work profession. That means contributing to social work's knowledge base and involves being competent to make conference presentations and prepare articles for publication in professional journals.

Frequently Utilized Social Work Competencies

Six additional clusters of activity were regularly performed by most social workers, but were especially emphasized in work in one or more of the job functions. The competencies to perform these tasks, however, are sufficiently important for all social workers to master.

Case Planning and Maintenance.   The case planning and maintenance cluster requires the worker to be competent to perform ongoing case planning, coordinate any additional services the client requires, monitor and evaluate case progress, obtain case consultation when appropriate, and complete required paperwork for case records.

In addition to using the basic interpersonal helping skills required to perform these tasks, the particular competencies required for case planning and monitoring include the following:

1. *Expertise in service planning and monitoring.* Social work practice often involves oversight of a battery of services being offered to an individual or family. With the client, the social worker identifies the services already being provided and those still needed, and helps to develop plans for clients to gain access to resources that might prove helpful. Once the service plan is in operation, the social worker then monitors the progress of the case to ensure that the plan, in fact, is working. This may include reviewing case records, consulting with other service providers both within the employing agency and elsewhere, and maintaining a professional relationship with the client to assess his or her ongoing perception of the helpfulness of the services being provided.

2. *Ability to carry out the employing agency's programs and operating procedures.* Agency-based social workers are agents of the organizations that employ them. Whether the programs are social provisions, social services, or social action, they are important tools for helping, and the social worker must know how to access those resources to benefit their clients. Often agencies require a frustrating amount of paperwork, but it is, nevertheless, essential to complete the required forms and recording in order to ensure that funds continue to be generated by the agency, continuity can be achieved should the social worker assigned to a case change positions, and appropriate monitoring by supervisors can take place.

3. *Knowledge of client background factors.* The social worker involved in case planning must gather specific background information that can be used in creating a comprehensive approach to helping. Included among this information is the identification of such resources as friends, family, neighbors, co-workers, teachers, clergy, and other personal contacts that may offer assistance. The social worker must also obtain information from the client about current or past experiences with the human services delivery system in order to make judgments about the merits of connecting clients to particular resources as part of a package of helping services. Finally, the social worker is responsible for ensuring that clients are informed of their rights and that confidentiality regarding their situation is properly protected even though services are being provided by several agencies.

4. *Skill in interagency coordination.* The social worker must also be knowledgeable about the availability of various resources and the requirements for gaining access to them and be capable of making sound professional judgments about their potential helpfulness. Further, the social worker must be skilled in communicating with persons with various professional backgrounds and creating networks among agencies and professionals to facilitate a coordinated approach to client services. This may mean exchanging information among agencies, planning and leading case

conferences, securing case consultation when needed, and negotiating decisions about who will provide which services to an individual or family—and, importantly, who will pay for them.

5. *Ability to engage in case advocacy.* At times, clients in crisis are placed on an agency's waiting list, an agency's eligibility requirements may be rigidly interpreted in a way that does not fit the uniqueness of a particular client's situation, or many other factors may interfere with clients receiving needed services. In those cases, the social worker becomes an advocate for the client and makes appeals to his or her own or another human services agency to help clients obtain needed services. This involves activities such as informing clients about an agency's appeal process, making a personal appeal to a social worker in another agency, or even representing a client before an agency's appeal board.

Individual and Family Treatment.   Another set of tasks frequently performed by social workers in direct service positions involves providing treatment to individuals and families. Individual and family treatment requires that the social workers select and use clearly defined formal treatment modes or models to help individuals and/or families improve their social functioning or resolve social problems. Activities include the use of any of a wide array of interventive techniques and strategies ranging from nondirective to confrontational approaches.

In addition to the basic interpersonal helping skills, the worker must also possess the following:

1. *Sufficient knowledge of human development to make in-depth psychosocial assessments.* The social worker engaged in clinical or treatment activities with individuals and families is required to have considerable knowledge about human functioning. He or she must be prepared with sufficient information about expected functioning for persons at different developmental levels to make a valid psychosocial assessment on which treatment plans can be developed. In addition to knowledge of normal development, the social worker must have sufficient knowledge to diagnose pathology, recognize deviance, and help clients recognize their own or others' dysfunctional behaviors.

2. *In-depth knowledge of family functioning.* Just as the social worker must be skilled at assessing normal and problematic individual social functioning, he or she must also be prepared to diagnose factors affecting the functioning of families and other households. A rather substantial literature exists that identifies various types of family structures including the two-parent, single-parent, postdivorce, remarried or blended, and gay/lesbian households. Each has particular issues it must address if it is to attain stability and offer a positive environment to its members. Clinical social workers, especially, need to recognize that interactional patterns of families can have a profound and lasting impact on family members and that, with professional help, harmful patterns can often be corrected.

3. *Skill in the selection and application of individual and/or family treatment modalities.* To engage in individual and family treatment, the social worker must have mastered one or more specific treatment approaches. The range of specific

approaches that a social worker might draw from is quite broad. Sheafor and Horejsi, for example, identify the following as some of the practice frameworks social workers typically use:[4]

Psychosocial therapy	Task-centered model
Behavior modification therapy	Solution-focused model
Cognitive–behavioral therapy	Clubhouse model
Person-centered therapy	Self-help approach
Reality therapy	Family systems approach
Interactional model	Family therapy approach
Structural model	Family problem-solving approach
Crisis intervention	Family preservation model

This list would be extended considerably if one were to compile a list of all of the specialized individual and family treatment models and approaches that might be a part of a clinical social worker's repertoire.

Delivery System Knowledge Development.   The tasks included in the delivery system knowledge development cluster suggest that the social worker must learn about the community's service delivery system and develop an understanding of various regulations, policies, and procedures that affect social programs. The focus of this cluster is on the gathering of information about the network of services and service resources within the social worker's geographic area. Activities include visiting agencies, attending meetings, and making contacts in order to become acquainted with or keep up-to-date with changes in the services provided, developing cooperative service arrangements among agencies, and keeping current on regulations, organizational policies, and agency guidelines.

Developing knowledge about the human services delivery system is an *indirect service*. It is work that develops important background information when serving clients, but it is usually conducted outside the presence of clients and is done without reference to a single client or group of clients. To carry out these activities the social worker must have the following competencies:

1. *Ability to maintain up-to-date knowledge of a variety of human services programs.* The effective social worker must know the community—or at least the human services delivery system in the community. The worker must read about local, state, and national programs, visit human services agencies to gain in-depth knowledge of their programs and procedures for gaining access to those services, and regularly attend interagency meetings where one can be updated about changing programs.

2. *Skills in building interagency coordination and linkage.* Rarely is merely acquiring information sufficient for social work practice. Social workers often develop linkage arrangements to facilitate information-sharing processes among agencies that regularly interact when serving clients. Sometimes that takes the form of interagency teams, such as a domestic violence team, where social workers must be skilled at interagency and interprofessional team building.

Staff Information Exchange.   As an agency-based profession, social workers must also be thoroughly versed about the programs and operating procedures in their own agencies. In addition, a worker must be prepared to contribute to the effective operation of that organization by working to resolve problems in agency functioning and contributing to decisions that strengthen the agency. To be effective in information exchange, the social worker must be prepared to organize and/or participate in meetings or use other means of communication to exchange information with staff members, resolve job-related problems, and/or make decisions that affect agency functioning. The following competencies are required of the social worker when performing these tasks:

1. *Ability to prepare and consume written and oral presentations regarding agency programs.*   Much of the information about agency operation is transmitted through written communication or formal staff meetings. This activity can consume considerable time, and, if it is not to detract from client services, the social worker must learn to read and write such materials quickly and accurately. Oral communication skills, too, are important. Knowing how to make formal presentations that are interesting and lively, yet emphasize the important content, facilitates effective communication of in-house materials.

2. *Capacity to facilitate staff members' ability to make decisions and resolve problems.*   In addition to sharing information, the members of an agency staff must regularly engage in activities that help the agency resolve problems and find ways to function more effectively. Typically this activity occurs through staff meetings, committee assignments, or team meetings. Knowledge of group dynamics, parliamentary procedure, and skill in moving group processes ahead all help to facilitate this activity. At times, the social worker may be required to use skills in consensus building, mediation, or negotiation in order to complete the work in this cluster of tasks.

3. *Ability to facilitate interdisciplinary collaboration.*   In agencies that use the talents of several professions or disciplines in delivering their social programs, problems in interdisciplinary collaboration inevitably occur. Although the professions have carved out their boundaries or unique missions in general terms, in practice there are overlapping areas. Further, individual practitioners often drift in their practice activities toward the orientation of their colleagues, blurring even further the boundaries between the disciplines. When professional drift becomes excessive, clients lose the advantage of the perspective that each discipline offers and, sometimes, services are given by persons without sufficient preparation.

Risk Assessment and Transition Services.   All direct service providers have to make judgments about the urgency for services or the consequences of not providing services. Based on that assessment they determine the type of services needed, facilitate the transition of clients from one service to another, and/or decide on the appropriateness of terminating the helping process. To perform these tasks, the worker must have the competence to assess a case situation to determine its difficulty (i.e., risk, urgency, or need) and engage clients either in making use of services or preparing them for transition or termination of services. Tasks include the observation of individuals and the gathering of information in order to decide if specialized services are required.

It takes considerable knowledge to accurately assess a practice situation. The social worker must learn the client's perception of the reasons services are required, the viewpoints of significant people in the client's immediate environment, and, if working as part of an interdisciplinary team, obtain information others have collected. To engage in these assessment activities, the social worker should have the following competencies:

1. *Ability to apply general systems and/or ecosystems theory when assessing factors affecting a practice situation.* The perspective one brings to the assessment process will affect the conclusions that are eventually reached. Due to the need for social workers to assess both personal and environmental factors, social workers have increasingly found system-based theories particularly valuable because they allow the social worker to address interactions between systems (e.g., individual, family, neighborhood). The focus of the ecosystems perspective, for example, is on interaction among five elements in a practice situation: (1) individual(s) characteristics; (2) family lifestyle and dynamics; (3) cultural values and beliefs; (4) environmental-structural factors such as racism, sexism, or ageism; and (5) historical experiences that have contributed to the client's situation.

2. *Skill in engaging clients in examining problems in social functioning.* An important part of social work practice involves helping clients explore the severity and intensity of the situation being addressed and determining if routine or emergency service is required. The most critical source of information for making such judgments is the client. The worker must be skilled in engaging clients in problem analysis.

3. *Skill in utilizing social work assessment techniques.* The ability to use specific assessment tools effectively is critical if a social worker is to make valid judgments about the severity of a particular case situation or is to make a decision about terminating service and/or helping clients with transition to other services. Examples of assessment competencies include mastery of techniques such as ecomaps, genograms, or life history grids; the competence to help clients accurately identify and specify the problems to be addressed; and the ability to prepare clear and concise social functioning assessment reports for agency records and communication with other professionals.

4. *Skill in the use of crisis intervention.* If a risk assessment determines that a client (i.e., individual or family) is in crisis, the social worker must be prepared to act immediately. Crisis intervention requires rapid response over a limited time that is focused on a specific client emergency. The worker's focus is on helping the client make decisions that will resolve the crisis, and, if necessary, crisis intervention may require taking action that will protect the client as well as others.

5. *Ability to facilitate client transitions between services and/or to terminate service.* Helping clients make transitions from one service to another also requires considerable care and planning. Transitions might involve, for example, moving from one's own home to a foster home, from a hospital to a nursing home, from one agency to another, or simply from one social worker to another. Workers must be sensitive to the difficulty of such transitions for clients and carefully prepare them for these changes. When the service activity is completed, or if for some reason a different social worker is assigned to a case, clients must be prepared for the termination of the professional relationship.

Staff Supervision.   Agency-based human services practice often requires supervision of a variety of personnel with differing qualifications and job assignments. Some may be volunteers, others may be staff members such as custodians and clerical staff, and still others are other social workers or human services providers. To provide staff supervision, one must be prepared to guide the day-to-day work of staff members by orienting them to the organization and its requirements, by assigning work and teaching them to perform their jobs, as well as by monitoring and assessing their performance. The tasks in this cluster encompass the array of tasks typically associated with supervision, including the provision of job orientation and training, clarification of job duties and work expectations with individuals and groups, and the evaluation, interpretation, and feedback of job performance evaluations.

One must be skilled at collecting pertinent information, developing productive working relationships, assessing situations, and so on. In addition, the social worker engaged in staff supervision must have the following competencies:

1. *Knowledge of the literature regarding the supervisory process.* A rather abundant literature has emerged that confirms there is an administrative or monitoring component to supervision, a role in providing professional support to the worker, and an educational component through which the worker is helped to grow and develop in practice competence. This literature also suggests ways to structure supervisory learning processes so that it is of maximum value to the worker and yet is efficient in terms of the time invested by both the worker and supervisor.

2. *Capacity to facilitate the work of supervisees.* The ultimate payoff from good supervision is having supervisees who can perform their work efficiently and effectively. The supervisor must be clear about the job assignments of the workers and able to assess their strengths and limitations related to performing various assignments. When necessary, supervisors also teach the workers practice skills and/or facilitate their attendance at training sessions or professional seminars in which their competence can be enhanced.

3. *Ability to conduct worker evaluation and guide professional development.* The work of supervisees must be constantly monitored to ensure that high-quality service is provided and agency policies and procedures are appropriately carried out. In addition, the supervisor must be prepared to formally evaluate worker performance, discuss that overall evaluation with the worker in a manner that will enhance professional growth, and supply the results of the evaluation for the agency's personnel records. Since these evaluations often become the basis for job promotion and salary increments, or possibly even job termination, they require accurate, fair, and sensitive interpretation and feedback from the supervisor.

Competencies Occasionally Needed by Social Workers

The following seven task clusters of social work practice activity are occasionally performed by most social workers and more regularly required in one or more specialized job functions or practice areas. The competencies required to perform these activities should be a part of each social worker's repertoire of knowledge and skill.

Group Work.   Group work requires the social worker to use small groups as an environment for teaching clients skills for effective performance of daily living tasks, communicating information to enhance social functioning, or for facilitating problem resolution or therapeutic change. In these tasks, the worker consciously uses the group process in order to teach individuals how groups work and how to act as a member of the group.

Group skills appear to be used most as a method of treatment by MSW-level social workers, but they also have application when teaching skills to clients or staff and in team meetings or other agency-related activities. Competencies required to perform these tasks include the following:

1. *Knowledge of group structure and function.*   Groups may be formed in social work practice for such varied purposes as therapy, training, mutual support, or social action. Some will be structured to maximize members' input into deliberations, while others will be focused on accomplishing specific tasks or making decisions. All, however, will be concerned with interaction among members as they engage in their work. The social worker needs knowledge of the phases of group development and skills in handling the power issues that characteristically arise in groups.

2. *Capacity to perform the staff role within a group.*   Social workers are often responsible for constructing groups. They must be able to identify the criteria for selecting clients or others to participate in the group, recruit and screen potential members, and conduct the initial planning activities (e.g., arrange time and place to meet, invite members) that allow the group to come together. Depending on its purpose, when the group does meet, the social worker is most likely to perform such functions as helping the group determine its goals, providing information, teaching particular skills to the members, building consensus, discouraging those who tend to dominate and encouraging those who are reluctant to become involved, supporting group leaders, and so on.

3. *Ability to engage in group therapy.*   In therapeutic groups, a social worker is likely to be particularly active in guiding the group's process. The worker should have considerable knowledge about each member and guide the process to ensure that his or her goals for being in the group are met while, at the same time, the group's goals are being attained.

Dispute Resolution.   Disputes inevitably arise in human services agencies. At times those disputes are between clients and the agency. For example, a client may have expected resources that were not provided in a timely manner, or a staff member may have been viewed as discourteous or unhelpful. It is within a client's rights to dispute these matters or even to file a formal grievance. Disputes may also exist between staff members or between a staff member and the administrator or board of an organization. Such disputes must be resolved if the agency is to devote maximum attention to client services. To be prepared to help resolve disputes, the social worker should be prepared to use advocacy, negotiation, and mediation to resolve such problems.

In addition to using basic interpersonal helping skills to assist in dispute resolution, a social worker must also have the following two additional competencies:

1. *Understanding of agency procedures and its decision-making structure.* To address disputes, the social worker must be prepared to accurately relate client concerns to the agency's functioning. If a client's rights have been violated, the worker must understand how that relates to agency policies and procedures in order either to correct the problem or explain why it occurred. The worker also needs to understand the agency's structure so that the correct person or persons can be approached to address the problem or a strategy can be developed to correct agency procedures and prevent similar problems from occurring in the future.

2. *Skill in advocacy, negotiation, and mediation.* The social worker involved in dispute resolution is often in a position to help resolve the issue by advocating for the client's or another worker's interests, mediating the problem between the affected parties, or helping to negotiate a resolution of the matter. These skills should be a part of the repertoire of all social workers, but most specifically those who hold administrative or supervisory positions.

Service Connection.   As brokers for the human services who link clients with community resources, social workers must be prepared to employ techniques that help clients to connect with established services and take action to eliminate barriers that prevent them from receiving those services. Activities in this cluster center on the linkage function, although some advocacy on the part of the worker may be required.

Service connection tasks overlap with some of those used in case planning and maintenance, but they differ to the extent that the worker engaging in service connection helps the client make the desired connection with a community service and then drops out of the picture. Additional competencies that are particularly important in this cluster of activity are the following:

1. *Maintaining an ongoing critical assessment of the battery of social programs in the community and region.* Social programs change rapidly. When making service connections, social workers must be careful to provide accurate information because clients can become frustrated and discouraged if a referral is inappropriate and may not follow through and thus not receive needed assistance.

2. *Ability to make an accurate intake assessment of a client's needs and to skillfully refer clients to appropriate resources.* When clients enter the human services delivery system they often are not clear about just what services they need or where to get them. A familiar agency is sometimes the starting point, and the social worker must be prepared to help clients gain clarity about the issues that concern them and the services they require. Sometimes the social worker or others in the agency can provide the needed services, but at other times referrals must be made elsewhere. A social worker must make judgments regarding how directive to be when making a referral and might use techniques ranging from giving the client the name and telephone number of an agency, to making an appointment for the client, to arranging for transportation, or even to taking the client to the appointment.

3. *Expertise in advocating for clients with human service programs.* Efforts to connect clients with services often fail because clients are placed on lengthy waiting lists or agencies are unwilling to make flexible interpretations of eligibility requirements that might permit serving the client that has been referred. It is important that social workers follow up with clients who have been referred elsewhere to be sure that the connection was made. If the client has not received service, the worker may elect to actively advocate for that client with that agency.

Program Development.   Social workers who hold administrative or management positions often carry responsibility for either modifying existing programs or creating new ones. They must have the competence to document and interpret the need for additional human services programs, develop working relationships with relevant resources for program support (e.g., boards, funding sources, legislative bodies, referral sources), oversee implementation of new programs, and evaluate program success. Workers convert program goals and concepts into specific plans, develop budgets and staffing plans, "sell" the program(s) to funding sources and other decision makers, and compile data for evaluation purposes.

The competencies required to successfully carry out this indirect service activity include:

1. *Skill in community and organizational data collection and analysis.* Social workers engaged in program development must do their homework carefully to ensure that client services are not jeopardized by the enthusiasm for innovation. The skills required for program development include collecting and analyzing data about the adequacy of programs offered in their own agencies, as well as the ability to conduct community needs assessments that will help to place their programs in the context of the battery of human services in the community.

2. *Skill in the design and implementation of social programs.* Once a careful analysis of information regarding existing programs is completed, the social worker engaged in program development must create a plan for new or revised programs that will more adequately respond to the community's needs. The program must be carefully designed and issues addressed as to who will be eligible, where services will be provided, what it will cost, who will deliver the service or social provision, what practice approach will be used, and how its effectiveness will be evaluated. The social worker must then develop a budget identifying the anticipated income and expenditures required to start the operation of the program and describe specific plans for its implementation.

3. *The capacity to obtain agency and/or community support for new or revised programs.* The social worker promoting either program modification or the creation of a new program must have the support of the staff and board (or responsible legislative body) where it will be located. Securing such support requires knowledge of organizational change processes and typically, requires a long period of planning and involvement of board and staff members in the process.

Obtaining support for new programs from the community often requires coalition building among human services agencies and other interested parties. Program development, at times, involves the social worker in the preparation of grant applications for initial support of the program, and in public education activities such as speaking before community groups, preparing news articles, conducting radio and TV interviews, and lobbying individuals for support.

Instruction.   Most social workers engage in a certain amount of teaching. Much of their teaching is in informal work with clients to help them learn skills for addressing the issues they face in life. However, many social workers also engage in instructional activities in which a planned curriculum is delivered to groups of clients, agency staff members or volunteers, students, or community groups. To provide instruction effectively, the social worker must be prepared to plan, arrange, conduct, and evaluate educational programs. Activities involve course planning, syllabus design, test construction, and course evaluation.

Several special competencies are required to fulfill the formal teaching roles of social workers and include the following:

1. *Capacity to develop curriculum for instruction or training programs.* Whether helping parents learn more effective ways to deal with the inevitable problems their children experience or teaching foster parents about expected phases of child development, the curriculum must be based in the best available literature and delivered in a carefully sequenced and organized manner.

2. *Skill in planning workshops, seminars, or classroom sessions.* Once a curriculum is developed, it must be delivered. The logistics of announcing the meetings, recruiting the participants, ensuring that there is a meeting space with plenty of parking, arranging for refreshments, having the necessary instructional materials available, and so on, all call for careful planning. Failure to attend to these planning matters can negate even the best content.

3. *Ability to engage students, trainees, or groups of clients in learning activities.* Social workers' skills in group work, adapting to client interests, and basic communication skills serve them well when teaching. Because the content is typically aimed at helping the audience learn how to do something, the teaching style is likely to be more interactional than the styles used in standard classroom instruction where the goal is more oriented to transmitting information.

4. *Capacity to assess and evaluate instructional activities.* Instructional programs tend to be repeated and critique of instructional activities provides an important base for the next round of instruction. The competent instructor, therefore, must develop or adopt instruments that accurately assess the students' learning experience and invite suggestions for ways to improve the value of the experience for participants.

Staff Deployment.   Human services agencies are labor intensive, that is, they work with relatively few tangible products and most of their resources are invested in people. Therefore, an important activity is the deployment of staff in a way that makes efficient use of staff time and ensures that the appropriate personnel are available to serve clients. To perform this set of tasks effectively, a social worker must recruit and select staff, arrange staffing patterns and workload assignments, monitor staff productivity, and oversee compliance with organizational policies. Tasks in this cluster concentrate on the ensurance of staff coverage and equitable workload distribution, along with scheduling and coordinating working hours, leave, and vacation, and monitoring service demands. These tasks require the following competencies:

1. *Capacity to match personnel with job assignments.* To accurately select and assign staff and volunteers to the various tasks that must be performed, it is necessary to have considerable knowledge of the work to be done and the capacities of available staff members. If needed skills are not present, it is necessary to then seek that competence through additional personnel or, the replacement of existing personnel. Thus, the social worker in this capacity must be skilled at personnel selection and recruitment, as well as in matching the personnel capacities to the needs of the agency.

2. *Ability to create a clear organizational structure for conducting the work of the agency and a fair means of assigning the workload.* It is important that those social workers involved in personnel deployment are skilled at maintaining an equitable plan for assigning workload, a clear and fair set of personnel rules and regulations that provides for both professional autonomy and agency responsibility, and a reasonable plan for monitoring the performance of the staff members. Specific activities that might be performed to accomplish these goals include assigning tasks, coordinating working hours, planning vacation time, making arrangements when personnel are on sick leave, and so on.

3. *Skill in the development of instruments for the evaluation of worker performance.* It is important to monitor changing service demands and worker competencies in order to determine staffing requirements. Worker performance evaluation requires carefully constructed performance measures that can be applied to workers throughout the organization and will yield valid information for assessing the agency's effectiveness.

Protective Services.   The very young and the very old are among the most vulnerable members of U.S. society, and social workers are often in a position to protect them from potential physical, mental, or economic abuses. Some social workers are employed to offer protective services when there is suspected abuse. To provide those services, the social worker is required to collect and analyze data to be used in assessing at-risk clients and presenting information to appropriate authorities if clients are judged to be in danger or of having their basic rights violated. As part of this process, the worker may be expected to start legal proceedings and testify or participate in court hearings involving custody, competence, outplacement, or institutionalization.

The following special competencies are required to provide effective protective services. These specific competencies need to be used in addition to the competencies already described, especially those associated with interpersonal helping, individual and family therapy, case planning and maintenance, and risk assessment:

1. *Capacity to identify at-risk factors such as physical and emotional maltreatment.* Abusive situations are difficult to identify because abuse often occurs within a family and is not readily evident to outsiders. The abusers attempt to conceal the maltreatment, and the persons being abused are often intimidated to the point they are fearful of reporting or even admitting they have been abused. Literature and workshops are available to help social workers providing protective services develop the needed competencies to work in these situations.

2. *Knowledge of the law and legal processes concerning protective services.* In most states it is mandatory that any helping professional report suspected abuse or maltreatment. When abuse is suspected, the legal and human services systems join to investigate and, when appropriate, take action to prevent further abuse and resolve issues that contribute to the abuse. The social worker not only needs good clinical skills but must also be thoroughly familiar with the relevant laws and legal processes that apply.

3. *Knowledge of local resources to be contacted if clients are in danger.* In some abusive situations the client is in immediate danger and the social worker must be prepared to seek police protection, make arrangements for temporary placement outside the home, or take other needed actions to protect the client. The worker engaged in child protection work must be thoroughly informed about the available resources and how to gain access to them.

4. *Ability to deal with conflictual situations.* People are typically frightened and angry when a social worker enters an abusive situation. The worker must be able to diffuse situations where high levels of conflict are present and assist clients to attempt resolution of issues in a calm and peaceful manner.

Organizational Maintenance. Organizational maintenance activities require a social worker with the necessary knowledge and skills to manage the ongoing operation of a program or administrative unit to ensure its efficient and effective functioning by securing, allocating, and overseeing the utilization of its resources (e.g., staff, funds, supplies, space) and marketing its services. Some of the tasks required for this cluster center on financial operations, for example, estimating budgets, documenting and reviewing expenditures, and compiling billings, cost reimbursement, and cost control documents. Other tasks deal with the maintenance of a physical plant, control of inventory, and working with staff and vendors in order to ensure smooth program operations.

The following competencies are necessary to conduct the activities associated with organizational maintenance:

1. *Understand the operation of basic business systems and the requirements for oversight of agency resources.* Public scrutiny of these agencies is typically high, requiring that administrators create and implement carefully developed measures of accountability. Systems must be developed for such activities as estimating budgets, documenting and reviewing expenditures, compiling billings, managing funds, maintaining the physical plant, securing necessary supplies, and so on.

2. *Skill in creating and managing agency paperflow.* At times the excessive demand for accountability in human services agencies creates an enormous amount of paperwork. Programs that maximize staff efficiency require workers with knowledge of computer word processing and administrators who are knowledgable about or skilled in data analysis, the collection and storage of agency records, and the implementation of cost control programs.

3. *Skill in marketing and fund-raising for human services organizations.* Organizational maintenance also requires that the social worker be prepared to make the services of the agency known in the community. Potential clients need to be made aware of the services that might be secured from the agency, and the general public needs to be informed on a regular basis about the important role the agency plays in the community. This public relations activity is also a prerequisite for securing funds to operate the agency's programs. In addition to documenting, justifying, and monitoring the regular flow of funds from client fees, tax sources, and/or United Way allocations, effort must also be made to generate supplemental funds through such sources as foundation grants, agency benefit events, and personal bequests.

Low Utilization Competencies for Most Social Workers

The final two task clusters, research and policy development and tangible service provision, were central to social work in its historical development but appear to be a secondary activity for social workers today. The low scores for research and policy development, when combined with somewhat low scores for program development and public education (i.e., instruction), generates an important question for social work. Has this profession abandoned its mission to address the societal causes of social dysfunction? The even lower scores for tangible service provision also raises a question. Has social work abandoned its commitment to the most vulnerable members of the society, that is, those who are in need of the most basic resources of food, clothing, and housing?

Research and Policy Development.   If social workers are to assist communities to improve social conditions or contribute to improved social conditions through influencing laws or regulations at the state or federal levels, they must be skilled at collecting data about those social conditions and assist policy makers as they apply that knowledge to various social policies and programs. In short, the worker must be prepared to collect, analyze, and publish data; present technical information to the general public, legislators, or other decision makers responsible for changes in human services programs or community conditions; and/or interact with community groups. The worker must be able to collect and compile information, conduct surveys, present or publish findings from studies, testify as an expert witness, or organize and take part in campaigns or demonstrations.

What competencies does a social worker need to perform the research and policy development tasks? The following are necessary:

1. *Ability to develop and implement program and needs assessment research.* An important mechanism for minimizing the effect of political manipulation in policy and program decisions is fact. If social workers simply bring emotion to the bargaining table, helpful social policy is unlikely to emerge. Thus, social workers must be prepared to collect accurate data to serve as the foundation for social policy analysis.

2. *Skill in social policy analysis and influencing decisions of policy makers.* With a sound data base, social workers are then prepared to assess existing and proposed social policies to determine a proposed policy's potential for resolving social problems and/or enhancing the overall quality of life. Armed with a solid analysis, the social worker then carries out a strategy to influence the outcome through actions intended to influence the decisions of those who finally establish the policy or program.

3. *Capacity to inform the public regarding social problems and potential solutions.* Social workers are often in a position to see the effects of existing social policies as they affect their clients in positive or negative ways and, therefore, it is important for them to share that knowledge through speaking to public groups, working with the media, and so forth.

Tangible Service Provision.   At the heart of social work's self-image is its concern that the poor and most at-risk members of the society have their basic needs met. These activities focus on meeting the basic needs of clients as they cope with everyday life. Tasks include teaching budgeting, money management, food preparation and homemaking skills; helping clients find jobs and housing; and putting clients in touch with people of similar backgrounds and experience. Workers may visit clients to assess the suitability of living arrangements and take part in leisure activities to help them reduce loneliness.

Those social workers who are involved in tangible service provision need to be competent in the following areas:

1. *Knowledge of local resources that provide clients with social provisions such as shelter, food, clothing, money, and employment.* In virtually all communities and in most legislation creating social programs, the responsibility for implementing programs is assigned to several different human services agencies. "One-stop shopping" is rare in the human services. The social worker, then, must be familiar with the social provisions that are available and know how clients can gain access to them.

2. *Ability to develop positive helping relationships with clients requiring basic social provisions.* Social stigma is often attached to needing these basic services. To help clients make use of these provisions and, where possible, become self-supporting, social workers need to establish good working relationships characterized by empathy and trust.

3. *Competence in teaching clients to use resources effectively.* It is said that the successful social worker works himself or herself out of a job. Indeed, the competent social worker can teach clients to do many things for themselves—including how to gain access to resources when needed and how to use those resources in a way that helps them achieve independence from the human services.

Concluding Comment

For a profession with the broad mission of helping people interact more effectively with their environments, it is not surprising that the identification of common features that bind social work practitioners into one profession has proven difficult. It is only at the somewhat general level of defining its mission that social workers have gradually moved toward consensus. Agreement at this broad conceptual level, however, does not necessarily indicate that at the more concrete level of day-to-day practice there is sufficient similarity in the work performed to consider this a single profession.

Drawing on data from a national task analysis study of social work and examining the clusters of work activity regularly performed by social workers, it has been possible to obtain a reasonably clear picture of social work practice. One can reasonably conclude that in practice, as well as in theory, social work can stand as a single profession. Many tasks are regularly performed by most social workers, supporting the view that a common core of activities exists in the many expressions of practice.

In the preceding pages, we identified a set of competencies social workers are expected to possess. It is important for the new social worker to begin the process of mastering these competencies, as was evident in Demetria's work in Chapter 1. At least a few of the competencies displayed by Demetria are highlighted in Box 9.1.

Box 9.1

Some Competencies Displayed by Demetria

As evidenced by Demetria's work with the Miles family (see Chapter 1), social work practice requires even the beginning worker to possess many competencies. Demetria's BSW program had provided her with many of the basic competencies needed to begin her work in child welfare, and she will no doubt develop them further through her practice experience and by attending relevant professional conferences and workshops in the future. Demetria's *primary job function* was that of a *direct practitioner,* i.e., working directly with Joseph and Mrs. Miles, although she benefited from the *indirect practice* insights of her supervisor.

Examples of Demetria's competencies in the most universal cluster of social work practice tasks, the *Interpersonal Helping Cluster,* were evident in her *ability to develop professional helping relationships.* In her beginning contacts with both Joseph and Mrs. Miles, Demetria did not rush the conversation and allowed time to chat, not for fear of getting to the point and possibly facing conflict, but rather to establish some mutual connections that would yield sufficient rapport to move ahead in addressing the tough issues. Demetria was also competent in *client information gathering.* Through a relatively sparse amount of interviewing, she was able to accumulate a substantial amount of information about this family, which assisted her in understanding the family dynamics and, perhaps, the root causes of the issues Joseph was experiencing.

Among the frequently used clusters of competencies, Demetria was effective in the *Case Planning and Maintenance* tasks. She formalized her *Service Planning* tasks by presenting her plan to the staff team for consultation, and in the process of conducting her investigation demonstrated the *ability to carry out the employing agency's programs and operating procedures.* Demetria also demonstrated good *Delivery System Knowledge.* She had an adequate degree of *up-to-date knowledge of a variety of human services programs* and used that knowledge to help the Miles family find the resources to begin addressing their issues. Finally, Demetria was engaged in providing a *Risk Assessment Service.* The school had reported the possibility that child abuse and/or neglect had occurred, and Demetria's job was to first determine the degree to which this child was at-risk and then to attempt to help resolve the issues that were detrimental to the child's well-being. In the process, she *engaged the clients in examining their problems in social functioning* and demonstrated *skill in utilizing social work assessment techniques.*

KEY WORDS AND CONCEPTS

Competence
Universal practice competencies
Primary job function
Direct practice

Task analysis
Cluster of practice activity
Indirect service activities

SUGGESTED INFORMATION SOURCES

Sheafor, Bradford W., and Horejsi, Charles R. *Techniques and Guidelines for Social Work Practice,* 7th Edition. Boston: Allyn and Bacon, 2006.

Teare, Robert J., and Sheafor, Bradford W. *Practice-Sensitive Social Work Education: An Empirical Analysis of Social Work Practice and Practitioners.* Alexandria, VA: Council on Social Work Education, 1995.

ENDNOTES

1. Robert J. Teare and Bradford W. Sheafor, *Practice-Sensitive Social Work Education: An Empirical Analysis of Social Work Practice and Practitioners.* Alexandria, VA: Council on Social Work Education, 1995. (Also available on-line free to CSWE members at http://www.cswe.org.)
2. Teare and Sheafor, pp. 97–117.
3. Bradford W. Sheafor and Charles R. Horesji, *Techniques and Guidelines for Social Work Practice,* 7th Edition (Boston: Allyn and Bacon, 2006), pp. 246–335.
4. Sheafor and Horesji, pp. 82–118.

PROTECTING THE HOMELAN
PROTECTING THE HOMELAND
SEAL OF THE PRESIDENT OF THE UNITED STATES

The Role of Social Work in Prevention*

Prefatory Comment

The practice of social work has been able to demonstrate flexibility in meeting public needs within the context of political and economic opportunities and constraints, especially in the early stages of the twenty-first century. Assisting social work practice in this regard are intervention concepts such as *prevention* originally developed by the medical and public health professions. The social work profession is challenged to develop its own prevention theories grounded in psychosocial concepts as demonstrated in this chapter. Following an in-depth discussion of prevention, the remainder of the chapter will examine the potential role of social work intervention in the prevention of violence and homicide in gangs, the risks of over zealous prevention efforts as evidenced by the U.S. Department of Homeland Security following the 9/11 attacks, and the continued development and testing in the courts or *class action social work* as a primary mental health prevention strategy.

Prevention: An Evolving Concept in the Twenty-First Century

As human services budgets were drastically reduced during the 1980s and into the 1990s, an increasing number of people continued to need services. Substance abuse, child abuse, crime and delinquency, homelessness, AIDS, and the breakdown of the family are social problems that also continue to increase. Even in the most favorable economic periods for the human services, the mental health needs of the U.S. population have far surpassed the nation's financial and manpower resources to meet these needs. For example, it is estimated that there are anywhere from 1 to 2 million children in the United States each year who suffer physical or sexual abuse or neglect. Considering that each case could cost society $7,000 to treat, the total treatment

---

* Chapter written by Armando T. Morales.

expenditure might amount to $14 billion. The Department of Health and Human Services, however, spends less than $30 million per year for the treatment of child abuse and neglect. Federal and state agencies spend approximately $500 million per year for alcohol treatment services and yet treat less than 10 percent of all addicted alcohol abusers.[1] To live with increasingly limited financial and professional personnel resources while not losing sight of the potential of progressive health and welfare policies, were they to be someday passed by Congress, could result in less costly interventive approaches impacting larger numbers of people. Theories of prevention, therefore, have to be developed and applied to practice.

Prevention

Contemporary mental health conceptual formulations of prevention have as their foundation in public health prevention theories and practice. In public health terms, prevention, as previously noted, has three stages. *Primary prevention* indicates actions taken prior to the onset of a problem to intercept its cause or to modify its course *before* a person is involved. It is the elimination of the noxious agent at its source. Through systematic spraying of affected ponds, for example, malaria-carrying mosquitoes, their eggs, and larva are destroyed before they have the opportunity to infect humans. *Secondary prevention* involves prompt efforts to curtail and stop the disease in the affected persons and the spreading of the disease to others. *Tertiary prevention* involves rehabilitative efforts to reduce the residual effects of the illness, that is, reducing the duration and disabling severity of the disease. In its most succinct form, therefore, prevention has three stages: prevention, treatment, and rehabilitation.

In 1977, the National Institute of Mental Health established an Office of Prevention to stimulate and sponsor large-scale programs of research on prevention. This office has also assisted the Council on Social Work Education to prepare curriculum materials about prevention.[2] The director of the Office of Prevention developed the following definition of primary prevention within a mental health context:

> Primary prevention encompasses activities directed towards specifically identified vulnerable high risk groups within the community who have not been labeled psychiatrically ill and for whom measures can be undertaken to avoid the onset of emotional disturbance and/or to enhance their level of positive mental health.[3]

Primary preventive programs were for the promotion of mental health, as educational rather than *clinical* in conception and practice, with their ultimate goal being to help persons increase their ability for dealing with crises and for taking steps to improve their own lives.[4] Goldston identifies two goals in primary prevention: (1) to prevent needless psychopathology and symptoms, maladjustment, maladaptation, and "misery" regardless of whether the end point might be mental illness; and (2) to promote mental health by increasing levels of wellness among various defined populations.[5] This places an emphasis on strength and positive qualities, in contrast to the problem-centered focus found in the medical model.

In applying primary prevention to child abuse, for example, intervention program efforts can be developed at three different levels. On a macro, social-reform level, prevention interventions may include legislation to protect children's rights, abolishment of corporal punishment, advocacy for abortion, and a more equitable economic distribution of resources. A second level of primary prevention intervention, also macro in impact, may utilize educational approaches aimed at a variety of audiences. This may include, for example, educating and sensitizing society to basic issues in child abuse and its deterrents, the use of newsletters and "crash courses" to provide helpful information to young families, and teaching adolescents in public schools essential skills needed in their future parental roles. A more focused primary prevention practice strategy, which is directly concerned with the operation of intrafamilial variables, involves utilizing homemaker and home visitor services to provide support and crisis assistance to at-risk families with young children. The visitors could be hospital-based personnel, day care, child support workers, or community volunteers.[6]

Gang Violence and Homicide Prevention

Numerous polls show that the nation's number one problem is youth violence. In addition to pending crime bills, former President Clinton advocated proposals that would limit the availability of guns and attempted to influence the media to show less violence on the screen. U.S. Attorney General Janet Reno threatened a "crackdown" on Hollywood over television violence.[7] Reno went even further when she stated that the United States had passed white South Africa as having the highest number of people in jail per capita. She was described as being "remarkably" interested in *preventing* crime rather than just punishing it, reflecting a shift in priority that, if she succeeded, could have left a lasting mark on law enforcement nationally.[8] President George W. Bush and Attorney Generals John Ashcroft and Alberto Gonzales to date have not shown an interest in crime prevention. Rather, they prefer increasing penalties for crimes.

Youth violence is increasing dramatically. According to the Department of Justice between 1987 and 1991 the number of adolescents arrested for homicide in the nation increased by 85 percent. In 1991 youths from ten to seventeen accounted for 17 percent of *all* violent crime arrests. Youths are not only the perpetrators, they are also the victims. Violent youth gangs, which are now present in 126 cities across the nation, are responsible for many of these homicides.[9] Like the nation, the president, and the U.S. attorney general, the profession of social work has to be concerned and challenged and has to address this national problem of gang violence and homicide with its own psychosocial-based theories of prevention. What follows is one approach in addressing this problem, first anticipated and reported in social work in this text in the late 1980s.

A seventeen-year Chicago study involving 12,872 homicides reported that more than half of Hispanic youth victims were killed in gang-related altercations.[10] In 1985, 10.5 percent of 2,781 homicide victims in California were killed by gangs, and in Los Angeles 24 percent of 1,037 homicides were gang-related.[11] Other large urban areas with gangs also have significant numbers of persons being assaulted and/or killed by gangs. This violence exacts an extremely high toll in injuries, death, and emotional pain and adversely impacts the quality of life for thousands of poor people residing in the inner cities.

The public health profession, with its focus on epidemiologic analysis and prevention, believes it can make a substantial contribution to solving problems of interpersonal violence. Former Surgeon General C. Everett Koop stated that "violence is every bit a public health issue for me and my successors in this century as smallpox, tuberculosis, and syphilis were for my predecessors in the last two centuries."[12] The health professions are making their initial bold entry into this major problem area, following in the footsteps of criminology, sociology, and the criminal justice system. Psychiatry and psychology have been investigating the issue primarily from a biological (brain chemistry) and behavioral (modifying the behavior of individuals) perspective. Chapter 13 demonstrates how the social work profession, with its micro- to macrolevel knowledge and skills base, is ideally suited to apply its techniques with individual gang members, gang groups, and the community to reduce urban gang violence and homicide. In addition to employing social work's traditional approaches in dealing with the problem, the present task is to devise ways in which prevention theory, with corresponding intervention models, can be applied.

It was stated earlier that *primary prevention* in a public health context involves averting the initial occurrence of a disease, defect, or injury. Primary prevention in homicide requires national efforts directed at the social, cultural, educational, technological, and legal aspects of the macro environment, which facilitate the perpetuation of the country's extremely high homicide rate—indeed a tall order. A national strategy would involve public education on the seriousness and ramifications of violence, contributing factors, high-risk groups, and need for social policy as a physical health and mental health priority in the United States. The topic must become a higher priority in medical schools and schools of nursing, social work, and psychology. At the community level community self-help groups, social planning councils, and other civic groups need to work toward educating U.S. citizens about the causal relationship of alcohol, illegal drugs, firearms, and television violence to homicide and violence.[13] In theory these strategies, when directed at high-risk populations, are supposed to reduce those conditions that are seen as contributing to violence and homicide.

Secondary prevention in a public health context concerns the cessation or slowing down of the progression of a health problem. It involves the early detection and case finding by which more serious morbidity may be decreased. Applying this concept to homicide, such case finding requires the identification of persons showing early signs of behavioral and social problems that are related to increased risk for subsequent homicide victimization. Variables such as family violence, childhood and adolescent aggression, school violence, truancy or dropping out of school, and substance abuse are early indicators of many persons who later become perpetrators of violence and homicide. Secondary prevention intervention strategies with individuals already exhibiting these early symptoms interrupt a pattern that may later result in serious violence or homicide.[14]

Tertiary prevention pertains to those situations in which a health problem is already well-established, but efforts can still be made to prevent further progress toward disability and death. In the case of homicide, the problems of greatest concern are those of interpersonal conflict and nonfatal violence, which appear to have a high risk for homicide. Aggravated assault is one early significant predictor related to homicide.[15] In a study in Kansas, in 25 percent of the homicides either the victim or the perpetrator had previously been arrested for an assault or disturbance.[16] Victims of aggravated assault, such as spouses or gang members, are at especially high risk for becoming homicide cases.

Attempts have been made to develop program models aimed at preventing youth violence and homicide, although some of these programs are not specifically aimed at *gang* homicide prevention. These educational-, court-, and community-based programs seem to be functioning mainly at the primary (reducing conditions contributing to homicide) and secondary (identifying persons showing early signs of sociobehavioral problems) prevention levels. A few of these programs, as examples of prevention models, will be discussed.

Educational Prevention Models

The *Boston Youth Program* instituted in four Boston high schools had a curriculum on anger and violence. The ten-session curriculum provided (1) information on adolescent violence and homicide; (2) the discussion of anger as a normal, potentially constructive emotion; (3) knowledge in developing alternatives to fighting; (4) role-playing and videotapes; and (5) the fostering of nonviolent values. Following the completion of the program, an evaluation of a control group (no curriculum) and an experimental group (curriculum) revealed that there was a significant, positive change of attitude in the experimental group. The researchers cautioned, however, that further study had to delineate the actual impact the curriculum would have on actual *behavior,* and the longevity of the impact.[17] The Boston Youth Program was directed at minority students, but it was not indicated whether any of these students were gang members.

Peer Dynamics is another school-based program, sponsored by the Nebraska Commission on Drugs, which was designed to reduce the incidence of destructive risk-taking behaviors associated with juvenile delinquency and substance abuse among high school adolescents in fifty-six public schools. With the goal of developing improved self-esteem and better communication skills, the program trained and supervised students who participated in group interaction activities with other students. A follow-up evaluation found that in relationship to other students, program participants showed a noticeable drop in discipline referrals. The final evaluation noted that Peer Dynamics affected both sexes equally and that the greatest changes were noted in eighth-, tenth-, and eleventh-grade students. No significant change in attitude toward themselves or others was reported in the control group.[18] Again, this was not a program designed specifically for gang youths, although some gang members may have been participants. The question remains, however, whether improved *attitudes* result in less violence and homicide.

A third school-based prevention program functioning in the city of Paramount in Los Angeles County is called the *Paramount Plan*. This was designed to be a "gang-prevention" model and, unlike the Boston Youth Program and Peer Dynamics that target high school youths, it is an educational model directed at *all* fifth and sixth graders in the school district. The program consists of neighborhood parent meetings and an antigang curriculum taught to students in school for fifteen weeks. Prior to the program, 50 percent of students were "undecided" about joining gangs. After the fifteen weeks, 90 percent said they would not join gangs.[19] No mention was made of the 10 percent of students who did not change their minds about joining gangs. In poor urban areas where there are gangs, only 3 to 5 percent of youths become delinquents and/or join gangs. In other words, at least 95 percent of youths do not join gangs even without a gang-prevention program such as the Paramount Plan. Further research is needed to determine if those in the 10 percent who did *not* change their minds about joining gangs actually do, and second, whether they later become either perpetrators or victims of gang homicide. Perhaps one of the major research challenges is to be able to measure what was prevented.

Court- and Community-Based Programs

In Baltimore, Maryland, *Strike II* was developed as a court-based program linking juvenile justice with health care. Its "clients" were court adjudicated first-time offenders (secondary prevention) for violent crimes, assault, robbery, arson, and breaking and entering. Noninstitutionalized probationers were eligible for the program, which was a probation requirement. This multidisciplinary program employed paralegal staff, counselors, social workers, and psychiatrists. The juvenile probationers were involved in five programs: recreation, education, job readiness, and ongoing counseling and medical care as needed. These services were in addition to traditional probation supervision.

The recidivism rate for Strike II clients was only 7 percent, compared to 35 percent statewide and 65 percent for those leaving corrections institutions. The basic cost (excluding medical and job readiness services) was $100 per client.[20] With impressive results, the Strike II program dealt largely with violent juveniles in a physical health/mental health, educational, employment, juvenile justice program. Although gang members were not mentioned specifically, it would appear that with a reduction in recidivism these perpetrators would also have been at reduced risk for becoming violence/homicide victims.

Another community-based program, aimed specifically at gangs, was called *House of Umoja*. It was developed in Philadelphia by two inner-city black parents whose son had joined a gang. His fellow gang members were invited to live with the family, following the model of an extended African family. In response to increased gang-related homicides in 1974 and 1975, the House of Umoja spearheaded a successful campaign to reduce gang violence by obtaining peace pledges from eighty youth gangs. From this experience evolved a community agency called Crisis Intervention Network that worked toward reducing gang violence through communication with concerned parties and organizational efforts.[21] This approach later was called the *Philadelphia Plan.*

In 1978 the state of California Youth Authority reported its findings concerning its *Gang Violence Reduction Project* in East Los Angeles. The project's basic strategy was to (1) promote peace among gangs through negotiation; and (2) provide positive activities for gang members. Directors maintain they reduced gang homicides in East Los Angeles 55 percent, from eleven homicides in seven months of one year down to five homicides during a similar seven-month period the following year. The project researchers admitted that "any judgment that a relationship exists between the changes in gang-related homicide and violent-incident statistics and the activities of the Gang Violence Reduction Project must be based on inference."[22]

Another community-based peace-treaty program targeting high-risk gang youth, patterned after the Philadelphia Plan, is the *Community Youth Gang Services Corporation* in Los Angeles. CYGS counselors in fourteen street teams were able to convince forty-four of 200 gangs they worked with to come to the table to develop a "peace treaty." During the period the peace agreement was in effect, from Thanksgiving of 1986 through the New Year's holidays of 1987, there was only *one* act of violence among the forty-four gangs. The peace-treaties model can "buy time" for all concerned, but if society does not respond with the needed resources (employment, job training, physical health/mental health services, education), peace treaties are very difficult to maintain. Obviously, *all* the above approaches are needed.

Gang Homicide Psychosocial Prevention Models

Continuing efforts have to be made in further refining homicide prevention models in order for them to correspond more closely with the specific type of homicide one wishes to prevent. There are different types of homicide that vary according to circumstances. Robbery, spousal, and gang homicide are all different and require different prevention strategies. If, for example, Asian Americans are at extremely high risk for being robbed and murdered at 2 A.M. in Uptown, U.S.A., through a community education effort Asian Americans would be informed about the high homicide risk in visiting Uptown at 2 A.M. Adhering to the warning could immediately reduce the number of Asian American homicide victims.

In addition to attempting to get a "close fit" between the prevention model and the specific type of homicide, it is equally important that the high-risk person be clearly identified in order to maximize the impact of the prevention model. In the educational- and community-based violence prevention models previously discussed, the focus of intervention appeared to be more on the perpetrator or the "pre-perpetrator" (the person showing early behavioral signs indicating he or she might become a perpetrator) who was at high risk for committing a violent act. In theory all potential victims in an unspecified population are spared victimization when the perpetrator ceases to be violent. Furthermore, there did not seem to be specific prevention programmatic strategies focusing on the violence victim or the person most likely to become a victim. What seems to be needed is a guideline or framework that assists in the identification of high-risk gang members.

Using California as an example, Table 10.1 represents a "general to specific" profile framework for identifying and "zeroing in" on the high-risk gang members who will be the target population for homicide prevention.

For our purposes, we will attempt to develop a hospital-based and community-based youth gang psychosocial homicide prevention model in which social workers play a key intervention role. The focus of these prevention models will be on the gang member who actually becomes a violence or homicide victim of a gang and goes or is taken to the hospital. In Table 10.1 these victims would be the gang members found in items 2b and 2c. In this respect the prevention models are largely tertiary in nature. However, they become primary prevention models when intervention strategies are aimed at younger children and latency-age siblings of the victim who are not yet gang members. By preventing children in high-risk families from becoming future gang members, the likelihood of the children being killed may be significantly reduced, because gang members are more than fifty times more likely to be killed than persons in the general population (519/100,000 versus 10/100,000).

Hospital-Based Model.   Health professionals in community clinics and hospitals are actually in the "trenches," dealing with thousands of violence and homicide casualties related to gang violence. These professionals are usually the first to touch these bodies, and in medical settings they function in a tertiary prevention role, literally trying to control bleeding and save lives. Wounded gang victims of gang violence are in reality a "captive audience," which creates an excellent intervention opportunity for secondary prevention.

Through the physician, social worker, nurse, or other health practitioners on the hospital emergency room team inquiring *how* the victim was injured (which may be confirmed by police, family members, or interested parties), professionals could ascertain if the incident was gang-related. Through in-service staff training concerning gangs and their culture, health staff would be able to determine whether the victim was a gang member. Specifically, dress codes, mannerisms, graffiti, language, tattoos, and other gang symbols could help establish or rule out the gang identity of the victim. Police, family members, peers, and/or witnesses could also be good sources for gang identity confirmation.

If the injuries were caused by gang members and the victim is a gang member, a designated health team member (the social worker) would be responsible for referring the matter to the hospital's SCAN Team. "SCAN Team" refers to Suspected Child Abuse and Neglect, or in some hospitals, Supporting Child Adult Network.[23] SCAN Teams, which are found in many hospitals, are composed of multidisciplinary health staff in which at least one member is a social worker. SCAN Teams were originally developed to investigate suspected child sexual or physical abuse or neglect cases coming to their attention in medical settings. In cases of suspected child abuse, for the protection of the child SCAN Teams are required to take immediate action by involving law enforcement and the child-welfare department.

Our gang-homicide prevention model would require that gang violence victims also become a SCAN Team intervention priority. However, one additional social worker on the SCAN Team would be a gang "specialist" and have primary

Table 10.1

Area and Demographic Characteristics Related to Homicide Risk

I. United States	One of the most violent countries in the world, ranked no. 5 out of 41 countries
II. California	Along with Southern states, ranks among the most violent states
III. Los Angeles	Among the more violent cities in the United States
IV. Inner City (L.A.)	The poorest areas, often the scene of most violent crime
A. Minority Groups	Overrepresented among the disadvantaged, poor, and those residing in the inner city
1. Profile of Perpetrators and Victims	
a. Males	4 to 5 times more likely than females to be killed
b. Age	15–25 age category at highest risk
c. Substance Abuse	Found in 50 to 66 percent of cases
d. Low Education	50 percent school drop-out rate not uncommon
e. Low Income	High unemployment, many living in poverty
2. Gangs	Quite prevalent in inner city and a product of social disorganization
a. Minor Assaults	Gang members are at high risk for being assaulted
b. Aggravated Assaults	Gang members are at high risk for being victims of aggravated assault; occurs 20 to 35 times more often than homicide
c. Homicide	Gang members are at high risk for becoming homicide victims, rate being 519 per 100,000 in the 150,000 gang-member population

Sources: M. L. Rosenberg and J. A. Mercy, "Homicide: Epidemiologic Analysis at the National Level," *Bulletin of the New York Academy of Medicine* 62 (June 1986): 382; H. M. Rose, "Can We Substantially Lower Homicide Risk in the Nation's Larger Black Communities?" *Report of the Secretary's Task Force on Black and Minority Health,* Vol. 5 (Washington, D.C.: U.S. Department of Health and Human Services, January 1986); I. A. Spergel, "Violent Gangs in Chicago: In Search of Social Policy," *Social Service Review* 58 (June 1984): 201–202; A. Morales, "Hispanic Gang Violence and Homicide," Paper presented to the Research Conference on Violence and Homicide in Hispanic Communities, Los Angeles, September 14–15, 1987, p. 13; *Los Angeles Times,* Wednesday, October 5, 1995, p. B-9; A. Morales, "Homicide," in Richard L. Edwards, ed., *Encyclopedia of Social Work,* 19th Edition (Washington, D.C.: NASW Press, 1995).

treatment-coordinating responsibility with the gang victim, his or her family, and the community.

Although not intentional, the emergency room provides access to a high-risk population (victims and families) that is often too embarrassed, frightened, or reluctant to seek assistance from traditional social work agencies. The anonymity of a large, busy, impersonal hospital can be less threatening.[24] Additionally, medical crises may make some persons psychologically vulnerable, hence more amenable to change during the crisis period.

In working with gang members who have been seriously injured as the result of gang assault, often this is when their psychological defenses are down because they are suffering adjustment disorder or posttraumatic stress disorder symptoms (PTSD). In the acute stage of PTSD symptoms, victims may have recurrent, intrusive, distressing recollections of the event, including nightmares, flashbacks, intense stress at exposure to events resembling the traumatic event, persistent avoidance of stimuli associated with the event, sleeping problems, hypervigilance, anxiety, and fear. They are sometimes reluctant to leave the home and even become fearful of their own friends in gang "uniform."

During this acute stage, which may last about six months, they are quite motivated to abandon "gang banging" (gang fighting). If the social worker is not the primary therapist, arrangements should be made for the youth to receive prompt treatment for PTSD while hospitalized, as untreated PTSD may become chronic and last for years. It is at this point that the social worker can also obtain needed employment, educational, recreational, or training resources for the vulnerable gang member. The parents may also be emotionally vulnerable, having just gone through an experience in which they almost lost their son or daughter. They may be more willing to accept services for themselves, if needed, and/or for younger siblings who might be showing some early behavioral signs of problems (deteriorating school performance, truancy, aggressiveness). Helping the family and young siblings is a *primary prevention* role, as these efforts may prevent future gang members (perpetrators or victims) from developing in this at-risk family.

There also may be situations in which the gang member arrives deceased at the hospital or dies during or after surgery. These cases would still be referred to the SCAN Team social worker for service. The focus of help would be—with the family's permission—helping the parents and other children deal with grief and providing any additional assistance they may need in burying their loved one. If there are adolescent gang members in the family, they may be quite angry and want to get even for their brother or sister's death. If not already involved, the social worker would call on community gang group agencies to assist in reducing further conflict. If there are younger siblings in the family, an assessment would be made of their needs, and efforts would be made to mobilize resources to meet these needs. These intervention strategies would have the objective of preventing future homicides in a high-risk family.

The preceding gang homicide prevention model operating from a medical-based agency is presented to illustrate how social work may be able to have intervention impact on a very serious problem shortening the life of many poor, inner-city youths. Figure 10.1 illustrates the various intervention strategies of the hospital-based gang homicide intervention model. Other models can be developed, such as the community agency-based model described in the following paragraphs.

Figure 10.1

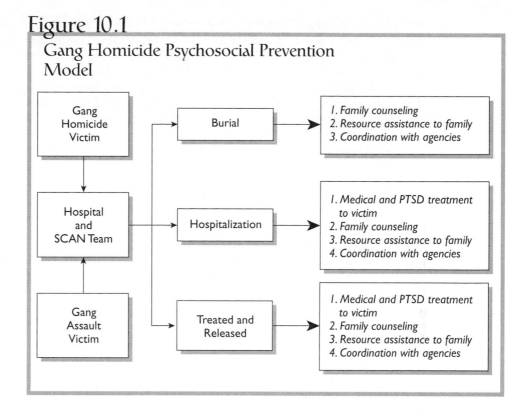

Gang Homicide Psychosocial Prevention Model

Community Agency-Based Model.   An example of an inner-city community agency-based model that the author developed and implemented with the help of a full-time social worker and a second-year clinical social work intern, was a clinical program funded by the Kellogg Foundation. The agency, Challengers Boys and Girls Club, founded in 1968 by Lou Dantzler, was located in South Central Los Angeles, a poor, predominantly African American area. This community was the hardest hit in all of Los Angeles as a result of the April 29, 1992, riot, which was this nation's most destructive and deadliest riot, resulting in sixty deaths and nearly a billion dollars of damage.

Within a three-mile radius of the agency are approximately 22,000 youths in a population of 379,000 persons, with 43 percent of the households headed by 15,000 single mothers over sixteen years of age with children up to eighteen years of age. This community has exceptionally high rates of school dropouts (56 percent of seventeen-year-old African American youths are functionally illiterate), AIDS, diseases of the heart, sexually communicated diseases, and homicide. Neighborhood homicide rates at 95 per 100,000 are almost twelve times the national rate, four times the Los Angeles rate, and at 600 per 100,000 in the neighborhood's gang population.

The agency, with 2,100 enrolled families, has an average daily attendance of 400 boys and girls (ages six to seventeen) during the summer months; 200 during the rest of the year. Program services, in addition to athletic and recreational services, include tutoring, classes in basic math, reading comprehension and computers, photography, woodshop, job application training, a new basic dental and health examination program, and mental health crisis intervention.[25]

In establishing a gang-homicide psychosocial prevention model, an assessment has to be made regarding the severity of the gang-related violence and homicide problem. Local law enforcement statistics are mandatory in this regard. Table 10.2 demonstrates the extent of the problem in the above targeted area.[26]

The target area is a very active, violent community, clearly contributing to making many young ethnic/racial youths an endangered species as they approach adolescence and young adulthood, being killed at the rate of 600 to 1,000 per 100,000 in the gang population, depending on the gang-related homicides for a given year.

The mental health crisis intervention program, staffed by the author as a mental health consultant, a full-time social worker, and a clinical social work trainee was available to those member families who experienced a sudden, severe crisis such as the premature death of a family member brought on by an accident, suicide, or homicide. These tragic events are known to leave a spouse or parent emotionally immobilized for months and, at times, even for years. The death of a child results in a more severe grief reaction for a parent than that of any other family member.[27] The surviving siblings' loss may be more than that of the surviving parent because they have lost not only an immediate family member but also the grieving parent(s) who is temporarily emotionally unavailable to them. During this time, depending on their prior adjustment, age, and emotional strength, these children are at high risk

Table 10.2

Prevalence of Gangs and Gang-Related Violent Crimes

Total No. of Gang Members	24,200
Latino Gangs	204
African American *Crips*	109
African American *Bloods*	45
Types of Gangs: *Criminal* (making $); and *Conflict* (turf-oriented)	
No. of Gang-related Crimes (5/1992 to 5/1993)	
Homicide	133
Attempted Homicide	247
Felony Assault	1259
Robbery	1034
Discharging Firearm into Inhabited Dwelling	61
Battery on Police Officer	19

Source: South Bureau, Los Angeles Police Department, 1993.

for emotional, educational, and behavioral problems. Prompt intervention (assessment, counseling, and possible referral in acute cases) may lessen and *prevent* a child from having more serious difficulties and problems of adjustment. In specific cases where the sibling was a gang member and the victim of a gang homicide, younger adolescent or preadolescent siblings are at especially high risk for becoming either future victims or perpetrators of gang violence and homicide.

In this inner-city, agency-based, gang-homicide psychosocial prevention model, nearly 100 high-risk African American and Hispanic elementary school children (mostly males) were referred for treatment for assaultive, fighting behavior directed at peers either at school, at home, in the neighborhood, or at Challengers. Of these, ten cases were more directly impacted by violence. For the purposes of brevity, only two of these cases will be commented on.

In one case, a fourteen-year-old Challengers member was the victim of a "drive-by" shooting outside his home by a gang group. The youth was not a gang member, yet met the general, stereotypic profile of a gang member held by many police and gang members; that is, he was a minority male adolescent residing in the poor, inner-city neighborhood. A bullet to his brain resulted in four months' hospitalization and permanent neurological impairments, including dependence on a wheelchair. Ongoing supportive visits were made with the youngster at the hospital, along with conversations with medical and social service staff and his guardian aunt. (His mother had passed away three years previously due to illness, and his father was in a correctional facility.)

On release, efforts were made to reintegrate the youngster into the Challengers program components, with supportive counseling as needed and assistance in applying for victim's assistance and Social Security benefits. The victim did not have younger or adolescent siblings, hence other family members were not at risk for gang homicide as future victims or perpetrators.

The second case concerned a 10-year-old suicidal boy, whose father had been killed by a robber twelve months previously, and his paternal uncle three months before. The boy was experiencing school behavioral problems, sleep disturbance, and some somatic complaints, including vomiting. The mother had already taken the boy to a child guidance-counseling program and was now enrolling the youngster in the Challengers recreational program. The agency made available to the mother an adult supportive counseling group, led by the mental health consultant and social worker, for family members who have lost a loved one due to a sudden, premature death. The mother herself was seen individually, with plans to later involve her in a group with similarly affected families. Such groups are also needed for children and adolescents. Additionally, outreach efforts are made with law enforcement and other community agencies, hospitals, and churches to identify high-risk families who had a child who was a gang member and was killed as the result of gang violence. These families, in their psychological state of vulnerability, were extended an invitation to become part of the Challengers program. As they began to participate in the program, they received a host of social, recreational, educational, dental, health, and mental health services. It was anticipated that the cycle of gang violence and trauma, with its accompanying sequelae of psychosocial problems, was lessened.

U.S. Homeland Security Department as a Prevention Effort

In response to 9/11, Congress enacted H.R. 5005 on January 23, 2002, called the "Homeland Security Act of 2002." Title I of the Act establishes the Department of Homeland Security (DHS), which has as its primary mission to:

a. *Prevent* [emphasis ours] terrorist attacks within the United States;
b. Reduce the vulnerability of the United States to terrorism; and
c. Minimize the damage and assist in the recovery from terrorist attacks that occur within the United States.

These three missions in the context of prevention theory could be seen as encompassing primary, secondary, and tertiary prevention. For example, the DHS operates through the following five main divisions:

1. Border and Transportation Security;
2. Emergency Preparedness;
3. Information Analysis and Infrastructures;
4. Management; and
5. Science and Technology. [28]

For the purposes of this prevention chapter, the focus will only be on Border and Transportation Security. At the primary prevention level, Border and Transportation Security strategies may involve the questioning and interrogation of vulnerable, at-risk persons who *might* be suspected of being possible terrorists even though they may have not committed any illegal act. The interrogation experience for these suspects could be quite stressful. They are not free to walk away from these interrogations. At this primary prevention level, these terrorist suspects could be released with no further official action taken by DHS.

Strategies in the secondary prevention level in achieving DHS terrorist prevention goals would involve the actual detention of terrorist suspects for investigation whether or not they have been perceived as having committed a minor to major criminal or policy violation as alleged by DHS authorities. Even if the suspects are U.S.-born American citizens, they could be detained in the United States without legal due process and without representation by an attorney.[29] This is in clear violation of the U.S. Constitution's Fourth Amendment (unreasonable search and seizure), Sixth Amendment (right to a speedy trial), Seventh Amendment (right to a trial by jury), and Fourteenth Amendment (equal protection under the law). The DHS investigation of the terrorist suspect could be indefinite. This experience could prove to be an emotional hardship both for the innocent suspect and his/her family.

At the tertiary prevention level, the suspect may not only be incarcerated indefinitely but if declared an "enemy combatant" by President George Bush, the suspect could be confined in a foreign country with lax laws considering the treatment of prisoners, and could possibly be subjected to mistreatment and torture. In such cases the suspect is not legally charged by the U.S. Justice Department. Rather, the person is turned over to the U.S. Military as an enemy combatant and is housed in the foreign country's prison. Such was the case, highlighted in Chapter 13, of U.S. citizen Jose Padilla, detained in Guantanamo without being charged and without access to a lawyer or the courts. He was indicted for crimes in December, 2005.[30]

Again, these detentions could result in severe psychiatric problems, especially if the subjects are subjected to torture.

Approving President Bush's detention of enemy combatants held incommunicado without due process, in a 102 page decision, U.S. District Court Judge Michael Mukasey concluded:[31]

"A formal declaration of war is not necessary in order for the executive to exercise its constitutional authority to prosecute an armed conflict—particularly when, as on September 11, the United States is attacked."

Kenneth Roth, the Executive Director of Human Rights Watch, had a different opinion, stating:[32]

"To permit a government that is at war in one part of the world to place people in military custody without charges elsewhere in the world without demonstrating participation in the armed conflict would create a gaping and dangerous loophole to basic human rights guarantees."

On August 29, 2005, U.S. Senators Richard Lugar and Barack Obama, who were members of the Foreign Relations Committee, were detained for three hours in a Moscow airport. Russian border guards demanded the search of their U.S. government aircraft carrying the Senators and their delegation. Russian authorities never did explain the reason for their three-hour search.[33] Could this happen in the United States?

Consider the following primary prevention case composite of Mrs. Kani Hadi, an American of Arab descent, age 33, and her two children, ages 10 and 8. Mrs. Hadi was born, raised, and college educated in the United States; and her husband, Muhammed, of Muslim, Arab descent, and was also born in the United States Mrs. Hadi's parents legally emigrated to the United States from Saudi Arabia 35 years previously and established a successful P.O. Box mailing business. Mrs. Hadi's husband was also doing quite well financially as an owner and manager of two Subway sandwich stores and a cellular phone retail store in West Los Angeles. Her husband had to attend a 7-day conference in Seattle during the children's school vacation. The mother took this opportunity to take her children on an educational vacation trip to visit the Canadian side of Niagara Falls.

After being processed through customs by U.S. and Canadian authorities, where they had to show their U.S. passports, they boarded Air Canada and flew directly from Los Angeles International Airport (LAX) to Toronto, where they stayed for five days in a luxury hotel. The next day they went on their all-day trip to Niagara Falls, which left them excited and almost breathless with the enormity and beauty of the Falls. The children were quite "hyper," playing with their miniature souvenir toys of Niagara Falls as they made their long bus trip back to the hotel.

A few days later after they showed their passports to both Canadian and U.S. authorities, they boarded their Air Canada flight back to Los Angeles and flew non-stop to LAX. As they were being processed through customs clearance, Mrs. Hadi and her children were called into the Immigration and Naturalization Office, where a ranking Department of Homeland Security representative by the name of Joe Hart was also present. Mr. Hart reported to Mrs. Hadi that they had been looking at her passport, which showed that she had made four trips to Saudi Arabia in the last ten years. He wondered what her motive was in visiting Saudi Arabia so often.

Mrs. Hadi was surprised by the question and was already feeling nervous after being signaled out by the authorities and transported to a distant, isolated office. She became a little teary and explained that her aging grandparents still lived there and she wanted to maintain contact with them, especially for the sake of the children who got to know them well. Mr. Hart looked at her skeptically with a raised eyebrow, and added that they had also confiscated her digital camera and wondered why she had not only taken many photos of Niagara Falls, but particularly photos of the large electric generators on the U.S. side of the Falls. Mrs. Hadi's eyes opened wide as she was now beginning to see where Mr. Hart was going with his questions. "Maybe they think that I am a Muslim terrorist spy," she thought to herself. Her worry was now turning into fear. "My son entered a 5th-grade school science fair and was required to do research on a science project. Because of his interest in electronics, he chose to demonstrate how water is used as energy to create electricity for cities. He was fascinated by the power of Niagara Falls and how it was generating electricity through massive generators, and since they were on the Canadian side of the Falls, the only visible generators were on the American side."

In attempting to defend herself, she added: "Look! I'm a U.S.-born American citizen and I have not done anything wrong." Mr. Hart replied: "That's another thing that I want to talk to you about. Your three passports are clever forgeries. We are going to keep them." Mrs. Hadi began to cry. She showed Mr. Hart her driver's license commenting, "Maybe this will prove my legal status." Mr. Hart quickly glanced at the license and said: "This is also a forgery and we're going to keep it." "But I need it to drive home," she pleaded. Mr. Hart replied that this was not his concern and that he was simply doing his job and following the spirit of the law since 9/11. He stood up and told her that she was fortunate that they did not arrest her and her children and that now she was free to leave. "Can I please have my cell phone so I can call my husband?" "No," we have to investigate all of the local and international calls you have been making," he replied.

Stunned, Mrs. Hadi walked slowly out of the office with her children, tears streaming down her cheeks. An Air Canada flight attendant recognized her and the children as passengers who had been in her First Class section and asked if she needed help. Mrs. Hadi explained the stressful experience she had just gone through. The flight attendant suggested that they walk over to the Traveler's Aid Office nearby, which was in the same terminal.

Travelers Aid Society (TAS) is a national nonprofit organization that originated in St. Louis, Missouri, in the mid-nineteenth century. It is the oldest, nonsectarian social welfare organization in the United States. By the beginning of the twentieth century, TAS began to expand and can now be found primarily in urban areas with a total population of 110 million people. In 2004, TAS served more than 5 million clients in 48 communities and thirty-six transportation centers (bus and train stations and airports) in the United States, Puerto Rico, and Canada. Their motto is "a helping hand along the way."[34] TAS is part of the network of social service agencies responding to travelers in need. For example, when a traveler becomes stranded, professional social workers step in to offer assistance. With the client and his or her family, they develop a plan that brings an end to the crisis and ensures a safe return home.[35]

The flight attendant introduced Mrs. Hadi to the social worker, Ms. Sue Kang, in the open, storefront office. Mrs. Hadi relayed her story to Ms. Kang, who replied that Mrs. Hadi's trying experience usually happens to undocumented persons with false passports arriving at LAX from Latin countries, certainly *not* U.S. born citizens. Mrs. Hadi asked if she could use Ms. Kang's phone to call her husband in Seattle, and Ms. Kang replied in the affirmative. She called her husband and left a message at his hotel room. With Mrs. Hadi's permission, they both walked over to Mr. Hart's office. Ms. Kang's questions made Mr. Hart defensive, and he still would not return Mrs. Hadi's documents. In viewing the documents, Ms. Kang's opinion was that the documents were legitimate.

Mr. Hart then replied: "This is the best I can do for Mrs. Hadi, *and* I'm doing her a favor. If she can show me the officially stamped, original birth certificates belonging to her and her children, I will return her documents." Mrs. Hadi informed Ms. Kang that she had the birth certificates at home. Ms. Kang suggested that she could drive Mrs. Hadi home to obtain them, drop off her children with her parents, and return to the airport to show Mr. Hart the birth certificates. Mrs. Hadi approved of the plan. When they returned to the airport, they presented the birth certificates to Mr. Hart, who quickly viewed them, then opened a drawer and handed the documents to Ms. Kang. He did not say a word. "What about my cell phone?" inquired Mrs. Hadi. Mr. Hart stated that the phone was going to be forwarded to DHS communications investigations and that it would be a while until they identified all of her international calls. As they walked back to the Travelers Aid office, Mrs. Hadi thanked Ms. Kang profusely and added that she could not have done it without her help. Ms. Kang minimized her effort and replied: "That's what we're here for, to help travelers in need."

Does the case of Mrs. Hadi who was of Arab descent, represent an act of racial profiling, or was she signaled out because of her digital photos of U.S. electric generators? Does DHS routinely inspect the digital photos of other passengers or was this again related to her ethnicity? Or was the reason for the DHS investigation related to her passport, which revealed four trips to Saudi Arabia (homeland of the majority of 9/11 airline suicide bombers) in the last 10 years? The post 9/11 *prevention* practices of the DHS may be designed for the protection and welfare of all Americans, but individuals like Mrs. Hadi illustrate the emotionally stressful burden that some persons, particularly certain ethnic-racial minorities, have to endure. In cases like that of Mrs. Hadi, the DHS prevention practices may actually cause psychiatric problems in persons who did not have these problems prior to their contact with the government. With the erosion of civil rights protections, these suspects cannot challenge the government's allegations. Rather than being innocent until proven guilty, they are judged guilty without an opportunity to prove their innocence in a court of law. The following racial profiling case example in "Class Action Social Work and Prevention" *does* represent an actual court case where the plaintiffs (injured party) were able to prove their innocence.

Class Action Social Work and Prevention

The enormous mission of social work is to enhance the quality of life for all persons. Some of the injustices and obstacles that damage the quality of life are poverty, racism, sexism, and drug abuse; there are many more.[36] Social work's impact on these problems is sometimes limited by the clinical model, by inappropriate interventive strategies, and by the fact that it becomes too time-consuming and inefficient to try to help people on a case-by-case basis. On other occasions a referred client with a "problem" may not really have a problem. The problem may be in the referral system.

For example, a school may refer a problem student to a social worker to help him or her adjust to the requirements of the school system. The school system, however, may have serious defects that are the primary cause of the student's problem. The goal of the social worker should then be to help tailor the school system to meet the educational needs of the student. The student in this situation may represent a *class* of people, that is, a number of students in a similar predicament. Rather than the social worker working individually with each student to document the deficiencies in the school system, one student can represent all students in a *class action* suit to improve conditions in the school. Class action is a legal concept that has promising implications for social work. Closer working relationships will have to be cultivated with the legal profession to enable lawyers to conceptualize broad social work concerns and to translate these into legal class action suits. Such an approach can be called *class action social work*. Victories in the courts could provide relief for thousands of poor people.

In some states social workers have already made pioneering efforts to enter the legal arena. In California, for example, the Greater California Chapter of the NASW presented an award to John Serrano, a social worker, for his actions as a concerned citizen in the widely publicized *Serrano v. Priest* case, which argued that the quality of a child's education should not be dependent on the wealth of a school district.[37] The California Supreme Court, in this class action suit filed by the Western Center on Law and Poverty, Inc., ruled 6 to 1 that the California public educational finance scheme, which relies heavily on local property taxes, violated the equal protection clause of the Fourteenth Amendment to the U.S. Constitution. The court held that the financing system invidiously discriminated against the poor. The court also asserted that the right to a public education was a fundamental interest that could not be dependent on wealth, and it therefore applied the strict equal-protection standard. Finding no compelling state interest advanced by the discriminatory system, the court held it unconstitutional.[38]

The significance of the *Serrano v. Priest* decision transcends California boundaries because all states except Hawaii use similar educational finance systems. Wealthier districts are favored to the detriment of poorer school districts. A direct relationship exists between the number of dollars spent per child and the quality of education available to that child. In *Serrano v. Priest* it was discovered that poor communities were paying two to three times as much school tax per $100 of assessed valuation as were wealthy communities, yet wealthy communities received two to three times as many educational dollars per child from the state as did the poorer communities.[39]

In *Serrano v. Priest* the court's policy considerations focused on the pervasive influence of education on individual development and capacity within modern society and on education's essential role in the maintenance of free enterprise democracy. It was considered that the combination of these factors sufficiently distinguished education from other governmental services for it to merit recognition as a fundamental interest.[40] No court had previously placed education within the framework of interests meriting strict equal-protection scrutiny, and this decision represented the first time any type of governmental service had been held to involve fundamental interests.[41]

Considering the *Serrano* precedent, might not the areas of welfare, health, and mental health services also represent a set of circumstances as unique and compelling as education? A right to public education may not be maximally enjoyed if a child is poorly housed, impoverished, malnourished, or in need of physical or mental health care. *Serrano v. Priest,* as a social work class action concept, has the potential to be the cutting edge of social reform in a wide range of governmental services, including several in which social workers already have knowledge and experience. In view of the regressive social and economic policies of Reagan, Bush, Clinton, and G.W. Bush, the opportunity for class action collaboration between law and social work as a significant tool of intervention is possible. The class action social work concept and its application was tested by one of the authors in the courts as a mental health primary prevention activity.

Class action is a legal procedural device for resolving issues in court affecting many people. Those persons actually before the court represent the unnamed members of the class in a single proceeding in equity, thereby avoiding multiple case-by-case actions. *Class action social work* is a forensic social work/legal profession collaborative litigation activity involving social work concerns, with the goal of obtaining a favorable court ruling that will benefit the social welfare of a group of socioeconomically disadvantaged persons. Class action social work in a mental health primary prevention context finds social workers and attorneys pursuing a court ruling that will have a positive psychosocial impact on a disadvantaged class of people who, prior to the ruling, were at risk in developing psychological or psychiatric disorders or symptoms. Among the requirements needed to accomplish the primary prevention goals are—to borrow from public health terminology—a small sample of "infected" organisms, an identification of the suspected toxic agent, and a laboratory procedural test to show whether the toxic agent caused the infection in the organism. Translating this into class action mental health primary prevention terms using an actual case (*Nicacio v. United States INS*), the "infected organisms" were thirteen Hispanic plaintiffs (the injured, complaining parties) who were exhibiting psychiatric symptoms, allegedly caused by stressful interrogations conducted by patrol officers of the United States Immigration and Naturalization Service (INS). The courtroom became the laboratory in which the suspected toxic evidence (behavior of the INS officers) was analyzed as to potential harm. If found to be harmful, the court could issue an order terminating the toxic behavior of the INS, which thus prevented psychosocial harm (psychiatric symptoms) in a specific at-risk population (millions of Hispanics residing in the Southwestern states or the State of Washington area, depending on court boundary definitions).

In *Nicacio v. United States INS*, Hispanic plaintiffs brought suit contending that (1) the border patrol agents of the INS were conducting roving motor vehicle stops in search of "illegal aliens" on the roadways of the state of Washington that were in violation of Fourth Amendment rights to be free from unreasonable searches and seizures; (2) that the actions of INS officials were unlawful; and (3) that the plaintiffs were entitled to monetary damages for humiliation, embarrassment, and mental anguish suffered as a result of a violation of their Fourth Amendment rights.[42] The facts of the case were that (1) all plaintiffs were of Mexican descent and were either born in the United States, U.S. citizens, or permanent resident aliens who resided in the Yakima Valley area of the state of Washington; (2) the plaintiff class was defined by the court as "all persons of Mexican, Latin, or Hispanic appearance who have been, are, or will be traveling by motor vehicle on the highways of the state of Washington"; (3) at the time litigation was initiated, INS agents were regularly conducting roving patrol motor vehicle stops, detentions, and interrogations in the Yakima Valley area; (4) many of the stops were based solely on Hispanic appearance, the agents' subjective feelings or intuition, or the suspected "illegal aliens'" innocuous behavior, appearance, or traits; and (5) persons stopped were required, in most cases, to provide identification or documentation of legal presence in the United States.[43]

In attempting to document the amount of humiliation, embarrassment, and mental anguish suffered by the plaintiffs as a result of their contact with INS officers, plaintiffs' attorneys contacted one of the authors as an expert witness to conduct a mental health evaluation of all the plaintiffs. Having been sworn in by the court and qualified and accepted as an expert witness, the author rendered a DSM-IV-R diagnosis of each plaintiff. The findings were that (1) not one of the thirteen plaintiffs had ever been hospitalized or treated on an outpatient basis for a mental health problem; (2) eleven of the plaintiffs suffered adjustment disorder symptoms, either with depressed mood, anxious mood, or mixed emotional features; (3) one plaintiff suffered acute posttraumatic stress disorder symptoms; and (4) one plaintiff was symptom-free.

The findings of the court were that (1) the INS border patrol practices were unlawful; (2) plaintiffs and class action members were entitled to a declaratory judgment covering future conduct of INS officers in stopping vehicles on public highways; and (3) plaintiffs were *not* entitled to recover monetary damages for their suffering, since plaintiffs were unable to specifically identify the officers.[44] The favorable court ruling affected *all* persons of Mexican, Latin, or Hispanic appearance residing only in the state of Washington, rather than in the Southwestern states, as had originally been requested by plaintiffs' attorneys. Even so, the court order stopped the noxious activities of the INS directed at Hispanics in the state of Washington. *All* Hispanics in the state of Washington, therefore, were spared INS-provoked psychiatric symptoms in future contacts with the INS. This case shows the growing potential of class action social work with a mental health primary prevention goal and outcome using social work psychosocial practice concepts.

Class action social work, as a macrolevel practice intervention prevention tool, can also be used to ensure that children at risk receive the welfare benefits and services to which they are entitled. Former President Clinton's welfare reform law could be a test case. As more children are growing up poor and without stable families, as Harris impresses on social workers and the social work profession, they must renew their commitment to child welfare and continue to play an important role in the development and formulation of public policy and child welfare services to strengthen the ability of vulnerable families to raise healthy children.[45]

In many instances, it is not necessary to develop and formulate new public policy concerning child welfare; simply creating new laws will not solve the problems. There may be many national and local situations in which child welfare laws and policies already exist to benefit children, but are not—for any number of reasons—being implemented. It is in these cases that class action social work intervention can be applied to prevent children from experiencing harm when they are not receiving the services to which they have a right.

Stein suggests that child welfare agencies are vulnerable to class action suits, alleging that clients are being deprived of constitutional guarantees or entitlements specified in federal or state policy. In this recession era of reduced spending at the continued expense of domestic programs, reductions in personnel and social services increase welfare agency vulnerability to class action suits, as the lack of funds *is not* a defense for failing to provide federal and state legally mandated services.[46]

Class action suits on behalf of children have charged that state agencies have failed to develop case plans; made inappropriate placements of children, ignoring racial/ethnic factors; failed to pursue adoptive placements; and failed to provide preventive services. Two other class action suits alleged state failure to provide preventive services, and one suit alleged maltreatment of children in foster care and failure to develop and implement permanent plans.[47] The specific role of social workers in these class action suits was not clear, that is, whether they were defendants, expert witnesses, or initiators and/or collaborators with the attorneys in the suits. It is when social workers are in the initiating, collaborating role with attorneys that it conforms to the earlier definition of class action social work.

Social workers need to pay careful attention to existing national and state benefits and welfare policies and to laws and regulations affecting vulnerable client groups, such as children, the homeless, welfare families, and institutionalized psychiatric and corrections populations, to ensure that they are receiving the services and benefits to which they are entitled. Continued denial of resources to clients by agencies, even after notification of mandated requirements, may have merits for attorney–social worker collaboration that eventually could result in a class action social work type of intervention. A favorable court remedy would prevent continued harm to the immediately affected client population (secondary prevention) and to future client populations (primary prevention).

Concluding Comment

Escalating costs, coupled with increasing need for human services and the fact that there will never be sufficient mental health practitioners to meet these needs, require the development and application of helping concepts, such as primary prevention, designed to benefit large numbers of persons *before* they are symptomatic. Because social work is one of the helping professions most involved in interacting with and helping communities, it is anticipated that the profession will play an increasingly vital role in applying primary prevention concepts.

Urban gang violence and homicide were highlighted in this chapter to indicate to the social work profession that, from a historical practice experience standpoint, it is best suited for the health and mental health professions to assume a leadership role in developing micro- to macro-intervention strategies to deal with a problem that is killing thousands of inner-city youths. Primary, secondary, and tertiary violence and homicide prevention programs were discussed and analyzed as to their impact on violence and gang homicide. A framework for identifying high-risk gang victims was developed to correspond to a suggested hospital-based prevention program. A challenge to President Bush and U.S. Attorney General Alberto Gonzaleo is a bold new approach to crime prevention dealing with urban violence. This is especially needed in the inner-city where thousands are killed due to urban gang terrorism as described in Chapter 13.

The prevention role of the Department of Homeland Security was discussed as a measure to protect U.S. citizens from terrorist attacks. However, as DHS carries out its mandated mission armed with the eradication of key civil rights amendments, some U.S. citizens will be denied their constitutionally guaranteed protections and incarcerated indefinitely. This can happen especially if they are labeled an "enemy combatant" by President Bush during the undefined period of time in undeclared wars in Afghanistan and Iraq. Prevention in this context becomes an iatrogenic (the healer makes the illness worse) "solution" as mental health problems may be created in persons who might have been in good health prior to exposure to the government's actions. This certainly was not the intention of prevention theories. How will social work respond?

Class action social work, shows promise as a macrolevel intervention strategy. *Serrano v. Priest*, a class action victory, established the precedent of the right to an equal education; it paved the road for the poor to fight for the right to health and welfare in order to maximize their new educational opportunity. Increasing an individual's opportunities through such assistance is in the best interests of the individual and society. The effectiveness of class action social work with a mental health primary prevention goal was demonstrated in *Nicacio v. United States INS,* in which a positive court ruling will have the effect of preventing literally thousands of at-risk Hispanics from developing psychiatric symptoms caused by discriminatory law enforcement practices. A rare opportunity for social work to help the poor on a broad scale seems very possible in light of *Serrano* and *Nicacio*. Examples were also provided to show how class action social work intervention can be applied on behalf of vulnerable client populations who are being denied legally mandated services. Collaboration with the legal profession should be vigorously pursued by social workers.

KEY WORDS AND CONCEPTS

Prevention
Primary prevention
Secondary prevention
At-risk population
Tertiary prevention

Class action social work
Gang homicide psychosocial prevention
    model
Department of Homeland Security

SUGGESTED INFORMATION SOURCES

"Homeland Security Act of 2002," at: http://www.dhs.gov/dhspublic/display

Durlak, Joseph A, and Wells, Anne M., "Primary Prevention Mental Health Programs for Children and Adolescents: A Meta-Analytic Review," *American Journal of Community Psychology,* 25, No. 2, April, 1997.

Howell, James C. "Youth Gang Programs and Strategies," Office of Juvenile Justice and Delinquency Prevention, U.S. Department of Justice, August 2000.

"Prevention as a New Direction: The Future of Social Work," in Morales, Armando, and Sheafor, Bradford W. *Social Work: A Profession of Many Faces,* 10th Edition. Boston: Allyn & Bacon, 2004.

ENDNOTES

1. H. John Staulcup, "Primary Prevention," in Aaron Rosenblatt and Diana Waldfogel, eds., *Handbook of Clinical Social Work* (San Francisco: Jossey-Bass, 1983), p. 1059.
2. R. A. Feldman, A. R. Stiffman, D. A. Evans, and J. G. Orme, "Prevention Research, Social Work, and Mental Illness," *Social Work Research and Abstracts* 18 (Fall 1982): 2.
3. Stephen E. Goldston, "Defining Primary Prevention," in George W. Albee and Justice M. Joffe, eds., *Primary Prevention of Psychopathology,* Vol. I: The Issues (Hanover, NH: University Press of New England, 1977), p. 20.
4. Ibid.
5. Ibid., p. 21.
6. Steven L. McMurtry, "Secondary Prevention of Child Maltreatment: A Review," *Social Work* 30 (January–February 1985): 43.
7. *Los Angeles Times,* Part I, Friday, October 22, 1993, p. 24.
8. "Truth, Justice, and the Reno Way," *Time,* Vol. 142, No. 2, p. 26.
9. "Teen Violence—Wild in the Streets," *Newsweek,* August 2, 1993, pp. 40–49.
10. Carolyn Rebecca Block, "Lethal Violence in Chicago over Seventeen Years: Homicides Known to the Police, 1965–1981," Illinois Criminal Justice Information Authority, p. 69.
11. Department of Justice, "Homicide in California, 1985" (Bureau of Criminal Statistics and Special State of California, 1985), p. 17; "Fiscal Year 1985–86 Statistical Summary," Los Angeles County Sheriffs Department; "Statistical Digest, 1986," Automated Information Division, Los Angeles Police Department.
12. Cited in N. Meredith, "The Murder Epidemic," *Science* 84 (December 1984): 42.

13. *Report of the Secretary's Task Force on Black and Minority Health*, Vol. 5, U.S. Department of Health and Human Services, January 1986, pp. 43–44.

14. Ibid., pp. 46–50.

15. Ibid., p. 50.

16. Police Foundation, *Domestic Violence and the Police: Studies in Detroit and Kansas City* (Washington, D.C.: The Foundation, 1976).

17. The Boston Youth Program, Boston City Hospital, 818 Harrison Ave., Boston, MA, cited in *Report of the Secretary's Task Force*, pp. 235–236.

18. C. Cooper, "Peer Dynamics, Final Evaluation Report, 1979–1980," Nebraska State Commission on Drugs (Lincoln: Nebraska State Department of Health).

19. "Early Gang Intervention," Transfer of Knowledge Workshop, Department of the California Youth Authority, Office of Criminal Justice Planning, 1985, pp. 11–12; also see Tony Ostos, "Alternatives to Gang Membership." (Unpublished paper, Paramount School District, Los Angeles County, California, October 1987.)

20. "Strike II," Hopkins Adolescent Program, Johns Hopkins Hospital, Park Building, Baltimore, MD, 1986.

21. Fattah Falaka, "Call and Catalytic Response: The House of Umoja," in R. A. Mathias, P. De Muro, and R. S. Allinson, eds., *Violent Juvenile Offenders: An Anthology* (San Francisco: National Council on Crime and Delinquency, 1984), pp. 231–237.

22. "Gang Violence Reduction Project, Second Evaluation Report: October 1977–May 1978," Department of the California Youth Authority, November 1978, pp. i, iii.

23. T. Tatara, H. Morgan, and H. Portner, "SCAN: Providing Preventive Services in an Urban Setting," *Children Today* (November–December 1986): 17–22.

24. Karil S. Klingbeil, "Interpersonal Violence: A Comprehensive Model in a Hospital Setting from Policy to Program," in *Report of the Secretary's Task Force*, p. 246.

25. Lou Dantzler, "Executive Summary, Challengers Boys and Girls Club" (Los Angeles, CA, 1990), brochure.

26. As reported to the author by the Los Angeles Police Department South Bureau, June 1993.

27. Barbara A. Soricelli and Carolyn Lorenz Utech, "Mourning the Death of a Child: The Family and Group Process," *Social Work* 30 (September–October 1985): 429–434.

28. http://www.dhs.gov/dhspublic/display

29. Phil Hirschkorn, "U.S. can hold 'dirty bomb' suspect," http://cnn.law.com

30. To avoid a U.S. Supreme Court review of Padilla's detention status, the Bush Administration has indicted him for criminal offenses and moved him to a federal prison awaiting a trial date (*Time*, December 5, 2005, p. 27).

31. Kenneth Roth, "U.S. Circumvents Courts with Enemy Combatant Tag," http://www.hrw.org/press/2002/06/us0612.htm.

32. Ibid.

33. *Los Angeles Times*, Monday, August 29, 2005, p. A-3.

34. "About Travelers Aid," http://www.travelersaid.org/about.html, p. 1.

35. Ibid., p. 2.

36. Scott Briar, "The Future of Social Work: An Introduction," *Social Work* 19 (September 1974): 518.

37. *NASW Newsletter*, Greater California Chapter, April 1975, p. 1.

38. Robert B. Keiter, "California Educational Financing System Violates Equal Protection," *Clearinghouse Review* 5 (October 1971): 287.

39. Ibid., p. 297.

40. Ibid., p. 298.

41. Ibid., p. 299.
42. *Nicacio v. United States INS*, 595 F. Supp. 19 (1984), p. 19.
43. Ibid., p. 21.
44. Ibid., pp. 19, 25.
45. Dorothy V. Harris, "Renewing Our Commitment to Child Welfare," *Social Work* 33 (November–December 1988): 483–484.
46. Theodore J. Stein, "The Vulnerability of Child Welfare Agencies to Class Action Suits," *Social Service Review* 61 (December 1987): 636–654.
47. Ibid., p. 640.

Social Work throughout the World

Prefatory Comment

People everywhere need assistance in addressing social issues that affect their lives, as well as help in resolving or reducing specific social problems that individuals from time to time confront. Thus, the need for social work, as the profession dedicated to both serving people and improving social conditions, is global.

The prior sections of this book focused on the ways in which social work evolved in the United States. Lest the reader assume that the functioning of social workers in the United States is the only model for this profession, this chapter is concerned with similarities and differences in the expressions of social work throughout the world. In addition, it reflects the growing globalization of social work and the evolving efforts to address international social issues.

Today's Global Social Concerns: A Context for Social Work

The distribution of wealth throughout the world illustrates the problems that social work and all of society must confront. The United Nations indicates that in the year 2000, 1.2 billion people, or one-fifth of the world's population, lived in extreme poverty (i.e., about $1 per day in 1995 U.S. dollars), and 2.8 billion people, or one-half of the world's population, lived below a poverty level of about $2 per day in U.S. dollars. Some good news is that this economic situation is improving for many. Between 1972 and 1999 the relative economic conditions improved 13 percent in Africa, 72 percent in Asia and the Pacific Islands, and 35 percent in Latin America and the Caribbean. Only the West Asia region declined (i.e., by 6 percent).[1]

Although the overall economic condition throughout most of the world is improving, the gap between the rich and poor countries continues. For example, according to the United Nations, in 2000 the 3.5 billion people living in the lowest income countries earned 20 percent of the world's income, while the 1 billion people in the richest countries earned 60 percent of that year's wealth.[2] Another illustration of this disparity is the fact that the richest 20 percent of the world's population:

▶ Accounts for 86 percent of the total private consumption of goods and services.
▶ Consumes 60 percent of the world's energy.
▶ Eats 45 percent of all fish and meat.
▶ Uses 80 percent of the world's paper supply.
▶ Owns 87 percent of the automobiles and 74 percent of the telephones.[3]

Indeed, relatively few segments of the world's population fully enjoy the benefits of the earth's resources. The projections for future population changes suggest a number of issues social workers should be particularly prepared to address.

World Population Changes: Creating a Global Demand for Social Work in the Future

It is estimated that as of mid-2005, the world's population totaled nearly 6.5 billion people, which is almost double the population as recently as 1965.[4] It had taken all of human history until 1804 to reach 1 billion people, and the earth easily supported this population. Now, even with vastly increased agricultural productivity, it is recognized that the world's food supply cannot indefinitely support a growing population. Nor can the air support increasing pollution, or the oceans produce a sufficient supply of fish, or the rivers provide drinking water for the people and animals, and so on. As Figure 11.1 indicates, this growth and the ensuing demands on the earth and its people will continue through at least the next fifty years.

There is encouraging news in the fact that worldwide the fertility rates are decreasing. Where in 1970 the annual rate of population growth was 2 percent, that figure has now dropped to about 1.25 percent, and by 2050 it is expected to be down to less than one-half percent. Although the growth trend looks favorable, the sheer number of people being added places great demand on the earth and its people to accommodate the increased population. To place this growth in perspective, consider the following: the Census Bureau estimates that in one month in 2005 there were 10.8 million births, 4.7 million deaths, and an overall population increase of 6.2 million people (approximately the number of people living in the entire Boston metropolitan area).[5] Population experts predict that the earth's carrying capacity for people is in the 7.7 to 12 billion range.[6] Within a relatively few years (i.e., by 2023) we will reach the lower limit of this estimate, and the projection for 2050 is above 9.4 billion people, well toward the middle of the estimated capacity of the earth to support its population. Virtually every country in the world will be challenged to find the means to purify the air, manage the forests, secure an adequate supply of water, protect the land to sustain necessary food production, provide required energy resources (e.g., for heat, light, and transportation), and—of special interest to social workers—develop social structures to allow the people to achieve quality lives and live peacefully in an overcrowded world.

Figure 11.1

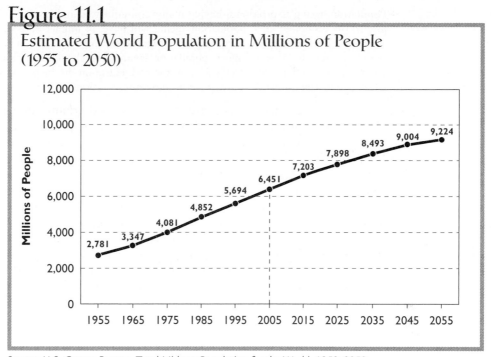

Estimated World Population in Millions of People
(1955 to 2050)

Source: U.S. Census Bureau. Total Midyear Population for the World: 1950–2050.
http://www.census.gov/ipc/www/worldpop.html

The problems associated with this growth are more than sheer increases in the number of people. The demographics, too, are shifting, which will require changes in many of our social institutions. Projections by the United Nations indicate that in the next one-half century the percentage of children will decline by 9.5 percent and the percentage of people age 60 and over will increase by 10.6 percent. Those in the "breadwinner" age group will remain about the same (around 60 percent of the population), supporting both the children and older people. What are the implications for these population changes? This aging of the population will have many social implications. For example, today only 10 percent of the older population is made up of those people who draw most heavily on health and human services, that is, individuals ages 80 and older. That percentage is expected to double by the year 2050 and will include approximately 400 million people worldwide. Also, as the population ages, a greater percentage of the survivors are female, who have a life expectancy much longer than that of males. At age 60, 55 percent of the population is female, at age 80 that portion increases to 65 percent, and by age 100 females make up 83 percent of the population.[7] Unique financial, social, and health issues will confront this growing number of older women.

The United Nations highlights three areas in which the changes in age structure will have an impact.[8]

> Population ageing is profound, having major consequences and implications for human life. In the economic area, population ageing will have an impact on economic growth, savings, investment and consumption, labour markets, pensions, taxation and intergenerational transfers. In the social sphere population ageing affects health and health care, family composition and living arrangements, housing and migration. In the political arena, population ageing can influence voting patterns and representation. (p. xxviii)

Similar patterns of change will occur related to increased urbanization and the issues associated with living in overcrowded conditions, the spread of communicable diseases, the protection of women and children from abuses, opportunities for employment and economic supports for those who cannot be employed, care for mentally disabled persons, and so on.

Such global population stresses call for world communication, collaboration, and planning to address impending problems. Social work has an important role to perform in helping the world address these and related issues, but action is sometimes hampered by the difficulty of speaking with a single professional voice. Hokenstad indicates that with increasing globalization, "social workers need to think about the equitable sharing of both its benefits and burdens so that the marginal sectors of society are not overlooked" and by advocating "on such matters as development, refugees, health care, human rights, discrimination, children's rights, and peacekeeping."[9]

Social Welfare Programs: A Varied Response to Human Need

Each country, according to its own resources and the extent of its human needs, has developed a unique mix of social welfare programs. The structures of those programs affect what services can be provided and, for social workers, the roles they will perform. No two countries have evolved identical human services, although they have borrowed ideas from each other.* Some approaches have proven more successful than others in preventing social problems such as poverty, providing health care and crime prevention, and so on, and thus the functions performed by social workers vary considerably.

Several social welfare philosophies characterize the different approaches to human services throughout the world. For example, in preindustrial or agriculture-based societies, social needs are met primarily by families, churches, the few wealthy persons in the society, and various guilds (e.g., agricultural trade groups and civic organizations). This type of society is typically found among developing countries in

---

* A particularly informative source when examining social work in several different countries is M. C. Hokenstad, S. K. Khinduka, and James Midgley, eds., *Profiles in International Social Work*. Washington, D.C.: NASW Press, 1992. London: Routledge, 1994. Included in this book are descriptions of social work in Chile, Great Britain, Hungary, India, Japan, Hong Kong, Singapore, South Korea, Taiwan, South Africa, Sweden, Uganda, and the United States.

Africa, Latin America, Asia, and elsewhere. In these societies, direct human services are most likely to be provided on a natural helping or volunteer basis, and social work practice tends to evolve as a macro social change profession. In these societies, social workers' efforts have been orientated toward *social development,* that is, social, economic, and political change to improve basic human conditions.

Another philosophy tends to emerge when industrialization begins to occur in a country. When this happens, individual and family mobility is required, urbanization increases, and people are viewed as commodities whose time and talent can be bought and sold. There is reliance on the market system to provide people with needed resources because the extended family may not be present or have the capacity to meet its members' social needs. Thus a set of social programs and persons to deliver these programs evolves. It is in these postindustrial societies that professional levels of social work are most likely to develop.

Epsing-Anderson has developed a typology of three distinct social welfare systems that have emerged in postindustrial societies. Epsing-Anderson's typology is based on the analysis of the degree to which the social welfare system (1) treats people as having a right to services, and not just as commodities used in the production of goods and services; (2) redistributes money and other resources to achieve greater equality and reduce poverty; and (3) maintains a balance between the government and private sectors having responsibility for the well-being of people.[10] Examination of how countries differ on these three points (i.e., comparative social welfare) yields the following distinct variations in postindustrial welfare approaches—or social welfare states.

First, the *corporatist welfare state* is designed to maintain existing social class differences and the distribution of resources by the system. Services are distributed primarily by private or corporate entities, and people are not viewed as having the right to services. This approach to social welfare is at the most conservative side of the continuum of approaches and attempts to maintain the status quo. Examples of countries where this approach is dominant include France, Italy, Spain, and Austria. In these countries, social workers' activities are primarily related to delivering social provisions and resolving marriage and family issues. Social work practice under this system is highly specialized, and most recognized social workers are required to hold a social work credential, usually with training at the vocational level.[11]

Second, the *liberal welfare state* is best represented by the United States, Canada, Great Britain, Australia, India, and Japan—although these countries differ in the degree to which each of the criteria for comparing welfare systems is embraced. These programs typically focus on redistributing income to the low-income population; are designed to reinforce the work ethic and view peoples' labor primarily as an economic commodity; maintain minimum standards of well-being through government programs, yet also subsidize the private for-profit and nonprofit welfare programs; tend to stigmatize people receiving services, thus maintaining social stratification; and only minimally treat people as having a right to services. In these countries social workers provide a range of services, from direct practice interventions to efforts to facilitate at least incremental change in social structures. Most professional social workers in these countries hold a professional social work credential at the undergraduate or graduate level.

Last, the *social democratic welfare state* provides universal services and contends that the peoples' work should not simply be treated as another commodity. Social programs in countries that have adopted this model (e.g., Norway, Sweden, the Netherlands) attempt to achieve maximum standards of human well-being through universal health insurance systems and are designed to socialize the costs of family living through governmental transfers such as children's allowances, sharing costs of caring for the aged and handicapped, and guaranteeing full employment to all who can work. In this type of welfare system, relatively few of the service providers hold a social work credential. Those who have credentials are prepared at the vocational or secondary levels, except when offering therapeutic services typically related to child behavior issues and parenting problems.[12]

In reality, no country exactly fits into any one of the welfare states in this typology and, indeed, social welfare systems are constantly changing. A country may move from one type to another, or closer to or more distant from any form of welfare state over time, yet understanding where this country stands at any one time is essential if there is to be a successful social technology transfer (e.g., adopting or adapting maternal leave programs or crisis intervention techniques).[13]

The Emergence of Social Work Training and Education

It is difficult to mark the beginning of a profession. In the United States, for example, the National Association of Social Workers designated 1998 as the centennial year for the profession, presumably because in 1898 the New York Charity Organization created a six-week training program known as the New York School of Philanthropy. If one holds social work up to all the criteria for professions proposed by Abraham Flexner and other experts on the sociology of professions (see Chapter 4), it is more likely that social work in the United States met the criteria to become a recognized profession somewhere around the late 1920s. Nevertheless, the initiation of education and training programs is usually documented and thus is used to signal the advent of professions. It is informative, therefore, to note a few of the dates when significant training or education in social work was introduced in a partial list of countries throughout the world as a means of marking when social work began in each.*

1898	United States	1924	South Africa
1899	The Netherlands	1931	Ireland
1903	England	1932	Spain
1908	Germany	1936	India and Egypt
1920	Belgium	1963	Uganda
1921	Sweden	1989	Hungry
1922	Chile	1992	Italy

---

* The literature is somewhat inconsistent regarding the starting dates of educational programs and, therefore, the dates included in this list should be viewed as approximate.

Social work also varies in different countries in the educational levels recognized as preparation for practice. In some countries it is *training,* with no particular academic preparation (not even a high school diploma required). In others, high school or specific community college vocational training is the requisite preparation, while in many countries college-level *professional education* is the requirement to enter social work. In a few countries a professional master's degree is the terminal practice degree. Nowhere is a doctoral degree the expected preparation for social work practice.

Barretta-Herman's analysis of social work education throughout the world suggests that the educational programs are relatively consistent in the content they offer.[14] More than two-thirds of the respondents to her survey from 35 different countries indicated that the schools required coursework in the following areas: personal communication, research, social and public policy, community intervention, ethnic or culturally focused content, organizational theory, and bio-psycho-social theory. In the social work practice areas, there was again considerable consensus in requiring content regarding work with groups, case work, work with communities, marital and family counseling, and work with social agencies. These data indicate there is relatively high consistency throughout the world regarding the fundamental content required for social work practice.

A Global Approach to Social Work

As recently as the late-1900s, a worldwide perspective on social work was accurately termed *international social work* and was concerned with comparing social work as it existed in the different countries and how the different social welfare conceptions shaped social work practice. As social work has matured it has become possible to address social work from a *global perspective,* that is, as one profession practicing in different countries. However, in some countries social work is almost entirely offered through government agencies; in others it is mostly in the private sector; and in yet others it is balanced between the two. Sometimes it is highly clinical and oriented toward change in the person, and in other countries it is mostly focused on changing the structure of the society and the human services delivery system.

Is there a common set of knowledge, values, and/or competencies to unite this set of activities into a single worldwide profession? In 2005, Weiss[15] published the results of a study in which she surveyed 781 BSW-level student social workers from 10 countries reflecting all three social welfare conceptions defined by Epsing-Anderson (above) and located in North and South America, Europe, Africa, Australia, and the Middle-East. The results of this study pinpoint (statistically significant at the < .001 level) three fundamental perspectives that serve as the theoretical and value center of social work:

> The major finding of this study is the substantial similarity in the students' perceptions of the source of poverty, the way to deal with poverty, and the goals of the profession. . . . The similarities in students' views are indicative of a common understanding of poverty as rooted in social or structural, rather than individual, causes and as requiring state

intervention for its alleviation. The similarities also reflect the dual commitment of the profession to social justice, understood as the need for the redistribution of resources for the benefit of those who have been deprived, and to (enhancing) individual well-being. (p. 108)

In a world in which people and countries are highly interdependent, the existence of a global social work profession is a step toward addressing the major issues that shape the world. To facilitate the development of and advocacy for positions to address these global issues, to encourage sharing of relevant knowledge and skills for social work practice, and to educate social workers who can strengthen the human services throughout the world, several important steps have been taken.

International Professional Organizations

Two international organizations provide the basic leadership for the globalization of social work. One, the International Federation of Social Workers (IFSW), is structured to work through various national professional membership organizations such as the National Association of Social Workers and the professional trade unions of social workers that exist in some countries. Begun in 1928 following the International Conference on Social Work held in Paris, today organizations from approximately 80 countries, representing 470,000 social workers, participate in the IFSW. The activities of IFSW include publication of a newsletter, maintaining a commission that advocates for the protection of human rights throughout the world, the development of a statement of ethical guidelines for social workers, and maintenance of updated policy positions on twelve global social welfare issues.[16]

The second important international social work organization is the International Association of Schools of Social Work (IASSW), which was also formed in 1928. This organization now includes more than 400 member social work education associations (e.g., Council on Social Work Education) and individual schools from 90 countries. The IASSW is concerned with facilitating the inclusion of international content into social work education programs, providing consultation to the United Nations and the United Nations Children's Fund, and facilitating the transfer of academic credit among schools from different countries. With the IFSW, it publishes the journal *International Social Work*.[17]

Defining Social Work Globally

Arriving at a generally accepted definition to describe social work in the United States proved difficult (see Chapter 3). Finding a definition that embraced the common features of social work throughout the world was even more challenging. However, in 2000 the IFSW adopted a definition of social work that encompassed the many expressions of this profession throughout the world. This definition was a major accomplishment that makes it possible for social work to act as a single profession in addressing global issues, to allow workers to gain employment in other countries, and to create educational programs that transfer from country to country. The strong social justice and humanitarian emphasis of social work is evident in the IFSW definition.[18]

The social work profession promotes social change, problem solving in human relation-ships and the empowerment and liberation of people to enhance well-being. Utilising theories of human behaviour and social systems, social work intervenes at the points where people interact with their environments. Principles of human rights and social justice are fundamental to social work.

Although this definition is similar to the NASW definition that characterizes social work in the United States, the strong orientation toward changing the social structures that affect people, as opposed to the U.S. emphasis on individual change, is evident.

Values and Ethics Held by Social Workers Globally

The underlying beliefs about the inherent value of people and the responsibility of societies to create conditions in which people can thrive are perhaps the glue that binds social workers together. These basic principles transcend the particular cultures and social welfare systems in various parts of the world and are the most universal expressions of the common beliefs that characterize social work globally.

The International Federation of Social Workers has devoted considerable effort to developing an international code of ethics and, at its conference in Adelaide, Australia, in 2004, adopted a revised code of ethical principles. Underpinning the statement of principles is recognition that "Ethical awareness is a necessary part of the professional practice of social workers. Their ability and commitment to act ethically is an essential aspect of the quality of the services offered to those who use social work services."[19] This code then addresses three sets of basic principles that characterize social work practice throughout the world:

▶ *Human Rights and Human Dignity.* Social work is based on respect for the inherent worth and dignity of all people and the rights that follow from this. Social workers should uphold and defend each person's physical, psychological, emotional, and spiritual integrity and well-being, e.g., including respecting the right to self-determination, promoting the right to participation, treating each person as a whole, and identifying and developing client strengths.

▶ *Social Justice.* Social workers have a responsibility to promote social justice, in relation to society generally, and in relation to the people with whom they work, e.g., challenging negative discrimination, recognizing diversity, distributing resources equitably, challenging unjust policies and practices, and working in solidarity with others to break down barriers to an inclusive society.

▶ *Professional Conduct.* Social workers should act in accordance with the ethical code or guidelines current in their country that will provide more nationally relevant guidance to ethical practice. However, several universal guides to conduct are suggested including, for example, maintaining practice competence, acting with integrity and maintaining appropriate boundaries, giving priority to the interests of clients over personal interests, maintain confidentiality, and so on.

Global Views of Social Issues

One direct result of the similar values held by social workers is that agreement has been reached regarding understanding and developing approaches to resolving social problems that are experienced throughout the world. Social workers can make comparative analyses of issues and adopt or adapt solutions that have been successful in other countries.

Social workers and organizations of social workers are concerned with such worldwide issues as achieving and preserving peace, distributing human and economic resources more equitably, protecting the rights and preventing the exploitation of children and youth, enhancing women's status and safety, facilitating international adoptions, and so on. Evidence of these concerns is found in the issues addressed in the IFSW policy statements that have been adopted to date.*

▶ Health
▶ Human Rights
▶ Older Persons
▶ Refugees
▶ Women
▶ Peace and Social Justice
▶ Globalization and the Environment

▶ HIV-AIDS
▶ Migration
▶ The Protection of Personal Information
▶ Conditions in Rural Communities
▶ Youth
▶ Displaced Persons
▶ Indigenous People

The value of these position papers is not only to identify topics for which social workers are in general agreement, but also to provide a more influential voice to international organizations such as the United Nations (UN). In that venue, social workers have been actively involved with a number of UN-related agencies including the United Nations Children's Fund (UNICEF), the UN Development Program, the Department of Policy Coordination and Sustainable Development, the UN High Commission for Refugees, and the World Health Organization.

Social Workers Act Globally: The Tsunami Disaster

The real payoff from social work's international linkages is the ability to apply social work knowledge and skills when events occur that affect whole regions of the world. A case in point was the December 26, 2004, tsunami waves generated from an earthquake in the Indian Ocean that devastated coastal areas of South Asia and East Africa. There were confirmed deaths of nearly 300,000 people.[20]

In response to the 2004 tsunami, a number of social workers from various countries were sent to the damaged area to provide crisis recovery services. Established relationships with the American Red Cross, CARE (Cooperative for Assistance and

---

* All position papers are available from the International Federation of Social Workers Secretariat, Postfach 6875, Schwarztorstrasse 20, CH-3000 Berne, Switzerland, in English, French, and Spanish. They are also available at the IFSW website http://www.ifsw.org.

Relief Everywhere), and other international organizations provided an organized way to reach social workers who were soon on-sight to help people find food, clothing, and temporary housing; gain access to emergency health care; and address mental health issues resulting from the trauma through therapeutic approaches. A class of MSW students from the University of Maryland's School of Social Work was heading for India at the time of the tsunami as part of an international exchange with Rajagiri College. Dean Jesse Harris, who was accompanying the students, provided consultation to local social workers in India regarding assistance to disaster victims, and the students helped tsunami victims through such activities as distributing water-purification tablets, assisting them in securing other needed supplies, and raising money from friends and family to assist in ongoing disaster relief efforts.[21]

The International Association of Schools of Social Work quickly created a program, the "Rebuilding Peoples' Lives Network," to help connect schools of social work in nonaffected areas of the world with those in regions experiencing the tsunami. Through this program, social workers throughout the world learned of the needs of people linked through the network and were able to provide needed physical and emotional resources, create a communication channel for consultation and other assistance, and assist in accessing resources through national and international relief organizations.[22] To capture the lessons learned from this experience, a special edition of the journal *International Social Work* has been planned. Articles in this edition of the journal will help improve crisis recovery efforts in the future by developing an effective means for providing disaster relief to the people in need and by suggesting ways that social work education programs might build some of disaster response content into their curricula.

When responding to a disaster, either manmade or natural, social workers can assist through *crisis recovery work*, i.e., actions to help people recover from the crisis; actions to assist in rebuilding people's lives, i.e., *disaster relief*; and *disaster preparedness and prevention*, i.e., responding to what is learned from the experience to establish policies and practices that will prevent a similar occurrence in the future or, if that is not possible, to improve the ability to respond to the disaster.

Employment in International Social Work

Four forms of international practice are possible for a social worker. One form is to secure a position in an international organization that advances human services on a worldwide basis. The UN serves as the primary agency to coordinate the efforts of the various countries to overcome oppression, facilitate the delivery of health and welfare services that cross international boundaries, and promote social justice. Social work with UN-related agencies such as UNICEF, the Economic and Social Council, the World Health Organization, and the UN High Commission on Refugees are examples of such positions.

Second, the U.S. government, too, has positions concerned with international social welfare issues. The Department of Health and Human Services maintains an international affairs staff to give attention to worldwide human services issues, and its Office of Refugee Settlement is actively involved in promoting the safety, welfare, and rights of refugees. The International Development Cooperation Agency (USAID) administers foreign aid programs in approximately 100 countries throughout the world, and the Peace Corps has provided developing countries with the human and technical resources to improve their physical infrastructure (e.g., water, sanitation, roads), health care, and human services.

Third, perhaps the most common form of international employment for social workers is to find a social work job in a government or voluntary agency in another country. These roles typically include service provision, consultation, and teaching or training activities. Particularly for countries that are in the process of developing services to individuals and families, the skills possessed by most U.S. social workers are highly valued. The reverse is true, too, for social workers from developing countries, who often have a strong social development background and bring a helpful expertise not typically found among U.S.-educated social workers.

Last, some international social work positions exist in multinational corporations or the U.S. military, which locate personnel in foreign countries. When families are relocated (or left behind), there are inevitable social adjustments to be made. As in other social work practice in business and industry, social workers provide direct services to help individuals and families to deal with their social problems, assist the company in sharpening its cultural sensitivity, and represent the company as a participant in the local community, making contributions to and interfacing with the human services delivery system.

How does one become prepared for international social work? Certainly, the demands on workers differ depending on the nature of a country's social welfare system and/or the type of position that the social worker holds. Specific preparation, then, cannot be identified that is essential for all positions. However, a few fundamental areas of preparation are somewhat universal.

First, become informed and stay current regarding international affairs, particularly issues of social and economic justice, human rights, and peace. Careful reading of both the social work literature on international issues and the general news sources is essential.

Second, develop competence in the use of one or more foreign languages. Although English is used for general communication in most parts of the world, it is respectful to others to attempt to speak to clients in their language (however faltering) and, particularly if providing direct services, much subtle meaning in communication is lost if one does not know the language.

Third, it is also essential to develop knowledge of the host county's culture. This is prerequisite to helping to avoid the tendency to believe that one's own culture is superior and, therefore, to force his or her way of doing things into the other culture. The concept of "the ugly American" reflects the reputation persons from the United States have developed by reflecting such cultural insensitivity. Just as in other forms of insensitivity (e.g., racism, sexism, ageism), the study of the other's culture and experience is a first step in increasing awareness and avoiding inadvertent acts of insensitivity.

Finally, the unique contribution that a professional social worker brings is his or her professional knowledge and skill. Experience in practicing social work after completing one's professional education is prerequisite for most international social work positions.

Although all the above competencies are necessary for successful international social work practice, one research project identified the basic social work principles of "individualizing the client," "maximizing client empowerment," "maximizing client participation," and "maximizing client self-determination"[23] as the factors most associated with successful Peace Corps and USAID projects. Ghavam's study of 74 projects throughout the world, found that "the greater the villagers' role and participation in start-up, assessment, and design phases of the projects resulted in more overall success of the development projects." This study also found that the project director's technical preparation for the position, experience in international work, and adequacy in the culture and language of the area were also associated with the overall success of the projects.[24] In short, good social work practice, plus orientation to the language and culture of the specific country, corresponds with successful international practice. The competent social worker already has a good start for international practice.

Concluding Comment

As technology advances, the world shrinks. The presence of a worldwide economy makes countries increasingly interdependent. The ability of the media to immediately transmit information around the globe creates an unprecedented awareness of events as they occur in even remote areas of the world. And the availability of the World Wide Web and e-mail allows human services agencies and human services providers to exchange information through a virtually cost-free and instantaneous process. Although some parts of the world have not yet fully experienced the Technological Revolution, in many ways international boundaries have become less significant.

Parallel to the diminishing isolation of individual countries, social work, too, is beginning to blur national distinctions and think of itself as a global profession. Writing for the *NASW News,* Sheryl Fred suggests that global social work might accurately be considered an emerging field of practice:

> Counseling victims of the tsunami disaster. Helping immigrants and refugees in the United States receive the services they need. Empowering tribal communities in India to fight for their land rights. All of these are direct practice examples of the international field of practice in social work, a career path that has long been in practice but is only recently gaining attention from the social work profession as a whole.[25]

A challenge for the next generation of social workers will be to evolve a concept of social work that will bridge the differing philosophies of society's role in meeting human needs and yet maintain the social worker's unique mission as the profession that addresses individual and family needs and, simultaneously, is concerned with changing the society to reduce or eliminate factors that contribute to people's problems in social functioning.

KEY WORDS AND CONCEPTS

Crisis recovery
International social work definition
International Declaration of Ethical
   Principles for Social Work
Corporatist welfare state
Liberal welfare state
Global social work

International Federation of Social
   Workers
Social democratic welfare state
International Association of Schools of
   Social Work
Disaster preparedness and prevention
Disaster relief

SUGGESTED INFORMATION RESOURCES

Brinkerhoff, Derick W., and Brinkerhoff, Jennifer M. *Working for Change: Making a Career in International Public Service.* Bloomfield, CT: Kumarian Press, 2005.

International Federation of Social Workers. http://www.ifsw.org

Robb, Matthew. "International Social Work: Go Global!" *Social Work Today* (January/February) 2005, pp. 15–18.

Rosenfeld, Lawrence B., Caye, Joanne S., Ayalon, Ofra, and Lahad, Mooli. *When Their World Falls Apart: Helping Families and Children Manage the Effects of Disasters.* Washington, D.C.: NASW Press, 2005.

Ramanathanm, Chathapuram S., and Link, Rosemary J. *Principles and Resources for Social Work Practice in a Global Era.* Belmont, CA: Brooks/Cole-Wadsworth, 1999.

ENDNOTES

1. United Nations, *Global Economic Outlook 3: Past, Present and Future Prospects* (New York: United Nations Environment Programme, 2002). http://www.unepo.org
2. Ibid.
3. Ibid.
4. U.S. Census Bureau. Total Midyear Population for the World: 1950–2050. http://www.census.gov/ipc/www/worldpop.html
5. U.S. Census Bureau. World Vital Events Per Time Unit 2005. http://www.census.gov/cgi-bin/ipc/pcue
6. Geoffrey Gilbert, *World Population: A Handbook* (Santa Barbara, CA: ABC-CLIO Press, 2001), pp. 16–17.
7. United Nations, *World Population Ageing 1950–2050* (New York: United Nations Population Division, 2001).
8. Ibid.
9. M. C. Hokenstad, cited in Peter Slavin, "Profession Has a Global Role," *NASW News* 47 (March 2002): 1–2.
10. Gøsta Epsing-Anderson, *The Three Worlds of Welfare Capitalism* (Princeton, NJ: Princeton University Press, 1990), pp. 21–29.
11. Matthew Colton, Ferran Casas, Mark Drakeford, Susan Roberts, Evert Scholte, and Margaret Williams, *Stigma and Social Welfare: An International Comparative Study* (Brookfield, VT: Ashgate, 1997), pp. 138–140.
12. Ibid.

13. Norma Berkowitz, Lowell Jenkins, and Eileen Kelly, "Reaching Beyond Your Borders: Social Technology Transfers." In Ka-Ching Yeung, chief editor, *Proceedings: Joint World Congress of the International Federation of Social Workers and International Association of Schools of Social Work, 1996*, p. 176 (publisher not identified, 1998).

14. Angeline Barretta-Herman, "A Re-Analysis of the IASSW World Census 2000." Unpublished manuscript. St. Paul, MN: University of St. Thomas, 2002, pp. 16 and 18.

15. Idit Weiss, "Is There a Global Common Core to Social Work?" *Social Work* 50 (April, 2005): 101–110.

16. International Federation of Social Workers, "General Information." http://www.ifsw.org

17. International Association of Schools of Social Work, "Welcome." http://www.iassw.soton.ac.uk

18. International Federation of Social Workers, "Definition of Social Work." http://www.ifsw.org

19. International Federation of Social Workers, "Ethics in Social Work, Statement of Principles." http://www.ifsw.org

20. Tsunamis.Com. http://www.tsunamis.com/tsunamis-death.html

21. Sheryl Fred. "Members React to Tsunami Disaster." *NASW News* 50 (March 2005), p. 10, and personal conversation with Dr. Jesse Harris, 7/14/05.

22. Lena Dominelli. "Social Work's Response to the Tsunami Disaster." *Social Work Education Reporter* 53 (Spring/Summer 2005), pp. 15 and 17.

23. Bradford W. Sheafor and Charles R. Horejsi, *Techniques and Guidelines for Social Work Practice*, 7th Edition. Boston: Allyn and Bacon, 2006, pp. 68–81.

24. Hamid Reza Ghavam, "Characteristics of External Activators in Third World Village Development." Unpublished Doctoral Dissertation, Colorado State University, Fort Collins, CO, pp. 148–149.

25. Sheryl Fred. "Building an International Field of Practice." *NASW News* 50 (April 2005), p. 4.

12

The Challenges for Social Workers in Rural America

Prefatory Comment

One of the many faces of social work can be found in rural America. It is estimated that 56.4 million people, or 24.7 percent of the U.S. population, live in a rural area. This one-fourth of the people live on four-fifths of the land and expect to enjoy such quality of life factors as open space, relatively uncrowded conditions and, typically, a sense of community not found in more populated areas. However, the reality in rural America is that the incidence of social problems is high, human services providers are scarce, and the quality of community interaction has diminished.

Indeed, rural life is changing. Products of the land that once tied people to rural life are less central to rural economies: crop lands have been consumed by urban sprawl; mineral deposits have been depleted; excessive timber cutting has decimated forests; and most family farms have given way to corporate agriculture. In addition, the isolation once experienced in rural America has been modified by modern technology; for example, cell phones provide relatively inexpensive access to people throughout the United States; satellite dishes offer entertainment and instant information about world events; and the growing availability of high-speed internet connections allows many people to work from their homes (a trend known as *telecommerce*), making it possible for urban dwellers to move to rural communities. For social workers employed in rural areas, practice must be adapted to meet the changing needs of rural communities and to serve this different mix of people and interests.

The *context* in which social work practice is conducted can have a substantial influence on what a social worker does—or is able to do. Indeed, the environment part of the person/environment equation that defines social work is different in different regions of the country, and even within more or less populated areas in the same region. The people, too, vary from region to region as culture and values are far from uniform across the United States. These differences shape the practice of social work in any location, but particularly in rural areas.

In the past, rural people were bound together through their dependence on the land for their livelihood; their involvement with the local school, church, and community events for social interaction; and even their faith in local health and community service providers when in need. Once thought to be the last bastion of the good life, the romanticized perception of rural life is no longer valid. Young people don't find sufficient excitement in rural town activities; a large number of adults spend many hours commuting to and from city jobs; and the residents experience social problems just as severely, and sometimes more severely, as their urban counterparts. Even school violence, once thought to be an urban phenomenon, reached rural America in March 2005 when a teacher and six schoolchildren were gunned down in tiny Red Lake, Minnesota.

Like the rest of the United States, rural areas are becoming increasingly diverse and multidimensional. Addressing these changes and solving the resulting problems is especially difficult because as rural economic conditions deteriorate, the tax base diminishes and the relatively small population is unable to find the resources to create needed programs. In addition, the limited population simply cannot support the highly specialized services from physicians, social workers, and other professionals that are taken for granted in today's urban society. It is within the context of these changing conditions that rural social workers provide their services.

Characteristics of Rural Areas

What, then, are the unique characteristics of rural areas? The ingredients of most definitions of a rural area include a relatively small population that is located at a distance from a population center, and a culture that typically differs from urban life. In the 2000 Census, the U.S. Census Bureau captured the population and distance ingredients with a complex formula based primarily on population density. The Census Bureau defines an *urban center* as an area with more than 1,000 persons per square mile and an *urban cluster* as an area with a density of at least 500 persons per square mile that is located near an urban center. By default, all areas external to these urban areas and clusters are considered rural or nonmetropolitan areas.[1] Of course, there are varying degrees of ruralness. Clearly, the person who must commute 30 minutes to reach an urban center has very different access to the resources available in that center than someone two hours away. The rural/urban boundaries have been further blurred because as the number of jobs has declined in rural areas, it has become necessary for rural residents to commute to urban centers for employment. The same boundary diffusion exists in reverse for people who have lived and worked in a metropolitan area, but have moved to rural areas due to the freedom of location created by technological advances and their desire for the quality of life thought to exist in less populated areas. Are people rural because of where they live or where they work?

In addition to population and space, we can further refine our understanding of rural life by understanding the people. A study commissioned by the W.K. Kellogg Foundation in 2002 identified the following traits that tend to be highly valued by people live in rural communities: 1) self-reliance and a strong work ethic, 2) a fairly conservative approach to money and to taking care of the land, 3) a highly religious faith, and 4) a reliance on teamwork to get things done.[2] A study by Waltman further documented that *rural* connotes "a way of and an outlook on life characterized by a closeness to nature, slower pace of living, and a somewhat conservative lifestyle that values tradition, independence and self-reliance, and privacy."[3] Thus, it would be a mistake for a social worker to assume that he or she could simply transfer the skills acquired in an urban or suburban setting to practice in a rural area. Social work practice must be adapted to this different environment.

Historically, rural people have been exceptionally family oriented because the demands of farm life required that all family members help with preparing and tilling the land, planting and harvesting the crops, and maintaining the equipment and farm. Today, the reality of rural life is that the advancement of corporate agriculture has forced millions of farm families to abandon agriculture and commute to cities and towns for employment. Unfortunately, the manual labor of farm work has not been a good background for changing to the "high tech" jobs in the urban areas. Some differences between rural people and the residents of suburban and urban areas are reflected in Table 12.1. Rural people tend to be older, less frequently of minority background, have less income, experience more unemployment, and are more likely to live in poverty conditions. In relation to other social problems, rural residents now show patterns similar to urban residents in the incidence of single-parent families, dual-employment families, substance abuse, higher divorce rates, family violence, and adolescent pregnancies.

Despite the increasing similarities with urban America, rural economies continue to be intertwined with the land. A too-wet or too-dry planting or harvest

Table 12.1

Comparative Characteristics of Rural and Urban Dwellers

Characteristic	Rural	Urban
Total population (2001, millions)	56.4	228.4
Median age (2000, years)	38.0	34.0
Population age 60 and older (percent)	19.7	14.8
Minority population (2000, percent)	17.0	24.9
Median household income (2000, dollars)	$32,837	$44,984
Per capita income (2000, dollars)	$17,510	$23,470
Unemployment rate (2001, percent)	4.9%	4.7%
Poverty rate (2000, percent)	13.4%	10.8%
Food insecure household (2000, percent)	11.5%	10.2%

* Sources: Economic Research Service, "Rural America at a Glance," Washington, D.C.: U.S. Department of Agriculture, September 2002. http://www.ers.usda.gov/publications/rdrr94–1/rdrr94–1.pdf; and Economic Research Service, "Rural Population and Migration: Rural Elderly," Washington, D.C.: U.S. Department of Agriculture, June 2002. http://www.ers.usda.gov/briefing/Population/elderly.

season, an early frost, a hailstorm, a forest fire, the presence of pollutants in a river or lake, and a mineshaft cave-in are all examples of events that happen without warning, and that, in the short-term, can dramatically affect a rural economy. More long-term trends, too, are affecting rural America. Changing employment patterns in agriculture and the extractive occupations (e.g., timber, mining), as well as the continuous encroachment of urban boundaries into rural lands, has changed a once stable way of life into one that must adapt to unanticipated conditions. Rural life inevitably involves a certain amount of economic risk that the individual cannot control, and there is limited ability to support community-based human services to assist people experiencing the fallout from economic difficulties. It is for this reason that rural services are most frequently supported by government programs, since a broader funding base can provide stability that a local area cannot.

Small towns have traditionally served, and continue to serve, as the center of rural life. Community activities tend to center around schools (especially school sports), churches, retail stores, post offices, and outlets where necessary equipment or products grown in the area are brought and sold (such as, the local co-op grain elevator or farm implement store). All rural communities, however, are not alike. In fact, there are four distinct types of rural communities; 1) the farm/ranch trade center, 2) the mining/energy/timber company town, 3) the tourist center, and 4) the bedroom community for a metropolitan area. Each type of community faces unique problems, but all are undergoing rapid transition and experience difficulties in adapting to this change.

 ## Social Welfare in Rural Areas

A primary task for the social worker in a rural area is to help the community and its residents address the social issues that result in part from this changing environment. A particular difficulty is that human services have typically been designed in an urban mode, where it is assumed that people will seek help when it is needed, can do so without excessive transportation problems, and, further, can readily have access to human services professionals with highly specialized skills to provide assistance.

In rural areas, there are obstacles to the inhabitants receiving the types of professional services developed in the urban mode. A study by Martinez-Brawley and Blundall identified the following reasons that farm families are reluctant to use human services: concerns about families' reputations in the community; lack of understanding about what services do and how they work; family tradition of not asking for help from social agencies; feeling that one must bear one's problems; fear of being perceived as lazy or incapable of taking care of oneself; feeling that no one has useful answers to life's problems; fear of social workers; and pride.[4] When people do ask for services or are required by courts, schools, or others to receive help, the potential clients often find a limited battery of services available and few, if any, qualified professionals to provide services. Also, because of the cost of transportation, as well as the time it takes to reach social agencies, persons in genuine need of services often elect not to ask for help. Thus health and social problems go unattended—or family and friends are left to address the problems as best they can.

Unfortunately, serious social problems that go unattended usually don't get better. Therefore it is especially important that social workers are versatile in their practice with clients and are prepared to create innovative and, sometimes, unconventional approaches to providing services. At the same time, these social workers must devote considerable attention to working with the community to develop prevention programs (see Chapter 10) and to build linkages among the few existing services to maximize their effectiveness.

Characteristics of Social Work Practice in Rural Areas

Although social work practice in rural areas may not require substantially different competencies than those typically required for most social workers (see Chapter 9), the mix of activities is surely different. Often the rural social worker is one of a very few professionals in a community, and this requires the worker to possess wide-ranging knowledge to improve conditions for both individuals and communities. The "all-purpose" rural social worker must be innovative, resourceful, self-motivating, and able to function with minimal supervision.

Employing agencies must recognize that rural practice requires more than just transporting urban social workers and urban-oriented approaches to service delivery to rural areas. Social workers in rural areas must be prepared to provide counseling to individuals and families; to build support networks and engage natural helpers in providing services; to work with local and county officials or other community leaders to create needed services; to be a spokesperson for the most vulnerable people in the community; and, increasingly, to be able to provide services at a distance through telecommunication vehicles.

The Social Policy Statement on "Rural Social Work" adopted by the National Association of Social Workers in 2002 highlights the general nature of social work practice in rural areas:

> Social work practice in rural communities challenges the social worker to embrace and effectively use an impressive range of professional interventions and community skills. It is critical that the social worker have practice experience in multiple areas . . . including clinical and health practice, community organization, administration and management, public welfare, and community-based services. . . . The skills of professional social workers are uniquely suited to helping rural people organize their lives, families, communities, and organizations to overcome adversity, identify and develop resources, and change lives for the better.[5]

The most relevant practice approach for most rural social work is labeled *generalist*. This approach prepares the social worker by giving him or her a broad range of knowledge and skills to assess a particular situation, recognizing that it may be necessary to intervene at several levels (e.g., individual, family, community); to select from a number of possible ways of helping the client(s) address their issues;

and to actually intervene in people's lives to help them achieve their goals. Four elements characterize generalist practice:

1. A multidimensional orientation that emphasizes the interrelatedness of human problems, people's life situations, and specific social conditions;
2. An eclectic approach to assessment and intervention, i.e., one that draws from many different practice frameworks and considers several possible actions that might be effective in this practice situation;
3. The selection of intervention strategies and social work practice roles based on the unique client situation and the usefulness of involving various client and community systems in the process; and
4. A knowledge, value, and skill base that is versatile enough to support alternative approaches when addressing the unique client, problem, goal, or situation.[6]

To achieve the breadth required in the generalist approach, the social worker must sacrifice a certain amount of depth in working with clients. It would be rare to find a highly focused clinician or a specialized social policy analyst in rural social work practice because the population base simply doesn't yield enough demand to support practice that uses only a narrow repertoire of interventions, no matter how competent the provider may be.

Generalist practice is not unique to rural areas. In fact, it is the most universal practice approach used in social work. The *1995 Encyclopedia of Social Work* begins the section on generalist practice with the statement, " . . . social work is inherently generalist."[7] Further, the Council on Social Work Education's curriculum policy statement and accreditation standards require the generalist practice orientation in all undergraduate social work programs and for the foundation or initial part of master's programs. The good news for rural human services agencies is that if they hire a professional social worker, he or she will have the basic knowledge and skill required for generalist practice.

A Glimpse of Rural Social Work Practice

In practice, the rural social worker translates the concept of generalist social work into action. Usually practice starts at the individual level, takes into consideration the client's family and cultural background, and often ends with an effort to affect community change to address large-scale issues that become evident in the case situation. The case of Mary offers some insight into a rural social worker's practice activities.

Mary, a 20 year-old, unmarried college student, grew up in a coalfield county in central Appalachia. She became pregnant and was referred to a social worker who staffs the county human services department's satellite office. Mary was referred by the college's health center, where the pregnancy was confirmed. Mary was very reluctant to make contact with the county department, as she didn't want to be seen going into the offices, even to ask for help addressing her issue. She thought seriously about suicide as a way out of this trouble before finally deciding to contact the social worker.

In the initial interview the social worker learned that as a first-generation college student, Mary fears she will let her family down if she doesn't complete a college degree. She sobbed, "They have made sacrifices in order for me to attend college and I can't disappoint them now." When exploring the availability of resources, the social worker learned that for generations the family has lived in poverty and that Mary's mother has no marketable employment skills, her father is disabled because he contracted black lung disease from his years in the coal mines, and her youngest sister has a chronic health problem that constantly drains the family's financial resources. When the social worker inquired if Mary wanted information about obtaining an abortion in the nearest large community, Mary flatly refused, indicating that the family belongs to a fundamentalist church and an abortion would be unthinkable. She would have to live with her mistake.

The social worker considered several practice activities that would be important when working with Mary. First, she would need to give Mary ongoing support as Mary deals with the family's disappointment and the expected negative reaction from church and community members. Second, she would need to assist Mary in deciding if she would keep the baby or place him/her for adoption. If Mary decides to keep the baby, will this become another burden for a family already stretched beyond its financial and emotional capacity? Or will Mary attempt to strike out on her own and live independently? What role might the baby's father play in the future? If she decides to place the baby for adoption, Mary will need help in placing the child and will need emotional support through that process. Third, to improve Mary's chances of delivering a healthy child, it will be necessary for her to begin receiving prenatal care from a physician, who will need to determine if Mary's lifestyle (a nutritious diet, no tobacco, no alcohol or other substances) is compatible with the child's healthy development. This will require not only Mary's commitment and discipline, but will also require supplemental financial resources.

One of the social worker's first actions was to arrange for Mary to have an appointment every other Wednesday morning, when the mobile clinic from the county health department was in town. Mary was told that the clinic opened at 8 A.M. and she could appear when it was convenient with her schedule. Mary indicated that she had a 9:00 A.M. class and would plan to be there at 8:00 A.M. sharp so that she would not jeopardize her success in college. "After all, my family would be even more disappointed in me if I don't succeed in college," she told the social worker.

The social worker was doing her job. She helped Mary assess her situation; clarified choices Mary needed to make; offered her support in dealing with anticipated responses from her family, church, and community; and referred her to other services she would need to access as the pregnancy proceeded. The social worker also agreed to meet with Mary and her family, as well as Mary and the baby's father, to talk through the situation and the implications of various decisions they might make—giving Mary added strength to move forward with her planning. In addition to this practice activity, a problem arose that required the social worker to attempt to bring about change in the procedures of another human services agency.

> During one of her interviews with the social worker, Mary volunteered that she was on the brink of failing one of her courses. It was the 9:00 A.M. class on Wednesdays that she kept missing because the appointment at the health department was never completed on time. Mary reported that two other girls going to the clinic had the same problem and one even lost her job because she was always late to work. Upon further investigation, the social worker learned that the mobile van usually rolled into town 10–15 minutes late and by the time the staff got organized for the day and finished their coffee, it was after 8:30 before they saw any patients. Mary and the social worker then went to the clinic and asked the staff to adjust their practices so that they could begin providing the services when the clinic was scheduled to open. Although the staff promised to correct this problem, nothing changed, and by the end of the semester Mary failed her 9:00 A.M. class. A trip to the clinic's central office, facilitated by the social worker, made it possible for the worker, Mary, and the other two girls having the scheduling problem with the clinic to strongly advocate to the county health director for action to correct this problem.

The social worker is not in this business to be popular. When the effort to work directly with the clinic staff failed to fix the problem, this generalist social worker elevated the issues to the next higher level of authority and thus was able to at least prevent this problem from affecting future patients of the clinic. In this case, the interests of her client took precedence over the risk of angering the clinic staff.

Special Considerations in Rural Practice Today

In the various contexts in which social workers are employed, the practice requires adaptations to changing factors in that environment. In rural areas, social workers face several especially perplexing problems.

Access to Well-Prepared Professionals

Having convenient access to services has long been a problem for rural residents. The sparse population, distance from population centers, and conservative values that discourage seeking assistance all work against rural residents receiving needed services from social workers or other helping professionals. At the same time, highly educated professionals such as doctors, dentists, nurses, and social workers often prefer to live in urban areas where specialized resources to support their practice are available, schools for their children's education are more adequate, and cultural enrichment opportunities are more plentiful.

In the health care field, for example, diagnostic and treatment equipment has become so expensive and personnel so highly specialized that a large population is required to justify the cost of the services. In the various settings in which individual and family counseling services are provided, the equipment is not expensive, but there is an increasing expectation that clients will have access to personnel equipped with expertise to perform an ever increasing range of specialized interventions (e.g., from psychotherapy to strategic family therapy to social planning) without traveling a great distance. When few alternatives exist, the pressure to provide services for which one is not adequately prepared is too often a temptation experienced by the rural social worker.

Transportation

Even with improved roads and highways, easy physical access to specialized services is not an option for most rural residents. For people living in rural areas, having access to an automobile is virtually a necessity as public transportation is almost nonexistent. People must usually travel some distance for jobs, daycare, to attend church or other community events, or to purchase groceries and other necessities. Low-income people living in rural areas experience the problem of automobiles being expensive to purchase and maintain, and the cost of fuel for commuting a distance to receive health or human services places an excessive burden on them. Many choose to not seek help until the problems reach crisis proportions and are more difficult to resolve.

The fact that service delivery is often based on the urban model, where clients are expected to go to an agency for services, is efficient for the professionals but costly in time and travel expense for the clients. Human services agencies too often ignore the transportation problem, but they do have some options. Some agencies are returning to the use of visits to clients' homes as the primary location of services, thus placing the travel costs and expenditure of time in travel on the agencies and workers. Other agencies are using "circuit-riding" workers who visit a distant community periodically, utilizing space in churches, schools, or county extension offices to meet with clients. Increasingly, rural social workers are looking to the use of technological advances to facilitate their work with clients who otherwise would have limited access to their services.

Technology

It is not uncommon for specialized medical personnel to have direct links to rural hospitals and general practitioners in rural communities where they provide telephone or televised consultation regarding medical procedures. For social workers, there is considerable debate over how much social work practice can be conducted at a distance from the client. Some of the questions to be addressed are the following: How much is lost when counseling with a client by telephone rather than in person, or with the use of webcams or similar inexpensive interactive home video equipment, or even through e-mail or client chatrooms? Might clients be connected into support groups around specific issues or problems? If electronic communication tools are used, what are the risks of confidential information being obtained by other parties? Would clients experience a greater sense of impersonality? Would these losses, if there are losses from use of electronic technology, be greater than the client receiving no services at all? Not only must social work address these issues, but there is an increasing need for technology-competent social workers who can creatively develop ways to use the burgeoning technology to improve client access to services.

On the positive side, technology has decreased some of the professional isolation of rural social workers. Vast sources of information to inform and support their practice are at the fingertips of rural social workers. On-line searches, for example, can instantly provide background data to inform practice decisions through search engines such as the NASW website (www.helpstartshere.org) or the University of South Carolina's many links to resources (www.cosw.sc.edu/swan). In addition, rural social workers can have access to considerable information through on-line journals and university libraries, as well as through Google (www.google.com), Google Scholar (www.scholar.google.com), MSN Search (www.msn.com), Yahoo (www.yahoo.com), or other word searches. Once again, the promises of our advanced society do not fully carry to rural areas. Where most rural social workers can have internet access by dial-up telephone lines, the opportunity for high-speed internet connection is almost nonexistent, making it time-consuming to take full advantage of this resource.

Affordable Housing

Because of the lack of population density in rural areas, the housing problems are not as visible as in urban settings. Tucked away in isolated areas are a large number of mobile homes and dilapidated single-family dwellings. Although the average value of a home is less than for suburban and urban dwellings, homes tend to sit on large parcels of ground that makes even minimal housing expensive to purchase. It is reported that nearly 71 percent of poor rural families spend more than 30 percent of their income on housing.[8] When the cost of housing is factored in with the cost of transportation and the higher level of unemployment, it becomes evident why rural families have a much higher poverty rate.

One outcome of these conditions is the often unnoticed homelessness in rural areas. Like the urban homeless, the rural homeless are largely single men living in their cars or abandoned structures, yet 15 percent are families who have experienced foreclosures on their homes. These families tend to experience short-term homelessness (i.e., 3 to 4 months), but have few options such as homeless shelters to provide them with temporary housing and to support them in addressing this problem.[9]

Methamphetamine Use

Substance use and abuse has been viewed as primarily an urban problem, but today it has entered rural life—particularly in the form of a high incidence of methamphetamine (meth) production and use. A 2000 report found that

> rural and small-town youth were more likely than urban juveniles to become substance abusers and that an eighth grader in a rural town is more likely to use illicit drugs than an urban eighth grader. More specifically, when compared to urban eighth graders, rural eighth graders are 104 percent more likely to use amphetamines in general. They are 59 percent more likely than their counterparts in large cities and 64 percent more likely than eighth graders in small metropolitan areas to use methamphetamine specifically.[10]

Unlike some substances such as cocaine that must be imported, meth is a synthetic drug that is easily produced in the United States using products (e.g., anhydrous ammonia) that are commonly used in agriculture and found in farm supply stores. Most methods of meth production require a heat process that produces a distinct odor which is not easily disguised in densely populated areas, making rural sites particularly attractive for clandestine meth labs.

Methamphetamine is a highly addictive drug, and the fallout from this addition affects the work of many rural social workers. The National Center on Addiction and Substance Abuse at Columbia University estimated that in 2001 the cost of substance abuse accounted for an additional $41 billion in education costs as a result of ensuing violence, special education for children of addicts, truancy, and counseling costs.[11] Child welfare workers in rural America attribute a considerable amount of child abuse and neglect, HIV infections, and stress on Medicaid and financial assistance programs with meth addictions. The successful treatment of meth users in mental health settings requires very specialized professional skills that are rarely found in rural areas, forcing those persons who are addicted and seek rehabilitation to travel great distances in order to receive services—or worse, to not receive services at all.

Concluding Comment

Rural social work practice requires the adaptation of urban programs and practices to meet the needs of rural people. Although rural jobs have been lost, the population remains at nearly one-fourth of the U.S. population because many people displaced from rural employment continue to live in rural areas and commute to cities for jobs. Others who formerly worked in cities have found that they can live in rural areas and conduct their work from home—bringing with them expectations for the same services they had access to in urban areas.

The sparse population in rural areas makes it difficult to finance the specialized services that are increasingly expected and to attract the specialized professionals needed to provide those services. Therefore, it is important that social work education programs produce a sufficient supply of social workers with a generalist practice orientation in order to meet the demand in rural areas. Of particular importance for these workers today is the ability to address issues related to transportation and housing, the use of informational technology to reach clients, and the basic knowledge needed to address the meth crisis in rural America.

KEY WORDS AND CONCEPTS

Context of social work practice
Definition of "rural"
Dependence on land and nature
Generalist social work
Housing and homelessness in rural areas

Information technology in social work practice
Methamphetamine use in rural America
Rural culture and values
Rural transportation issues

SUGGESTED INFORAMTION SOURCES

Carlton-LaNey, Iris B., Edwards, Richard L., and Reid, Nelson P., eds. *Preserving and Strengthening Small Towns and Rural Communities.* Washington, D.C.: NASW Press, 1999.

Ginsberg, Leon H. *Social Work in Rural Communities,* 4th Edition. Alexandria, VA: Council on Social Work Education, 2005.

Lohmann, Nancy and Lohmann, Roger A., eds. *Rural Social Work Practice.* New York: Columbia University Press, 2005.

National Association of Social Workers. www.helpstartshere.org.

Rawson, Richard A., Anglin, M. Douglas, and Ling, Walter. "Will the Methamphetamine Problem Go Away?[11] *Journal of Addictive Diseases* 21(1), 2002.

Rural Human Services. Welfare Information Network. www.financeprojectinfo.org.

ENDNOTES

1. U.S. Census Bureau. "Census 2000 Urban and Rural Classification" Retrieved 4/12/2005 from http://www.census.gov/geo/www.ua/ua2k.html

2. W.K. Kellogg Foundation, *Perspectives of Rural America: Congressional Perspectives,* Retrieved 4/8/2005 from www.wkkf.org. pp. 3–4.

3. Gretchen H. Waltman, "Main Street Revisited: Social Work Practice in Rural Areas," *Social Casework,* 66 (October 1968): 467.

4. Emilia E. Martinez-Brawley and Joan Blundall, "Farm Families' Preferences toward the Personal Services," *Social Work* 34 (November 1989): 513.

5. National Association of Social Workers, "Rural Social Work," *NASW News,* 47 (March 2002): 10.

6. Bradford W. Sheafor and Charles R. Horejsi. *Techniques and Guidelines for Social Work Practice,* 7th Edition (Boston: Allyn and Bacon, 2006), pp. 87–88.

7. Pamela S. Landon, "Generalist and Advanced Generalist Practice." In Richard L. Edwards, ed., *Encyclopedia of Social Work*, 19th Edition, Vol. 2. Washington, D.C.: National Association of Social Workers, 1995, p. 1101.
8. Pamela Friedman, "Current Issues in Rural Housing and Homelessness." Rural Assistance Center. Retrieved from http://www.financeprojectinfo.org/rural/ruralhousing.asp.
9. Ibid.
10. Pilar Kraman, "Drug Abuse in America—Rural Meth." *Trends Alert: Critical Information for State Decision Makers*, Lexington, KY: The Council of State Governments, March 2004, p. 3.
11. Ibid., p. 1.

13

Domestic and International Gang Terrorism*

Prefatory Comment

This new chapter replaces "Urban, Suburban, and International Terrorist Gangs," which appeared in the 10th edition of this book in 2004. That chapter had a strong clinical emphasis for readers seeking a deeper social work, psychological, and psychiatric understanding of violent behavior among gang members, both in the United States and the Middle East.

The twentieth century could have been characterized as the "Age of Anxiety," given the overwhelming episodes of deliberate human carnage that caused anxiety for millions of people in the United States and around the world. To name a few of these events, for example, there were two world wars, Hitler's genocide of six million Jews, World War II ending with the atomic bomb, and the Korean and Vietnam Wars. The "Cold War" that followed, between nuclear super-powers Russia and the United States, did not detract from this anxiety.

Now in the twenty first century, especially with America's experience following the 9/11 terrorist attack in New York resulting in the death of 3,200 citizens, coupled with countless terrorist attacks around the world, this era could be called the "Age of Fear." Many now feel they might become victims of terrorism. Following 9/11, Congress and President Bush established the Department of Homeland Security in 2002 to focus the full resources of the American government on the safety of the American people. The new Department even established terrorist threat colors to warn U.S. citizens, ranging from Green—low risk of terrorist attack, to Red—severe risk of terrorist attack.[1]

But what do we actually know about domestic terrorists *in* the United States and those originating in the Middle East, such as Osama bin Laden and his terrorist group called al-Qaeda, who claimed responsibility for the terrorist attacks of 9/11? In reality, these groups are terrorist *gangs* that have contributed to the deaths of

---

*Chapter written by Armando T. Morales.

thousands of Americans, leading to social disorganization, economic hardship, psychological trauma, grief, and family dysfunction. *All* of these human consequences are in social work's practice arena. This new chapter will define terrorism and exactly what domestic terrorist groups and the al-Qaeda terrorist group have in common, and how they now are beginning to join forces to carry out their goals.

Many social workers deal daily with people suffering the effects of social, psychological, economic, and political oppression and dehumanization, some of whom eventually become either victims or perpetrators of violence and homicide. June Hopps argued that social workers are in the best position to articulate the relationship of micro to macro psychosocial forces to violence and to contribute recommendations for positive change. Offering a challenge to social work, Hopps asked: "If we in the social work profession don't, who will?"[2] Hopps was right on target because now there are more clinically trained social workers than members of other core mental health professions combined (192,814 clinical social workers; 73,018 psychologists; 33,486 psychiatrists; 17,318 psychiatric nurses).[3]

Defining and Understanding Terrorism

Anyone who has experienced intense fear understands the feeling of terror and what it is. The definition of terrorism has been changing over time and might be related to the social context in which terrorism finds itself at any particular time. Webster defined a *terrorist* as a person, usually the member of a group, who uses or advocates terrorism; a person who terrorizes or frightens others.[4] These definitions apply well to domestic and international terrorist gangs.

Terrorism by the State

There can be occasions in which a formal government can subject its citizens to terrorism to achieve a desired social control outcome. For example, in October 2002, Russian President Vladimir V. Putin ordered the use of a special gas to aid in the killing of fifty Chechen militants who had taken a Moscow theater audience of 750 civilians captive. The Chechen militants were threatening to blow themselves up along with the 750 Russian civilians if Russian troops did not leave their homeland. Russian law enforcement personnel charged into the facility using firearms and lethal gas. In addition to the Chechen terrorists, approximately one hundred Russian civilians were killed by the gas.[5]

A controversial case in which federal law enforcement intervention exposed U.S. civilians to terrorism involves the burning of the Branch Davidian compound in Waco, Texas, in 1993, under the authority and direction of U.S. Attorney Janet Reno. A deadly standoff between the Branch Davidians led by David Koresh and the Bureau of Alcohol, Tobacco and Firearms (ATF), who were attempting to serve weapons warrants, resulted in the deaths of four ATF agents and six Davidians. What followed was a 51-day siege led by the FBI, which ended in a fierce fire that destroyed the compound on April 19, 1993. Among the dead were Koresh and approximately eighty Davidians, which included forty-one women and children.[6]

Domestic Terrorism as Retaliation

Timothy McVeigh, a onetime member of the Ku Klux Klan and a highly decorated soldier in the Gulf War, became disillusioned about how the U.S. military treated Iraqis and its own troops with the use of chemicals. He was also outraged by the lethal actions taken by federal law enforcement at Waco. He claimed that he waited patiently for two years for justice for the victims of Waco, which never came. He therefore chose to bomb the Murrah federal building in Oklahoma City on April 19, 1995, which was the second anniversary of Waco. He stated in his letters: "Foremost the bombing was a retaliatory strike; a counterattack for the cumulative raids and subsequent violence and damage that federal agents had participated in over the preceding years, including, but not limited to Waco."[7]

McVeigh and three associates bombed the federal building, killing 168 people, including nineteen children; 642 people were injured. Was McVeigh simply another disturbed war veteran trained to kill who acted out his pathology upon U.S. citizens (many federal employees) and in the process modeled the behavior of his government? Did he represent a domestic militant terrorist group that is still active? McVeigh tells us that the reason for his heinous act was retaliation. In turn, the government retaliated against McVeigh and executed him on May 16, 2001.[8]

In Search of a Functional Definition of Terrorism.   There is no universally accepted definition of terrorism. The case examples cited above are acts of terrorism, but they may not be defined as such by the perpetrators. McVeigh, for example, might have defined his act not as terrorism but rather as the behavior of a true American patriot who was trying to bring attention to what he perceived as the eroding civil liberties of U.S. citizens. On the other hand, government bodies as alleged perpetrators of terrorism, whether in Russia or in the United States, may not view their acts as terrorism. Rather, they, such as the FBI, view the casualties of these violent confrontations as had occurred in Waco as criminals.

Terrorism is defined in the *Code of Federal Regulations* as ". . . the unlawful use of force and violence against persons or property to intimidate or coerce a government, the civilian population, or any segment thereof, in furtherance of political or social objectives" (28 C.F.R. Section 0.85). When citizens living in the United States commit such acts, it is known as *domestic terrorism*. When these acts are committed against the United States by persons external to U.S. boundaries, for example, non-U.S. citizens (foreigners), the acts are defined as *international terrorism*.[9] The Code definition appears general enough to capture most terrorism acts. The extensive trauma and lethality visited upon urban and suburban areas by gangs, for example, fit neatly into the definition.

Gang Terrorism as Defined by a State Legislature

In responding to the increasing gang terrorism problem, the California Legislature enacted the California Street Terrorism Enforcement and Prevention Act in 1988. This was known as the STEP Act and was the first in the nation addressing street gang terrorism. Section 186.21 of the Penal Code outlines the Legislative Finding and Declaration as the Legislature: ". . . further finds that the State of California is in a state of crisis which has been caused by violent street gangs whose members threaten, terrorize, and commit a multitude of crimes against the peaceful citizens of their neighborhoods. These activities, both individually and collectively, present a clear and present danger to public order and safety and are not constitutionally protected."[10] This Declaration, which defines what it considers gang terrorism, has even more descriptions of terrorism than the federal code. Four other states experiencing gang terrorism have since enacted STEP Acts similar to that of California. These states are Florida, Georgia, Louisiana, and Illinois.[11]

In a national survey of 368 state prosecutors' offices, of 175 counties with populations exceeding 250,000 people, 84 percent reported gang problems. In 193 smaller counties with populations ranging from 50,000 to 250,000, 46 percent reported gang problems.[12]

 ## Defining and Understanding Gangs

There is no one accepted standard definition of a "gang." In this respect, this chapter is a pioneering effort to label al-Qaeda as an international terrorist gang. Al-Qaeda was selected as a "model" of an international terrorist gang first because of its deadly terrorist acts and second because of the abundance of information available on al-Qaeda.

Al-Qaeda is not a juvenile gang, and efforts have to be made to clarify the types of gangs—especially terrorist gangs—that exist currently. Most of the gang literature focuses on youth gangs. Over 90 percent of juvenile crime is committed in groups, but not all of these groups could be considered gangs. Being a gang member is not a crime! Nor is it a crime to have gang tattoos, gang attire, and other symbols or colors or to use hand signs and language related to gang culture. Court convictions for gang-related crimes, whether juvenile or adult, are the most significant determining factor in establishing whether a gang member or the gang is criminal and violent.

Gang Researchers and Penal Code Definitions of Gangs

Gang researchers frequently use five criteria to define gangs: (1) formal organizational structure; (2) identifiable leadership; (3) identification with a territory; (4) recurrent interaction; and (5) engaging in serious or violent behavior.[13] Within this definition, a group could qualify to be defined as a gang but not engage in serious or violent behavior, which then would make it a nonviolent gang. Prosecutors in some states rely on penal code definitions and criteria as to which groups are defined as gangs because confirmation of gang membership can enhance the penalty significantly for a gang-related crime. For example, in California's Penal Code Section 186.22 (Street Terrorism Act) a gang is:[14]

A. Any ongoing organization, association, or group of three or more, having as one of its primary activities commission of one or more of the following crimes:
   1. Assault with a deadly weapon
   2. Robbery
   3. Homicide or attempted homicide
   4. Sale or possession of narcotics
   5. Shooting at a house or vehicle
   6. Arson
   7. Vehicle grand theft
B. Has a common name, sign, or symbol; whose members individually or collectively engage in a pattern of criminal gang activity

The above legally defined criteria almost exclusively apply to lower-class, inner-city *street* gangs since the street is usually where the members associate and/or commit crimes. White non-Hispanic suburban gangs, on the other hand, usually commit their crimes at *schools*, as was the case with the Trench Coat Mafia gang comprised of fourteen members. The STEP Act criteria therefore might be an example of racial profiling since most inner-city gang members are African American and *Latinos*. The Trench Coat Mafia "white" suburban terrorist gang in Littleton, Colorado, which killed 13 students and a teacher, does not meet the above criteria with the exception of having committed homicides and attempted homicides with deadly assault weapons. Perhaps a more equitable description and application of the STEP Act would be to call it the *"SSTEP"* (Street, Schools Terrorism Enforcement and Prevention) Act. Like the Trench Coat Mafia, international terrorist gangs do not fit the STEP Act definition with the exception of homicidal behavior and use of deadly weapons. Therefore, a more comprehensive and encompassing definition needs to be conceptualized.

A New Definition of Domestic and International Gang Terrorism

In attempting to focus on terrorism and terrorist gangs, the author offers a more general definition that is not biased against any ethnic or racial group, age level, social economic class, or location of terrorist crime, yet captures the essence of its violent, deadly behavior as follows:

A *terrorist gang* is a peer group of persons in a lower-, middle- or upper-class domestic or international community of any age who participate in unlawful terrorist activities and violence against persons or property to intimidate or coerce a government, the civilian population, or any segment thereof, in furtherance of domestic or international political or social objectives. Such violent behavior may be harmful to themselves (e.g., suicide bombings, crashing vehicles or planes into structures, suicide by gang) and/or others (killing of civilians and/or military personnel) in society.

This definition has elements of the definitions discussed in the previous section, yet it is specific enough to exclude about 95 percent of gangs that do not subject their neighborhoods, schools, or communities to deadly terrorism.

The Ethnic and Racial Burden of Minorities in Gang Identification

Many young people because of their psychosocial stage of development and their need to be in groups, to conform, and at times to dress in provocative clothing and hairstyles, often draw attention upon themselves by adults and especially police officers. Whether in the inner city, city, or suburbia, it is difficult to determine who is actually a violent threat to the community. Today, because of 9/11, many "Arab-looking" males of all ages are under suspicion and greater surveillance by citizens and law enforcement alike. Middle-class youth, particularly non-Hispanic white youths, are given the benefit of the doubt by police and are not interrogated or arrested. For example, following the Oklahoma City bombing, which prior to 9/11 was the greatest single act of domestic terrorism in the history of the United States, young adult non-Hispanic white males were not under suspicion as possible future bombers or associates of the McVeigh group. Inner-city, city, and suburban lower- or middle-class African American, Asian, and Hispanic youth, however, are overly suspected of being gang members and considered a genuine threat to society, and hence are often arrested as a *preventive* tactic. This controversial practice is known as "profiling," that is, that "criminal suspects" meet the arrest profile of certain offenders.

Gang Behavior Career Continuum

To assist the social worker to be able to distinguish which "ducks" are actually the dangerous ones, since they "all look, walk, and talk alike," the author has prepared a *Gang Behavior Career Continuum* to apply criteria to differentiate the degree of members' violent commitment to the gang. The brief vignettes and profiles used to describe the various gang behaviors in the different career levels are based on the author's 12,000 or so of treatment interviews of gang members since 1977. As can be seen in the *Gang Behavior Career Continuum*, (see Figure 13.1), there are seven career levels of involvement in the aspects of gang behavior and participation. Descriptive behavior pertaining to mid-Eastern youths is based on newspaper and magazine accounts and adapted to the gang behavior career continuum. Female gang members are not included in the following because 95 percent of U.S. gang members are males. Female gang members are even less represented in terrorist gangs.

The "Non-Gang" Level

In the United States, in the least involved level, referred to as "non-gang," are found the largest numbers of youth, up to 70 to 80 percent in some inner-city areas, who have consciously or unconsciously, knowingly or unknowingly, as impressionable

Figure 13.1
Gang Behavior Career Continuum: U.S. Gangs and International Gangs

U.S. GANGS

Gang Terrorism Begins Here

Non-Gang	Pre-Gang	Wannabe	Soft-Core	Moderate Core	Hard-Core	Super-Hard-Core
Exhibits some gang culture traits, no contacts with police, no arrests or convictions.	Some gang culture and contacts with police. No convictions.	Unpredictable, few police contacts to major convictions.	Few contacts, arrests, and convictions for minor gang crimes, on probation, in school.	Arrests and convictions for violent gang crime, institutionalized at local and state level, on probation/parole, rarely in school, unemployed. Will take risks for "hood."	Arrests and convictions for attempted and/or homicide, long-term placement in juvenile or adult state prison, no school or job. Shot caller. Will kill or die for gang.	Adult court convictions for one or more homicides, long-term prison or death row, poor school and work history. Shot caller in and out of prison. Will kill or die for gang.

INTERNATIONAL GANGS

Gang Terrorism Begins Here

Non-Gang	Pre-Gang	Wannabe	Soft-Core	Moderate Core	Hard-Core	Super-Hard-Core
Plays at "war," casts stones at U.S. military; imitates violent behavior of older children.	First contacts with U.S. military. Curfew violations and associating with known activists.	Idolizes al-Qaeda, takes risks without authorization, unreliable, not al-Qaeda talent. Not recruited.	Detained for stealing ammo or rifle from U.S. soldier; caught with gasoline and empty bottles.	Recruited into al-Qaeda, indoctrinated to al-Qaeda perspective of religion. Caught with Molotov cocktails.	Trained to fight and make bombs. Assists in bomb attacks, leaves homeland for terrorist assignments "somewhere." Learning to be a "shot caller." Wants to be a martyr.	Has been leader in bombing attacks. Supervising several al-Qaeda cells, has direct contact with top shot callers, including bin Laden. Willing to die for cause and become a martyr.

This *Gang Behavior Career Continuum* for U.S. gangs was developed by Armando T. Morales, UCLA Neuropsychiatric Institute and Hospital, School of Medicine, Los Angeles, California, in May, 1990. The *Gang Behavior Career Continuum* for International gangs was developed in 2002. Terrorist gang behavior for both U.S. and international gangs begins at the moderate-core level.

preadolescents and adolescents, incorporated the gang culture prevalent in their community. Understandably they have accepted some of the gang music (e.g., gangsta rap), clothing, walk, talk, hairdo, tattoos, and even knowledge and skills in writing and understanding graffiti; but they have no arrests or juvenile court convictions for offenses related to gang involvement. In Afghanistan and Palestine, for example, preadolescents and young adolescents who cast stones at American troops or Israeli army tanks and are not apprehended might fit into this category. They are imitating the behavior of older youth and young adults who are protesting against "the enemy."

The "Pre-Gang" Level

At the "pre-gang" level, these U.S. youths have also absorbed some of the gang culture previously mentioned, but now they are beginning to have some contacts (field interrogation cards) with police and a few arrests and taken to the police station for being with more sophisticated gang members. But no petitions (charges) are filed in juvenile court. In Afghanistan or Palestine, these youngsters might be having their first formal contacts and warnings by U.S. or Israeli authorities for suspicious behavior, curfew violations, or associating with known "troublemakers."

The "Wannabes" Level

The "Wannabes" (want-to-bes) are in the next level on the gang career continuum. These U.S. youths at times are quite disturbed and unpredictable and very much want to be in the gang. But they are not respected by legitimate gang members, nor are they wanted in the gang because they lack the consistency, dedication, and loyalty expected of "good" gang members. Wannabes have been known to abandon their pursuit of the gang when they experience their first incarceration or first real fight with rival gang members. Some are manipulated by the gang to "prove themselves" by asking them to carry out an assigned gang homicide. Afghanistan adolescent Wannabes might be those youngsters who look up to and want to be part of al-Qaeda, for example, but who have not yet been formally accepted due to their inexperience, lack of intelligence, impulsivity, or unreliability. U.S. gangs, as is the case with al-Qaeda, are looking for "good" soldier material to help carry out their goals.

The "Soft-Core" Level

The soft-core level finds the young U.S. gang member with his first minor gang-related arrest for group drinking or drugs, or perhaps a gang related "joy ride" (auto theft), or misdemeanor gang assault requiring an arrest, probation investigation, juvenile court appearance, and a sustained petition (conviction). The soft-core gang member is now placed on probation and continues going to school. A budding Afghanistan teenage terrorist at this level might have his/her first detention by authorities for having attempted to steal a military rifle from an American soldier or being caught with an unlit gasoline "Molotov cocktail" near a U.S. Army base camp. Individuals and gangs in the first four levels of the gang behavior career continuum are rarely involved in serious violent behavior, as is the case with most gangs, and hence could not be considered terrorist gangs.

The "Moderate-Core" Level

The moderate-core U.S. gang member is a lot more experienced and a little older and rarely attends school. By now he has had two or three convictions in juvenile court for gang-related violent offenses and has tasted incarceration at least two or three times in local or state youth correctional facilities. His multiple tattoos not only advertise his local gang, but also represent an affiliation with state-wide northern or southern gangs. He is also beginning to have contact with ex-convicts who are the "shot callers" (give orders) for the gang. While institutionalized, the moderate-core gang member is further indoctrinated into the values, norms, and expectations of gang culture.

A bright, talented, older Afghanistan adolescent or young adult at this level might feel honored that he is being recruited into al-Qaeda and will be receiving a modest salary that will keep his family from starving. He will be indoctrinated with the al-Qaeda perspective of Muslim religion and will learn about the importance of bringing *jihad* (holy war) to Christian Western nations.[15] Instead of being incarcerated, he will have to leave his home for intensive training in guerilla warfare by al-Qaeda. Rather than boasting his membership in al-Qaeda through tattoos, gang colors, and a shaved head like many American gang members, the new recruit will learn how to make himself inconspicuous. He will have a more formidable "code of silence" than U.S. gang members. He will assume a low profile as he is prepared for a terrorist assignment "somewhere" in the Middle East, South or North America, or elsewhere in the world. Gang members at the moderate-, hard-, and super hard-core level *are* participating in violent behavior causing harm to others, and therefore would be considered members of terrorist gangs.

The "Hard-Core" Level

The hard-core gang member is similar to the moderate-core, except that the hard-core gang member has higher status and respect in the gang. He is one of the "shot callers." Not only has he been incarcerated in local and state juvenile facilities, but he now has convictions in adult court for gang-related offenses, including attempted homicide and homicide. Some hard-core gang members had their first experience at being sentenced to state prison as adults even though they might have been only 16 or 17 years old when they committed their first serious crime. Usually the hard-core members are a little older (18 to 25) and are among the local leaders of the gang, have impressive respect and "juice" (power) in the gang, and often are "shot callers" (give orders). Hard-core gang members not only have injured others in battle, but also wear their "war medals" (knife and/or bullet wound scars) proudly.

An al-Qaeda member at this level has been taught how to prepare bombs and other tools of mass destruction (biological and chemical warfare) and has assisted in some smaller terrorist bombing activities involving a handful of victims somewhere in the Middle East. By now, those closest to him (family, wife, or girlfriend) have no knowledge of his al-Qaeda involvement or where he lives. He occasionally might write to them to let them know he is "fine" and will see them soon. Subsequent strong emotional messages may indicate that he has been assigned to a suicide bombing mission.

The Super-Hard-Core Level

Finally, the most violent, terrorist level of the gang career continuum is the "super-hard-core" gang member. In the United States, they have adult court convictions for gang-related terrorist offenses, such as one or more homicides, "three strikes," or witness/victim intimidation including the killing of potential witnesses. Some have even killed police officers or prison guards. They continue to have close ties with local gangs and are well established in the prison gang hierarchy. Following parole, some may attempt to serve a liaison function under orders from the state prison gang to conduct "business" (e.g., drugs, extortion, executions) in the community of the local gang. They are not only respected by the local gang, but also feared because they might be in a position to carry out contracted "green light" hits (executions) locally or even order "hits" on gang members not complying with their wishes, such as not paying "taxes" (protection money) to the prison gang. The federal government and some states have successfully prosecuted well-organized violent criminal gangs such as the Italian and Mexican Mafia under "RICO" (Racketeering Influenced Corrupt Organizations) statutes. Some of the super-hard-core terrorists are serving sentences of 10 to 20 years or life without the possibility of parole, and a few are on death row for multiple gang-related homicides. Dozens of the super-hard-core gang terrorists have been legally executed by the state.

An international gang terrorist at this level would be someone like Imam Samudra, age 35, an alleged al-Qaeda member. He admitted that he was the organizer and leader of the October 12, 2002, bombing that killed 191 people at a Bali entertainment facility. The victims were mostly foreign tourists, but among the dead were seven Americans. Samudra claimed that he received training in making bombs in Afghanistan when he was about 25 years of age.[16] Osama bin Laden, alleged leader of al-Qaeda, certainly would fit in this category as an ultimate "shot caller."

 ## Theories of Gangs

Five theoretical perspectives explaining the causes of gangs will be examined. The first theory is similar to Thrasher's classic description of gangs in the 1920s, in which gangs are seen as a natural progression from, and the consequence of, a youth's search for excitement in a frustrating and limiting environment. They are usually a result of a general breakdown of social controls and are characterized by persons with few social ties, such as immigrants, the mentally ill, and the destitute, and by a corresponding lack of parental control over the young.[17] The majority of U.S. gangs—with the exception of some non-Hispanic white suburban gangs—are found in the poorest neighborhoods. Likewise, in the world community, particularly in the Middle East, international terrorist gangs are found in the poorest areas. Al-Qaeda recruitment, with promises of food, salary, and religious glory, provides some hope for desperate youths and young men. Dying with dignity in fighting the enemy might be preferable to starving to death on the desert sand.

A second causal factor has been proposed by anthropologist Miller, who studied lower-class gangs in Boston. He describes gang members as males who usually were reared in female-dominated households, and consequently, in adolescence, the gang, Miller maintains, "provides the first real opportunity to learn essential aspects of the male role in the context of peers facing similar problems of sex role identification."[18]

A third perspective is suggested by social scientists such as Cohen, Cloward, and Ohlin. They maintain that the gang is the collective solution of young, lower-class males to a situation of stress wherein opportunities for the attainment of wealth and/or status through legitimate channels are blocked. In response, the gang develops a subculture or *contra-culture*. The gang, therefore, must be explained in terms of social conditions in which lower-class youths are placed by the dominant society.[19] Although these authors do not mention it specifically, classism and racism are the forces that block and lock in minority youth to the social conditions that produce gangs.

A fourth perspective is advanced by Matza, who challenges the "blocked-out" subculture theory, stating that it explains too much delinquency. He believes that gangs exist because adolescents are in a state of suspension between childhood and adulthood; hence, they spend most of their time with peers and are anxious about both their identity as males and their acceptance by the peer group (gang). They conform to the norms of the gang because not to do so would threaten their status.[20] This "anxious about their identity" theory might not be applicable to Afghanistan young men in international terrorist gangs such as al-Qaeda. Rather, they are anxious about being able to provide food and other resources to their families. All of the above theories have merit and are applicable in many instances, as gangs are very heterogeneous and complex and cannot be explained by any *one* theory. What they all have in common is a group contagion, cohesion, loyalty, and dedication, and a deep feeling of the old Musketeers saying: "One for all, and all for one."

The author proposes a fifth theoretical perspective. In a study of East Los Angeles *Latino* gang and non-gang probation juvenile camp graduates, gang members, significantly more than non-gang members, came from families exhibiting more family breakdown, greater poverty, poorer housing, more alcoholism, more drug addiction, more major chronic illness, and more family members involved with law enforcement and correctional agencies.[21] In the face of these overwhelming problems, the youngster turns to the gang as a *surrogate family*. Here, the gang member receives affection, understanding, recognition, loyalty, and emotional and physical protection. In this respect the gang is psychologically adaptive rather than maladaptive. Many terrorist gang members will often die or kill rival gang members for their gang, turf, political mission, or neighborhood. When this occurs, membership then becomes maladaptive.

The story when it concerns young Afghanistans and Palestinians and their families is a little different. Afghanistan families have been exposed to so much war, terror, and trauma on their soil, and they do not have many resources to offer their children. In the past 21 years of conflict, they have suffered catastrophic losses. In this time period, 1.5 million have died as the result of conflict, along with a total destruction of their country.[22] In this respect, young men who leave their families are not searching for a surrogate family; rather, they are seeking a way to survive and in turn hope to help their families survive.

The Prevalence of Gangs

As far as can be determined, to date there has not been a solid, data-based gathering of information comparable to Thrasher's classic work as to the numbers of gangs currently in large cities. This is largely due to there not being a national reporting system with precise information. A major problem is attempting to find agreement as to who really are gang members and if they are, are they still active or in *remission* (no longer participating in gang violence)? Without a precise definition, the data therefore are difficult to interpret. The best *national* effort is found in the 1996 National Youth Gang Survey of 2,629 responding agencies, with 53 percent reporting that gangs were active in their jurisdiction. Respondents in large cities claimed the highest level of gang activities, 74 percent, followed by suburban areas (57%), small cities (34%), and rural counties (25%). Based on this response, the researchers concluded that up to 4,824 U.S. cities were experiencing gang problems, and that there may be as many as 31,000 gangs, with a total membership of 846,000.[23] There are no solid data to determine how many of these gangs are actually deadly terrorist gangs.

Relatively accurate information exists with regard to the prevalence of terrorist groups—which we are calling international terrorist gangs—around the world. Following "9/11," President Bush signed Executive Order 13224 on September 23, 2001, which gives the U.S. government authority to block the assets of organizations and individuals linked to terrorism. The Order lists 189 such groups and individuals. At the top of the terrorism list is al-Qaeda and Osama bin Laden and the Palestine Islamic Jihad. U.S. government global terrorism research includes data concerning the number of terrorist attacks by region, as shown in Table 13.1.[24]

As can be seen in this table, compared to other nations, the United States has by and large been spared the rage of international terrorism, that is, until 9/11. From the standpoint of terrorist threats to the United States, it would appear that 31,000 U.S. gangs, with 846,000 members, might potentially present a greater danger to Americans than 189 international terrorist groups, including the 9/11 attacks that claimed about 3,000 lives. Consider the fact that gang group terrorism in Los Angeles alone took the lives of 9,196 Americans between 1986 and 2001. (See Figure 13.3 on p. 261.)

Table 13.1

Total International Attacks by Region, 1996–2001	
Latin America	831
Western Europe	353
Asia	319
Middle East	188
Africa	184
Eurasia	149
North America	19

Types of Gangs

Most social scientists investigating gangs today would agree that there are at least three types of gangs: the *criminal*, the *conflict*, and the *retreatist*. The author suggests that a fourth type of gang is emerging in recent years, which could be called the *cult/occult gang*.

The *criminal gang* has as its primary goal material gain through criminal activities. Success is obtained through the theft of property from premises or persons, extortion, fencing, and obtaining and selling illegal substances such as drugs. In the 1920s Thrasher discovered that some of the wealthiest youth gangs—which he called *beer gangs*—were involved in the liquor business during Prohibition.[25] Today, some former gang members are making their money in drugs in criminal racketeering organizations.

The *conflict gang* is very turf oriented and will engage in violent battle with individuals or rival groups that invade their neighborhood or commit acts they consider insulting or degrading. Respect is highly valued and defended. Hispanic gangs, in most cities, are highly represented among conflict gangs. Their mores, values, rituals, and codes are highly consistent in various neighborhoods and cities throughout the nation and have existed in some areas for almost seventy years.

The predominant feature of the *retreatist gang* is the pursuit of getting "loaded" or "high" on alcohol, marijuana, heroin, acid, cocaine, or other drugs. Retreatism is seen by Cloward and Ohlin as an isolated adaptation, characterized by a breakdown in relationships with other persons. The drug user has a need to become affiliated with other retreatist users to secure access to a steady supply of drugs.[26] What distinguishes the criminal gang involved in drugs from the retreatist gang is that the former is primarily involved for financial profit. The retreatist gang's involvement with drugs is primarily for consumption.

The fourth type of adolescent delinquent group is the *cult/occult gang*.[27] The word *cult*, as used here, pertains to a system of worshiping the devil or evil. *Occult* means something hidden or secret, or a belief in mysterious or supernatural powers. Not all cult/occult devil or evil worship groups are involved in criminal activity or ritualistic crime. The Ku Klux Klan, for example, may be seen as a cult group, and some chapters, in spite of their hate rhetoric, are law abiding, whereas other chapters have committed criminal acts.

The majority of occult groups, whether criminal or law abiding, are composed of adults. However, some juvenile groups are becoming interested in satanic and black magic practices and are using them for their own gratification of sadistic, sexual, and antisocial impulses. Their knowledge and application of rigid, ritualistic occult practices, however, is often haphazard. Los Angeles has perhaps the largest number of these adolescent cult/occult gangs, numbering about thirty-two.[28] These gangs are composed predominantly of white, non-Hispanic middle-class youths and a few middle-class Hispanics. They are not turf-oriented like conflict gangs, but are found in several middle-class locations.

A neo-Nazi subtype of white cult/occult gang groups are the Skinheads, whose racist, anti-Semitic, homophobic "gay bashing," and other violent behavior has appeared in the South, Midwest, and West Coast. According to Spergel, their group structure and behavior comply with the gang pattern, including use of colors, tattoos, common dress and hairstyle, name, drug use, and criminal behavior (usually "hate" crimes). The majority of Skinheads come from middle-class and/or working-class white families.[29] The gothic-cultural Trench Coat Mafia, a terrorist gang, could have fitted in with the Skinhead neo-Nazi cult gang.

The four types of gangs previously discussed have a predominant pattern of behavior, such as turf-territorial conflict gang with rivals, criminal behavior for profit, retreating into drug and alcohol consumption, and devil-evil worship (cults). This would not prevent some gang members, however, from participating in behaviors outside of the four traditional "domains" identified above. For example, a turf-conflict gang might be involved in some drug dealing to benefit the gang, but this would not be the gang's primary pattern of behavior. Or an individual turf-conflict gang member might be an entrepreneur and sell drugs to benefit himself, not the gang. It is also possible for a gang to participate in activities covering several domains of behavior and not fit neatly into any one pattern of activities. Such is the case of the international terrorist gang al-Qaeda.

First of all, al-Qaeda conforms to the requirements of the criminal gang as it is involved in receiving financial benefits from the drug trade in Afghanistan to help finance its terrorist activities. In 1999, Afghanistan produced 5,000 tons of opium, which was more than 70 percent of the world's supply. The group in power at that time, the Taliban, helped finance several international terrorist groups and their leaders, including bin Laden.[30]

Secondly, al-Qaeda certainly represents a conflict, turf-oriented gang at a macro level as their international terrorist acts are acts of retaliation intended to discourage all U.S. military occupation and presence in Arab nations. Al-Qaeda views U.S. presence in Arab nations as an act of imperialism with a specific interest in their extensive oil resources.

Thirdly, bin Laden could clearly be perceived as having a cult-like following concerning his personal violent interpretations of the Quran, a thirteenth-century Arab bible or doctrine, regarded as the eternal words of God himself by at least 1.3 million Muslims around the world. The Quran is a book of divine revelation by the eternal words of Allah himself. Like all religions, these bibles and doctrines are subject to interpretation. Many moderate interpreters of the Quran condemned 9/11 and other terrorist acts resulting in the killing of civilians. These moderates believe that these atrocities are antithetical to the teaching of the Quran.[31] The charismatic bin Laden, however, interprets the Quran as providing him the spiritual authority to participate in "jihad" (holy war) against those he considers enemies of Islam. *Jihad* has other meanings, such as "effort."

In February 1998, bin Laden, as head of al-Qaeda, issued a manifesto stating:

> The ruling to kill the Americans and their allies—civilian and military—is an individual duty for every Muslim who can do it in any country in which it is possible to.[32]

According to Afghanistan scholar Rashid, the subsequent bombings by al-Qaeda in August 1998 of the U.S. embassies in Kenya and Tanzania, killing 220 people, made bin Laden a "household word" in the Muslim world and the west.[33]

The Ecosystems Model

The Ecosystems Model highlighted in Part Five of this book is particularly helpful in examining the gang problem in more depth as gangs cover all of the main points and five levels of the model, that is, historical, environmental–structural, culture, the family, and the individual. More specifically, what might be the *historical* issues related to gangs and why have they been with us for over 160 years? What might be the historical gang picture as it concerns Afghanistan? Might the existence of gangs be related in part to the impact of *environmental–structural* issues and how they might alleviate or aggravate the problem even more? The gang exists and perhaps thrives in American *culture,* and what is it about our culture that might be contributing to gangs in America? Is there something in Afghanistan culture that cultivates and fosters the formation of gangs?

What about the role of *the family*; is it in any way contributing to the gang problem, and why are parents having more difficulty in raising sons than daughters? What went wrong in Littleton, Colorado, with the family of the Trench Coat Mafia gang members in white, affluent suburbia? Or perhaps extreme poverty is a contributing factor to the destruction of the family and in turn the growth of gangs as one Afghanistan father, Akhtar Muhammad, who sold two of his young sons for bags of wheat, stated: "I miss my sons, but there was nothing to eat."[34]

The final level of the ecosystems model pertains to *the individual*. Here we try to understand why a person does what he does. Why does the preadolescent or adolescent join the gang, and what distinguishes the violent, homicidal, and at times suicidal gang member from others who are not so violent? Are they emotionally disturbed or fiercely dedicated to their cause, or both? Is there a difference between a U.S. gang member who dies in gang conflict protecting his "hood" and an Afghanistan youth terrorist who is shot to death while hurling a Molotov Cocktail at a U.S. Army tank? Figure 13.2 demonstrates the areas of inquiry discussed above. Following a discussion of these five levels, a *micro* psychosociocultural case analysis and comparison of domestic, urban, suburban, and international gang terrorism will be made.

History of Gangs

Gangs have been with us since the beginning of civilization, with the concept of gangs first reported in the literature by former gang member St. Augustine (AD 354–430) about 1619 years ago. In his book *Confessions,* St. Augustine described his father as a gambler, alcoholic, and womanizer and his mother as a pious Christian who seemed to have a chronic or major depression. Without parental control, adolescent St. Augustine associated with neighborhood delinquents and committed crimes.[35]

The first youth gangs in the United States made their appearance in the national turf-oriented atmosphere of "manifest destiny"—the rationale for the forceful takeover of the Mexican-owned Southwest—in the mid 1800s. These gangs first appeared in Philadelphia in the 1840s, evolving from volunteer fire companies. The tough firemen—the Super Bowl heroes of the era—were the idols of neighborhood adolescents, who looked upon them with awe. These teenage groupies, who likewise identified with the company's turf, engaged in physical fights with rival fire company youth groups. These early gangs had names such as the Rats, the Bouncers, and the Skinners. They defaced walls, fences, and buildings with graffiti, similarly to what gangs do today in urban and suburban areas. The *Philadelphia Public Ledger,* on August 13, 1846, described them as being "armed to the teeth with slug shots, pistols, and knives." The biggest provocation to violence was the intrusion of rival gangs into their turf.[36]

Arab nations have a much longer history with groups that could be called gangs. One of the oldest reported cult gangs was called the Order of the Assassins, a sect of the Ismaili founded by Hassan bin Sabbah in 1090 in Alamut, Persia. A bright, dynamic person who attended university, through religious study and teachings he elevated himself to the supreme position of *Imam*—God's personal representative on earth. The Order of the Assassins was known for its fondness of hashish, which made his "band" or gang of followers more impressionable to his commands. His gang of followers were so fanatically loyal to him that they were prepared to kill for and die for their *Imam.* Bin Sabbah would set out to dispose of his enemies by dispatching his Assassins to infiltrate the ranks of his prospective victims. Sometimes they would remain under cover for years before killing their assigned victims. Bin Sabbah had a following of 70,000 loyal Assassins.[37] Bin Sabbah's use of religion and his use and sale of drugs, which provided economic support for his followers, do not seem too different from what bin Laden is accomplishing a thousand years later. If bin Laden does not have 70,000 followers, he certainly has many followers located in several parts of the world.

Figure 13.2

Ecosystems Model for Psychosocial Analysis of Factors Impacting Gangs

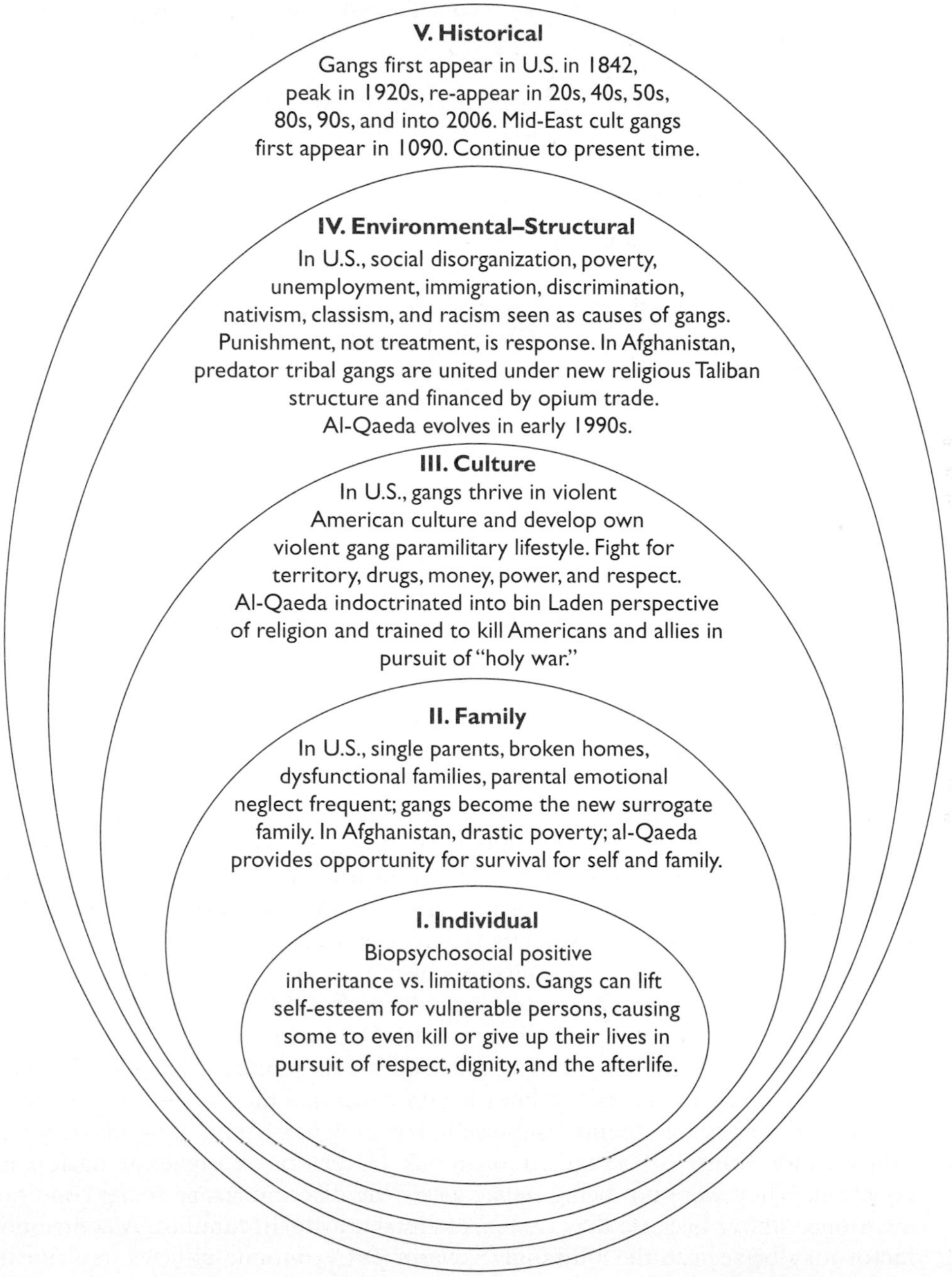

V. Historical

Gangs first appear in U.S. in 1842, peak in 1920s, re-appear in 20s, 40s, 50s, 80s, 90s, and into 2006. Mid-East cult gangs first appear in 1090. Continue to present time.

IV. Environmental–Structural

In U.S., social disorganization, poverty, unemployment, immigration, discrimination, nativism, classism, and racism seen as causes of gangs. Punishment, not treatment, is response. In Afghanistan, predator tribal gangs are united under new religious Taliban structure and financed by opium trade. Al-Qaeda evolves in early 1990s.

III. Culture

In U.S., gangs thrive in violent American culture and develop own violent gang paramilitary lifestyle. Fight for territory, drugs, money, power, and respect. Al-Qaeda indoctrinated into bin Laden perspective of religion and trained to kill Americans and allies in pursuit of "holy war."

II. Family

In U.S., single parents, broken homes, dysfunctional families, parental emotional neglect frequent; gangs become the new surrogate family. In Afghanistan, drastic poverty; al-Qaeda provides opportunity for survival for self and family.

I. Individual

Biopsychosocial positive inheritance vs. limitations. Gangs can lift self-esteem for vulnerable persons, causing some to even kill or give up their lives in pursuit of respect, dignity, and the afterlife.

Environmental–Structural Factors

Periodic government reports responding to social crises are useful in highlighting the environmental–structural factors impacting gangs in the United States. For example, after studying the causes of hundreds of riots in 150 cities across the United States in the mid 1960s, the U.S. Riot Commission, known as the Kerner Report, issued its findings, stating:

> White racism is essentially responsible for the explosive mixture which has been accumulating in our cities since the end of World War II. . . . The ghettos too often mean men and women without jobs, families without men, and schools where children are processed instead of educated, until they return to the street—to crime, narcotics, to dependency on welfare, and to bitterness and resentment against society in general and White society in particular.[38]

Similar environmental–structural factors were reached in a report by the Congress of Mexican American Unity and Chicano Moratorium Committee as the causes of five *Latino* community riots in East Los Angeles in 1970 and 1971.[39] These oppressive conditions were attributed to white racism.

But Thrasher did not conclude that the existence of 1,313 gangs in Chicago in the 1920s was the result of white racism because 95 percent of the gangs *were* "white" (not Hispanic). However, Thrasher cited similar underlying causes as the Kerner and Webster Commission (L.A. Riots of 1992) reports, that is, the failure of social institutions to function efficiently in a youngster's experience, as indicated by disintegration of the family, "inefficiency of schools," political indifference, low wages, unemployment, and lack of recreational opportunities.[40] Thrasher, taught us over seventy years ago that the gang was a function of specific conditions and does not tend to appear in the absence of these conditions. Perhaps the core problem is societal discrimination against the poor (*classism*), which in turn is combined and exacerbated by ethnic and racial prejudice and *racism*. The "conditions" nevertheless continue to exist, as do the gangs in these communities, that being the bottom line.

In comparison to the United States, environmental–structural factors concerning the people of Afghanistan appear unfathomable. Former U.N. Secretary General Boutros-Ghali stated in 1995 that Afghanistan became one the world's orphaned conflicts ignored by the West in favor of Yugoslavia. World powers turned away from Afghanistan, permitting civil war, ethnic fragmentation, and polarization to become state failure. Afghanistan was seen to no longer exist as a viable nation, and according to *New York Times Bestseller* correspondent-scholar Rashid, when this happens, civil society is destroyed and that generations of children grow up rootless, without identity or reason to live except to fight. He adds that adults are likewise affected by being traumatized and brutalized knowing only war and the power of warlords.[41]

But how does the "white" suburban Trench Coat Mafia gang massacre and other white suburban gangs fit into this traditional gang explanation and equation? They were not being impacted by the discriminatory social conditions mentioned above because they came from intact, affluent families. A contributing factor may be seen in the antifamily government economic policies implemented over the past twenty-five years by both Republican and Democratic administrations expounding "family values," making it more stressing and difficult for parents to have more options available for them to spend more time with their children. These regressive family policies particularly impacted mothers. For example, working mothers with children under the age of 3 years increased from 33.8 percent in 1976 to 61.8 percent in 1997. For working mothers with children under the age of 6 years, there was an increase from 39.8 percent in 1976 to 65 percent in 1997.[42] In other words, increased taxes, mortgages, and other expenses passed on to families by government forced parents to spend less time at home nurturing and supervising their children. Their children, therefore, experienced the same emotional neglect and rejection felt by poor inner-city and Afghanistan youths, many of whom then join or create gangs to fulfill their psychosocial needs. This neglect may really be the root of the problem—emotional neglect and lack of supervision whether in poor *or* affluent families.

Cultural Factors

Compared to other nations around the world, the United States is perceived as a violent nation with an ultraviolent culture. A nation founded on violence, preoccupied with power and oppression of Native Americans and other minorities including women and the poor, occurring within the powerfully violent modeling context of wars, advocating the practice of capital punishment, and having an obsession with the possession and use of firearms, all contribute to the creation of a violent citizenry.

There is evidence of an association between war and individual violence as a society at war is teaching its members that such behavior is acceptable under certain circumstances. Warring nations are more likely to experience increases in homicide rates than are nations not involved in war. The U.S. homicide rate more than doubled (4.5 per 100,000 in 1963 to 9.3 in 1973) during the Vietnam War years. Researchers found the fact of war to be the most plausible explanation and the most influential variable in the causal equations.[43] Vietnam veterans, especially combat veterans, are more likely than nonveterans to be violence-prone and to evidence more social, psychological, and substance abuse problems than nonveterans.[44] Although the Persian Gulf War had only about 200 U.S. military casualties, scores more were wounded and/or witnessed violence. The traumatic psychological consequences of combat for U.S. male and female military personnel may visit violence upon their families, neighbors, and communities for many years to come. Oklahoma City bomber Timothy McVeigh and Washington, D.C., suburb sniper John Allen Muhammed, both decorated combat veterans of the Gulf War, appear to be carrying on the pathological tradition of acting out their deadly violence upon the community.

Like war and the possession of firearms and assault rifles by the public, capital punishment is another expression of violent behavior valued by the majority of Americans, which, in turn, contributes to further violence. One study concluded that publicized executions by the state, instead of deterring further violence, incites imitative execution-like behavior in society.[45] With nearly 700 executions since

1977, the United States, with the exception of China, leads the world in executing its citizens: approximately 70 to 100 per year. Former Supreme Court Justice Blackmun called capital punishment a failed experiment in deterrence fraught with arbitrariness, discrimination, caprice, and mistakes.[46]

The U.S. media also play a significant role in modeling and influencing young minds. Children spend more time watching television than in any other single activity, and by the age of 18 the average person has witnessed over 18,000 homicides on television. Sixty percent of prime-time TV programs contain violent solutions to conflict situations, with cartoons being among the most violent.[47]

Since wars and violence are seen as contributing to a culture of violence, Afghanistan, an impoverished country of 20 million people fraught with countless wars and civil conflict and with 1.5 to 2 million deaths and countless wounded over the past 23 years, would be even more adversely impacted than the United States. It truly has been an apocalyptic experience and existence for the people of Afghanistan. The total Afghan population has been displaced several times over, and its capital city, Kabul, has been partially destroyed. Vulnerable Kabul, with many rich archaeological treasures dating back to prehistoric times, such as charting the presence of Alexander the Great, and historic pieces tracing the development of Buddhism, Islam, Mongolians, and Aryans, has been looted by Afghanistan Mafia-style criminal gangs.[48]

In short, there is little semblance of an infrastructure to sustain Afghanistan society. According to Rashid, the only productive factories in Afghanistan were those where prostheses, wheelchairs, and crutches are manufactured.[49] Will we ever be able to measure the amount of violence that the Afghan population generates as the result of living in such a violent cultural environment? Could this be one of the factors accounting for Afghanistan being the world's capital of international terrorism?

The Family

It was seen earlier that the percentage of U.S. working mothers with children under the age of 6 years increased from 40 percent in 1976 to 65 percent in 1997, thereby making it more difficult for mothers to be home nurturing and supervising their children. The situation appeared worse for fathers. Prompted by the Trench Coat Mafia gang killings, a June 1999 national poll of children ages 12 to 14 living in twenty-five cities revealed that 60 percent of sampled respondents reported that they wanted to spend more time with their parents. Households with two wage earners and those headed by a single parent obviously make the child's wishes difficult to fulfill. Forty-one percent of the respondents stated they spent an equal amount of time with both parents; 47 percent spent more time with the mother; and 11 percent spent more time with the father.[50] It would appear that African American and Hispanic youths coming from poorer families would have even less contact with fathers, since the majority of these families are headed by a single parent (mother).

The last twenty-three years of civil war and conflict in Afghanistan has produced up to 50,000 widows in Kabul alone. These conflicts killed between

1.5 and 2 million men, which would increase the number of widows to hundreds of thousands nationwide. The widows ranged in age from 20 to 40 years of age, and 90 percent of the widows had children. Their homes reflected bare, dirt floors, and a perpetual hunger for these families was not uncommon. Following the fall of the Taliban in 2001, the political and social conditions for widows improved slightly. However, the basic needs for this fragmented family group remained unfilled. Five years of strict Taliban rule left widows and their families on the receiving end of harsh fundamentalist edicts such as women could not work, go to school, or leave their homes unless escorted by a male relative. As the most isolated victims of the Taliban, many resorted to begging in the streets to obtain food for their children. Some even sought employment in the oldest profession.[51] How would an Afghanistan child be psychologically impacted by the loss of a father due to war and being raised by a widowed mother living in abject poverty and experiencing starvation? Given these conditions, again, the message is clear—suffer and die or fight!

The Individual

Here, for both U.S. and al-Qaeda gang members, the ecosystems model focuses on the individual level, examining the biological and psychological factors of each person, with specific attention to what makes certain persons vulnerable to not only joining gangs, but also to becoming terrorists members of the gang. The terrorist behavior does not appear in a vacuum and is in many ways related to the previously discussed historical context in the person's background, the environmental–structural conditions in which the violence occurs, the violent cultural condition of society, marital and family vulnerabilities exacerbating the individual's psychosocial condition, and finally the individual's biological and psychological endowment interacting with the former factors.

A significant amount of controversy exists in attempting to link biological factors to violence. At best it can be said that some biological factors, such as genetic conditions, hormonal imbalances, brain diseases, and chemistry dysfunctions, may predispose some individuals toward violence under certain circumstances. One cannot predict who will be violent with any high degree of accuracy, only that given certain biological predisposition factors, the potential for violence exists.[52]

 ## The Origin of Domestic and International Gang Terrorism

A neuropsychological study of psychosis, psychopathy, and homicide of twenty-six hospitalized male patients produced two distinct groups. One group was high in psychosis but low in psychopathy. The other group was low in psychosis but high in psychopathy.[53] This study renewed the old controversy as to whether murderers are "mad" or "bad." Might some just be "normal," such as soldiers, gang members, or al-Qaeda, killing others for a cause they believe in? Or is it possible that they reflect the whole spectrum of mental health? Discussing a few of the deadly acts by gang terrorists in the following might shed some light on this issue.

The "Kroth," a white, suburban, middle-class gang in Pearl, Mississippi, with a population of 22,000, were involved in a plot to rid themselves of their enemies at high school and win the respect they felt they deserved. The Kroth, a name garnered from satanic verses and whose members were admirers of Adolf Hitler, was a small suburban gang of only seven or eight members. On October 1, 1997, 16-year-old Luke Woodham, one of the Kroth members and a sophomore at Pearl High School, entered the school with a .30–30 hunting rifle and opened fire, killing two students and wounding seven others in an 11-minute terrorist rampage. He had no prior criminal record.[54]

Consider the case of al-Qaeda gang terrorist Mohamed Atta, the organizer and leader of the 9/11 catastrophe. Atta did not experience rejection in his two-parent middle-class home in Cairo. Always ambitious, even as a boy, he excelled academically, graduating from prestigious Cairo University, and thereafter he attended graduate school in Hamburg, where he earned a graduate degree in urban planning. Friends and professors described him as a stoic, very disciplined man and enormously respectful of authority, always doing what he was told. His father described him as a very sensitive man, yet one with a sense of humor.

In Hamburg, Germany, he joined an Arab Al Quds mosque and became quite politicized, especially after U.S. soldiers forced the Taliban to flee Kabul. In 1998 and 1999 he received "training" in Afghanistan by al-Qaeda. He became interested in being part of an airline hijack team. He learned to fly a jet airliner; then came 9/11.[55] Atta did not seem to be a disturbed man; perhaps he was somewhat of an extremist but someone who was very religious and angry at what he perceived as American injustice in Afghanistan and other Arab nations. The indoctrination by bin Laden's interpretations of the Quran (Koran) focused his anger and provided him a solution. The result was predictable. His death appeared to be more of an altruistic suicide, that is, dying for a cause, similar to the Japanese Kamikaze pilots of World War II.

Prior to 9/11, a couple of teenagers had the same idea as the 9/11 terrorists. Eric Harris and Dylan Klebold, leaders of the Trench Coat Mafia, Littleton, Colorado, massacre in April, 1999, which resulted in the killing of thirteen persons including a teacher, wrote in their journal that had they survived the school slaughter. "We will hijack a hell of a lot of bombs and crash a plane into New York City with us inside firing away as we go down. Just something to cause more devastation. Hate! I'm full of hate and I love it. I hate people and they better fear me if they know what's good for them."[56] These adolescents were definitely disturbed, willing to kill and die for respect and validation by others. They committed suicide after the murders. Harris was under psychiatric care and taking psychiatric medication.

Like the "Kroth," the Trench Coat Mafia was another suburban neo-Nazi white, middle-class gang with some gothic characteristics. They were attracted to Marilyn Manson's industrial gothic, death metal music. Prior to the Columbine High massacre, the Trench Coat Mafia gang was like most gangs in the country, neither homicidal nor suicidal. Furthermore, it is uncommon for a gang to commit a homicide on school grounds. Most white suburban gangs such as neo-Nazi hate groups, commit their crimes in the community. From February 1996 to May 1999, 37 students and one teacher were killed on campus; 55 students were wounded and three committed suicide.[57] All of the above sixteen homicide and suicide perpetrators, with one exception, were adolescent "white males." The one exception was a "black male" who asked his female friend to carry his gun in her backpack. While reaching for a pencil, the gun accidentally went off in the classroom, wounding her in the leg. These 37 deaths burst into a national psychosocial outcry and a demand for immediate answers for this problem. On the other hand, to date, there hardly has been a whimper concerning the thousands of inner-city youths being killed each year by terrorist gangs in the nation. Consider the 9,196 deaths of Americans due to gang terrorism between 1986 and 2001 in just one U.S. urban area, Los Angeles, illustrated in Figure 13.3.

Los Angeles, with a population of nearly ten million people, has 150,000 gang members in approximately 1,000 to 1,200 gangs, with the majority being *Latino* and African American conflict and criminal gangs. Figure 13.3 shows that they commit about 400 to 800 gang-related homicides per year, but only a small percentage of these involve homicide followed by suicide. These are not detected or reported as such. It is not suggested that the vast majority of gang members suffer from serious mental illness—it might be mainly those who actually commit the 400 to 800 homicides each year, which represents less than half of 1 percent of the

Figure 13.3

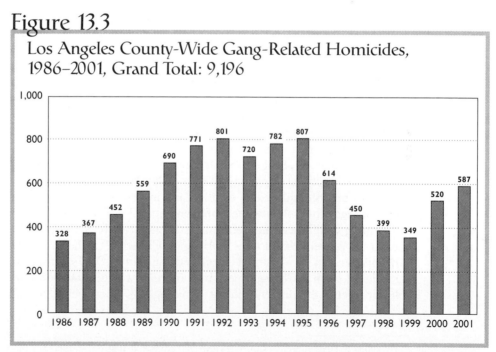

Source: L.A. Co. Sheriff's Dept.: Operation Safe Streets, December, 2002.

150,000 gang members. Those who commit homicide and then suicide, as was the case with the Trench Coat Mafia, are the most emotionally disturbed.

Al-Qaeda membership and gang culture require its members to place their primary loyalty and allegiance to the gang and/or their "cause," rather than to their family. Some, especially the more disturbed gang members, will actually kill and/or die for their gang, turf, religious cause, or respect. The importance of "respect" is also related to how secure they feel about themselves. The more vulnerable and inadequate they feel, often exacerbated by depression, the more drastic actions they believe are required to reestablish that respect.

Some gang members who seek more psychological strength abandon the gang and join forces with a greater power such as becoming "born again Christians." This was the case of 31-year-old al-Qaeda member Jose Padilla, an American of Puerto Rican descent and former gang member. He was raised in the Hispanic Logan Square neighborhood of Chicago. As a child he was not a bully but had the reputation that if someone started trouble with him, he would finish it. In his early teens he became a member of the Puerto Rican gang called the Latin Disciples. At age 14, he and co-gang members assaulted and robbed three men. One of the victims gave chase but Padilla and his "homies" killed him. Padilla was convicted of this crime and spent four years in a juvenile detention facility. Upon release he continued his criminal career, which consisted of assaults, thefts, resisting arrest, attacking police officers with knives, and firing his gun at a motorist.

Padilla became interested in the Muslim religion because he longed for the inner peace he observed among religious Muslims. He moved to Florida and in 1994 joined two mosques and was eventually converted, radicalized, and recruited into an extremist group along with other young Muslims. He married in 1996 but suddenly left his wife in 1998 and moved to Egypt, stating to family and friends that he was going to learn Arabic. His education was going to be sponsored by "friends." The CIA, who had been investigating Padilla, caught up with him in Cairo and arrested him as a known al-Qaeda terrorist. CIA investigators reported that Padilla was in Pakistan six months after 9/11 and met with al-Qaeda leaders and presented a proposal involving the development and detonation of a nuclear-type "dirty bomb" in the United States. Senior U.S. officials described the instructions as laughable and inaccurate, more of a parody than a plan. Nevertheless, former U.S. Attorney General Ashcroft had Padilla arrested and incarcerated indefinitely at Guantanamo without legal counsel as an "enemy combatant."[58] Padilla is still at Guantanamo.*
Obviously, Padilla, as other reformed gang members have done, should have reached out to the power of God as a "born again Christian" rather than Osama bin Laden and his version of Muslin religion and the Quran. We see therefore that Padilla graduated from a Chicago gang to a more powerful international terrorist gang. He represents the poster child or "missing link" between U.S. and international

*To avoid a U.S. Supreme Court review of Padilla's detention status, the Bush Administration has indicted him for criminal offenses and moved him to a federal prison awaiting a trial date (Time, December 5, 2005, p. 27).

terrorist gangs. Might there be others? In May 2005, the Departments of Justice and Homeland Security began a series of initiatives to confront a new domestic and international gang terrorism threat involving a juvenile and adult Salvadorian gang known as *Mara Salvatrucha*, or MS-13. Fostered by political and economic factors in the mid-1980s in Los Angeles, it has between 30,000 and 50,000 members in six countries, including 10,000 members in 33 states in the United States.[59] Law enforcement authorities report that al-Qaeda has met with leaders of MS-13 for recruitment purposes.[60] Apparently the link between domestic and international terrorist gangs is becoming more of a dangerous reality since the pioneering efforts of Padilla.

Another apparently disturbed al-Qaeda international gang terrorist was Englishman Richard Reid, the "shoe bomber" who attempted to light his explosive shoes on American Airlines Flight 63 in December 2001. His father was British born of Jamaican descent and married a white English woman who was the daughter of a magistrate. Richard Reid was born in London in 1973 at a time when his father was in prison for car theft. The father spent a total of twenty years in prison for various offenses. His parents divorced when he was 11. Reid left school at age 16 and, like his father, became involved in street crime and car theft. He spent several years in and out of prison. His father had converted to Islam in prison and advised his son to do the same while in prison because "Muslims treat you like a human being." After his next incarceration, Reid converted. He later became politicized at London's Finsbury Park at the center of extremist Islamic culture. Some of the extremists were members of al-Qaeda. By 1998 Reid was committed to "Jihad," the holy war. He reportedly traveled to Pakistan and later to the Afghanistan al-Qaeda terrorist training camp. He returned to London in the summer of 2001. It is presumed that during these summer months until October of 2001, the plan to bomb Flight 63 were finalized. To date it is not known who built Reid's very sophisticated shoes. The shoes contained very powerful explosives, and had Reid been successful in detonating them, they would have destroyed the plane, passengers, and Reid.[61] Reid's juvenile and adult criminal history, much like that of Padilla, would have been consistent with a diagnosis of conduct disorder of adolescence and, later as an adult, antisocial personality disorder.

Macro Intervention with Domestic Terrorist Gangs

It would be difficult to specifically target and impact homicidal–suicidal gang members through a macro intervention approach because they use the gang and its culture (often "packing" a firearm and being hypersensitive to being disrespected) to vent and express their violent pathology. Their homicidal–suicidal terrorist behavior can, however, serve as an indicator for individual special attention as described in the preceding section for U.S. gang members. If they have already committed and been convicted in court of serious gang-related terrorist acts against others, such as homicide, attempted homicide, and aggravated assault, incarceration will protect the community and make their gang less violent. Hopefully there are mental health resources available in the institution to provide them the necessary treatment.

An absence of these programs and a failure to identify these disturbed young people in the institution places them at suicide risk and other inmates at great risk for terrorizing victimization and even death. Rather, macro preventive intervention for this U.S. population would involve the creation and provision of community mental health programs for children. These could assist in the early elementary school detection of problem behavior symptoms such as attention deficit disorder (ADD), attention deficit hyperactivity disorder (ADHD), fetal alcohol syndrome (FAS), "crack cocaine babies," and childhood conduct disorder and depression.

For the majority of healthier, higher functioning gang members with greater ego strength who are not in the mod-core, hard-core, or super-hard-core career levels where gang terrorism behavior begins (described in Figure 13.1), and who are involved with gangs as a temporary, acting-out developmental phase, community-based macro-type programs can be successfully designed and implemented. One such program, called "The Little Village Project," was developed by social workers Spergel and Grossman in Chicago, Illinois. This community approach to the prevention and control of gang violence was based upon the following six key interrelated intervention strategies:[62]

1. *Community mobilization* (involvement of local residents, agencies, police, and youth).
2. *Opportunities provision* (jobs, special education, and training programs).
3. *Social intervention* (outreach to gang youths in the streets).
4. *Suppression* (controlling the gang in order to suppress its criminal behavior).
5. *Organizational change and development* (agency collaboration to reduce crime).
6. *Targeting* (multidiscipline team targets specific to youths and gangs).

The results of this macro, social work, community organization, gang-intervention program was positive. An analysis of 125 targeted youth over a three-year period indicates that 98 percent had contact with community youth workers and 95 percent received some kind of informal counseling or support from project staff.

 ## Macro Intervention with International Terrorist Gangs

In 1947, Secretary of State George C. Marshall advanced the concept of a European self-help program to be financed by the United States. The motivation for this idea, later called the "Marshall Plan," was a self-serving policy for the protection of the United States by helping Germany and other European nations rebuild their infrastructure and economies. The United States feared that without this help, poverty, unemployment, and dislocation would continue and make these countries vulnerable to a new Hitler-like fascism or communism, as occurred after World War I. Between April 1948 and December 1951, $13 billion worth of economic aid was distributed to various European nations, including Germany. The Marshall Plan was very successful.[63] A similar plan was followed in Japan after World War II.

In July 2002, President Bush promised a Marshall Plan–style program to rebuild Afghanistan. Again, this is a self-serving policy for the protection of the United States to prevent fragments of the deposed Taliban and the al-Qaeda terrorist network from finding sympathetic Arab public support and sections of Arab countries in which to regroup.[64] The United Nations has outlined a $14.9 billion goal over a ten-year period, and $5 billion over the next five years; $1.7 billion was needed immediately. The United States pledged $296.7 million for 2002 in addition to the $400 million in humanitarian aid already allocated.[65] Whether or not the United States will still honor these commitments following the March 2003 military invasion and occupation of Iraq in search of the still missing "weapons of mass destruction," remains to be seen. U.S. Forces captured Saddam Hussein on December 13, 2003.

Nevertheless, the successful Marshall Plan concept has set a social policy precedent and model for financial assistance to impoverished areas fostering terrorist gangs such as al-Qaeda. Afghanistan will receive financial assistance to reduce this problem thereby offering more protection to U.S. citizens. Could there not be a U.S. domestic Marshall Plan for the economic development of inner-city areas to reduce the thousands of Americans killed each year by gang terrorism? Or would they, because the majority are poor black and brown people, be considered "expendable"? The 1960s' U.S. Riot Commission's (Kerner Report) conclusion that: "White racism is essentially responsible for the explosive mixture which has been accumulating in our cities since the end of World War II," is, 45 years later, still very relevant to understanding the causes of urban gang terrorism in many of our cities across the country.

The Marshall plan policy is different than the victim compensation plan provided by Congress in 2002. The families of approximately 3,200 persons killed on 9/11 will be financially compensated from a $6 billion federal budget. First of all, each family will receive $250,000 for pain and suffering. Second, additional monies will be forthcoming based on the personal financial distinctions of the deceased. In other words, families of decedents with a higher income will receive more financial compensation. For example, the family of a 30-year-old stockbroker decedent with a wife and child who was earning $80,000 per year could potentially receive $2,521,241 in economic losses. On August 7, 2002, Ken Feinberg, director of the 9/11 Victim Compensation Fund provided by Congress, issued his first award. He awarded $1.04 million to the family of an unmarried recent college graduate who earned $60,000 per year and died at the World Trade Center.[66] The Victim Compensation Fund for the families who lost a family member due to international terrorism set a policy precedent. The $250,000 pain and suffering compensation, although never a replacement for the loss of a loved one, does assist families in reestablishing their lives emotionally and economically.

Whereas 9/11 claimed approximately 3,200 lives as a result of international gang terrorism, urban gang terrorism in Los Angeles alone claimed nearly three times that number, specifically, 9,196 lives between 1986 and 2001. Most of the victims were in some way associated with gangs, having either an active or inactive status. But also a significant number of victims were innocent children, adolescents, and adults without gang connections. Extrapolating the 9,196 Los Angeles gang terrorism murders and assuming that each decedent came from a family with at least four persons, 36,784 family survivors were therefore psychologically impacted by PTSD (among the thousands who witnessed the murders), grief, and bereavement—in short, pain and suffering. In comparison to the middle- and upper-class victims of 9/11, the majority of gang terrorism family survivors come from poor, single-parent, low-income families and neighborhoods. Should such a victim compensation policy be available only to victims of international gang terrorism, or should it be expanded to also include the victims of urban and suburban gang terrorism? Compensation of $250,000 for pain and suffering to the families of domestic gang terrorism would have a significant economic impact on their lives and, more importantly, provide them the resources to improve their quality of life, thereby reducing the risk of future premature deaths of their children due to domestic gang terrorism.

Concluding Comments

Today, 94 percent of U.S. urban and suburban areas with 100,000 people or more (177 of 189 areas) report that they have youth gangs.[67] For the past 20 to 30 years, Americans have shown a callousness and indifference to the thousands of predominantly African American, Hispanic, and Asian American inner-city gang killings occurring each year nationally but received a shocking "wake-up call" when the white neo-Nazi Trench Coat Mafia gang massacred thirteen people (twelve students, one teacher) at Columbine High in affluent white suburbia. The suicide of these two perpetrators, who were also the gang's leaders, "cooled off" the violence potential of the remaining twelve to fifteen Trench Coat Mafia gang members.

The Bush administration received a majority of support from both Republican and Democratic elected officials and the general public for spending billions of dollars for a war with Iraq. A total of 124 U.S. soldiers were killed from the beginning at the war in 2002 to March 2003, when President Bush declared "Mission accomplished." There are two major conclusions to draw from these facts: (1) Americans value war as a solution to international problems and are willing to spend billions toward this end; and (2) having lost 124 lives out of 300,000 military personnel in Iraq represents a death rate of 41.3 per 100,000. The annual death rate for 500 gang members in a population of 100,000 Los Angeles gang members represents a rate of 500 per 100,000. In other words, our soldiers were nearly 13 times safer on the battlefields of Iraq than gang members walking in the streets of Los Angeles. However, since President Bush announced the "end of the Iraq war" in March 2003 an additional 2211 U.S. soldiers were killed by Iraqi insurgents from March 19, 2003 to January 15, 2006.[68] With these additional deaths *and* the reduction of U.S. troops from 300,000 to 138,000, the current rate has now increased to 1,348 death per 100,000 population, far more than the Los Angeles gang homicide rate. Hopefully, the military death rates will not in any way reach the 9,196 gang-related deaths reported earlier in this chapter.

The federal government has established a precedent of social policies concerning international gang terrorism and economic compensation for the families of international gang terrorism. The implementation of a domestic "Marshall Plan" for those cities with terrorist gangs can enhance the economic development of afflicted areas and reduce the terrorist gang problem. As Secretary of State Colin Powell stated at the World Trade Forum in February, 2002, ". . . terrorism really flourishes in areas of poverty, despair, and hopelessness where people see no future" (see Endnote 2 in Chapter 1). Powell was speaking about the Mid East, but it certainly is relevant to U.S. gang terrorism.

Additionally, like the 9/11 survivor families, the families of domestic gang terrorists should receive $250,000 each for "pain and suffering" to help them escape distressing, dangerous environments. Otherwise, we are only compensating victims of international gang terrorism, which are far fewer in number than the victims of domestic gang terrorism. We, as taxpayers, are footing the bill for all of these programs.

The National Association of Social Workers, with its Washington, D.C., influence, could begin a political process by appealing to politicians, Mexican American Legal Defense and Education Fund, National Association for the Advancement of Colored People, American Civil Liberties Union, and other civil rights attorneys concerning this important issue. Such a social work and attorney collaboration on behalf of a class of people, highlighted in Chapter 10, "Class Action Social Work" might be the legal concept and theory to apply to this problem. It might sound like a "pie in the sky" plan, but unless we make an initial attempt and get the ball rolling, it will never happen. Our profession is strategically in position to have this effort as one of its highest priorities for the rest of the decade. It will reestablish social work's commitment to special populations in dire psychosocial need on a macro public policy level. We cannot afford to lose another 10,000 to 20,000 young Americans to gang terrorism in the coming five to ten years.

KEY WORDS AND CONCEPTS

Conflict gangs
Retreatist gangs
Criminal gangs
Cult/occult gangs
Neo-Nazi gangs
al-Qaeda

Marshall plan
Domestic and international gang terrorism
Super-hard-core gang member
Macro gang intervention
Victim compensation fund

SUGGESTED INFORMATION SOURCES

Li, Xiaoming, Stanton, Bonita, Pack, Robert, Harris, Carole, Cottell, Lesley, and Burns, James. "Risk and Protective Factors Associated with Gang Involvement Among Urban African American Adolescents," *Youth and Society* 34, No. 2 (December, 2002).

Morales, Armando T. "Urban Gang Violence: A Psychosocial Crisis," in Armando T. Morales and Bradford W. Sheafor, *Social Work: A Profession of Many Faces*, 8th Edition. Boston: Allyn and Bacon, 1998.

Morales, Armando T. "Urban and Suburban Gangs: The Psychosocial Crisis Spreads," in Armando T. Morales and Bradford W. Sheafor, *Social Work: A Profession of Many Faces*, 9th Edition. Boston: Allyn and Bacon, 2001.

Morales, Armando T. "Urban, Suburban, and International Terrorist Gangs," in Armando T. Morales and Bradford W. Sheafor, *Social Work: A Profession of Many Faces*, 10th Edition. Boston: Allyn and Bacon, 2004.

Patterns of Global Terrorism. U.S. Department of State, Publication #10940, Office of the Coordinator of Terrorism, May, 2002.

Rashid, Ahmed. *Taliban.* New Haven: Yale University Press, 2001.

"Terrorism in the United States 1999," Federal Bureau of Investigation, U.S. Department of Justice, Washington, D.C., U.S. Government Printing Office, 1999.

Thrasher, Frederick M. *The Gang: A Study of 1313 Gangs in Chicago.* Chicago: University of Chicago Press, 1963.

ENDNOTES

1. "What Terrorist Threat Colors Mean," http://usgovinfo.about.com.
2. June Gary Hopps, "Violence—A Personal and Societal Challenge," *Social Work* 32 (November–December 1987): 467–468.
3. Kelley O. Beaucar, "The Violence Has Come Home to Roost," *NASW News* 44, No. 6 (June, 1999): 3.
4. *Webster's Encyclopedic Unabridged Dictionary of the English Language* (San Diego, CA: Thunder Bay Press, 2001), p. 1960.
5. John Daniszewski and David Holley, "At Least 90 Captives Die in Moscow Raid," *Los Angeles Times* (October 27, 2002): A1.
6. http://www.amarillonet.com/stories/032900/usn
7. "The McVeigh Letters: Why I Bombed Oklahoma," http://www.papillonsartpalace.com/timothy.htm (p. 2).
8. "The McVeigh Letters," p. 3.
9. "Terrorism in the United States 1999" (Federal Bureau of Investigation, U.S. Department of Justice, Washington, D.C.: U.S. Government Printing Office, 1999), pp. i, ii.
10. "Chapter 11, Street Terrorism Enforcement and Prevention Act, 186.21, Legislative Finding and Declaration," *Penal Code 2002, Unabridged California Criminal Justice Edition* (San Clemente, CA: LawTech Publishing Co., 2002), p. 47.
11. Claire Johnson, Barbara Webster, and Edward Connors, "Prosecuting Gangs: A National Assessment," Series: National Institute of Justice, Research in Brief, February, 1995, p. 10. Available at http://www.ncjrs.org/txtfiles/pgang.txt

12. Claire Johnson et al., p. 3.
13. James C. Howell, "Youth gangs," *Fact Sheet #12* (Washington, D.C.: U.S. Department of Justice, Office of Juvenile Justice and Delinquency Prevention, December, 1997).
14. Penal Code Section 186.22, Participation in a criminal street gang, *West's California Juvenile and Court Rules 1993* (St. Paul, MN: West Publishing Co., 1993).
15. Associated Press, "Suspected al-Qaeda Appointee Is Revealed," *Los Angeles Times* (November 24, 2002): A44.
16. Richard C. Paddock, "Indonesia Seizes Alleged Planner of Bali Bombing," *Los Angeles Times* (Friday, November 22, 2002): A3.
17. Frederick M. Thrasher, *The Gang: A Study of 1313 Gangs in Chicago* (Chicago: University of Chicago Press, 1963), pp. 31–35.
18. W. B. Miller, "Lower Class Culture as a Generating Milieu of Gang Delinquency," *Journal of Social Issues* 14 (1958): 5–19.
19. See A. K. Cohen, *Delinquent Boys: The Culture of the Gang* (Glencoe, IL: Free Press, 1955); and R. A. Cloward and L. E. Ohlin, *Delinquency and Opportunity* (New York: Free Press, 1960).
20. D. Matza, *Delinquency and Drift* (New York: Wiley, 1964).
21. A. Morales, "A Study of Recidivism of Mexican American Junior Forestry Camp Graduates," unpublished Master's Thesis (School of Social Work, University of Southern California, 1963).
22. Ahmed Rashid, *Taliban* (New Haven: Yale University Press, 2001), p. vii.
23. J. Moore and C. P. Terret, "Highlights of the 1996 National Youth Gang Survey," *Fact Sheet #86* (Washington, D.C.: U.S. Department of Justice, Office of Juvenile Justice and Delinquency Prevention, November 1998).
24. "Patterns of Global Terrorism" (U.S. Department of State, Publication #10940, Office of the Coordinator of Terrorism, May 2002), pp. 145–147.
25. Thrasher, p. 117.
26. Cloward and Ohlin, p. 178.
27. *Report on Youth Gang Violence in California*, The Attorney General's Youth Gang Task Force, June 1981, p. 8
28. M. Poirier, "Street Gangs of Los Angeles County," unpublished pamphlet, 1982.
29. Irving A. Spergel, "Youth Gangs: Continuity and Change," in *Crime and Justice* (Chicago: University of Chicago Press, 1990), p. 613.
30. Rashid, p. 6.
31. K. L. Woodward, "In the Beginning There Were the Holy Books," *Newsweek* (February 11, 2002): 50–57.
32. Rashid, p. 134.
33. Rashid, p. 134.
34. "Verbatim," *Time* (March 18, 2002): 29.
35. Saint Augustine, *Confessions* (New York: The Modern Library, 1949), p. 34.
36. A. Davis and M. Haller, eds., *The People of Philadelphia* (Philadelphia: Temple University Press, 1973), p. 78.
37. B. Lane, *Killer Cults: Murderous Messiahs and Their Fanatical Followers* (London: Headline Book Publishing, 1996), pp. 16–17.
38. *Report of the National Advisory Commission on Civil Disorders* (New York: Bantam Books, 1968), p. 206.

39. A. Morales, *Ando Sangrando: I am Bleeding: A Study of Mexican American–Police Conflict* (La Puente, CA: Perspectiva Publications, 1972), pp. 91–122.

40. Thrasher, p. 33.

41. Rashid, p. 207.

42. U.S. Bureau of the Census, Current Population Survey, Special Studies P23–194, 1997.

43. I. L. Kutash, S. B. Kutash, and L. B. Schlesinger, eds., *Violence Perspectives on Murder and Aggression* (San Francisco: Jossey-Bass, 1978), pp. 219–232.

44. "Ounces of Prevention: Toward an Understanding of the Causes of Violence," *1982 Final Report to the People of California,* Commission on Crime Control and Violence Prevention, State of California, p. 137.

45. I. L. Kutash, p. 138.

46. *Callins vs. Collins,* No. 93–7054 (1994), Justice Harry Blackmun dissenting opinion, p. 1.

47. R. S. Brabman and M. H. Thomas, "Children's Imitation of Aggressive and Pro-Social Behavior When Viewing Alone and in Pairs," *Journal of Communication* 27 (1977): 199–205.

48. "Mafia Gangs Threaten Afghanistan's Archaeological Treasures," ABC News Online, Nov. 3, 2002. http://www.abc.net.au/news/newsitems 717558.htm.

49. Rashid, p. 207.

50. C. Wallis, "The Kids Are Alright," *Time* (July 5, 1999): 56–58.

51. "Afghanistan: Focus on the Plight of Widows," UN Office for the Coordination of Humanitarian Affairs, Sunday, December 1, 2002, p. 1. Also available at http://www.irinnews.org

52. Final Report, pp. 81–82.

53. P. Nestor, M. Kimble, I. Berman, and J. Haycock, "Psychosis, Psychopathy, and Homicide: A Preliminary Neuropsychological Inquiry," *The American Journal of Psychiatry* 159, No. 1 (January 2002): 138.

54. B. Hewitt, J. Harmes, and B. Stewart, "The Avenger," *People* (November 3, 1997): 116–120.

55. T. McDermott, "A Perfect Soldier," *Los Angeles Times,* Part One (January 27, 2002): 1, 10, 11, 12, and 13.

56. K. Nicholson, "Harris Wrote of Massacre Plan," *Denver Post* (Wednesday, December 5, 2001).

57. "Violence in U.S. Schools," List of School Shootings, ABC News, Internet Ventures, www.abcnews.com

58. A. Ripley, "The Case of the Dirty Bomber," *Time* (June 24, 2002): 28–32.

59. Chris Kraul, et. al., "L.A. Violence Crosses the Line," *Los Angeles Times*, May 15, 2005, p. 1.

60. Rick Connel and Robert J. Lopez, "MS 13 Leaders reportedly met with al-Qaeda," *Los Angeles Times*, March 15, 2005, p. 1.

61. M. Elliott, "The Shoe Bomber's World," *Time* (February 25, 2002): 46–50.

62. I. Spergel and S. F. Grossman, "The Little Village Project: A Community Approach to the Gang Problem," *Social Work* 42, No. 5 (September 1997): 456–470.

63. 1994–2001 *Encyclopedia Britannica.* "Marshall Plan," p. 1., file://C\Britannica\ 2001\ cache\info-97-html

64. S. Efron, "U.S. to Push for Promised Afghan Aid," *Los Angeles Times* (July 26, 2002): A3.

65. M. Magnier, "Nations Promise Funds to Afghans," *Los Angeles Times* (January 21, 2002): A1, A6.

66. J. Tyrangiel, "Holding the Checkbook," *Time* (September 11, 2002): 62–65.
67. M. W. Klein, "The Gang's All Here, There and Everywhere," *USC Trojan Family Magazine* 26 (1) (1997), p. 14.
68. http://www.cnn.com/SPECIALS/2003/iraq/forces/casualties/

chapter 14

Social Work with U.S. Casualties of the Middle East Wars*

Prefatory Comment

Since the beginning of World War II the United States has been at war more than 40 percent of the time. In terms of human sacrifice 375,000 soldiers have been killed in action and another 940,000 severely injured and maimed.[1] These data do not include the uncounted millions of civilian casualties in countries where the fighting occurred. And the devastation doesn't end with the death or injury of a soldier. It continues to affect individuals and/or their families for decades. Recent wars in the Middle East (i.e., Afghanistan and Iraq) present a unique challenge for social workers charged with meeting the needs of warfare survivors—those who were injured as well as surviving family members—needs that will continue for many years to come.

Social workers in hospitals and veterans' outreach centers play a central role in the recovery process—for both survivors and their loved ones. Social workers in military hospitals help patients and their families maintain communication. They arrange for transitions to other forms of care that might be necessary for rehabilitation or for the development of new job skills. They also address psychological injuries. Social workers in other human service agencies, too, have a role in the aftermath of war. They play a critical role in helping survivors and their families overcome the often unrecognized long-term consequences of war.

Social Work and Survivors of War

Working with survivors of war is not new for social workers. The first paid social workers in the United States were appointed to help with issues experienced by soldiers and their families in the 1860s, during the Civil War (see Chapter 4).

*This chapter was prepared by Joanne E. Clancy, Clinical Social Worker with the Trauma Recovery Team, Veterans Affairs Medical Center, Houston, Texas, and Bradford W. Sheafor, Professor of Social Work, Colorado State University.

Trattner notes that, "Like all wars, the 'War Between the States' created enormous relief problems, not only for wounded and disabled soldiers but for bereaved families who lost their male breadwinners during the conflict."[2] Social workers continued to provide these important services not only during the seven wars subsequent to the Civil War, but also during the intervening years when physical and emotional scars persisted.

Today and in the foreseeable future, social workers will attend to survivors of wars. Some will serve as social workers in the military. Others will be civilians employed by the Veterans' Administration and other veterans' organizations. Social workers employed in schools, hospitals, courts and prisons, mental health centers, child welfare agencies, drug and alcohol rehabilitation centers, nursing homes, and other practice settings will also serve survivors or families impacted by war. Because survivors of warfare present for services in multiple settings, all social workers should develop skills in grief counseling and management of trauma survivors' complex needs.

As in other areas of the human services, social workers are the professionals most likely to make referrals. They must not only know the general resources available to clients, but must also be informed about services specifically designed for veterans and their families. If needed services are not available social workers must advocate for their creation. Social workers, unlike individuals in the general population, are in a position to observe the far-reaching aftermath of war as it affects members of society for years after the hostilities have ceased. It is from this vantage point that social workers have special insights to contribute regarding the prevention of wars.

Social Work with Soldiers and Veterans

The recent wars in Afghanistan and Iraq are the most sustained combat efforts initiated by the United States since the Vietnam War. This new generation of combat veterans requires the focused energies of many service providers (physicians, nurses, psychologists, occupational and physical therapists, and social workers) as the veterans strive to reintegrate into society. The social work profession has a unique opportunity to take the lead in this stabilization and recovery process because the systemic manner through which social workers approach problems, coupled with their ability to provide multiple levels of service in a variety of settings, maximizes their ability to impact the lives of both veterans and their families.

People die in wars. An even greater number survive but sustain serious, life-changing injuries on the battlefield. During World War II one out of every three wounded soldiers died. In Vietnam one out of four wounded soldiers died. Soldiers serving in Iraq have even better odds of surviving; only one out of every eight wounded soldiers die.[3] Despite this "good news," many surviving soldiers return home with catastrophic injuries that disfigure and emotionally scar them for life. Advances in field medicine may save their lives but, as one former medic quite eloquently stated, "I'm not sure we did them any favors. These men and women were young, healthy people in the prime of life. They went home with missing arms, legs, and eyes. A lot of them have psychological problems as well. Even the lucky ones, the ones who have people to help and support them, face decades of physical and emotional pain, discrimination, and the challenge of learning to live a life very different from the one they planned. Yeah, I'm not sure we did them any favors."

Adjustment to the traumatic loss of one's physical integrity, especially when functional ability is seriously compromised, is a long and painful process. Simple tasks once taken for granted become impossible or require Herculean effort to accomplish. Depending on the nature and severity of the loss, the affected individual may require months or years of physical therapy to regain even a fraction of his or her former independence. Dramatic changes in body image, coupled with others' reactions to the veteran's altered physical appearance, further complicate the recovery process. One young soldier, a quadriplegic, stated, "I want to commit suicide but I can't move my arms or legs. No one will help me do it. My mother keeps telling me things will get better if I just have patience. I'm 21 years old . . . how can things ever get better? I was an athlete. I planned to become a physical therapist. I wanted to get married and start a family someday. Who would want me now? I am completely helpless until someone cleans me up and sits me in my motorized chair. All my dreams are gone, what's the point?"*

Sustained exposure to potentially life-threatening experiences escalates the risk for psychological problems. This is especially true in a war zone where death and serious injury are not only feared, but also expected. In a recent study targeting the effects of combat on the mental health of soldiers in Afghanistan and Iraq,[4] researchers discovered a strong correlation between combat experiences (being shot at, handling dead bodies, witnessing the death of a peer, killing enemy combatants) and the prevalence of posttraumatic stress disorder (PTSD). The presence of PTSD increased proportionally with the number of battles in which soldiers engaged during their deployment. Mental illnesses most commonly identified among study participants include acute stress disorder, posttraumatic stress disorder, generalized anxiety disorder, major depression, and alcohol abuse.

Despite the high incidence of mental distress among combat troops, few soldiers express interest in pursuing mental health treatment. This holds true even when the soldiers are presented with opportunities to visit "wellness tents" in the field, participate in debriefings post-deployment, or meet with mental health professionals in more formal settings. Researchers in one study[5] determined that only 38 to 45 percent of soldiers who met criteria for a mental disorder were interested in receiving help. Even more startling, only 23 to 40 percent of those expressing a desire for assistance actually sought help post-discharge. The stigma of mental illness (i.e., "I am weak, crazy, not normal") and the fear that seeking mental health care will adversely impact future career opportunities were primary factors in their decision-making process.

---

*All stories told by soldiers and veterans throughout this chapter were reported to social workers in veterans' centers and hospitals.

Social Work with the Families of Soldiers and Veterans

Combat survivors struggle to escape traumatic memories that assault them through intrusive thoughts and nightmares. At the same time, their loved ones struggle to understand what happened to the individual they sent to war. The person who returns is altered in ways that cannot always be seen or explained. One soldier's mother poignantly stated, "I sent my son to war. The person they sent back is not my son . . . it is a shell that looks like my son. He is angry and distant. My heart is breaking because nothing I say or do can recapture what he, and we, have lost."

When soldiers receive orders for deployment into a combat zone, a kaleidoscope of emotional reactions emerge from both the soldier and from his or her family members: Denial, "this isn't really happening. . . it is?"; Fear, "what if he or she is seriously injured, crippled, or killed in combat?"; Anger, "I never really thought he or she would be sent to war."; Confusion, "what will become of our family before, during, and after my loved one's deployment into a war zone?" The emotional impact of impending deployment is magnified by the reality that war, even under the best of circumstances, results in death and sacrifice.

The free-floating sea of emotional reactions within and between family members can wreak havoc on a family's ability to prepare for, endure, and recover from the deployment experience. Individuals process and cope with emotional distress in ways uniquely their own. Age, gender, and past experiences influence each family member's willingness and ability to openly challenge and move through their collective emotional experience. During this critical time in the family's life cycle, forging a united front is crucial to the healthy adjustment of all involved. Without adequate guidance and support, many of these "at risk" families will become "collateral casualties" of war.

Social Programs for Soldiers and Veterans

In the event of the death of a soldier, family members not only must deal with the death of a loved one, but most families will also be poorer. Initially, government programs help to offset expenses and the wages of the soldier who died, but these resources are designed to decline over time, thus challenging social workers to help the families develop alternate sources of income.

> The National Military Families Association calculated the benefits for the family (a wife and children ages 1 and 3) of an enlisted man with a salary of $38,064 a year, including a housing allowance and combat pay. Apart from the lump-sum payments (i.e., $12,420), his wife would receive the equivalent of an annual income of $ 57,624, falling to $ 45,804 after two years, then declining in steps as the children reach adulthood. By the time the younger child turns 23, the wife's check would amount to only about a quarter of her husband's active-duty salary.[6]

Further, many families require emotional assistance as they experience the grief process. Social workers in hospice agencies and mental health centers regularly provide valuable counseling to parents, siblings, spouses, and children of soldiers killed while performing military duty.

Social workers also encounter soldiers returning from a war zone who experience problems meeting basic social needs. If the individual is a professional soldier who has not yet fulfilled his or her commitment to military service, reassignment to a new duty station often occurs. This forestalls any immediate concerns about housing and income. If, however, the individual has fulfilled his or her military obligation, an additional challenge of separation from service and transition to civilian life ensues. Housing and finances may or may not be an issue for these individuals. The presence or absence of extended family support during this time of transition is a primary variable in determining post-discharge outcomes.

The financial issue is more complex for reservists and National Guard personnel mobilized to an active duty status. Although job security is guaranteed, many of these individuals incur significant financial reversals while on active duty. The military cannot, and does not, match the salaries these individuals receive from their civilian employers. This disparity in income often generates far-reaching consequences for these individuals and the family members they leave behind. In one instance a young mother of three stated, "What does the military expect us to do? My husband made over $100,000 a year as a computer analyst. I am a housewife. How am I supposed to pay the mortgage and keep our household running on what the Army is paying him? We will probably have to file bankruptcy. So much for supporting those willing to serve their country!"

Social Work Practice during Reintegration Efforts

Outreach and Resource Mobilization

Although several disciplines work with active duty military personnel and veterans, social workers are best qualified to address their subsequent emotional and social needs. Historically what sets the social work profession apart from other disciplines is the willingness to meet individuals "where they are," emotionally and geographically. Social workers display great flexibility in their willingness to engage in outreach efforts designed to identify and engage elusive populations. This willingness to aggressively pursue populations most at risk "where they work, live, and play" allows social workers to intervene early on, before the problems escalate.

Social workers assigned to active duty military positions, and those working civilian contracts for the Department of Defense or other divisions of the federal government, play a critical role in outreach efforts. Their presence at military bases, in the field, and at veterans' outreach centers and hospitals across the country provide opportunities to identify the needs of soldiers and veterans at each stage of the deployment process. The following case study highlights the role social work plays in promoting a health transition for soldiers and their family members.

Mr. X is a 22-year-old, married Marine sergeant recently discharged from the military after a tour of duty in Iraq. He was discharged approximately 2 months before the social worker's initial contact with him at a local veterans' outreach center. The social worker assigned to his case identified a number of problem areas. The veteran had limited income and needed temporary financial assistance. He was interested in securing employment and in returning to school, but had no idea how to access vocational services. He and his spouse were experiencing a variety of marital problems they had not been able to resolve on their own. Both partners had little understanding of the emotional problems this soldier was experiencing.

The social worker immediately set forth to identify and mobilize available resources. The veteran and his wife received referrals to community-based agencies for financial services. A referral to the vocational counseling department at the local veterans' hospital was initiated to assess his readiness for training and/or job placement services. The social worker also initiated a referral to the hospital's PTSD program so the veteran and his spouse could receive assistance coping with the veteran's psychiatric problems. The couple also received a list of Internet referrals where they could download information pertinent to issues encountered by veterans of Middle Eastern wars.[7]

The social worker met with this couple weekly at the outreach center for several months. She provided emotional support and monitored their progress accessing identified resources. When the couple expressed frustration due to snags in the referral process to several agencies, the social worker assumed an advocacy role. Several months later when the veteran returned for follow-up services at the veterans' hospital he was asked what had been most helpful during the initial months following his military discharge. The veteran replied, "The Vet Center social worker. We felt lost, alone, and confused. Our social worker was very kind. She guided us through a maze of resources we would never have figured out on our own. She seemed to really care about what happened to us and gave us hope that, in time, things would get better. I don't know where we would be if this caring professional had not stepped up to bat for us."

Education and Skill Building

The transition from soldier to civilian, especially after serving in a war zone, is challenging. If physical and/or mental disabilities factor into the equation, the adjustment process becomes even more complicated. Through individual, group, and family sessions social work professionals provide knowledge about specific conditions, identifying existing treatment options and introducing coping skills so those affected can more readily navigate the challenges at hand. The simple act of "naming the problem" brings relief and provides direction. As one veteran so aptly stated, "Now that I know what the problem is, I can begin identifying ways to attack it."

Skill building is another critical piece of the recovery process. The majority of combat veterans are young and they possess a limited range of coping skills. Exposure to a variety of problem-solving techniques, offered through educational classes and skill building sessions, provides them with a "toolbox for recovery."

These tools, once acquired and reinforced, empower individuals to assume the lead in creating their own solutions. The social worker's role during this process is to impart knowledge and guide individuals through role-play sessions designed to enhance their effectiveness in skills application. The case of a young female amputee clearly illustrates this point.

> Ms. P is a 23-year-old female soldier severely wounded during a terrorist attack in Iraq. She was standing guard when a jeep carrying explosives crashed into a building near her position. She lost both legs below the knees. Emotionally devastated by her loss, this young veteran had no idea how to cope with the drastic life changes brought about by her amputations. Her family was equally at a loss. The social worker assigned to her case provided information about typical reactions experienced by amputees and their family members. He invited them to attend a support group with other amputees and their families. This provided opportunities for mutual support and the exchange of ideas and information. He also invited the family to attend a series of classes that focused on independent living skills. During these classes the veteran developed strategies to assertively communicate her needs. Role-plays where family members assumed the role of amputee helped sensitize them to the challenges faced by their loved one on a daily basis. The veteran and her family also received instruction on the variety of prosthetic devices she would need to normalize her life. Stress management and play therapy classes introduced healthy alternatives for coping with distress inherent after traumatic losses.
>
> When asked to describe this educational experience Ms. P replied, "My first reaction . . . this is a big waste of time. I didn't see how going to classes would help me or my family deal with the fact I have no legs. I attended grudgingly at first to humor the social worker. Then, as the weeks went by, I realized things were getting better. We were learning new ways to get things done that really worked. I learned to communicate with my family more productively and they stopped being afraid to tell me how they really felt. We have even learned to laugh together when the going gets tough. Meeting with other amputees and their family members was also helpful. We learned a lot from each other and made some new friends, too. I never realized how important these classes would be to my recovery. I hope all the other veterans coming back with injuries like mine have a chance to participate in this kind of program. The classes made me realize I still have a life to live, but it is up to me to get out there and live it."

Supportive Interventions

Taking a human life or witnessing the traumatic death of another human being produces far-reaching consequences for even the most psychologically sound individual. Although loss is a normal part of the life cycle, most humans never encounter the type of traumatic losses identified above. During the heat of battle most soldiers report feeling numb. One young soldier described his experience by saying, "I was on auto-pilot. I saw people dying all around me and all I could focus on was staying alive. I had to kill several enemy soldiers and didn't think much of it at the time."

The psychological impact of one's actions in combat may take days, weeks, even months to surface. Another young veteran reported the following experience. "I was a helicopter door gunner in Iraq. My job was to kill enemy soldiers on the ground. One day we came across a band of rebels and they started shooting at our helicopter. I returned fire, knowing I would kill at least some of them. After the battle we landed to do a body count. Among the dead were a young woman and her baby. As we flew back to base camp it felt like I was dying inside, one piece at a time. Things have never been the same since that day."

Survivors of combat trauma face three significant challenges as they strive to recover from traumatic losses incurred on the battlefield. First, taking human life, even in the name of self-preservation, transforms them into "old souls." An *old soul* is a young person who has seen the darkest side of him- or herself. Although all humans have the capacity to kill when confronted with life and death situations, few of us ever cross this line. Thinking you can kill someone, and knowing you have, are very different experiences.

Second, the taking of a human life generates tremendous conflict between one's beliefs and values, and actions taken during the heat of battle. One young soldier participating in a PTSD program expressed the following thoughts. "I grew up in the church. I learned that harming others was a mortal sin. I remember one day, when my unit was preparing for battle, a preacher stopped by our tent to pray with us. He asked God to protect us and keep us safe. Then he told us to go out there and kill those bastards. His comment really confused me. He sanctioned behavior that is in direct conflict with what I spent the first 18 years of my life believing. It really messed me up. Now I question if God even exists. I also worry about my soul . . . if there is a God, am I doomed to hell because of what I did in Iraq?"

Finally, returning combat soldiers often experience profound guilt. This guilt stems not only from taking human lives, but also for surviving when others do not. One young man, traveling in a convoy, described the following experience. "My buddies and I were driving supplies between two base camps. My truck was scheduled to take the lead, but the other driver begged me to let him go first. He was new in country and wanted to prove himself. I said yes against my own better judgment. We were on a narrow road with a steep ravine on one side. The truck in front of me hit a mine. All I could do is watch in horror as the truck plunged over the cliff. Bodies flew everywhere. I stopped my truck and we scrambled down the cliff to rescue survivors. There weren't any . . . we ended up collecting dead bodies instead. If I had refused to let the new guy lead the way this wouldn't have happened. It's a hell of a burden to carry around each day."

Social workers provide the bulk of mental health services to individuals seeking assistance from veterans' outreach centers, hospitals, and mental health trauma programs. The focus of treatment is empowering veterans to identify, process, and move beyond their traumatic experiences. Social workers conducting individual and group therapy sessions encourage trauma survivors to "remember and let go" of traumatic memories, since forgetting is not a realistic option. Multifamily group therapy adds yet another dimension to the recovery process. Allowing veterans and family members to share their common experiences provides hope and encouragement that life can, and will, go on. A final case study illustrates the social worker's role as change agent when addressing veterans' mental health concerns.

Mr. M. is a 25-year-old, married combat veteran who served two tours of duty in Iraq. During the second tour his unit encountered a group of insurgents, which resulted in intense hand-to-hand combat. Several of his buddies were killed during the attack. Mr. M. sustained only minor injuries. Unfortunately, his traumatic experience continued to haunt him after discharge. He reported a great deal of inner conflict about having killed several enemy soldiers during the battle. He also felt guilty for surviving when many of his peers did not. During his first session with a social worker in an outpatient trauma program he shared the following information. "I have been a wreck since I got back from Iraq. I have nightmares about killing and being killed. I think about the war all the time and have to avoid watching the news or I get all stressed out. I am irritable a lot of the time and don't want to be around anyone. Life just doesn't seem worth living anymore."

The social worker's first intervention involved consultation with the clinic psychiatrist. The psychiatrist prescribed medication to help alleviate Mr. M.'s symptoms. Next, Mr. M. was enrolled in both individual and group therapy. The goal of individual therapy was to provide a milieu where the veteran could discuss the most painful aspects of his combat experience. The social worker identified a number of techniques to aid him in redirecting painful thoughts when they occurred. Mr. M. was also assisted in challenging self-defeating thoughts about his survival and reframing his feelings about killing enemy soldiers in the line of duty.

During group therapy sessions the focus was helping Mr. M. realize he is not alone in his struggle. Opportunities to process thoughts and feelings with other veterans experiencing similar reactions helped him develop a new appreciation of his own situation. It also provided exposure to others' coping strategies, some of which he adopted with great success. During one session he remarked that things at home were not going very well between him and his spouse. This resulted in a referral to a multifamily group. In this context Mr. M. and his wife learned how to join forces so they could combat symptoms of the veteran's PTSD instead of fighting with one another.

After 3 months of treatment the veteran and his wife met with the treatment team to discuss his progress and identify ongoing issues for work. Both expressed great relief that things were beginning to improve. Mr. M. was less irritable and anxious. His nightmares were less frequent and intense. He noted a return of optimism about the future. His wife reported that participating in the multifamily group was the best possible thing that could have happened. She felt supported and validated both by the social work leader and other members of the group. She stated, "Attending family group made me realize we are not in this alone. I heard our story coming out of the mouths of other veterans and their wives. Some of them have been in treatment longer that we have. Their testimonies gave us hope that things can and will get better if we just hang in there. I don't know what might have happened if we hadn't come in for help. We still have a long way to go, but at least we are moving in the right direction!"

Special Considerations Regarding Today's Victims of War

It is clear that social workers have an important role to play in assisting individuals and families who are survivors of war. There is, however, special knowledge and unique insights required of social workers as they serve these individuals?[8]

Serving an All-Volunteer Force

Previous generations of soldiers resulted from a combination of draftees and enlistees. Present-day soldiers are members of an all-volunteer force who have elected to spend at least part of their careers in the military. This difference affects the characteristics of who is in the military and how they respond when they face physical or mental injuries, presenting special challenges for the social workers who serve them. For example, over 50 percent of soldiers serving in Afghanistan and Iraq are between the ages of 20 and 29. Although early intervention and outreach efforts are much improved since the Vietnam War, youth often deters returning soldiers from accepting available support. Young veterans tend to minimize symptoms and avoid seeking professional help. When problems are psychiatric in nature, these problems are even more difficult to identify and young soldiers are more reluctant to engage in treatment.

Also, this group of war veterans is more educated than veterans from previous wars. Ninety-five percent of active duty soldiers have either a high school diploma or have passed the General Education Equivalence Exam (GED). This challenges clinicians to develop new and creative ways of selling the idea that early intervention, for both medical and psychiatric conditions, can assist with the re-integration process.

Further, over 50 percent of service members are married, and about 11 percent of marriages are to other service members. This generates serious concerns when married couples are simultaneously deployed to high-risk areas, especially when minor children are involved. Complex issues facing couples in this situation include: the constant worry that one's partner will be injured or killed; child care during the parents' deployment; the impact of separation from parental figures on offspring at critical points during the developmental process; and reestablishing family ties once members reunite. Of even greater concern are the consequences for children when one or both parents die in combat.

Finally, the ability to choose whether or not one engages in military service impacts post-discharge adjustment, especially for individuals deployed to a war zone. When an individual is free to choose whether or not to join the military it creates a sense of self-determination (i.e., "This is something I elected to do, and going to war may or may not be part of the package"). When one is conscripted it generates a sense of powerlessness and anger, especially when bad things happen (i.e., "I had no choice . . . the government ruined my life").

Women in the Military and Associated Gender Issues

During previous wars female soldiers were forbidden to participate in direct combat. Present-day women can and do select military occupation specializations (MOS) that place them on frontlines of the battlefield. As a result, female combat veterans face the same physical and mental health risks as their male counterparts. This role transition creates far-reaching consequences in regard to treatment. Patients currently treated by veterans' hospitals are predominately male. When females do seek treatment, the primary focus, until now, has been military sexual trauma and health-related issues. The influx of females joining the military is changing the face of post-military intervention. As female veterans become a larger percentage of those seeking care, clinicians must create and implement programming designed to meet the unique needs of this population.

The Need for Cultural Competence When Serving Returning Troops

In the 1960s the civil rights movement was a major focus of the American people. The inequity between racial groups in the 60s was nowhere more evident than for those serving in the military. Soldiers of color were drafted and sent to fight in foreign lands for freedoms they were themselves denied back home. One African American veteran stated, "I fought a war to free the South Vietnamese people from oppression. Then I came home and had to use separate facilities instead of the restrooms white folks used. I had to enter restaurants from the back or was refused service altogether. Many privileges white people took for granted were not even an option for me. I am still angry that I was drafted to fight for something I could not even enjoy myself."

America has made great strides in addressing racial discrimination since the 1960's. Today, ethnic minorities make up a portion of military personnel that is very close to the minority distribution in the United States. As of September 30, 2004, combined deployment lists from the Afghanistan and Iraq wars report the following racial analysis of troops: 70 percent white, 15 percent African American, 9.5 percent Hispanic, and 5 percent other/unknown. These figures do not include soldiers deployed within the United States.[9]

Despite these gains, in addressing racial discrimination, however, prejudice is still very much present in certain segments of the population. Professionals working with returning veterans of color must be careful to avoid assumptions based on race or ethnicity. It is imperative to remember that strategies applied to the dominant culture with great success might fail miserably with minority groups. Cultural and racial sensitivity affords clinicians the opportunity to learn, from their patients, what is most and least helpful during the reintegration process.

The Affects of Guerrilla Warfare and Acts of Terrorism

As opposed to the more traditional forms of battlefield warfare, in Iraq and Afghanistan the greatest sources of danger are guerrilla warfare and terrorist acts, not direct combat.[10] In an urban war threats are ambiguous. Anyone, any-where, might be the enemy. This lack of an "identified enemy" places soldiers in a constant state of alert. During the Iraq War the ratio of seriously wounded to those killed in action was the highest in U.S. history.[11] Ninety-four percent of soldiers in Iraq reported exposure to hostile small arms fire, 86 percent reported knowing someone who was seriously injured or killed, and 68 percent reported seeing dead or seriously injured Americans. The majority of these losses were the result of random acts of violence. One young Iraq veteran relayed his feel-ings by saying, "I never felt safe over there. I was a truck driver, not a combat soldier, but every time I got in my vehicle I worried about being ambushed or hitting a mine. I saw too many of my friends die that way . . . I always worried I might be next."

Social Work and the Prevention of War

Social workers serve the survivors of war, but it is important to also address the broader issues that are the causes and consequences of war. Identifying the cause of war is a complex issue. Surely one factor is the grossly unequal distribution of wealth and resources throughout the world. As identified in Chapter 11, "Social Work throughout the World," a few rich and developed countries (and especially the United States) possess a significant part of the world's wealth and use a sub-stantial proportion of the earth's natural resources (e.g., oil, timber, minerals), allowing their people to enjoy a substantially higher quality of life than exists else-where. It is not surprising that others who experience the social consequences of such poverty (i.e., poor housing, inadequate diet, poor health, limited transporta-tion, etc.) are willing to go to war to correct this inequality. Another factor contributing to wars is growing religious fanaticism, both in the United States and throughout the world, in which one extremist religion attempts to force its religious beliefs onto others. This condition polarizes people and leaves little room for compromise, often preempting efforts to address other human concerns. Finally, excessive emphasis on "nationalism" and "patriotism," although laudable in spirit, too often leads to a false sense of superiority and unwillingness to compromise national desires for the greater good of the world's people.

The cost of war in terms of both human and economic resources is enormous. The loss of life and the maiming of human beings not only have a substantial emotional impact on those affected, but also have a significant economic drain on the nation. Resources that might have been devoted to resolving the social, health, and economic issues discussed elsewhere in this book are diverted to maintaining a military presence throughout the world, protecting homeland security, and absorb-ing the direct costs of active battle. For example, the following 10-year change in U.S. expenditures reflects the diversion of resources from before the Afghanistan and Iraq wars to FY2004 (see Table 14.1).[12]

Table 14.1

Increase in U.S. Expenditures for National Defence (1994 to 2004) Compared to Expenditures for Domestic Social Program			
	1995	**2004**	**Increase**
National defense	$ 273.6 Billion	$ 454.1 Billion	66.0 %
Training/employment/social services	13.7 Billion	20.4 Billion	48.0 %
Income security	39.2 Billion	52.3 Billion	33.3 %

Clearly, the cost of war has shifted resources away from meeting the needs of vulnerable U.S. citizens. The spiraling national debt resulting from this action must be paid off by future generations—with financial interest.

In its policy statement on "Peace and Social Justice,"[13] the National Association of Social Workers takes a stand on three issues related to war.

▶ Although we have recently gone through a new military buildup and actions against terrorist groups and the countries that harbor them, the United States needs to emphasize economic support rather than Western dominance. . . . Whenever possible, the United States must foster cooperation in its foreign policy rather than unilateral military action. A long-range goal should be the reduction of military spending and diversion of the subsequent savings to social needs.

▶ Even in the face of overt terrorist attacks on the United States, it is still vital that we work in creative ways with other nations and international organizations to reduce violence against innocent civilians.

▶ The United States needs to continue using qualified professional social workers to serve the armed forces and military dependents to ensure that a high priority is given to human values and social welfare needs in those settings.

Concluding Comment

War has far-reaching consequences for combat soldiers, their family members, and society as a whole. Without timely and effective intervention, soldiers returning from Afghanistan and Iraq are at risk for a lifetime of maladjustment and misery. Social work professionals, acting as teachers, guides, and advocates, can significantly reduce this risk. Strategic placement of social workers during all stages of the recovery process will enhance soldiers' potential to move beyond their combat experiences. Although social workers cannot stop wars, prevent deaths during combat, or undo physical and/or psychiatric injuries incurred during war, they can empower survivors to live happier, more productive lives. Further, they can use their advocacy skills to help prevent wars and improve the quality of life for all people throughout the world.

KEY WORDS AND CONCEPTS

Role of social work during reintegration efforts

Effects of guerrilla warfare and terrorist acts on combat troops

Social implications of war for returning veterans

Consequences of deployment for families

Challenges imposed by traumatic physical injuries

Impact of combat on soldiers' mental health

Women in the military

Cultural competence in social work practice with soldiers

SUGGESTED INFORMATION SOURCES

Riverbend. *Baghdad Burning: Girl Blog from Iraq.* New York: Feminist Press at the City University of New York, 2005.

Roberts, Cheryl A. *Coping with Post-Traumatic Stress Disorder: A Guide for Families.* Jefferson, NC: McFarland, 2003.

Skiba, Katherine M. *Sister in the Band of Brothers: Embedded with the 101st Airborne in Iraq.* Lawrence, KS: University of Kansas Press, 2005.

ENDNOTES

1. Ross Doutkat, Abigail Cutler, and Terrence Henry, "Casualties of War," *Atlantic* 29 (March 2004): 50.
2. Walter I. Trattner. *From Poor Law to Welfare State: A History of Social Welfare in America,* 6th Edition. (New York: Free Press, 1999), p. 77.
3. Nancy Gibbs, "The Lucky Ones," *Time Magazine* 165 (March 21, 2005): 36.
4. C. Hoge, C. Castro, S. Messer, D. McGurk, D. Cotting, and R. Koffman. "Combat Duty in Iraq and Afghanistan, Mental Health Problems, and Barriers to Care," *New England Journal of Medicine* 351: 13–22.
5. Ibid.
6. Jerry Alder, "Children of the Fallen." *Newsweek* 145 (March 21, 2005): 26.
7. The National Center for Posttraumatic Stress Disorder, www.ncptsd.org, identifies multiple links to Internet sites offering education materials, support networks, and benefits/resource information.
8. For detailed information refer to: National Center for PTSD and Walter Reed Army Medical Center. *Iraq War Clinician Guide,* 2nd Edition. (Washington, DC: Department of Veterans Affairs, June, 2004) and *VHA Office of Public Health and Environmental Hazards Analysis of VA Health Care Utilization among Southwest Asian War Veterans Combined. Operation Iraqi Freedom/Operation Enduring Freedom.* (Washington, DC: Department of Veteran's Affairs, March 2005).
9. Han Kang, Director of Epidemiology Services, Department of Veterans Affairs, e-mail communiqué on May 9, 2005.
10. "The unique circumstances and mental health impact of the wars in Afghanistan and Iraq: A National Center for PTSD fact sheet." Retrieved 5/3/2005 from http://www.ncptsd.va.gov.

11. T. Ricks, "Where Does Iraq Stand Among U.S. Wars? Total Casualties Compare to Spanish-American, Mexican, and 1812 Conflicts," *The Washington Post* (May 31, 2004): A16.

12. *The U.S. Budget for Fiscal Year 2006: Historical Tables.* "Table 8.7—Outlays for Discretionary Programs: 1962–2006." (Washington, DC: Office of Management and Budget, 2005):145–146.

13. National Association of Social Workers, *Social Work Speaks: National Association of Social Workers Policy Statements, 2003–2006,* 6th Edition, (Washington, DC: NASW Press, 2003): 267–269.

part five

Social Work Practice with Special Populations

The term *special populations* has a particular meaning in this book. Dictionary definitions note that "special" is something "additional to the regular." Like all people, the populations addressed in the following chapters have the same universal needs as all humans, but in addition they experience the need for special attention by social workers. These are population groups who are characterized by uniqueness based on race, ethnic origin, gender, age, a handicapping condition, or other characteristics that make them more vulnerable to problematic social conditions or second-class status.

In addition to helping people individually address the issues they confront, the social worker also addresses the forces in American society that keep these groups disadvantaged. The underlying philosophy of social work is that the individual and the society are interrelated. For example, poor physical and mental health, premature death, chronic substance abuse, and inadequate nutrition are all factors that are correlated with, and which contribute to, people living in poverty. Some people would argue that these special population groups are disadvantaged because they are biologically or emotionally inferior to the majority—leading to a view labeled "isms," i.e., a perspective representing racism, sexism, classism, ageism, and so on. Social workers reject the "isms" and conclude that when a group consistently experiences a social condition more severely than others, there is systematic bias built into the society's structure that can, and should, be changed.

In working with special population clients, a combination of a generalist practice approach and specialized clinical skills are often required. People who have experienced the "isms" often experience multiple areas of problematic social functioning, requiring a generalist approach, but some issues would likely be of such a serious nature that specialist skills are needed to affect change. In the following chapters, important practice considerations for several special population groups are identified as a means of sensitizing the new social worker to the unique characteristics and experiences of each group.

The eleven chapters in Part Five each address a different special population. Chapters 15 through 19 address groups that are disadvantaged because of physical characteristics such as gender, age, sexual orientation, and physical disability. Chapters 20 through 25 address populations who experience discrimination and oppression due to race, ethnicity, and culture—including the experiences of the Muslim American community (especially since 9/11), Asian Americans, American Indians and Alaskan Natives,

Mexican Americans, African Americans, and Puerto Ricans. For special populations in which the authors did not have sufficient expertise, nationally recognized experts in working with that population were commissioned to write those chapters. To bring continuity to the chapters, each author was provided with guidelines that suggested including demographic information about that population, analyzing the group's experience in U.S. society through a five-level ecosystems model (see Box P5.1), discussing issues in social work practice when

Box P5.1

An Ecosystems Model for Assessing Special Populations

The practice of social work involves a focus on the interaction between the person (individual, couple, family, group, organization, community, or larger societal structure) and the environment. A social work intervention might be directed at the person or the environment, or both. The goal of the social worker is to enhance and restore the psychosocial functioning of persons or to change noxious social conditions that impede the mutually beneficial interaction between persons and their environment. The ecosystems model derived from ecological theory,[1] and general systems theory[2] provides a structured way to examine system interactions that should be considered during a social work practice intervention. In these chapters, the model is applied to the analysis of each special population—although it can be utilized in most social work practice situations. This ecosystems model offers a structure to allow the social worker to focus on five levels, as presented in Figure P5.1.

First, at the *individual level,* the focus is on the biopsychological endowment each person posesses, including personality strengths, level of psychosocial development, cognition, perception, problem-solving skills, emotional temperament, habit formation, and communication and language skills. Additionally, it is important to be knowledgeable about the person's attitudes, values, cultural beliefs, lifestyle, skills, and abilities; their view of the world; and how they respond to and cope with physical and psychological stress and problems. This only represents the highlights of factors at the individual level; the list is by no means exhaustive. The same brief format will be seen in the other levels of analysis.

Second, at the *family level,* the focus is on the nature of family lifestyle, culture, organization, family, division of labor, sex role structure, and interactional dynamics. Within a cultural context each family is unique. It is therefore important to know its values, beliefs, emotional support capacity, affective style, tradition, rituals, overall strengths and vulnerabilities, and how it manages internal or external stress. The nature and quality of the spousal relationship and the depth of connectedness to children and extended family are other areas requiring examination.

Third, in civilizations, cultures have evolved for survival purposes. Each culture develops behavioral responses influenced by the environment, historical and social processes incorporating specific structures such as language, food, kinship styles, religion, communications, norms, beliefs, and values. At the *cultural level* of the ecosystems model, therefore, the focus should be on understanding the cultural values, belief systems, and societal norms of the host culture and, in the case of minorities, their original culture. There may exist a conflict of cultures that, in advanced form, may result in mental-emotional impairment due to culture

(Continued)

Figure P5.1
Ecosystems Model for Analysis of Psychosocial Factors Impacting Special Populations

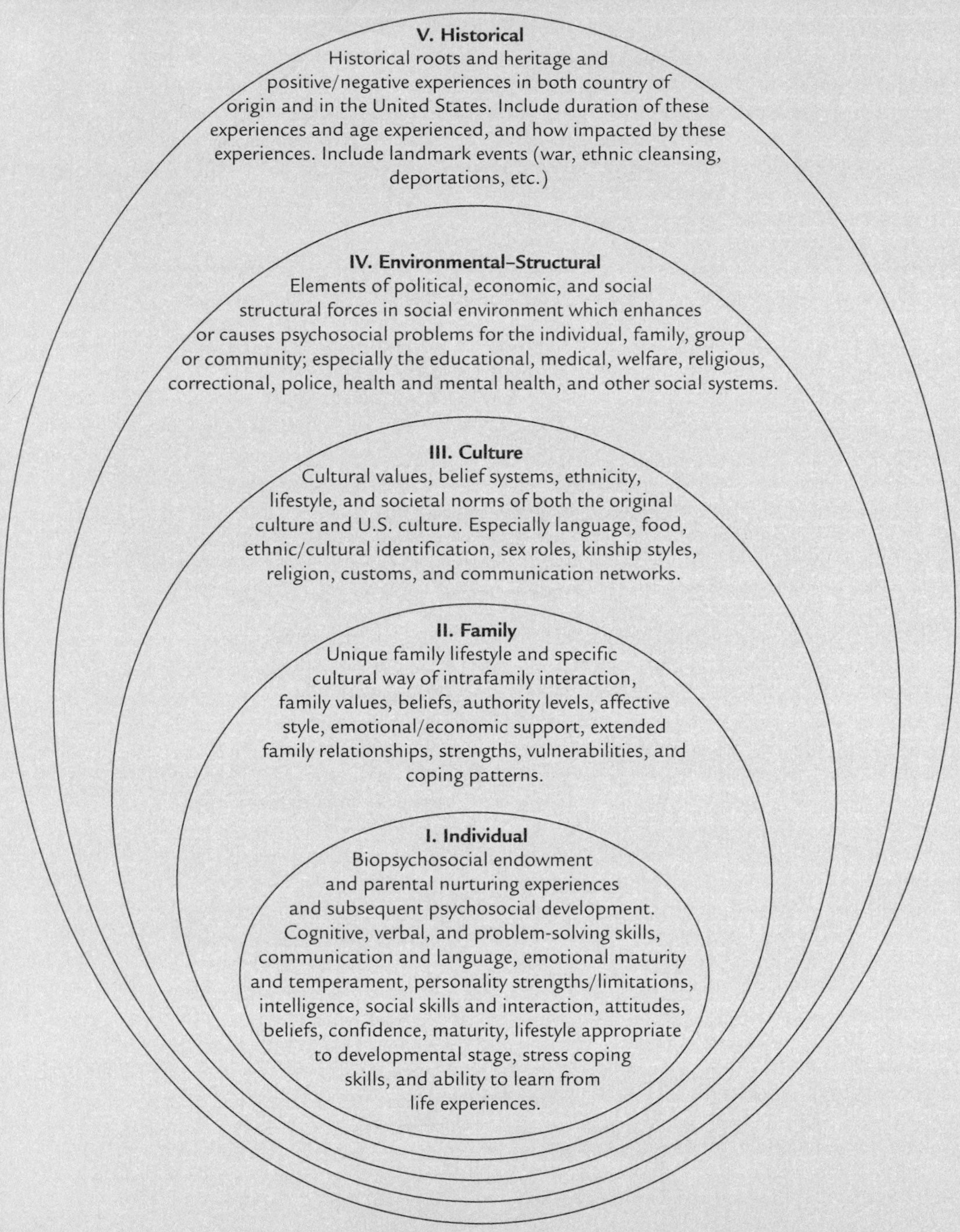

V. Historical
Historical roots and heritage and positive/negative experiences in both country of origin and in the United States. Include duration of these experiences and age experienced, and how impacted by these experiences. Include landmark events (war, ethnic cleansing, deportations, etc.)

IV. Environmental–Structural
Elements of political, economic, and social structural forces in social environment which enhances or causes psychosocial problems for the individual, family, group or community; especially the educational, medical, welfare, religious, correctional, police, health and mental health, and other social systems.

III. Culture
Cultural values, belief systems, ethnicity, lifestyle, and societal norms of both the original culture and U.S. culture. Especially language, food, ethnic/cultural identification, sex roles, kinship styles, religion, customs, and communication networks.

II. Family
Unique family lifestyle and specific cultural way of intrafamily interaction, family values, beliefs, authority levels, affective style, emotional/economic support, extended family relationships, strengths, vulnerabilities, and coping patterns.

I. Individual
Biopsychosocial endowment and parental nurturing experiences and subsequent psychosocial development. Cognitive, verbal, and problem-solving skills, communication and language, emotional maturity and temperament, personality strengths/limitations, intelligence, social skills and interaction, attitudes, beliefs, confidence, maturity, lifestyle appropriate to developmental stage, stress coping skills, and ability to learn from life experiences.

A special thanks to Professor Lois Miranda and social work faculty and students at the University of Wisconsin, Oshkosh, for assisting in the further refinement of the ecosystems model.

(Continued)

shock. The enhancing, nurturing aspects of the culture(s) should be noted as well as noxious elements such as sexism, ageism, and racism.

The fourth level of analysis involves *environmental-structural* factors and the positive or negative impact they have on special populations. Environmental-structural theories postulate that many of the problems of affected oppressed groups, such as special populations, are caused by the economic and social structure of U.S. society. Women, for example, are not poorer as a group than men because of biological or cultural inferiority. Rather, sexism is a U.S. male cultural value that is expressed and reinforced through the structure of economic, political, educational, and other social institutions. Ryan states that when U.S. white society looks at the poorly educated minority group child in the ghetto or *barrio* school, blame is placed on the parents (no books in the home), the child (impulse-ridden, nonverbal), minority culture (no value on education), or their socioeconomic status (i.e., they are socially and economically deprived and don't know any better). In pursuing this logic, Ryan adds, no one remembers to ask questions about the collapsing buildings, old, torn textbooks, insensitive teachers, relentless segregation, or callous administrators—in short, the environmental structure imposed upon the person with its accompanying negative consequences.[3]

The fifth and final level of the ecosystems model concerns positive and noxious factors in the *historical experience* of the special population member(s). The historical roots and experience of female subordination by males, for example, will affect the nature and quality of women's interaction with all agencies and their representatives. The male social worker may not be aware of his unconscious sexist behavior—the result of decades of conditioning—as he attempts to "help" female clients with their problems. Years of minority group oppression and exploitation, at times including genocide, lynching, and "police executions without trial," have left deep scars on minority group members and will affect the way they relate to human services agency representatives. Some elderly whites may recall very positive historical experiences remembering how supportive and encouraging U.S. social institutions had been, only to become depressed and discouraged when abandoned by the government when old. In addition to knowing about the U.S. historical experience, it is also of value to know the historical experience of immigrants and the countries they came from.

working with this population, and providing case material that would help readers recognize the application of these materials to social work practice.

How does use of this ecosystems model play out when working with an individual client? The following example illustrates how to fully assess a client's situation by considering factors at the five levels provided in this model.

CASE EXAMPLE

José is a small, frail-looking 14-year-old Spanish-speaking youngster brought into the community mental health center by his mother because he began to yell, cry, and scream and then threw himself under a table at a public laundromat. The Anglo-American psychiatrist who saw José was able to speak some Spanish. José told the doctor that he was at the laundromat with his mother the day before and that he had seen a police car slowly pass by the laundromat. He insisted the police officer on the passenger side of the car pointed his machine gun at the laundromat. At that time, fearing for his life, he threw himself under one of the tables and began screaming.

The mother confirmed that a police car had passed the laundromat but stated that the officers merely passed and did not expose any firearms. Other symptoms José was exhibiting were fear of going to school (where he was failing), fear of leaving the house, nightmares (people trying to kill him), insomnia, fear of being arrested by immigration officials and deported, depression, agitation, increasing suspicion of people, and irritability, especially toward his mother, stepfather, and siblings. This progressively deteriorating behavior had been going on for about six months. The doctor concluded that José was, at times, incoherent, delusional, having visual hallucinations, and displaying disorganized behavior. This clinical picture was consistent with DSM-IV 298.8, Brief Psychotic Disorder. He was prescribed antipsychotic medication. He continued in treatment for two weeks but his symptoms did not subside. The medication was not having any effect.

An Hispanic bilingual–bicultural mental health consultant was asked to see José and his mother and make an assessment and treatment recommendation. José was born in "Muy Lejos," a rural, agricultural village in Guatemala. His parents were both farm laborers, as were his grandparents. He was raised in a very traditional, religious, rural culture where sex roles, division of labor, and respect for the elderly, extended family, and authority figures were valued. When José was six, his father was suspected of being a guerrilla and was killed by right-wing government forces. Sensing her life was also in danger, José's mother left him with his grandparents and came to the United States without documents in order to obtain employment and then send for José and other relatives. José felt abandoned and cried on the phone whenever his mother was able to call him,

which was once every three or four months. Frequently, José would have to join other villagers and escape into the hills, sometimes for several months. José saw many killings, including decapitated bodies placed in the village by the right-wing forces to intimidate villagers.

In the meantime, the mother struggled for several years as a low-paid domestic and began to live with a documented Hispanic male. They had two children, two and four years younger than José. Finally, the mother was able to save enough money to send for José. He had been brought to the United States by a secret, underground system some six months previously. Initially he was happy to be reunited with his mother, but then the previously discussed symptoms began to surface.

José presents a difficult, complex case, although in no way is his situation unique. Rather than presenting one clearly identifiable problem for the mental health practitioner to treat, as is often the case with many middle-class clients, José brings at least five major problems that need to be prioritized in terms of severity and treated in a sequential manner. First, José is suffering acute *posttraumatic stress disorder* symptoms that have to be treated, including appropriately prescribed medication that will reduce his anxiety and fear, and permit him to sleep. Second, he is experiencing *culture shock,* having abruptly left an agrarian environment and come to the central cities area of Los Angeles. He doesn't understand the language or the requirements of school; he is being chased by urban gangs. Third, he is experiencing *separation anxiety* pain, having left his loving grandparents, who were really his substitute parents. It is also painful to be separated from relatives, friends, and one's country, never knowing if one will return. Fourth, he harbors a significant amount of unresolved anger toward his mother, who he believes *abandoned* him at a critical point in his life. These unresolved issues are intensified at his current psychosocial developmental level of adolescence. Finally, young José is confronted with a *reconstituted family*. He has to learn to deal with a stepfather who is taking the place of his beloved father. He also has to learn to live with a ten- and twelve-year-old stepsister and stepbrother. In short he is a complete outsider in all respects.

Following the treatment of the psychiatric symptoms, José then will have to work on cultural shock issues, separation anxiety, and unresolved matters related to his mother. At the appropriate time family therapy should also be initiated to help them function more positively as a family unit. The social worker may also have to help José resolve school and community-stress problems and link him up with community social-recreation programs.

In working with special population groups, once a sound knowledge base is established through the use of a concep-tual tool such as the ecosystems model, the social worker has to intervene at both micro- and macro-intervention levels. In cases such as that of José, a detailed biological, psychological, sociological, cultural, and historical assessment has to be made in order to know what is needed and, more important, what has to be done. This case highlights more micro-intervention strategies than macro. Macro-intervention approaches would have utilized the helping concepts of client advocacy, empowerment, social action, networking, and class action social work which involves collaboration with the legal profession on behalf of oppressed, disadvantaged special populations.

ENDNOTES

1. Urie Bronfenbrenner, "Toward Experimental Ecology of Human Development," *American Psychologist* 32 (1977): 513–551.
2. Lars Skyttner, *General Systems Theory: Ideas and Applications*. (River Edge, NJ: World Scientific, 2001).
3. William Ryan, *Blaming the Victim* (New York: Pantheon Boks, 1971), p.4.

Social Work Practice with Women

Diane Kravetz

Prefatory Comment

Dr. Diane Kravetz, Professor of Social Work, School of Social Work, University of Wisconsin, Madison, has provided us with a comprehensive chapter on social work practice with women. This national social work scholar, who has few if any equals concerning women's issues in social work, furnishes us with current (2000) demographic data pertaining to women. Dr. Kravetz, for example, reports that life is very stressful for single mothers. For example, the median income for married couples with children under 18 was $63,110; and for single mothers with children under 18 it was $24,693. For African American and Hispanic women, the problem was even worse. Further, of 900,000 Americans living with AIDS, 20 percent are women. Most HIV-infected women are poor and do not have the resources to gain access to new treatment programs that have led to dramatic declines in AIDS cases. Violence also is a major issue for women, especially partner violence, with approximately 1.5 million women being raped and/or assaulted each year by an intimate partner. Dr. Kravetz points out that gender is an economic determining factor in families. For example, fathers who have higher education and employment than mothers use this fact as justification for their exerting power and control over wives and children. Correspondingly, women have primary responsibility for the unpaid work of childrearing, caretaking, and maintaining the household, thus ensuring their subordinate status within the family.

The special needs and concerns of women are relevant for every field of practice, social problem area, and level of intervention. This chapter reviews the political, social, economic, and personal problems of women in the United States; it highlights women's personal strengths and political accomplishments; and it presents the principles and methods of practice that provide the foundation for effective and ethical social work practice with women. Over the past four decades, dramatic changes have occurred in women's status and roles. The ecosystems model provides an excellent framework for understanding these changes and the current conditions of women's lives. The model ensures that we fully understand how women's personal issues and problems are inextricably connected to larger social, political, and economic structures and cultural beliefs.

Current Demographics

In 2000, 143.4 million females constituted 51 percent of the population of the United States. White women accounted for 70 percent of the female population; black women, 13 percent; Hispanic women, 12 percent; Asian American/Pacific Islander women, 4 percent; and American Indian/Alaska Native women, 1 percent. The median ages for American Indian/Alaska Native women (29) and Hispanic women (26) were significantly lower than those of Asian American/Pacific Islander (34), black (32), and white (40) women. Just over half (53%) of all women ages 15 to 64 were married. A majority of women (61%) were in the paid labor force.[1]

Gender differences have largely disappeared at the high school and college levels. Of women 25 years and older in 1998, the large majority of white women (88%), black women (78%), Asian American/Pacific Islander women (83%), and American Indian/Alaskan Native women (80%) had graduated high school. Only Hispanic women had low rates of completing high school (56%). Disparities were more pronounced among women who had graduated college. Asian American/Pacific Islander women had the highest rates (39%); white women (25%) were also more likely to graduate college than black women (16%), Hispanic women (11%), and American Indian/Alaskan Native women (17%).[2] Differences in graduation rates have major implications since median weekly earnings vary significantly by educational level. In 2001, college graduates earned $924 per week, while high school graduates earned $520 and those with less than a high school diploma earned $378.[3]

Gender differences are significant, however, at the advanced degree level, where women received only 28 percent of professional and doctorate degrees in 1996. Of all advanced degrees earned by women in 1996, over one-third (35%) were in education. Women earned the majority of advanced degrees in literature (72%), education (66%), foreign language (58%), liberal arts (58%), and nursing and public health (85%). Although their numbers have increased, women continue to receive a relatively small proportion of advanced degrees in business (26%), engineering (8%), law (21%), medicine and dentistry (27%), natural science (27%), and philosophy (19%).[4]

The percentage of women 16 years and older in the labor force has doubled from 30 percent in 1950 to 61 percent in 2000. Labor force participation differs somewhat among black women (64%), white women (61%), Asian American/Pacific Islander women (59%), Hispanic women (57%), and American Indian/Alaskan Native women (55%). The traditional arrangement—married couple, wife not in the paid labor force—accounts for less than one-third (29%) of married-couple families with children under 18. Large numbers of mothers with children under 18 were employed, including married mothers (70%) and unmarried mothers (79%). In 2000, 79 percent of women with children 6 to 17 years of age and 65 percent of women with children under 6 years of age were in the labor force. In 1972, less than 45 percent of children ages 6 to 17 and less than 30 percent of children under age 6 had working mothers.[5]

Even with their advances in education and increased participation in the labor force, women still earn much less than men. In general, women earn about 73 cents for every dollar men earn. In 2000, the median earnings for men who worked full time were $37,339; for women with similar work experience, median earnings were $27,355. In married-couple families, women's employment reflects not only changing social attitudes and their increased access to higher education but also the economic advantage of two incomes. Most high-income households (79%) have two or more wage earners, compared to only a small number (7%) of low-income households. In 2000, the median income for married-couple families ($59,346) was significantly higher than the median income for a family maintained by a man without a spouse present ($42,129) and more than double the median income for a family maintained by a woman without a spouse present ($28,116). The median income for married couples with children under 18 was $63,110; for single mothers with children under 18, it was $24,693.[6]

In 2000, the large majority of family households (77%) continued to be married-couple households. The proportion of married-couple families differed among racial groups, with whites (83%) and Asian American/Pacific Islanders (80%) having the highest rates, and Hispanics (68%), American Indian/Alaskan Natives (65%), and blacks (48%) having the lowest. Female-householder families represented 17 percent of all families in 2000, whereas they made up 10 percent of all families in 1959.

The most significant change in American families has been in the marital status of the parents with whom children live. Married-couple families with children represented 69 percent of all families with children in 2000, compared to 87 percent in 1970. At the same time, the proportion of single-mother families has more than doubled, increasing from 12 percent of all families in 1970 to 26 percent in 2000, while single-father families have increased from 1 percent to 5 percent. High divorce rates and childbearing outside of marriage are the primary reasons for the rise in female-headed households. White single mothers are more likely to be divorced (50%) than never married (30%). Black single mothers are more likely to be never married (65%) than divorced (17%). Hispanic single mothers, who represented 17 percent of single mothers in 2000, were more likely to be never married (44%) than divorced (25%). The majority (51%) of single mothers are white.[7]

Most often, children living with an unmarried parent are living only with their mother (83%). Only 9 percent live with their father without their mother being present, with a portion (16%) of these fathers cohabiting with an unmarried partner. An additional 8 percent of these children live with their unmarried fathers and mothers. In 1996, many Hispanic (73%) and black (54%) children and about a third (35%) of white children living with their unmarried fathers also lived with their mothers.[8]

One significant factor for the increase in families maintained by women has been the increased birth rate among unmarried women. In 1950, 4 percent of all births involved single women. By 2000, the proportion of births to single women increased to 31 percent. Of these births, 87 percent (1,063,000) were to never married women, and 13 percent (163,000) were to widowed or divorced women. Among African Americans, births to unmarried women represented 38 percent of births in 1970 and 69 percent in 2000. Among whites, the rates of birth to unmarried women increased fourfold between 1970 and 2000, from 6 percent to 27 percent. Rates for American Indian/Alaskan Natives increased from 22 percent to 58 percent.

From 1980 to 2000, rates of birth to unmarried Cuban American women increased from 10 percent to 27 percent; Mexican American women, from 20 percent to 41 percent; and Puerto Rican women, from 46 percent to 60 percent. While rates among unmarried Chinese and Japanese American women have ranged between 3 percent and 11 percent, rates increased from 33 percent in 1980 to 50 percent in 2000 among Hawaiian unmarried women. Among teens, 83 percent of births were out-of-wedlock; over half (54%) of out-of-wedlock births were to women who had not graduated from high school.[9]

The increase in female-headed families has also been caused by increasing rates of divorce. For men and women born from 1925 to 1934, only about 15 percent were divorced by age 40. In contrast, for those born from 1945 to 1954, 34 percent of the women and 3 percent of the men were divorced by age 40. By 1996, 40 percent of ever-married white and Hispanic women, 48 percent of black women, and 24 percent of Asian American/Pacific Islander women had divorced from their first marriage. Most separated (64%) and divorced (57%) women live with their own children under age 18, whereas only about 18 percent of separated and divorced men do.

Highly limited employment options, social norms that assign women primary responsibility for caring for children, and high rates of divorce and out-of-wedlock childbearing are largely responsible for the feminization of poverty. In 1998, black (27%), Hispanic (26%), and American Indian/Alaskan Native (21%) women were most likely to be poor, compared with Asian American/Pacific Islander (13%) and white (9%) women; but most women living in poverty were white (about 7 million).[10] Female-headed families are particularly at risk of poverty, with women of color being most vulnerable. In 2000, for families maintained by single women, the poverty rate was 25 percent, more than double the rate for families maintained by men without a spouse (11%) and five times the rate for married-couple families (5%). Among families maintained by single mothers, black women (34%) and Hispanic women (36%) had the highest rates of poverty, while white women (18%) and Asian American/Pacific Islander women (22%) had somewhat lower rates. Among families maintained by men without spouses present, black men (16%) and Hispanic men (14%) had the highest rates of poverty; white (9%) and Asian American/Pacific Islander (5%) men had the lowest. In every case, the poverty rates for men were substantially lower than those for women of the same race.[11]

With separations and divorce, most women experience drastic declines in their standard of living and income, with their financial problems compounded by inadequate or unpaid child support, divorce settlements that fail to take into account wives' investments in their husbands' careers rather than their own, reductions in welfare programs, and limited employment options. In 1996, 29 percent of separated and 21 percent of divorced women were living in poverty, more than twice the rates of separated (12%) and divorced (9%) men. A large majority (73%) of divorced men had incomes at least twice the poverty level, while just over half (52%) of divorced women did.[12] Still, children living with divorced mothers are generally more economically secure than children living with never-married mothers, because divorced women tend to be older, have more education, and have higher incomes.[13] In 1995, about 45 percent of children raised by divorced mothers and 69 percent of children raised by never-married mothers lived in or near poverty.[14]

Women constitute the majority of older Americans. In 2000, women accounted for 59 percent of the population age 65 and over.[15] Significantly more older women than men live alone due to women's greater longevity and the fact that widowed or divorced men are more likely to remarry. Because of their relatively low incomes and greater likelihood of being widowed, older women have higher rates of poverty than do older men. In 2000, among people ages 65 years and over, 12 percent of women were poor compared with 7 percent of men.[16] Many older women lack adequate health care since Medicare does not fully cover, for example, prescription drugs and long-term care; and Medicaid provides additional benefits to only one-half of Medicare recipients who are poor. Older women spend 22 percent to 53 percent of their income on out-of-pocket health care expenses.[17]

Health and Mental Health Risk Factors

Across the life span, women's health and mental health concerns differ from those of men. There are also differences among racial/ethnic groups of women, but these are largely due to economic factors.

Cardiovascular disease is the number one cause of death and disability among American women, with African American women having the highest rates. While the incidence and mortality rates of lung cancer for men have declined, between 1960 and 1990 lung cancer deaths among women have increased by more than 400 percent. Approximately 80 percent of lung cancer cases in women are thought to be attributable to cigarette smoking. Breast cancer is the most frequently diagnosed cancer in women. The incidence is higher for white women than for women in other racial/ethnic groups, but the mortality rate for breast cancer is highest for black women, most likely because until the mid-1990s they had lower rates of having a mammogram.[18]

An estimated one-fourth of the 800,000 to 900,000 Americans living with HIV/AIDS are women. Throughout the 1990s there were significant declines in AIDS-related deaths and in the numbers of new AIDS cases, but these decreases have been much greater for men than for women. Most HIV-infected women are poor and do not have the resources to take advantage of the treatment advances that have led to the dramatic declines in new AIDS cases and AIDS-related deaths. Women account for 30 percent of new HIV infections, which are primarily due to heterosexual sex (75 percent), followed by injection drug use (25 percent). In 1999, African American women made up 63 percent of new AIDS cases among women; white women and Hispanic women each accounted for 18 percent; Asian American/Pacific Islander women and American Indian/Alaska Native women each accounted for less than 1 percent. Girls were the majority (58 percent) of new AIDS cases among teenagers.[19]

Large numbers of women are victims of physical, psychological, and sexual abuse. More than half of all working women are sexually harassed on the job, and between 30 percent and 50 percent of female students are harassed at college.[20] Over half (52 percent) of all women have been physically assaulted either as a child or as an adult. One in six women (18 percent) has experienced an attempted or completed rape at some time in their lives. Many of these women (22 percent) were under 12 years old when they were first raped; 32 percent were 12 to 17 years old. Approximately 1.9 million women are physically assaulted and approximately 302,100 women are forcibly raped each year.

Violence against women is primarily partner violence. Approximately 1.5 million women are raped and/or physically assaulted each year by an intimate partner. Of women raped and/or physically assaulted since the age of 18, 76 percent were assaulted by a current or former husband, cohabiting partner, or date; 17 percent were victimized by an acquaintance; and 9 percent were victimized by a relative other than a husband. Only 14 percent were victimized by a stranger. In contrast, men are primarily raped and physically assaulted by strangers (60 percent) and acquaintances (32 percent), not by intimate partners (18 percent). Most of the violence against women (93 percent) and against men (86 percent) is perpetrated by men. Almost one-third of murdered women are killed by an intimate partner, compared to about 4 percent of men. More than one million women are stalked each year, and about half of these women are stalked by an intimate.[21]

Ecosystems Model

The statistical picture painted above highlights important changes that have taken place in women's lives over the past four decades. It reveals progress as well as serious problems and inequities. The ecosystems model provides a framework for understanding the beliefs, norms, institutional arrangements, and social roles that define and maintain women as a subordinate social group. Each of the five interconnected levels of the ecosystems model (historical, environmental–structural, culture, family, and individual) is discussed below in relation to the role it plays in the social and personal problems of women. Each level helps us understand the persistent and pervasive inequality between the sexes.

Historical Factors

Throughout history, women have been defined as innately and inevitably different from and inferior to men. This androcentric view is supported by socially constructed definitions of woman as biologically destined to be dependent, nurturant, and domestic. *Patriarchy* is the term used for the social, economic, and political arrangements that emerge from these cultural assumptions and that give males authority over females and formal power over public policies and practices. Patriarchy is evident in the privileging of male perspectives and needs throughout society.

Historically, women had few legal rights; they were viewed as the property of their fathers or husbands and in need of male protection. Securing women's rights began when the right to vote was extended to women in 1920 through ratification of the Nineteenth Amendment to the Constitution, after 51 years of advocacy by feminists in support of women's suffrage.

Until the middle of the twentieth century, social norms viewed paid work as deviant for married women. As a result, most female workers were young, single, and primarily from white working-class, immigrant, and African American families. Some college-educated women chose to remain single in order to pursue careers as teachers, librarians, caseworkers, settlement house workers, and nurses. Also, employment was more common for married African American women and married immigrant women.[22]

A series of changing social conditions made employment socially acceptable and necessary for women, including middle-class married white women. These included "labor-saving" devices in the home; recruitment of female labor during the World Wars and expanded employment opportunities post–World War II in "pink-collar" work (clerical work and sales); increased economic need for two-income families; increased educational opportunities for women; a rising divorce rate and increasing numbers of female-headed households; and women's increased control of reproduction. The organized efforts of feminists resulted in new antidiscrimination laws in education and employment; changing views of gender roles; and sweeping changes in women's status and in their roles in public life, work, and in the family.[23]

Cultural Factors

The *gender system* organizes society in terms of gender differences and then values one gender over the other, giving males more power, more prestige, more resources, and more privilege. Cultural ideology serves to "normalize" the ways in which men and women are viewed and valued differently, so that the domination of one gender over the other becomes unquestioned, as does the power of the gender system to define individual behavior, interpersonal relationships, and formal roles. While popular views about women's capacities and proper place in the social hierarchy have been transformed over the past four decades, there is still considerable resistance to the principle of equality between the sexes.

New options [...] rtunities have opened for women in every arena. For example, in 1981, [...] years after the founding of the first women's rights organization, the National Organization for Women (NOW), Sandra Day O'Connor was named as the first woman appointed to the U.S. Supreme Court. Two years later, Sally Ride became the first American woman in space. In 1985, Wilma Mankiller became the first woman elected to lead a major Native American tribe when she was elected principal chief of the Cherokee Nation of Oklahoma. Barbara Harris, an African American, was ordained as the first female bishop in the Episcopal Church in 1989.

Still, evidence of the persistence of traditional, patriarchal beliefs about women's rights and roles is abundantly clear in the antifeminist efforts of the New Right.[24] Their first victory was the defeat of the simple proposition that women should have the same citizenship rights as men. The Equal Rights Amendment (ERA), which read: "Equality of rights under the law shall not be denied or abridged by the United States or by any state on account of sex," remained three states short of the number required for ratification when the deadline for ratification expired on June 30, 1982. To defeat the ERA, opponents promulgated numerous myths about the ERA, including claiming that it would force women into combat. Ironically, one indicator of social change is that during the Gulf War in 1990–1991, 11 percent of the armed forces on active duty were female, two women were taken as war prisoners, and 15 women died serving their country. By 1994, women were no longer barred from combat in the air and on the sea, and in the Iraq War about 20 percent of the combat support troops are women.[25]

The interconnections of patriarchy with other social inequalities create different systems of subordination for different groups of women. The concept of *triple oppression* is particularly useful in understanding the experiences of many women of color. This concept recognizes "the interplay among class, race, and gender, whose cumulative effects place women of color in a subordinate social and economic position relative to men of color and the majority white population . . . Their inferior status is reproduced concurrently in the home and in all other social arenas."[26] Within every subgroup of every major racial/ethnic group, female and male experiences differ significantly, with women in each group having problems related to gender inequality within their own group and in society at large. For women of color, issues related to gender must be understood in terms of the overwhelming influence of racism, ethnic prejudice, and class discrimination.

Lesbians are oppressed not only by sexism but also by heterosexism, that is, the belief that heterosexuality is superior to and more natural than homosexuality. As a lifestyle and subculture in which women function relatively independently of men, lesbianism challenges the cultural mandates that women seek personal fulfillment and economic security through heterosexual bonding. By creating hate and fear toward lesbianism, heterosexism maintains gender inequality. Homophobia and fear of being labeled homosexual serve to keep women (and men) within the confines of traditional gender roles. Since the Stonewall riots in New York City in 1969, there has been a proliferation of gay- and lesbian-centered organizations and businesses, the inclusion of sexual orientation in nondiscrimination legislation, increased visibility of gays and lesbians in public life, and broader acceptance of gays and lesbians and their lifestyles. Still, discrimination, stigmatization, violence, and invisibility continue to define the lives of gays and lesbians. Just as there has been organized resistance to the progress that has been made toward gender equality, there has been a backlash against gay rights, including vicious condemnation by the Christian Right and an increase in hate crimes against gays and lesbians.[27]

Environmental–Structural Factors

Women's Legal Rights.   Federal legislation and Supreme Court decisions have played a critical role in women's having the opportunity to pursue equality. They have provided the necessary leverage for women's gaining access to and demanding fair treatment in public institutions; changes in public attitudes and behaviors have followed.

Between the early 1960s and the late 1970s, there was substantial progress in advancing women's rights in higher education and in the workforce. For example, Title VII of the 1964 Civil Rights Act prohibited sex discrimination in hiring, firing, promotions, and working conditions. The 1963 Equal Pay Act required equal pay for women and men holding the same jobs. Under pressure from NOW and other women's rights organizations, President Lyndon Johnson signed Executive Order 11375 in 1967, which strengthened Title VII of the Civil Rights Act. This order directed employers who received federal contracts to provide equal employment opportunities for women and to develop affirmative action programs to redress the effects of past discrimination. Other far-reaching legislation included the 1974 Equal Credit Opportunity Act, which allowed married women to obtain credit in their own names, and Title IX of the 1972 Education Amendments Act, which prohibited sex discrimination in education by institutions that received federal funding. Abortions became legalized through the 1973 *Roe v. Wade* decision, although court decisions and legislative policies have greatly restricted access to abortion for many women.

More recent legislation benefiting working women includes the Civil Rights Act of 1991, which extended the protection of Title VII to victims of intentional discrimination to allow recovery of damages previously limited to victims of racial discrimination; and the 1993 Family and Medical Leave Act, which granted unpaid time off to care for a sick child or relative without losing one's job. There has also been some degree of reform in the laws and policies governing the treatment of victims of rape, domestic violence, and sexual harassment. For example, in 1980, sexual harassment in the workplace was included as a violation under Title VII of the Civil Rights Act of 1964. The Civil Rights Act of 1991 permitted compensatory and punitive damages for victims of sexual harassment in the workplace; and in 1992, the U.S. Supreme Court ruled that sexual harassment in educational settings was a form of gender inequality and thus was covered by Title IX of the 1972 Educational Amendments Act.

Women in the Labor Force.   With higher levels of educational attainment, women have increased their presence in the higher-status managerial and professional occupations. In 2001, women accounted for 47 percent of those in executive, administrative, and managerial occupations, compared with 34 percent in 1983. In professional occupations, their proportion increased from 47 percent to 52 percent. However, within each group, many more men than women are in the higher-paying occupations. Women earn just 67 percent as much as men in the executive, administrative, and managerial occupations and just 73 percent as much as men in the professions. Most women are in lower-paying jobs, where they also earn less than men in those same job categories. Women accounted for 45 percent of the sales jobs and earned 62 percent as much as men. They made up 77 percent of workers in administrative support, including clerical, where their earnings were 81 percent of men's. For private household work, which includes child care workers, cleaners, and servants, no earnings comparisons were calculated since very few men (4 percent) work in this area.

Earnings differences between the sexes cannot simply be attributed to differences in degrees and jobs. Women earned less than men at every degree level. With a high school degree or less, women earned about $600 less per month than comparable men. With a bachelor's degree, women earned, on average, $1,400 less per month than men. With an advanced degree, women earned about $2,000 less per month. The fact that men entered higher-paying fields only partially accounts for their overall higher earnings. For example, if women with bachelor's degrees had entered the same fields at the same rates as men with bachelor's degrees, the earnings gap would be only slightly reduced, from $1,380 to $1,250.[28]

In schools of social work in 2000, in graduate and joint graduate/baccalaureate programs, 10 percent of the women and 24 percent of the men were at the rank of professor. The median salary of full-time female faculty with a doctorate at the rank of professor was $68,503 for whites and $61,516 for minorities. For comparable male faculty, salaries were $76,435 for whites and $72,000 for minorities. In baccalaureate programs, 9 percent of women and 20 percent of men were professors. The median salaries of white male and female professors with a doctorate were $57,445 and $57,985, respectively. For comparable minority faculty, female salaries were $45,000; male's were 54,735.[29]

The Family

As in other social institutions, the gender system is a determining factor in family life. It is in the family where children learn gender role expectations and obligations; it is generally where heterosexuality is taught and enforced. Although there are specific differences based on race and class, gender is the primary basis for determining family roles and responsibilities and for distributing family resources. In the past in most families, men's participation in public life has determined their privileged status in their families. Men's achieving higher levels of education and employment than women provided justification for their exerting power and control over women and children. Correspondingly, women's having primary responsibility for the unpaid work of childrearing, caretaking, and maintaining the household has determined their subordinate status within the family.[30]

However, women's employment has disrupted patriarchal family norms and roles, regardless of class and race. Contributing financially to the household increases women's self-esteem, assertiveness, and independence. At the same time, paid work can be a source of stress. Many husbands resist and resent their wives' increasing autonomy; and although men's involvement in family life is increasing, the balancing of work and family roles is still primarily an issue only for women.

Despite women's expanded responsibilities as wage earners, they continue to have primary responsibility for household tasks and for meeting the needs of husbands, children, and older relatives. Taking care of young children and providing long-term care for the elderly are stressful and time-consuming and can have damaging consequences for women's paid work, social lives, personal relationships, and mental health. Women assume these family responsibilities with no financial compensation, little recognition, and few public supports. Leaving the labor force at various times in order to care for children and/or elderly family members places women at a disadvantage in competing for jobs and reduces their earnings and retirement benefits.[31]

With increased education and labor force participation and wider availability of contraception and abortion, women are marrying at a later age, delaying childbearing, and having fewer children. In 1970, the median age at the time of first marriage was 21 years for women and 23 years for men. Now, men and women are marrying in their late twenties (median ages 27 and 25 years, respectively).[32] In 1998, births to women in their twenties and early thirties represented 75 percent of all births. Women 35 to 44 years of age (13%) and women 15 to 19 years of age (12 percent) accounted for the remaining births. Almost half of women with a college education gave birth to their first child after age 30.[33] Among women 40 to 44 years old in 2000, Hispanic women had the highest average number of births (2.5). Black women had an average rate of 2.0 births; and white women and Asian American/Pacific Islander women averaged 1.8 births. Among women 40 to 44 years old, 19 percent were childless in 2000, compared to 10 percent of the same age in 1980.[34]

About half of the approximately 5.4 million pregnancies occurring in the United States each year are unintended, and slightly over half (54 percent) of these unintended pregnancies ended in abortion in 1996. The actual percentage is probably higher, given the underreporting of induced abortions in population surveys. The rate of abortion was highest in 1980, at 29.4 per 1,000 women, and has declined consistently since then. In 1996, the overall induced abortion rate was 22.9 per 1,000 women aged 15 to 44 years. Most abortions (88 percent) are performed in the first twelve weeks of pregnancy; 54 percent occur in the first eight weeks. One-third of women having abortions are 20 to 24 years old, and 48 percent are 25 years old or older; 83 percent are unmarried; 41 percent are white; 61 percent have given birth before. About 14,000 women have abortions each year following rape or incest. It is estimated that by age 45, 43 percent of women in the United States will have had an abortion.[35]

Lesbian Families.   Lesbian women have always created families as lesbian couples, with or without children, and as lesbian mothers with children. It has been estimated that gay and lesbian families make up at least 5 percent of all families.[36]

On the 2000 U.S. Census, 594,391 households self-identified as same-sex, unmarried partners, of which 49 percent were lesbian couples. Of the lesbian couples, 73 percent were white; 12 percent, Black; 12 percent, Hispanic; 2 percent, Asian American/Pacific Islander; and 1 percent, American Indian/Alaska Native. Same-sex unmarried partner households were reported in 99.3 percent of all counties in the United States and accounted for 0.6 percent of all households.

Like many heterosexual women, many lesbians choose to be mothers. In a recent study of Black gay, lesbian, bisexual, and transgender people, 40 percent of women, 18 percent of men, and 15 percent of transgender people reported having at least one child.[37] Estimates of the number of lesbian mothers have ranged from one to five million. Beginning in the 1990s, more lesbians are choosing to adopt or to have children through heterosexual sexual intercourse or artificial insemination. Like other families, lesbian mothers create support networks of men and women to assist them in raising their children. Their extended families of choice, consisting of gays and non-gays, serve the same functions that extended families have traditionally served.[38] Of the research on the psychosocial development of children of gay men and lesbians, "not a single study has found children of gay or lesbian parents to be disadvantaged in any significant respect relative to children of heterosexual parents . . . home environments provided by gay and lesbian parents are as likely as those provided by heterosexual parents to support and enable children's psychosocial growth."[39]

Although there has been some progress, lesbian families continue to be stigmatized and marginalized. Lesbians confront discrimination in employment, housing, education, medical care, and credit with little or no legal protection. Only twelve states and the District of Columbia prohibit sexual orientation discrimination.[40] A majority (62 percent) of the U.S. population has no legislative protection at the state or local level against sexual orientation discrimination in private employment. Lesbian couples are denied the legal and economic benefits and protections extended to married couples, including hospital visitation rights, Social Security spousal benefits, inheritance rights, health insurance coverage, and being able to stay together legally in the United States under immigration provisions for family reunification. In 1996, President Clinton signed the "Defense of Marriage Act," which prohibits federal recognition of same-sex marriages. In addition, 35 states have specific anti–same-sex marriage laws. Only eight states and 83 municipal governments offer domestic partner benefits.[41]

Without the option of marriage, partners of biological parents are seeking joint custody or second-parent adoptive rights. Four states now have laws or regulations prohibiting gays and lesbians from adopting or being foster parents. In 23 states and the District of Columbia, the state adoption law permits second-parent or stepparent adoptions by same-sex couples.[42]

With all of these legal and social concerns, lesbians create families that are not much different than others of their race and class in many respects. However, lesbians and their children are likely to be much more open to diversity. Lesbian (and gay) couples tend to have more egalitarian relationships than heterosexual couples. Their approaches to parenting are less likely to promote traditional gender role ideologies in children.[43]

Families of Women of Color.   For women of color, women's roles and experiences in the family are shaped by the culture of a specific racial/ethnic group as well as by the values, traditions, and social circumstances of the particular subgroup to which they belong. Women of color have always had the primary responsibility for transmitting cultural, spiritual, and family values from one generation to the next and thus have been in the center of the inevitable tensions between preserving cultural identity and accommodation to mainstream American values. Their family life can be profoundly influenced by the effects of prejudice, discrimination, poverty, and, for some, language barriers. Differences in family members' levels of acculturation can add considerable conflict and strain. Extended family households are more prevalent among people of color, partially due to cultural histories and partially due to the necessity of sharing resources with and providing support to new immigrants, the elderly, single mothers and their children, and other family members with financial difficulties.

African American women share many common values and a history of racial oppression in the United States even though they may represent different subgroups, including those who are U.S.-born descendants of slaves from Africa and those who have immigrated from the Caribbean, Great Britain, Africa, and other countries. African American two-parent families were common during and after slavery until a sharp decline occurred, beginning in the 1960s.[44] By 2000, 48 percent of African American families were headed by married couples, as compared to 56 percent in 1980 and 68 percent in 1970. Social and economic forces have severely limited the number of African American men available for economically and emotionally secure marriages. These forces have included the decline of manufacturing jobs in the cities of the Northeast and Midwest and the accompanying decline in employment opportunities; high rates of unemployment or employment in jobs that offered very low pay and little security; and high rates of male mortality and incarceration.[45] Unmarried mothers had less incentive to marry unemployed men; and married women no longer had economic security as a reason to stay married.

Institutionalized racism has placed extraordinary burdens on many African American women, including poor housing, lack of education opportunities, and poor health care; high rates of unemployment and limited job opportunities; and racial violence. Nonetheless, they have managed to create and maintain strong family and community networks. Because of their long-standing tradition of participation in the paid labor force, African American women are less tied to stereotypic female roles and behaviors and view paid work as compatible with family roles. Of course, their success in the labor force poses the same challenges in terms of balancing multiple roles as it does for other women.[46]

African American families often consist of immediate and extended family members, both kin and non-kin, who have strong bonds and share roles in egalitarian and flexible ways. Single mothers and single grandmothers are most likely to be the heads of households, while the extended family provides support and resources over several households. Grandmothers are held in high esteem and play critical roles, often assisting parents by caring for children and by providing emotional support and financial assistance to all members of the family. The responsibility for caring for children is generally shared by older siblings. When necessary, it is not unusual for children to be adopted informally by extended family members.[47]

African American grandmothers are currently facing a new set of challenges as a result of a growing number of "skipped generation" families in which grandparents are raising grandchildren with no parent in the home. This trend has been linked to increased rates of teen pregnancy; AIDS; mental and physical illnesses and drug abuse among parents; and incarceration of parents. In 1997, African American grandmothers accounted for over half (54 percent) of "skipped generation" families. White grandmothers constituted the next largest group (28 percent), while Hispanics made up the smallest group (16 percent). Of the grandchildren who lived only with their grandmothers, 63 percent were black. Parenting grandmothers do not expect or plan to mother their grandchildren and have few models or established services to help them deal with the needs of their grandchildren, the parents of their grandchildren, their other adult children, and their own needs as older African American women.[48]

Although Hispanic women may share linguistic, religious, and family traditions, they belong to groups with very different histories in the United States. Many Cuban American women came to the United States as political refugees, beginning in 1959, and are now middle- and upper middle class. Cubans who arrived since 1980 are more likely to be economically disadvantaged. Mexican Americans represent many different groups, including for example, U.S.-born descendants of the original settlers in the Southwest, U.S.-born descendants of Mexicans who migrated to the United States, and documented and undocumented migrant farm workers. Many Mexican American and Puerto Rican women are relatively uneducated and work in low-status, low-paying jobs. Conversely, Mexican American women (16 percent) and Puerto Rican women (20 percent) also hold the higher-status and higher-paid managerial and professional positions. Of all Hispanic women in the United States, 38 percent are foreign born; most (73 percent) of these women are not U.S. citizens.[49]

The family has traditionally been the center of Hispanic life. *Familismo* refers to the traditional Hispanic view of the family as a source of strength and support. It stresses the importance of family loyalty, mutual assistance, and preserving the family's honor. **Familismo** refers to relationships within the extended family and includes kin beyond the nuclear family, godparents, and friends who lend emotional and economic support. Within the traditional Hispanic family, *Machismo* refers to a man's strong sense of obligation to and responsibility for family and his expectation that he will provide for and protect his family. Men are viewed as the heads of the household and expect to have final authority in family decision making. The complement of **Machismo** is *Marianismo*, which emphasizes women's self-sacrifice for the sake of family members. Mothers, and often grandmothers, have responsibility for raising children and maintaining strong families. **Marianismo** promotes female dependence on men and devotion to husbands and children, and discourages education and employment for women. Thus, for Hispanic women, preserving their own culture has meant preserving gender roles that are much more restrictive and subservient than those of other women in the United States. The contradiction between economic and educational accomplishment and "proper" conduct for Hispanic women is particularly stressful for women who pursue higher education.

Hispanic women who work outside the home may be isolated by language barriers and in low-status, low-paying jobs with few opportunities for advancement. Their employment is most often viewed by their husbands as an extension of their traditional gender roles, as simply one more way for them to contribute to the well-being of the family. However, with employment, the perspectives and family roles of many Hispanic women have changed. Differences in gender expectations between employed women and their husbands have created considerable stress in Hispanic families. Men's continuing expectations of dominance and control and women's increased independence have contributed to increased incidences of domestic violence and rates of divorce. Divorce itself is seen as a failure to fulfill the appropriate role for women in the Hispanic community and thus as a failure to preserve the family's honor. Divorced women often find themselves blamed and stigmatized by their ex-husbands and by the larger Hispanic community as well.[50]

Asian American/Pacific Islander women represent ethnic groups that differ by race, language, and culture. Women of Asian ancestry have come to the United States under very different circumstances, with some groups having been in the United States for several generations (e.g., Chinese and Japanese) and others being comparatively recent immigrants (e.g., Hmong and Vietnamese). Although they are often stereotyped as the "model" minority, only some groups of Asian American/Pacific Islander women are highly educated and in high-status occupations. Asian American/Pacific Islander women (41 percent) are more likely than white women (26 percent) to have earned a college degree but also more likely to have less than a ninth grade education (11 percent compared with 4 percent). A higher proportion of Asian American/Pacific Islander women (19 percent) than white women (15 percent) have incomes over $50,000 but also are more likely to be poor (11 percent as compared with 9 percent). Overall, 62 percent of Asian American/Pacific Islander women are foreign born, and over half (54 percent) of these women are not citizens.[51]

Over one-third (39 percent) of Asian American/Pacific Islander women are in the higher-paid managerial and professional occupations.[52] Their upward mobility has been limited, however, by stereotypes of Asian women, by discrimination, and by racism.[53] Other groups of Asian American women who came as refugees or immigrants have limited education, occupational skills, and proficiency in speaking English. Regardless of the number of generations in the United States, many traditional values are upheld, including rigidly defined hierarchical family structures. It is expected that Asian American women will be unassuming, deferential, and subservient to their husbands, to their husbands' fathers, and to their sons, who will become the heads of their families after the father's death. Mothers and daughters are expected to serve as the nurturers and caretakers of the household. Family welfare and status are considered more important than those of the individual. Traditional Asian taboos against taking problems outside the family reinforce traditional gender expectations, since deviating from tradition brings dishonor to the family, not only to the individual woman.

In Asian communities, maintaining large kinship networks is very important, but those networks generally disappear in the United States. Problems are magnified for many refugee women whose families were disrupted through war, refugee camps, and resettlement. Asian American refugees experienced the personal tragedies and traumas of war, including malnutrition, disease, and sexual abuse; the deaths of husbands and children; and the loss of their country, home, family, and friends. With little education, few urban job skills, and poor facility with the English language, many Asian American women rely on their children to negotiate their interactions with U.S. society. The discrepancies between the levels of acculturation between parents and children add additional burdens to women.

Much like Hispanic men, Asian American men consider women's work in small family-run businesses or in other jobs to be an extension of their family obligations. However, women who are working to supplement the family's income are exposed to U.S. values of independence and individualism, which are in stark contrast to traditional Asian values of emotional restraint, social conformity, and altruism; and many begin to recognize that their family system is more responsive to the needs of men than for the needs of women. Tension in the family increases with women's new sense of independence. Asian American men's loss of power in the family can lead to domestic violence and divorce, especially if they are also suffering from a much reduced socioeconomic status as immigrants or refugees.[54]

American Indian/Alaska Native women represent over 500 federally recognized tribes, many having different histories, geographic locations, languages, political and economic structures, and kinship systems. It has been estimated that a third live in urban areas, a third live on reservations, and a third move back and forth between the two.[55] Those who live on reservations have particularly high rates of poverty, poor-quality housing, and health problems.

American Indian/Alaska Native societies were cooperative, clan-based systems in which women had considerable authority over political and social life. When the U.S. government assumed control, they imposed capitalism, the nuclear family, and patriarchy. American Indian/Alaska Natives were forcefully removed from their lands, and their children were placed in U.S. government–run schools where native language, dress, and spiritual practices were prohibited. American Indian/Alaska Natives were again relocated from 1945 to 1968 by the Bureau of Indian Affairs from tribal lands into the cities.[56] All of these changes disrupted large, extended kinship networks and women's roles as the transmitters of culture and custom.

Federal policies and practices have contributed to American Indian/Alaska Natives having low rates of graduation from high school, high rates of unemployment, and high rates of drug and alcohol abuse, which have led to high rates of homicide, suicide, and motor vehicle–related injuries and fatalities. Being in the center of family and tribal life, women have suffered the consequences of these social conditions. American Indian/Alaska Native women have the highest mortality rates from alcoholism and illicit drug use of all American women and a higher mortality rate from suicide than the other three minority populations. Their rate of violent victimization is also significantly higher than that found among all other women.[57]

Depending on the tribe, American Indian/Alaska Native women still have considerable influence. Mothers, grandmothers, and other older female members of the tribe are responsible for teaching younger women, passing on tribal traditions and customs. "Grandmother" refers to a number of female elders, not necessarily kin, or medicine women who are considered wise and deserving of great respect. Women are often involved in the day-to-day leadership of their tribes and in political work related to treaty rights and the protection of native resources. The Apache still operate within a matrilineal extended family system in which the grandmother plays a central role and the family is the center of cultural and political life. In this tribe, wife abuse is practically nonexistent. In other tribes and in out-marriages, where women marry men of other races, family structures are patriarchal, and women face the problems and powerlessness that traditional gender roles present.[58]

The Individual

Because gender is a central determinant of social status and socialization, it influences all of the individual's experiences, including those that contribute to the development of psychological disorders. The influence of conventional gender roles and female socialization can be seen especially clearly in disorders prevalent among women. Two primary examples are eating disorders and depression.

About one in five women will experience an episode of major depression during her lifetime, twice the rate seen in men. Each year, about 13 percent of women have a diagnosable depressive disorder. Suicide is the fourth leading cause of death among women ages 15 to 24 years and the fifth leading cause of death among women ages 25 to 44 years. Depression is almost twice as likely to be reported by female teens than by male teens. Girls are 80 percent to 90 percent more likely than boys to consider suicide or attempt suicide and 50 percent more likely to make an attempt that requires medical attention.[59]

Biological processes and hormonal changes do not explain sex-related differences in rates of depression; they may play a role, however. For example, an increase in depression among girls at the time of puberty is more likely if there are pre-existing risk factors, like rape or sexual abuse.[60] Similarly, postpartum depression is more likely among women struggling to be the ideal mother, wife, and homemaker: self-sacrificing, patient, and always in control. Other risk factors for postpartum depression include being less educated and poor and having less social support, including less support from the baby's father.[61]

For most girls, depression in adolescence is related to their beginning to feel the pressures of conforming to the female gender role. As teens, girls learn the importance of maintaining an attractive physical appearance and are exposed to sexual harassment and dating violence.[62]

Married women are at greater risk for developing depression than are single women. Their primary roles as nurturer, caretaker, and homemaker have low social status and can be socially isolating. Striving to conform to culturally idealized notions of the intensely involved mother can be a source of low self-esteem and anxiety for women who do not have the time, physical ability, social support, or material resources necessary for such intense mothering, which describes the social and economic situations of most women. Stress from combining work and family roles can also lead to depression. Finally, since women tend to be concerned with personal relationships and caretaking, they are likely to be more aware of and affected by the stressful events experienced by family members, co-workers, and friends.[63]

More than 90 percent of people with bulimia nervosa, anorexia nervosa, and binge eating disorder are female. Cultural pressures are related to the prevalence of these disorders. Women are still evaluated based on the extent to which their physical appearance conforms to cultural standards of beauty and femininity; women are still socialized to be dependent on the external approval of others.[64] Eating disorders have also been linked with racism, homophobia, and sexual abuse. Restrictive dieting, bingeing, and purging are common among white women and among women of color.[65]

Low-income women have a high rate of mental health problems, with low-income single mothers particularly at risk. Social and economic stresses contribute to low-income women's heightened risk of distress and disorder. They are more likely to experience crime and violence, the illness or death of children, and the imprisonment of husbands, and to suffer from chronic life conditions such as inadequate housing, dangerous neighborhoods, and financial insecurities.[66]

For older women, the stresses of poverty, widowhood, and increased dependency on family members often result in loneliness, isolation, depression, alcoholism, and drug abuse. Also, women are at higher risk of elder abuse than are men.[67]

Racism, ethnic prejudice, discrimination based on race and sex, and racial violence exacerbate the mental health problems of women of color. Many women develop physical and psychiatric disorders because of traumatic experiences as refugees and immigrants. Also, the high levels of stress associated with the process of acculturation may produce a higher prevalence of mental illness and alcohol and drug abuse.[68]

For lesbians, the pervasive homophobia and heterosexism of society can create psychological distress. Lesbians often experience rejection, ridicule, and actual or threatened physical violence. Other stresses include the risk of unwanted exposure and the ongoing process of coming out; discrimination in housing, employment, and child custody; and the lack of legal protection for and social recognition of their partnerships and parental status. These problems contribute to higher rates of depression, alcoholism, and suicide.[69]

Finally, victimization creates profound emotional difficulties for many women. Many victims of sexual harassment, physical assault, rape, stalking, and domestic violence experience high levels of fear and anxiety, shame, social and sexual withdrawal, low self-esteem, and depression. As compared with nonassaulted women, rape survivors are more likely to develop posttraumatic stress disorder and have higher rates of depression, nightmares, physical health problems, and suicide. A history of physical, emotional, and sexual abuse increases the likelihood that women will abuse alcohol and other drugs, which can lead to other serious health problems, including HIV infection.[70]

Intervention Strategies

For every level of intervention, social workers can use the ecosystems model to frame their understanding of how sexism affects the psychosocial problems experienced by women and the social conditions that enhance or restrict their lives. Social workers must analyze and evaluate the personal, social, and economic consequences of gender inequality to determine appropriate goals, targets of change, and interventions with women clients.

To counter the pervasive influence of incomplete, inaccurate, or biased information about women, it is essential that social workers be knowledgeable about current research on gender differences, gender roles, differences in the socialization and life experiences of women and men, and the nature of institutionalized inequality and female oppression. Social workers also need to understand the effects of sexism on their own beliefs, values, expectations, and behavior. They need to identify the range of ways gender bias can influence every phase of the planned change process.

In social work practice, issues related to female socialization and *gender inequality* will be of varying significance, depending on the specific problem or issue. In every situation and for every client, the social worker needs to evaluate (1) the relationships between traditional gender roles and gender inequality and the presenting problem; (2) the ways in which gender bias affects the established knowledge base about that problem and contaminates traditional services and treatments; (3) the relevant theories and research on women, especially those that address explicitly the intersections of gender, intragroup variance among racial and ethnic groups, class, sexual orientation, and other sources of oppression; and (4) the range of methods and approaches that have been developed to deal with the gender-related aspects of the presenting problem and desired outcomes. At best, ignoring the realities and complexities of women's lives, fails to provide clients with the opportunity to reduce their social and economic powerlessness and vulnerability. At worst, social work practice that ignores the social circumstances of women may actually promote female subordination and victimization.

Micro Practice with Women

Social workers use a range of microlevel interventions to help women deal with problems in psychosocial functioning. In the assessment phase, a social worker needs to evaluate women's functioning at home, at work, and in the community in terms of existing gender-role norms and discriminatory practices. Although the immediate target of change is the woman and/or her family, there must be ongoing recognition of the ways in which a woman's personal problems are shaped by her social, economic, and legal circumstances. Social workers must be realistic about the many ways in which discriminatory employment practices, sex-biased community attitudes, and restrictive family roles create barriers and place limits on women's options for change.

Understanding the full range of factors that shape women's lives, a social worker can extend the range of solutions and life changes to be considered and select interventive strategies that will help clients reach their goals. Social workers should incorporate knowledge concerning female oppression and gender-role socialization in the same manner that they incorporate knowledge concerning all other aspects of clients' problems and situations selectively and sensitively, taking into account the values, needs, concerns, and goals of their clients.

With an awareness that women's lack of social power can generate passivity and dependence, workers should include female empowerment as a central goal. This can be accomplished by sharing resources, power, and responsibility with clients. Interventive strategies consistent with these principles include appropriate self-disclosure by the worker, having the client take an active part in goal-setting and outcome evaluation, making the worker's own values explicit, and emphasizing the client's strengths and assets. Such strategies minimize clients' dependency on the worker, increase the likelihood that clients feel free to reject the values and approaches of the worker, and concretely demonstrate the belief that women are capable of being autonomous and in control of their own lives.

As with all oppressed groups, it is empowering for women to understand the influence of social factors on their personal lives. Social workers can incorporate *gender-role analyses* into their work with women to encourage clients to evaluate the ways in which social roles, norms, and structural realities limit female autonomy and choice. Through this process, women can come to understand how, by internalizing cultural values about women, they sometimes act as coconspirators in their own oppression.

All-women groups can be used to deemphasize the authority of the social worker and help members share and understand the experiences that have influenced them as women. Such groups facilitate the respect and trust of women for one another and help them to develop a sense of solidarity with women as a group. Finally, workers can encourage their clients to participate in social action on their own behalf. It is growth-producing for women to engage in social actions designed to change those conditions at work and in their community that most directly have negative effects on their lives.

Being female increases the worker's ability to empathize with clients and to understand and share experiences related to being female in a male-dominated society. In their practice, male social workers must develop ways to ensure that traditional male–female power relationships and interactive strategies do not characterize their work with women clients. They need to recognize that there are limitations in their ability to empathize with women and to serve as role models, and that the male worker–female client combination reinforces cultural views that women are dependent on male authority.

In working with groups, workers must be aware of the intersection of gender issues with group dynamics. This includes recognition of the differences between mixed groups and all-female groups in stages of group development, goals and structure, leadership, interpersonal relations, and communication patterns. Workers should be aware of the ways in which groups have been especially useful in work with women with common issues; for example, with substance-abusing women, women with eating disorders, lesbian mothers, unwed teenage mothers, women of color, and low-income women.

Work with families must take into account the social, economic, and political realities that shape family roles and relationships, and conversely, how women's roles and responsibilities in their families support or constrain their participation in public life. In working with families, social workers can provide support and direction to help mothers and their female children become more assertive and self-directed. They can help clients challenge gender-role stereotypes in the family, examine more flexible and nontraditional roles, and equalize power.

In establishing goals, in planning interventive strategies, and in evaluating outcomes, workers and clients must recognize that some changes *will* increase women's self-esteem, feelings of autonomy, and social functioning, but at the same time produce new stresses and conflicts. Presenting a self-image and behaviors that deviate from traditional roles and norms may incur difficulties for women. Some relationships may become more satisfying, but others are likely to become more stressful. Parents, spouses, children, friends, relatives, and co-workers may be ambivalent, if not hostile, toward a woman's desire to make nontraditional changes in her life. Also, because of sexism in education and employment as well as in other social institutions, women may not be able to fully or easily achieve the changes they desire; assessment and evaluation must focus, therefore, on whether women are behaving in a self-directing, autonomous manner and whether their behavior is the result of a conscious understanding of available options and a deliberate weighing of costs and benefits.

Macro Practice with Women

The principles and methods that are incorporated into nonsexist micro practice are also used in nonsexist approaches to macro practice. Empowerment of women and the development of responsive policies and services require that workers emphasize client participation, egalitarian relationships, and collaborative decision-making and that they reduce the power and status differences between themselves and their clients.

At the macro level, workers' tasks include assessing the impact of sexism, heterosexism, racism, and poverty on female clients; analyzing the unmet service needs of women and their children; evaluating the presence of bias in the design and delivery of existing services; and developing and/or modifying programs and services to meet the special needs of women. Neighborhood organizing, community development, and social action provide a range of methods that workers can apply to provide and/or improve local resources for women. Social planning, program development, and policy analysis engage higher-level political processes and public education efforts on behalf of women.

Empowering women includes helping them to gain the power to control their own lives. Community organization skills can be used to help women build and maintain their own groups, organizations, and agencies. Social workers can help women to translate their concerns into specific objectives and goals; to develop their organizational and leadership skills; to increase the resources available to the group; and to identify and evaluate strategies that will help them to reach their goals. Workers' knowledge of funding and resource development can be particularly valuable to such groups.

In community and organizational practice, as in micro practice, there are some circumstances in which a female social worker is likely to be more effective than a male. For example, in the areas of physical abuse, child sexual abuse, and teen pregnancy, a female social worker is likely to be trusted more. Women workers' experience as women, and often as mothers, helps them identify women's needs and concerns and may enhance their credibility. Also, women community organizers, planners, and administrators can work with female client systems without the power-status differential that is inherent when men work with women.

For female social workers, macro practice requires recognition that the workers themselves are likely to be influenced by the sexism pervading both the systems in which they work and those they want to influence. Administration and community organization are viewed as male domains and rely primarily on male models. Further, the policies, programs, and services that are targets of change are most likely controlled and administered by men. Women who enter these domains as workers or who attempt to change them on behalf of their clients often encounter gender-role stereotyping, devaluation, exclusion, suspicion, prejudice, sexual harassment, and discrimination.

Micro Practice with a Battered Woman

The following case illustrates the ways in which women's problems involve social, economic, and legal factors; role socialization; and interpersonal and psychological distress and dysfunction. It demonstrates how micro practice can be used to improve the lives of battered women.

BACKGROUND

Tracy was brought to the shelter for battered women from the emergency room of the local hospital. She had been severely beaten by her husband, who had also threatened to kill her. She had two black eyes, two broken ribs, severely bruised legs and arms, and a broken finger on her left hand. According to Tracy, her husband pulled the phone from the wall when she tried to call the police; it was then that she sustained the black eyes. Fortunately, a cousin came by for an unexpected visit, at which time Tracy's husband fled the house. The cousin drove Tracy and her three-year-old daughter, Jane, to the hospital. Tracy's husband had taken her purse when he fled from the house. The only possessions Tracy and her daughter had with them were the clothes that they had on.

INITIAL CLIENT CONTACT AND ENGAGEMENT

When she met with the social worker, Tracy expressed much concern about whether this was really the right thing to do. She was angry, confused, and very worried about how she would manage for herself and her child. The worker reassured Tracy that her feelings were common to many of the women when they first came to the shelter. The worker emphasized that the shelter would provide Tracy with safety and security; no decisions about other services or goals would be made until Tracy was ready. The worker's goals were to communicate her caring and her willingness to help; to reduce the fears and anxiety associated with being in this new situation; and to assure Tracy of safety and confidentiality. The worker explained that she would be meeting with Tracy and that Jane would have her own social worker and be part of the children's play group at the shelter.

IDENTIFYING NEEDS AND OBTAINING RESOURCES

At their second meeting later that same day, the worker began to collect information about Tracy's situation and needs for service. Tracy was severely depressed and on antidepressants. Following their session, the worker contacted Tracy's psychiatrist to coordinate services. She also began to work with the county social service department to obtain financial assistance for Tracy's medical and psychiatric care. The worker told Tracy about the range of resources and services available at the shelter and in the community.

PROMOTING CLIENT SELF-DETERMINATION

The worker explained that her role was to help Tracy make decisions about her life, not to make decisions for her. Tracy would need to decide what she wanted to do and what would be in her best interests. The worker emphasized that she would support, encourage, and advocate for Tracy throughout, but that it was Tracy's right and responsibility to make her own decisions.

EMPATHY AND EMPOWERMENT

Tracy told the worker that she was very confused, that she trusted the worker, and that she would like the worker to develop a plan for her to leave her husband. The worker reassured Tracy that she appreciated her trust and that she understood her anxiety, but that Tracy would be able to determine her own needs and set her own goals, with the worker's help. Not taking over at this point, although this was the request of the client, began the process of empowering Tracy to take control of her own life.

FACILITATING EMPOWERMENT THROUGH GROUP SUPPORT

The worker encouraged Tracy to join the shelter's counselor-facilitated support group. Here, Tracy was able to see that she was not alone. She saw the ways that other women were able to come to terms with their abuse; she heard from women who had begun to work with lawyers and to find housing; and she began to see some commonalties between her experiences and those of other battered women. The group helped her to feel more optimistic about her own ability to change and to become more assertive. She felt less isolated and received support for her attempts to help other women deal with their issues.

ENHANCING SELF-ESTEEM THROUGH VALIDATION

Tracy particularly liked group discussions about how they had been raised as females and brought up to expect that a happy marriage was a certainty and their most important goal. They described the pressures they felt from family to remain married no matter what. Tracy felt increasingly free to talk and express her own opinions, since she felt support and acceptance from the other members of the group. She became active in helping think through problems and possible alternatives for herself and other group members. The support group provided Tracy with opportunities to share experiences, overcome her social isolation and lack of female friendships, and find hope and strength by seeing the successes of others.

TRANSFORMING FEELINGS INTO ACTION

In their individual sessions, the worker progressed from encouraging Tracy to express her feelings and helping her to clarify emotions, to encouraging Tracy to take steps to improve her situation. The worker reassured Tracy that she was not to blame. She was neither the instigator of the abuse nor a willing participant; she was not responsible for her husband's violence. She helped Tracy believe she had the right to be safe and that no one had the right to abuse her.

DEVELOPING CLIENT INSIGHT

The worker also wanted Tracy to recognize that, with new information and options, she was responsible for protecting herself and her child. The worker helped Tracy to understand the dynamics of wife abuse and the ways in which social factors contributed to her abuse. In discussing social factors and common patterns of domestic violence, it was important that the worker not reinforce Tracy's feelings of helplessness. Instead, by understanding these social factors, Tracy could take increased responsibility for the choices she made, thereby gaining a sense of personal power.

PLANNING FOR CHANGE

In considering Tracy's leaving her husband, they discussed her needs for housing, employment, child care, and improved parenting skills, as well as financial aid to cover transportation, medical and psychiatric expenses, and legal assistance. Tracy did decide to leave her husband, although she was worried about her actual ability to do so. As Tracy set her goals, she and the worker outlined the steps that would be necessary, including Tracy's spending time with workers in other agencies. The worker also introduced Tracy to the legal advocate who worked for the shelter program. She would explain her legal rights, including arrest policies and the legal process of obtaining a restraining order.

Macro Practice on Behalf of Battered Women

Macro social work practice finds the social worker providing services on behalf of people, as opposed to micro practice in which the worker provides a direct service on a face-to-face basis with an identified client. In macro practice, the worker attempts to make organizations, neighborhoods, and communities responsive to the needs of clients. Macro practice may also involve developing or changing policies, regulations, and laws to help people. This can be seen in the following macro case.

DEFINING THE PROBLEM AND NEED

Shelter staff had already established community education programs with business leaders and church groups, and they had recruited volunteers to assist with the twenty-four-hour crisis line. However, several problems were constantly confronting the staff and their clients. All the workers at the shelter were frustrated with the ineffectiveness of restraining orders. Also, they increasingly saw ties between domestic violence and substance abuse, but their programs could not deal with the substance abuse, and the alcohol and drug programs did not address the battering. Finally, they knew that therapists in their community continued to offer battered women marital therapy when it is now widely accepted that it places women in danger to provide relationship counseling or mediation where there has been battering.[71]

DEVELOPING STRATEGIES

The shelter staff decided to meet with workers from the mental health and health, social service, and substance abuse treatment systems to discuss approaches for addressing the psychological, social, medical, and financial needs of women and their children.

The shelter workers also decided to develop a coordinated community response to the problem of domestic violence. They were aware that this is a strategy being applied across the country to improve services and to develop community-wide public awareness campaigns and primary prevention efforts in the schools.[72] "This activity is propelled by an understanding that, in spite of legal advances, unless there is a coordinated community response, batterers will take advantage of the fragmentation, misunderstanding, and bias of the criminal justice system to avoid prosecution and subsequent consequences for their acts of violence, often further isolating, manipulating, and controlling their victims in order to do so."[73] They would involve several key agencies, including battered women's shelters, prosecutors' offices, police and sheriff's departments, programs for men who batter, and other human service agencies.

SYSTEMS ADVOCACY

Staff evaluated what changes in policies they should address at the macro level, advocating on behalf of an entire population rather than advocating only on behalf of individual women.

With workers from other agencies, they reviewed the changes that systems advocacy has accomplished elsewhere. These included: waivers to the work requirement for battered women applying for welfare; collaborations between advocates and child welfare agencies to prevent abusers from using children to punish victims for leaving or to coerce them to return; routine screening for domestic violence in medical settings; and provision of immediate advocacy initiated by the advocacy program upon notification by law enforcement, instead of waiting for the victim to initiate contact. They discussed the need for new arrest policy legislation that distinguishes victim's self-defense violence from the primary aggressor assault and battering. They were aware that police are increasingly arresting battered women for allegedly assaulting their partners, which makes battered women much more vulnerable to future abuse.[74]

PLANNING/IMPLEMENTATION/EVALUATION

Over the next months, representatives from each agency will meet together to establish a common philosophy and a set of policies and procedures that will provide individual and systems advocacy as part of a coordinated community response to domestic violence. The group will be responsible for developing strategies to implement policy changes and to obtain feedback from advocates and victims on the impact of these changes.[75]

Emerging Issues and Trends

There have been profound changes in women's rights and status in the United States. Women from many social groups have more freedom to make choices about education, sexuality, marriage, childbearing, parenting, and paid employment. There is less tolerance of violence against women. There is more acceptance of lesbians and lesbian lifestyles. There is increased understanding of the common and unique experiences of different groups of women.[76] Still, we are far from achieving equality for women. Women who are not attached to men are poorer than those who are, and women of color are poorer than white women. Health care is inaccessible and inadequate for many women. Most employed women continue to be in sex-segregated, low-wage jobs. Compared with men, women continue to have less independence and fewer resources.

The profession of social work has a major role to play in the design and implementation of social policies, programs, and services. The feminization of poverty will continue to dominate the focus of social welfare policies and programs. Divorce and out-of-wedlock pregnancies, sex segregation and discrimination in the labor force, and the lack of federal family-support policies will maintain women's disadvantaged status. Our challenge is to find ways to support the needs of employed women and at the same time create alternate approaches to support childrearing and caregiving. By developing strategies for eliminating traditional gender role socialization and inequality, social workers can alter the conditions that contribute to female victimization as well as debilitating health and mental health problems for women.

Concluding Comment

Throughout the 1980s and 1990s, legislation and court decisions on affirmative action, abortion rights, discrimination in education and employment, and welfare narrowed women's rights and options. With the increased strength of the New Right and the backlash against feminism at the beginning of the new millennium, it will be important that social workers join with other groups concerned with social justice to protect the gains of the past.

Most important, social workers need to eliminate gender inequality within the profession as it impacts on the lives of female clients and workers. In evaluating services and programs, workers need to understand gender, race, class, sexual orientation, age, and disability status as interconnected sources of female subordination; and that meaningful change for women must take into account the multiple systems of domination that operate in women's lives. Social workers must be knowledgeable about the relationships between female subordination, women's problems, and social work services. They must proactively work to eliminate male dominance in schools of social work and in social work agencies and organizations. Until these conditions are met, we cannot presume that we have the theoretical, empirical, and ethical base for our practice with women. To develop meaningful and nonoppressive policies, services, programs, and interventions for women, social workers must work to eliminate stereotyping and discrimination for clients and women social workers as well.

KEYWORDS AND CONCEPTS

Women's legal rights
Gender system
Gender inequality
Gender-role analysis

Lesbians
Triple Oppression
Violence against women
Patriarchy

SUGGESTED INFORMATION SOURCES

Adams, D., ed., *Health Issues for Women of Color: A Cultural Diversity Perspective.* Thousand Oaks, CA: Sage, 1995.

Bricker-Jenkins, M., Hooyman, N., and Gottlieb, N., eds. *Feminist Social Work Practice in Clinical Settings.* Newbury Park, CA: Sage, 1991.

Julia, M. *Constructing Gender: Multicultural Perspectives in Working with Women.* Belmont, CA: Wadsworth, 2000.

Renzetti, C., Edleson, J., and Bergen, R., eds. *Sourcebook on Violence Against Women.* Thousand Oaks, CA: Sage, 2001.

Rosen, R. *The World Split Open: How the Modern Women's Movement Changed America.* New York: Viking Press, 2000.

Straussner, S., and Brown, S., eds. *The Handbook of Addiction Treatment for Women: Theory and Practice.* San Francisco: Jossey-Bass, 2002.

Van Den Bergh, N., ed. *Feminist Practice in the 21st Century.* Washington, D.C.: NASW Press, 1995.

ENDNOTES

1. U.S. Census Bureau, *Women in the United States: March 2000* (PPL-121), Internet Release date: March 15, 2001.
2. Henry J. Kaiser Family Foundation estimates based on Urban Institute analyses of the March 1999 Current Population Survey, U.S. Bureau of the Census.
3. U.S. Department of Labor, *Highlights of Women's Earnings in 2001,* Report 960 (Washington, D.C.: U.S. Government Printing Office, May 2002).
4. U.S. Census Bureau, *What's It Worth? Field of Training and Economic Status,* Current Population Reports, Series P70-72 (Washington, D.C.: U.S. Government Printing Office, April 2001).
5. U.S. Department of Labor, *Employment Characteristics of Families in 2001,* Current Population Survey, Internet Release date: March 29, 2002; S. S. Dhooper and S. E. Moore, *Social Work Practice with Culturally Diverse People* (Thousand Oaks, CA: Sage, 2001).
6. U.S. Census Bureau, *Money Income in the United States: 2000,* Current Population Reports, Series P60-213 (Washington, D.C.: U.S. Government Printing Office, September 2001).
7. U.S. Census Bureau, *America's Families and Living Arrangements: 2000,* Current Population Reports, Series P20-537 (Washington, D.C.: U.S. Government Printing Office, June 2001); U.S. Census Bureau, *Census Facts for Native American Month (November 1–30, 1997),* Press Release, October 31, 1997.
8. U.S. Census Bureau, *Living Arrangements of Children: 1996,* Current Population Reports, Series P70-74 (Washington, D.C.: U.S. Government Printing Office, April 2001).
9. U.S. Census Bureau, *Fertility of American Women: June 2000,* Current Population Reports, Series P20-543RV (Washington, D.C.: U.S. Government Printing Office, October 2001); National Center for Health Statistics, *Chartbook on Trends in the Health of Americans. Health, United States, 2002* (Washington, D.C.: U.S. Government Printing Office, 2002).
10. D. Misra, ed., *Women's Health Data Book: A Profile of Women's Health in the United States* (Washington, D.C.: Jacobs Institute of Women's Health and The Henry J. Kaiser Family Foundation, 2001).
11. U.S. Census Bureau, *Poverty in the United States: 2001,* Current Population Reports, Series P60-219 (Washington, D.C.: U.S. Government Printing Office, 2002).
12. U.S. Census Bureau, *Number, Timing, and Duration of Marriages and Divorces: 1996,* Current Population Reports, Series P70-80 (Washington, D.C.: U.S. Government Printing Office, February 2002).
13. U.S. Census Bureau, *America's Families and Living Arrangements: 2000.*
14. U.S. Census Bureau, *Marital Status and Living Arrangements: March 1995 (Update),* Current Population Reports, Series P20-491 (Washington, D.C.: U.S. Government Printing Office, December 1996).
15. U.S. Census Bureau, Census 2000. Summary File 1. Table 1. Total Population by Age and Sex for the United States: 2000.
16. U.S. Census Bureau, *Women in the United States: March 2000* (PPL-121), Internet Release date: March 15, 2001.
17. Misra, 2001.
18. Misra, 2001.
19. The Henry J. Kaiser Family Foundation, *Fact Sheet: Women and HIV/AIDS,* May 2001.

20. B. M. Britton, "Sexual Harassment," in S. Ruzek, V. Olesen, and A. Clarke, eds., *Women's Health: Complexities and Differences* (Columbus: Ohio State University Press, 1997), pp. 510–519.

21. U.S. Department of Justice, *Intimate Partner Violence,* Bureau of Justice Statistics, NCJ 178247, (Washington, D.C.: National Institute of Justice, May 2000); U.S. Department of Justice, *Full Report of the Prevalence, Incidence, and Consequences of Violence Against Women: Findings from the National Violence Against Women Survey,* NCJ183781 (Washington, D.C.: National Institute of Justice, November 2000); U.S. Department of Justice, *Extent, Nature, and Consequences of Intimate Partner Violence: Findings from the National Violence Against Women Survey,* NCJ 181867 (Washington, D.C.: National Institute of Justice, July, 2000).

22. V. Sapiro, *Women in American Society* (Mountain View, CA: Mayfield Publishing, 1994); M. Zinn and D. Eitzen, *Diversity in Families* (New York: Addison Wesley Longman, 1999).

23. A. Kessler-Harris, *Securing Equity* (New York: Oxford University Press, 2001); R. Rosen, *The World Split Open: How the Modern Women's Movement Changed America* (New York: Viking Press, 2000); Sapiro, 1994; Zinn and Eitzen, 1999.

24. S. Faludi, *Backlash: The Undeclared War Against American Women* (New York: Crown, 1991).

25. "Women in Combat: Lawmakers Draw New Line." MSNBC News Services. http://www.msnbc.com/id/7909442/

26. D. Segura, "Chicanas and Triple Oppression in the Labor Force," in T. Cordova, N. Cantu, G. Cardenas, J. Garcia, and C. Sierra, eds., *Chicana Voices: Intersections of Class, Race, and Gender* (Austin, TX: CMAS Publications, 1990), pp. 47–65.

27. G. Appleby and J. Anastas, *Not Just a Passing Phase: Social Work with Gay, Lesbian, and Bisexual People* (New York: Columbia University Press, 1998); C. Tully, *Lesbians, Gays, & the Empowerment Perspective* (New York: Columbia University Press, 2000).

28. U.S. Census Bureau, *What's It Worth? Field of Training and Economic Status.*

29. T. Lennon, *Statistics on Social Work Education in the United States: 2000* (Alexandria, VA: Council on Social Work Education, 2002).

30. P. Boss and B. Thorne, "Family Sociology and Family Therapy: A Feminist Linkage," in M. McGoldrick, C. Anderson, and F. Walsh, eds., *Women in Families: A Framework for Family Therapy* (New York: W. W. Norton and Company, 1989), pp. 78–96; M. M. Ferree, "Feminism and Family Research," in A. Booth, ed., *Contemporary Families: Looking Forward, Looking Back* (Minneapolis: National Council on Family Relations, 1991), pp. 103–121.

31. N. Chappell, "Aging and Social Care," in R. Binstock and L. George, eds., *Handbook of Aging and the Social Sciences* (San Diego, CA: Academic Press, 1990), pp. 438–454; N. Hooyman and J. Gonyea, *Feminist Perspectives on Family Care* (Thousand Oaks, CA: Sage, 1995); D. Spain and S. Bianchi, *Balancing Act* (New York: Russell Sage Foundation, 1996).

32. U.S. Census Bureau, *America's Families and Living Arrangements: 2000.*

33. Misra, 2001.

34. U.S. Census Bureau, *Fertility of American Women: June 2000.*

35. Misra, 2001.

36. J. Stacey, "Gay and Lesbian Families: Queer Like Us," in M. Mason, A. Skolnick, and S. Sugarman, eds., *All Our Families: New Policies for a New Century* (New York: Oxford University Press, Inc., 1998), pp. 117–143.

37. J. Battle, C. Cohen, D. Warren, G. Fergerson, and S. Audam, *Say It Loud: I'm Black and I'm Proud* (Washington, D.C.: The Policy Institute of the National Gay and Lesbian Task Force, March 2002).

38. Appleby and Anastas, 1998; C. Patterson, "Children of Lesbian and Gay Parents," *Child Development*, 63 (1992): 1025–1042; Tully, 2000.

39. Patterson, 1992, p. 1036.

40. Data from the National Gay and Lesbian Task Force.

41. W. van der Meide, *Legislating Equality* (Washington, D.C.: The Policy Institute of the National Gay and Lesbian Task Force, January 2000); Data from the National Gay and Lesbian Task Force.

42. Data from the National Gay and Lesbian Task Force.

43. K. Allen and D. Demo, "The Families of Lesbians and Gay Men: A New Frontier in Family Research," *Journal of Marriage and the Family*, 57 (February 1995): 111–127; M. Allen and N. Burrell, "Comparing the Impact of Homosexual and Heterosexual Parents on Children," *Journal of Homosexuality*, 32 (1996): 19–35; L. Kurdek, "The Allocation of Household Labor in Gay, Lesbian, and Heterosexual Married Couples," *Journal of Social Issues*, 49 (1993): 127–139; L. Lott-Whitehead and C. Tully, "The Families of Lesbian Mothers," *Smith College Studies in Social Work*, 63 (1993): 265–280; C. Patterson and R. Redding, "Lesbian and Gay Families with Children," *Journal of Social Issues*, 52 (1996): 29–50.

44. W. Devore, "'Whence Came These People?' An Exploration of the Values and Ethics of African American Individuals, Families, and Communities," in R. Fong and S. Furuto, eds., *Culturally Competent Practice: Skills, Interventions, and Evaluations* (Needham Heights, MA: Allyn & Bacon, 2001), pp. 33–46; Zinn and Eitzen, 1999.

45. Zinn and Eitzen, 1999.

46. G. Winbush, "African American Women," in M. Julia, *Constructing Gender: Multicultural Perspectives in Working with Women* (Belmont, CA: Wadsworth, 2000), pp. 11–34.

47. Dhooper and Moore, "Understanding and Working with African Americans," 2001, pp. 98–134.

48. U.S. Census Bureau, *Coresident Grandparents and Grandchildren*, Current Population Reports, Series P23-198 (Washington, D.C.: U.S. Government Printing Office, May 1999); D. Burnette, "Grandparents Raising Grandchildren in the Inner City," *Families in Society* (1997): 489–501; P. Gibson, "African American Grandmothers: New Mothers Again," *Affilia: Journal of Women and Social Work*, 14 (Fall 1999): 329–343.

49. U.S. Census Bureau, Current Population Survey, March 2000, Ethnic and Hispanic Statistics Branch, Population Division. Internet Release Date: March 6, 2001.

50. G. Acevedo and J. Morales, "Assessment with Latino/Hispanic Communities and Organizations," in Fong and Furuto, 2001, pp. 147–162; H. Burgos-Ocasio, "Hispanic Women," in Julia, 2000, pp. 109–137; L. Negroni-Rodriguez and J. Morales, "Individual and Family Assessment Skills with Latino/Hispanic Americans," in Fong and Furuto, 2001, pp. 132–146.

51. U.S. Census Bureau, Current Population Survey, March 2000, Racial Statistics Branch, Population Division. Internet Release Date: June 28, 2001.

52. U.S. Census Bureau, Current Population Survey, March 2000, Racial Statistics Branch, Population Division. Internet Release Date: June 28, 2001.

53. Dhooper and Moore, 2001.

54. Y. Song-Kim, "Battered Korean Women in Urban United States," in S. Furuto, R. Biswas, D. Chung, K. Murase, and F. Ross-Sheriff, eds., *Social Work Practice with Asian Americans* (Newbury Park: Sage, 1992), pp. 213–226; Dhooper and Moore, 2001; A. Zaharlick, "Southeast Asian-American Women," in Julia, 2000, pp. 177–204.

55. W. Leigh and M. Jimenez, *Women of Color Data Book* (Washington, D.C.: National Institutes of Health, 2002).

56. Dhooper and Moore, "Understanding and Working with Native Americans," 2001, pp. 174–211; B. Neal, "Native American Women," in Julia, 2000, pp. 157–175; W. Leigh and M. Jimenez, *Women of Color Data Book* (Washington, D.C.: National Institutes of Health, 2002).

57. Office of Justice Programs, *Promising Practices and Strategies to Reduce Alcohol and Substance Abuse Among American Indians and Alaska Natives,* An OJP Issues & Practices Report, U.S. Department of Justice (Washington, D.C.: National Institute of Justice, August 2000); Office on Women's Health, *The Health of Minority Women* (U.S. Department of Health and Human Services, May 2000); H. Weaver, "Native Americans and Substance Abuse," in S. Straussner, ed., *Ethnocultural Factors in Substance Abuse Treatment* (New York: Guilford Press, 2001), pp. 77–96.

58. Dhooper and Moore, 2001; S. Evans, "Women," in F. Hoxie, ed., *The Encyclopedia of North American Indians* (New York: Houghton Mifflin, 1996), pp. 665–689; T. LaFromboise, J. Berman, and B. Sohi, "American Indian Women," in L. Comas-Diaz and B. Greene, eds., *Women of Color: Integrating Ethnic and Gender Identities in Psychotherapy* (New York: Guilford Press, 1994), pp. 30–71.

59. Misra, 2001; *Health, United States, 2001* (National Center for Health Statistics, 2001).

60. S. Nolen-Hoeksema and J. Girgus, "The Emergence of Gender Differences in Depression during Adolescence," *Psychological Bulletin,* 115 (1994): 424–443.

61. A. Dunnewold, *Evaluation and Treatment of Postpartum Emotional Disorders,* Practitioners Resource Series (Sarasota, FL: Professional Resource Press, 1997).

62. B. Levy, ed., *Dating Violence: Young Women in Danger* (Seattle: Seal Press, 1991); S. Nolen-Hoeksema, "Sex Differences in Depression During Childhood and Adolescence," in *Sex Differences in Depression* (Stanford, CA: Stanford University Press, 1990), pp. 178–196; J. Stoppard, "Depression in Adolescence: Negotiating Identities in a Girl-Poisoning Culture," in *Understanding Depression: Feminist Social Constructionist Approaches* (New York: Routledge, 2000), pp. 113–136.

63. E. Galinsky and J. Bond, "Work and Family: The Experiences of Mothers and Fathers in the U.S. Workforce," in C. Costello and B. Krimgold, eds., *The American Woman, 1996–97* (New York: W. W. Norton, 1996), pp. 79–103; Nolen-Hoeksema, 1990; S. Nolen-Hoeksema, "Epidemiology and Theories of Gender Differences in Unipolar Depression," in M. Seeman, ed., *Gender and Psychopathology* (Washington, D.C.: American Psychiatric Press, 1995), pp. 63–87; A. Rhodes and P. Goering, "Gender Differences in the Use of Outpatient Mental Health Services," in B. Levin, A. Blanch, and A. Jennings, eds., *Women's Mental Health Services: A Public Health Perspective* (Thousand Oaks, CA: Sage, 1998), pp. 19–33; Stoppard, "Women's Lives and Depression: Marriage and Motherhood," 2000, pp. 137–160.

64. S. Bordo, *Unbearable Weight: Feminism, Western Culture, and the Body* (Berkeley, CA: University of California Press, 1993); K. Halmi, "Eating Disorders," in M. Goldman and M. Hatch, eds., *Women and Health* (San Diego: Academic Press, 2000), pp. 1032–1041;

S. Raeburn, "Women and Eating Disorders," in S. Straussner and S. Brown, eds., *The Handbook of Addiction Treatment for Women: Theory and Practice* (San Francisco: Josse-Bass, 2002), pp. 127–153.

65. B. Thompson, "'A Way Outa No Way' Eating Problems among African-American, Latina, and White Women," *Gender & Society* 6 (1992): 546–561; Office on Women's Health, *The Health of Minority Women* (Washington, D.C.: U.S. Department of Health and Human Services, May, 2000).

66. D. Belle, "Poverty and Women's Mental Health," *American Psychologist* 45 (1990): 385–389; G. Brown and P. Moran, "Single Mothers, Poverty, and Depression," *Psychological Medicine* 27 (1997): 21–33.

67. C. Beck and B. Pearson, "Mental Health of Elderly Women," in J. Garner and S. Mercer, eds., *Women As They Age: Challenge, Opportunity, and Triumph* (New York: Haworth Press, 1989), pp. 175–193; M. Hudson, "Elder Mistreatment: Its Relevance to Older Women," *Journal of American Women's Association* 52 (1997): 142–146, 158; D. Padgett, B. Burns, and L. Grau, "Risk Factors and Resilience: Mental Health Needs and Services Use of Older Women," in Levin, Blanch, and Jennings, 1998, pp. 390–413; B. Turner and L. Troll, *Women Growing Older: Psychological Perspectives* (Thousand Oaks, CA.: Sage, 1994).

68. D. Adams, ed., *Health Issues for Women of Color: A Cultural Diversity Perspective* (Thousand Oaks, CA: Sage, 1995); E. Cole, O. Espin, and E. Rothblum, eds., *Refugee Women and Their Mental Health: Shattered Societies, Shattered Lives* (New York: Haworth Press, 1992); Comas-Diaz and Greene, 1994; S. Straussner and S. Brown, eds., *The Handbook of Addiction Treatment for Women: Theory and Practice,* Part Four: "Addictions Issues for Ethnically Diverse Women" (San Francisco: Jossey-Bass, 2002), pp. 299–374; C. Willie, P. Rieker, B. Kramer, and B. Brown, eds., *Mental Health, Racism, and Sexism* (Pittsburgh: University of Pittsburgh Press, 1995).

69. C. Alexander, ed., *Gay and Lesbian Mental Health: A Sourcebook for Practitioners* (New York: Harrington Park Press, 1996); Appleby and Anastas, 1998; Tully, 2000; K. Van Wormer, J. Wells, and M. Boes, *Social Work with Lesbians, Gays, and Bisexuals: A Strengths Perspective* (Needham Heights, MA: Allyn & Bacon, 2000).

70. S. Covington and J. Surrey, "The Relational Model of Women's Psychological Development: Implications for Substance Abuse," in S. Wilsnack and R. Wilsnack, eds., *Gender and Alcohol: Individual and Social Perspectives* (New Brunswick, N.J.: Rutgers University Press, 1998); J. Newmann, D. Greenley, J. Sweeney, and G. Van Dien, "Abuse Histories, Severe Mental Illness, and the Cost of Care," in Levin, Blanch, and Jennings, 1998, pp. 279–308; C. Renzetti, J. Edleson, and R. Bergen, eds., *Sourcebook on Violence Against Women* (Thousand Oaks, CA: Sage, 2001); B. Schell and N. Lanteigne, *Stalking, Harassment, and Murder in the Workplace: Guidelines for Protection and Prevention* (Westport, CT: Quorum Books, 2000); K. Stout and B. McPhail, *Confronting Sexism & Violence Against Women: A Challenge for Social Work* (New York: Longman, 1998).

71. J. Austin and J. Dankwort, "A Review of Standards for Batterer Intervention Programs," *Violence Against Women Online Resources,* 1997, www.vaw.umn.edu; D. Saunders, "Interventions for Men Who Batter: Do We Know What Works?" *In Session: Psychotherapy in Practice,* 2/3 (1996): 81–94.

72. D. Saunders, "Domestic Violence: Legal Issues," in R. Edwards, ed., *Encyclopedia of Social Work,* 19th edition (Washington, D.C.: NASW Press, 1995), pp. 789–795.

73. R. Thelen, "Advocacy in a Coordinated Community Response: Overview and Highlights of Three Programs," *Violence Against Women Online Resources,* 2000, www.vaw.umn.edu.
74. Thelen, 2000.
75. S. Riger, L. Bennett, S. Wasco, P. Schewe, L. Frohmann, J. Camacho, and R. Campbell, *Evaluating Services for Survivors of Domestic Violence and Sexual Assault* (Thousand Oaks, CA: Sage, 2002).
76. This chapter focused primarily on differences among women based on race/ethnicity and sexual orientation. However, a fuller discussion would examine, for example, the unique experiences and needs of women with disabilities, older women, and women of different religions.

16

Social Work Practice with Lesbian, Gay, and Bisexual People

*George A. Appleby and Jeane W. Anastas**

*Dr. George A. Appleby is Professor of Social Work and Dean of the School of Health and Human Services, Southern Connecticut State University, and Dr. Jeane W. Anastas is Professor, School of Social Work, New York University.

Prefatory Comment

A social work intern came to realize that a significant number of her clients were lesbian or gay youth who had been kicked out of their homes or who had run away from home because of parental reactions to their gayness. As she got to know each individual, she was struck by recurring themes: the individuals' recognition of their sexual orientation; family rejection; hostility of peers and friends; verbal and physical abuse; and the resulting confused, angry, and fearful feelings that increased their self-doubt. Homophobia and discrimination can create problems with self-esteem and self-image for people who do not fit comfortably into the heterosexual majority.

Our intern, like all good social workers, attempted to formulate an assessment and intervention plan based on her knowledge of the clients' life situations. Unfortunately, she was unable to recall any required readings related to this topic, and she did not remember an in-depth discussion about lesbians or gays in her social work classes. She did recollect, however, that once someone in class said that "faggots and dykes" should not be allowed to work with children because what they did was sinful and would have a bad influence on the development of those in their care. The professor did not say much, and the subject was dropped. She thought this seemed consistent with a NASW workshop she had attended where the presenter confirmed that there is homophobia among social work students and faculty.[1]

However, this intern knew that the NASW Code of Ethics encouraged her to further the cause of social justice by promoting and defending the rights of persons suffering injustice and oppression. Gays and lesbians certainly met this requirement. She recalled that the Code was translated into NASW policy statements that prescribed the practice behavior of members. In it, social workers are enjoined to view discrimination and prejudice directed against any minority as adverse to the mental and social health of the affected minority as well as a detriment to society. Furthermore, social workers are urged to work to combat discriminatory employment practices and any other form of discrimination that imposes something less than equal status on bisexual, gay, or lesbian individuals. NASW, she recalled, affirmed the right of all persons to define and express their own sexuality. All persons are to be encouraged to develop their individual potential to the fullest extent possible.

Our budding Jane Addams, while highly motivated to act ethically and to give the most effective help, had no idea where to start. After some thought, she decided to ask her supervisor for assistance. Her supervisor had received her MSW over a decade ago and knew little herself. She suggested that the intern do a literature review on this topic.

 ## Current Demographics

An understanding of the lesbian, gay, and bisexual population in the United States must begin with a presentation of the current demographic picture.* There is a significant gap in our knowledge because scholars, like the general public, have been affected by the societal myths and taboos surrounding homosexuality. Thus, they have often avoided the objective analysis of this aspect of human functioning entirely. When the topic has been studied at all, its science has often been limited by moral and social doctrines, seldom debated, about the ways humans ought to behave. Twenty years ago public discussion of homosexuality was minimal, very little research existed, and available studies were usually limited to the investigation of individuals who sought treatment or attempted to change their sexual orientation; thus, the studies were not helpful in understanding the vast majority of gay, lesbian, and bisexual people who were not in treatment.

Even today, a process of selective attention in the study of gay, lesbian, and bisexual people continues to limit our knowledge. However, while few national studies include information on sexual identity or sexual orientation, the 2000 Census for the first time generated data on same-sex households in which respondents called themselves "unmarried partners."[2] While such data excludes anyone not living with a partner or not describing themselves in those specific terms, it is the first time that the existence of gay and lesbian households has been acknowledged in our national self-enumeration.

---

*Transgender issues, while an emerging and very important topic in social work, are not addressed in all parts of this chapter to keep its length manageable.

Because oppression has resulted in the invisibility of gays and lesbians as a whole until recently, and because it is hard to define and describe an invisible population, much of the data we have about the homosexual population today comes from local surveys and ethnographic studies. Developing representative samples of lesbian, gay, and bisexual populations for research is notoriously difficult.[3] The data we do have suggest, however, that there is greater similarity than difference between gay and straight people.

Defining a Gay, Lesbian, or Bisexual Identity

Because of the myths and lack of knowledge that have surrounded this topic, it is especially important that we discuss who is and who is not lesbian, gay, or bisexual. A young graduate student has a crush on her female professor. She manufactures numerous ways to be near her. Is she a lesbian? An army captain is discharged from the service for having sexual relations with an enlisted man. Is he gay? Two adolescent boys masturbate one another to orgasm. Are they homosexual? While having sexual intercourse with her husband, a woman frequently fantasizes about having sexual relations with other women. She has never had actual sexual contact with another woman. What is her sexual orientation? Because human sexuality occurs on a spectrum of feelings, thoughts, and behavior, the answers to these questions are not so easy.

Categorization can lead to understanding—or to stereotyping. For example, if a woman is labeled a lesbian, it may be assumed that she will only date women, be involved in many tempestuous short-term relationships, wear pants, play sports, raise dogs, and drive a truck. Likewise, if a person is a gay male, then he may be assumed to be sexually promiscuous, be overly concerned about his body and youth, obsess about fashion and style, frequently flick his wrists, and become a hairdresser or decorator. These are common stereotypes, but in reality attributes such as these are seldom so predictable or clear.

Despite these dangers, the task of understanding any phenomenon starts with naming and defining, and the terminology has been changing. The term *lifestyle* has been confused with the definition of homosexuality. The term is used more appropriately to describe certain forms of lesbian, gay, and bisexual social and cultural expression, not fundamental sexual orientation, but is usually rejected as trivializing a core sense of identity. Also problematic for similar reasons is the term *sexual preference*, once widely used. Same-sex emotional, affectional, and sexual feelings and behavior are not something that is consciously and freely chosen. Thus, the more appropriate terms are *sexual orientation* or *sexual identity*.

The term *homosexual*, once the most common, is now sometimes rejected because it denotes a category first imposed from a medically oriented, heterosexual perspective. *Gay* is now the most commonly used term in contrast to the term *straight*. While *gay* is sometimes used to describe both men and women, many women prefer to call themselves *lesbians*.

Contemporary definitions of being gay, lesbian, or bisexual emphasize affectional and emotional ties as well as sexual behavior. *Lesbian* is thus defined as "a woman who has **primary** [emphasis added] emotional and sexual attraction to other women." Similarly, "*gay* most commonly refers to men who **primarily** [emphasis added] have emotional and sexual attraction to men." In both cases, however, it is noted that in either case cross-gender sex may sometimes occur as well. The term *bisexual* refers to "a man or woman with sexual and emotional and affectional orientation toward people of both sexes," meaning that neither same- nor opposite-sex orientation is primary but same-sex feelings and behavior is acknowledged. Therefore, in the health field, it is common to refer to *MSMs*, meaning "men who engage in same-sex behavior, but who may not necessarily self-identify as gay."

A sexual orientation or sexual identity as gay, lesbian, or bisexual "involves acknowledging the significance" of same-gender feelings and sexual behavior. What a person does, how he or she defines who he/she is, how others define the person, and the social scripts into which a person fits him-or herself are all influences on sexual orientation and sexual identity.[4]

All of these definitions take into account that self-definition and sexual orientation do not always conform with sexual behavior. The National Opinion Research Center at the University of Chicago reported that approximately 5 percent of the male population and approximately 4 percent of the female population claimed to have had sex with a same-sex partner since the age of eighteen, while almost 8 percent reported experiencing attraction to persons of their own sex. However, when respondents were asked to self-identify as either heterosexual, homosexual, or bisexual, only about 3 percent of the males and less than 2 percent of the females stated "homosexual." The same study reported a homosexual or bisexual identity of 9.2 percent for men and 2.6 percent for women among residents of the twelve largest American cities.[5] Thus, population estimates differ substantially depending on geography and on whether the questions are related to sexual conduct, enduring attraction, or sexual orientation and identity.

Young people are increasingly using the terms *queer* and *questioning* (for an individual "who may be experiencing lesbian, gay, bisexual, or transgender feelings or urges, but has not yet identified his or her sexual orientation or gender identity," known by the acronym LGBTQ). These newer terms reflect the stance that lesbians and gay men will no longer allow the heterosexual majority to name and define them.

Given the complexities of terminology and definitions just described, it is essential to be sensitive to language, culture, and geography. Ask clients or colleagues what they mean when you are uncertain of how they are defining themselves or what aspects of sexual identity or orientation they are talking about. Such a question will be interpreted more often as a demonstration of respect and concern than as ignorance.

Population Characteristics

Lesbians, gays, and bisexuals live in every area of the United States, but they appear to be found in larger numbers in urban areas where there is relative tolerance for diversity. They are represented in all occupations and socioeconomic groups. They are white, African American, Hispanic, Asian, and American Indian. They reflect the same demographic characteristics as found in the general population except that there may be higher levels of education among gays and lesbians than are found in the general population. Although there are limits to our knowledge base, failure to acknowledge the variety of lesbians', gays', and bisexuals' social situations only adds to the marginalization of their lives.

Using census and other data and recognizing the complexities in defining and counting the gay and lesbian population in the United States, the Urban Institute estimates that between about 2 percent and 3 percent of the United States population was gay and lesbian in 2000—that is, between 3.9 million and 5.9 million individuals.[6] This translates to between one in fifty and one in about thirty people. Because there are more gay men than lesbians, between 2.5 percent and 3.8 percent of men in the United States are likely gay and between 1.3 percent and 1.9 percent of women are likely lesbian. If we were to consider the typical size of an individual's network of family, friends, work colleagues, and others, these data suggest that most probably know someone who is lesbian, gay, or bisexual, whether or not they are aware of it.

Whatever the true numbers, it is important to recognize that there are a breadth of living situations and a number of subpopulations within the group, many of which overlap. Any community will have different social networks based on age, class, ethnicity, language, race, sex, and special interests. Among gay and lesbian couples identified in the 2000 Census, more than one quarter included at least one person who identified as a member of a racial or ethnic minority. Hidalgo warns that class differences and racism do divide lesbian, gay, and bisexual communities.[7] Some observers suggest, however, that there is a greater commitment to democratic structures and an integration of subgroups than is commonly seen in heterosexual communities, which is confirmed by the 2000 Census findings that gay and lesbian couples are more likely to live in neighborhoods with non-white and non-English speaking people than married, heterosexual couples. This may be true because the individuals who live in these communities may be more accepting of diversity in both sexual orientation and in racial and ethnic diversity, since the need for affiliation is often met in a group of similarly oriented people who share the common experience of oppression.

However, racial and ethnic factors do have an impact on associations. African American and Hispanic gays, for both economic and cultural reasons, often maintain residence with or near their families, unlike many white gays, who establish homes away from relatives, often in one of the larger urban areas. This has an impact on the amount and intensity of association with other gays. Smith suggests that is another factor in determining the level of association of African Americans with the gay community: "Gay whites are people who identify first as being gay and who usually live outside the closet in predominantly white gay communities. . . . black gays, on the other hand, view our racial heritage as primary and frequently live 'bisexual front lives' within black neighborhoods."[8] While there are no empirical data on the subject, the observation has been made that identification is equally important in other racial and ethnic groups.

Carballo-Dieguez notes that religion and folk beliefs strongly influence the Hispanic culture. Conservative and traditional values are barriers to an openly gay lifestyle.[9] Of the various religions, fundamentalists and Baptists seem most likely to condemn homosexuality, and African Americans, as Mays and Cochran point out, hold membership predominantly in these denominations.[10] Newby would concur with the importance of social structure, values, and religion on the public expression of sexual orientation in the African American community and proposes that this may explain the higher rate of bisexuality and lower percentage of gay exclusivity than is found among whites.[11] Thus, African American and Latino gays are a double minority, often stigmatized by being in both the minority of color and being gay, while lesbians of color are in "triple jeopardy" because of being women as well.

Ecosystems Framework

Social work addresses the interaction between the person and the environment. The goal of practice is to enhance and restore the psychosocial functioning of persons, or to change the oppressive or destructive social conditions that negatively affect the interaction between persons and their environments. The ecosystems model of practice, the framework of this text, consists of five interconnected domains or levels: (1) historical; (2) environmental-structural; (3) cultural; (4) family; and (5) individual. The lives and social conditions of lesbians, gay men, bisexuals, and transgender people (LGBT) are now assessed in relation to each of these domains.

Historical Factors

The ecosystems model is concerned with both positive and noxious factors in the historical experience of members of the population of interest. The history of minority group oppression and exploitation has already been noted. It has taken form in religion, culture, law, and social sanction. The United States, strongly influenced by interpretations of Judaic and Christian moral codes, is one of the most homophobic of societies. While change is in fact taking place in each of these areas, not one of these social structures could be characterized as nurturing. At best, they are benign.

The Stonewall rebellion in 1969, in which a group of gays and lesbians resisted and protested against police harassment and brutality at a gay bar in New York, is usually regarded as the birth of the modern Gay Liberation Movement. Since that time, lesbian, gay, and bisexual individuals have become increasingly visible in our society. They are fighting for equal protection under our laws and for access to the same benefits afforded heterosexuals, such as civil marriage, domestic partnership, and civil unions.

Religious groups have been in the forefront of opposition to homosexuality. However, not all religions oppose it. Biblical interpretations vary widely, with advocates of both sides quoting scriptures as their defense. Presently, each of the major Judaic and Christian denominations has begun to recognize the spiritual and civil rights needs of their lesbian, gay, and bisexual members but often not without controversy. The Metropolitan Community Church, a nondenominational group founded to minister to homosexuals, has over one hundred member churches throughout the country.

While some members of the gay community choose to remain invisible in an attempt to isolate themselves from the effects of oppression, others have committed themselves to action and self-realization. Many lesbians and gays recognized the community's potential political clout in the 1960s as they became aware of their size as a minority group and their significance as a voting bloc. This led to the enormous growth of gay political and advocacy organizations on local and national levels since the 1970s and 1980s, continuing to the present time. Currently, lesbian, gay, and bisexual civil rights issues, including partnership and/or marriage rights, foster-parenting protections, custody rights, and access to all available health care and treatment options, especially in relation to the AIDS epidemic, are being addressed at both the state and local levels. For example, gay activists have helped to bring about a general reassessment of federal ethical guidelines in experimental medical treatment and research in order to bring potentially life-saving treatments to patients sooner than in the past. However, there are still no federal protections for gay rights in housing, employment, or in any other area. As efforts to address numerous legal and policy issues continue under the banner of human rights, the visibility and influence of the lesbian, gay, and bisexual minority will continue to grow.

Environmental-Structural Factors

Heterosexism, homophobia, and "homohatred" or homonegativity are probably the most relevant environmental or structural issues affecting lesbian, gay, and bisexual persons, and this chapter has already described some of the ways in which homophobia has been institutionalized as a barrier in this society. Compounded with sexism and racism, they have generated additional barriers to the healthy development and well-being of lesbian, gay, and bisexual persons.

Heterosexism is defined as the belief that heterosexuality is or should be the only acceptable sexual orientation. Blumenfeld suggests that heterosexism, which is encouraged by fear and hatred, results in prejudice, discrimination, harassment, and acts of violence and hatred.[12] These are the wide-range impacts of giving cultural precedence to heterosexuality.

The impact of environmental-structural factors gives a specific social form to this population. Paul and Weinrich identified three such factors: social invisibility, social diversity, and social and personal differentiation.[13] The great majority of gay, lesbian, and bisexual people are not easily identifiable. There are as many kinds of gays as there are kinds of straights.[14] Finally, the ways in which people adapt to having a gay or lesbian orientation vary according to the relative tolerance or hostility of the immediate social environment.

Social invisibility makes it possible for the general public to be ignorant of diversity as it really exists. One result has been widely held inaccurate stereotypes. An example would be the assumed connection between male heterosexuality and involvement in sports. Garner and Smith reported significantly higher rates of homosexual activity in several samples of athletes than had been previously found.[14] The current passion among some gay men for bodybuilding and athletic club membership also serves to challenge this stereotype.

Gays and lesbians have always been the victims of homicides, gay bashing, and extortion because of religious sanctions and legal discrimination. The social acceptance of homophobia, homohatred, racism, and sexism in our society serves only to exacerbate prejudice. And the incidences of hate, violence, and harassment have increased significantly as a result of the HIV/AIDS epidemic.[15] This oppression has had a significant impact on the health and mental health status of lesbians and gay men. The National Education Association (2005) reported that a third of LGBT students drop out of high school because of harassment, and four of five of them face daily verbal and physical harassment at school.[16]

Because of these various forms of homonegativity, myths and stereotypes about LGBT people are widespread. Tully (2001) identifies twenty-five commonly held beliefs of this kind, noting how research shows them to be untrue.[17] These include that long-term relationships are uncommon among lesbians and gay men; that most gays and lesbians abuse alcohol and other drugs; that children raised in gay or lesbian families are more likely to be gay or lesbian than those raised in non-gay homes; that it is possible to identify gay or lesbian people by commonly held physical characteristics; that lesbians and gay men are more promiscuous than non-gays; that most pedophiles and child molesters are gay men; and that homosexuality is a mental illness. Institutionalized discrimination unfortunately helps such misconceptions to survive.

Culture

Popular images often suggest that gay and lesbian people are involved with a specific subculture or lifestyle. As a result, gays and lesbians may be thought to be readily identifiable by styles of dress or behavior, or to be invested only in activities or institutions designated as exclusively gay and/or lesbian. However, as a stigmatized group, lesbians and gays are in fact an invisible minority, only some of whom choose to make themselves and their interests visible individually and collectively in the gay and/or lesbian community and queer subculture.

Access to such gay- or lesbian-identified institutions and organizations is often very important for individuals who have affirmed, are exploring, or are consolidating a gay or lesbian identity. People who live in rural or small communities far removed from these centers of activity may sometimes be disadvantaged in making connections with others like themselves, in developing ways to receive affirmation for significant parts of their lives, or in finding help or support in coping with homophobia.

Contact with the gay community, however, will quickly dispel any notion that gay and lesbian people are similar to each other in appearance or lifestyle beyond the sexual orientation that they share. Diversity within the identifiable lesbian, gay, and bisexual community is as great as among heterosexuals as a group. As in any other social group, these differences can be a source of tension, which may disappoint those looking to "the community" for an ideal way of life to emulate; or for a conflict-free environment as they work on developing their own identities or seek refuge from the discrimination from the community at large. The relationship between the individual and the community can thus be either a mutually enhancing or a conflicted one. Many lesbians and gays, however, draw essential support and affirmation from the culture.

In addition, many gay and lesbian people do not participate in the identifiable gay and lesbian subculture even when it is available to them. Their political, social, and recreational pursuits may not be related to their sexual orientation at all, and their social and emotional supports may come exclusively from friends and/or family. Sometimes this choice may stem from a wish to remain private or "closeted" (or selectively "out") in their sexual orientation out of fear; at other times it may result from a choice to give other dimensions of their lives and identity priority. Thus, the degree of an individual's involvement with the gay or lesbian community is itself a dimension of diversity among lesbians and gays.

The concept of *biculturality* has recently been used to describe the socialization processes that lesbians and gays undergo.[18] Acceptance of a gay or lesbian identity means adopting new norms and values and being rejected by and/or rejecting old standards. Dating and coupling, definitions of family, celebrations and ritual participation, both secular and religious, and political and social interests are all affected by sexual orientation. For lesbians and gay men of ethnic- and racial-minority background, the cultural issues are even more complex.

This concept of a homosexual culture is viewed as controversial by some, because intergenerational transmission of this culture and socialization into it does not ordinarily take place in the family of origin, as it does in cultures as defined in other contexts. In fact, gay and lesbian individuals are usually first socialized into majority, heterosexual culture. However, applying the concept of culture to gay and lesbian ways of life highlights the inclusiveness of a lesbian or gay identity, the shared experiences of gay and lesbian people over time and across societies, and the diversity of gays and lesbians on other dimensions such as race, class, and gender. The related notion of biculturality points out that gays and lesbians live to differing degrees in multiple worlds, with the attendant opportunities and stresses of negotiation and boundary maintenance.[19]

Family Factors

Lesbians and gay men have been categorized by society as people without families, uninterested in creating families, and threatening to family life. Despite this perception, the fact is that at least 2 million lesbians and gay men are parents of minor children.[20] Census data from 2000 found that one in five same-sex male couples identified and one in three lesbian couples enumerated had one or more children under 18 living with them, although it is assumed that this is likely an undercount. Large numbers of the gay, lesbian, and bisexual population live in long-term, committed, coupled relationships.[21]

Achtenberg notes that discriminatory treatment, misunderstanding, and prejudices often pose social and legal barriers to the recognition and protection of families created by lesbians and gay men.[22]

Many gays and lesbians credit their family of origin as the source of their emotional support and strength as well as their positive belief and value system. Yet for other gays and lesbians, the family is a source of interpersonal tension and conflict, hardly the basis for self-acceptance or a healthy adjustment to a hostile society. Many gays credit their "chosen family"—family of design consisting of lovers and friends—as the buffer that has had the greatest impact on their adaptation.

The gay, lesbian, or bisexual person, his or her parents, and the spouse and their children are all confronted daily with stereotyping and social rejection. The images of homosexuality are all negative: the "sinner," the "drag queen," the "child molester," the "bull dyke." By the time one reaches adulthood, the association (not necessarily conscious) between homosexuality and the stereotype is formed. These dehumanizing stereotypes are perpetuated by the peer group, the mass media, and cultural tradition. The individual may feel pressure to establish distance from homosexuality. Few people, then, are socially prepared to deal with this issue when it arises.

"Passing" is a second consequence of stigma. Anyone who does not fit the stereotype can "pass," while those who meet the stereotyped expectations become visible. An individual may come to recognize his or her special sexual orientation without realistic models of what this means. The reaction may be, "I'm the only person in the world like this," or "I'm not like them, thank God." Parents, other family members, and friends are also likely to avoid or deny disclosure when their loved one does not fit the stereotype. Gay, lesbian, and bisexual youths are reared in heterosexual families, peer groups, and educational institutions. Thus, these youths grow up learning the same stereotypes and negative judgments as their straight peers, threatening the sense of self. Because "passing" is so pervasive, they are deprived of positive role models to prepare them for dealing with their sexual orientation. Sustaining self-esteem and a sense of identity becomes problematic at best.

Rejection is the third consequence of stigma, which produces distancing between those with the stigma and those without. Disclosure can become a critical issue within the family. The gay or lesbian child may lose the sense of authenticity characteristic of family relationships if he or she keeps the secret, or face rejection if he or she seeks understanding and emotional support by disclosing his or her sexual orientation. This potential alienation from the family is one way in which the homosexual minority is different from other minority groups, who generally can count on support within the family in the face of stress from the outside world. This same dynamic will be true with friends and work colleagues. Bell, Weinberg, and Hammersmith note that secrecy brings about a different sort of distancing, offering the example of a gay person who appears outwardly popular and well liked by the group yet feels alienated and isolated.[23]

The development of a subculture, a separate space that allows a sense of community and naturalness, is the fourth consequence of stigma. The subculture may be an opportunity to develop a special kinship with fellow victims of stigma. The stronger the disapproval by the majority culture, the more attractive a subculture is as a source of mutual support.

The final consequence is that of the self-fulfilling prophecy or "secondary deviance." This means that features of the stereotype may be embraced in protest or defiance or for lack of support for more normative styles of life. "Drag," "camp," and "leather" are stereotypic styles reflecting theatrical and humorous responses to society's arbitrary distinctions between masculine and feminine cultures. This poking of fun at gender roles by flouting them is often seen by non-gays as confirmation of their worst stereotypic fears.

Forming Families: Myths and Realities

Numerous studies have been made of children being reared by lesbians to determine what effects on development there may be. Because alternative insemination and access to adoption by gays are relatively new phenomena, the studies to date have generally compared children of divorced lesbian mothers to those of divorced women who are not lesbians. Taken together, the studies have consistently shown that gay men and lesbians who parent do not differ in child-rearing practices or lifestyle from other parents and that the children of lesbian mothers and gay men have no more problems in adjustment or development than do others.[24] There is no evidence of gender-role confusion or higher rates of gay or lesbian orientation among them, as had initially been hypothesized. In fact, there is some evidence that children of lesbians have a greater appreciation for diversity of all kinds and value tolerance more highly than others, having seen first-hand the toll that prejudice like homophobia can take.

The concern that a child who grows up with a homosexual parent will develop a gay orientation appears to be a widely held myth. The assumption that children develop their sexual orientation by emulating their parents is false. Remember that the vast majority of lesbians, gays, and bisexuals were raised by heterosexual parents.[25]

Another myth is that children who grow up with a gay or lesbian parent are at risk of molestation or abuse by either the parent or the parent's friends. However, research on the sexual abuse of children shows that the offenders are, in disproportionate numbers, heterosexual men.[26] It is also a common assumption that children in the custody of a lesbian or gay parent will be harmed by social stigma, but there are no clinical reports or research of stigma or unusual emotional problems in these children.[27] The practitioner must also realize that the coping and adaptational qualities of gay people in families are also tempered by economics, ethnicity, race, and class identity.

Individual Factors

The study of why people become gay or lesbian usually starts with an exhaustive review of biological theories focusing on genetic and hormonal factors and on psychoanalytic and behavioral theories addressing pathology and dysfunction. The conclusions of these studies are seldom supported by the data presented. Thus, the attempt to identify etiological factors has a long history, but with close inspection one must conclude that no specific genetic, intrapsychic, or interpersonal causative factors can be generalized to the lesbian, gay, and bisexual population.[28] However, there is knowledge about individual development that has value for practice intervention. One way to improve our understanding or our definitions of sexual orientation is to correct the myths and inaccuracies surrounding homosexuality. One myth, which represents the popular version of an outmoded psychoanalytic explanation of homosexuality, is that male homosexuality represents a fear or hatred of women. (The reverse is also sometimes said of lesbian women.) This myth has led to ineffective treatment based on the assumption that gay men can be converted to heterosexuality simply by having sexual experiences with women. This simplistic view is contradicted by the large proportion of gay men who have had or continue to have sexual experiences with women but retain a positive gay identity.

Another myth is that gay people are compulsively sexual. The Kinsey Institute's estimates of gay sexual activity are probably overstated. Like straights, most gays spend most of their time doing things other than looking for sex or having it. Since 1981, the HIV/AIDS epidemic has struck a large number of gay and bisexual men. The widespread awareness in the gay community that the virus believed to cause AIDS is transmitted through unprotected sex (i.e., without condoms) has led to significant changes in sexual practices and thus, for some years, a reduction in sexually transmitted disease and the rate of HIV infection among gay men.

Finally, while lesbians and gay men may often be accused of flaunting their sexuality, in fact, most conceal their sexual orientation at least part of the time. Stigma and the consequences of discrimination in many areas of daily living are convincing reasons for concealment.[29] Berger suggests that because lesbians and gay men are generally indistinguishable from other men and women, public attitudes are formed on the basis of those who are most open about their sexual orientation.[30] "Straight" heterosexuals apply a double standard to same-sex and opposite-sex behavior, in that public displays of affection between a man and a woman are taken for granted while even holding hands in public is considered "flaunting" when it occurs between two women or two men.

Identity Formation.   Sexual orientation may change over time. A woman who is primarily homosexual in early adulthood may become more heterosexual in later life or vice versa. In his study of older gay men, Berger found that it is not uncommon for a man with an essentially heterosexual orientation in early adulthood to develop predominantly homosexual interests in middle age.[31] These observations lead us to the view that homosexuality is an identity formation process occurring over time. This formulation has much promise for social work assessment and intervention.

Berger proposed a model wherein homosexual identity results when a person completes three tasks that are independent of one another. The first in this process is the sexual encounter; that is, physical contact of a sexual nature with someone of the same sex. Second is the social reaction; that is, the process of labeling the individual by others as homosexual. The last component in this model is the identity task; that is, the individual experiences identity confusion (the discomfort felt between a same-sex experience and a heterosexual self-image) and works to come to terms with this in some way.[32]

Viewing lesbian, gay, or bisexual orientation as the result of an identity-formation process has important implications for social work intervention. First of all, and most important, there is no empirical justification for the belief that homosexuality, in and of itself, is a psychiatric illness or a result of poor psychological adjustment. Practitioners who continue to advocate illness models based on "conversion therapies" are ignorant, irresponsible, or both.[33]

Social Stress and Social Supports.   Like Berger, other theorists have adopted an interactionist perspective to examine the intricate linkage between social life and personal experience. Human beings cannot escape the influence of social position and social expectation on their development and self-perception. Bradford and Ryan note that "those who are discriminated against or who expect to face discrimination if their 'condition' were to become known are different from those who do not occupy stigmatized or 'deviant' social positions. The connection between living on the margins of society and the impact of this upon daily life and an adequate sense of psychosocial security" is yet to be fully documented. However, we do know that lesbians and gay men always live with this tension.[34]

This stress and lack of support—rather than stresses related to sexual orientation—may result in higher rates of alcoholism among lesbians, gays, and bisexuals. Gay bars are among the few public places where gay men and lesbians can meet to socialize. Drinking can also provide emotional insulation from homophobic or racist attitudes.[35] It is estimated that one-third of lesbians are alcoholics. Gay men and MSMs also have higher rates of alcohol and drug use than straight men do. Legal, health, and social service agencies, often insensitive to lesbian, gay, and bisexual persons, have tended to focus on sexual orientation as the cause of this phenomenon, despite evidence that they do not differ in psychosocial functioning from heterosexuals. Lesbians of color, like their male counterparts, have a higher incidence of alcoholism than straights.[36]

Brooks emphasizes the importance of social support networks for lesbians and gay men. These are relationships with significant others, developed as a result of sharing a history of common experience through which people create environments of caring and support for each other.[37] While recognizing that the importance of supportive interactions among people is not new, Bradford notes that research evidence of social supports helping people in health crises is recent. Maintenance of good health is related to the number of people in a social network.[38] Alcalay adds that the number of contacts, the frequency and intensity of contacts, as well as the presence of family and friends within the network, are all related to health.[39] In other words, friends can be "good medicine."

Bradford and Ryan have synthesized the research related to social support and crisis in relation to lesbian health. They conclude that supports encourage preventive behavior, provide needed resources, increase a sense of personal control over one's environment, and reduce the social marginality of one's minority status. Supports are buffers against the distress of traumatic life events. Lesbians, gay men, and bisexuals without sufficient supports are especially vulnerable to commonplace stressors as well as the monumental stress related to minority status.[40] It is within the context of stress, social marginality, and minority status that the impact of a hostile, discriminatory environment should be understood. This approach to understanding developmental issues focuses our attention on life adaptations and thus is consistent with the ecosystems perspective.

Macro Practice with Lesbian, Gay, and Bisexual People

Germain and Gitterman, in their advancement of the ecological model, treated stress as a psychosocial condition "generated by discrepancies between needs and capacities, on the one hand, and environmental qualities on the other. It arises in three interrelated areas of living: life transitions, environmental pressures, and interpersonal processes."[41] The social work interventions related to support, empowerment, psychoeducation, consultation, case advocacy, and self-help seem appropriate for most clients while case management, individual, group, couple, and family therapy might be the preference of some gay, lesbian, and bisexual clients.

Oppression, power, heterosexism, and homophobia form the macro environmental context in which lesbians and gay men develop and function. These social dynamics are experienced as nonnurturing social behaviors and as barriers to optimal social functioning, such as discrimination, prejudice, bias, and violence, and therefore are appropriate environmental or macro social change targets of social work intervention.

Social workers should act to expand access, choices, and opportunities for all oppressed people. Community development, organizational change, staff training, coalition building, program and policy development, class advocacy, and social action are appropriate for change that will benefit lesbian, gay, and bisexual people as well.

Social workers should help gay and lesbian activists to organize their communities with the intent of developing educational and political strategies and of forming coalitions of advocacy groups, such as the Human Rights Campaign, and *class action social work* alliances with groups such as the American Civil Liberties Union, Lambda Legal Defense, and the National Gay and Lesbian Task Force. Goals are to advance civil rights legislation, to defeat efforts to limit civil rights, to advocate for programs to eliminate hate crimes and antigay violence, and to enhance education, treatment services, and research related to lesbians, gay men, and bisexuals. The intent is that homosexuals are entitled to the same Fourteenth Amendment equal rights, liberties, and privileges as are other citizens, such as in housing, employment, public accommodation, inheritance and insurance, domestic partnership or marriage, child custody, adoption, foster care, and property rights.

The constitutional rights of privacy free from government regulation or intrusion and equal treatment before the law should be afforded to all lesbians, gay men, and bisexuals. This is basic to U.S. citizenship. Criminalization of homosexual acts is a violation of the right of individual privacy, which has recently drawn action from the U.S. Supreme Court. Criminal statutes proscribing adult homosexual behavior create an environment of oppression arising from fear of prosecution and provide the means of blackmail. These statutes are most reprehensible when linked to enforcement by entrapment. Such laws perpetuate discrimination against homosexuals. Discrimination on the basis of homosexuality violates an individual's right of privacy and denies the person equal protection of the law.[42]

Achtenberg reminds us that to favor lesbian, gay, and bisexual rights or to support an end to discrimination must mean to deplore the ways in which society undermines the formation, preservation, and protection of the lesbian, gay, and bisexual family.[43] Gay rights must also include support for custody and visitation statutes that ensure strict neutrality with regard to the sexual orientation of the parent. Advocacy for adoption and foster parenting laws and administrative practices that are strictly neutral are needed. Joint adoptions by same-sex couples should be permitted when it is in a child's best interests and when the parent-child relationship has been cemented. Laws permitting delegation of personal and health care duties to non-relatives should be created, as well as provision for fair determination of the guardian or conservator for an ill person. The same sentiment should inform the laws of intestate succession. Equity, not sexual orientation or marital status, should become the value undergirding the distribution of work-related and governmental benefits.

The National Gay and Lesbian Task Force (NGLTF) and the Human Rights Campaign (HRC), two leading GLBT civil rights organizations, have refocused their attention to civil marriage, domestic partnerships, and civil unions. Grassroots energy has been redirected to the state level to organize against the federal bill, the Defense of Marriage Act (DOMA), which defines this institution as the exclusive domain of heterosexuals, and to build constituencies in support of gay marriage. The focus of this highly emotional debate is on economic issues, illustrating how same-sex couples are discriminated against by not having access to over one thousand benefits, protections, and responsibilities granted only through civil marriage. The NGLTF's analysis, using Connecticut as an example, points out that same-sex couples are denied equal treatment under Social Security policy, federal tax laws, immigration, inheritance, and health care protocols that allow married couples to protect their families, as under the Family and Medical Leave Act. Analysis clarifies that by allowing same-sex couples to marry, no one is harmed, and couples and their children will access benefits and programs designed by the government to promote family stability and financial security.[44]

A nonjudgmental attitude toward sexual orientation allows social workers to offer optimal support and services, thus empowering lesbian, gay, and bisexual people through all phases of the coming out process and beyond. The outcome of interpersonal intervention, however, is also contingent on the agency's policies and procedures. Social workers must first focus on the level of staff knowledge and commitment before introducing gay-affirming programs. Agency policies and procedures should address the needs of lesbian, gay, and bisexual clients and staff.

Legislation embodying the above principles should be the goal of the social work profession. Passage of such legislation on state or national levels requires building coalitions of like-minded civil rights advocacy groups and extensive public education. Social workers are skilled in problem identification and resolution through organization building and strategy development. These are the needed macro skills if environments are to be supportive of positive gay identity development and no longer barriers to healthful functioning and psychosocial adaptation.

Micro Practice with Lesbian, Gay, and Bisexual People

Failure to consider that a client may be lesbian, gay, or bisexual is the most common mistake made by social workers. Despite stereotypes, most lesbian, gay, and bisexual clients are not visually identifiable as such, and many may not identify themselves as lesbian, gay, or bisexual at first, especially when the problem for which they are seeking assistance may not have much to do with sexual orientation.[45] However, the social worker is unlikely to get a full enough picture of the client's situation to be helpful without keeping an open mind to the possibility of gender identity issues.

Effective work with lesbians and gay men requires what Hall has termed a dual focus: "The practitioner must be able to see the ways in which the client's presenting problem is both affected by and separate from her sexual orientation."[46] Damage to self-esteem resulting from oppression and stigmatization must always be considered, but at the same time the client probably occupies roles, works on developmental tasks, and experiences feelings in which being lesbian, gay, or bisexual is incidental. For example, the teenage prostitutes our intern met through her work at the AIDS service organization must deal with the rejection they experienced from families because they were gay or lesbian. At the same time, these teens have the same developmental needs for the support and approval of adults and peers that others do and would be seeking a way to separate and differentiate themselves from their families even if rejection based on their sexual orientation had not occurred. Thus, a worker counseling any of them might expect to hear both a longing for the love and approval of their parents, despite their rejecting behavior, and a simultaneous longing to be completely free of parental restraint or control.

Whether or not the client seeks help with an issue involving sexual orientation or during the "coming out" process, the worker's feelings, attitudes, and comfort with a lesbian, gay, or bisexual identity or orientation must be examined; they require self-exploration over time.[47] It is the homophobia gay and lesbian individuals may encounter that is likely to be a problem, not the homosexuality itself. Rather than seeking causes or explanations for homosexuality, this perspective leads the social worker to explore and help the client to overcome the obstacles, internalized or external, that may stand in the way of healthy functioning as a lesbian, gay, or bisexual person.

Psychological and psychoanalytic theory have given more attention to male than to female homosexuality over the years.[48] From a contemporary psychoanalytic standpoint, there are many varieties of both heterosexual and homosexual functioning, and homosexual or heterosexual object choices are not viewed in themselves as healthy or unhealthy. Nevertheless, studies suggest that negative attitudes toward homosexuality and homosexual clients persist among some social workers and social work students.[49] Such attitudes create barriers that keep lesbian, gay, and bisexual persons from seeking or receiving effective mental health services in times of need.

When homosexuality was viewed as pathological, it was assumed that some critical experiences early in life produced an outcome, same-gender object choice, which was thought to be immutable without psychological treatment. Not only has it proven very difficult to identify any experiential or developmental "causes" or antecedents of homosexuality with any confidence,[50] but the treatment of homosexuals in psychological distress was usually distorted to mean treatment of the homosexuality itself.[51]

On the one hand, adult developmental theory now tells us that personality and life course are not "cast in stone" in childhood. Additionally, close study of the sexual practices of both heterosexual and homosexual people and attention to the life histories of lesbian, gay, and bisexual people suggest that sexual practices and self-identification may change over time. On the other hand, to self-identified lesbian, gay, or bisexual individuals the homosexual identity may feel immutable, essential, and core to their sense of themselves as persons. Psychological treatment is thus focused on addressing whatever distress a self-identified lesbian, gay, or bisexual person may be experiencing, rather than on the sexual orientation itself.[52]

Contemporary theory emerging from research and clinical work with lesbians, gays, and bisexuals, then, suggests that the developmental pathways to their sexual identity are numerous. This identity is no longer assumed to be pathological. The task of the worker is to understand and accept these varieties of sexual identity and experience that exist and to assist the lesbian, gay, or bisexual client to deal with any problems that may accompany or simply coexist with his or her particular sexual orientation.

Common Problems

As with other minority groups, oppression that may be visited on gay and lesbian people because of their sexual orientation can be destructive to individual self-esteem and well-being. At early stages of the coming-out process, many people actively resist acknowledging, even to themselves, that they are sexually attracted to or active with others of their own gender. This resistance is often the product of negative attitudes toward homosexuality they themselves have absorbed, as everyone does, from the society as a whole; or of negative reactions they fear from significant others such as parents, children, friends, associates, or authority figures such as teachers, coaches, or religious leaders. It is essential that the social work services lesbians, gays, and bisexuals receive be free of the homophobia and heterosexism that would add to or reinforce these fears and attitudes.

CASE EXAMPLE

Lynn, who was seventeen and a high school senior, was referred to a social worker for treatment following a brief psychiatric hospitalization. She had been admitted to the hospital after friends of hers, becoming alarmed, reported to her parents that she had ingested a number of pills and was "acting funny." This episode was viewed as a suicidal gesture by both the young woman and her parents. It followed a period of several months during which arguments between the girl and her parents had been growing in frequency and intensity. The arguments were over such issues as Lynn's style of dress, her social activities, her "lack of respect" for her parents, and the fact that she had stopped attending church with the family. Lynn was the youngest of three children and the only one still living at home. Her father owned his own small business and worked long hours; her mother worked as a nurse. Both parents were fundamentalist Christians, and their recreational activities, which were few, were centered on the church. The family lived in a suburban community on the outskirts of a large metropolitan area in the Northeast.

From the beginning of counseling, Lynn announced firmly that she was a lesbian, and she always appeared for her appointments dressed in tight blue jeans, studded leather jacket, and black boots. Her manner appeared angry and "tough," and the image she cultivated was that of the stereotype of the "dyke." Lynn had also told her parents she was a lesbian. Her father was extremely rejecting of homosexuality, which he regarded as sinful; her mother was slightly more sympathetic. Because she had also spoken openly about her sexual orientation in the hospital, Lynn had been referred to a worker who was also a lesbian, although Lynn was not aware of that fact.

Starting with what Lynn had said was important about herself, the worker began exploring Lynn's sexual orientation and what it meant to her. Lynn had begun heterosexual dating at fifteen and had enjoyed a relationship with a boy she liked very much. However, as time went on she realized she experienced her relationship with him as a "good friend" and not as a "boyfriend" like her friends did. About this time, she also became aware of her attraction to other young women. She had her first sexual experience with a woman at sixteen, which she described as her coming out. After this point, for her "there was no going back."

The worker began exploring what being gay meant to Lynn. It turned out that Lynn knew only two other lesbians, both "tough kids" from her hometown. The worker then asked Lynn if she would be interested in making contact with an organization for lesbian and gay youth in the city. Lynn began to meet a much more varied and congenial group of peers with whom she could begin to talk about the pain of isolation and disapproval she was experiencing at school and at home. She also used the group to talk about her plans for college and her worries about what it would be like to be identified as a lesbian on campus.

As Lynn gained social support from the group and a sense of personal support and acceptance from her social worker in their meetings, her appearance and style of dress began to change somewhat. She also began tentatively to share with her worker some painful feelings she had about being gay, especially her parents' reactions to her and the religious beliefs she still heard from them that regarded her orientation as a sin. Lynn's presentation changed from angry and tough to depressed and vulnerable as she struggled to understand the painful feelings she was dealing with. During this stage, the worker was glad she had not shared information about her own sexual orientation with Lynn, who had never asked about it, thinking that doing so might have made it harder for Lynn to feel comfortable talking about the negative side of her feelings about her own homosexuality.

The more Lynn talked about her experiences in the family, however, the more it became clear that Lynn's parents had been distant from her in other ways for quite some time. It also became clear that her low self-esteem went back to early childhood. Lynn's father was quite rigid in his beliefs and standards and was rarely home because of his work; her mother was alcoholic and thus not reliably available to Lynn. Lynn increasingly expressed interest in understanding things in her family that had been going on long before her sexual orientation became an issue. In order to deal with these issues and to help prepare Lynn to leave home, Lynn and her parents were referred for family therapy as well.

Lynn continued in counseling until the time came for her to leave for college. Although she continued to suffer some periods of depression, no further suicidal gestures were made, and the conflict at home was somewhat reduced. When she left, Lynn was able to imagine herself meeting others at college who might share both her sexual orientation and some of her other interests as well.

This case illustrates the importance of attending to a range of issues in working with a lesbian, gay, or bisexual client. Clearly, comfort with the client's lesbian identity and understanding the homophobic reactions of others was essential to working with this case. This comfort must encompass both the positive and negative feelings a client will most likely experience in coming out. Second, the typical developmental issues and concerns of the age or stage of development must be considered as well. Here, the anxiety of an impending separation as Lynn "grew up" and went off to school was upsetting to parent and child alike. Third, it was important to be aware of the problems and vulnerabilities of both the individual and the family as they met the challenges of coming out and their life-stage transitions. Finally, the role of social supports and ways to reduce isolation for lesbians and gays—lesbian and gay youth in particular—cannot be overestimated. Lynn's contact with peers provided validation for her sexual orientation and role models for the many ways in which people incorporate and express a gay or lesbian identity.

Working with Couples

Dating and coupling behavior is often what exposes gays and lesbians to their greatest risk from homophobia. It is not simply walking down the street alone but wanting to walk down the street holding a partner's hand that most often produces panic in the individual or fear of abuse from others. Going to a bar or expressing affection to a lover in public may, in fact, even precipitate a gay-bashing attack. With the incidence of such violence on the rise, gay and lesbian relationships are sometimes actually, as well as metaphorically, under assault.

The lack of formal and informal social sanction for the relationship is a source of strain for all gay and lesbian couples. Even if the relationship is one between partners whose lesbian or gay identity has long been established, the lack of valida-tion of the relationship itself can produce a range of reactions, including sorrow and anger, that would otherwise be marked by joy. Holidays, for example, may find the partners separated as they fulfill commitments to families that may not welcome them together. Rituals of courtship and commitment may be lacking entirely or may be limited to the context of the gay community. Family and friends who are prepared to be generally supportive of the individual may react negatively to any steps taken by the couple to make the relationship public or legally sanctioned. Socializing in work or other contexts in which a husband or wife may be automati-cally included will leave gay and lesbian couples to decide whether to ask for the recognition and inclusion of a partner, or to give up validation of the relationship and the opportunity to be together in order to feel more private or more safe.

In the face of these strains, gay and lesbian couples have invented customs and rituals to sustain themselves and have adapted available supports to their own needs. Small groups of couples or friends may celebrate holidays together as faith-fully as many families do. Some churches celebrate the vows of gay and lesbian couples, and some couples have chosen to invent their own spiritual or secular cele-brations of commitment. Anniversaries are often carefully observed, although the date chosen is usually that of some significant event signifying involvement other than marriage.

Without the mechanisms of legal marriage (except in Massachusetts, in Canada, and in a few European countries), couples may register as domestic partners where permitted; may enter into joint financial ventures and arrangements, including home ownership; may write wills to benefit one another; and may seek devices such as a durable power of attorney or a living will to give to one another the right to make medical decisions and other legal arrangements on each other's behalf, as married couples can. In the absence of such an instrument as a will, next of kin, who may be estranged, can dispossess a lover of long standing in the event of a death, which can be a significant worry to one or both partners. Laws governing such arrangements and the limits on their use differ from state to state, and people may need assistance in finding information about resources for developing these supports in their own area.

Because these are same-sex couples, sex roles usually do not define the patterns within gay and lesbian couples to the extent they may among mixed-sex couples. In the absence of more common norms, patterns of work-sharing and relating may be more egalitarian, or they may follow some reciprocal pattern invented by the partic-ipants. As in all couples, rigid and inflexible roles may come to feel burdensome or stifling to one partner or the other, or both may be unaware of the habits that have developed. As with heterosexual couples, what couples do and what they say they do about roles and work-sharing may not be the same.[53] The role of the social worker, then, is to explore the wishes and feelings of both members of the couple and to help them design whatever arrangement for living seems most comfortable.

While sexuality does not define the lives or adjustment of gay and lesbian peo-ple any more than it does for heterosexuals, problems in sexual functioning can affect gay and lesbian relationships. Some of these may relate to social pressures, as partners who must suppress the expression of love and attachment outside the home may have difficulty in expressing tenderness and sexuality spontaneously and comfortably at home as well. Patterns of sexual behavior are often quite different in gay and lesbian couples. On average, lesbian couples often experience low levels of sexual activity after the first few years, and most are monogamous. Although ideologies about monogamy differ among lesbians, an affair often seems to precede the break up of a relationship. Gay couples, on average, enjoy higher levels of sexual activity for longer and have often been stably nonmonogamous. For gay couples, sexual behavior within and outside the couple relationship has been changing because of the AIDS epidemic, and the new patterns emerging may call for new adjustments. What is important, of course, is to assist each gay or lesbian couple in achieving open communication, mutually satisfying sexual expression, and acceptable negotiation of any differences that may exist between the partners in the context of their emotional relationship. It is common, however, for the breakup of a couple relationship to precipitate a crisis, when a gay or lesbian person may seek professional help, and the experience of loss of a significant relationship is a piece of personal history for many, if not most, lesbians, gays, and bisexuals.

Working with Lesbian, Gay, and Bisexual Parents

There are some special issues lesbian, gay, and bisexual parents and their children must deal with that the practitioner must be prepared to respond to. Divorced parents and their children often worry that the other biological parent (or even a grandparent) may seek custody, claiming that the custodial parent is unfit simply because of sexual orientation. These fears can have profound effects on how the family represents and conducts itself, both outside and inside the home.

Each lesbian, gay, or bisexual parent must decide how to talk with the children about his or her identity. Children too young to understand much about sex understand clearly about love; a gay or lesbian identity may best be explained in terms of loving other men or women and by differentiating love between adults from the love of an adult for a child. Sex need not be the center of the discussion, any more than it would be if a heterosexual parent were talking about his or her relationship with another parent or lover. In addition, because children identify so strongly with parents, they do need to hear that they will not necessarily grow up to be gay or lesbian just because a parent is gay or lesbian. Most of all, the parent must try to help the child ask any questions or express any fears he or she may have. The meaning of the parent's lesbian, gay, or bisexual identity is not a topic that can be dealt with once and set aside; rather it must be revisited and reinterpreted as children grow older and their questions change.

In gay and lesbian families with children, the definition of the role of the parent who did not bear or legally adopt the child is usually an issue for the partners. What to call the "other mommy" or the "other daddy" may be a unique challenge, and the lack of language reflects the normlessness that gay and lesbian families face. In other ways, however, the issues of how childcare, housework, and employment responsibilities will be managed and shared may differ little from what heterosexual couples who become parents go through. The issues for blended families in which each partner brings offspring into the relationship may be similar as well. Asking the family about the role of each parent and how each is named and defined will validate both partners and reveal much about how the family has organized and represented itself at home and in the wider world of the extended family, the school, the workplace, and the community at large.[54]

An emerging concern within the child welfare system is the number of LGBT youth in out-of-home care and the problems they are having within it. Some kids are "pushed out" into street life or into the child protection system by parental rejection when they begin to explore or express a non-heterosexual identity. However, LGBT adolescents are often harassed or rejected in congregate care settings, which in some progressive child welfare systems has led to the creation of gay-specialized facilities. However, placement with foster parents who will accept and embrace an emerging gay identity is usually the best option, both to avoid the problems often encountered in group care and to offer positive role models.

Working with Older Lesbians, Gays, and Bisexuals

Lesbians and gays are an invisible minority in general, and older bisexual, gay, and lesbian people may feel invisible both in the gay and lesbian community and among older people. Ageism keeps them marginal to the gay community; homophobia keeps them marginal to elder service agencies and programs. Research has shown that stereotypes of the older lesbian or gay man as isolated, depressed, and unfulfilled are untrue; health, access to needed material resources, and social contacts that reduce loneliness all contribute to life satisfaction among older gays and lesbians, just as they do among the non-gay elderly.[55]

Today's older lesbians, gays, and bisexuals came of age in the pre-Stonewall era, and most had to come to terms with their sexual identity at a time when homophobia was even more widespread and overt than it is today. Professional mental health services were then more likely to be a source of stress than of support to lesbians and gays. Some elders may only have discovered or affirmed their gay or lesbian identity later in life, but they may still carry with them residues of the attitudes that were pervasive in their younger years.

Despite these obstacles, older lesbians and gays of today have much to offer the community. Their life stories are often tales of survival and affirmation that can instruct and inspire their younger counterparts.[56] Life review is often useful to the elderly, whose task is to consolidate a sense of the meaning of their individual lives and to understand them in the context of the historical events that have framed them. Because of the oppression they have confronted and survived, gay and lesbian elders may wish to share their stories with younger gays and lesbians as well as with family and non-gay friends.

The common challenges of aging—retirement, ill health, the death of a lover or close friends—affect older gays and lesbians as well. Although many have strong social support systems, the majority will not have children to turn to when meeting these crises. Those who are sick, who care for a sick or disabled partner, or who are bereaved may find that access to the support services available to other older people in similar circumstances is not so easy for them. How can gay or lesbian partners provide for each other in retirement, illness, or after death? Will the hospital, nursing home, physician, or nurse give the gay or lesbian partner the same consideration and access to the patient a husband or wife would get? Will the widows' or widowers' group or the caregivers' support group accept a gay or lesbian member? Will the gay or lesbian elder feel comfortable in reaching out for the support that is needed?

Emerging Issues and Trends

The future of social work practice with lesbians, gays, and bisexuals will build on the advances in understanding gained in the recent past and highlighted in this chapter. There are some emerging issues and trends we know about today that will take the practice of social work in new directions in the years to come.

Health Disparities

The major United States government report on health and health care needs, Healthy People 2010, discussed many population groups whose health lags behind others but did not address health disparities for the LGBT population. However, the Gay & Lesbian Medical Association (GLMA) issued their own report on health disparities using government and other data to outline the major issues for gay, lesbian, bisexual and transgender people.[57] Only a few areas will be outlined here, and because HIV/AIDS still affects so many gay men and MSMs, a separate section is devoted below to that topic.

Mental Health

Although homosexuality itself is no longer regarded as a psychiatric disorder, its history has left traces of distrust among LGBT people and of substandard care on the part of some providers. In fact, some mental health professionals still offer conversion or reparative therapies (designed to change a gay or lesbian's sexual orientation to a straight one) despite the fact that all major mental health organizations have denounced such treatments as ineffective and even harmful.[58] However, effective treatments are now available for such problems as depressive and anxiety disorders, and gay and lesbian people are high utilizers of mental health treatment. In addition, much more needs to be known about the resilience of LGBT people in the face of stigma and discrimination.

Although data are limited, gay men are more likely than straight men to suffer from depression and anxiety disorders.[59] They may also be more likely than other men, and than lesbians, to suffer from an eating disorder. Some studies suggest that depression is also common among lesbians. For example, the National Lesbian Health Care Survey,[60] polling almost 2,000 lesbians, reported that the most common health problem experienced was depression or sadness. Other stress-related illnesses (such as weight problems) were reported by significant percentages. More than half the sample reported that they had been too nervous to cope with ordinary responsibilities sometime during the year. Twenty-one percent had suicidal thoughts, and 18 percent had actually made a suicide attempt. Three-fourths of those surveyed were in counseling. The mental health symptoms reported appear similar to those of other high-stress groups. This study has since been replicated, with similar findings, although other studies suggest that depression rates are no higher among lesbians than among straight women. Being coupled is a protective factor for lesbian women, while being married is a risk factor for heterosexual women. Both lesbians and gay men are at high risk for suicidal ideation and suicide attempts (although not completed suicides).[61]

Mental health problems may be especially common and severe for youth who are gay-, lesbian-, bi-, or trans-identified or who are questioning such an identification. Suicidal thoughts and attempts are alarmingly high among LGBT youth (much higher than among non-gay adolescents), and experiences of victimization contribute to this risk.[62] Since social workers provide the majority of mental health services in the United States, these are all areas in which culturally competent social workers can make a big difference.

Substance Use and Abuse

As noted earlier, lesbians and gay men have high levels of alcoholism and drug abuse, perhaps two to three times the rate as in the general population. However, LGBT face problems with access to gay-affirmative drug and alcohol treatment resources (SAMSHA, 2001); this problem occurs in a national context in which there is not enough treatment available overall for people with drug and/or alcohol problems. Two other areas that need attention are treatment options for those with co-occurring mental health and substance abuse problems and prevention approaches that are tailored for use with LGBT people and communities. In addition, rates of tobacco use are higher among gay and bisexual men and among lesbians than among comparable straight men and women, a problem that has not yet been well addressed despite the many well-known health risks associated with smoking. Finally, it should be noted that drug and alcohol problems among LGBT people are associated with other serious health risks, such as HIV/AIDS, other STDs, violence, and cirrhosis and other diseases of the liver.

Cancer

Gay and lesbian people are disproportionately affected by some types of cancer, such as breast cancer (lesbians), cancers associated with the HIV virus, lung cancer, and cancers associated with the human papilloma virus (GLMA, 2001). The higher rates of breast cancer among lesbians is thought to be related to higher rates of general risk factors for the disease including not bearing children, alcohol use, and obesity. Gay and bisexual men are currently at higher risk for non-Hodgkins lymphoma, Hodgkins disease, and anal cancer, the last of which may be due to human papilloma virus (HPV) exposure in anal sex. HIV co-morbidity may be involved in these higher rates of occurrence (and lower survival rates) among these men. In addition, lesbians are less likely than heterosexual women to receive regular gynecological care, which means lower rates of screening for cervical cancer via the pap test and later detection of ovarian cancer. Finally, the elevated rates of cigarette smoking among LGBT people contribute to higher rates of lung cancer.

Violence and Victimization

While there are many forms of violence that affect people's health and well-being, one is hate crime. While the most common form of hate crime is against African Americans, and while many groups can be victims (for example, other racial groups, women and Jews), "the most socially acceptable" type of hate crime is targeting LGBT people, especially among young people.[63] However, since many states do not include crimes motivated by sexual orientation or gender expression in their definition of a hate crime and hence in their reporting to the federal government, it is likely that current estimates of its occurrence are low. In surveys of gays and lesbians carried out in several localities, 1 to 5 percent of lesbians reported experiencing physical violence based on their sexual identity, while about 25 percent of gay and bisexual men reported a similar experience. When physical assaults against gays and lesbians result in homicide, the specific acts committed tend to be more violent than similar bias crimes against other groups. Among young people, rates are much higher, and many heterosexual youth also experience such harassment in the mistaken belief that they were gay. Much of the verbal and physical abuse of gay, lesbian, and queer youth actually takes place in schools. Obviously, greater efforts at prevention are needed along with better data on these incidents from both criminal justice and health facilities like hospital emergency rooms.

Impact of AIDS

Since the epidemic began, more than a million Americans have developed AIDS; three of five have died. The majority have been gay men. The psychological and social impact on gay men and the gay community has been deep and profound. We are more than 20 years into the HIV/AIDS pandemic, and the myth that lesbians are not living and dying with the disease persists. Unfortunately this perception is held by the general public, the lesbian, gay, and bisexual communities, and many health care providers and researchers, and even educators and activists believe that lesbians are at the lowest or no risk. This false belief is fueled by a narrow focus upon woman-to-woman transmission, limitations of HIV/AIDS surveillance data, the notion that "real" lesbians don't get AIDS, and the failure to recognize differences between "identity" and "behavior."[64]

AIDS is now the leading cause of death of men and women between the ages of 25 and 44 years in the United States. The number of cases is increasing most rapidly among women and among those infected through heterosexual contact. Some

40,000 to 50,000 Americans are infected with HIV yearly. Half are under the age of 25. Worldwide, 8,500 people are infected daily.[65]

After several years of decline in new HIV cases in the gay, bisexual, and transgender communities due to successful safer sex prevention campaigns, the rates are again rising among young gay men and minorities of color. Some common, erroneous beliefs are that AIDS is a chronic disease, reasonably managed by medication, and that HIV infection can be avoided by not having sex with men over thirty. In addition, the context of AIDS education has shifted. A politically conservative Christian right wing has forced public policy to focus on abstinence, not evidence-based and targeted safer sex programs (like sero-sorting) and to use faith-based initiatives, which are often anti-gay and may include reparative therapy.

Gay men and lesbians have experienced the death of lovers, friends, and associates in staggering numbers, and, given the numbers of those infected but not yet ill, this experience will no doubt continue until a cure is found. Many have not had the opportunity to process these multiple losses. In addition to the fear of AIDS, which may bring chronic anxiety akin to posttraumatic stress disorder (PTSD), there is a pervasive sense of mourning and depression in the homosexual community, which affects many aspects of life, including sexuality, and a real risk exists of reverting to more negative attitudes about homosexuality, among lesbians, gays, and bisexuals themselves as well as among straights. This backlash has resulted in some bitterness and despair in the gay community, and fear that hard-earned gains and increased acceptance may slip away in the face of AIDS.

For many homosexuals, the stresses of being different in a nonaccepting, nonunderstanding society are intensified by the AIDS health crisis. The irrational fear of AIDS, exacerbated by contradictory information along with the actual threat, has resulted in a population of "worried well."[66] These are persons at risk of AIDS because of past or present sexual activity or intravenous (IV) drug use but without a known exposure to the virus, and those who have tested HIV positive but have not developed symptoms. Quadland and Sattles suggest that it is extremely important for mental health and other health professionals to clearly convey the message that homosexuality and sexual behavior did not cause AIDS and not allow society to blame the victims of this tragedy.[67] Without a significant effort to expand affirming mental health services, the emotional needs of lesbians, gays, and bisexuals will continue to be met primarily through organized self-help groups.

In response to the epidemic, lesbians, gays, and bisexuals combined their political energy and skill and assumed leadership of the nation's efforts by organizing local, state, and national self-help efforts, developing services, advocating for patients, lobbying for expanded research and treatment funds, and pressing for protective legislation. Most local AIDS service organizations were founded by gays and continue to be influenced by gays.[68] However, in recent years, there has been concerted effort to move AIDS planning, education, and service into the mainstream of health and welfare programs. This is happening as more health care providers accept their professional responsibility for the epidemic and as the profile of those infected changes from primarily white gay and bisexual men to African American and Latino IV drug users, their sexual partners, and their babies. Presently the fastest growing categories of victims are adolescents and minority women and their children. Because this process of main-streaming services is quite slow and requires considerable experience, lesbians, gay men, and bisexuals will continue to provide leadership and financial support in this effort.

Lesbian, Gay, and Bisexual Professionals

Many social workers are themselves lesbian, gay, or bisexual, some being openly identified to their colleagues as such, others not. Thus, the professional social worker must consider sexual orientation issues in relation not only to clients and the community but also to professional relationships with students, supervisors, peers, and employers. As the Gay Liberation Movement and the professions come of age, the number of openly lesbian-, gay-, and bisexual-identified professionals is likely to grow.

Whether to "come out" when seeking employment or once on the job is a major dilemma that every lesbian, gay, and bisexual social worker must face. Fear of losing one's job is widespread and a major factor affecting their decisions to remain closeted on their own or a partner's behalf.[69] Although documented instances of such discrimination are scant, except in the military, few states have civil rights legislation explicitly protecting gays and lesbians from discrimination in hiring and other aspects of employment. Despite the provisions of the NASW Code of Ethics, few social work agencies and institutions have antidiscrimination policies of their own that explicitly mention sexual orientation, and most schools of social work also lack such protections. Workers who retain their jobs may experience social and/or professional isolation, mild harassment, or especially close scrutiny of their performance on the job.[70] For example, a recent survey of supervisors at one school of social work's field placement agencies suggested that the responses to a social work intern's "coming out" on placement might be quite variable.[71]

Providing training to all staff and support to those working with clients who are lesbian, gay, or bisexual, or who are from families with lesbian, gay, or bisexual members, are ways both to legitimate the issues and to remove pressure from identified lesbian, gay, or bisexual staff to be the resident experts. Such practices are not just affirming for staff; they are therapeutic for clients as well, some of whom may be dealing with issues of sexual orientation themselves.

The profession, through its associations (e.g., NASW, Societies for Clinical Social Work, American Association of Black Social Workers, as well as other ethnic and specialty groups), has begun to respond to minority group pressure by increasing membership education, establishing state-level lesbian and gay caucuses, and supporting civil rights legislation. Many more social agencies, such as child and family services and mental health clinics, have broadened their mission to serve this population. The Council on Social Work Education has added lesbian and gay content to the required human diversity curriculum standards and, with an exception for religious institutions, sanction against those programs that continue to discriminate against lesbian, gay, and bisexual students, staff, and faculty. The profession has responded to similar changes in cultural ideology in the past and will continue to do so in the future.

Concluding Comment

In recent decades, a revolution has taken place in gay people's perception of themselves. The notion of homosexuality as an individual illness has been discredited and replaced with a political and social definition that posits that to be gay is to be a member of an oppressed minority, similar in many ways to racial and ethnic minorities.[72] In response to oppression, lesbians, gays, and bisexuals have organized to reinforce this new self-view and to press for civil rights that are currently denied. The future political agenda of lesbian, gay, and bisexual communities will include macro level, state and national activity around each of the following issues: (1) civil rights (e.g., the repeal of state sodomy laws, passage of antidiscrimination statutes, and legal recognition of relationships); (2) violence/hate crimes (e.g., protection against gay bashing, harassment, and abuse); (3) substance abuse (e.g., increased awareness of, access to, and the development of lesbian- and gay-sensitive drug and alcohol services); (4) health care (e.g., ensuring access to and the quality of gay sensitive services, sexually transmitted disease and AIDS care, reproductive rights, new reproductive technologies such as alternative insemination, and women's health equity); (5) mental health service based on gay-affirmative models; (6) community, family, and social life (e.g., custody, child, and foster care rights); (7) youth services (e.g., education, support services, and legal protections); (8) elder care (e.g., expansion of services to reflect the increase in numbers and the different life histories and expectations of the elders of the future); and (9) equal protection in the workplace, including the right to serve openly in the military without harassment and discrimination.

Same-sex marriage and equal treatment in the military will continue to be the battleground for civil rights activism. Both engage core social institutions where blatant discrimination and breach of a gay or lesbian citizen's privacy and equal protection rights persist. Recently, the State Supreme Court of Hawaii asked for compelling reasons why the state should not permit legal same-sex marriage. Congress, in anticipation of an affirmative decision, passed a "Defense of (heterosexual) Marriage Act" (DOMA) intended to block the state's recognition of same-sex marriages. Many states have followed suit.

Since 2005, however, Massachusetts became the first state to allow same-sex marriages. Vermont and Connecticut have legalized civil unions while 10 states and the District of Columbia offer domestic partnerships. Hawaii, California, Oregon, and New Jersey have enacted variations of these arrangements. While "domestic partnership" recognition has also been advanced in industry and in some municipalities, these alternatives to marriage can only confer "second-class" rights and privileges in comparison to those awarded with marriage. Because of the Defense of Marriage Act (DOMA), however, even those married in Massachusetts cannot avail themselves of the federal benefits, like spousal Social Security benefits, that marriage usually guarantees.

The "Don't ask, don't tell" military policy is being challenged successfully in the federal courts because of its apparent violation of the Constitution's equal protection and privacy clauses. The legal process is slow, however, and the gains that have been made appear to be made at the margins, for example, more states promulgating administrative policy allowing for gay and lesbian foster parenting and adoptions. These advances are hardly secure in that the 'Religious Right' and political conservatives are scapegoating gay men and lesbians as they targeted communists and Jews only decades ago.

Social visibility of lesbian, gay, and bisexual people will become the norm. Social acceptance and integration will be illusory in some sectors of society while a reality in others. Social work professionals are in a position to have an influence on many of the issues facing lesbians, gays, and bisexuals today and in the future: civil rights, access to health and reproductive services, child custody, adoption and foster care, and mental health and substance abuse services, to name but a few. We will all be challenged to use that influence for the good.

KEY WORDS AND CONCEPTS

Gays
Lesbians
Bisexuals
Homophobia

Heterosexism
Oppression
Conversion therapy

SUGGESTED INFORMATION SOURCES

Appleby, G.A., and Anastas, J.W. *Not Just a Passing Phase: Social Work with Lesbian, Gay and Bisexual People*. New York: Columbia University Press, 1998.

Comstock, G.D. *Violence Against Lesbians and Gay Men*. New York: Columbia University Press, 1991.

D'Augelli, A.R., and Patterson, C.J., eds. *Lesbian, Gay, and Bisexual Identities over the Lifespan*. New York: Oxford University Press, 1995.

Edwards, R.L., ed. *Encyclopedia of Social Work*, 19th Edition. Washington, D.C.: NASW Press, 1995: following articles: Berger, R. ML, and Kelly, "Gay Men: Overview," pp. 1064–1074; Hunter, J., and Schaecher, R., "Gay and Lesbian Adolescents," pp. 1055–1063; Gochros, J.S., "Bisexuality," pp. 299–304; Laird, J., "Lesbians: Parenting," pp. 1604–1615; Morales, J., "Gay Men: Parenting," pp. 1085–1094; Shernoff, M., "Gay Men: Direct Practice," pp. 1075–1084; Tully, C.T., "Lesbians: Overview," pp. 1591–1596; Woodman, N.J., "Lesbians: Direct Practice," pp. 1597–1603.

Garnets, L.D., and Kimmel, D.C., eds. *Psychological Perspectives on Lesbian and Gay Male Experiences*. New York: Columbia University Press, 1993.

Gay and Lesbian Medical Association (GLMA). (2001). *Healthy People 2010: A Companion Document for Lesbian, Gay, Bisexual and Transgender Health*. San Francisco, CA: Author. Available at www.glma.org

Geller, T., ed. *Bisexuality: Theory and Research*. New York: Haworth Press, 1991.

Gonsiorek, J.C., and Weinrich, J.D., eds. *Homosexuality: Research Implications for Public Policy*. Newbury Park, CA: Sage, 1991.

Herek, G.M., and Berrill, K.T., eds. *Hate Crimes: Confronting Violence Against Lesbians and Gay Men.* Newbury Park, CA: Sage, 1992.

McWhirter, D.P., and Mattison, A.M. *The Male Couple: How Relationships Develop.* New York: Prentice-Hall, 1984.

National Association of Social Workers. "Lesbian, Gay, and Bisexual Issues," *Social Work Speaks: NASW Policy Statements,* 4th Edition. Washington, D.C.: NASW Press, 1997.

Nava, M., and Dawidoff, R. *Created Equal: Why Gay Rights Matter to America.* New York: St. Martin's Press, 1994.

Slater, S. *The Lesbian Family Life Cycle.* New York: Free Press, 1995.

Sullivan, A. *Virtually Normal: An Argument About Homosexuality.* New York: Alfred A. Knopf, 1995.

Vaid, U. *Virtually Equal: The Mainstreaming of Gay and Lesbian Liberation.* New York: Anchor Books, 1995.

ENDNOTES

1. A.P. Weiner, "Racist, Sexist, and Homophobic Attitudes among Undergraduate Social Work Students and the Effects on Assessments of Client Vignettes," unpublished doctoral dissertation (New Brunswick, NJ: Rutgers University, 1989); also see G. Appleby. "Hearing: Gay Bashing and Harassment," unpublished conference proceedings (San Francisco: NASW Annual Program Meeting, 1989).

2. Ost, J., & Gates, G.J. *The Gay & Lesbian Atlas* (Washington, DC: The Urban Institute Press, 2004).

3. Martin, J., & Meezan, W. *Research Methods with LGBT People* (Binghamton, NY: Harrington Park Press, 2003).

4. Appleby, G.A., & Anastas, J.W. *Not Just a Passing Phase: Social Work with Gay, Lesbian, and Bisexual People* (New York: Columbia University Press, 1998), p. 57.

5. A.P. Bell and M.S. Weinberg, *Homosexualities: A Study of Diversity among Men and Women* (New York: Simon & Schuster, 1978).

6. Urban Institute, 2001, p. 49.

7. H. Hidalgo, "Third World," in H. Hidalgo, T. Peterson, and N.J. Woodman, eds., *Lesbian and Gay Issues: A Resource Manual for Social Workers* (Silver Spring, MD: National Association of Social Workers, 1985), pp. 14–16.

8. M.C. Smith, "By the Year 2000," in J. Beam, ed., *In the Life: A Black Gay Anthology* (Boston: Alyson Press, 1986), p. 226.

9. A. Carballo-Dieguez, "Hispanic Culture, Gay Male Culture, and AIDS: Counseling Implications," *Journal of Counseling and Development* 68 (September–October 1989): 26–30.

10. V.M. Mays and S.D. Cochran, "Black Gay and Bisexual Men Coping with More Than Just A Disease," *Focus* 4 (January 1988): 1–3.

11. J.H. Newby, "The Effects of Cultural Beliefs and Values on AIDS Prevention and Treatment in the Black Community," a paper presented at the Annual Program Meeting of the National Association of Social Workers, San Francisco, October, 1989.

12. W.J. Blumenfeld, *How We All Pay the Price* (Boston: Beacon Press, 1992).

13. W. Paul and J.D. Weinrich, "Whom and What We Study: Definition and Scope of Sexual Orientation," in *Homosexuality*, pp. 26–27.

14. A.P. Bell, M.S. Weinberg, and S.K Hammersmith, *Sexual Preference: It's Development in Men and Women* (Bloomington: Indiana University Press, 1981).

15. B. Garner and R.W. Smith, "Are There Really Any Gay Male Athletes? An Empirical Survey," *Journal of Sex Research* 13 (1977): 22–34.

16. GLSEN. July 11, 2005. www.glsen.org. Jeremy Townsley. (2001). Health Risks of Gay Youth. IUPUI. www.jeremyt.org

17. Tully, C.T. *Gay and Lesbian Persons*, in A. Gitterman, ed., *Handbook of Social Work Practice with Vulnerable and Resilient Populations*. (New York: Columbia University Press, 2001).

18. C.A. Lukes and H. Land, "Bicuiturality and Homosexuality," *Social Work* 35 (1990): 155–161.

19. Ibid.

20. N. Hunter and N. Polikoff, "Custody Rights of Lesbian Mothers: Legal Theory and Litigation Strategy," *Buffalo Law Review* 25 (1976): 691–733.

21. M. Mendola, *A New Look at Gay Couples* (New York: Crown, 1980); also see D. McWhirter and A. Mattison, *The Male Couple: How Relationships Develop* (Englewood Cliffs, NJ: Prentice Hall, 1984).

22. R. Achtenberg, "Preserving and Protecting the Families of Lesbians and Gay Men," in Shernoff and Scott, *The Sourcebook on Lesbian/Gay Health Care*; also see S.K. Hammersmith, "A Sociological Approach to Counseling Homosexual Clients and Their Families," in E. Coleman, ed., *Integrated Identity for Gay Men and Lesbians: Psychotherapeutic Approaches for Emotional Well-being* (New York: Harrington Park Press, 1988), pp. 174–179.

23. Bell, Weinberg, and Hammersmith.

24. M. Kirkpatrick, K. Smith, and R. Roy, "Lesbian Mothers and Their Children: A Comparative Study," *American Journal of Orthopsychiatry* 51 (1981): 545–551; also see B. Miller, "Gay Fathers and Their Children," *The Family Coordinator* 28 (1979): 544–552; F. Bozett, "Gay Fathers: Evaluation of the Gay Father Identity," *American Journal of Psychiatry* 51 (March 1978): 173–179; R. Green, "Thirty-five Children Raised by Homosexual or Transsexual Parents," *American Journal of Psychiatry* (1978): 135; B. Hoeffer, "Children's Acquisition of Sex-Role Behavior in Lesbian Mother Families," *American Journal of Orthopsychiatry* 51 (March 1981); S. Golombok, "Children in Lesbian and Single Parent Households: Psychosexual and Psychiatric Appraisal," *Journal of Child Psychology and Applied Discipline* 24 (1983); E.F. Levy, "Lesbian Mothers' Coping Characteristics: An Exploration of Social, Psychological, and Family Coping Resources," unpublished doctoral dissertation (Madison: University of Wisconsin, 1983).

25. Kirkpatrick, Smith, and Roy.

26. R.M. Berger, "Homosexuality: Gay Men," in A. Minahan, ed., *Encyclopedia of Social Work*, 18th Edition (Silver Spring, MD: National Association of Social Workers, 1987).

27. S. Susoeff, "Assessing Children's Best Interests When a Parent Is Gay or Lesbian: Toward a Rational Custody Standard," *UCLA Law Review* 32 (April 1985); M. Kirkpatrick and D. Hitchens, "Lesbian Mothers/Gay Fathers," in *Emerging Issues in Child Psychiatry and the Law* (New York: Brunner & c Mazel, 1985).

28. N.J. Woodman, "Homosexuality': Lesbian Women," *Encyclopedia of Social Work*

29. M.S. Weinberg and C.J. Williams, *Male Homosexuals: Their Problems and Adaptations* (New York: Oxford University Press, 1974).

30. R.M. Berger, "What Is a Homosexual?: A Definitional Model," *Social Work* 28 (February 1983): 132–135.

31. Ibid.
32. Ibid.
33. E. Coleman, ed., *Integrated Identity for Gay Men and Lesbians: Psychotherapeutic Approaches for Emotional Well-being* (New York: Harrington Park Press, 1988), p. 19.
34. Bradford and Ryan, p. 4.
35. L. Icard and D.M. Traunstein, "Black Gay Alcoholic Men: Their Culture and Treatment," *Social Casework* 68, no. 5 (1987): 267–272.
36. S.C. Anderson and D.C. Henderson, "Working with Lesbian Alcoholics," *Social Work* 30 (June 1985): 518–525.
37. V. Brooks, *Minority Stress and Lesbian Women* (Lexington, MA: D.C. Heath, 1981).
38. J.B. Bradford, "Reactions of Gay Men to AIDS: A Survey of Self-Reported Change," unpublished doctoral dissertation (Virginia Commonwealth University, 1986).
39. R. Alcalay, "Health and Social Support Networks: A Case for Improving Communication, "*Social Networks* 5 (1983): 71–88.
40. Bradford and Ryan, pp. 3–5.
41. C.B. Germain and A. Gitterman, *The Life Model of Social Work Practice* (New York: Columbia University Press, 1980).
42. M. Coles and W. Rubenstein, "Rights of Gays and Lesbians," paper presented at the Biennial Conference at the University of Wisconsin, Madison, June 15–18, 1987.
43. Achtenberg, p. 244.
44. Dougherty, T. (2005). Economic benefits of marriage under Federal and Connecticut Law. National Gay and Lesbian Task Force Policy Institute. wwwthetaskforce.org
45. M. Hall, "Lesbian Families: Cultural and Clinical Issues," *Social Work* 23 (1978): 380–385.
46. Hall, p. 380.
47. Ibid.
48. K. Lewes, *The Psychoanalytic Theory of Male Homosexuality* (New York: Simon & Schuster, 1988).
49. A. Rosenthal, "Heterosexism and Clinical Assessment," *Smith College Studies in Social Work* 52 (February 1982): 145–159.
50. A.P. Bell and M.S. Weinberg, *Homosexualities: A Study of Diversity among Men and Women* (New York: Simon & Schuster, 1978).
51. J. Krajeski, "Psychotherapy with Gay Men and Lesbians: A History of Controversy," in T.S. Stein and C.J. Cohen, eds., *Contemporary Perspectives on Psychotherapy with Lesbians and Gay Men* (New York: Plenum, 1986).
52. C. Golden, "Diversity and Variability in Women's Sexual Identities," Boston Lesbian Psychologies Collective, ed., in *Lesbian Psychologies: Explorations and Challenges* (Urbana: University of Illinois Press, 1986).
53. A. Hochschild, *The Second Shift* (New York: Viking Press, 1989).
54. S. Crawford, "Lesbian Families: Psychosocial Stress and the Family-Building Process," in *Lesbian Psychologies*.
55. R.M. Berger, "Realities of Gay and Lesbian Aging," *Social Work* 29 (January 1984): 57–62; also see M. Kehoe, "Lesbians over Sixty Speak for Themselves," *Journal of Homosexuality* 16 (March–April 1988): 1–78.
56. M. Adelman, ed., *Long Time Passing: Lives of Older Lesbians* (Boston: Alyson Publications, 1986).
57. GLMA, 2001.
58. Smith, G., Bartlett, A., & King, M. "Treatments of Homosexuality in Britain since the 1950s—an Oral History: The Experience of Patients," *British Journal of Medicine*

(2004), and King, M., Smith, G., & Bartlett, A. "Treatments of Homosexuality in Britain since the 1950s—an Oral History: The Experience of Professionals," *British Journal of Medicine* (2004).

59. GLMA, 2001.
60. Bradford and Ryan.
61. Ibid.
62. Ibid.
63. Ibid. p. 383.
64. N.A. Humphreys and J.K. Quam, "Middle-Aged and Old Gay, Lesbian and Bisexual Adults," in G.A. Appleby and J.W. Anastas, eds., *Not Just a Passing Phase: Social Work with Gay, Lesbian and Bisexual People* (New York: Columbia University Press, 1998).
65. L. Daimant, ed., *Homosexual Issues in the Workplace* (Washington, D.C.: Taylor &: Francis, 1993); C. Kitzinger, "Lesbians and Gay Men in the Workplace: Psychosocial Issues," In M.J. Davidson and J. Earnshaw, eds., *Vulnerable Workers: Psychosocial and Legal Issues* (New York: John Wiley &: Sons, 1991), pp. 223–257.
66. K.J. Harowski, "The Worried Well: Maximizing Coping in the Face of AIDS," in Coleman.
67. M.C. Quadland and W.D. Sattles, "AIDS, Sexuality, and Sexual Control," in Coleman.
68. G.A. Appleby, "What Social Workers Can Do," in S. Alyson, ed., *You Can Do Something about AIDS* (Boston: The Stop AIDS Project, 1989).
69. M.P. Levine and R. Leonard, "Discrimination against Lesbians in the Work Force," *Signs: Journal of Women in Culture and Society* 9 (April 1984): 700–710.
70. J. Rabin, K. Keefe, and M. Burton, "Enhancing Services for Sexual-Minority Clients: A Community Mental Health Approach," *Social Work* 31 (April 1986): 292–298.
71. K. Lewes, *The Psychoanalytic Theory of Male Homosexuality* (New York: Simon & Schuster, 1988).
72. W. Paul, "Social and Cultural Issues," in *Homosexuality: Social, Psychological, and Biological Issues* (Beverly Hills, CA: Sage, 1982).

chapter 17

Social Work Practice with Children and Youth

Armando T. Morales and Bradford W. Sheafor

Prefatory Comment

Children and youth in the United States have been thought of as cherished beneficiaries of America's past, symbols of the quality of the society, and conveyors of the nation's hopes for the future. Unlike many nations, the United States invests considerable resources in social, recreational, and educational programs to benefit its youngest members. Political and philosophical differences may exist about how to best enhance the quality of life for children and youth, but there is little disagreement that their physical, psychological, and intellectual development is important. Morales and Sheafor demonstrate the key roles social workers play in each of these forms of human development.

Children were once exploited as a source of labor in the sweatshops of urban America and on family farms in rural areas. At one time it was not uncommon for poor white families to abandon their children to the urban streets during hard economic times, for black slave children to be sold away from their parents for a profit, for children of Mexican migrant families to toil each day in the hot sun doing backbreaking farm labor, and so on. The condition of housing in which children lived was often crowded, unsanitary, and dangerous in urban tenements, Appalachian coal towns, and migrant camps, largely because wealthy owners were in complete control and their priority was to make a profit for themselves and their corporations. Children's education, too, was viewed as a luxury and was often made available to them only before they were old enough to provide productive labor in factories or, in rural areas, at the times of the year when crops were dormant and the children were not needed in the fields.

In the early 1900s, concerns about the damaging conditions experienced by children became a national issue. The public was gradually made aware of the plight of children, and sentiment that this important resource should be protected and nourished began to evolve. Committees concerned about housing quality, child labor, the excessive placement of children in orphanages and other institutions, and basic child health issues contributed to President Theodore Roosevelt calling a White House Conference on the Care of Dependent Children in 1909. The subsequent formation of the U.S. Children's Bureau, which, under the direction of social worker Katherine Lenroot, initiated government oversight and advocacy in the interest of children, was a milestone in social welfare history.[1] As a result, child labor legislation was passed, mother's pensions (later public assistance) were provided, minimum housing quality was required, and public education mandated.

Current Demographics

Compared with conditions prior to the twentieth century, the quality of life for children and youth in the United States has improved considerably. Yet, more is needed. Based on an analysis of the 2000 Census data, Kominski, Jamieson, and Martinez identified seven conditions experienced by school-age children that are strong indicators of undesirable outcomes later in life. Some of these at-risk factors are related to the individual and others to the family. The at-risk factors and the percentages of the 5- to 17-year-old population experiencing these conditions were as follows:

- At least one disability, 7.6 percent
- Retained in grade at least once, 8.1 percent
- Speaks English less than "very well," 4.9 percent
- Does not live with both parents, 30.8 percent
- Either parent emigrated to the United States in past five years, 2.3 percent
- Family income below $10,000 annually, 8.5 percent
- Neither parent/guardian employed, 10.5 percent

Although 54 percent of the children and youth experienced none of these risk factors, 28 percent were affected by one factor and 18 percent experienced more than one of these conditions.[2]

There are, of course, many factors that increase risk for children and youth. The following pages present estimates from current data regarding the number of children that experience a variety of conditions that place them at greater risk for problems—both now and in the future. Given the Census Bureau estimate of more than 72.5 million children and youth in the United States, the sheer numbers are often so large they are not meaningful unless we can translate them to a population with which we are familiar, such as the community in which we live. To make such a translation possible, data are provided in Boxes 17.1 through 17.7 that reflect the expected incidence in a community of 100,000.*

---

*Children and youth make up 25.465 percent of the total U.S. population, and thus in our mythical community of 100,000, they become 25,465 young people. If, for example, you should live in a community of 500,000, simply multiply the numbers in the boxes by five and, if your community is 50,000, multiply by .5 to get an estimate of the incidence of each condition where you live. Of course, each community is unique and the national average provides only a rough indicator of what might be expected in your community.

Personal Characteristics

As indicated in Box 17.1,** in this age group there are slightly more males than females and more youth (i.e., in the 12- to 17-year-age group) than there are children in the two younger age categories. The racial/ethnic distribution in the United States is changing with the percent of the Hispanic population increasing, the white population decreasing, and the other groups remaining about the same as in the past. Also, the percent of foreign-born children is getting larger, and it is likely that the number who have difficulty speaking English (a risk factor) is also increasing, although more recent data than 1999 are not available.

Family Composition and Housing

The varying family structures in the United States affect the opportunities and experiences of children and youth. As Box 17.2 indicates, less than 65 percent of the children and youth live with two biological parents; another 6.7 percent live with their biological mother and a stepparent. As will be evident in examining Box 17.4, the 22.7 percent of this population group living with a single mother increases the

Box 17.1

Personal Characteristics of U.S. Children and Youth

(per 100,000 population with 25,465 ages 0–17)

Gender (2003)

► Male, 51.2% = 13,035
► Female, 48.8% = 12,430

Age (2004)

► 0–5 years, 32.8% = 8,353
► 6–11 years, 32.6% = 8,302
► 12–17, 34.6% = 8,811

Race/Ethnicity (2004)

► White (non-Hispanic), 59% = 15,024
► Hispanic, 19% = 4,838

► African American (non-Hispanic) 16% = 4,074
► Asian American/Pacific Islander, 4% = 1,019
► Native American, 1% = 255

Foreign Born (2002)

► 4.2% = 1,070

Difficulty Speaking English (1999)

► Ages 5–17, 5.0% = 941

**Data presented in Boxes 17.1 through 17.7 are selected from the following sources:

- Child Trends, "Child Trends DataBank," http://www.childtrendsdatabank.org
- Federal Interagency Forum on Child and Family Statistics. *America's Children in Brief: Key National Indicators of Well-Being, 2004.* http://www.childstats.gov/ac2004/intro.asp
- U.S. Census Bureau, *Income, Poverty, and Health Insurance Coverage in the United States: 2003.* http://www.census.gov/prod/2004pubs/p60–226.pdf
- U.S. Department of Health and Human Services, *Trends in the Well-Being of America's Children and Youth: 2003.* http://aspe.hhs.gov/hsp/03trends
- U.S. Office of the Surgeon General, *Mental Health: A Report of the Surgeon General: 2000.* http://www.surgeongeneral.gov/library/mentalhealth/chapter3/sec1.html

Box 17.2

Household Composition and Housing of U.S. Children and Youth

(per l00,000 population with 25,465 ages 0–17)

Household Composition (2002)

▶ Living with biological parents, 64.2% = 16,349
▶ Living with one biological parent and stepparent, 6.7% = 1,706
▶ Living with biological mother only, 22.7% = 5,781
▶ Living with biological father only, 2.5% = 637
▶ Living with grandparent(s), 1.8% = 458
▶ Living with no biological family, 1.9% = 484 (including 186 in foster care)

Quality of Housing (2001)

▶ Live in housing with severe physical problems, 11% = 2,801
▶ Live in crowded housing, 6% = 1,528
▶ Live in household where rent/payments and utilities requires more than 50% of family income, 11% = 2,801

chances of growing up in poverty more than 4.5 times. Another evident trend is the increasing number of children who live with their grandparents. When these arrangements are made (i.e., kinship care), social workers are often involved in securing financial resources and legal sanction to assure the safety and well-being of the children. Similarly, social workers are also involved in placements where no biological family is present—especially when foster care is being provided.

One in nine children lived in a house or apartment with severe physical problems. This dilapidated housing, for example, is characterized by the absence of complete plumbing, unvented room heaters as the primary heat source, water leakage, broken plaster or open cracks or holes in walls, and signs of rats. Often, too, the housing is crowded with more people than the space can accommodate. Also, 11 percent of the families pay more than one-half of their income just for housing, leaving relatively little money for food, clothing, medical care, and transportation. In short, for many children and youth, "home" is not conducive to their well-being, but nevertheless is a substantial financial drain on family resources. Warm and safe housing is essential for meeting the very basic needs of people, and social workers are often involved in promoting and helping people secure affordable housing.

Family Income and Employment

A child's well-being is improved if the family income is adequate to support good-quality housing, health care, food, clothing, and so on. The median income for all households in the United States in 2003 was $43,318. However, as Box 17.3 reveals, 29.0 percent of the families had less than $25,000 income. With the poverty threshold for a typical family of two adults and two children under age 18 at $19,157 per year,[3] it is clear that many families live below the expected quality of life standards in the

Box 17.3

Income and Employment Status of Families of U.S. Children and Youth

(per 100,000 population with 25,465 ages 0–17)

Household Annual Income Distribution (2003)

▶ Less than $25,000, 29.0% = 7,385
▶ $25,000 to $49,999, 26.9% = 6,850
▶ $50,000 to $74,999, 18.0% = 4,584
▶ $75,000 to $99,999, 11.0% = 2,801
▶ $100,000 and above, 15.1% = 3,845

Median Family Income (2003)

▶ White family = $47,777
▶ Hispanic family = $32,997

▶ Black family = $29,645
▶ Asian family = $55,699
▶ Married-couple family = $62,405
▶ Single-female headed family = $29,307
▶ Single-male headed family = $41,959

Mother Employed (2001)

▶ Full-time, 52% = 13,242
▶ Part-time, 18% = 4, 584
▶ Not employed, 30% = 7, 640

United States. The disparity in income is perhaps best captured by the fact that the 20 percent of households with the lowest income had a 3.4 percent share of the total U.S. income, while the 20 percent of the households with the highest income received 49.8 percent, that is, one-fifth of the families received almost one-half of the income.[4]

It is also evident in Box 17.3 that a variety of risk factors are associated with a family's income level. Where Asian and white families have an average income above the national median, black and Hispanic families fall well below the norm. Married couple families, many having two employed members, average nearly $62,500 per year, and even the household headed by a single male is close to the median for all families. It is the single-female headed family that on average is experiencing poverty. More specifically, it is the Hispanic or black family headed by a single mother that places the children at greatest risk of having low income. Increasing income, however, comes at a cost. With more than one-half of the mothers working full-time and another 18 percent working part-time, the parent's ability to devote the necessary time and energy to the child's growth and development often decreases, becoming a trade-off for additional income.

Poverty and Hunger

The single most clear predictor of social problems for children and youth is to live in poverty. When discussing the impact of poverty on children in a substantial study of child poverty funded by the independent David and Lucile Packard Foundation, Lewitt, Terman, and Behrman[5] conclude:

> Not only do poor children have access to fewer material goods than rich or middle-class children, but also they are more likely to experience poor health and to die during childhood. In school, they score lower on standardized tests and are more likely to be retained in grade and to drop out. Poor teens are more likely to have out-of-wedlock births and to experience violent crime. Finally, persistently poor children are more likely to end up as poor adults. (p. 8)

Kearnsey, Grundermann, and Gallicchio[6] estimate that without the income supports of various social programs, the child poverty level would double. Thus, social workers are committed to at least maintaining the level support for children and their families through the U.S. income maintenance programs. The social action agenda of the National Association of Social Workers supports this view.

Poverty and its associated problems do not fall equally on children and youth (see Box 17.4). In a wealthy country such as the United States, it is troubling that 8.2 percent of the white population and 11.8 percent of the Asian population experience poverty. Yet, that figure pales when compared to the 22.5 percent poverty rate for Hispanics and the 24.4 percent rate for the black population. Being Hispanic or black is a risk factor for children in the United States. In addition, as indicated above, living with a single mother is another high-risk factor. Although 9 percent of the children living with married parents experience an income below the poverty line, the chances of living in poverty increases more than four-fold when living with a single mother.

Poverty-related factors such as inadequate health care and substandard housing typically have a long-term negative impact on the well-being of children. Hunger has an immediate impact on poor people because it represents a threat to one's very survival. Approximately 13 percent of all children and youth experience a level of hunger classified as "food insecurity," a condition in which there is difficulty obtaining enough food, reduced quality of diet and therefore improper nutrition, and anxiety about a continuing food supply. More than 3 percent of the families report food insecurity with accompanying periods of hunger, and another one-half percent experience severe hunger where there is simply not enough food for the children and adults in the family.

Box 17.4

Poverty and Hunger Status of U.S. Children and Youth
(per 100,000 population with 25,465 ages 0–17)

Ethnicity of Children in Families at or below Poverty Level (2003)

▶ White, 8.2% = 1,232
▶ Hispanic, 22.5% = 1,089
▶ Black, 24.4% = 994
▶ Asian, 11.8% = 120

Marital Status of Family at or below Poverty Level (2003)

▶ Living with married parents, 9% = 1,625
▶ Living with single mother, 42% = 2,428

Household Sometimes or Often Reporting "Not Enough to Eat" (2002)

▶ Food insecurity without hunger, 13.1% = 3,367
▶ Food insecurity with moderate hunger, 3.3% = 848
▶ Food insecurity with severe hunger, 0.5% = 128

Learning Stimulation and Educational Status

In many ways, hope for a nation's future depends on the education of its children and youth. In an increasingly high-tech universe, persons with limited education find it difficult to compete for jobs and earn the income necessary to support themselves and their families. From the basic learning provided in families or child care facilities through formal education in elementary and secondary schools, the learning potential of children and youth is developed. Box 17.5 contains data describing the day care arrangements for children up to age 6 who have not begun kindergarten. Nearly 4 in 10 children in this age group are cared for by their parents during the day, another 23 percent receive day care from a relative, and 16 percent are in the care of nonrelatives.

A valuable source of preparation for children to enter schools is care in early childhood education programs such as day care centers, Head Start programs, preschools, nursery schools, and other early childhood programs. For 3- to 5-year-olds in 2001, black (non-Hispanic) children were the most likely to attend these programs (63.7 percent) and Hispanic children were least likely (39.8 percent). Almost 60 percent of the children at or above the poverty line were enrolled in a center-based early childhood education program, as compared to 48 percent of children from families below the poverty line. By reading to children, parents can further help them develop the prerequisite skills to succeed in school. Approximately 58 percent of the 3- to 5-year-old children are read to daily, although this experience is somewhat lower for black and Hispanic children, those from families below the poverty line, single-parent families, and those with mothers who have only a high school or lower educational level.

Box 17.5

Educational Status of U.S. Children and Youth

(per 100,000 population with 25,465 ages 0–17)
Day Care Arrangements for Children Not yet in Kindergarten (2002)
[Note: Some children participate in more than one non-parental care arrangement.]

- ▶ Parental care only, 39% = 2,175
- ▶ Care in a home by a relative, 23% = 1,283
- ▶ Care in a home by a non-relative, 16% = 892
- ▶ Day-care center, 33% = 1,840

Early Childhood Education Program, Ages 3–5 (2001)

- ▶ 56.4% = 2,342

Daily Family Reading to Children, Ages 3–5 (2001)

- ▶ 58% = 2,408

High School Dropout in Last Year, Ages 15–17 (2000)

- ▶ 5% = 220

High School Completion during Last Year (2001)

- ▶ White, 93.3% = 807
- ▶ Hispanic, 63.2% = 176
- ▶ Black, 87.0% = 205

Each year, approximately 5 percent of the students in high school drop out. The decision to drop out not only precludes gaining a high school diploma, but unless the student completes a general education diploma (GED), he or she is also ineligible for college enrollment. Advanced education adds much more to the quality of one's life than income, yet the long-term impact on annual earning power is also evident. In 2004, for persons ages 18 and over with no high school diploma, the average income was $18,734. That amount increased to $27,915 if one completed high school and rose to $51,206 if at least a bachelor's degree was completed.[7] The fact that 93.3 percent of the white students complete high school, as compared to 87.0 percent of the black students and only 63.2 percent of the Hispanic youth, partially accounts for the family income differential described above. It is evident that one goal for social workers should be to help all children remain in school whenever possible.

Health Status and Chronic Physical Conditions

A critical factor in the successful growth and development of children and youth is their health. As Box 17.6 indicates, the health care system in the United States has failed many of the nation's young people. The high cost of health care places at risk the 11 percent of the families who have no health insurance and, to a lesser degree, the 29 percent who are dependent on Medicaid or other government-financed health programs. Lack of adequate health insurance usually means there will be little attention to preventing health problems or even for early treatment when illnesses can be more readily treated. Evidence of the long-term impact of not having adequate health care can be seen in the fact that more than twice as many poor people have less than "good" or "excellent" health, as compared to those above the poverty line.

Three broad indices of health issues experienced by children and youth provide a snapshot of the prevalence of these conditions. Nearly 17 percent of all children ages 5 through 17 experienced at least one chronic health problem that limits their activities—with males experiencing these conditions at a much higher rate than females. Social workers often work with these children and youth because the conditions affect their social, psychological, physical, and educational functioning. In addition, an estimated 21 percent of the children and youth ages 9 through 17 experience a diagnosed mental health problem that requires intervention—including 11 percent with a *significant functional impairment* (i.e., affecting interaction at home, school, or with peers) and 5 percent classified as experiencing an *extreme functional impairment*. Finally, a problem of particular national significance today affecting young people concerns the food-related problems of either an eating disorder (i.e., anorexia or bulimia) or the problem of being excessively overweight, with physical and mental health problems often associated with these conditions.

Child maltreatment, too, can have devastating emotional and physical impact on children and youth. As the primary profession providing child welfare services, social workers often deal with the victims, as well as the perpetrators, of child abuse. Of the substantiated child abuse cases in 2003, males and females were almost equally victims. The rates of victimization were highest among the youngest and most vulnerable, i.e., children age 3 and under were almost three times more

Box 17.6

Health Status of U.S. Children and Youth

(per 100,000 population with 25,465 ages 0-17)

Family Health Insurance* (2003)

▶ Private 66% = 16,807
▶ Government (e.g., Medicaid), 29% = 7,385
▶ None, 11% = 2,801

Health Status Less Than "Very Good" or "Excellent" (2002)

▶ Below poverty line, 29% = 1,270
▶ Above poverty line, 13% = 2,741

Activity Limited by Chronic Condition, Ages 5-17 (2002)

▶ Males, 10.7% = 1,014
▶ Females, 6.2% = 560

Mental Health Problems, Ages 9-17 (2000)

▶ Mental health problem needing intervention, 21% = 2,717
▶ Functional impairment, 11% = 1,423
▶ Extreme functional impairment, 5% = 647

Eating Problems, grades 9-12 (2003)

▶ Eating disorder, 6% = 705
▶ Overweight, 85% above recommended body mass index
  ▶ Ages 6-11, 15.8% = 1,312
  ▶ Ages 12-17, 16.1% = 1,419

Victim of Child Maltreatment, (2003)

▶ 1.2% = 306

Deaths per Year (2003)

▶ Infant deaths, 0.72% = 10
▶ Children ages 1-4 deaths, 0.31% = 17
▶ Children ages 5-14 deaths, 0.17% = 24
▶ Youth ages 15-17 deaths, 0.68% = 30
▶ From motor vehicle accidents (ages 15-17), 0.28% = 12
▶ From homicide (ages 15-17), 0.93% = 4
▶ From suicide (ages 15-17), 0.74% = 3

*Some children are covered by both private and government insurance

likely to be abused than youth ages 16 and 17. Further, among the substantiated cases of child maltreatment, 63.2 percent experienced neglect, 18.9 percent were physically abused, 9.9 percent were sexually abused, and 4 to 9 percent were emotionally or psychologically maltreated. An estimated 1,500 children died of abuse or neglect in 2003—2 out of every 100,000 children in the United States.[8]

Other factors also contributed to the deaths of children and youth. The death rates were highest for infants and youth ages 15–17. The infant deaths were typically medically or abuse related, and the additional factors causing death among the older youth were motor vehicle accidents, homicide, and suicide.

At-Risk Social Behaviors

In addition to the above risk factors, various social behaviors place children and youth at further risk. In some ways it is surprising that so many youth survive adolescence. For example, as Box 17.7 indicates, a high number of 8th through 12th graders regularly smoke cigarettes (a long-term health risk factor), binge drink, and use various

Box 17.7

At-Risk Social Behavior of U.S. Children and Youth

(per 100,000 population with 25,465 ages 0–17)

Cigarette Smoker, smokes daily (2004)

▶ 8th grader, 4.4% = 65
▶ 10th grader, 8.3% = 122
▶ 12th grader, 15.6% = 229

Binge Drinker, 5 or more drinks in a row in past 2 weeks (2004)

▶ 8th grader, 11.4% = 167
▶ 10th grader, 22.0% = 323
▶ 12th grader, 29.2% = 429

Illicit Drug Use, used in past 30 days (2002)

▶ 8th grader, 10.4% = 153
▶ 10th grader, 20.8% = 306
▶ 12th grader, 25.4% = 373

Sexually Active (had intercourse) in Last Three Months (2003)
      (Note: 63% reported condom use and 17.0% reported use of birth control pills)

▶ 9th grader, 21.2% = 311
▶ 10th grader, 30.6% = 450
▶ 11th grader, 41.1% = 604
▶ 12th grader, 48.9% = 718

Females and Pregnancy (ages 15–17) (2000–2003)

▶ Pregnancies, 5.4% = 115
▶ Abortions, 1.5% = 32
▶ Live births, 4.3% = 91
▶ Unmarried parents, 88.5% of births = 80
▶ Late or no prenatal care, 6.6% of births = 6
▶ Low-birthweight child, 7.8% of births = 7

Involvement with Violence, ages 14–17 (2003)

▶ Committed a violent crime, 5.2% = 303
▶ Carried a weapon at school, 17.4% = 1,005
▶ Victim of dating violence, 8.9% = 523
▶ Victim of serious crime, 1.5% = 88

illicit or illegal drugs. Many are also sexually active, and 5.4 percent of the women in the 15- to 17-year age group become pregnant each year. Most of these children were born to unmarried parents (a risk factor for the child); nearly 7 percent had late or no prenatal care (another health risk factor); and almost 8 percent were of low birthweight (i.e., below 5.5 pounds), thus increasing the chance of serious medical and developmental problems. Violence is also a part of life for many 14- to 17-year-olds, with more than 5 percent committing a violent crime in 2003, 17 percent carrying a weapon to school, 9 percent becoming victims of dating violence, and another 1.5 percent being a victim of a serious violent crime.

The Ecosystems Model

One way of attempting to organize an enormous amount of social, cultural, and physical and mental health data is to apply the ecosystems model discussed in Part Five. For example, at the *historical level,* when one considers historical issues impacting children and youth in the United States, it is clear that this country has come a long way from the days of exploiting children during the Industrial Revolution and into the 1930s and even the 1940s. This practice is almost nonexistent today, except for migrant farmworker children who do not attend school in order to earn income to help their underpaid parents support the family. Authorities, business owners, and schools seem to look the other way when this is happening. There are areas of progress, yet at the same time there are many examples of humanitarian violations and lack of compassion toward troubled youths. One improvement concerns the capital punishment of juveniles. In the 1940s, the United States executed forty-nine youths ages 16 and 17 for homicides. Today, as a result of *Roper V. Simmons* in 2005, the Supreme Court ruled that no person under the age of 16 can be executed and no person can be executed for having committed a capital crime while under the age of 16.

Applying the ecosystems model at the *environmental/structural level*, it is evident that the quality of life has improved significantly for most children and youth in the nation. This, however, is directly related to affluence; that is, the higher the affluence, the better the child's environment. The structure of the environment is largely determined by policies, laws, rules, regulations, and allocation of resources by those in political power. Again, families with the most influence receive the best treatment for their surroundings. For example, when the Los Angeles earthquake struck in January 1992, the areas that received the quickest relief; police and fire services; street, freeway, and building repairs; and food and water were the affluent areas of Los Angeles. American-born children and youth of undocumented parents were denied assistance, even though the poorest families lived in the hardest hit areas. Twenty and thirty years ago, such a dynamic would have been called either racism or institutional racism, terms that are considered obsolete today; however, these types of discriminatory behaviors and practices are very much alive. Social workers need to develop the critical and analytical skills to assess these issues, which cause children and youth harm.

At the *cultural level* in the ecosystems model, the focus is on the values, belief systems, and societal norms of American culture; but care must be given to not ignoring the cultural heritage of children and parents who were born and raised in other cultures. In most cases, children and youth possessing more than one culture are viewed as enriched, because they speak more than one language and have more than one culture to draw on as prescriptions for life and survival. In some states, however, this is viewed as anti-American, and efforts are made to discourage children and youth from using other languages in school or being taught in their own language as a transitional learning phase into English. In some states these programs are called "English as a second language" programs. Social workers therefore need to understand local and state policies that enhance educational development, as well as those that place additional burdens on children and youth, because poor academic performance is the highest predictor related to crime and delinquency.

Culture also determines the way in which families raise and discipline their children. For example, American culture condones corporal punishment of children and youth by their parents. Some cultures outlaw this practice, yet some countries practice severe forms of corporal punishment that Americans would consider criminal. Social workers need to understand these differences and assess whether the practice is traumatic for the specific recipient of the punishment, as opposed to the rationale provided by the person administering the discipline.

At the *family level* in the ecosystems model, emphasis is placed on the nature of the specific family lifestyle, culture, organization, division of labor, sex role structure, and interactional dynamics. Each family *is* unique. For children and youth raised in one intact, nuclear family, the task of incorporating all these potential benefits is far less difficult than it would be for children who are raised in foster or group homes, with relatives, or in separate two-parent families. Consider the often complex issues faced by minors in the *reconstituted* family, which finds two newly wed parents, each with his or her own children from a prior marriage (each child with its own sibling rivalry issues), moving into "one happy home." Each parent has his or her way of raising children, and the children in turn might resist the authority of the new parent, who might have different ideas of the role of children in the family and how they should be disciplined. Because of their complex developmental stage, adolescents sometimes are found to rebel in these types of families. It becomes even more complicated in reconstituted families when the new parents each come from a different culture. However, the majority of these families find ways of surviving in spite of all the obstacles.

Finally, the ecosystems model calls for an analysis at the *individual level,* focusing on the biological and psychological endowment of each person. In the case of children and adolescents who are beginning to show symptoms of the risk behaviors mentioned earlier in the chapter, it is especially important to investigate the biological, genetic, and psychosocial factors in the family history, such as addictions, behavioral problems, hospitalizations (health and mental health), juvenile/adult corrections history, and psychiatric histories, such as depression, anxiety disorders, schizophrenia, and developmental disabilities. A thorough assessment will find the social worker asking questions about pertinent family history and obtaining this information from each parent, their parents, and, if possible, even their parents, which, in effect, would be the children's great-grandparents. Such family histories can offer extremely important clues to understanding the current problem behavior of a child or adolescent. Figure 17.1 highlights some of the factors discussed in this section.

Figure 17.1

Ecosystems Model for Analysis of Psychosocial Factors Impacting Children and Youth

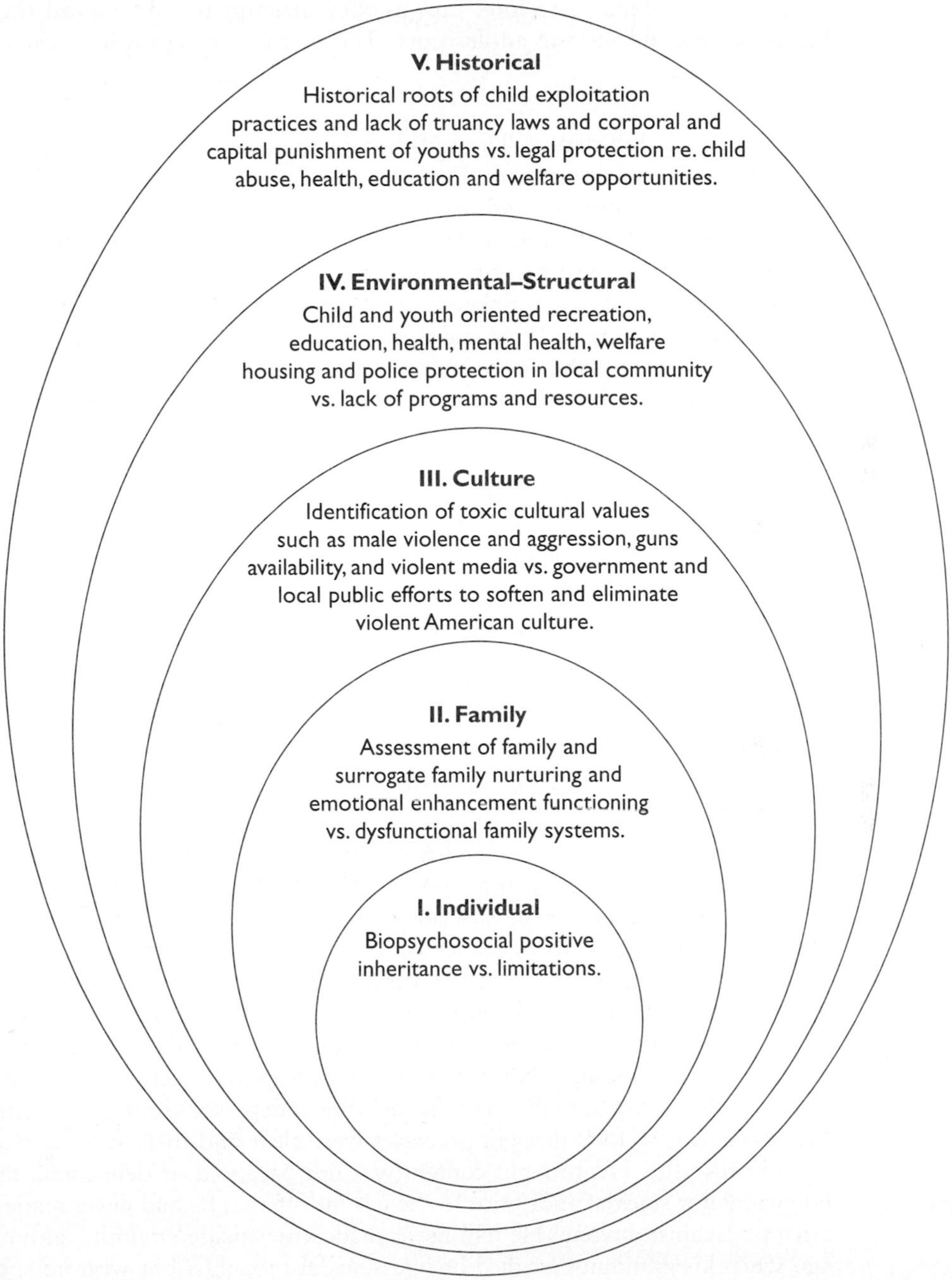

V. Historical

Historical roots of child exploitation practices and lack of truancy laws and corporal and capital punishment of youths vs. legal protection re. child abuse, health, education and welfare opportunities.

IV. Environmental–Structural

Child and youth oriented recreation, education, health, mental health, welfare housing and police protection in local community vs. lack of programs and resources.

III. Culture

Identification of toxic cultural values such as male violence and aggression, guns availability, and violent media vs. government and local public efforts to soften and eliminate violent American culture.

II. Family

Assessment of family and surrogate family nurturing and emotional enhancement functioning vs. dysfunctional family systems.

I. Individual

Biopsychosocial positive inheritance vs. limitations.

A Micro Case Analysis

The following represents a micro case composite to assist social workers in understanding what factors to look into as they attempt to understand the high-risk behavior of children and adolescents. The discussion will follow the ecosystems model format.

The High-Risk Behavior.   The high-risk behavioral problem in our case composite concerns a 17-year-old named "Joe," a biracial male who, upon being discovered in his girlfriend's apartment, hid in a closet while armed and shot through the door when called out by the police. He wounded one of the police officers. Upon the minor firing first, the officers (including the wounded officer) retaliated in self-defense and fired 20 shots through the door, of which twelve bullets hit Joe. Joe's explanation was simply, "I wanted them to kill me. I shot at them so they would kill me." Is this normal behavior for adolescents? Is this a form of homicide, suicide, or both? What factors led to this tragic confrontation, which resulted in the adolescent being tried as an adult for assault to commit murder upon police officers? Joe could join nearly 2 million other troubled people in prison in the United States whose high-risk behavior began in childhood and adolescence. To assist the court and jury in understanding the reasons for this behavior, a social worker was appointed by the court to address these issues.

The Individual.   Joe was interviewed in jail in English, which is his only language. He is of Anglo and African American descent, 6 feet 3 inches, very slim, about 143 pounds, and has light, olive-complexioned skin. He was dressed in the traditional bright orange jail clothing with one hand only showing out of his uniform. His right hand had been amputated as the result of wounds he received during his violent confrontation with the police. He exhibited excellent verbal skills and vocabulary and was of above average intelligence with an IQ of 118, although he dropped out of school in the eleventh grade. He had fifteen prior contacts with police since age eleven, most of these for minor offenses such as trespassing, running away, vandalism, curfew, and theft from a neighbor. His most serious offense previously was for stealing a car and reckless driving in this stolen vehicle while being pursued by the police.

During the entire interview, Joe was attentive, socially comfortable, and friendly, made good eye contact, was cooperative, and answered all questions without hesitation, even elaborating in some of his responses. He was well-oriented to time, person, place, and surroundings. No distortions in perceptions were noted, nor was there evidence of psychosis, hallucinations, delusions, depersonalization, or other perceptual disturbances. Joe's thought processes were clear and there was no evidence of a thought disorder. His thought content was not paranoid or delusional. He was not homicidal nor suicidal and, prior to the instant offense, he had never made homicidal attempts against anyone. He had never made any suicide attempts, although a year ago when his grandmother died he had suicidal thoughts, but with no specific plan.

Now, while in jail, he has had occasional suicidal ideation, but with the absence of a specific plan. No brain disorder symptoms were present. He has always had sleeping problems, going to bed very late and getting up very late in the morning, almost at noon. In jail he is required to get up early and go to bed early, but he still suffers from insomnia. He has a poor appetite, and while in jail he has lost 30 pounds in one year. The weight loss and sleep disturbance could be related to depression and trauma, which then become an important area for further assessment.

Depression can also be caused by alcohol and drugs. In Joe's case, it is seen that he began using alcohol at age 12 with regular use by age 13, usually two to three 40-ounce bottles of beer nightly. He smoked marijuana "like cigarettes." In his case, the marijuana lifted his depressed mood caused by the alcohol.

The Family.   Joe's parents were never married, although they always lived in the same city. They lived together for the first four or five years in a stormy relationship. The mother's parents never approved of her "being with a black man." The mother, age 34, a part-time waitress of Anglo American descent, gave birth to Joe when she was 16 years of age. She still lives with her parents. Teenage motherhood can place a child at high risk for future psychosocial problems. Joe's father, age 35, is of African American descent and is a periodically employed auto mechanic. He reports that he is an alcoholic, as are his parents and three brothers and sisters. Joe's mother also admits to an occasional drinking problem and has used cocaine in the past. She reports that her only brother is dying of alcoholism. Addiction and depression genes run in families and can be inherited. Joe received a double genetic loading of addiction genes from both sides of the family, which certainly contributed to his alcoholism.

Joe did not have a stable childhood and really was never happy. He cried often as a child and was always angry as he got older. He was raised by at least three family groups: first by his mother and father; later by his mother and her parents; and thereafter by his mother, at times by his father when his mother could not tolerate him, and in later adolescent years by his maternal grandparents. After his maternal grandmother died, he lived with his maternal grandfather. Discipline was inconsistent and confusing for Joe as a child and later as an adolescent. For punishment, his mother would make him stand in a closet for hours as a "time-out;" his grandparents felt sorry for him and did not set any limits or form of discipline; and his father spanked him and on occasions hit him with his fists to counterbalance the grandparents' permissiveness.

Culture.   Joe is multicultural, having absorbed both the positive and negative elements of African and Anglo American culture. Although his parents did not complete high school, they valued education and tried to persuade Joe to do his homework, even to the point of severely punishing him, which made him resent school, education, and authority even more. A "drinking culture" and an acceptance of firearms were valued by all three family units, and each family had firearms in the home. At times Joe would go target shooting with his mother or rabbit hunting with his father. Only the maternal grandparents attended church regularly—Joe's parents had different religions and they fought about which religion Joe should incorporate into his moral value system. The problem was "solved" by Joe not being exposed to any religion. Corporal punishment is also determined by the cultural values of a society. Joe's three family units believed in corporal punishment, but only the father actually used it. Joe felt that both the father's corporal punishment and the mother's lengthy time-outs were equally stressing.

Being raised in the U.S. culture that has embraced racism for centuries, it was especially painful for Joe as a child to hear his white grandparents' rejection of his father because he was "black." Some of the heated arguments between his parents involved the "race card," with the mother calling the father *nigger* and the father calling the mother "dirty white trash."

Such conflict in his early years contributed to an identity crisis in Joe; his mother recalls him frequently crying at home until nine or ten years of age, wishing he were "white." As he entered adolescence, he rejected the white in him, which he perceived as weakness, and instead accepted the "black" in him, which brought him power and respect. He began to dress in black-gang-oriented clothing, with *Raiders* logos. He founded a gang called the *HBRs* (Half-Breed Rainbows) comprised of biracial adolescent males (Japanese Anglos, Mexican Anglos, African American Anglos, Filipino Anglos, and American Indian-Anglos). Apparently, these biracial youths, or "half-breeds" as Joe preferred that they be called, were experiencing the same stresses and identity conflicts as Joe; together, they were a surrogate family.

Environmental–Structural Issues.   Joe's three family units resided in either white lower middle class or the poor African American community. Through elementary school, when living with his mother or grandparents, he was only one of just a handful of biracial children in a 95 percent plus white school. Almost on a daily basis, his mother reports that he would come home crying because the "white kids" called him *nigger*. It was not much better for him in the elementary school when he stayed with his father, because then he was rejected by the African American children because he was not "all black." When he formed his gang and dressed in black, he intimidated white high school students and earned some "respect." In the poor environment where juvenile gang culture was almost everywhere, it was not difficult to establish his gang. Frequent police harassment of gangs and Joe for being "black" only added to his defiance toward authority. Joe was never referred for counseling or mental health services in the middle-class community he was residing in, and these services did not exist in the African American section of town.

Historical Issues.   Joe received a sentence of 25 years to life in state prison for attempted murder of a police officer. Had he killed the officer, he would have automatically received the death penalty, because his state required this for the killing of a law enforcement official. Our penal code laws have evolved over a period of centuries for the protection of society and properly serve this function. Historically, Americans strongly believe in deterrence and the value of corporal punishment in meeting this end. It might work in some of the cases with the appropriate person! In other words, it is a practice that is risky, with no scientific proof that it does or does not work. Time-outs can also be harmful and psychologically torturing, as seen in Joe's case— again it depends on how it is perceived and felt by the recipient of the punishment.

Our historical values encourage firearms, drinking, and male assertiveness and masculinity. These factors were also very much present in this case. The centuries-old presence of white *and* black racism also played a significant role in this case. Joe was literally caught in the middle of this powerful, toxic, painful issue from birth up until the present. Historically, our nation finds it very difficult to have, as a budget priority, the provision of quality mental health services in poor communities, whether white or African American. The nation maintains a chronic indifference to the plight of the poor and prefers instead to spend billions of dollars on incarceration. In Joe's case, when he comes out of prison in 25 years, the government will have spent at least $1 million for his incarceration, and not one cent for prevention.

The Social Worker's Psychosocial Impressions. The social worker diagnosed Joe as suffering from a conduct disorder, adolescent type, alcohol and cannabis dependence in full remission because of incarceration, and a recurring major depression, moderate type without psychotic features. Current stressors adding to his depression include incarceration and the loss of his hand. The initial depression, which might have had a biological origin, was present since childhood and could also have been caused by trauma (corporal punishment and time-outs in a closet).

Perhaps the stressor that exacerbated his depression was the painful loss of his grandmother, who he felt was really his mother. Following this loss, he was very depressed and talked with friends about being killed in a shoot-out with rival gangs (suicide by gang) or the police (suicide by cop). Persons who are suicidal are ambivalent about dying. Prior to being shot, he was attempting to avoid a confrontation with police by hiding in the closet, which unconsciously also represented his old familiar chamber for punishment. However, the confrontation escalated, and he forced the police to shoot him (suicide by cop). Psychoanalytically, he was expressing his rage at his own parents (police) for all the punishment they had administered to him. Now he was seeking the ultimate punishment from these parent figures, death! The social worker recommended treatment for him, but neither the jail nor prison had these mental health resources available, because the primary goal of such facilities is detention and punishment.

A Macro Case Example

Although Joe clearly made decisions that negatively affected his life, he was also a victim of his genetic makeup, his family and environment, and the culture of U.S. society that tolerates racism and fails to actively prevent human problems. Like Joe, many children are highly vulnerable to social problems. Social workers are often involved in programs that provide treatment or rehabilitation for such children and youth.

Some children and youth, however, attempt to become part of the solution to human problems. It is not uncommon, for example, for a child to befriend an elderly neighbor, to develop a special caring relationship with a person experiencing a handicapping condition, or to become an active volunteer providing services in hospitals, schools, churches, or synagogues and in other forms of human services organizations.

Youth sometimes also become involved in the macro side of human services. Although human services agencies do not uniformly engage young people in making policy and program decisions, those that do—and particularly those programs that provide services to youth—find that the engagement of representatives of their consumers can lead to programs that are more relevant to today's youth. Just as effective school principals and teachers actively involve students and student organizations in important decisions about their schools, so too should social workers and human services agencies.

One macro function that supports human services that is frequently performed by children and youth has been fund-raising to support an agency cause. Children selling cookies, candy, and magazines to support schools and human services agencies have become an accepted part of U.S. society. Similarly, people are asked to pledge contributions for agencies based on a child's distance in running, skating, swimming, or biking. Certainly, children and youth have a great deal to contribute to society, particularly to the human services. Social workers and other human services providers too often overlook this important resource that cannot only enhance the services and also help tomorrow's adults prepare for their role as citizens.

Concluding Comment

Growing up in America as an infant, child, and adolescent can be stressful for many and deadly for a small number of young people, with traffic accidents, suicide, and homicide being the major causes for premature death. Poverty, ill health, lack of stimulation, inadequate housing, and other social problems can diminish the quality of life for many others. However, in spite of the many problems and barriers outlined in this chapter, almost 95 percent of our young people survive and become productive citizens.

For the social worker to be effective in his or her intervention with young clients and their families, in-depth knowledge about the issues they face is necessary. The ecosystems model can guide the worker in organizing the direction of the case inquiry so that the information is organized in a form relevant to an accurate assessment and helpful to the client. A detailed micro (or direct service) case was presented to help the reader to understand the many bio-psychosocial issues that may appear in one case and to identify the dynamic interplay of these factors. Effective macro interventions to address the lack of social and mental health services in poor communities, the absence of youth delinquency services, and the lack of attention paid by elementary, middle, and high schools to the prejudice, discrimination, and racism directed at very vulnerable children and adolescents, such as Joe, might have helped to prevent his situation.

In a very different form of macro intervention, social workers can play a vital role by involving young people in establishing and critiquing existing programs and policies, raising funds for social programs, and preparing for responsible citizenship. Perhaps social workers and others have done too little to engage youth in community activities, allowing the 5 percent who are troubled, destructive, or harmful to others to become inaccurately viewed as representative of the young people in the United States today.

KEY WORDS AND CONCEPTS

U.S. Children's Bureau
Child maltreatment
At-risk social behavior
Biracial children and adolescents

Biracial families
Reconstituted families
Corporal punishment
White and black racism

SUGGESTED INFORMATION SOURCES

Annie E. Casey Foundation, *2004 Kids Count Data Book: Moving Youth from Risk to Opportunity*, http://www.kidscount.org

Children's Defense Fund, http://www.childrensdefense.org

Hamilton, Stephen F. and Mary Agnes Hamilton, eds., *The Youth Development Handbook: Coming of Age in American Communities*. Thousand Oaks, CA: Sage Publications, 2004.

Health Resources and Services Administration, "National Survey of Children with Special Health Care Needs, http://mchb.hrsa.gov/chscn/index.htm

McWhirter, J. Jeffries, ed. *At-Risk Youth: A comprehensive Response*. Belmont, CA: Brooks/Cole, 2004.

National Institute of Child Health and Human Development, "National Children's Study: 2005," http://nationalchildrensstudy.gov/

Quinn, William H. *Family Solutions for Youth At Risk: Applications to Juvenile Delinquency, Truancy, and Behavior Problems*. New York: Brunner-Routledge, 2004.

ENDNOTES

1. Robert H. Bremner, *From the Depths: The Discovery of Poverty in the United States* (New York: New York University Press, 1969), pp. 204–229.
2. Robert Kominski, Amie Jamieson, and Gladys Martinez. "At-Risk Conditions of U.S. School-Age Children." U.S. Census Bureau. http://www.census.gov/population/www/documentation/twps0052.html
3. U.S. Census Bureau, *Poverty and Poverty Thresholds 2004*. http://www.census.gov/hhes/porerty/threshld/thresh04.html
4. U.S. Census Bureau, *Income, Poverty, and Health Insurance Coverage in the United States: 2003*. Table 1. http://www.census.gov/prod/2004pubs/p60–226.pdf
5. Eugene M. Lewitt, Donna L. Terman, and Richard E. Behrman, "Children and Poverty: Analysis and Recommendations," in Richard E. Behrman ed., *The Future of Children: Children and Poverty* (Los Altos, CA: Center for the Future of Children, 1997), p. 8.
6. John R. Kearnsey, Herman F. Grundmann, and Salvatore J. Gallicchio, "The Influence of Social Security Benefits and SSI Payments on the Poverty of Children." *Social Security Bulletin 57* (Summer 1994): 27–38.
7. U.S. Census Bureau, *Education and Annual Earning Power: 2001*. http://www.census.gov/Press-Release/www/releases/archives/education/004214.html
8. Administration for Children and Families, *Child Maltreatment: 2003*, U.S. Department of Health and Human Services, http://www.acf.hhs.gov/programs/cb/publications/cm03/cm2003.pdf

chapter 18

Social Work Practice with Older Americans

Manuel R. Miranda, Armando T. Morales,

and Bradford W. Sheafor

Prefatory Comment

The most rapidly growing segment of the U.S. population is its older people. Estimated at 35 million people in 2000, the number of older Americans is expected to increase to more than 71.5 million in 2030 and to nearly 87 million in 2050. Even more dramatically, the population age 85 and over is expected to increase five-fold from 2000 to 2050. Although many older Americans are healthy, active, and productive, many face declining physical and mental health, erosion of financial resources, and loss of friends and family. Drs. Manuel Miranda (California State University, Los Angeles), Armando Morales (University of California, Los Angeles), and Bradford W. Sheafor (Colorado State University) examine the significant role social workers can perform in assisting older people as they deal with the common issues of aging. The chapter includes a case example involving an elderly couple that demonstrates how micro- and macro-level practice can benefit older clients.

Many older people enjoy good health, positive interaction with friends and family, and have adequate income to help achieve a favorable quality of life. Yet, the phrase "old age isn't for sissies" reveals the inevitable decline in social, physical, and emotional conditions people experience as they approach the ending phase of the life cycle. This period of life typically involves a series of transitions: from enjoying an active and healthy lifestyle to dealing with accumulating health conditions that may be limiting or even life-threatening; from meaningful employment and adequate income to retirement and sharply reduced financial resources; and from being surrounded by an intimate group of family and friends to increasing loneliness created by a declining set of loved ones as illness and death take their toll. These transitions take place at different rates and with different degrees of problems for each individual. We are buoyed by visions of successful athletes in the

"Senior Olympics," and saddened by reports that the highest suicide rate of all people in the United States is among males ages 65 and over. The roles for social workers in working with elderly people along this continuum from the healthy to the frail are many and varied—but all are important.

Population demographics indicate that social work practice with older people is likely to be the social work profession's most substantial growth industry. While this population has been growing in both numbers and as a portion of the U.S. population for more than a century, as the "baby boomers," sometimes referred to as "senior boomers," begin to reach this age the demand for social work services will expand even more rapidly. Further, people now live substantially longer and thus the population of older people will inevitably grow even more rapidly. For example, a person born in 1900 was expected to live an average of 47.3 years; by 2002 that expected life span had increased by 30 years—to 77.3 years.[1] The result of this growth in the number of older people is the associated demand for a variety of health and human services.

Indicators of Social and Economic Well-Being

The elderly population increased more than eleven-fold from 1900 to 2000, compared to only a three-fold increase for those under age 65, and now includes over 35 million people. That number is projected to increase to 40.2 million by 2010, 71.5 million by 2030, and to reach 86.7 million by mid-century. This 12.4 percent of the total U.S. population in 2000 is projected to become 20.6 percent in 2050. Further, the 85 and over population that draws most heavily on social workers and human services is increasing even more dramatically. The 4.2 million people 85 years and older identified in the 2000 U.S. Census is expected to double by 2030 and to reach 21.0 million people—or 5 percent of the U.S. population, by 2050.[2] Indeed, the demand for new social programs and social workers prepared to address the needs of this increasingly frail population inevitably will increase.

Women live an average of five years longer than men and make up 58 percent of the age 65 and over population and 69 percent of those age 85 and over.[3] Because women are more likely to survive to the oldest ages, the problems of the oldest-old are primarily the problems of women. Because of the increased life expectancy for women, they are much more likely to spend part of their older years as widows living alone (i.e., in 2003, 54 percent of the women age 75 and older lived alone, as compared to only 23 percent of the men[4]) and often without the benefit of pension income from the husband's employment that was characteristically the primary retirement income source for that generation. This fact requires a significant shift in existing income maintenance, health care, and other social programs to address the needs of elderly women more adequately.

Due to adverse social conditions for African Americans (and other minority population groups) in the United States, the white population lives an average of five years longer than African Americans.[5] However, whites will decline as a percentage of older people—from an estimated 83 percent in 2003 to a projected 61 percent in

2050. Among the minority racial groups, the Hispanic population is expected to triple by 2050 (from 6 percent to 18 percent of the older population), and the black and Asian groups are also expected to show substantial growth.[6] The need for culturally relevant programs for seniors will increase dramatically during this period, and social workers with Spanish language facility will no doubt be in increased demand.

The average income in 2003 for households headed by older persons was much less than for households of persons under age 65—$23,787 as compared to $50,171.[7] Poverty rates, however, reflect an adjustment for family size, and the poverty rate for older people (i.e., 10.2 percent) in 2003 was slightly below that of the total population (12.5 percent). Given that the poverty rate for older people was higher in 1959 (35.0 percent), the effort to reduce poverty among older people through Social Security, Medicare, prescription assistance, senior housing, and other programs indicates that if political forces can be activated to address a social problem, dramatic results can follow. Nevertheless, poverty among older adults has not been eliminated, and more than 3.6 million older people continue to live at or below the poverty line. Thus many older people experience economic vulnerability.[8]

Like other age groups, the wealth is unevenly distributed, and among the elderly the very wealthy are becoming even wealthier. Although the percent of older people living in poverty was reduced by 4.2 percent between the years 1974 and 2002, during that period the percent of older people with high income increased by 8.0 percent.[9] Further, the increase in income among older people was disproportionately related to the white population, where between 1984 and 2001 there was an increase of over 81 percent, while the comparable black population experienced only a 60 percent increase. More importantly, the median net worth of an older white household ($205,000) was five times larger than for older black households ($ 41,000).[10] Although it is not realistic to expect equal income distribution among the various population groups in a capitalistic society such as the United States, clearly there are factors of systematic bias in this culture that disadvantages certain population groups—and the condition is not improving over time.

Where do older people get their income? The importance of Social Security as an income source for many older people is evident in the fact that 39 percent of their total income is from that source, with earnings generating 25 percent, pensions 19 percent, income from assets held by the older people 14 percent, and other income sources 3 percent. A comparison of the income sources for the lowest one-fifth of the older population and the highest one-fifth (see Table 18.1) reveals why there is relative disinterest among the powerful high-income population for support of Social Security and public assistance, as these programs have relatively little direct effect on the wealthy older people.[11]

When income is inadequate for older people, full- or part-time employment provides a way to supplement one's income. Employment, however, is often dependent on a person's educational level—particularly if the older person is not able to engage in physically demanding labor. Over the past fifty years, there has been a substantial change in the educational background of older people. In 1950, for example, only 17 percent of the population had as much as a high school diploma or more, and only 3 percent had a college degree. In 2003 more than 72 percent of

Table 18.1

Income Sources for Highest and Lowest Quintile of Older People

Income Source	Lowest 1/5th	Highest 1/5th
Social Security	82.6%	19.8%
Public Assistance	8.9	0.1
Pensions	3.5	20.4
Asset income	2.4	8.9
Earnings	1.1	38.4
Other	1.5	2.4

the older population had completed a high school degree or more, and 17 percent had at least a bachelor's degree. Again, there is substantial disparity among the racial and ethnic groups. Where 76 percent of the white and 70 percent of the Asian members of the older population had completed high school or more, only 52 percent of the black and 36 percent of the Hispanic older population had achieved that educational level.[12] Thus the chance for black and Hispanic older people to compete for jobs is limited by educational attainment.

Indicators of Health

Often the emphasis on the health problems experienced by older people masks the fact that most older people consider themselves to be healthy and vibrant participants in life. In a survey conducted by the Centers for Disease Control and Prevention, 73 percent of the people age 65 and over rated their health as good to excellent relative to others their age. Health statistics, like other indicators of well-being, reflect the toll of adverse social conditions on minority groups. Where there was a positive health assessment by 76 percent of the older white population, that was true for only 59 percent of the black and 63 percent of the Hispanic older Americans.[13] As opposed to prevailing perceptions about the clients and activities involved in gerontological social work, much of this practice involves helping older people improve the quality of their lives through social and recreational activities, as well as preventing and/or adapting to declining health.

The positive attitude many older people report regarding their health, however, should not minimize the fact that many older people experience one or more chronic health conditions and that the costs of health care for older people is a major factor in the soaring health care expenditures in the United States. Chronic health problems and sensory impairments increasingly affect people as they get older and affect men and women at different rates. The following list reveals the incidence of a selected set of physically and socially limiting health conditions for persons age 65 and older.[14]

Table 18.2

Physical Problems Explained by Older Men and Women

Physical Condition	Men	Women
Hypertension	47%	52%
Trouble hearing	47	30
Heart disease	37	27
Arthritic symptoms	31	39
Obesity	30	32
No natural teeth	26	29
Cancer	25	18
Diabetes	18	14
Trouble seeing	16	19

Social workers employed in nursing homes, hospitals, and other health-related human service agencies must be knowledgeable about the limitations in social functioning associated with these conditions.

Mental health problems, too, plague older people. Moderate to severe memory impairment, including Alzheimer's disease, affects 15 percent of the men and 11 percent of women age 65 and older, and clinically relevant depressive symptoms are evident in 11 percent of the men and 18 percent of the women. These factors increase among the oldest part of this age group: at age 85 and older, one-third of both the men and women have moderate to severe memory loss, and the depressive symptoms increase to 15 percent for men and 22 percent for women.[15] The problems of older people is one of the most neglected areas in the field of mental health in the United States and demands more research and knowledge/skill development among social workers. Nevertheless, social workers in many settings, including nursing homes, mental health centers, and psychiatric hospitals, can expect to work with older people experiencing mental health issues.

Physical and mental health problems among older people are costly. Payments to physicians, hospitals, and prescription drugs are major expenses for older people. The average cost for health care per year in 2001 for persons age 65 and over was $10,948. For low-income people who typically do not have adequate health insurance and thus neglect prevention and early intervention with health problems, the average cost was $14,692. People with no chronic conditions incurred only an average of $3,837 in health costs as compared to those with five or more conditions generating $15,784 in total costs. If a person was required to have care in a nursing home or other institution, the cost increased to $46,810 per year.[16] These expenditures are not only a drain on the affected individuals, but on the U.S. economy as a whole.

Ecosystems Model Analysis

The ecosystems model developed for this volume by its authors provides a useful analytic scheme for the social worker wanting to learn more about the practice demands when working with older people. By examining aging from the various perspectives defined in the model (i.e., historical, environmental, cultural, family, and individual) an understanding of the complex needs of this population emerges.

Historical Factors

The diseases of the aged, the quality of their lives, their ability and willingness to care for themselves, their capacity to cope with stress—all these are shaped not only by individual histories, such as hereditary and early family life, but also by the society in which the aged people lived as they were growing up. What were work conditions like? What was family life like? What social services were provided? Were there economic calamities, such as a severe depression?

Certainly, the milieu of today's aged is very different from that in 1900. There were fewer aged then, both in absolute numbers and as a percentage of the total population: 4 percent in 1900 (3 million) versus 12.4 percent in 2000 (35 million). Work was usually a lifetime affair in 1900, with formal retirement and a pension an oddity. Today, work is more a stage of life, one that is increasingly entered at an older age and left at a younger one. Social Security is now usual, with two pensions per retiree becoming more frequent.

Less quantifiable changes have also occurred. The belief that the aged are the fittest survivors and the mystiques of old age as a time when cares are gone were shattered early in the twentieth century as the realities of the lives of many of the aged became more widely known. Poverty was often the reward of a lifetime of labor, since there were no pensions and no room for elderly workers in an increasingly efficiency-conscious industrial society. Illnesses often went untreated, either because the older people could not afford to pay, because illness was considered inevitable in old age, or because the medical profession preferred to treat the problems of younger people.

In the early twentieth century, with public support perceived as charity, with poorhouses and homes for the aged usually considered nothing more than warehouses for the unfit and the dying, with steady employment uncertain, and often with parents and older children all working, the family was essential for survival. Grandparents, parents, and children assumed various roles in ensuring the integrity and well-being of the family. The elderly maintained their property rights, in part as insurance that they would always be cared for. There was no clear distinction between family life and work; no formal retirement age.

The elderly today reflect different experiences. Various forces on the family—social legislation giving individuals more independence and greater mobility, more emphasis within the family on raising children, and more mothers working outside the home—have distorted the traditional interdependencies between the elderly and their children and grandchildren. The Great Depression left its economic and psychological scars. A lifetime of relatively low earning now shows up as relatively low pensions for many of the elderly. The family today is radically different from what it was thirty-five years ago, and there is evidence of further forces for change. For example, single-parent families have become a significant phenomenon. Also, the proportion of families living with a relative such as a grandparent (extended families) has dropped appreciably in the past fifty years, and the majority of mothers now work or seek work outside the home when their children reach school age.

The needs and demands of the future aged will be different from those of today, but we are uncertain of what those differences will be. Many of the future older people will be better educated. Their Social Security pensions, increasingly supplemented by a second pension, should enable them to sustain a tolerable standard of living, although paradoxically the gap between their employment earnings and their pensions may be greater than it is for many of today's aged.

All in all, an understanding of the terrain in which the aged have lived and are living is needed if the field of social work is to perform its task of providing the information and insight needed by society to optimally serve its current and future aged.

Environmental–Structural Factors

How do the elderly maximize the quality of their lives? What perceptions do different groups of the elderly have of their lives—of health, of their status in society, of their regard to younger people? How are these perceptions formed, and what do they imply about the services needed by the aged? How do these perceptions square with their needs as seen by others? How does this pattern of life prepare the individual for retirement, for the change in income and often in status that may accompany it? How does the individual who has worked for thirty or forty years find new values to replace economic ones?

Infusing these and other questions pertaining to the aged in society are attitudes toward the aged and aging—attitudes held by the aged themselves and by the younger population. Prejudice against the aged—*ageism*—is displayed in several ways: (1) in our obsession with youth (although that may wane as the average age continues to rise); (2) in the emphasis by the media on extraordinary achievements of the aged, rather than on their ordinary, often satisfying lives; and (3) in the poor general understanding of the contributions older people can make to society.

Anthropologists have found that the aged are regarded differently in different cultures. Views of the aged widely held in Western societies, including the notion that the old have little to contribute to society, are not shared by other societies. Bias against the old is not inevitable; rather, it is shaped by various, only partly known forces.

One important element affecting the Western attitude toward the elderly and becoming old is the materialistic economic valuation of human worth—how much money a person makes, how big his or her house is, how valuable are his or her material possessions. In retirement, income drops markedly for most Americans, and there may be the false perception that with retirement one's income is no longer determined by work, but by pension policies. Such changes in level and source of income may result in a loss of esteem among the elderly.

In addition to ageism and the potential loss of status as a result of reduced income with retirement, the elderly generally face a number of additional stresses during the later years of life. As stated by Butler and Lewis, "The elderly are confronted by multiple losses, which may occur simultaneously: death of a partner, older friends, colleagues, relatives; decline of physical health and coming to personal terms with death; loss of status, prestige, and participation in society; and for large numbers of the older population, additional burdens of marginal living standards."[17]

The process of aging, even in the absence of health problems or loss, can be acutely distressing. Confusion and uncertainty confront the elderly as they attempt to deal with the variety of changes accompanying the aging process. Some of these changes occur slowly, such as physical appearance and social status, whereas others occur much more dramatically, such as catastrophic health problems or forced retirement. The process of aging should be visualized as a continuous stream of changes occurring within an environmental–structural setting that more or less dictates how the changes will affect the elderly. The increasing unpredictability and loss of physical and/or mental control accompanying aging, plus the inevitability of death, contribute to making this life stage one of considerable difficulty.

The sensitivity of one's environment in responding to the multitude of physical, economic, and social needs accompanying old age symbolizes its valuation of its elderly population. The diseases of the aged, the quality of their lives, their ability and willingness to care for themselves, their capacity to cope with stress—all these are shaped not only by individual histories, but also by the environmental–structural setting in which the elderly live. Social workers must advocate for more effective policies, planning for the future, enabling both society and the elderly to make optimum use of available resources and, above all, enriching the lives of the elderly.

Culture

The question as to whether an elderly culture exists remains unclear in the social science literature. Seeking to identify comparability to other minorities, such as ethnic or racial subgroups, as well as other age groups (e.g., teenagers), is seen by some researchers as inappropriate because of the special role of the aged in our society. This can be noted in the following excerpt:

> The aged do not share a distinct and separated culture; membership in the group defined as "aged" is not exclusive and permanent, but awaits all members of our society who live long enough. As a result, age is a less distinguishable group characteristic than others such as sex, occupation, social class, and the like. True, many aged persons possess distinctive physical characteristics. But even here there is a broad spectrum, and these "stigmata" do not normally justify differential and discriminatory treatment by others.[18]

With the rapid increase in the number of individuals 65 years of age and older, as well as the dramatic rise in their percentage of the general population, the social and political visibility of the elderly has never been higher. A multitude of political, economic, and social organizations representing the elderly have developed, forcing an increased focus on both social service and political action. The tremendous heterogeneity among our elderly (e.g., race, ethnicity, economic status, health, sex, education level, and geographic location) makes it quite difficult to think of them as an age-segregated subculture.

It would seem more appropriate to think of the elderly as a group with many common concerns related to their physical, social, and economic status; and that our social service delivery systems should become more cognizant of these needs in developing effective intervention modalities. The fact that the elderly are often economically vulnerable and beset with health and social problems are factors associated with the aging process, as opposed to cultural organization or process. The concept of a distinct subpopulation, however, does assist in the reorganization and development of social policy, planning, and service delivery.

Family Issues

With the increase in life expectancy, separate generations of children, parents, and grandparents will share such experiences of adulthood as work, parenthood, and even retirement. The fact that contemporary parents and children will spend a greater proportion of their lives together as adults than ever before in history speaks directly to the opportunity to form deep bonds of rapport and empathy. In addition, with reduced fertility rates, there are fewer individuals within the family network, thus affording the opportunity for not only a more extensive intergenerational network but a more intensive one as well.

As a result of the reduction in fertility, our society is currently confronted with a situation in which, for the first time in history, the average family has more parents than children.[19] With a significant reduction in the number of childbearing years, as well as a reduction in the number of years between the first- and last-born child, generation demarcations have become clearer. For most women, the active years of child raising are over by the time they become grandmothers. And with the extension of life, grandparents are now typically living independently of their children for twenty-five years or more. The implications of this are not totally clear, but serving as some familial stabilizing force due to their experience, wisdom, and economic resources is a distinct possibility.

The elderly are frequently portrayed as a frail and dependent group who create a drain on our national resources and are a strain on family caregiving. There is no doubt that the oldest-old, those 85 and above, are in greater need of medical assistance and long-term care. Meeting the physical and social needs of our rapidly growing oldest-old represents one of the major social welfare concerns of the future. However, there are a vast number of our elderly who are healthy, independent, and willing to contribute to the enhancement of their families' well-being. In fact, available research indicates that the elderly in industrialized societies tend to give more economic assistance than they receive.[20]

The ability of the elderly to serve as a "safety valve" within the family network can express itself in a variety of ways. They sometimes serve as arbitrators between their children and grandchildren, specifically assisting grandchildren in understanding parental responsibilities, as well as give economic backup during the usual family problems of home ownership, educational expenses for children and grandchildren, and unexpected financial burdens. With the increasing number of separations, divorces, and single-parent households, grandparents are frequently called on to serve as stress buffers for their children, as well as serving as substitute parents for their grandchildren (i.e., in 2002 the U.S. Census Bureau estimated that 1.8 percent of all children lived with their grandparents).[21]

Clearly, the changing roles of the elderly in family life include an increasing degree of multigenerational networking. The opportunities for more extensive and intensive bonding within families in an aging population could provide the basis for the strengthened interdependency necessary for meeting an individual's needs in the final decades of the life cycle.

Individual Issues

Self-concept among the aged has shown some interesting changes throughout history. In preindustrial eras, the elderly generally enjoyed revered status, although their numbers were much smaller than is the case today. With the advent of the industrial and post-industrial eras, however, the value placed on accumulated historical knowledge and experience has given way to innovation, creativity, and productivity. At this point, the elderly were increasingly perceived as outdated, a burden on society's overall economic development. Over time, more and more employers developed strategies to remove older individuals from the workforce with early retirement incentives or outright dismissal. As a consequence, the perception of growing old frequently implied being unproductive, not retrainable, and physically incapable. Many of the elderly accepted these negative stereotypes, thus creating a diminished sense of self-worth and low motivation to continue to engage society in a meaningful manner.

With the increased life span of our population, these negative stereotypes are beginning to change. What it means to be 65 and older in today's society differs significantly from what it meant in earlier periods. The majority of those over 65 today are healthy, youthful in outlook, and willing to remain actively involved in the world of work, family, and community affairs. Clearly, the elderly in contemporary society are redefining the concept of being old, particularly as it applies to societal norms of age-appropriate behavior. Old age should be seen as a fluid concept, defined by the traits and abilities of each generation as it becomes older, not determined by past expectations and norms. Perhaps for the specific *individual*, being "old" is more related to "lifestyle" or "attitude" rather than chronological age. For example, a 40-year-old "couch potato" might be older *mentally* than a 65-year-old who jogs, roller skates, plays the guitar and keyboard, and is raising a 2-year-old daughter or grandchild.

With better health and independence in the later stages of life, becoming 65 does not have to begin a period of withdrawal and decline. On the contrary, this period of the life cycle should represent the opportunity for renewal, with the development of new skills and goals for leading a productive life. Being productive does not necessarily imply working full time. Many of today's elderly seek part-time employment and/or volunteer work. Never before has there been such a need to keep our older individuals actively involved in our society. Likewise, with the lengthening of their lives, the elderly in turn need more than ever to remain meaningfully engaged in productive activity. The development of opportunities in our society that contribute to a continuing sense of self-worth and overall good health among our elderly citizens is a challenge for social workers and our human services agencies.

Intervention Strategies with Older People

The ecosystems model provides an excellent framework for the development of both macro and micro practice with the elderly. The inclusion of a set of factors representing the internal as well as external influences on the elderly client provides the necessary guide in structuring an effective intervention strategy. In addition, the profession of social work, with its values and interactional approach, is ideally suited to effectively serve our elderly population. With the variety of changes and needs confronting the elderly client (e.g., financial stability, acute and long-term health care needs, adequate housing, loss of a spouse and other family members, etc.), a profession such as social work, with its focus on making changes in the environment as well as within the individual, provides the necessary practice base for effectively developing intervention strategies.

As a field of practice, the profession of social work has enjoyed a longer period of involvement with the elderly than other practice professions.[22] However, social work, as is the case with other professions, is frequently guilty of ageism. Butler has defined *ageism* as a "process of systematic stereotyping of and discrimination against people because they are old, just as racism and sexism accomplish this with skin color and gender. Old people are categorized as senile, rigid in thought and manner, old-fashioned in morality and skills."[23] The categorization of all elderly by a simple set of stereotypes leads to their exclusion from the more advanced techniques of social, mental, and physical health interventions and has generally left them excluded from both public and private mental health settings.[24] The great diversity among our elderly in terms of health, income, and educational, occupational, and familial status should immediately disallow any simplistic perception of who they are and what we can do for them. Although their health status may be more vulnerable, the elderly are more often than not very much as they were during earlier periods of their life cycle.

In general, the development of any intervention strategy for the elderly, whether macro or micro, should have as its basic objectives: (1) the promotion of independence to the maximum degree possible; (2) the assistance in obtaining the necessary resources for the maintenance of a good quality of life; (3) the facilitation of effective interaction between the elderly and others in their environment; and (4) the influencing of the development of social policy enhancing the elderly's lives. As noted by Cantor, "Basic to the concept of social care is the notion that assistance is provided as means of augmenting individual competency and mastery of the environment, rather than increasing dependency."[25] With these premises in mind, mental health services for the elderly will be discussed, accompanied by an example of a macro and micro intervention.

Micro Practice with the Elderly

What follows is a case example of social work practice with elderly clients. It highlights the special nature of the elderly's problems, which at times require a different intervention response from social workers than would be so with younger clients.

BACKGROUND

Mr. and Mrs. Soto, age 75 and 73, respectively, are an elderly Mexican American couple living in a lower-income Hispanic section of El Paso, Texas. Mr. Soto, who had six years of formal education, came to the United States as an immigrant laborer in his early twenties. He eventually settled in El Paso as a laborer with the Southern Pacific Railroad. Mrs. Soto, who also had six years of formal education, was raised as an orphan in Northern Mexico and immigrated to Los Angeles with an older sister in her late teens. The couple met in El Paso, married, and raised two sons and a daughter. The eldest son was killed in Vietnam, leaving the second-born daughter and the younger son.

STRAINED FAMILY RELATIONSHIPS

While the Sotos had a close and caring relationship, their children experienced severe difficulties with the acculturation process. Their daughter became pregnant in her middle teens, dropped out of high school, and eventually married.

Their son was heavily involved in gang activities as a youth and was in and out of the penal system. The son "grew out" of gang activities and now is supporting a wife and three children as a mechanic in a local El Paso auto shop. As a result of the children's problems during their earlier years, the relationship between Mr. Soto and his children is seriously strained. The son feels particularly rejected by his father, believing that he always favored the eldest son who was killed in Vietnam. In the early years, Mrs. Soto frequently attempted to intervene on behalf of her adolescent children, but was generally forced to accept Mr. Soto's negative perception of his children's behavior and lifestyle. Mr. Soto has not spoken with his daughter in over five years, and only rarely visits his son on holidays or special occasions. Mrs. Soto has maintained telephone contact with both of her children.

CULTURAL FACTORS

Although Mr. and Mrs. Soto are bilingual, they have always felt more comfortable speaking Spanish. Since Mr. Soto's retirement seven years ago, the couple has spoken Spanish almost exclusively. Neither has been actively involved in the political or social life of the community. They have been content during their married life to regularly attend the local Catholic church, as well as annual cultural events marking significant Mexican holidays. Both have always been actively involved in their garden on weekends, being proud of their skills. On retirement, Mr. Soto also began spending a couple of afternoons during the week at a social club developed for retirees (mostly Hispanic) by the Southern Pacific Railroad.

HEALTH CRISIS CHANGING TRADITIONAL ROLES

Mrs. Soto's activities mainly consisted of taking care of her husband, talking to her children and grandchildren on the telephone, maintaining her garden, and attending church on the weekends. Over a five-year period, Mrs. Soto's visits to the local comprehensive health clinic became more frequent because she suffered from osteoporosis and had fractured her hip in a fall six months before. Following two months of hospitalization, she was released to be cared for at home by her husband.

After fifty-one years of marriage, Mr. Soto was now placed in the position of being the caregiver instead of the care receiver. While at first assuring his wife and hospital staff that he could manage her care on his own, Mrs. Soto's minimal hearing and limited mobility began to overwhelm him. He began to feel guilty about his anger at her dependency and too proud to accept his estranged daughter's request that she be allowed to help out. Mr. Soto's son was having severe difficulties meeting his own family's needs and wasn't sure how to approach his father to offer whatever help he could give. Mr. Soto also was not particularly good in providing clarity to his son as to how he could assist.

PHYSICAL AND EMOTIONAL DECOMPENSATION

As the months passed and his wife's condition did not improve, Mr. Soto became withdrawn and depressed. Mrs. Soto had regressed to the point of requiring her husband's assistance in bathing and toilet needs. He found these activities particularly distasteful and became increasingly impatient with his wife's requests. Sensing her husband's discomfort and feeling increasingly guilty about her dependency, Mrs. Soto attempted to take care of her own toilet needs and fell, fracturing her hip. She was immediately re-hospitalized, with a prognosis of long-term nursing home care. She went home temporarily, awaiting Mr. Soto's decision.

LIMITED RESOURCES

The hospital social worker informed Mr. Soto that nursing home care would cost approximately $46,000 per year. Considering that Mr. Soto's total yearly income from his railroad pension and Social Security came to approximately $28,000, placing his wife in a private nursing home was out of the question. Because Mr. Soto, a homeowner, was not sufficiently impoverished to qualify for Medicaid, his only alternatives were to attempt to care for his wife in their home again, or spend down to the poverty level required to qualify for Medicaid. Neither of Mr. Soto's children was in a position to help financially. With their Medicare eligibility quickly reaching its limits, Mr. Soto became increasingly despondent. He stopped answering his telephone. Following a telephone call from the hospital social worker, Mr. Soto's son went to his father's home to find him in a deeply depressed state and cognitively disoriented. He kept mentioning that there was no hope and that both he and his wife would be better off dead, as they were now useless and of no benefit to society. "Ni para que vivir," Mr. Soto remarked.* Hearing this frightened the son, who the following day called his old parole officer asking for advice. The parole officer referred the son to the local community mental health program.

THE INITIAL PLEA FOR HELP

The son phoned the El Paso Community Mental Health Center (EPCMHC) and spoke to the intake worker, who in turn referred him to Ms. Lewis, a 27-year-old Anglo social worker. The son explained his father's situation and the fact that he wanted to die. Ms. Lewis explained that she did not speak Spanish and asked if the father spoke English. She was assured that the father spoke English but was more fluent in Spanish. Because the only Spanish-speaking therapist at the EPCMHC was already overextended with Spanish-speaking clients, and, because of the urgency of the case, Ms. Lewis decided to accept the case herself. Ms. Lewis asked the son to have his father call for an appointment.

CLIENT, WORKER, INTERVENTION MODEL, AND AGENCY RESISTANCE

The following day the son reported to Ms. Lewis that he had talked to his father but that his father did not want to see Ms. Lewis because he was not crazy. Ms. Lewis did not want to see the father unless he was motivated to ask for help. The son was very worried about his parents and pleaded with Ms. Lewis to visit his father at home. Ms. Lewis thought to herself that this would be counterproductive, might stimulate transference, and might be considered overidentifying with the client. Furthermore, the agency frowned on home visits. The son by now was near tears and was pleading for Ms. Lewis's help. Finally Ms. Lewis stated that she would make an exception to visit the father at home, if he agreed to join her for the visit. Sighing with relief, the son agreed.

VISITING THE INVOLUNTARY CLIENT

The son and Ms. Lewis arrived at the home unannounced, and the father seemed annoyed and made a comment in Spanish to the son. The son appeared to be pleading with the father. The mother's voice from the bedroom inquired as to what was going on. The son replied that he had asked Ms. Lewis to come over to see if she could be of some help. Mrs. Soto invited Ms. Lewis to the bedroom, and at this point the father criticized the son's bad manners and asked him to prepare coffee and Mexican bread for their guest. Mr. Soto observed how well Mrs. Soto and Ms. Lewis were interacting and began to smile, seeing how responsive his wife was. Ms. Lewis then involved the husband in the conversation and remarked in a supportive, concerned way that their life had certainly changed since Mr. Soto's retirement and Mrs. Soto's physical injuries. The son was standing at the door listening, prompting the father to reestablish his position of authority by asking his adult son not to listen in on "grown-up conversations." The son smiled and thanked Ms. Lewis for visiting the parents, adding that he had to return to work.

---

*In Spanish, "Ni para que vivir" means: There is no reason to live.

TRANSFORMING THE INVOLUNTARY CLIENT INTO A VOLUNTARY CLIENT

Ms. Lewis did not want to stay long, as she did not want to impose on the Sotos. She excused herself, stating she had to return to the office. Mr. Soto offered to walk Ms. Lewis to her car, commenting on how much she had helped his wife and made her smile again. Ms. Lewis said she noticed that he also had been smiling at times and wondered whether he sometimes felt lonely, isolated, unsupported, and overwhelmed with all of his responsibilities. He nodded in agreement. Ms. Lewis, handing her card to Mr. Soto, stated that if he wanted to talk more about these matters, he could phone her. He looked at the card, replied that he was not crazy, and said he had heard they saw "locos" at her clinic. Ms. Lewis stated that they did see a few people who needed medication to help them think more clearly, but that the majority of people were just like him and everybody else—struggling with problems of daily living.

ENGAGEMENT PHASE

A few days later Mr. Soto phoned for an appointment to see Ms. Lewis. Although he kept his first appointment, he was a little nervous and mostly spoke about his wife and her problems. He did not want his wife to know he was visiting Ms. Lewis. In the initial interviews Ms. Lewis assumed a tactful, supportive approach, not wanting to frighten or embarrass Mr. Soto. She observed him to be depressed and asked whether there were times when he just wanted to give up and run away. He became serious as his eyes reddened, stating firmly that he never would run away from anything, as a man always faces his responsibilities. The following week Mr. Soto stated that he wondered if not wanting to live, or wanting to die, was a form of running away. Ms. Lewis explored this further and made a determination that Mr. Soto had suicidal thoughts, but was not suicidal, as he did not have a specific suicide plan or give indications of a major depression. Ms. Lewis assured Mr. Soto that his depression was in response to his wife's physical condition. He denied this, stating that it was due "to other things," but would not elaborate, adding that she just would not understand.

TRANSFERENCE AND COUNTERTRANSFERENCE

The following week Ms. Lewis explored what Mr. Soto had meant about "other things." He became annoyed (transference), stating that she was too young to know, probably not married, and that this was something related to men and she could not help. Ms. Lewis became defensive (countertransference), stating that she was not too young, was married, had children, and knew something about male impotence. Mr. Soto was not familiar with the word impotence. Ms. Lewis, red-faced and in a clumsy manner, tried to explain what impotence was, using her index finger to demonstrate. Mr. Soto burst out laughing, stating that it had never happened to him, and that young Ms. Lewis looked funny explaining this to a man with sixty-three years of sexual experience. Ms. Lewis became aware of her embarrassment, anger, and anxiety, and recalled how once her own father had tried to speak with her about sex when she was a young adolescent. She also became aware of the fact that she was perhaps stereotyping Mr. Soto as an old man who had lost his sexual ability and desire.

CULTURE VERSUS SITUATION

This brief emotional confrontation "broke the ice," as Ms. Lewis by now was also laughing, pointing to her finger. She then said, "Really, tell me what is happening." Mr. Soto stated that he had always had a big sexual appetite but that since the injuries of his wife, she was not able to meet his sexual needs. He stated that he had taken younger women that he was meeting at the retirement club out for sex. Initially he enjoyed this, but then he began feeling guilty because it was against his religious and cultural beliefs. He was feeling unfaithful to his ill wife. The more he did this, the worse he felt, and he was unable to face her. Ms. Lewis had initially thought that Mr. Soto's "fooling around" was simply a Latin cultural requirement for males, but now realized that Mr. Soto was an honorable, religious man who was ashamed of his unfaithfulness. Ms. Lewis reminded him about how she had once raised the concept of "running away" from problems and asked if this wasn't an example of that. He seemed puzzled and replied that it could be seen that way. She also asked if whether, being overwhelmed with financial and caring responsibilities for his wife, "a person might not want to live?" He acknowledged that possibility but argued that taking one's life was more of a solution to a problem than running away. Ms. Lewis did not want to argue the point; she left him with his dignity and a sense of control over his life.

CLIENT INVOLVEMENT IN PLANNING

At the sixth session Ms. Lewis inquired about Mr. Soto's response to their meetings, and he commented that he found them helpful and that even though she was young and inexperienced in life, she had made him think about things in a different manner. He hadn't been "fooling around," but his desire for sex was building, he remarked with the wink of an eye. Prior to her medical condition, Mrs. Soto had been fulfilling his sexual desires. Ms. Lewis commented that with his and his wife's permission, she could speak to her physician about any possible limitations she might have. Mr. Soto thanked her for this, stating that he would just feel too uncomfortable discussing this with his wife, because he did not want to hurt her. Furthermore, he did not think he could talk to the physician because "they all use such big words." Ms. Lewis inquired if Mr. Soto wanted to continue with their weekly problem-solving meetings. He stated that they had been helpful for him but wondered how they could be more helpful for his wife, especially not knowing what to do if he couldn't take care of her at home. "I just don't understand it all. All these people and agencies talk so much about what they're going to do for my wife, but nothing gets done. That's when I feel down and useless." Ms. Lewis agreed that at times it became very complicated, but at the next meeting, together they would try and figure what had to be done.

Macro Practice with the Elderly

IDENTIFYING RESOURCES

Prior to her next meeting with Mr. Soto, Ms. Lewis set up a consultation with an EPCMHC social work colleague who was in charge of a senior citizens' day care program. On hearing of Mr. Soto's situation, the colleague informed Ms. Lewis of the services provided by the El Paso Area Agency on Aging (AAA), as mandated by the national Older Americans Act. Ms. Lewis was pleasantly surprised to learn that in addition to a neighborhood senior citizen center providing midday meals, AAA was capable of arranging homemaker support programs at the neighborhood Senior Citizen's Center. In addition, Ms. Lewis was informed that a national senior citizens' organization had recently set up a demonstration project in El Paso to provide special health services for the elderly Hispanic population.

SHARING INFORMATION WITH THE CLIENT
Following further information gathering on available support programs for the elderly population, Ms. Lewis scheduled her next meeting with Mr. Soto. The meeting proved to be a real "eye-opener" for Mr. Soto. He was delighted to learn that he could receive assistance, in the home, in meeting his wife's daily living activities as well as special transportation to ensure that she was able to keep her medical appointments. Of particular interest to Mr. Soto was Ms. Lewis's description of the special health demonstration projects being set up for the Hispanic elderly. These projects contained a physical rehabilitation program directed at reducing frailty among the elderly as well as increasing their independence. Mr. Soto inquired as to his wife's ability to benefit from such a service and was informed that she was a prime candidate, because one of the major goals of the rehabilitation program was building muscle mass and bone density. The prospect of reversing his wife's current state of dependency to that of increased mobility, physical strength, and independence brought a smile to Mr. Soto's face. Perhaps he really could have his wife back to the way she was prior to her hip fractures.

TOWARD CULTURALLY SENSITIVE PRACTICE
Ms. Lewis informed Mr. Soto that the rehabilitative process would take some time, but with the assistance of the in-home support services, daily meal, and transportation provided by the El Paso AAA, Mrs. Soto had a good chance of resuming her normal activities. Mr. Soto acknowledged his gratitude for such assistance but pondered his existing sexual needs and lack of social outlets, because he refused to return to the Southern Pacific social club due to his sense of guilt. Ms. Lewis mentioned that her agency sponsored a senior citizen day care program that included a weekly support group for senior citizens undergoing emotional stress. Mr. Soto inquired as to the composition of the group and was informed that it consisted of mostly white, elderly females, with an occasional Hispanic person. This disturbed him, and he relayed his disappointment to Ms. Lewis as to her agency's lack of cultural sensitivity in not sponsoring a support group for elderly Hispanics with problems similar to his. Ms. Lewis gave careful consideration to Mr. Soto's concerns and then asked what they should do about the problem.

BUILDING ON FAMILY STRENGTHS
Following several more individual sessions between Mr. Soto and Ms. Lewis, it was decided that Ms. Lewis would contact the national senior citizens' organization sponsoring the rehabilitation program in which Mrs. Soto was participating, to inquire

about helping with the problem. It was quickly discovered that although the rehabilitation project had been developed as a basic medical intervention strategy, they had received numerous requests for greater involvement of the healthy spouse in his or her mate's rehabilitation. A quick survey noted that approximately 70 percent of the patients were female, thus providing a cadre of Hispanic men who could be recruited to participate in a support group. The sponsoring organization quickly agreed to participate in organizing a support group and asked Ms. Lewis to assist them.

CLIENT INVOLVEMENT IN TREATMENT PLANNING

In further conversations with Mr. Soto, Ms. Lewis inquired as to whether he felt the support group should be all male or a mix of males and females. Ms. Lewis argued that a mixture of males and females would help the two sexes appreciate the differences and similarities in their problems as well as help them to resolve these problems. Mr. Soto argued that it would be culturally inappropriate to have Hispanic men and women openly discussing their sexual problems and opted for an all-male group.

GROUP SUPPORT

Mr. Soto entered an all male, English-speaking seniors' support group comprised of non-Hispanic whites and a few Hispanics. He was relatively quiet during the first few sessions, but at the third session he announced that he thought he had entered a sex therapy group but they had not been discussing sex. Mr. Green, the social worker who led the group, asked if he felt he had a sexual problem.

Mr. Soto replied that he had, in that he had "desires" and his ill wife was unable to fulfill his needs. One of the "old-timers," Mr. Gonzales, who had been in the group about a year, commented to Mr. Soto that a few members in the group had had a similar problem and solved it by having visits as needed with "Manuela." "Where do I find Manuela?" Mr. Soto innocently asked. "In either your right or left hand," whispered a laughing Mr. Gonzales. As the group laughed, Mr. Soto joined in, adding "Oh, *that* Manuela. I had forgotten about her!"

A DIFFERENT ENDING

In the following months, Mr. Soto felt increasingly supported and enjoyed "his group." He had now terminated his meetings with Ms. Lewis. Contributing to his improved morale was also the gradual but steady improvement of Mrs. Soto's health. It was hard for Mr. Soto to believe that just four months previously he had been thinking of taking his *and* his wife's lives!

Issues and Trends in Social Work with Older People

Several issues affecting the older population are of special concern. The overriding issue is, of course, the expanded life span and the related increase in older population—especially those labeled the oldest-old. Every social, economic, and health issue is magnified by rapidly increasing numbers of older people who are potentially affected by those issues. The challenge for social workers is to help deliver the needed services and, at the same time, advocate for changes in social policies and programs to ensure that older Americans can lead full, productive, and satisfying lives, with minimal dependency and physical and mental deterioration prior to death—and when the person's death is inevitable, can die with dignity.

Economic Conditions

The problem of economic deprivation among the older population can generally be traced back to their employment histories and retirement programs, including Social Security payments and benefits that are associated with the amount earned. This book has repeatedly documented the excessive income inequality that exists in the United States, which then translates to "pension inequality" when people retire. Those older people that were poor before retirement are typically even poorer after retirement. Three economic issues are of special concern to social workers.

First, as indicated in the initial section of this chapter, "Indicators of Social and Economic Well-Being," the poorest one-fifth of the population depends on Social Security retirement benefits for 82.6 percent of its income. Social Security retirement benefits are funded by payroll contributions from both workers and employers. However, rather than simply holding these funds until needed, like an individual who places money in a savings account, the U.S. government has spent most of the funds collected on other government programs with an actuarial plan devised to use payments by today's workers as the resources for benefits to those who are already retired. That scheme worked until the population demographics known as the baby boomers started retiring and, instead of paying into the Social Security Trust Fund, began drawing out of it. Predictions of the long-range implications vary, but it is likely that by 2012 the amount being contributed to Social Security will no longed exceed the amount being paid out, and by 2040 the excess that has accumulated will be depleted. At that point, Social Security will become insolvent unless there are changes in the contributions required (it is now based on a "social utilities" philosophy), reductions in the level of payments, or restrictions on which persons eligible for the benefits. As legislative efforts are made to fix this problem, social workers must be sure that the wealthiest one-fifth of the population who hold the greatest influence around such decisions (but only depend on Social Security for 20 percent of their income), do not succeed in reshaping Social Security to serve their own interests.

Second, the Supplemental Security Income (SSI) program represents the federal government's intention to provide a safety net of income support for the poorest and most vulnerable of our older, blind, and disabled citizens. However, this program only brings needy individuals up to 75 percent of the poverty level and currently reaches only one-half of those who are eligible. Many potentially eligible recipients of SSI fail to apply for the benefits due to the complexity of the forms and lack of publicity of its existence. In addition, SSI has an asset eligibility test, the cutoff for which has been cut in half by inflation since 1974. And there is an additional problem for those minority elderly unable to read, write, or speak English because they must provide their own interpreter at the local SSI office. Clearly, SSI revision is a must if we are to reduce the increasing percentage of our elderly living in poverty.

Third, legislative action to increase the minimum wage level would significantly assist those individuals currently working in these low paying positions, as many are older people. The income for an older person in 2005 working 36 hours per week for 50 weeks at the minimum wage of $5.15 per hour would generate income of only 71.5 percent of the amount required for an older couple to even reach the poverty level. Improved income throughout one's lifetime would also generate more Social Security benefits upon retirement.

Housing Improvements

The family and all its associated responsibilities are among the most treasured experiences for the elderly. Proximity to family members is significant in urban as well as rural settings. Proximity is particularly sought out by the elderly as they strive to maintain intergenerational continuity with their children and grandchildren. Thus, housing is of critical importance in affording the elderly the opportunity to remain in the community, near their families.

Existing federal housing programs have created barriers to the maintenance of extended family relationships. Low-income housing projects are generally located away from minority communities, with occupancy limited to an elderly couple or single person. Housing assistance in the form of vouchers requires searching for apartment units that are difficult to find, frequently unaffordable, and again located outside the community.

Clearly, significant modification of our national housing policies must be undertaken if we are to meet the needs of those elderly most in need of this form of assistance. The first general goal on an improved national housing policy for the elderly is freedom of choice. They must have the opportunity to choose the type of housing and living environment that best reflects their preferences and needs.

Thus, some elderly may prefer to stay in their own homes as long as possible, while others may prefer some type of group quarters. Likewise, some elderly prefer living in neighborhoods relatively balanced in age composition, while others prefer age-segregated retirement communities. The goal of freedom of choice means that a one-dimensional housing policy emphasizing only a few choices is unacceptable.

A second general goal, clearly related to freedom of choice, is that housing policy should be designed to preserve or sustain independent living situations as long as possible. There is considerable agreement that those elderly who prefer to remain in their own homes should be allowed to do so, and that public programs sustaining independent or noninstitutional living should be made available. This particular recommendation has great relevance for our minority elderly because it provides the opportunity to maintain intergenerational relationships and cultural continuity. This suggests that more attention be paid to services and support facilitating independent-living status.

A third goal provides for adequate housing assistance and services. These could take the form of direct financial or income support through housing allowances, or income supplements that enable the elderly to secure the type of housing that best meets their needs, while staying within their limited financial resources. Housing counseling programs for the elderly enable them to select the most appropriate living arrangements to maintain intergenerational continuity. In addition, service programs providing homemaker services, home repairs, home-delivered meals, and special transportation increase the ability of the elderly to maintain independent or semi-independent existences within their communities.

Effective housing assistance for the minority elderly must incorporate a multi-faceted and flexible set of policies and programs. Freedom of choice, coupled with effective support services, will greatly prolong the ability of minority elderly to remain in their communities, continuing the intergenerational dialogue so critically important to their cultural identity. Current housing policies limiting choices will only continue to fragment minority families. Future legislation must appropriate resources for the development of creative alternatives for and maintenance of aging "in place."

Enhancing Health: The Need for Continuing Care

Older peoples' ability to obtain adequate health care services is frequently reduced by their low-income levels and lack of health insurance. The relationship between income, the cost of care, and access/utilization of services is complex and not well understood. As the cost of health-related services continues to rise, people of limited financial means will obviously be at a disadvantage. Among the elderly, women, minorities, and those living alone are particularly vulnerable; their limited social support systems are unable to compensate for inadequate economic resources. Providers of continuing care services favoring self-paying clients find the elderly among the least attractive potential clients. Medicare and Medicaid are limited in the extent to which they cover continuing care services—particularly those delivered outside nursing homes, where the vast majority of the elderly reside.

Older people are often bounced from one provider system to another, each with its own (often conflicting) eligibility criteria. Recently there has been a significant promotion of case management to reduce the existing barriers and fragmentation in elderly health care services. Case management can be of help to the elderly, but only to the extent that they can access the services. The elderly need to be educated in case management as an effective tool in receiving services; and such services need to be developed in communities where the elderly reside. For case managers, a full understanding of the resources of continuing care, both formal and informal, within the community is a must. Case managers also need to fully understand those cultural factors influencing preferences for care arrangements within elderly minority populations.

Lack of cultural sensitivity in the design and delivery of services has a negative impact on the retention of minority elderly clients after they enter the service system. Use of appropriate language, traditional leisure activities, ethnically familiar foods, and acknowledgment and celebration of cultural holidays are examples of enhancements of the quality of life in continuing-care facilities for ethnic-minority elderly. Attention to these factors in the delivery of services to the home, adult day-care center, and nursing home would significantly improve the participation of the ethnic-minority elderly in these programs.

Strengthening Mental Health Services

While the problem of mental illness occurs in all age groups, the older population in the United States represents one of our more seriously afflicted populations. Between 15 and 25 percent of the 35 million Americans over the age of 65 suffer from some form of mental illness. As many as 8.5 million elderly Americans may be in need of mental health services, a figure that would be considered epidemic in any other health context. The factors responsible for the high degree of emotional disruption among the elderly are multiple, but the increasing degree of alienation from significant societal responsibility, fragmented family support system due to loss of spouse and mobility of children, and declining physical health and/or the demands of caring for a chronically ill spouse contribute to increased feelings of alienation and hopelessness. Depression, for instance, is a major problem whose seriousness cannot be overestimated, especially in light of the fact that elderly men over the age of 75 display one of the highest suicide rates of all age categories. Alcohol abuse is increasing in its degree of severity among the elderly, as is the misuse of prescription drugs. All of these represent reactions to feelings of severe stress and alienation. The elderly are also more likely than younger age groups to be afflicted with multiple health problems, thus creating a synergistic effect in increasing their degree of emotional despair. This problem is particularly acute in nursing home settings, which have increasingly become the dumping ground for many of our mentally ill elderly, as an alternative to state institutionalization. The degree of mental illness, coupled with the virtual absence of significant mental health treatment in nursing homes, represents one of the most neglected problems in the field of mental health services in this country.

Unfortunately, the lack of mental health services to the elderly is not limited to nursing home settings. The elderly, while comprising more than 12 percent of the American population, represent only 6 percent of all persons served by community mental health centers, and only 2 percent of those served by private therapists.[26] The underrepresentation of the elderly among recipients of mental health services, in both the public and private sectors, directly reflects the lack of sensitivity within the mental health system to the problems and needs of our elderly population. The depressed elderly female living alone, the severely stressed and overwhelmed elderly male attempting to care for his Alzheimer's-afflicted wife, and the economically deprived elderly couple forced to live with their children represent just a few examples of the multitude of life-stress situations the elderly confront. This increased vulnerability in the health, economic, and social areas of life would seem to justify the expectation that the elderly would be among the most active utilizers of existing mental health services. The fact that they do not use these services speaks directly to the various impediments preventing effective access.

Traditionally, ageism has prevented many mental health professionals from servicing the elderly, in the belief that therapeutic efforts with older people are likely to be difficult or unproductive. The focus on younger clients, both at the professional practice level and in the training setting, has prevented an understanding of and sensitivity to the special needs of the elderly client. Unfortunately, reversal of this trend is frequently confounded by the elderly themselves. Long-standing negative stereotypes of the mentally ill frequently prevent the current cohort of elderly from seeking needed services. The end result is that many of them are reluctant to admit to emotional problems and tend to recategorize the situation as either a moral problem, thus seeking assistance from the church, or as a physical problem, resulting in visits to a physician.

A number of practical barriers contribute to the limited access of the elderly to receiving mental health services. Misinformation, coupled with the lack of even the most basic knowledge about the availability of mental health services, contribute to the underutilization problem. Even the healthy, more mobile elderly are frequently discouraged from seeking mental health services due to poor service locations and/or settings lacking environmental sensitivity (e.g., not employing "seniors" in key staff positions) in helping the elderly to seek assistance. In addition, many of the elderly are intimidated by the often-confusing regulations and paperwork imposed by federal and state programs. The fragmentation of the service delivery system, encompassing the processing of each case only as part of a treatment plan and its accompanying red tape, provides a strong disincentive to continue treatment.

The lack of mental health services specifically for the elderly is particularly problematic, especially for ethnic/racial elderly. Recent research demonstrates that participation by the elderly in community mental health center programs could more than double if there were services specially designed for the elderly and staffed with trained mental health professionals.[27]

The health care system in this country must be strengthened and restructured so as to encourage the improved delivery of desperately needed mental health services to our nation's elderly. These services should include a variety of support systems for both the elderly and their families and caregivers. Mechanisms are needed to ensure not only that elderly persons and their families have access to the full range of needed services, but that these services be appropriately modified to meet the special needs of the various elderly populations. While admittedly a difficult task, increased cooperation between federally funded area agencies on aging and community-based mental health centers has dramatically improved service utilization rates, even among our most difficult-to-reach elderly. Coordination and cooperation among agencies whose responsibilities involve successful aging, health, and mental health services must be ensured if the elderly with mental health needs are to be served adequately.

Trends in Caregiving

Although a strong institutional structure for caregiving in nursing homes, hospitals, and mental health centers is required to meet the needs of older people, it should be recognized that most caregiving is informal and occurs within the family. In caring for ill or infirm older persons, it is typically a middle-aged daughter who takes on this responsibility and often she is also attempting to raise her own children and even maintain employment at the same time. The demands of this *intergenerational caregiving* can be overwhelming, and the assistance of social workers can be very beneficial as they perform this role. Caregivers, in particular, need information, referral contacts such as in-home nursing or adult day care, economic assistance, and access to respite care, as well as general supportive services from social workers.

It should also be recognized that another trend in intergenerational caregiving involves older people caring for younger generations. Older people often care for or provide financial assistance for their disabled, addicted, or poverty stricken children and, increasingly, when the parents are unable to care for their children, older people return to child-rearing responsibilities for their grandchildren. These are taxing duties for older people who often are experiencing health and financial issues themselves, and assistance from social workers can make a substantial difference in the older person's ability to carry out these responsibilities—and still maintain a high quality of life.

End-of-Life Issues

Although end-of-life issues may affect persons of any age group, social workers working with older people are far more likely to need to assist individuals and families in dealing with issues of death and dying, as well as the associated grief and sense of loss that ensues. In the United States positive strides have been made in the society generally, as we are becoming more open in discussing death and in helping those who are dying plan for death in a manner that meets their personal, family, and spiritual needs.

Social workers, along with nurses, physicians, and the clergy, often are a key discipline in hospice agencies that are dedicated to helping those persons who are terminally ill plan to close out their lives in a manner in which they are at peace with themselves and their loved ones. At the same time, social workers assist surviving friends and family members deal with the loss and appropriately grieve and move on with their lives. A particularly effective practice approach has been the engagement of survivors in groups that address grief issues; these support groups provide an opportunity to discuss the loved one who was lost, the death event, and the healing that can occur, and help individuals gain support from others having a similar experience. Grief takes different forms for individuals and for different cultural and religious groups. The social worker must be sensitive to these varied patterns of addressing death and grief.

Concluding Comment

Through generous support and effective leadership provided by the John A. Hartford Foundation and the Council on Social Work Education, the curricula of BSW and MSW educational programs are infused with content to prepare new social workers with the knowledge and skill to work more effectively with older people and the issues they face. This includes such preparation as understanding the upper end of the aging process; learning about programs such as Medicare, hospice, and Social Security; addressing the quality of life issues for both the healthy and infirm aged; being sensitive to cultural differences related to caregiving and grief; the importance of maximizing a client's end-of-life-autonomy, and dealing with one's own attitudes toward death and dying.

At the macro level, social workers must advocate the development of policies and programs that will further enhance the quality of life for older people. The NASW Policy Statement regarding "Senior Health, Safety, and Vitality" enumerates a number of areas where social workers are committed to seeking change.[28] Among these changes are policies related to economic stability, housing, health and mental health care, and so on. As indicated in this chapter, improvement in financial, health, and other conditions for older people benefits the society as a whole. This country cannot afford to think of fragmented subpopulations as separate from each other but must conceive of an intergenerational partnership providing the resources, time, and caring to ensure that those most in need receive the appropriate assistance.

KEY TERMS AND CONCEPTS

Older people
Agism
Oldest-old
Intergenerational caregiving

Elderly
Gerontology
Death with dignity

SUGGESTED INFORMATION SOURCES

Berkman, Barbara, and Harootyan, Linda, eds. *Social Work and Health Care in an Aging Society: Education, Policy, Practice, and Research.* New York: Springer, 2003.

Dreher, Barbara Bender. *Communication Skills for Working with Elders.* New York: Springer, 2001.

Keigher, Sharon M., Fortune, Anne E., and Witkin, Stanley, L. eds. *Aging and Social Work: The Changing Landscapes.* Washington, D.C.: NASW Press, 2000.

McInnis-Dittrich, Kathleen. *Social Work with Elders: A Biopsychosocial Approach to Assessment and Intervention.* Boston: Allyn and Bacon, 2005.

Neysmith, Sheila M., ed. *Critical Issues for Future Social Work Practice with Aging Persons.* New York: Columbia University Press, 1999.

The Future of Social Work with Older Adults. *Families in Society* 86 (July–September, 2005). http://www.familiesinsociety.org/new/SpecialIssue/OlderAdults/spissue2.asp

ENDNOTES

1. National Center for Health Statistics. *Chartbook on Trends in the Health of Americans: 2004.* http://www.cdc.gov/nchs/data/hus/hus04trend.pdf#027

2. Federal Interagency Forum on Aging-Related Statistics. *Older Americans 2004: Key Indicators of Well-Being.* Author. (Washington, D.C.: U.S. Government Printing Office, November, 2004), p. 68.

3. National Center for Health Statistics and Federal Interagency Forum, p. xiv.

4. Federal Interagency Forum, pp. 5 and 9.

5. National Center for Health Statistics.

6. Federal Interagency Forum, p. 4.

7. U.S. Census Bureau. *Income, Poverty, and Health Insurance Coverage in the United States: 2003.* (Washington, D.C.: Census Bureau), Table 1.

8. Census Bureau, Table 3.

9. Federal Interagency Forum, p. 77.

10. Federal Interagency Forum, p. 16.

11. Federal Interagency Forum, p. 78.

12. Federal Interagency Forum, pp. 6–7.

13. Federal Interagency Forum, p. 30.

14. Federal Interagency Forum, pp. 24–25.

15. Federal Interagency Forum, p. 90.

16. Federal Interagency Forum, pp. 44–46 and 102–103.

17. Robert N. Butler and Myrna I. Lewis, *Aging and Mental Health,* 2nd Edition (St. Louis, MO: CV. Mosby, 1977), p. 34.

18. G. F. Streilb, "Are the Aged a Minority Group?" in B.L. Newgarten, ed., *Middle Age and Aging* (Chicago: University of Chicago Press, 1968), pp. 46–47.

19. S. H. Preston, "Children and the Elderly in the U.S.," *Scientific American* (December 1984): 44–49.

20. Reuben Hill and Nelson Foote, *Family Development in Three Generations* (Cambridge, MA: Scheukman, 1970).

21. Child Trends. "Child Trends Data Bank," http://www.childtrendsdatabank.org.
22. Lewis Lowy, *Social Work with the Aging*, 2nd Edition (New York: Longman, 1985).
23. Robert N. Butler, *Why Survive? Being Old in America* (New York, Harper & Row, 1975), p. 12.
24. D. I. MacDonald, ADAMHA Testimony before the U.S. House of Representatives Committee on Appropriations, Subcommittee on Labor-Health and Human Services Education (Washington, D.C.: Congressional Record, 1987).
25. M. H. Cantor, "Social Care: Family and Community Support Systems," *The Annals* 503 (May 1989): 100.
26. A. S. Flemming, L. D. Richards, J. F. Santos, and P. R. West, Report on a Survey of Community Mental Health Centers," Vol. 3 (Washington, D.C.: Action Committee to Implement the Mental Health Recommendations of the 1981 White House Conference on Aging, 1986).
27. MacDonald.
28. *Social Work Speaks: National Association of Social Workers Policy Statements* 2003–2006 (Washington, D.C.: NASW Press), pp. 320–326.

Social Work Practice with People with Disabilities

*Celia Williamson**

*Dr. Celia Williamson, a social worker, is Associate Professor in the Department of Rehabilitation, Social Work, and Addiction, University of North Texas, Dentron, Texas and currently serves as the faculty assistant to the Provost.

Prefactory Comment

Social work students trickled into the classroom on the first day of class to take the required course called "Social Work Practice with People with Disabilities." Among the last to arrive was the professor, Dr. Sue Gary, who used a joystick to guide her electric wheelchair deftly around the trash can and podium to settle in at the desk.

"I am Professor Gary," she said, "and, please, on this first day of class I would like for you to tear out a sheet of notebook paper and write your name and today's date." She continued, "When you have done that, write 'First Exam,' at the top of your paper in block letters." After the groans subsided she read out a short series of true/false questions. Below are the actual questions. See how you would do:

1. True or False: A person can have a disability and not be handicapped.
2. True or False: There are many more people with mental retardation than there are with mental illness.
3. True or False: People with disabilities demonstrate unusual courage and determination as they work within the limitations of their disabilities.
4. True or False: People with disabilities are appropriately described as a minority group.
5. True or False: The medical condition is the foremost factor in determining how well a person with a disability will carry out the activities and responsibilities of life.
6. True or False: The majority of people 65 to 74 years old have a disability.
7. True or False: The United States has never had a president with an obvious physical disability.

Social Work Practice with People with Disabilities

The phrase, "people with disabilities" is now familiar to many in the United States. During the 1980s, the debate surrounding the Americans with Disabilities Act (ADA) and its final passage in 1990 helped to cultivate a growing awareness of disability. Since that time, social work literature has increased its focus on disability issues. Introductory and human behavior textbooks now address disability issues and social work journals have increasingly engaged in discussions of this emerging area.

But why would this be considered a relatively new area for social work practice? Disability is certainly not new. Since the beginning of time, individuals and families have encountered illness and injury and, as a result, have had to adjust their lives. Social work, from its inception, has been involved in helping people to deal with a wide variety of life's problems, including those that come from disability. In fact, a close look at early social work history shows a clear involvement with people impacted by disability. The settlement house movement grew up around immigrants who were drawn to cities during the industrial revolution and was vitally involved in issues surrounding occupational injuries, workers' compensation, and public health. Social workers have long played prominent roles in advocacy and service delivery for people with mental and physical disability.[1]

The phrase "people with disabilities" first began appearing in literature in the 1980s.[2] Its appearance is more than just a matter of semantics, more than simply a new term to address old problems. It represents a significant change in the understanding of how disability impacts individuals and society—one that conceptualizes people with disabilities as a minority group, instead of as isolated individuals with specific disorders.

Before this change occurred, discussions about disability emphasized medical conditions. The "problem" was the disorder itself, and interventions were directed at the micro level, at helping individuals to correct, compensate, or cope with their own specific medical conditions. In the wake of the civil rights movement, however, people with disabilities began to gain an awareness of how the environment played a role in their disability. They began to address their situations in light of what they had learned from civil rights advocates and racial minority groups. They took a more "macro" look at the situation and it changed the whole approach. Suddenly solutions could be found by changing the environment as well as by changing the individual.

This is a clear application of the Morales-Sheafor ecosystems approach,[3] because it allows for a comprehensive examination of the problems and resources by directing attention to each of five different levels of systems, nested one inside the other. These include the individual level, the family level, the level of culture, the level of environmental and structural influences, and the historical level. Each of these levels impacts the development and the resolution of human problems.

Consider this example. As you walk across town, you happen to pass a man without legs who is sitting in a wheelchair outside a restaurant. There are five steps up to the front door of the restaurant and no ramp. How would you describe this problem?

The medical model would focus on the fact that the man cannot walk. It would seek to fix his condition or find him prosthetic legs. The ecosystems model, on the other hand, might just as easily see the lack of a ramp as the problem. The environment could be adjusted so that the man could use his wheelchair to get into the restaurant, as could other wheelchair users and mothers with strollers. In fact, today this would be a legal problem, as well, because public access to restaurants is covered by the ADA.

When the ecosystems viewpoint is used, the problem no longer resides solely with the individual. The focus moves to a much broader issue: the right of all citizens to access the benefits of society and the obligation of society to remove barriers to that access. There is a distinct civil rights ring to it, eloquently voiced by 12-year-old Jade Calegory in his 1988 testimony before Congress in support of the ADA:

> I guess my teacher was right about history repeating itself. I learned in school that black people had problems with buses, too. They had to sit in the back of the bus, but some of us with disabilities cannot even get on the bus at all. Black people had to use separate drinking fountains and those of us using wheelchairs cannot even reach some drinking fountains. We get thirsty, too. Black people had to go to separate theaters, schools, restaurants, and some of us have to, also. That is not because we want to, but because we cannot get in.[4]

Defining Disability

Language is a powerful vehicle for the expression of our cultural understanding. The words we speak convey both overt and covert meanings and subtly impact the way we think. Thus, it is not surprising to see that the reconceptualization of disability from a medical condition to a civil rights issue is reflected in the words we use in discussing it.

In everyday discussions, the terms "impairment," "disability," and "handicap" are often used interchangeably, a reflection of the earlier medically based emphasis, where the impairment and the handicap were one and the same. A broader understanding of disability requires a careful delineation of these terms, and an understanding of how they differ.[5]

The term *impairment* refers to loss or abnormality at the level of body system or organ. Examples might include a distortion in vision caused by a weakening of blood vessels in the retina or the loss of a limb by amputation. A medical diagnosis is often used in describing an individual's impairment and the focus is not on the whole person, but on the specific part of the anatomy that is impacted.

A *disability* results when an impairment causes a restriction in the ability to carry out normal life activities. For example, the loss of a leg, the impairment, results in limitations to mobility. The weakening of the blood vessels in the retina results in an inability to read standard size print. The focus here is on the *functional results* of the impairment for the individual. Because short-term medical problems have a more limited impact on individuals, the term disability is usually reserved for discussions related to functional limitations which are long-term or result from chronic conditions.

The term *handicap* takes an even broader perspective and looks at the barriers that are created by an interaction between the disability and the environment. If a restaurant does not have large-print menus and if the waiters have not been trained to assist patrons by reading the menu to them, individuals with visual disabilities might be handicapped in regard to eating out. The combination of poor vision and lack of accommodation results in a loss of public access for the individual and a loss of revenue for the restaurant.

It is very possible for a person to have a disability but not to be handicapped. In fact, this is the focus of the new approach—to remove barriers so that people with disabilities are not handicapped in regard to their life activities.

It should be noted that, in addition to clearly delineating the meaning of words, it is also important to understand the emotional impact words can carry. The word "handicap" is a good example of this. In the 1970s "handicap" was the politically correct term. It was seen as a term that helped to normalize the experience of disability. After all, golfers were given a handicap to compensate for differences in ability levels so that all could compete from an equal starting point. When the historical roots of the word were discovered, however, it lost its political correctness. Historically, it referred to beggars, seeking handouts with "cap-in-hand." This was certainly not the image that people with disabilities wished to reinforce. Although the term handicap can still be appropriately used to denote the interplay between environment and disability, the term "barrier" is more often used today. In fact, "barrier" places the problem even more squarely in the environmental context.

Other changes in our language have also occurred in this process of reconceptualizing disability. One of the most important is the delineation of the principle of "people first language." The underlying concept is that the structure of verbal expression itself can reinforce either the predominance of the disability as the defining characteristic of an individual (retarded child) or relegate the disability to only one element among many that define that person (child with mental retardation). By putting the disability in the secondary position, the preeminence of personhood is emphasized: people with disabilities are always *people first*.

In choosing words that honor personhood, derogatory terms, such as imbecile or cripple or deformed, should be avoided altogether, as should the implication that people with disabilities are inevitably victims. For example, people are not "confined" to wheelchairs, they use them. In fact, wheelchairs are liberating devices. To refer to people with disabilities as afflicted, unfortunate, or stricken places them in a disempowered position. Even suggesting that they are unusually courageous because they live with a disability sets them apart. It broadens the impact of the disability from its specific functional implications and places an aura over the whole character and life circumstance of the individual. When people with disabilities are assumed to be essentially *un*able, the societal stigma turns out to be much more of a barrier to effective functioning than the specific limitations of the disability itself.[6]

Demographic Considerations

The 2000 U.S. Census indicates that 47.9 million people in the United States live with a disability or some other long-lasting condition.[7] Figure 19.1 shows the distribution of various types of disability based on the functional impact. The numbers across these columns add up to considerably more than 48 million because many individuals experience more than one disability. This means that nearly one in five Americans has a disability or other long-lasting condition. Clearly, social workers will be involved with people with disabilities in every type of agency or service setting.

It should be noted that the incidence of disability is not evenly spread across the population. Figure 19.2 shows that older individuals are much more likely to

Figure 19.1

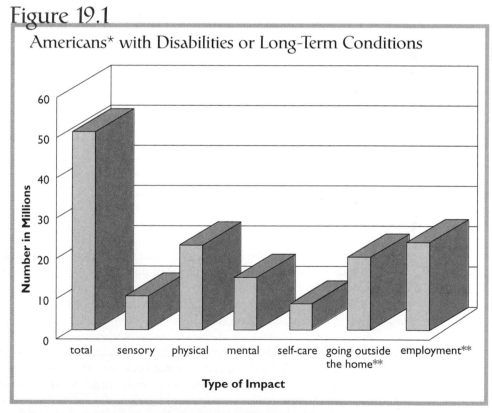

Americans* with Disabilities or Long-Term Conditions

*Civilian Noninstitutionalized Population of the United States aged 5 and older
**Includes only individuals aged 16 and older

Source: J. Waldrop & S.M. Stern. (March 2003). Disability Status: 2000. U.S. Census Bureau, Retrieved on 9/6/05 from http://www.census.gov/prod/2003pubs/c2kbr-17.pdf

Figure 19.2

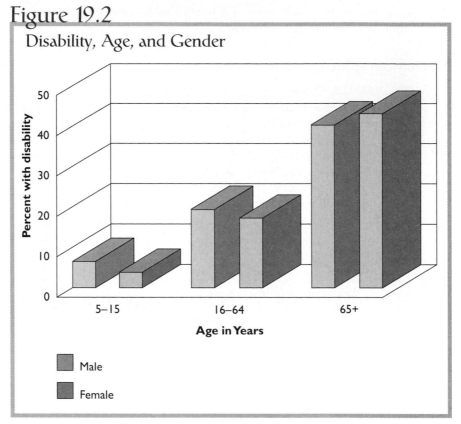

Disability, Age, and Gender

Note: This includes the Civilian Noninstitutionalized Population.

Source: J. Waldrop & S.M. Stern. (March 2003). Disability Status: 2000. U.S. Census Bureau. Retrieved on 9/6/05 from http://www.census.gov/prod/2003pubs/c2kbr-17.pdf

experience disability than younger ones. It makes sense that the longer one lives, the more chances one has of encountering illness or injury. Lifelong choices about smoking, drug use, diet, and exercise have a cumulative effect, impacting function more in later years. Notice, though, that even in the highest age group, not all individuals experience disability. It is important not to assume that aging and disability are inevitably related. This figure also illustrates that males are somewhat more likely to be impacted by disability in early and midlife. In maturity, females are more likely to be affected.

Figure 19.3 reveals some correspondence between race, ethnicity, and disability. This is a complex relationship that is not yet fully understood. Some disorders are hereditary and thus more likely to appear in genetically related populations. Health conditions that result in disability may be positively or negatively impacted by dietary and other cultural practices. Beliefs about medical practices, access to culturally relevant health care, and economic disparities among various racial groups also impact the prevalence and persistence of disability. Even the likelihood of

Figure 19.3

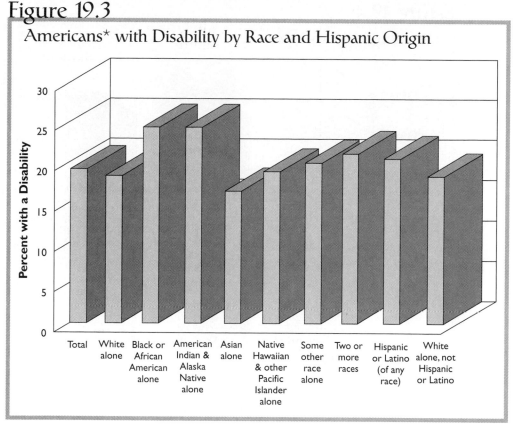

Americans* with Disability by Race and Hispanic Origin

Y-axis: Percent with a Disability (0 to 30)

Categories: Total, White alone, Black or African American alone, American Indian & Alaska Native alone, Asian alone, Native Hawaiian & other Pacific Islander alone, Some other race alone, Two or more races, Hispanic or Latino (of any race), White alone, not Hispanic or Latino

* Civilian Noninstitutionalized Population of the United States aged 5 and older

Source: J. Waldrop & S.M. Stern. (March 2003). Disability Status: 2000. U.S. Census Bureau. Retrieved on 9/6/05 from http://www.census.gov/prod/2003pubs/c2kbr-17.pdf

reporting disability may vary among different groups. Although the membership in a racial or ethnic group may be biologically based, the impacts may be sociologically grounded. Clearly, disability must be addressed within the cultural context of the individuals who feel its impact.

There is also a correlation between earnings and disability,[8] which is revealed in Figure 19.4. Lower income is associated with higher rates of disability. The data does not necessarily reveal a causal link, however. Individuals with lower earnings are less likely to have access to health care and may be more likely to be employed in high-risk jobs. This makes them more subject to incurring disability. On the other hand, a person with a disability is less likely to be employed (Figure 19.5). So, the interplay of income and disability is complex. This same reciprocal causality is evident in the relationship between education and disability (Figure 19.6). Mental retardation and other significant disabilities that impact individuals early in life may reduce access to higher education. At the same time the jobs that are open to those with lower educational levels are

Figure 19.4

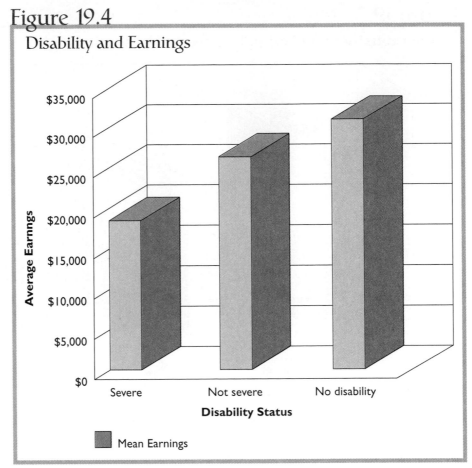

Disability and Earnings

Note: This includes individuals in the United States who are 21–64 years old.

Source: U.S. Census Bureau, 1996 Survey of Income and Program Participation, August–November 1997, as reported by McNeil, 2001.

more likely to involve physical labor and/or risk of injury, meaning those with lower educational levels may be more likely to become disabled later in life. In income, employment, and education, people with less severe disabilities reflect patterns more similar to the nondisabled population than those with severe disabilities.

Two things seem very evident in looking at the statistics that reflect disability patterns in the United States. The first is that disability impacts a large proportion of the population—nearly one in five individuals—making it an extremely important consideration for the social work profession. The second is that the medical model, which focuses on the physical impact of the disabling condition, can only partially explain the differences across populations. Biological explanations are insufficient. Factors in the social environment must also be taken into consideration. Even age, which seems so firmly rooted in the biological perspective, is subject to the impact of

Figure 19.5

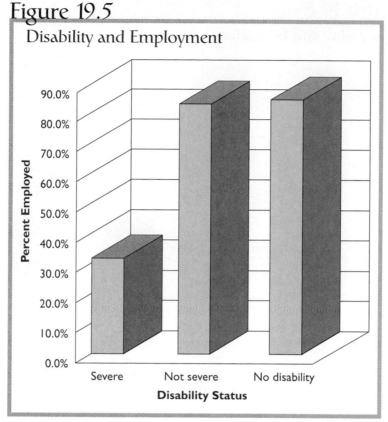

Disability and Employment

Note: This includes individuals in the United States who are 21–64 years old.

Source: U.S. Census Bureau, 1996 Survey of Income and Program Participation, August–November 1997, as reported by McNeil, 2001.

societal perceptions. Several researchers have suggested that older people are less likely to receive rehabilitation services than younger ones.[9] Ageism allows people to assume that dysfunction is simply part of getting older. So, for example, instead of treating urinary incontinence we sigh and talk of getting older and just change the sheets. In fact, incontinence is often reversible. In such cases, it is not so much the medical condition but the attitude that is the problem.

Other Risks Associated with Disability

It is important to briefly mention some additional risks that are associated with disability. Some studies have suggested that children and adults with disabilities are more often the targets of physical and sexual abuse than people without disabilities, though other studies have failed to support this finding.[10] It is clear that injuries resulting from abuse, including child abuse, and other forms of family and societal violence can cause disability.

Figure 19.6

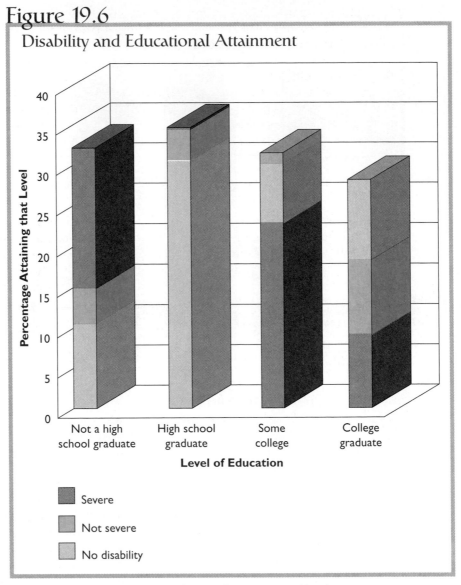

Disability and Educational Attainment

Note: Includes individuals in the United States who are 25 years old and over.

Source: U.S. Census Bureau, 1996 Survey of Income and Program Participation, August–November 1997, as reported by McNeil, 2001.

While chemical dependency is itself a disability, studies indicate increased rates of substance abuse and chemical dependency among people with other disabilities. Again, reciprocal causality makes it difficult to fully interpret these figures. Although it is true that many traumatic head injuries occur as a result of intoxication and as many as 62 percent of injuries resulting in mobility impairments are substance abuse related, there are also indications that substance abuse rates are higher among people with congenital disabilities,[11] indicating that disability may also precede chemical dependency.

Disability and each of these other variables—education, income, abuse, and addiction—are interrelated in a complicated fashion. No straight-line cause and effect pattern can be established. Instead, there is a circular interaction pattern, where each variable impacts all other variables. This pattern of interaction requires an ecosystems approach because that model provides a framework in which to examine these complicated interrelationships.

Disability and the Minority Model

It is clear from the demographic information presented above that people with disabilities comprise a large subgroup of the American population, larger than any single racial or ethnic minority group. But is it really appropriate for people with disabilities to think of themselves as a minority? Dworkin and Dworkin describe four essential criteria for a group to be accorded minority status.[12] A minority group:

1. is *identifiable,* either in terms of appearance or behavior;
2. experiences *less access to power* so that fewer resources, influence, and control are afforded to it;
3. experiences *discriminatory treatment,* often evidenced by segregation and stereotyping; and
4. *sees itself as a separate group.*

Many people with disabilities are readily identifiable in terms of appearance. A difference in physical appearance itself, such as the body posture of a person with cerebral palsy, or the visibility of the accommodations, such as braces or a white cane, announce the presence of a disability. Behaviors, such as the use of sign language or the onset of a seizure, also serve to identify the person as someone with a disability.

Some individuals may choose not to disclose or to hide their disability, and thus avoid probing questions, stereotypes, and other issues of discrimination. During the 1930s President Roosevelt was rarely photographed in his wheelchair or using his crutches. In the 1996 presidential campaign Senator Robert Dole incorporated his disability into his public image, neither hiding nor emphasizing its presence. The very fact that one would have to choose whether to talk about a facet of themselves because of possible discrimination reinforces the group's separate identity.

If one considers income and education as indices of power,[13] then people with disabilities clearly fit the second criteria for minority group status. Figures 19.4 and 19.5 clearly illustrate that lower levels of income and education are highly associated with disability.

The discriminatory treatment of people with disabilities is also easy to establish. When diagnostic terms can be hurled as insults, as "retarded" and "spastic" often are, the presence of stereotyping becomes very apparent. Federal law recognizes that "individuals with disabilities continually encounter various forms of discrimination in such critical areas as employment, housing, public accommodations, education, transportation, communication, recreation, institutionalization, health services, voting and public services."[14] Attitude surveys of human service providers, employment rates, and research in basic patterns of social interaction suggest that American society harbors significant prejudice against people with disabilities.[15] Physical barriers result in de-facto segregation. People with disabilities clearly meet the third criteria for designation as a minority group.

It is the fourth criteria that has most recently been met. Until the late 1960s, the medical model dominated the conceptualization of disability and separate diagnostic groups often found themselves competing with each other for limited federal funds. People may have labeled themselves with a particular diagnosis and joined in advocacy activities to support services for that group, but they did not necessarily see themselves as objects of discrimination. "Object" is the correct term here—discrimination denies personhood.

The 1960s, however, focused public attention on civil rights, feminism, deinstitutionalization, and consumerism. It was in the context of these social movements that the conceptualization of disability began to change.[16] In 1972, in Berkeley, California, a group of students with disabilities banded together to demand access to classes on the University of California campus and to pool their resources for transportation and attendant care. They developed the first Center for Independent Living, building it on the principles of consumer sovereignty, self-reliance, and political and economic rights.

As people with disabilities began to recognize that they were being treated differently based on the stigma associated with being disabled, rather than merely in regard to differences in functional abilities, they began to see similarities that spanned across disability areas. This cross-disability awareness led to coalitions between groups that previously saw each other as competing for the same funds. This alliance of various disability-specific advocacy groups provided the political muscle which helped to bring about the passage of the ADA.

Thus, the minority perspective holds some distinct advantages for people with disabilities. It allows the cultivation of cross-disability alliances that results in increased political power. It provides a vehicle for identification with a group that looks at itself with pride, as self-reliant survivors, and it expands the pool of potential solutions, because environmental change as well as personal change is now an option.

Societal Responses to Disability

In addition to broader sociocultural influences, the way a society responds to disability is influenced by its perceptions about the causes of disability, the threats that it perceives to be related to the disability, and the amount and kinds of resources that are available to deal with the disability.[17]

The perceived causes of disabilities have shifted dramatically over the course of history. Early explanations often centered on spiritual dimensions. Mental and physical disorders alike were often viewed as punishment from the gods and those with disabilities were often shunned or even tortured. In the latter half of the eighteenth century, when genetics was seen as the cause of mental deficiency, laws prohibiting marriage or providing for sterilization of people with mental or emotional disorders were passed in half of the states.[18] Later, the perception that disability was essentially a medical condition came to prominence and medical interventions were the preferred course of action.

When society was seen as the cause, there was increased pressure for the society to provide solutions. Historically, services for people with disabilities have been afforded first to soldiers injured in war because societal responsibility was clear. Indeed the first federal-level public aid program in the United States established pensions for soldiers who were disabled during the War for Independence.[19]

Society also responds differently to specific impairments based on perceived cause. People with mental retardation or congenital disorders are not often seen as responsible for their disorder, and public willingness to provide services is relatively high. Visible volunteer efforts and fund raising keep these disabilities before the public eye and encourage increased private and public support. Mental illness or chemical dependency, which are still perceived by many as resulting from character flaws, receive less public attention and support, although the prevalence of either mental illness or chemical dependency far exceeds that of mental retardation.[20]

The potential threat of a disability can also greatly influence societal response. The polio scare of the late 1940s and early 1950s brought significant governmental and volunteer response. The March of Dimes was born out of the impetus to stop this public threat and government as well as private research efforts helped to eradicate the virus. Once the vaccine was developed, the presence of a clear and decisive medical intervention helped to mobilize the community response to the disease. Here, a "guilt-free" cause, a substantial threat, and an effective technology combine to shape society's response in a positive way. It should be noted that the disease itself and the disability resulting from it are different. Society mobilized primarily against the disease, but the wave of public sentiment carried over into the provision of services for those who became disabled because of the virus.

The Acquired Immune Deficiency Syndrome (AIDS) epidemic reveals an interesting, though distressing, interplay between perceived cause and perceived threat and resources. It stands in contrast to the polio epidemic. Early on, those who were identified as "responsible for" the spread of the Human Immunodeficiency Virus (HIV) that causes AIDS were seen as the only ones threatened. The general public response was low. Later, when the extent of the threat was realized, efforts at prevention and intervention were intensified. Now, ironically, the potential threat is an economic one as well as a medical one and the level of economic resources that might be required to provide services for individuals with AIDS makes the public somewhat uneasy about committing itself to a specific level of care. The fact that no clear medical response is yet available also complicates efforts to gain public and governmental support in combatting the disorder.

Social Workers and People with Disabilities

Social workers will encounter people with disabilities in all aspects of their lives—as friends, colleagues, clients, and even in the mirror. All service settings should provide access to people with disabilities, and social workers should not assume that a client with a disability is seeking services in relation to the disability. Some service systems, however, are designed to address issues specific to disability. Social workers can find active roles within these systems of services.

Five major areas of legislation address disability issues specifically. These include workers' compensation, rehabilitation, social security, education, and civil rights. In addition, a distinct service system exists to serve veterans with disabilities. Each of these legislative areas addresses different issues and addresses them from a unique viewpoint that grew out of the historical context in which they were formulated. They do not always complement one another.

Workers' compensation laws were passed on a state-by-state basis during the early 1900s. This means that many different workers' compensation laws exist, and a disability incurred in California may be addressed very differently from one incurred in Mississippi. Most of these laws address disability from within the medical model, with specific impairments resulting in specific reparations. In some states, each part of the anatomy is assigned a percentage, so that, for example, the loss of the index finger on the dominant hand results in a particular percentage of disability for the individual.[21] Other states allocate a lump sum payment of a specified amount for each body part lost. Social workers, along with nurses and rehabilitation professionals, often fill roles in medical case management as a part of the workers' compensation service system.

On the heels of World War I, the federal government enacted the 1918 Soldier's Rehabilitation Act. It authorized vocational rehabilitation services for veterans whose disabilities were a result of military service. The first civilian rehabilitation services followed two years later, in 1920, under the Smith-Fess Act. This separation of veterans' and civilian services continues to this day. Although veterans are not excluded from the civilian system, veterans' services often provide for more extensive benefits. Social workers fill positions in Veterans' Administration hospitals and may work extensively with veterans with disabilities and their families in the process of adjustment to disability and in finding the resources to support employment and independent living.

The overriding purpose of the civilian act, which has since been designated as the Rehabilitation Act, is to help people with disabilities become employed. Each state provides vocational rehabilitation services under the auspices of this act. Vocational rehabilitation counselors purchase a range of services for people with disabilities in order to help them to secure employment. These may include medical services, vocational assessments, training or education, counseling services, adaptive equipment, supported employment, and job placement services. Social workers may contract to provide services directly to the consumers of the vocational rehabilitation program.

The act also has provisions for funding independent living centers, which are charged with promoting consumer control, self-help, and self-advocacy and with assisting communities to meet the needs of people with disabilities. Services provided by independent living centers include peer counseling and individual and community advocacy. Typically the staff of independent living centers are, themselves, individuals with disabilities. Social workers with disabilities can play a vital role in bringing both professional training and personal experience to bear in these service settings.

The Social Security Act provides important income and medical insurance supports for people with disabilities through the Supplemental Security Income (SSI) and the Social Security Disability Insurance (SSDI) programs. Special work incentive programs are available through SSI and SSDI to help individuals with disabilities make the transition from Social Security income supports to employment. Social workers are often employed by SSI/SSDI programs to assist people in accessing these services.

The Individuals with Disabilities Education Act mandates that all children with disabilities have access to a free, appropriate public education designed to meet their unique needs. These educational services are provided through the local school district and school social workers often assist in the process of determining just what services are needed and then help families and schools to access those services. Efforts are made to keep children involved with their non-disabled peers, avoiding isolated, "special" settings.

Although there are provisions in other laws to help secure the civil rights of people with disabilities, the ADA is the seminal piece of legislation in this area. There are no services provided under this bill, but social workers need to be aware of its provisions in order to help people with disabilities to maintain their full rights as citizens of this country. Social workers can also take an active role in ensuring that the services they provide are available to all people, regardless of disability.

In addition to these government programs, social workers may provide disability-specific services in private for-profit and private not-for-profit service systems. Today many companies are taking a proactive stance toward work-related injuries, establishing their own disability management programs that are focused on making accommodations that allow workers to quickly return to work after an injury. Social workers find active roles in this arena, both through positions in disability management programs themselves and through involvement of employee assistance programs.

Social workers can also be found in private not-for-profit organizations that often contract with government agencies to provide services in relation to disability. Disability-specific organizations and foundations, such as United Cerebral Palsy or the Arthritis Foundation, employ social workers. In addition to direct services that may be provided by these organizations, social workers are involved in extensive public education and advocacy campaigns. It is clear that there are many roles that social workers can fill in providing services to people with disabilities, their families, and the communities in which they live.

The Ecosystems Model and People with Disabilities

The ecosystems framework[22] provides the opportunity for a broader conceptualization of disability, recognizing that the history of discrimination against people with disabilities, the structural impact of governmental policies, the cultural assumptions about what people with disabilities can and cannot do, and the impact of disability on the family, as well as the individual psychological and biological specifics of the disorder all play a part in determining both problems and solutions. Figure 19.7

Figure 19.7

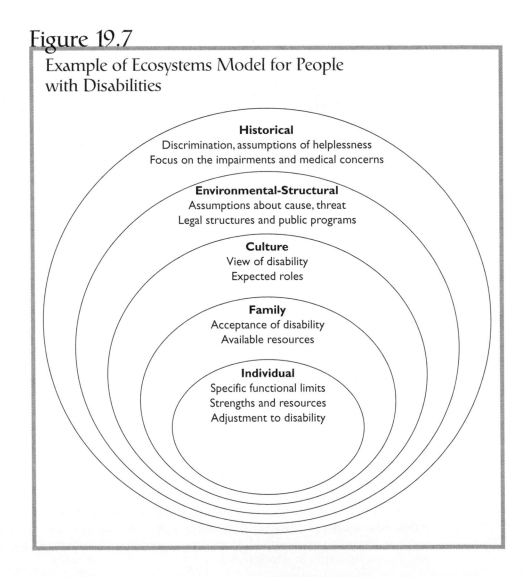

Example of Ecosystems Model for People with Disabilities

Historical
Discrimination, assumptions of helplessness
Focus on the impairments and medical concerns

Environmental-Structural
Assumptions about cause, threat
Legal structures and public programs

Culture
View of disability
Expected roles

Family
Acceptance of disability
Available resources

Individual
Specific functional limits
Strengths and resources
Adjustment to disability

frames some of the issues specific to disability that must be considered within each level of the concentric spheres of the ecosystems model.

Social workers may focus the intervention at any one of these levels or at several levels at the same time. Wherever the intervention is focused, its success will be dependent on the social worker's understanding of the impact at all levels. This is clearly illustrated in the case example below.

THE INDIVIDUAL

Jerry Desoto is almost ready to be discharged from a rehabilitation hospital where he spent the past two months. He was injured three days after his eighteenth birthday when he crashed his motorcycle, a birthday gift from his parents, into a telephone pole. He was intoxicated at the time of the crash. His spinal cord injury resulted in paralysis from the waist down.

Jerry had been a starter on the high school basketball team. School began three weeks ago. Jerry has been working with a tutor and will be able to return to school on a part-time basis. Between attending classes and continued tutoring he should be able to finish his senior year with his class. His superb physical condition before the injury has greatly helped his recovery.

Jerry is counting the days until discharge. For him, it represents a milestone in his recovery, a move back into the "real world" and a chance to reestablish his friendships. For Jerry's social worker, Chris, the process of discharge began as soon as Jerry was admitted to the rehabilitation hospital.

At the micro level, the biopsychosocial factors that impact Jerry are many and varied. Jerry has lost all sensation and all voluntary use of all his muscles below the waist. His friends are aware that he can no longer walk and that he would need a specially equipped car in order to drive. Only his family and closest friends are aware that he has also had to learn new ways to control bowel and bladder elimination. He has learned to handle the catheter well, but still has occasional difficulties with bowel control. That is one of his major concerns about returning to school. Jerry has also lost sexual function, though he has not yet allowed himself to admit it. He is having enough trouble adjusting to the fact that he will not be the school's top basketball player, and is not ready to address the way his sexual function will impact his self-image.

Jerry had been looking forward to leaving home at the end of the year. This accident has placed him back in a more dependent mode, at least temporarily, and it irritates, even angers, him that he will have to look to his mother for assistance. He cannot even go to town without getting someone to take him. His mother is too eager to help. She wasn't really ready for her youngest to leave home, anyway.

THE FAMILY

Jerry's father is a line worker in an automobile assembly plant and his mother teaches fifth grade. He has an older brother, Jake, who works in an autobody repair shop and has just moved out into an apartment. Even with good medical insurance coverage, the costs of this accident have been substantial and Jerry's father takes every opportunity to work overtime. His mother has been primarily responsible for working with the hospital in regard to Jerry's rehabilitation.

Jerry is acutely aware of the additional financial burden that the accident has placed on the family. He blames himself because he had been drinking. His parents could not afford to give him a car, so they had compromised when his father found the used bike. Now they blame themselves for being stingy with his safety. In addition to medical expenses, there were renovation expenses. Jerry's home had to be modified so that he could live there. The strain over finances has surfaced some old issues in the marriage.

CULTURAL ISSUES

Jerry's buddies have been attentive but Jerry is a bit wary of the town's response. It's not that he is afraid that they will not welcome him, it's just that he is afraid of their expectations. They raised money for renovations to his home by putting a change jar in the local hamburger joint. They want to see him happy, but he is often angry, depressed, and discouraged. The church youth group has asked him to speak about his "courageous recovery" and how his faith has helped him through. He hasn't been to church in two years.

Jerry's status in his community to this point has been built on American youth cultural issues such as his athletic abilities, his ability to drink and go out with his buddies, and his ability to charm the girls in his class. While there are accommodations that can help him to overcome the biological limitations of his condition, he must also come to terms with how his status as a person with a disability has impacted the way people expect him to act. Society has proscribed certain "sick roles" that require that he play the part of an always optimistic, grateful recipient of the kindness of others. In his community, it would be selfish for him to expect accommodations to be made on his behalf and it would be presumptive of him to think that any girl's parents would be willing to have their daughter date someone who is "damaged."

ENVIRONMENTAL–STRUCTURAL ISSUES

Jerry is fortunate that his injury occurred after the passages of the Individuals with Disabilities Education Act and the Americans with Disabilities Act. These important pieces of legislation provide a legal framework to ensure his access to education, transportation, and governmental and public services. His legal rights and the physical realities of his community environment do not always match, however, and there is pressure on him not to pursue the issue. "Surely," his old girlfriend's mother confides in a friend, "he does not expect the school to spend all that money putting in a lift so he can get into the weight room in the school basement when that means they will have to delay buying new band equipment another year. After all, it's so much money to spend on only one person."

HISTORICAL ISSUES

Historical patterns of discrimination have left a deep mark on the lives of people with disabilities, particularly in the area of employment and economic self-sufficiency. Even with the non-discrimination assurances in the ADA, Jerry will have to counterbalance years of Labor Day telethons and pity-based pleas with a strong message of his own competence if he is to convince employers to truly consider his job application. The history of discrimination is ensconced not only in employer attitudes but in legislation, such as the Social Security Act, that defines disability as an *in*ability to work; and in the very brick and mortar of our cities, in stairs and curbs without cuts. Changes are not realized with the stroke of a legislative pen. History is impacted only by living life differently day to day, building tomorrow's history with today's actions.

MULTILEVEL INTERVENTIONS

Chris, Jerry's social worker, has begun to work with Jerry's mother, both to ensure that she knows how to assist Jerry, and also to help her see how important it is for Jerry to take charge of his life, to make his own decisions. Chris was also able to involve Jerry's father in renovating the house. She arranged for a staff member from an independent living center to visit the home and work with the father to develop a common-sense and cost-effective plan for renovation that the family can afford. The independent living center also offered the services of a peer counselor to help Jerry learn how to negotiate his town in a wheelchair and do minor wheelchair repairs. The peer counselor can also talk to Jerry on a personal and practical level about using catheters and facing stereotypes, including Jerry's own stereotypes, about what life is like from a wheelchair.

At the time of discharge, several issues hang in the balance. Jerry has learned to handle the biological demands of his condition within the context of the hospital, but the community brings new challenges. He must also find a new place for himself socially, within his high school and community, and come to terms with the impact of his injury upon his sense of who he is. Despite the fact that this accident had been related to alcohol use, Jerry has been looking forward to drinking with his buddies once he gets out. He figures, if nothing else, he can still drink with the best of them. In addition, both Jerry and his mother have important lifecycle steps to accomplish, which his accident has complicated. Family finances may also require changes in his plans for college.

When Chris attended Jerry's high school graduation several months later, she could point to several specific interventions that helped to tip the balance in Jerry's favor. With Chris's encouragement, Jerry's mother turned her attention from its intense focus on Jerry to a broader look at the community's, and particularly the school's, accessibility issues. Mrs. Desoto enlisted the help of a sixth-grade student who had spina bifida and had used a wheelchair all his life. Together, they made a survey of all the local schools and delivered a list of needed accommodations to the school board. Mrs. Desoto was encouraged by this student's easy acceptance of his disability and his clear enjoyment of life.

Chris used a macro perspective to work with Mrs. Desoto to understand the provisions of the ADA and the best tactics to take in advocating change. The top priority was to make the high school weight room accessible. When Jerry began using the weight room, he was able to reduce his outpatient trips for physical therapy to once a month. It gave Jerry an opportunity to work out with his friends and reestablish the easy camaraderie he had with them in the context of sports. The coach asked him to help manage the basketball team.

Chris had also referred Jerry to vocational rehabilitation to assist him in finding employment. A combination of student loans, grants, and assistance from vocational rehabilitation will make it possible for Jerry to attend a community college next year and receive training specifically targeted to his vocational goals. His brother will move to an accessible unit in his apartment complex and they will share expenses.

As is true in any situation, each level of analysis in the ecosystems framework impacted Jerry's recovery and adaptation process, from individual factors of biology to the presence of federal laws that ensure the availability of accessible educational opportunities and housing options. For Chris, once again micro and macro practice dovetail. In her experience, it is often the energy and insight gained from personal experience that give direction and focus to larger advocacy efforts.

Emerging Issues for Social Work Practice with People with Disabilities

Health care has been an important political issue for the nation as a whole and is a predominate concern for people with disabilities. Although many individuals with disabilities are quite healthy and one should be careful not to confuse illness with disability, portability of health insurance and coverage of pre-existing conditions has a particular impact on many people with disabilities. Often insurance packages only cover acute care, leaving the continuing costs associated with a chronic condition uncovered. Specific disorders, such as mental illness, may be poorly covered, or not covered at all. In addition, because work is the primary vehicle in the United States for access to health insurance and many people with disabilities are unemployed, a large percentage of individuals with disabilities do not have health care coverage at all.[23]

Employment itself is a major concern. Employment rates for people with severe disabilities are the lowest of any minority group, making full participation in society more difficult. Work provides not only the financial means for participation, but it also accords adult status and establishes networks for building friendships and community connections. Not only is employment important for people with disabilities, it is vitally important for the economic health of the nation as well. When individuals with disabilities move from Social Security rolls to active roles in the workforce, the economy profits from their productivity and avoids the cost of the income support.

Unfortunately, disincentives exist within the Social Security legislation, often making it difficult for people with disabilities to move from SSI and SSDI rolls into the workforce. Insurance availability is one such issue. People who move from SSI or SSDI to a job will eventually lose access to Medicare or Medicaid, though current provisions allow for a transition period. Individuals must have an assurance of other sources of health care coverage before they can risk moving off Social Security rolls.

The Americans with Disabilities Act was signed into law in 1990, but people with disabilities continue to face issues of access and equality. Inaccessible work, education, and recreational environments continue to present barriers to full participation in society, and those who push for changes may be seen as "ungrateful" or "selfish" because they have moved outside of the expected "sick role" of passive acceptance. Other attitudinal barriers also persist. Old stereotypes of helplessness and incapacity continue to limit the opportunities open to people with disabilities and reduce their contributions to their communities and to the nation. Many people incur a disability later in life and may, themselves, hold some of these assumptions about incapacity. Discrimination, therefore, must be fought at all levels—from self-image to societal image.

Concluding Comment

While medical advances hold great promise for the treatment of many disabling conditions, the impact of disability on American society is likely to increase greatly over the next five to ten years. At this time, medicine has advanced further in the area of emergency services than it has in rehabilitative care. More people are surviving head injuries and other traumas, but often with multiple disabilities. In addition, the American population is becoming older—and age increases the risk of disability. Add to this the number of infants affected by fetal alcohol syndrome and the ingestion of other chemicals of abuse during pregnancy. Add, again, the number of individuals who may be impacted by AIDS. It is clear that, in the near term, the number of people with disabilities in the United States is likely to increase substantially.

The need for services will also increase dramatically. Medical professionals will continue to address the biological issues, and vocational rehabilitation counselors will focus on issues of employment, but social workers will bring a unique focus that includes interventions at all system levels. Social workers must join hands with the disability rights movement in recognizing that disability issues should not focus exclusively on the medical problem or the individual's skills for a particular job. Disability issues are civil rights issues. Social workers must work to ensure that public policies and service programs are made more responsive. They must help individuals, families, and their communities to find room within their own cultural frameworks to value the lives and contributions of people with disabilities. In this way, social workers can truly work *with* people with disabilities, enhancing their lives and enriching society.

KEY WORDS AND CONCEPTS

ADA
People with disabilities
Medical model

Reciprocal causality
People first language
Impairment vs. disability

SUGGESTED INFORMATION SOURCES

Asch, A., and Mudrick, N. R. "Disability," in Richard L. Edwards, ed., *Encyclopedia of Social Work,* 19th Edition. Washington, D.C.: NASW, 1995.

Ferguson, P., Ferguson, D., and Taylor, S., eds. *Interpreting Disability: A Qualitative Reader.* New York: Teachers College Press, 1992.

Nagler, M., ed. *Perspectives on Disability: Text and Readings,* 2nd Edition. Palo Alto, CA: Health Markets Research, 1993.

ENDNOTES

1. N. Groce, *The U.S. Role in International Disability Activities: A History and a Look Towards the Future* (New York: Rehabilitation International, 1992).

2. J. Blaska, "The Power of Language: Speak and Write Using 'Person First,'" in M. Nagler, ed., *Perspectives on Disability*, 2nd Edition (Palo Alto, CA: Health Markets Research, 1993), pp. 25–32.

3. A. Morales, "Social Work Practice with Special Populations," in A. Morales and B. Sheafor, eds., *Social Work: A Profession of Many Faces*, 7th Edition (Boston: Allyn & Bacon, 1995), pp. 287–293.

4. United States Congress, Senate Committee on Labor and Human Resources, Subcommittee on the Handicapped, *Americans with Disabilities Act of 1988: Joint hearing before the Subcommittee on the Handicapped of the Committee on Labor and Human Resources, United States Senate, and the Subcommittee on Select Education of the Committee on Education and Labor, House of Representatives*, One Hundredth Congress, second session on S.2345, September 27, 1988 (Washington, D.C.: USGPO, 1989).

5. World Health Organization, *International Classification of Impairments, Disabilities and Handicaps* (Geneva: World Health Organization, 1980).

6. Blaska, pp. 25–32.

7. J. Waldrop and S.M. Stern (March 2003). *Disability Status: 2000*, U.S. Census Bureau, Census 2000 Brief, # C2KBR-17 (Washington, D.C.: U.S. Department of Commerce, Economics and Statistics Administration). Retrieved 9/5/2005 from http://www.census.gov/prod/2003pubs/c2kbr-17.pdf

8. J. McNeil (February 2001). *Americans with Disabilities: Household Economic Studies*, U. S. Census Bureau, Publication # P70–73 (Washington, D.C.: U.S. Department of Commerce, Economics and Statistics Administration). Retrieved 9/5/2005 from http://www.census.gov/prod/2001pubs/p70–73.pdf

9. G. Becker and S. Kaufman, "Old Age, Rehabilitation and Research: A Review of the Issues," *Gerontologist* 28 (August 1988): 459–468; B. Holland and D. Falvo, "Forgotten: Elderly Persons with Disability—A Consequence of Policy," *Journal of Rehabilitation* 56 (April, May, June, 1990): 32–35.

10. J. Garbarino, "The Abuse and Neglect of Special Children: An Introduction to the Issues," in J. Garbarino, P. Brookhouser, K. Authier, eds., *Special Children—Special Risks: The Maltreatment of Children with Disabilities* (New York: Aldine DeGruyter, 1987), pp. 3–14.

11. D. Corthell and J. Brown, "Introduction," in *Substance Abuse as a Coexisting Disability*, Eighteenth Institute on Rehabilitation Issues (Menomonie, WI: Research and Training Center, Stout Vocational Rehabilitation Institute, 1991), pp. 1–25.

12. D. Stroman, *The Awakening Minorities: The Physically Handicapped* (Lanham, MD: University Press of America, 1982), pp. 6–8.

13. D. Stroman, p. 7.

14. Americans with Disabilities Act of 1990 (Preamble) 42 U.S.C.A. Section 12101 *et seq.* (Washington, D.C.: West, 1993).

15. United States Congress, House of Representatives, Committee on Small Business, *Americans with Disabilities Act of 1989*, One Hundred First Congress, Serial No. 101–45, February 22, 1990 (Washington, D.C.: usgpo 1990).

16. G. DeJong, *The Movement for Independent Living: Origins, Ideology, and Implications for Disability Research* (East Lansing: University Centers for International Rehabilitation, Michigan State University, 1979).

17. S. Rubin and R. Roessler, "Historical Roots of Modern Rehabilitation Practices," in *Foundations of the Vocational Rehabilitation Process,* 4th Edition (Austin, TX: Proed, 1995), pp. 1–40.
18. Rubin and Roessler, pp. 15–16.
19. President's Committee on Employment of the Handicapped, "Disabled Americans: A History," *Performance* 27 (November–December, 1976, January 1977): 8.
20. LaPlante, p. 2.
21. Rubin and Roessler, pp. 23–24.
22. Morales, pp. 287–293.
23. A. Asch and N. Mudrick, "Disability," *Encyclopedia of Social Work,* 19th Edition (New York: NASW), pp. 752–761.

chapter 20

Social Work Practice with Muslims in the United States

David R. Hodge

Prefatory Comment

The attack on Pearl Harbor on December 7, 1941, shocked and angered the United States and thrust Americans into more than a three-year war with Japan. Domestically, *all* Japanese immigrants and U.S.-born Japanese Americans were perceived as dangerous enemies and were placed in relocation centers for the duration of the war. They lost their land, property, and possessions. Sixty years later, nineteen Muslim al-Qaeda terrorists crashed three civilian airliners into the Pentagon and New York World Trade Centers, killing approximately 3,200 American citizens. This launched the United States into a brief war in Afghanistan in search of Osama bin Laden, who was believed to have masterminded the attacks on the United States, and into a more prolonged war in Iraq. Foreign-born Muslims were spared the extreme public backlash visited upon Japanese, but, nevertheless, American Muslims were and still are being subjected to prejudice, discrimination, and stereotyping.

In adhering to the proactive spirit of this text in guiding students and practitioners into uncharted waters requiring the profession's attention, David R. Hodge was commissioned to write this original chapter. David R. Hodge is uniquely qualified as a social work scholar with several publications concerning practice with Muslims in the United States. He teaches us through examples how Muslims are stereotypically depicted in the social work literature and how social workers perceive Muslims through the lens of the dominant culture. He also provides micro and macro practice interventions and suggestions in working with this unique population ignored far too long by social work.

Muslims in America

Muslims have existed in American society since the founding of the United States.[1] In the past few decades, the size of the Muslim population has grown dramatically.[2] At least three factors underlie this growth: high levels of immigration, comparatively high birth rates among Muslim women, and Americans converting to Islam. Ascertaining the exact size and composition of the Muslim population in the United States is problematic, however, as U.S. law prohibits the Census Bureau from inquiring about respondents' religion. Although estimates vary, a number of observers believe that Muslims may now be the second largest spiritual tradition in the nation.[3,4]

As the Islamic community continues to grow, social workers will increasingly be called upon to provide services to this discrete cultural group. Islam, however, represents a distinct worldview that differs substantially from the dominant secular worldview that informs American society. Consequently, widespread concern exists among Muslims that helping professionals trained in secular educational settings will have little knowledge or understanding of Islamic values.[5–9] Indeed, although this textbook represents a step in the right direction, research indicates that most social work students receive no educational content on religious diversity during their education.[10]

It is important to note that social workers are ethically mandated to develop and exhibit spiritual competency.[11] *Spiritual competency* can be understood as a more specific, faith-based form of cultural competency.[12] Accordingly, spiritual competency can be thought of as the process of developing (1) an empathic understanding of the client's spiritual worldview; (2) intervention strategies that are appropriate, relevant, and sensitive to the client's worldview; and (3) knowledge of one's own biases that might affect the proper implementation of steps one and two.[13] It is helpful to think of spiritual competency as a lifelong endeavor in which no one ever achieves complete competency. All of us are in process.

The ecosystems model cited in the introduction to Part Five of this text is particularly useful in developing spiritual competency with Muslims. This method represents a holistic approach in which four environmental systems—family, culture, environmental/structural factors, and history—are viewed as salient aspects in the client's life. Flowing from the European Enlightenment's emphasis upon the rational, autonomous person, the secular culture tends to accent the role of the individual *apart from* environmental systems. Conversely, Islamic culture tends to view the individual as a person who is *part of* environmental systems.[6] In other words, the ecosystems model offers the advantage of understanding reality in a manner that is congruent with how Muslims tend to view the world. As the following section implies, Islam is not as much an individualistic belief system as it is a way of life that unifies the metaphysical and material systems.[14]

A Preliminary Understanding of Islam

Islam is commonly understood to mean submission, specifically submission to Allah, the supreme and only God. Individuals who practice this submission are called *Muslims*. Both terms, Islam and Muslim, appear repeatedly in the Quran, making Islam the only world religion to have a built-in name from its inauguration.[15] The Quran was revealed to the honored founder of Islam, the Prophet

Muhammad (570/580–632), the "Messenger of God." The Quran is held to be God's revelation to humankind. While the Quran states that Allah communicated with other prophets, recognized by Jews and Christians, the Quran is God's final, immutable revelation.

Out of gratitude for Allah's goodness and compassion, Muslims seek to follow the straight path of God's precepts, the *shari'a*. The common western demarcation between the personal, which may incorporate the spiritual, and the public, which is secular, is foreign to Islam. The shari'a governs all aspects of one's life. In other words, Islam offers adherents a holistic way of life in which the personal and the public are integrated. The primary basis for the shari'a is the Quran. The shari'a is also informed by the *hadith*, the recorded collections of the sayings of the Prophet.[16]

Significantly, Muslims date their history from the creation of the Islamic community, or *ummah*, rather than from their founder's birth or death or the inception of the Quran.[17] Two significant expressions of Islam characterize the worldwide Islamic community. Approximately 90 percent of Muslims are *Sunnis*. The remaining 10 percent are *Shiites*, who form the overwhelming majority in Iran.[15] Renard suggests a helpful comparison can be made between Protestantism and Sunni Islam and Roman Catholicism and Shiite Islam.[18] In Sunni Islam and traditional Protestantism there is an emphasis upon a direct relationship between the believer and God, unmediated by external authority structures. Similar to Roman Catholicism, Shiites have a hierarchical authority structure of legal scholars, based upon the consensus of the Shiite community, who hold an added responsibility for interpreting the Word of God for the faithful.

Since the time of the Prophet Muhammad, the Islamic community has grown to approximately a billion people.[16,19] Islam is frequently associated with the predominantly Islamic Arab nations of the Middle East where the faith originated. Yet, among the global Islamic community, Arab Muslims are a minority.[20] The largest populations of Muslims are found in South and Southeast Asia.[15] Indeed, the Islamic community encompasses the globe.

Local culture, political concerns, issues of interpretation, and other factors all function to shape the expression of Islam among self-identified Muslims. While there is extensive agreement that the shari'a should govern all facets of one's conduct, the practices that exemplify a "true Muslim" are contested throughout the Islamic world.[15] In reality, the Islamic community comprises many smaller Muslim communities, each with its own distinct characteristics.

Consequently, readers should bear in mind that no particular set of beliefs and values are representative of all Muslims. Many individuals who self-identify as Muslims are likely to disavow a number of the perspectives presented in this chapter. Rather than offering the final word on Islam, this chapter is better viewed as providing readers with an initial, tentative understanding of Islam.

Although much diversity exists within Islamic discourse, it is important to acknowledge that a number of commonalities also exist that serve to demarcate Muslims from other populations. Perhaps the most significant of these distinguishing commonalities are the "five pillars" upon which the Islamic faith rests.[21]

The Five Pillars of Islam

The five pillars of faith are widely affirmed by Muslims as central facets of Islam. These practices can be thought of as the heart of a wider set of beliefs and practices.[17] While the wider framework of beliefs and practices is often influenced by local cultural factors, the five pillars are viewed by Muslims around the world as providing a basic outline for the expression of Islamic spirituality.[21]

The first and most fundamental tenet of the Islamic faith is the Declaration of Faith.[22] The declaration is the method by which individuals enter into the worldwide Islamic community. Individuals simply profess, "There is no god but God and Muhammad is His Messenger." The declaration testifies to the absolute, singular theism of Islam and the primary role of Muhammad as his last prophet.[17] Thus, it serves to remind Muslims that they are part of a worldwide community of believers under the care of a compassionate, merciful God who is personally involved with his creation.

The second pillar of faith is the performance of ritual prayers. Prayer is preceded by symbolic physical cleansing and is understood to be a holistic practice that encompasses body, mind, and emotions. Different positions are adopted, including standing straight, bending over at the waist, and kneeling with the head to the floor. The prayers are performed five times throughout the day, with the individual facing Mecca, the holy city of Islam, in Saudi Arabia, where God first entered into a covenant with the Islamic people. The offerings of prayers at dawn, midday, mid-afternoon, sunset, and an hour after sunset reinforce the concept that daily life and faith are continuously intertwined.[22] Similarly, for many Muslims the uniformity of practice embodied in the ritual observance symbolizes the equality of humankind before God.[15]

The third pillar is charity or alms giving. Each year a percentage, typically 2.5 percent of accumulated wealth, is given to address economic inequalities and promote the general welfare of the Islamic community.[19] Individuals who are poor are exempt from giving. The act of giving helps to ameliorate materialistic desires and reminds the giver that the source of all wealth is God rather than oneself.[18] Put differently, giving fosters a sense of thanksgiving to God for his goodness and a sense of community identity and responsibility.[17]

The fourth pillar is the yearly fast held during the month of Ramadan. Since Ramadan is based upon the lunar calendar instead of on the solar calendar, Ramadan occurs roughly 10 days earlier each year. Able-bodied adults abstain from eating, drinking, smoking, and sexual activity from sunrise to sunset to foster spiritual renewal.[15] In addition to facilitating a closer relationship to God, the Ramadan fast also encourages Muslims to empathize with those less fortunate than themselves.[5]

The final pillar of faith is the pilgrimage to Mecca. At least once during their lifetime, individuals are expected to make the pilgrimage unless financial or physical impediments exist.[17] During the pilgrimage, individuals often experience a oneness with God and recognize the equality of all people before God, as Malcolm X's experience illustrates.[5] The pilgrimage was instrumental in changing Malcolm X's hatred of whites into an affirmation of the equality of all races.[23]

In many cases, the degree to which individual Muslims practice the five pillars may be a good indication of the salience of faith in their lives. Conversely, it is also important to note that Muslims may say extra prayers later in the day or trust in God's benevolent understanding when faced with circumstances that make compliance difficult (e.g., an employer refusing to allow time for prayer during work hours; restrictive school policies; child care responsibilities, etc.).[24,25] For Muslims in the United States, this may be a particularly important consideration, as the cultural context in the United States often differs radically from that experienced in one's culture of origin.

The Demographics of Muslims in the United States

Obtaining data that accurately reflect the status of Muslims in the United States is difficult due to the methodological limitations associated with surveying relatively small, faith-based communities that may not be evenly dispersed across the nation. For instance, perhaps the most representative survey to date, the American Muslim Poll based upon a national sample of 1,781 self-identified Muslims in 2001, may have underweighted the views of African Americans, nominal Muslims, and perhaps Anglo converts. With these limitations in mind, the American Muslim Poll indicates that close to two-thirds (64%) of Muslims in the United States were born outside of the country.[26]

In 1965, the United States immigration policy was changed so that the needs of the labor market replaced racial/ethnic criteria.[1] The implementation of a more equitable immigration policy allowed highly skilled Muslims from around the world to join previous generations of European immigrants in seeking a better life for themselves and their families in America. This has led to the development of a richly diverse community. Currently, the Islamic community in the United States is composed of individuals from at least 80 nations.[26] In many ways, American Muslims are a microcosm of the global Islamic community, with significant numbers arriving in recent decades. Among those born outside the United States, 36 percent arrived between 1980 and 1989 and 24 percent between 1990 and 2001.[26]

Estimates of the number of Muslims in the United States range from one million[27] to eleven million,[3] with most authorities suggesting a population of four to six million.[4,15,23,25,28] Approximately 80 percent of American Muslims are Sunnis.[25] Although most major cities have Muslim populations, large concentrations are located in Boston, Chicago, the Detroit–Toledo corridor, Houston, Los Angeles, and New York City.[1,25,28,29] Shiites, who constitute the remaining 20 percent, form significant communities in Chicago, Detroit, Los Angeles, New York City, and Washington D.C.[1,30] While almost every state has a Muslim population of some size, particularly heavy concentrations exist in California and New York.[27]

Reflecting global demographics, the American Islamic community is composed of significant populations from Asia and the Middle East/North Africa, as well as African Americans.[26,28] Data on ethnicity from the American Muslim Poll are reported in Table 20.1. As implied above, this survey may underestimate the number of African

Table 20.1

Demographics of Muslims in the United States ($N = 1,781$)

Ethnicity		Age Group	
South Asian	32%	18–29 years	23%
Pakistani	17%	30–49 years	51%
Indian	7%	50–64 years	20%
Bangladesh	4%	65 + years	7%
Afghan	4%	Education	
Arab	26%	< High school	6%
African American	20%	High school graduate	12%
African	7%	Some college	24%
Other	14%	College graduate	58%
Unsure	1%	Income*	
Gender		<$15,000	10%
Male	59%	$15,000–$24,999	10%
Female	41%	$25,000–$34,999	13%
Marital Status		$35,000–$49,999	17%
Married	69%	$50,000–$74,999	22%
Single, never divorced	19%	$75,000 or more	28%
Divorced, separated, widowed	11%		

*Seventeen percent of respondents declined to report their income.

Source: American Muslim Poll (Washington, D.C.: Project MAPS, 2001).

American Muslims since the survey methodology specified that 20 percent of the respondents were African Americans. Estimates of the number of African Americans in the Islamic community tend to be higher, typically in the 30 to 40 percent range.[1,4,25,27]

The vast majority of African American Muslims, who are largely converts to Islam, are Sunnis.[2,25] Although the Nation of Islam, headed by the charismatic Louis Farrakhan, is often portrayed in the media as representative of African American Muslims, it speaks for only a small portion of African American Muslims. The Nation of Islam, which has an estimated membership of 10,000[2] to 50,000[31] is widely considered by other Muslims to be outside the bounds of mainstream Islam.

As the demographic data in Table 20.1 suggest, Muslims in the United States tend to be highly educated and financially secure.[26–28] Over 40 percent work in managerial, medical, or professional/technical occupations, and half earn more than $50, 000 annually.[26] Foreign-born Muslims in particular tend to be members of the middle to upper middle class.[28]

Concurrently, it is important to recall that many Muslims are disadvantaged. There tends to be a significant cultural, occupational, and economic gap between foreign-born and African American Muslims. In addition, some immigrants are quite poor, such as those individuals who were forced to immigrate because of political unrest in their country of origin. Roughly a quarter of regular mosque participants live in households with incomes below $20,000, less than half the level of the median household income.[32]

As one might expect, given the diversity that exists among American Muslims, some degree of tension exists within the Islamic community.[1,28] These tensions are frequently mitigated, however, by the community's need to face the dominant secular culture with a united front. As they struggle to preserve their faith, Muslims often focus on points of shared interest that are particularly important to the Islamic community at large, such as the family.

Muslim Families

Family plays a central role in Islamic culture. The word *family* can be used in a more expansive sense than is typical in western secular culture. Within secular culture, the image that the term family tends to bring to mind is that of the "nuclear family," two adults and possibly one or more children. Within Islamic culture, the term family is often associated with what the secular culture would refer to as the extended family or kin network. In its broadest usage, family can even refer to the local, national, or global Islamic community.[33]

Marriage is perceived, not just as the joining of two individuals, but also as a union of two extended kin networks. The concept of lifelong singleness is foreign to Islam, and divorce, while permitted, is strongly discouraged. Marriage is viewed as a means of spiritual and personal fulfillment that fosters the social good.[34] In contrast with the secular culture's emphasis upon appearance, qualities such as education, spirituality, and quality of character are emphasized in mate selection. As is the case with many other important decisions in life, many Muslims seek the wisdom of the wider kin networks for advice on appropriate marriage partners.[25] In some cases, this trust may be exemplified by marriages that are arranged by the kin networks. The family also bears responsibility for ensuring that the marriage succeeds and that all parties are content.

The American *egalitarian marriage model* held up as an ideal in secular culture generally holds little appeal to Muslims, who value mutual respect rather than secular notions of equality.[14] Husbands and wives are traditionally held to be of equal worth but also to have complementary roles.[5] Men are responsible for the material provision and leadership of the family, while women have the primary responsibility for maintaining the home and raising the children. Men generally oversee and have the final word on decisions in the public sphere, while women make the decisions about child-rearing and household concerns.

Affirmation of a *complementary marriage model* does not necessarily mean that women are precluded from working outside the home or that men do not participate in housework.[14] In actuality, women commonly work outside the home and men frequently assist with housework. As a mark of mutual respect, spouses often consult with each other when faced with important decisions.[7]

Women's employment outside the home is typically held in tension with providing a nurturing environment for the family, particularly young children. Children are considered a blessing from God, and large families are generally encouraged. A secure mother/child attachment is held to be critical to children's well-being and, by extension, the future health of the Islamic community. Mothers generally prefer to spend as much time as possible with their children, which also allows them the opportunity to enculturate Islamic values and preserve their heritage.[25]

Parents often play a role in the lives of their children that is analogous to the role played by peer groups in the lives of children in the secular culture.[35] Girls participate with their mothers in various activities and boys often accompany their fathers. Children typically bond closely with their parents, siblings, and other family members. Youth are considered to be men and women upon reaching puberty, at which point they often begin practicing the five pillars of faith. Furthermore, little concern is expressed that post-puberty youth differentiate from the family unit as interconnectedness among family members is valued.[6] Youth are encouraged to care for other family members, and it is common for parents to role model this value by having elders stay with the family rather than placing them in an institutional setting.[7] Elders are respected for their wisdom and experience and often function as mediators for other members of the kin network when family problems arise.

Families are typically marked by a strong sense of cohesion and interdependency. Group counseling may be seen as a violation of family privacy and consequently is not widely accepted among Muslims.[36] Family and individual counseling is usually advised. Utilizing spiritual ecomaps,[37] which highlight existential relationship with environmental resources, and spiritual genograms,[38] which focus on family relationships over time, can be useful in identifying personal and environmental assets.

For social workers socialized to view secular norms as "universal," Muslim families can seem to be enmeshed in a maladjusted, unhealthy manner.[6] As an expression of spiritual competency, it is important for social workers to work within the family's value system to find solutions to problems. Practitioners must refrain from imposing, either explicitly or implicitly, secular values that popular culture may affirm as "normal" and "universal." Social workers must ensure that they respect complementary marriages, cohesive family units, and other Islamic values that Muslims may hold.

Common Cultural Values in Islamic Discourse

Muslims commonly affirm a number of values including: community, God's sovereignty, modesty, virtue, and nutrition. Rather than understanding these values as a series of separate entities, they should be viewed as interrelated constructs reflecting the unified, holistic Islamic cosmology.

Community

Community is a significant Islamic value.[39] Flowing from the belief that all people are equal under God, Muslims tend to see themselves a part of an extended, faith-based family—the Islamic community. As occurs with a family, members care for and are responsible to the community and the community is responsible for and cares for its members in a reciprocal relationship.

Since Muslims see themselves as part of a larger community, individual aspirations are held in tension with the preferences of others. Muslims tend to emphasize benevolence, care for others, cooperation between individuals, empathy, equality and justice between people, the importance of social support, and positive human relatedness.[8] As part of being in a community, individual preference is often circumscribed so as not to harm other members of the community. Consequently, in contrast to the explicit, overt communication valued in the secular culture, Muslims often prefer implicit forms of communication that are highly sensitive to others' needs and concerns.[6] Similarly, secular individualistic values such as personal success, self-actualization, self-reliance, and personal autonomy hold somewhat less attraction for Muslims, who tend to find meaning in group success, community development, interdependence, and consensus.[8]

Much like the extended family, the community protects and empowers the individual.[40] For instance, African American women report finding a safe social space from the inequalities they experience in the larger culture and this empowers them to redefine themselves in a positive manner.[41] Similarly, immigrant Muslim women report that the Islamic community provides a haven of safety that is instrumental in helping them cope with the stresses of adapting to a new societal context.[42]

Since individual identity is intertwined with the community's identity, every individual has a responsibility to protect the community.[39] In school settings, for instance, Muslim students may feel responsible to defend siblings, family, and faith when these dimensions of community are attacked.[9] Similarly, as an expression of their desire to protect the well-being of the community, elders often mentor other community members.

God's Sovereignty

Muslims believe that God brought the Islamic community into being. God is understood to be omnipotent and personal—at the center of the Muslim's existence.[5] Nothing happens to the Muslim apart from God's will. While this belief is sometimes thought to engender fatalism, more properly it prepares Muslims to face hardship and fosters perseverance during trials. Further, since life is a transitory journey on the road to eternal life, Muslims can face the future with optimism. The eternal perspective can foster a sense of existential meaning that facilitates coping during difficult situations.[43]

In keeping with the centrality of God in the Muslim's life, cognitive interventions based upon the shari'a may be particularly effective. While traditional psychotherapy and group counseling may not be widely accepted among Muslims,[43] cognitive therapy, in which unproductive beliefs are identified and replaced with God's precepts, has been demonstrated to be at least as effective as traditional forms of therapy with anxiety disorders,[44] bereavement,[45] and depression,[46] while concurrently ameliorating problems at a faster rate.

In addition to God, the Muslim cosmology includes belief in Satan, angels, and supernatural beings referred to as *jins*. Possession by a jin is a legitimate possibility in the Muslim cosmology and, accordingly, should not automatically be taken as an indication of psychosis.[19] As noted in the DSM, it is important to take cultural norms and values into account when conducting an assessment.[47]

Modesty

Another cultural value that is widely affirmed is modesty, particularly around members of the opposite sex.[35] While there is wide agreement in the Islamic community that modesty is an important value, much debate has occurred regarding how this value should be operationalized in American society. For men, the issue is not as keenly felt since Islamic standards regarding what is considered modest clothing for men overlap with secular views. The issue is more significant for women. Views on what constitutes modest apparel for women range from what secular culture deems modest to clothing that covers everything except the hands and face. Thus, many Muslim women wear a headcovering of some type, such as a scarf, a practice referred to as veiling or *hijab*. Since the practice of veiling has no mainstream cultural counterpart, women who choose to veil often face ridicule and discrimination.[14]

Related to modesty are Islamic views on social relationships between the sexes. Many Muslims feel that men and women should not mix socially with members of the opposite gender.[9] Some Muslims feel that, outside of interactions that occur within the family, the sexes should be separated after kindergarten.[48] Others believe that interaction between the sexes is permissible in a group context. When working with youth in particular, social workers should be careful to respect Islamic norms about mixing with members of the opposite gender. In cases where it is necessary to meet with someone of the opposite gender, holding the meeting in an open, public forum may be acceptable.[49]

Secular dating patterns are widely seen as problematic, especially for youth. Dating can be a contentious issue in Muslim households, particularly when parents and youth hold different views of what constitutes proper Islamic behavior.[49] While social workers may be tempted to side with a youth's desire for greater freedom, it is advisable to explore solutions that are congruent with the family's value system.

Virtue

Modesty can be seen as one dimension of virtue. In classic Islamic thought, virtue provides the foundation for human happiness.[50] Islam affirms a set of moral and ethical norms that have much in common with other theistic faiths. Behavior that is injurious to others, whether mentally, physically, or morally, is forbidden.

The equality of all individuals before God is upheld, along with the need to treat others with respect and honesty.[35,51]

Muslims also affirm the sanctity of human life, generally from conception to natural death. Thus, euthanasia, suicide, and abortion, except in instances when the mother's life is at stake, are not permitted.[35] Homosexuality, which is understood to be socially constructed, is not sanctioned.[52] Sexual activity is reserved for marriage and is viewed as a gift from God.[19]

Nutrition

As part of a holistic cosmology, Muslims generally follow a dietary code to promote physical and spiritual well-being. Many Muslims only eat meat that is considered *halal*, a term used to describe beef, poultry, and sheep that have been lawfully slaughtered according to Islamic specifications.[25] Some Muslims adopt a vegetarian diet to avoid meat that is not halal.[53] Others may accept kosher-prepared meals, which, although not the same as halal food, may be similar enough to be acceptable to some Muslims.[7] Still others will eat items from a standard western menu as long as the food does not contain pork. The dietary code also prohibits mind-altering substances, such as alcohol.

As an aid to developing spiritual competency with Muslims, Table 20.2 delineates a number of values that are commonly affirmed in Islamic discourse and secular discourse. As emphasized above, social workers should not assume that Muslims or secularists will affirm all the delineated values. Many secularists, for example, hold pro-life views and many self-identified Muslims exhibit explicit communication styles that clearly express their opinions. In addition, many of the values listed in Table 20.2 are held in tension with one another. Muslims retain a sense of individualism, for example, while conceiving of themselves as a community. In short, Table 20.2 should not be viewed as a rigid typology, but rather should be seen as a visual means of creating awareness regarding possible value differences that may exist between adherents of an Islamic worldview and a secular worldview.

Structural Factors in the Social Environment

Social work theory on oppression states that a difference in worldviews in conjunction with a power differential between the worldviews tends to foster bias toward the worldview without access to power.[54,55] In other words, the dominant culture tends to oppress the subordinate culture in areas where a conflict in worldviews or value systems occurs. As Gilligan's[56] work illustrates, females and males affirm different value systems; consequently, females tend to encounter discrimination in settings where males have more power.

Diaphobia and Religious Stereotypes

Just as the term sexism was developed to describe gender-based bias, the term *diaphobia* has been used to describe animosity that is directed toward a divine

Table 20.2

Value Differences in Secular and Islamic Discourses*

Secular Discourse	Islamic Discourse
Individualism	Community
Separateness	Connectedness
Self-determination	Consensus
Independence	Interdependence
Self-actualization	Community actualization
Personal achievement and success	Group achievement and success
Self-reliance	Community reliance
Respect for individual rights	Respect for community rights
Self-expression	Self-control
Sensitivity to individual oppression	Sensitivity to group oppression
Identity rooted in sexuality and work	Identity rooted in culture and God
Egalitarian gender roles	Complementary gender roles
Pro-choice	Pro-life
Sexuality expressed based on individual choice	Sexuality expressed in marriage
Explicit communication that clearly expresses individual opinion	Implicit communication that safeguards others' opinions
Spirituality and morality individually constructed	Spirituality and morality derived from the shari'a
Material orientation	Spiritual/eternal orientation

*Table adapted from D. R. Hodge, "Social work and the House of Islam: Orienting practitioners to the Beliefs, and Values of Muslims in the United States," *Social Work* 50 (2005): 162–173.

worldview in which a transcendent God serves as the ultimate point of reference.[57] As adherents of a subordinate, theistically based culture in the dominant secular culture, Muslims often encounter bias. Diaphobia is manifested in the formation of spiritual prejudices and religious stereotypes among secularists. The beliefs, values, and practices of Islamic culture are not evaluated on their own terms. Rather they are evaluated according to the criteria established by the secular culture. Secular culture functions as the final arbitrator of right and wrong. Values falling outside of the secular value system are implicitly characterized as morally deficient. In short, diaphobic tendencies manifest themselves most prominently in areas where Islamic values differ from those affirmed by the secular culture.[58]

Muslims consider prejudice and stereotyping to be one of the most important issues facing the Islamic community in the United States.[26] Spiritual prejudices and religious stereotypes are disseminated throughout American society via the media, educational sector, and other culture-shaping institutions. Research has documented that secular actors, such as the *New York Times,* exhibit bias toward Muslims.[59,60] Observers have delineated how the rich diversity of Islamic culture is frequently transformed in media depictions of Muslims into denigrating images connoting ignorance, oppression, fanaticism, and violence.[61,62] Muslims are acutely aware of how they are characterized. Over two-thirds (68 percent) think that the media is unfair in its portrayal of Muslims and Islam and almost eight in ten (77 percent) think that Hollywood portrays Muslims and Islam unfairly.[26]

Similar tendencies have been documented in the social work literature. Research has explored how people of faith, including Muslims, are portrayed in social work textbooks.[63] The small amount of material devoted to faith groups tends to reflect the worldview of the dominant secular culture rather than the perspective of Muslims and other people of faith. In other words, Muslims are not depicted as they would tend to characterize themselves, a practice that leaves social workers unequipped to work in a spiritually sensitive manner. Rather, texts tend to depict Muslims as they are seen through the lens of the dominant secular culture, a practice that sets social workers up to reinforce the diaphobic stereotypes and prejudices that exist in the larger secular culture.

For instance, one social work textbook reports that the Muslim world abounds with "horror tales of crimes against humanity," and that the "moral agenda" of Middle Eastern countries "is the complete enslavement of women."[64] Such portrayals do not represent the self-descriptions of most Muslims. The Muslim world, of course, is not completely devoid of human atrocities, but then neither is the secular world free of "crimes against humanity." As Gellner[65] has observed, the secular worldview flowing from the European Enlightenment directly fostered the French Revolution, communism, and, indirectly, National Socialism. These movements have resulted in the deaths of tens of millions of human beings and inflicted untold suffering upon millions of others. It is noteworthy that human atrocities of this magnitude are essentially without parallel in the Muslim world.

Research that has examined the relationship between Islam and human rights has found that governments rooted in Islam do not foster the abuse of human rights.[66] An examination of 23 predominantly Muslim countries with a control group of non-Muslim nations found that both upheld the same level of human rights. Highlighting examples of human depravity in Muslim nations while simultaneously downplaying or even ignoring instances of human depravity flowing from a secular worldview does little to foster understanding between people.

As implied above, similar dynamics occur when discussing women. The issue of veiling in particular is a flashpoint in secular discourse. In some western nations, secularists have even worked to abrogate Muslims' rights by attempting to ban girls from wearing the hijab in public schools.[58,67] For many in the secular culture, hijab has come to symbolize the oppression of women that is believed to occur in Islamic culture.[67]

Muslim women, however, frequently view the situation quite differently. From the perspective of many Muslim women, it is secular culture that oppresses women.[14,68] Secular culture is viewed as fostering lack of respect for women by, for example, reducing women to sexual objects, engendering high levels of debilitating eating disorders, promoting a hedonistic, narcissistic climate in which men walk away from their commitments to their wives and children, producing popular music that glamorizes the humiliation of women, and creating a milieu in which rape, sexual assault, and physical violence against women are everyday occurrences. Such degradation of women is comparatively rare in Islamic communities where, it is held, women are treated with respect.[18,69]

Counter to secular assumptions, many women view the practice of hijab as liberating.[14,68] Veiling is seen as emancipation from a secular culture that celebrates immodesty. Donning hijab communicates that the woman is to be elevated above the level of a sexual object, and that she is to be treated with respect based upon her abilities. It is also important to note that veiling occurs for many other mutually compatible reasons. For example, as an expression of their spirituality, many women veil to express their obedience to God. Many Muslims veil for the sense of safety and peace that the practice engenders. The practice may also symbolize pride in Islam.

Social workers must guard against reducing complex, multifaceted issues to simplistic caricatures. Portraying secular values as liberating and Islamic values as oppressive does little to foster understanding. To work effectively with Muslims, it is important to be able to see the world through an Islamic lens. Spiritually competent practice occurs at the point where social workers have developed an empathetic understanding of how Muslims view the world.

The biased characterizations in the secular culture have fostered a sense of mistrust and dislocation among Muslims in the United States. These portrayals also help create an atmosphere in which discrimination against Muslims is legitimated in schools, workplaces, and other public forums.[70] Employers, for instance, may fire Muslims for praying during lunch hour. Public school teachers may attempt to abrogate Muslims' constitutional rights by banning students from wearing the hijab or discriminating against papers that deal with Islamic topics.

Due to fear that they will be misunderstood or discriminated against, Muslims may be reluctant to seek assistance from social workers and other human services professionals.[5,6,8,9,71] Social workers can address this concern by showing interest in Islam[9] and becoming familiar with Islamic values.[8] Emphasizing traditional empathetic qualities, such as care, genuineness, respect, support, and warmth, can also help overcome initial concerns.[72] Similarly, meeting practical needs, such as advocating on behalf of oppressed Muslims, can also help build bridges.[73]

Civil Rights

To advocate for Muslim concerns, social workers must be aware of the environmental resources that exist. Social workers should take the time to familiarize themselves with relevant statutes, organizations, and institutions, so that the appropriate resources can be brought to bear in a given context. The free exercise clause of the U.S. Constitution protects individuals' right to freely express their faith in public settings. The web sites of the U.S. Equal Employment Opportunity Commission (EEOC) and the Department of Education contain information on, respectively, employees' and students' free exercise rights. Particularly useful is the updated version[74] of former President Clinton's[75] memorandum on the free exercise rights of students in public schools.

School social workers in particular should also be aware of the Equal Access Act (P.L. 98-377) and Protection of Pupil Rights Amendment (PPRA) (20 U.S.C. §1232h). The Equal Access Act ensures that students of faith have the same right to school facilities as secular students. Schools cannot, for example, allow an environmental club to meet in an empty classroom and refuse to provide a classroom for Muslim students to perform daily prayers.[74] The PPRA provides federal protection for parents' and students' rights whenever federal funding is involved. Under PPRA, parents have the right to inspect instructional material that addresses a number of controversial areas, including content on sexuality, to ensure that it conforms to their values. To prevent the imposition of secular values, schools must make parents aware that such material is being presented and obtain written consent from parents before exposing children to any of the material.

Muslim Organizations

Social workers should also be aware of the institutions that Muslims have developed to cope with living in a secular culture. Perhaps the most prominent is the *masjid*, or *mosque*. Over 1,200 mosques exist in the United States, and almost 90 percent were founded since 1970.[32] The services offered by mosques in the United States have evolved substantially to meet the unique needs of the Islamic community. In traditional Muslim countries, mosques tend to be places where Muslims have the option of gathering for prayer, particularly Friday midday prayers. In North America, to provide a greater degree of social support to the Islamic community, mosques have tended to expand the range of services they offer. In addition to traditional prayer services, mosques often function as centers for an increasingly diverse array of services, including education for children and adults, counseling services, prison programs, daycare, and youth activities.[25,32,51]

The Muslim Student Association (MSA) is the largest student organization serving the Islamic community in the United States. According to Altaf Husain (personal communication), president of the MSA, there are currently more than 500 chapters in the United States. They offer a number of religious and cultural services, including, perhaps most importantly, social support to the hundreds of thousands of Muslims enrolled on American college campuses.[1]

As an outgrowth of the MSA, former students founded the Islamic Society of North America (ISNA), perhaps the most prominent Muslim organization in the United States.[28,32] The ISNA attempts to foster a degree of commitment and community among American Muslims, both through its own actions and by facilitating a large number of locally based organizations throughout the country.[25,76] ISNA activities are diverse and address most dimensions of Muslim life in America. Services include the provision of instructional materials, journals, workshops, library facilities, housing assistance, a charity fund, women's services, and a marriage bureau that operates a computerized database for matching single individuals with potential partners. Although ISNA attempts to serve all segments of the Muslim population, it tends to be perceived as an organization tailored primarily to meet the needs of immigrants.[25] The Muslim American Society performs many of the same functions for African American Muslims, and numerous additional Muslim organizations have been founded in recent years, with varying degrees of support among the general Muslim population.

Recently emigrated Muslims may be unaware of the range of programs available, since many of the services that have evolved are unique to the American Islamic community. Social workers who are familiar with the array of services in a given area can often function as brokers, linking Muslims to extant programs. The resources and social support such programs provide are often crucial in helping Muslims deal with the stress associated with religious stereotypes, racism, gender inequality, and immigration.[41,42]

Similarly, many Muslims may be unaware of the legislative statues that protect their religious liberties in the United States. The history of their own people in their nation of origin may incline Muslims to believe that the justice system in this nation is also partial and prejudiced. While the court system in the United States is far from perfect, perpetrators of violence and discrimination against Muslims are regularly convicted.

Historical Factors

While historical influences are critical to any population, they may be especially salient with Muslims who have recently immigrated to the United States. As noted above, Muslims in the United States originate from at least 80 different nations.[26] Traumatic events, such as war, famine, and persecution in individuals' culture of origin, can shape how individuals interact with governments, the extent to which they trust "the system," and even their willingness to trust social workers. Similarly, African American Muslims are shaped by a history of racism that often affects their ability to trust European American institutions.

Social workers who regularly work with Muslims from a particular ethnic/national background should consider learning more about that cultural group and the historical influences that shape its interpretation of Islam. For instance, social workers who regularly work with African American Muslims might review Solomon's article on African Americans.[77] Even though the article does not specifically address Muslims, readers are likely to find many of the historical/cultural insights useful in work with African American Muslims. The ramifications of events from previous eras echo down through time, influencing present attitudes and practices.

In tandem with culturally specific influences, it is also important to develop an awareness of historical developments that have shaped the collective Islamic identity. In attempting to work out the implications of an Islamic worldview, Muslims have provided numerous scientific, literary, and artistic contributions to the world. Social workers are unlikely to be familiar with many of these developments since the dominant secular culture tends to highlight advancements that flow from the European Enlightenment. Consequently, social workers might consider familiarizing themselves with some of the major Islamic innovations in these fields.

September 11th

Another historical influence that all Muslims in the United States share is the legacy of the terrorist attacks on American facilities, the most prominent being the September 11, 2001, attacks on the Pentagon and the World Trade Centers. The effects on the Islamic community and the general population have been complex. The fact that the terrorists were Arab and self-identified as Muslims played into lingering stereotypes and prejudices with the result that innocent law-abiding Muslims were often victimized in the immediate aftermath of the attacks.[78] In a series of high-profile appearances, President Bush stressed that Islam is a religion of peace, emphasized that Muslims should be treated with respect, and defended the right of Muslim women to wear the hijab in public settings without fear.[79] Subsequently, public perceptions of Muslims became significantly more favorable. In fact, the general public's view of Muslims was more favorable six months after September 11, than they were before the terrorists' attack.[80]

These developments seem generally congruent with the experience of Muslims in the United States in the months after the attack. When asked to give their opinion on Americans' attitudes toward Muslims since September 11, approximately three-quarters (74 percent) stated that, in their personal experience, Americans had been respectful and tolerant of Muslims.[26]

Concurrently, it is important to note that September 11 fostered an increase in anti-Muslim discrimination. Incidents of alleged discrimination filed by Muslims with the Equal Employment Opportunity Commission (EEOC) from September 11, 2001, to May 7, 2002, more than doubled compared to the number filed one year previously (497 vs. 193).[81] Muslim organizations that track reports of bias reported a threefold increase, including incidents of murder, with reports of discrimination being particularly prominent at airports and ports of entry.[70] Just over half of Muslims (52 percent) know of at least one incident of anti-Muslim discrimination in their community since September 11.[26]

While incidents of discrimination may have declined in the months following September 11,[78] a more long-term concern may be The Uniting and Strengthening America by Proudly Appropriating Tools Required to Intercept and Obstruct Terrorism Act of 2001 (H.R. 3162), better known by its acronym, the USA Patriot Act. The USA Patriot Act was passed by congress in the aftermath of September 11 with little debate. Criticized by members of both the political right and the left, the legislation expands government powers, critics argue, at the expense of civil liberties, while the erosion of civil liberties diminishes everyone's freedom, and many Muslims are concerned that they will be unduly targeted.

Implications for Micro and Macro Practice

The ecosystems approach helps social workers look beyond the level of the individual to complex environmental realities that shape Muslims' existence in the United States. More specifically, it is important to remember the following: the Muslim client is part of an extended family that is informed by Islamic values, which exists in a social environment animated by both detrimental and beneficial structural factors, which in turn is influenced by culturally specific historical events such as September 11. As noted above, Figure 20.1 encapsulates some of the issues that should be examined at each level of the ecosystems model when working with Muslims.

In assessing problems and designing solutions, social workers should consider each of the concentric spheres of the ecosystems approach. Interventions can be aimed at any single level or combination of levels. Clients, however, are much more likely to own and apply suggested interventions if social workers have considered the multiple facets of existence that are represented by the ecosystems model. As the following example illustrates, developing intervention strategies that are appropriate, relevant, and sensitive to the client's worldview typically requires consideration of each level of the ecosystem model.

THE INDIVIDUAL

Mustafa, a 12-year-old boy, was in danger of being expelled from public school for fighting. A Sunni Muslim, Mustafa was born in Detroit, to where his parents had emigrated from Turkey. In previous years, Mustafa had attended a private Islamic school. When Mustafa's father was transferred to California, the family decided to enroll Mustafa in a public school since there were no Islamic schools in the local vicinity. Bright and articulate, and in previous years an excellent student, Mustafa's grades had dropped considerably since he started attending public school a few months ago.

Although Kerry, the school social worker, initially found Mustafa to be somewhat uncommunicative, Mustafa became increasingly open as Kerry wondered about the difficulty Mustafa must have encountered switching from an Islamic school to a public school. Mustafa slowly began sharing some of the problems he was facing as a student of faith in a secular environment. He often found himself going hungry on days the cafeteria served food that contained pork. On Earth Day, one of his teachers had led the class in a meditation session in which students were to visualize themselves as part of Mother Nature, a practice that made Mustafa extremely uncomfortable due to its spiritual overtones. Another teacher had given a writing assignment in which students could write about any subject and then rejected Mustafa's paper, which argued for the sanctity of life from an Islamic perspective, on the grounds that it was "too religious." Although he got along with most students, some ridiculed his faith, called him a "terrorist," and disparaged his mother, who wears a veil, when she came to pick him up at school. Mustafa felt that he had to defend his faith and family, with his fists if necessary.

Figure 20.1

Example of Ecosystems Model for Muslims
in the United States

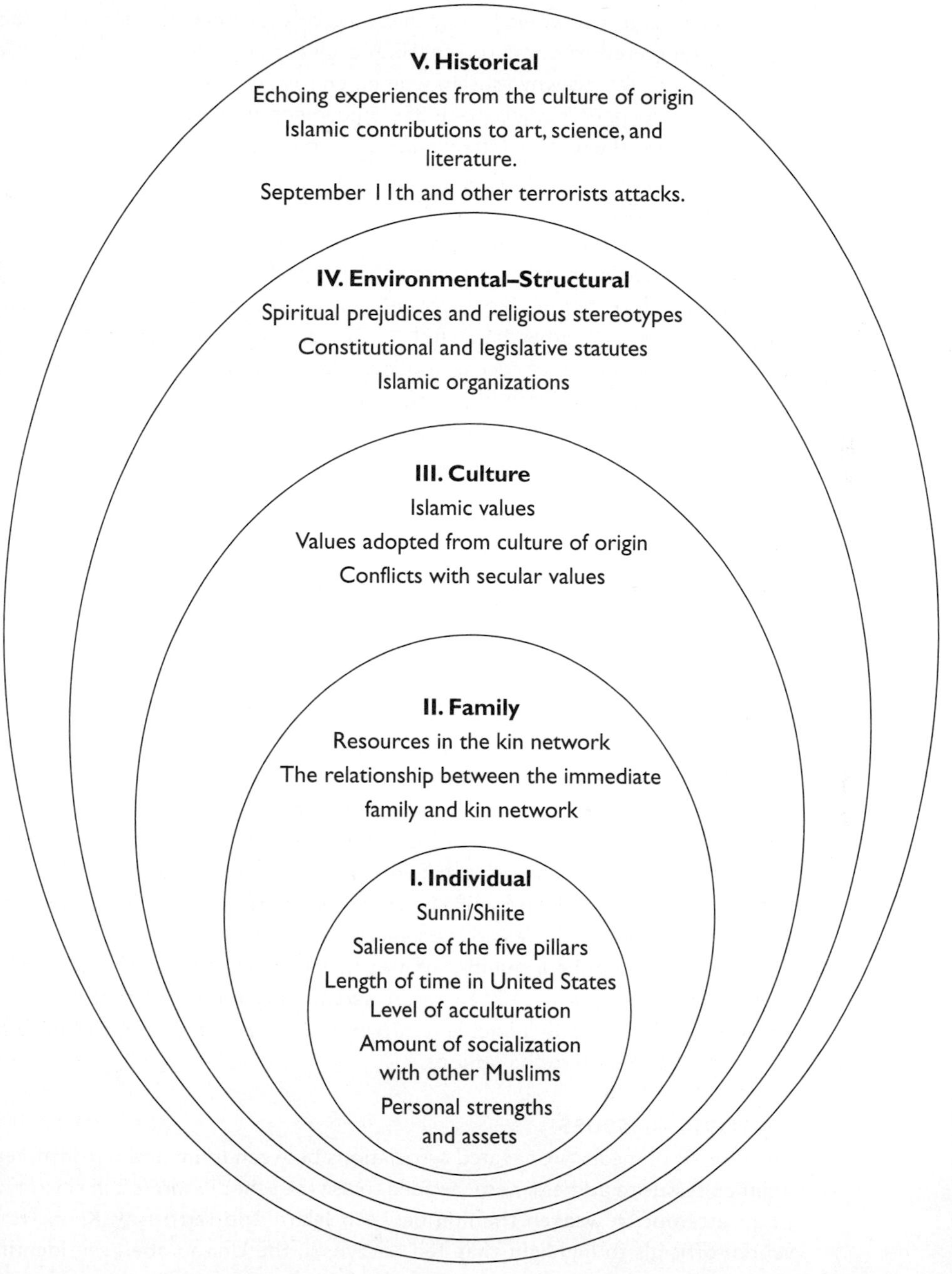

V. Historical

Echoing experiences from the culture of origin

Islamic contributions to art, science, and
literature.

September 11th and other terrorists attacks.

IV. Environmental–Structural

Spiritual prejudices and religious stereotypes

Constitutional and legislative statutes

Islamic organizations

III. Culture

Islamic values

Values adopted from culture of origin

Conflicts with secular values

II. Family

Resources in the kin network

The relationship between the immediate
family and kin network

I. Individual

Sunni/Shiite

Salience of the five pillars

Length of time in United States

Level of acculturation

Amount of socialization
with other Muslims

Personal strengths
and assets

THE FAMILY

Kerry arranged a meeting between Mustafa and his main system of social support, his immediate family. His family was surprised at the situation. Mustafa had not shared the problems he encountered at school because he felt that he had to stand up for the Islamic community on his own. His parents resolved to support Mustafa and communicated to him that they would handle the situations together, as a team. His mother and sisters volunteered to come to school and give a classroom presentation on hijab, explaining the reasons why Muslim women choose to veil. His father offered to share some of his experiences at his place of employment along with strategies he had developed to address the religious stereotypes and prejudices he encountered at work.

CULTURAL ISSUES

Upon meeting Mustafa's family, Kerry built trust by addressing the husband first and then, later in the conversation, asking his permission to speak to his wife and daughters. Kerry also wore modest attire and used more indirect forms of communication (e.g., "In my professional judgment . . . " rather than "I feel . . . "). Adopting a slightly more directive approach, Kerry explored a number of concrete options that might meet the family's goals. Sensitivity was shown to nonverbal forms of communication, as Kerry worked toward coming to a consensus regarding how to tackle the situation. Trust was enhanced by Kerry's demonstrated willingness to advocate with school officials on the family's behalf in a number of areas.

To address the dietary issues concerning pork, Kerry contacted the food services personnel. They arranged for school menus to be sent to Mustafa's mother a week in advance. With prior notice, she was able to prepare a lunch for Mustafa to take to school when the menu consisted of food that was not halal.

ENVIRONMENTAL-STRUCTURAL ISSUES

After contacting the U.S. Department of Education and obtaining constitutional guidelines on the free exercise of religion, Kerry set up a meeting with school officials. In the ensuing discussion, Kerry emphasized two points that directly addressed Mustafa's situation. First, the establishment clause of the U.S. Constitution stipulates that schools must maintain neutrality between competing spiritual belief systems. The classroom implementation of New Age forms of visualization and meditation are prohibited. Second, Kerry noted that the free exercise clause protects students' right to express their religious beliefs. Teachers cannot discriminate against a student's paper just because it presents a religious perspective.

Kerry also phoned a number of mosques in the wider vicinity to ascertain if any offered youth programs or knew of any Islamic organizations that sponsored youth programs. After locating a couple of programs, Kerry sent a letter to Mustafa's father, drawing his attention to the options.

HISTORICAL ISSUES

The historical, media-propagated associations between Islam and terrorism represented a difficult issue to address. Kerry decided to use the school's interest in environmentalism in an attempt to weaken the link between Islam and terrorism. Kerry worked with school officials to highlight that Ted Kaczynski, the Unabomber, self-identified as an environmentalist and was in a significant following in the environmental movement. Yet, because environmentalists generally affirm a value system that resonates with the dominant secular worldview, the media carefully distinguished between the majority of self-identified environmentalists, who advocate for the environment peacefully, and self-described environmentalists that use terrorist tactics in the name of environmentalism. Consequently, few people associate environmentalism with terrorism.

Kerry pointed out that the media adopts a different agenda with Muslims since their spiritual value system fails to resonate with the secular values held by most members of the media. Even though the overwhelming majority of Muslims condemn the use of violence in the name of Islam, the media often fail to distinguish between peaceful Muslims and those who commit acts of violence. Yet, just as it is inappropriate to judge all environmentalists by those who commit violence, so too it is inappropriate to judge all Muslims by those who commit violence. We must deconstruct the ethnocentric discourse propagated by the dominant culture, Kerry argued, and welcome the enriching perspectives Muslims bring to our school, society, and nation.

From one perspective, Kerry's interventions met with mixed results. Having access to the school menus resolved the dietary issues. The presentation by Mustafa's mother and sisters on veiling, in conjunction with Kerry's coupling of Islam and environmentalism, helped foster a more tolerant environment at the school. Conversely, while the school eventually implemented a policy to end the imposition of New Age religious practices on the student population, some teachers still exhibited reluctance to accept spiritually themed papers and Mustafa often felt that he received lower grades when his work presented an Islamic perspective. Although this discrimination was grounds for a lawsuit, Mustafa's parents declined to press the issue in court.

From the perspective of Mustafa's parents, however, Kerry's combination of micro and macro level interventions was a success. Mustafa's grades had improved to their former level. While Mustafa's peers at school still didn't always accept or agree with his Islamic views, they were more respectful and, consequently, fights were a thing of the past. As is the case in other situations, consideration of each level of the ecosystems model is vital for effective, spiritually competent work with Muslims.

Conducting Comment

Muslims in the United States face an uncertain future. International events over which individual Muslims have little control, such as the U.S. military attack and occupation of Iraq, have the potential to dramatically affect the well-being of innocent, law-abiding Muslims. In addition to living with this unpredictability, Muslims must continually deal with the oppression that people of faith encounter in the dominant secular culture.

As a minority population in a hostile cultural environment, Muslims are often in need of advocacy on their behalf. Individual initiatives, legislative efforts, and international actions are needed to ensure that the rights of Muslims and other people of faith are protected. Social workers, due to their unique skill sets, are often ideally situated to provide this advocacy.

Unfortunately, in at least some instances, the social work profession itself has adopted the stance of dominant culture, propagating diaphobic stereotypes that foster misunderstanding and bias toward Muslims. Social workers, however, are called to deconstruct the assumptions of the dominant culture that affect their ability to provide services. Personal biases must be identified and addressed.

As an ethically based profession, the NASW Code of Ethics provides clear guidelines regarding the stance that social workers must adopt toward Muslims and other people of faith. More specifically, social workers should educate themselves about the oppression religious people encounter, avoid derogatory religious language, and refrain from facilitating any form of religious discrimination while actively working to prevent and eliminate religious discrimination. As the NASW Code of Ethics states, social workers are to foster respect for cultural and social diversity within the United States and globally, seeking to ensure justice for *all* people.

KEY WORDS AND CONCEPTS

Muslim
Islam
Hijab
Mosque

Diaphobia
The Five Pillars
Spiritual competency

SUGGESTED INFORMATION SOURCES

Aswad, B. C., and Bilge, B., eds. *Family and Gender Among American Muslims*. Philadelphia: Temple University Press, 1996.

Carolan, M. T., Bagherinia, G., Juhari, R., Himelright, J., and Mouton-Sanders, M. "Contemporary Muslim Families: Research and Practice," *Contemporary Family Therapy* 22, No. 1 (2000).

Esposito, J. L., ed. *The Oxford Encyclopedia of the Modern Islamic World*. New York: Oxford University Press, 1995.

Hodge, D. R. "Social Work and the House of Islam: Orienting Practitioners to the Beliefs and Values of Muslims in the United States," *Social Work* 50(2005):162–173.

Mahmoud, V. "African American Muslim Families," in M. McGoldrick, J. Giordano, and J. K. Pearce, eds., *Ethnicity and Family Therapy*, 2nd edition. New York: Guilford Press, 1996, pp. 122–128.

Smith, J. I. *Islam in America*. New York: Columbia University Press, 1999.

ENDNOTES

1. Yvonne Yazbeck Haddad and Jane I. Smith, "United States of America," in John L. Esposito, ed., *The Oxford Encyclopedia of the Modern Islamic World*, vol. 4 (New York: Oxford University Press, 1995), pp. 277–284.
2. J. Gordon Melton, *The Encyclopedia of American Religions*, 6th Edition (London: Gale Research, 1999).
3. Yvonne Yazbeck Haddad, "Make Room for the Muslims?" in Walter H. Conser Jr. and Summer B. Twiss, eds., *Religious Diversity and American Religious History* (Athens: The University of Georgia Press, 1997), pp. 218–261.
4. P. Scott Richards and Allen E. Bergin, *A Spiritual Strategy* (Washington, D.C.: American Psychological Association, 1997).
5. Belkeis Y. Altareb, "Islamic Spirituality in America: A Middle Path to Unity," *Counseling and Values* 41, no. 1 (1996): 29–38.
6. Manijeh Daneshpour, "Muslim Families and Family Therapy," *Journal of Marital and Family Therapy* 24, no. 3 (1998): 355–390.
7. Anahid Kulwicki, "Health Issues Among Arab Muslim Families," in Barbara C. Aswad and Barbara Bilge, eds., *Family and Gender Among American Muslims* (Philadelphia: Temple University Press, 1996), pp. 187–207.
8. Eugene W. Kelly, Amany Aridi, and Laleh Bakhtiar, "Muslims in the United States: An Exploratory Study of Universal and Mental Health Values," *Counseling and Values* 40, no. 3 (1996): 206–218.
9. Vanessa Mahmoud, "African American Muslim Families," in Monica McGoldrick, Joe Giordano, and John K. Pearce, eds., *Ethnicity and Family Therapy*, 2nd Edition (New York: Guilford Press, 1996), pp. 122–128.
10. Edward R. Canda and Leola Dyrud Furman, *Spiritual Diversity in Social Work Practice* (New York: The Free Press, 1999).
11. NASW Code of Ethics, 1999, www.naswdc.org/Code/ethics.htm (accessed January 20, 2000).
12. David P. Boyle and Alyson Springer, "Toward a Cultural Competence Measure for Social Work with Specific Populations," *Journal of Ethic and Cultural Diversity in Social Work* 9, no. 3/4 (2001): 53–71.
13. Derald Wing Sue, Patricia Arredondo, and Roderick J. McDavis, "Multicultural Counseling Competencies and Standards: A Call to the Profession," *Journal of Counseling and Development* 70, no. 4 (1992): 477–486.
14. Marsha T. Carolan, et al., "Contemporary Muslim Families: Research and Practice," *Contemporary Family Therapy* 22, no. 1 (2000): 67–79.
15. Dale F. Eickelman, *The Middle East and Central Asia*, 3rd Edition (Upper Saddle River, NJ: Prentice Hall, 1998).
16. David Waines, *An Introduction to Islam* (Cambridge: Cambridge University Press, 1995).
17. John L. Esposito, *Islam* (New York: Oxford University Press, 1988).
18. John Renard, *Responses to 101 Questions on Islam* (Mahwah, NJ: Paulist Press, 1998).
19. Syed Arshad Husain, "Religion and Mental Health from the Muslim Perspective," in Harold G. Koenig, ed., *Handbook of Religion and Mental Health* (New York: Academic Press, 1998), pp. 279–291.
20. Paul Lawrence and Cathy Rozmus, "Culturally Sensitive Care of the Muslim Patient," *Journal of Transcultural Nursing* 12, no. 3 (2001): pp. 228–233.

21. Mahmoud M. Ayoub, "United States of America," in John L. Esposito, ed., *The Oxford Encyclopedia of the Modern Islamic World*, vol. 3 (New York: Oxford University Press, 1995), pp. 333–334.

22. Gamal Abou El Azayem and Zari Hedayat-Diba, "The Psychological Aspects of Islam: Basic Principles of Islam and Their Psychological Corollary," *The International Journal for the Psychology of Religion* 4, no. 1 (1994): 41–50.

23. Akbar S. Ahmed, "Popular Religion in Europe and the Americas," in John L. Esposito, ed., *The Oxford Encyclopedia of the Modern Islamic World*, vol. 3 (New York: Oxford University Press, 1995), pp. 354–358.

24. Elise Goldwasser, "Economic Security and Muslim Identity: A Study of the Immigrant Community in Durham, North Carolina," in Yvonne Haddad and John L. Esposito, eds., *Muslims on the Americanization Path?* (Atlanta: Scholars Press, 1998), pp. 379–397.

25. Jane I. Smith, *Islam in America* (New York: Columbia University Press, 1999).

26. American Muslim poll (Washington, D.C.: Project MAPS: Muslims in the American Public Square, 2001).

27. Barry A. Kosmin and Seymour P. Lachman, *One Nation Under God* (New York: Harmony Books, 1993).

28. Frederick Mathewson Denny, "Islam in the Americas," in John L. Esposito, ed., *The Oxford Encyclopedia of the Modern Islamic World*, vol. 2 (New York: Oxford University Press, 1995), pp. 296–300.

29. Carol L. Stone, "Estimate of Muslims Living in America," in Yvonne Yazbeck Haddad, ed., *The Muslims of America* (New York: Oxford University Press, 1991), pp. 25–36.

30. Raymond Brady Williams, "South Asian Religions in the United States," in John R. Hinnells, ed., *A New Handbook of Living Religions* (New York: Penguin Books, 1997), pp. 796–818.

31. Jonah Blank, "The Muslim Mainstream," *U.S. News and World Report* 20, 7 (1998): 22–25.

32. Ihsan Bagby, Paul M. Perl, and Bryan T. Froehle, *The Mosque in America: A National Portrait* (Washington, D.C.: Council on American-Islamic Relations, 2001).

33. Elizabeth Warnock Fernea, "Family," in John L. Esposito, ed., *The Oxford Encyclopedia of the Modern Islamic World*, vol. 1 (New York: Oxford University Press, 1995), pp. 458–461.

34. Dena Saadat Hassouuneh-Phillips, "'Marriage is Half of Faith and the Rest is Fear of Allah,'" *Violence Against Women* 7, no. 8 (August 2001): 927–946.

35. Yvonne Y. Haddad and Jane I. Smith, "Islamic Values Among American Muslims," in Barbara C. Aswad and Barbara Bilge, eds., *Family and Gender Among American Muslims* (Philadelphia: Temple University Press, 1996), pp. 19–40.

36. Munir A. Shaikh, *Teaching About Islam and Muslims in the Public School Classroom*, 3rd Edition (Fountain Valley, CA: Council on Islamic Education, 1995).

37. David R. Hodge, "Spiritual Ecomaps: A New Diagrammatic Tool for Assessing Marital and Family Spirituality," *Journal of Marital and Family Therapy* 26, no. 1 (2000): 229–240.

38. David R. Hodge, "Spiritual Genograms: A Generational Approach to Assessing Spirituality," *Families in Society* 82, no. 1 (2001): 35–48.

39. Alphonso W. Haynes, et al., "Islamic Social Transformation: Considerations for the Social Worker," *International Social Work* 40 (1997): 265–275.

40. Mumtaz F. Jafari, "Counseling Values and Objectives: A Comparison of Western and Islamic Perspectives," *The American Journal of Islamic Social Sciences* 10, no. 3 (1993): 326–339.

41. Michelle D. Byng, "Mediating Discrimination: Resisting Oppression Among African American Muslim Women," *Social Problems* 45, no. 4 (1998): 473–487.
42. Fariyal Ross-Sheriff, "Immigrant Muslim Women in the United States: Adaptation to American Society," *Journal of Social Work Research* 2, no. 2 (2001): 283–294.
43. Rafic Banawi and Rex Stockton, "Islamic Values Relevant to Group Work, with Practical Applications for the Group Leader," *The Journal for Specialists in Group Work* 18, no. 3 (1993): 151–160.
44. M. Z. Azhar, S. L. Varma, and A. S. Dharap, "Religious Psychotherapy in Anxiety Disorder Patients," *Acta Psychiatrica Scandinavica* 90 (1994): 1–2.
45. M. Z. Azhar and S. L. Varma, "Religious Psychotherapy as Management of Bereavement," *Acta Psychiatrica Scandinavica* 91 (1995): 233–235.
46. M. Z. Azhar and S. L. Varma, "Religious Psychotherapy in Depressive Patients," *Psychotherapy and Psychosomatics* 63 (1995): 165–168.
47. *Diagnostic and Statistical Manual of Mental Disorders*, 4th Edition (Washington, D.C.: American Psychiatric Association, 1994).
48. Cyril Simmons, Christine Simmons, and Mohammed Habib Allah, "English, Israeli-Arab and Saudi Arabian Adolescent Values," *Educational Studies* 20, no. 1 (1994): 69–86.
49. Richard B. Carter and Amelia E. El Hindi, "Counseling Muslim Children in School Settings," *Professional School Counseling* 2, no. 3 (1999): 183–188.
50. Majed A. Ashy, "Health and Illness from an Islamic Perspective," *Journal of Religion and Health* 38, no. 3 (1999): 241–257.
51. Julia Mitchell Corbett, *Religion in America*, 2nd Edition (Englewood Cliffs, NJ: Prentice Hall, 1994).
52. J. Mark Halstead and Katarzyna Lewicka, "Should Homosexuality Be Taught as an Acceptable Alternative Lifestyle? A Muslim Perspective," *Cambridge Journal of Education* 28, no. 1 (1998): 49–64.
53. Charles Kemp, "Islamic Cultures: Health-Care Beliefs and Practices," *American Journal of Health Behavior* 20, no. 3 (1996): 83–89.
54. Tim Hamilton and Satish Sharma, "The Violence and Oppression of Power Relations," *Peace Review* 9, no. 4 (1997): 555–561.
55. Kathryn G. Wambach and Dorothy Van Soest, "Oppression," in Richard L. Edwards, ed., *1997 Supplement*, 19th Edition (Washington, D.C.: NASW Press, 1997), pp. 243–252.
56. Carol Gilligan, *In a Different Voice: Psychological Theory and Women's Development* (Cambridge, MA: Harvard University Press, 1993).
57. David R. Hodge, "Conceptualizing Spirituality in Social Work: How the Metaphysical Beliefs of Social Workers May Foster Bias Towards Theistic Consumers," *Social Thought* 21, no. 1 (2002): 39–61.
58. Bobby S. Sayyid, *A Fundamental Fear* (New York: St. Martin's Press, 1997).
59. Amal Omar Madani, "Depiction of Arabs and Muslims in the United States News Media," Dissertation, California School of Professional Psychology—Los Angeles, 2000, p. 9-B.
60. Nadege Soubiale and Nicolas Roussiau, "Social Representation of Islam and Changes in the Stereotypes of Muslims," *Psicologia, Teoria e Pesquisa: Brasilia* 14, no. 3 (September–December 1998): 191–202.
61. Greg Noakes, "Muslims and the American Press," in Yvonne Haddad and John L. Esposito, eds., *Muslims on the Americanization Path?* (Atlanta: Scholars Press, 1998), pp. 361–378.

62. Ronald Stockton, "Ethnic Archetypes and the Arab Image," in Ernest McCarus, ed., *The Development of Arab-American Identity* (Ann Arbor: The University of Michigan Press, 1994), pp. 119–153.

63. David R. Hodge, Lisa M. Baughman, and Julie A. Cummings, "Moving Toward Spiritual Competency: Deconstructing Religious Stereotypes and Spiritual Prejudices in Social Work Literature," Paper presented at the [Forty-Eighth Annual Program Meeting] Council on Social Work Education, February 24–27, Nashville, TN, 2002.

64. Katherine Van Wormer, *Social Welfare* (Chicago: Nelson-Hall Publishers, 1997).

65. Ernest Gellner, *Postmodernism, Reason and Religion* (New York: Routledge, 1992).

66. Daniel Price, "Islam and Human Rights: A Case of Deceptive First Appearances," *Journal for the Scientific Study of Religion* 41, no. 2 (2002): 213–225.

67. Esmail Shakeri, "Muslim Women in Canada: Their Role and Status as Revealed in the Hijab Controversy," in Yvonne Haddad and John L. Esposito, eds., *Muslims on the Americanization Path?* (Atlanta: Scholars Press, 1998), pp. 159–178.

68. Debra Reece, "Covering and Communication: The Symbolism of Dress Among Muslim Women," *The Howard Journal of Communication* 7, no. 35 (1996): 35–52.

69. Louise Cainkar, "Immigrant Palestinian Women Evaluate Their Lives," in Barbara C. Aswad and Barbara Bilge, eds., *Family and Gender Among American Muslims* (Philadelphia: Temple University Press, 1996), pp. 41–58.

70. Council on American-Islamic Relations Research Center, *The Status of Muslim Civil Rights in the United States 2002: Stereotypes and Civil Liberties* (Washington, D.C.: Council on American-Islamic Relations, 2002).

71. Zari Hedayat-Diba, "Psychotherapy with Muslims," in P. Scott Richards and Allen E. Bergin, eds., *Handbook of Psychotherapy and Religious Diversity* (Washington, D.C.: American Psychological Association, 2000), pp. 289–314.

72. Sarah Shafi, "A Study of Muslim Asian Women's Experiences of Counseling and the Necessity for a Racially Similar Counselor," *Counseling Psychology Quarterly* 11, no. 3 (1998): 301–314.

73. Alean Al-Krenawi, "Group Work with Bedouin Widows of the Negev in a Medical Clinic," *Affilia* 11, no. 3 (1996): 303–318.

74. Richard W. Riley, "Religious Expression in Public Schools," 1998, http://www.ed.gov/Speeches/08–1995/religion.html (accessed July 11, 2001).

75. William J. Clinton, "Memorandum for the U.S. Secretary of Education and the U.S. Attorney General," 1995, http://w3.trib.com/FACT/1st.pres.rel.html (accessed December 11, 1999).

76. Gutbi Mahdi Ahmed, "Muslim Organizations in the United States," in Yvonne Yazbeck Haddad, ed., *The Muslims of America* (New York: Oxford University Press, 1991), pp. 11–24.

77. Barbara Bryant Solomon, "Social Work Practice with African Americans," in Armando T. Morales and Bradford W. Sheafor, eds., *Social Work: A Profession with Many Faces*, 9th Edition (Needham, MA: Allyn and Bacon, 2001), pp. 519–539.

78. RNS Newservice, "Report: Anti-Muslim Violence May Be Declining," Religion News Service, October 26, 2001, http://pewforum.org/news/index.php3?NewsID-827 (accessed May 23, 2002).

79. Shelvia Dancy, "Bush Visits Mosque, Warns Against Anti-Muslims Violence," Religion News Service, September 17, 2001, http://pewforum.org/news/index.php3?NewsID=730 (accessed May 23, 2002).

80. Luis Lugo, "Muslim-Americans Gaining Respect," *The Atlanta Journal-Constitution,* March 25, 2002, http://accessatlanta.com/ajc/opinion/0303/0325muslims.html (accessed May 23, 2002).

81. U.S. Equal Employment Opportunity Commission, "EEOC Provides Answers About Workplace Rights of Muslims, Arabs, South Asians and Sikhs," U.S. Equal Employment Opportunity Commission, May 15, 2002, http://www.eeoc.gov/press/5-15-02.html (accessed July 23, 2002).

chapter 21

Social Work Practice with Asian Americans

Doman Lum

Prefatory Comment

One of the fastest growing segments of the U.S. population is the people of Asian background. The 2000 Census counted almost 10.7 million people of Asian descent (3.8 percent of the total population) and projects this will grow to 14.2 million people (4.6 percent) by 2010 and almost 18 million (5.4 percent) by 2020.[1] This population is difficult to describe because it is made up of people from many different Asian countries, such as, Korea, India, Japan, China, Laos, Vietnam, Cambodia, the Philippines, Guam, and others, and thus culturally competent social work practice with this population requires knowledge of and skill in working with many cultures. Doman Lum, Professor of Social Work at California State University at Sacramento, sorts out similarities and differences among these cultures. In addition, he highlights issues affecting practice to which the social worker should be sensitive.

The term *Asian American* may be seen as a geographical and political designation that covers a wide and diverse group of people whose country and culture of origin are from the continent of Asia and islands of the Pacific. The proper designation for this group is *Asian American/Pacific Islander*.

From a geographical perspective, there are thirty-eight Asian nations, which can be grouped into the five following entities: (1) China and India dominate the Asian population and land mass; (2) Japan is an island group; (3) Korea is positioned between China and Japan; (4) the Southeast Asian satellite primary countries are Vietnam, Thailand, Cambodia, Laos, and Malaysia; and (5) the island nations of Indonesia and Philippines, which are closer to Asia than the island regions of Micronesia, Melanesia, and Polynesia.

Demographics

The Asian population in the United States is projected to grow from 10.7 million people in 2000 to 33.4 million in 2050, increasing to 8 percent of the total U.S. population.[2] Driving the Asian population growth is Asian immigration. An estimated

63 percent of Asian Americans are foreign born; most speak English, with only 37 percent unable to speak English fluently or very well.[3]

Six countries of national origin made up nearly 90 percent of the U.S. Asian population, according to the 2000 U.S. Census. These countries were China (2.7 million people), the Philippines (2.4 million), India (1.9 million), Vietnam (1.2 million), Korea (1.2 million), and Japan (1.1 million). No more than about 200,000 Asian Americans were from any of the other Asian countries.[4] The regional distribution of Asians is approximately 2.1 million (18.8 percent) in the Northeast, 1.2 million (10.7 percent) in the Midwest, 1.9 million (17.0 percent) in the South, and 6.0 million, or 53.6 percent, in the West.[5]

Gender

Recently attention has been devoted to Asian American women due to a lack of information about their gender status and condition.[6,7] There is a high rate of interracial marriage among Asian American women, with Japanese American women outmarrying the most in the continental United States and Chinese Americans in Hawaii. Domestic violence against Asian battered women is often hidden due to family and marriage images portrayed to the Asian community. Asian women spousal abuse reveals factors such as extreme isolation; immigration dependency; reinforced powerlessness from society; traditional views of family and community, which place family before oneself; and a lack of economic and cultural resources to leave a violent situation.[8]

Socioeconomic Issues

Education is an important priority for every population group, and Asian Americans are better educated than any other racial/cultural group in the United States. The 2000 Census indicates that although the percent of Asian people who do not complete high school is about the same as the national average (19.6 percent), 44.0 percent complete a bachelor's degree or higher as compared to 24.4 percent for the total population.[9] These trends are due to the value placed on educational achievement by students' parents and the hard work ethic and willingness of Asian American students to make economic and social sacrifices to achieve academic success. Higher education is the gateway to professional jobs in such fields as science, medicine, engineering, law, business, and social work.

Linked to success in higher education and the value placed on industriousness in many of the Asian/Pacific Island cultures is a relatively high average income. In 2003, as compared to the total U.S. population with a median income of $45,572, the median income for Asian households was $55,699.[10] It was estimated that 6.1 million Asians (66.4 percent of the age 16 and older civilian population) were employed in 2003, and only 4.0 percent of those who wanted jobs were unemployed. The significantly higher median income and solid employment record should not obscure the fact that more than one out of ten Asian people were living in poverty.[11] Poverty was more common among recent immigrants from Southeast Asian countries who tend to lack education, are limited in speaking English, and have few marketable job skills. Thus Asian refugees tend to end up in deadend jobs, such as restaurant and garment factory workers, and often lack occupational mobility due to low levels of educational preparation.[12] Social work, therefore, has a role to play in addressing the socioeconomic issues of a substantial part of the Asian American population.

Housing and Health Status

In 2005, it was estimated that only 53.2 percent of the Asian American and 45.5 percent of the Native Hawaiian and Pacific Island populations own their own homes, as compared to the national average of 66.2 percent. In these cultures, priority is typically given to securing education and employment over home owner-ship. The lower level of ownership results in Asian Americans paying high rents (particularly on the West Coast), loss of the opportunity for tax write-offs on mortgages, and the necessity of living in crowded conditions. Statistics from the Asian Pacific American Community Development Data Center rate 14 percent of the Asian American homes as overcrowded, as compared to 3 percent of the housing units in the United States.[13]

Regarding health status, Asians have lower rates of infant mortality (4.8 deaths before age 1 per 1,000 live births) in 2002, compared with a total population indicator of 7.0 for all races. In addition, the age adjusted death rate, too, is sub-stantially lower: the national average is 853.3 per 100,000, while for Asian Americans it is only 299.5. However, there is an above average incidence of tuber-culosis (45.4 compared with a total population indicator of 9.4 per 100,000) due to the high number of Asian immigrants living in cramped quarters in metropolitan areas with poor air quality. The most recent life expectancy data indicates that Asians as a group were above average; they were expected to live an average of 80 years vs. 77.3 years for the general population.[14] Thus social workers are espe-cially needed to address the need for quality housing and assisting families as they support the older Asian people.

Health and Mental Health Risk Factors

Among the health and mental health problems of Asian Americans are depression, somatic complaints, anxiety disorders, adjustment disorders, and suicide.[15] Lee reports: "Work-related stress among the Asian American working class and under-class has exacerbated domestic tensions. Adjustment difficulties and challenges to traditional relations have troubled many marriages. Indeed, domestic violence afflicts all classes of Asian American families."[16] Hate crimes due to racism have compounded the environmental stress experienced by the Asian American commu-nity. Posttraumatic stress disorder is common among Southeast Asian refugees (par-ticularly Vietnamese, Cambodian, Hmong, and Mien), who fled their homelands and experienced atrocities (e.g., rape, murder, and robbery) in the process of leaving their countries, in refugee camps, and on entering the United States.

Ethnic Group Stressors

Loo has documented sustained racism against Asian Americans in the United States during recent decades.[17] She declares: "In the 1980s, Asian Americans became scapegoats for America's economic woes. Americans of Asian ancestry wore the mantle of foreignness, falsely blamed for the economic recession of the U.S. automobile industry. The 1982 race-hate murder of Vincent Chin in Detroit and rising incidents of anti-Asian violence in the 1980s were cases in point."[18] Later Loo observes: "The focus on suspected illegality of Asian donations to the Democratic Party campaign funds ha[s] reactivated racial stereotypes of the Chinese. Racist cartoons of President Clinton, Hillary Clinton, and Al Gore with slant eyes and clothed in Mandarin coats, appeared in the *National Review.* The cartoon was a startling throwback to anti-Asian cartoons of the 1800s."[19] Minority group racism against Asian Americans remains a national reality. Among older Americans, there are traces of racism against Japanese Americans, who were scapegoats during World War II. In many parts of the country where there are few Asian Americans, an individual experiences being an isolated and lonely minority person surrounded by invisible barriers of exclusion.

Intergenerational Asian American group stressors include the "parachute kid" phenomena of teenage children from upper middle class and wealthy Asians from Hong Kong, Taiwan, and other Asian areas who are dropped off in large metropolitan areas populated by Asian Americans, housed in exclusive-area homes, and left to attend American high schools on their own. Parents visit periodically from abroad or ask relatives in the United States to look after them. An alternative is to ask a sister or a brother in the United States to be a surrogate parent and to raise a teenage nephew or niece so that an Asian-born child can graduate from an American high school and enter an American university. Family development and raising a child are sacrificed for an American education. Parental responsibilities are abdicated by parents in their own country for a relative to assume teenage rearing in the United States.

Asian husband "astronauts" are depicted as businessmen who must travel abroad between their homes and family in the United States and various parts of Asia to maintain their business contacts and enterprises in, say, Hong Kong. Being left alone for months, Asian American families are stressed by the absence of the father, by the role of the mother as interim head of the household, and by the acting out of the children. Such families must constantly adjust and readjust to the husband and father who is coming and going.

The frail, elderly, single male in Chinatown who never married due to miscegenation laws lives alone in a small and dingy room. Early state laws prohibited the marriage of white women and nonwhite men. At the same time, immigration laws excluded admitting Chinese into the United States during the first half of the twentieth century. With no family to care and little government assistance, this elderly person struggles from day to day on small means, is isolated, and dies alone and forgotten.

Asian youth gangs in large cities with overseas-born members who are marginal students or school dropouts have been responsible for intimidating Asian businesses, such as restaurants and grocery stores, for protection money or have committed home invasion robberies, which target Asian families who keep large sums of money, jewelry, and other valuables in their homes. Some Asian families avoid putting assets in the bank for safe keeping and have them available at home for ready access. Brutal force (beatings or murder) is used to obtain "easy money."

Asian American gays and lesbians have experienced stress in coming out to their families. The homosexual lifestyle is against Asian cultural mores and the importance of perpetuating the next generation of the family and is still a source of shame for many traditional Asian Americans. Sexuality is a private matter. Social-support networks are needed to work with gay and lesbian persons, their families, and the attitude of the Asian American community.

 ## Service Systems

Service Delivery

Service delivery involves the detailed arrangements of programs, staffing, facilities, funding, and administrative management that take into account the unique features of the Asian community. Five principles are related to service delivery: (1) location and pragmatic services, (2) staffing, (3) community outreach programs, (4) agency setting, and (5) service linkage.[20] The following discussion explains the meaning of these service delivery areas.

It is important for the *location* of services to be within walking distance of the designated Asian American target group that the agency wishes to serve as a provider. Many Asian service centers are located in areas heavily populated by Asian Americans and are housed in storefronts, churches, ethnic associations, and agencies. Chinatown, Japantown or Little Tokyo, Koreatown, Little Saigon, and other designated areas reach Asian clients who live in the area, depend on public transportation, and are without private cars. Asian clients tend to avoid services labeled mental health center (mental illness is a social stigma) and are drawn toward services that have a pragmatic value (child and family education). An agency should select a location and a name that reflect these principles.

Bilingual and bicultural *staffing* should reflect the Asian American client population. In Asian American agencies, there are ethnic and linguistic skilled workers who are Chinese, Filipino, Japanese, Korean, Vietnamese, Hmong, and related groups and who have access to bilingual workers matching other clients. At the same time, a non-minority social worker who is both bilingual and bicultural can be an integral and effective part of the staff, if he or she is able to speak the language and is familiar with the culture.

Community outreach programs afford an agency staff exposure and credibility to the key institutions in the Asian American community. It is crucial to conduct educational workshops and set up information booths at ethnic festivals, language schools, ethnic churches, family associations, and related community groups. Planting the seeds of knowledge and service provision reap referrals and follow-up opportunities with community leaders.

The *agency setting* should reflect art and cultural items that communicate a message of sensitivity to the Asian community. A friendly bilingual receptionist, a welcome and relaxed atmosphere, and a plan to respond to walk-in clients create a conducive environment that sends a positive message to client and community.

Service linkage establishes a working relationship between existing agencies in the Asian community and institutions in the wider social service network. It is important to establish professional ties to key workers in grass-root ethnic organizations, churches, and service professional groups so that Asian clients are able to move easily through the service systems.

Role of the Social Worker

The role of the social worker in the service delivery system to Asian Americans involves the development of culturally specific services to meet the needs of specific Asian American client groups. There has been a debate between culture-common (etic) and culture-specific (emic) service delivery that can be framed around Asian American service agencies.[21] That is, should there be culturally common services that meet the needs of all clients or should there be culturally specific services to address the particular needs of Asian American people? Or, in a narrower perspective, should there be culturally common services for all Asian Americans or should there be single-ethnic agencies to meet the unique problems of a specific Asian American group? The social worker could advocate for a service agency to meet all types of Asian Americans, because it is cost effective and integrates the diversity of the Asian American community. At the same time, the worker might see the need for a service agency that addresses a particular group (e.g., Chinese, Japanese, Korean, or Vietnamese) due to the heavy community demands and ethnic leader support.

Sue, Mak, and Sue point out that the diversity in the Asian American community is becoming even more heterogeneous. There are Asians who have resided in the United States for many generations and those who immigrated here recently and cannot speak English, and their socioeconomic status is quite diverse, from those considered affluent to those far below the poverty line. They conclude: "Coupling these factors with the varying ethnicities (e.g., Asian Indian, Cambodian, Chinese, Filipino, Hmong, Japanese, Korean, Laotian, Samoan, Thai, Tongan, Vietnamese) it does not take much to conclude that any single theory of Asian American identity development would be an oversimplification and inadequate."[22] Discussion around focusing services on all Asian American groups housed under one roof or fostering single Asian group services is an interesting point of communication among social workers who are concerned with service delivery arrangements.

Service Gaps and Needs

Asian American communities in large metropolitan areas, such as Los Angeles, New York City, San Francisco, Seattle, and Sacramento, have nurtured clusters of Asian American social service networks that meet a variety of needs in their locales. Service delivery cooperation and coordination among Asian American service providers are crucial as funding diminishes or shifts toward specialized needs or new immigrant influx, and federal or state programs come on line to meet other needs.

Iglehart and Becerra offer a number of interesting agency linkage principles that are applicable to Asian American service delivery. They point out that ethnic agencies often receive funding for specialized services to ethnic groups from mainstream social services on the county or state levels. This means that Asian American agencies must conduct program evaluations to justify their existence and be accountable to government entities. Moreover, they must be cost effective and target funding wisely. In an interorganizational relationship, they observe that the ethnic agency has access to a particular ethnic population because of its presence in the ethnic community and its relationship with specific target populations.[23] In other words, Asian American agencies must cultivate good lines of communication, cooperation, and collaboration with the local Asian community, in general, and with particular groups if they want to continue serving them. Moreover, changing federal funding requirements develop partnerships between mainstream agencies and ethnic agencies, demand reduction in service duplication, and define special populations in need. Asian American agencies should cultivate working relationships with county, state, and federal officials who have special knowledge about service program trends affecting Asian American populations. There is a nucleus of important Asian Americans in the House of Representatives and the U.S. Senate who are willing to brief Asian service providers about legislative program development and funding that is anticipated or available. These are some of the ways that social workers in the Asian American community can proceed to close gaps and meet needs.

Micro Practice Perspectives

The Problem-Solving Approach

Chin reports that Asians who seek assistance expect a generalist helper or advice giver, an authority figure who takes a directive approach and provides concrete social services.[24] Lee asserts: "*A problem-focused, goal-oriented, and symptom-relieving approach* is highly recommended in the beginning phases of treatment. Rather than defining goals in abstract, emotional terms, goals may be best stated in terms of external resolution or symptom reduction."[25] Lee recommends the following treatment strategies with Asian American families:

1. Form a social and cultural connection with the family during the first session.
2. Acknowledge the family's sense of shame.
3. Establish expertise, power, credibility, and authority.

4. Define the problem.
5. Apply a family psycho-educational approach.
6. Build alliance with members with power.
7. Employ reframing techniques.
8. Assume multiple helping roles.
9. Restructure the social support system.
10. Integrate Eastern–Western health approaches.
11. Mobilize the family's cultural strength.
12. Employ the concept of empowerment as a treatment goal.
13. Understand the family's communication style.
14. Acknowledge countertransference and racial stereotypes.[26]*

The problem-solving, task-centered intervention is familiar to social work practitioners. Uba observes that Asian Americans expect the worker to give advice, recommend courses of action, and tell them how to resolve their problems. In a way, the social worker is asked to behave like a physician: to conduct an examination, make a diagnosis, and write out a prescription. This intervention strategy emphasizes a clear, detailed plan and straightforward solutions to concrete and immediate problems.

Problem solving is a rational, step-by-step procedure that requires cognitive mental comprehension and behavioral action. It involves six steps:

1. *Problem identification.* It is important for the Asian client to acknowledge and define the problem he or she is facing. It may be done in an indirect way ("I have a friend who has this problem . . . ") or the worker may have to piece together the problem and define the problem cluster or the interrelated set of problems for the client who may be too ashamed to articulate the problem directly.

2. *Problem analysis.* Analyzing a problem involves uncovering its history, placing the events and persons in chronological order, and assessing the needs of the person involved. It is important to find out what has happened in the past four to six weeks (acute crisis) and within the past six months to one year (important past history). Socioenvironmental stressors affecting the Asian client are an integral part of problem analysis.

3. *Solution alternatives.* Based on the identified problem, problem solving moves to examining a range of alternative solutions. The worker should ask the Asian client about possible solutions to the problem, several of which may be realistic and possible. The worker and the client should work on feasible solutions together, although the worker may have to generate some alternatives to initiate discussion. A potential solution is clear, realistic, specific, and attainable in a short period.

4. *Solution prioritization.* Each viable solution should be reviewed in order to find the most effective and realistic way to solve the problem. It is important to engage

---

*The reader is encouraged to read Evelyn Lee's Chapter 1, "Overview: The Assessment and Treatment of Asian American Families," in Evelyn Lee, editor, *Working with Asian Americans: A Guide for Clinicians* (New York: Guilford Publications, 1998).

the client in a discussion of the pros and cons of each potential solution so that the client may ultimately "own" the solution for him- or herself.

5. *Solution implementation.* After the client selects a solution, the next step is to implement the solution by constructing a number of task assignments that lead the client from the present situation to the changes needed. A task is a constructive action taken in response to a problem.

6. *Problem-solving evaluation.* It is important to observe and monitor behavioral and situational changes that have occurred in the process of implementing a problem solution. Keeping a diary or journal and logging who was involved, where and when the changes occurred, and what actually happened provide an opportunity for the worker and client to review progress at the next session.[27]

Ecosystems Model Framework

With the problem-solving, task-centered approach as a micro practice intervention for Asian Americans in mind, we turn to the ecosystems model framework, which involves gathering information and exploring and weighing dynamics in problem-solving processing. There are five dimensions of ecosystems problem solving: historical factors, environmental–structural factors, culture, the family, and the individual. Figure 21.1 illustrates the various levels.

Historical Factors

Asian Americans may incorporate a *psychohistorical reaction response.* That is, the history of oppression impacting this group may cause a psychological survival response from an Asian American client. Uba summarizes research on Asian American personality patterns regarding abasement, affiliation, anxiety, assertiveness, autonomy, conformity, expressiveness, extroversion, formality, locus of control, self-concept, and sex roles, with allowances for intraethnic variation in personality. The social worker should take a brief ethnic history of the client.[28]

During the mid-1800s and early 1900s, Asians of many nationalities came to the United States to pursue economic opportunities, to escape political oppression, and to migrate permanently to the West. Many Chinese and Japanese entered as laborers who expected to return to their homeland and retire in comfort after making their fortune in this country. As the Chinese succeeded in agricultural and mining endeavors, growing anti-Chinese sentiment spread among white gold miners and farmers. Riots, hangings, and evictions of Chinese spread throughout the West Coast. The Chinese were barred from entering the country through the Chinese Exclusion Act of 1882, denied American citizenship and the right to intermarriage, and contained in Chinatowns of major American cities. Similarly, the Japanese suffered limited immigration in the 1907 Gentlemen's Agreement and were denied ownership of land in the 1913 Alien Land Bill. The Immigration Act of 1924 closed the door to Asian immigrants and favored those from European countries. At the

Figure 21.1

Ecosystems Model for Analysis of Factors Impacting Asian Americans

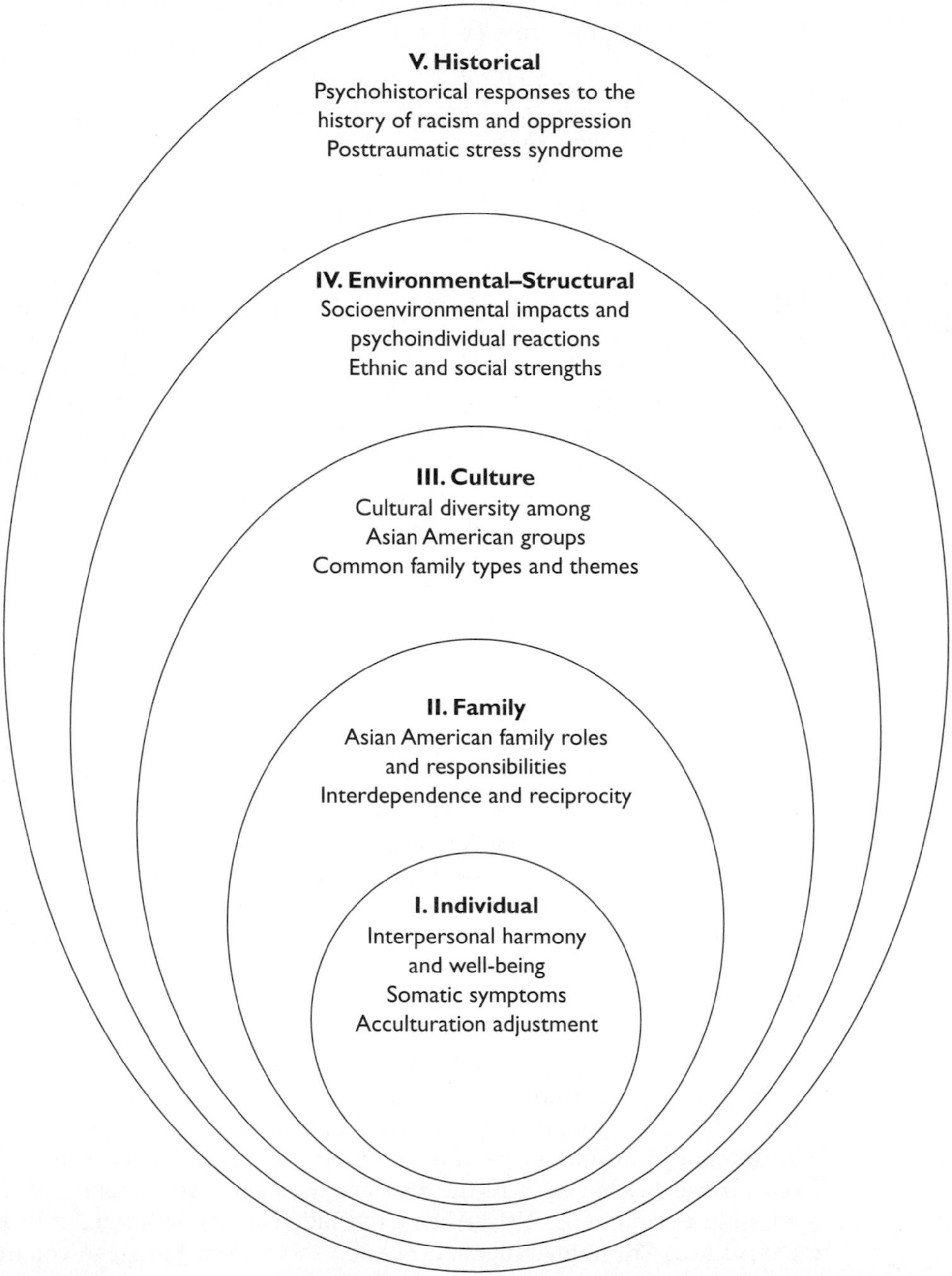

V. Historical
Psychohistorical responses to the
history of racism and oppression
Posttraumatic stress syndrome

IV. Environmental–Structural
Socioenvironmental impacts and
psychoindividual reactions
Ethnic and social strengths

III. Culture
Cultural diversity among
Asian American groups
Common family types and themes

II. Family
Asian American family roles
and responsibilities
Interdependence and reciprocity

I. Individual
Interpersonal harmony
and well-being
Somatic symptoms
Acculturation adjustment

early stages of World War II, President Roosevelt issued Executive Order 9066 on February 12, 1942, removing Japanese Americans along the West Coast from their homes and businesses to rural internment camps for the duration of the war. This had a major psychohistorical impact on all Japanese Americans, which is still felt today. However, since China was an ally during the war, war refugees from China were allowed into the United States for relief purposes.

The 1965 Immigration Act opened the United States to all countries. Asian immigrants from Hong Kong, Korea, the Philippines, and later from Southeast Asia after the Vietnam War (Vietnamese, Hmong, Mien, Laotians, and Cambodians) streamed into the United States.

Ho reports that the Filipino immigration population in the 1960s consisted of young professional males and females, many of whom experienced difficulties with obtaining U.S. professional licensure for foreign graduates. Moreover, many elderly Filipinos who came as unskilled laborers in the early 1920s are alone and isolated, with health care problems and living in cheap substandard housing. Korean immigration since 1965 has mushroomed due to political problems and the influx of Koreans who have been educated in the United States. The Korean American community is represented in the major West and East Coast metropolitan areas with small businesses (e.g., dry cleaning shops, convenience stores) and Christian churches. Pacific Islanders, particularly residents of American Samoa and Guam, have arrived in the United States because of their U.S. citizenship. Pacific Islanders from Tonga, Fiji, and Hawaii have been influenced by the Church of Jesus Christ of Latter-Day Saints, who believe that these regional groups are part of the lost tribe of Israel. Vietnamese, Cambodians, Hmong, and Mien entered this country as a result of the Vietnam War. Many Southeast Asian refugees have suffered posttraumatic stress in their flight from their homelands through holding camps in Thailand to their entrance into the United States. The first wave of refugees, mainly from Vietnam, consisted of highly professional and educated Vietnamese who integrated into this country, while succeeding waves were unskilled and minimally educated and became welfare dependent. Second-generation American-born Vietnamese have graduated from American universities and adjusted and acculturated in their communities.[29]

Part of taking an ethnic history incorporating psychohistorical factors is becoming aware of *acculturative stress* (e.g., loss of family members, role reversal, language handicaps) and related mental health needs. The social worker should look for the following signs of posttraumatic stress, even among Asian immigrants who have been in this country for several years, but who may have residual elements. The chief symptoms are the following:

1. Recurrent or intrusive recollections of past traumas
2. Recurrent dreams and nightmares
3. Sad feelings, as if the traumatic events are recurring
4. Social numbness and withdrawal
5. Restricted affect
6. Hyperalertness, hyperactive startled reaction
7. Sleep disorders

8. Guilt
9. Memory impairment
10. Avoidance of activities that might trigger recollection of events
11. Reactivation of symptoms caused by exposure to events similar to the original trauma

The psychohistorical dimension of ecological problem solving is a beginning point of reference for social work practice with Asian Americans, particularly immigrants and refugees.

Environmental–Structural Factors

Lum holds that there are external socioenvironmental impacts that cause a psycho-individual reaction of the client. Among these are basic survival needs (language barrier, reasonable housing, adequate employment, transportation, school for children), which trigger such psycho-individual reactions as culture shock (stressful adjustment to unfamiliar culture) and cultural conflict (e.g., loss of face, self-hatred, negative identity, and marginality).[30]

The task is to assess the environmental and social strengths of the client and the environment and to mobilize these potentials. Positive coping skills (e.g., the ability to restore cognitive commonsense problem solving in the client), cultural strengths (e.g., the mobilization of the extended family and ethnic community agencies, such as family associations and the local church), and other positive assessment areas are ways that the social worker can move rapidly to utilize environmental–structural support systems for the Asian American client.

Tran and Wright conducted a study of social support and well-being among Vietnamese refugees, underscoring the need for environmental and structural supports. According to their findings, a contented Vietnamese refugee seems to have stronger social supports, is not afraid to interact with Americans, has a relatively high family income, and is married. "To be happy in America," state Tran and Wright, "a Vietnamese person also needs good English communication ability, a high level of formal education, and a relatively long time of living in this country, and that person also needs to be in the younger age cohort."[31] The social worker should strive toward opening such environmental–structural doors as family and community groups, job training and employment opportunities, English as a second language classes, high school and technical school or college education, and a stable residence in a community.

Culture

Culture is the sum total of life patterns passed on from generation to generation within a group of people and includes institutions, language, religious ideals, habits of thinking, artistic expressions, and patterns of social and interpersonal relationships.[32] Asian/Pacific Islander cultures are varied and different from each other. On the Asian continent, the history of China as the Middle Kingdom and the dominant culture of Asia has influenced Japanese, Korean, and Southeast Asian cultural expressions (e.g., art, food, religion, and language), although each group has evolved its own variations. While it is important to acknowledge the uniqueness and difference of each Asian/Pacific Island group, there are common cultural themes that cut across the spectrum of Asian Americans.

Asian American parents who were born in an Asian country and their first-generation, American-born children have gone or are going through culture shock and bicultural conflict. Coming from an Asian country to the United States poses particular challenges to acculturate from a culture of origin to the dominant American society. Asian American families are in the process of integrating a meaningful life by selecting values and traditions from both societies. Often social workers help Asian American families resolve cultural tension and conflict and achieve bicultural integration.

Social workers must also learn *cultural boundaries* and protocols when working with Asian Americans. Cultural boundaries are lines of demarcations that separate an Asian American individual and/or family unit from the larger society. There may be personal matters that are kept within the family. Mental health problems, socioeconomic issues, and related family areas are withheld from the public. Cultural protocols are exercised in terms of formality, proper subject areas for discussion, and respect. To go beyond these spheres and to reveal personal problems affecting family well-being may require more time and patience on the part of the social worker, who must gain the trust and confidence of the Asian American person or family.

Asian Americans often operate in a *cultural duality*. They appear assertive, competent, and influential in their business dealings or on the job in the workplace, but they may exercise restraint, respect, and deference to their parents and elderly in the home situation. This is a cultural-integration example of how Asian Americans survive and cope with two related cultures that may require differing sets of expectations.

Maintenance of culture is important for many Asian Americans, who hold that the use of cultural beliefs, customs, celebrations, and rituals are a source of strength, renewal, and identity. Cultural values and practices are a means to cope with present and future life problems.

The Family

The family is the central value of the Asian American. Traditional Asian American families have specific roles and relationships. The family is patriarchal, with father as the leader of the family, mother as the nurturing caretaker, and sons with more value and status than daughters. The child is expected to obey parents and elders, while the parents are responsible to raise, educate, and support their children. The family's reverence for their ancestors is important for traditional families. Family members are interrelated with each other. The emphasis is on interdependence (caring for one's family and integration into the extended family). The family fosters positive life events and avoids negative shame. Modesty and reciprocity are important family characteristics to the extent of understating and minimizing individual achievement.

Children, particularly sons, are expected to bring honor to the family. The son carries on the family name. Family strengths include valuing respect, interacting with the extended family, and offering support for each other.

Lee identifies five types of Asian American families as follows:

Type 1: The Traditional Family.
All family members are born and raised in Asian countries and have limited contact with the mainstream of American society. Family members hold traditional values, speak their native language, and belong to family associations and other social clubs of people with similar cultural orientations.

Type 2: The Cultural Conflict Family.
The family consists of parents and grandparents with traditional beliefs and values and children with more Western acculturated perspectives, which are in conflict with each other. Issues are related to independence versus interdependence, obedience versus freedom, respect versus self-assertiveness. Arguments occur over dating, marriage, educational goals, and career choice. There is role reversal when the children speak better English and can broker problems for parents who have minimal English skills.

Type 3: The Bicultural Family.
Bicultural families consist of acculturated parents who are born in Asia or in America and are acculturated to the industrial Western society. Parents are usually well-educated and hold professional jobs, are bilingual, and have an egalitarian family structure in which problems are resolved through negotiation between family members. These families live in integrated middle-class neighborhoods and visit and care for grandparents on weekends.

Type 4: The Americanized Family.
Parents and children are born and raised in the United States, have a reduced understanding and practice of Asian culture, speak primarily English, and operate as individuals in an egalitarian relationship. Friends of the family may include Asians and non-Asians, and the mentality and attitude are more Americanized than Asian.

Type 5: The Interracial Family.
An Asian American has intermarried with another Asian American (e.g., Chinese with Japanese or Korean with Vietnamese) or has chosen a spouse outside the Asian American groups. There is a wide variety of family responses, from acceptance, resignation, indifference, to rejection, depending on the traditional and nontraditional spectrum of cultural values. Children of interracial families must shape their ethnic identity, ethnic group affiliation, and socialization.[33]

Cultural family types may be a useful vehicle for understanding the common dynamics of varying Asian American families, which transcend viewing separate but differing groups.

Yee, Huang, and Lew have also identified a number of common Asian American family concepts and themes, such as the following:

1. Strong family and social ties that buffer families from the consequences of life crises.
2. Family problem-solving skills, culturally shaped emotional responses and communication patterns.
3. Healthy identities with life and social skills to deal with life-span development challenges.
4. Interdependence, reciprocity, and collectivism in family patterns.
5. Cultural traditions that offer a prescription for living and a code of behavior.
6. A sense of autonomy and competence within close family relationships.
7. The importance of repaying parents for their sacrifices through high educational achievement and occupational aspirations.
8. A system of hierarchical roles based on age, birth position, and gender.
9. Marriage as the continuation of the husband's family line.
10. Reciprocity between generations based on emotional, financial, and child-care support exchanges.
11. Caring for elderly relatives as the family's responsibility.[34]

The Individual

The biopsychosocial dimensions of the Asian American client involve an examination of biological, psychological, and social aspects. From a biological health perspective, the Asian American concept of *interpersonal harmony* advocates minimizing conflict and maximizing getting along with each other. Health and healthy relationships in balance are interrelated to each other. Thinking "good thoughts" is more important than dwelling on sickness, mental illness, or death. The latter is a self-fulfilling prophecy for misfortune, whereas the former leads to good fortune. Somatic symptoms or the psychophysiological interaction between mind and body are important to uncover if an Asian American client has internalized stress and manifests physical problems. Often Asian Americans are taught to suppress negative feelings and reactions, rather than openly ventilate them. Mental health problems tend to be expressed as psychosomatic complaints (e.g., headaches, backaches, digestive troubles, and peptic ulcers). This goes back to maintaining harmony and cultivating a pleasant disposition. Physical problems are culturally acceptable expressions, but mental health problems are taboo areas that evoke a social stigma for the family in the eyes of the local Asian community. If there are biological health problems, the social worker should work with the client's physician to clear up somatic symptoms.

From a psychological perspective, it is important to assess the relation between the person's mental state and his or her behavioral interaction with significant others in the cultural community and the society as a whole. The level of motivation for change, as well as the resistance or unwillingness to cooperate or participate in the process of growth, are crucial to uncover from a psychological assessment.

Stressing positive change and acknowledging feelings of anger and disgrace change the psychological atmosphere. Prolonged silence may be part of the psychological mix. Asian Americans may remain silent as a sign of respect to the authority of the worker or as a culturally distinct way of relating and responding in an indirect manner. Significant others investigate the relationship of self and others, particularly family, peers, and other persons who are meaningfully related. The social worker needs to know the following:

1. Does the Asian client come from a nuclear, single-parent, blended, or extended family?
2. Are the parents foreign-born or American-born?
3. Does the family have a clear sense of parental authority and interdependence, a sense of democratic autonomy, or a mix of both?
4. Are the parents recent immigrants or refugees who are acculturating well or poorly to a new environment?
5. Are there differing value systems between the parents from their country of origin and their Americanized children?
6. Does the mother function as a go-between for an authoritative distant father and their children?

The answers to these questions may affect the psychological state of the Asian American client.

The social assessment of the Asian individual focuses on how the person interacts with group and community living. Lum identifies four aspects of social assessment:[35] (1) immigration history or the family's transition from the culture of origin to American society; (2) acculturation or the adjustment, change, and maintenance of culture in the family; (3) school adjustment or the academic and social experiences of children in their primary institution; and (4) employment or the primary work setting critical for adult self-esteem and respect in the ethnic community.

MICRO CASE EXAMPLE

Annie, a 15-year-old teenager from Hong Kong, was sent to relatives in Monterey Park, California, by her parents who have an import–export business and travel throughout Asia and the United States. Annie is the oldest of four siblings and has misgivings about leaving her friends in school behind. Her parents want her to graduate from an American high school and establish citizenship and residency so that she can be admitted to a University of California school. Her relatives in California consist of an uncle and his wife who are in their early thirties, without children, and married for five years.

Annie has had difficulties for several months adjusting to her new environment (living situation, school, peer relations) after arriving and entering school. She has cut classes, been in arguments with her uncle and his wife, and has made friends with some overseas-born Asians at school. She is a *parachute kid* (literally dropped into an American community from an Asian country of origin) who is separated from her primary nuclear family and is going through her teenage identity crisis with her surrogate parents, an uncle and aunt.

After repeated attempts by Uncle Chuck and Auntie Phyllis to resolve Annie's problems, they turn to the Asian American/Pacific Islander Counseling Center in Los Angeles for help. The social worker, David Lee of Chinese descent and Cantonese/English speaking, is assigned the case and has worked at the Asian Youth Center.

After becoming acquainted with the background and home situation of Annie and her uncle and aunt, the social worker obtains the following ecosystems dimensional information:

HISTORICAL FACTORS

Annie is reacting to her particular psychohistorical situation. It is common among upper-middle-class and wealthy families in Hong Kong and other Asian countries to send their children abroad for schooling. While Annie's friends remain in Hong Kong, the social worker finds out from Annie and her relatives that teen-age children have been sent to various large American cities, Canada, and England where there are relatives and friends of families. At the same time, Annie reveals that many of the American-born Asians have made fun of her since she is a FOB (fresh off the boat) or foreign-born Asian. This type of intragroup racism has isolated Annie from her school peer group and has caused her to gravitate toward some Asians who are marginal students. She also feels rejected by her parents and has flashbacks of being sent away by her parents, who have no time for her because of their business and social commitments.

ENVIRONMENTAL/STRUCTURAL FACTORS

Annie's present environment involves an uncle and an auntie who are trying to help her make a transitional adjustment to a new environment (Monterey Park, a predominately Asian American affluent suburb near east Los Angeles); a new school, which is academically demanding with few friends; and a new set of surrogate parents, who have tried to be flexible but firm with her. Her immediate reactions have been mixed: cutting classes and hanging out with other Asian high schoolers who are not interested in learning; testing her limits with her uncle and auntie, who previously allowed her freedom and space, but have misgivings about how to deal with Annie; and expressing her unhappiness about being away from her family and friends in Hong Kong, whom she dearly misses.

Yet Annie has some ethnic and social strengths. In Hong Kong she was a happy, serious, and bright student in her grade school. She was friendly and able to garner a variety of neighborhood and school mates. Yet in Monterey Park the opposite is true, because many of the Asian students are American born, speak English without an accent, and are Americanized in their behavior.

CULTURE

Annie is the product of a traditional Asian family who is a part of the Hong Kong business and social circles. Her parents could be termed "Asian jet setters"; they travel to nearby countries on business, pleasure, and shopping trips and leave their children in the care of nannies and relatives. Annie's Asian peers in California are either bicultural Asians who came from Hong Kong, Taiwan, and Malaysia many years ago or are American-born and Americanized to the point of speaking English without a trace of an Asian foreign accent and/or being unable to speak a Chinese dialect. Often these students are student body government leaders and model minorities, who academically compete well with their white counterparts and have Asian and non-Asian friends. Annie is painfully aware of the contrast and how she does not fit in with Asian American teenagers in terms of dress, makeup, language, conversational topics, and circle of friends.

FAMILY FACTORS

Annie's parents in Hong Kong have a role responsibility to be fulfilled on behalf of their daughter. Her father and mother need to come for a visit and to be aware of Annie's feelings and situation. Annie's mother could ease the transition by staying with her for an indefinite period until an adjustment has been made. A sense of interdependence and reciprocity should be established between parents and daughter. That is, Annie will try to make an adjustment to her new situation, and Annie's father and mother will each take turns staying with her in Monterey Park until everyone involved feels that there is progress in this transition. Otherwise, the family should agree that Annie may be happier and can thrive if she returns to her home, school, and friends in Hong Kong.

INDIVIDUAL FACTORS

Annie is painfully aware that she is unhappy, lonely, and somewhat depressed and that her sense of interpersonal harmony and well-being has been impaired by this move to California. Rather than dealing with her stress, she internalizes her feelings and keeps her personal thoughts to herself. At times the stress has been exhibited with such somatic symptoms as periodic outbreaks of acne, stomachaches, and headaches. When she is anxious or worried, Annie catches herself picking her lips, a nervous gesture. There are hole marks and raw patches in her lower lip as a result. Annie is an example of the acculturation adjustment for a growing number of teenage Asians from various countries of Asia who have been called parachute kids because they are dropped off the plane by their parents. As they parachute to various parts of the United States, their landing is at times rough and unwelcomed. They must fend for themselves alone or with the help of relatives and friends of their families of origin who are forced to become surrogate parents. One wonders whether the family disruption and resulting instability and crisis are worth the effort of fulfilling the American dream, without the necessary parental support that is necessary for growing up from childhood through adolescence to young adulthood.

As you review the ecological problem-solving approach, the ecological systems model, and the unique case study of Annie, brainstorm the various intervention strategies that you would employ as the social worker in this situation.

Macro Practice Perspectives

Macro practice with Asian Americans involves large regional and institutional change that results in social justice, new institutional structures, and the distribution of wealth and resources to meet the problems of this particular target group. Social policy, planning, and administration are macro intervention tools to affect social change in problem areas.

Of all the various Asian American groups in need, Asian refugees and immigrants have the greatest acculturation adjustment and socioeconomic survival needs. High-risk refugees face problems of underemployment, breakdowns in the family network, and changing family roles. Moreover, with the implementation of welfare reform (the 1996 Personal Responsibility and Work Opportunity Reconciliation Act), legal immigrants have partially lost medical and food stamp benefits. The previous Clinton administration proposed a $1.3 billion five-year restoration program that was to benefit 132,000 people, particularly Latino and Asian immigrants. The Balanced Budget Act of 1997 restored Supplemental Security Income for disabled persons and Medicaid benefits to 420,000 legal immigrants who were in the country before welfare legislation was enacted on August 22, 1996. The Agricultural Research Act of 1998 provided food stamps for 225,000 legal immigrant children, senior citizens, and the disabled who came to the United States before the new welfare law.[36] Asian American refugees and immigrants in the welfare system need to be trained in such jobs as gardeners, restaurant cooks, bakers, child-care workers, and other hands-on positions. These Asians are hard working and dependable if they are given the opportunities of employment.

On the local level, social policy, planning, and administration are tools to organize the indigenous Asian American community to meet the specific needs of Asian elderly, unemployed, new arrivals, and other target groups in need. Rather than waiting for federal and state assistance, it is more effective to identify Asian American leaders who have the social awareness and financial knowledge and skills to plan and implement local projects that benefit the Asian American community. An example of this was accomplished in Northern California.

In twenty-five years as an Asian American faculty member of California State University, Sacramento Division of Social Work, the author has witnessed a remarkable alliance between Asian American social work students, working professionals, and county officials. During the early 1970s, a nucleus of graduate Asian American social work students and faculty developed a National Institute of Mental Health (NIMH) training grant that offered field stipends and placed students in various Asian American field settings among the Japanese and Filipino elderly, downtown refugees and immigrants, and Asian residents of low-income public housing. As a result of these field placements and Asian American social work courses, MSW

(Master of Social Work) Asian American graduates founded a variety of Asian American social service centers as follows:

Health for All.   June Otow of Japanese descent researched the needs of Asian and other ethnic groups for adult day health care and started a downtown center that included nursing services, rehabilitation, and day-care programs for the disabled and a health screening program for preschool children.

Asian Liaison Worker.   Hach Yasumura of Japanese descent became the Asian liaison worker for Sacramento County Department of Social Services upon his graduation. His task was to establish a planning and program exchange network among the various Asian groups and grass-roots agencies in the county and to coordinate existing and future services to the local Asian community.

Asian Resource Center.   May Lee of Chinese descent began a job training and employment service for Asian Americans and focused on the growing Asian immigrant and refugee populations who need English as a second language training, job testing and training, and employment placement in the greater Sacramento area. Periodic job fairs for adults and career planning workshops for Asian high school youth have resulted in strengthening the economic stability of the Asian American community.

Asian/Pacific Counseling Center.   Harriet Taniguchi of Japanese descent was instrumental in founding, with a group of Asian mental health and health care professionals, an Asian multilingual counseling program with staff representing major Asian ethnic groups. Funding came from the United Way, the minority mental health advisory board that oversees Sacramento County mental health funding, and various short-term state and federal grants, which have been shaped to meet the medical problems of Asians.

Southeast Asian Assistance Center.   Ninh Van Nguyen, a social work graduate and ordained Presbyterian minister of Vietnamese descent, started the Southeast Asian Assistance Center, which focused exclusively on the employment and family needs of Vietnamese, Hmong, Cambodian, Mien, and Thai refugees. The emphasis is on responding to the practical, everyday living needs of these populations.

Asian American Nursing Home.   Under the leadership of the Asian Community Center, led particularly by Japanese and Chinese prominent professionals in Sacramento, funds were raised through community campaign drives, large-scale bingo, and federal grants for the construction and operation of a ninety-bed Asian nursing home that serves Asian food and promotes Asian family care involvement for bed-ridden elderly clients. A former social work graduate student, Calvin Hara of Japanese descent, recently became the administrator of the nursing home. Graduate Asian American social work students participated in a county-wide research assessment project to pinpoint the needs of the Asian elderly.

The Sacramento model for Asian American community planning brings together social work students who conduct research, participate in Asian field placements, and later assume agency roles in the Asian social service community; Asian American social work faculty, who foster an interest in academic and research projects that benefit the local Asian needs; and Asian community leaders, who are responsive to the changing social trends of the Asian groups in need. There is a unique town and gown arrangement that has borne the fruit of Asian American social service agencies that are affecting the lives and well-being of Asian clients today. On the drawing boards for the Sacramento Vietnamese community are two research proposals for a Vietnamese elderly adult day health care center, written by Vanessa Nguyen, and a Vietnamese senior center patterned after the On Lok program in San Francisco, by Lena Chon.

Asian American social workers in heavy populated Asian metropolitan areas of the United States may wish to adopt this cooperative macro practice model, which involves social work students, faculty, and community leaders in a creative partnership.

Emerging Issues

Asian Americans are an almost 11 million member minority group in the United States. There are heavy populations in the western United States in Los Angeles–Long Beach, San Francisco, Honolulu, and Seattle; on the East Coast, there are moderate populations in New York City, Boston, and Washington, D.C.; and they are modestly represented in the American heartland (Chicago and Houston). As indicated in this chapter, Asian Americans have been the subject of racism and racial stereotypes and acts of racial violence and hate crimes, and they continue to cope with this stress.

At the beginning of the twenty-first century, Asian Americans are still aware of their weak influence on the political scene in the United States. With few Asian American politicians on the state and national levels, there is no political or legislative force to advocate for the rights of this group. There have been no cabinet-level appointments of Asian Americans at the presidential level in the history of the United States. Asian Americans were the focus of investigation in the 1997 Senate and House investigation on presidential campaign reform and abuse as a result of the 1996 Clinton versus Dole election. The selection of a Chinese American, Bill Lee, as the civil rights head of the Department of Justice in 1998 was heavily contested by the Republican Congress and sent a message about conservative politics and Asian Americans. Chinese dissenters who were expelled from the People's Republic of China and came to the United States for political refuge were ignored in 1998 and 1999 by the Clinton administration and U.S. State Department officials for fear that their counsel may offend U.S. and China relations.

Asian Americans need to organize themselves in an effective way on a par with the Japanese American Citizenship League, which has chapters in major cities where there is a Japanese American constituency and is a lobbying force at the national level in Washington, D.C. As the population of Asian Americans exceeds the 11 million mark, Asian Americans will be heard as a formative political, financial, technological, and scientific force to shape and influence the American political, medical, and engineering scene. An Asian American governor, Gary Locke, was elected in the state of Washington in 1998, which is a major breakthrough. However, this offers a small glimmer of hope in a realm of dominant forces that intentionally exclude the presence of Asian Americans as full partners in promise of the American dream.

Concluding Comment

Asian Americans/Pacific Islanders are diverse groups of ethnic persons who were born in or whose parents came from the continent of Asia and the Pacific areas. Lee offers a sensible appraisal of Asian Americans in the United States when he reports that, with the dawn of the twenty-first century, Asian Americans undoubtedly will play an increasingly important and complex role in American society. With the growth and expansion of Asia's economy, some Asian Americans are intermediaries between the two continents, whereas others are continuing the fight for freedom and democracy in their homelands. Lee observes:

> Some are achieving high office as governors of states or managers in corporations, whereas others are barely surviving on poverty wages or hiding from the Immigration and Naturalization Service. All are grappling with the age-old issues of place and identity that inhabit the boundaries between disparate cultures. Coming to understand the forces and conditions that have created such diversity requires far-reaching and diligent efforts. The task will continue to challenge scholars in the years ahead.[37]

The paradoxes of economic influence versus political underrepresentation, political dissent versus democratic exile, and places of leadership versus illegal immigration fuel the fires of trying to figure out the place of Asian Americans in the United States. With such a disparity of diversity among Asians and such nonrecognition by the dominant political forces of America, it will be interesting to see how Asian Americans steer their course in human history.

In the year 2005, Asian Americans/Pacific Islanders are still aware of their weak influence on the political scene in the United States. However, as their population nears 11 million, this group will be heard as a formative political and financial force in shaping and influencing the American political scene. At the same time, hard work, education, the drive for achievement, thriftiness, and helping each other have been ethnic-group qualities that have caused this group to cope with racism, prejudice, and discrimination in spite of societal barriers.

KEY WORDS AND CONCEPTS

Acculturative stress
Asian American/Pacific Islander
Chinese Exclusion Act of 1882
Cultural boundaries

Cultural duality
Family types
Interpersonal harmony
Psychohistorical responses

SUGGESTED INFORMATION SOURCES

Fong, Rowena. "Cultural Competence with Asian Americans," in Doman Lum, ed., *Culturally Competent Practice: A Framework for Understanding Diverse Groups and Justice Issues.* Belmont, CA: Thomson Brooks/Cole, 2007.

Lee, Evelyn, and Mock, Matthew R. "Asian Families: An Overview," in Monica McGoldrick, Joe Giordano, and Nydia Garcia-Preto, eds., *Ethnicity & Family Therapy.* New York: Guilford Press, 2005.

Morelli, Paula T. "Tanemura. Social Work Practice with Asian Americans," in Doman Lum, ed., *Cultural Competence, Practice Stages, and Client Systems: A Case Study Approach.* Belmont, CA: Thomson Brooks/Cole, 2005.

Wong, Janlee. "Asian Pacific Islanders," in Krishna L. Guadalupe and Doman Lum, ed., *Multidimensional Contextual Practice: Diversity and Transcendence.* Belmont, CA: Thomson Brooks/Cole, 2005

ENDNOTES

1. U.S. Bureau of Census. "U.S. Interim Projections by Age, Sex, Race, and Hispanic Origin, 2004. http://www.census.gov/ipc/www/usinterimproj

2. Ibid.

3. Russell, C. *Radical and Ethnic Diversity: Asians, Blacks, Hispanic, Native Americans, and Whites* (Ithaca, NY: New Strategist Publications, 1998), p. 7.

4. U.S. Census Bureau, Census 2000. "U.S. Asian Population, Census 2000." Information Please Database: 2005, Pearson Education, Inc. http://www.infoplease.com/ipa/A0778584.html

5. Russell, p. 65.

6. R. Homma-True, "Asian American Women," in E. Lee, ed., *Working with Asian Americans: A Guide for Clinicians* (New York: Guilford Press, 1997), pp. 420–427.

7. M. P. P. Root, "Women," in L. C. Lee and N. W. S. Zane, eds, *Handbook of Asian American Psychology* (Thousand Oaks, CA: Sage Publications, 1998), pp. 221–231.

8. R. Masaki and L. Wong. "Domestic Violence in the Asian Community," in E. Lee, ed., *Working with Asian Americans: A Guide for Clinicians* (New York: Guilford Press, 1997), pp. 439–451.

9. "College Degree Nearly Doubles Annual Earnings, Census Bureau Reports." U.S. *Census Bureau News.* http://www.census.gov/Press-Release/www/releases/archives/education/004214.html

10. U.S. Bureau of Census. "Money Income and Earnings Summary Measures by Selected Characteristics: 2002 and 2003." Table 1. http://www.census.gov/prod/2004pubs/p60–226.pdf

11. U.S. Census Bureau, *Statistical Abstract of the United States: 2004–2005* (Washington, D.C.: U.S. Census Bureau), pp. 40 and 452.

12. F. T. L. Leong, "Career Development and Vocational Behaviors," in L. C. Lee and N. W. S. Zane, eds, *Handbook of Asian American Psychology* (Thousand Oaks, CA: Sage Publications, 1998), pp. 359–398.

13. Teresa Lewi, "Home Ownership Still Difficult to Attain for Many; AAPIs." http://www.asianfortune.com/aug05/Articles/apa%20housing.htm; and Freddie Mac and the National Coalition for Asian Pacific American Community Development, "Asian American Housing and Homeownership Trends," http://ncvaonline.org/archive/prj_GSE_APIHousing_Briefing_Chicago_080505.pdf

14. *Health, United States, 2004.* National Centers for Health Statistics, Tables 19 and 28. http://www.cdc.gov/nchs/data/hus/hus04trend.pdf#002

15. E. Lee, "Overview: The Assessment and Treatment of Asian American Families," in E. Lee, ed., *Working with Asian Americans: A Guide for Clinicians* (New York: Guilford Press, 1997), pp. 3–36.

16. L. C. Lee, "An Overview," in L. C. Lee and N. W. S. Zane, eds., *Handbook of Asian American Psychology* (Thousand Oaks, CA: Sage Publications, 1998), p. 16.

17. C. M. Loo, *Chinese America: Mental Health and Quality of Life in the Inner City* (Thousand Oaks, CA: Sage Publications, 1998).

18. Loo, xxii.

19. Loo, xxviii.

20. D. Lum, *Social Work Practice & People of Color: A Process Stage Approach* 5th ed. (Belmont, CA: Thomson, Brooks/Cole, 2004).

21. D. Lum and C. Guzzetta, "Should Programs and Service Delivery Systems be Culture-Specific in their Design?" in D. de Anda, ed., *Controversial Issues in Multiculturalism* (Boston: Allyn and Bacon, 1997), pp. 54–70.

22. D. Sue, W. S. Mak, and D. W. Sue, "Ethnic Identity," in L. C. Lee and N. W. S. Zane, eds., *Handbook of Asian American Psychology* (Thousand Oaks, CA: Sage Publications, 1998), p. 312.

23. A. P. Iglehart and R. M. Becerra, *Social Services and the Ethnic Community* (Boston: Allyn and Bacon, 1995).

24. J. L. Chin, "Toward a Psychology of Difference: Psychotherapy for a Culturally Diverse Population," in J. L. Chin, V. De La Cancela, and Y. M. Jenkins, eds., *Diversity in Psychotherapy: The Politics of Race, Ethnicity, and Gender* (Westport, CT: Praeger, 1993), pp. 69–91.

25. E. Lee, pp. 26–27.

26. E. Lee, pp. 28–33.

27. L. Uba, *Asian Americans: Personality Patterns, Identity, and Mental Health* (New York: Guilford Press, 1994).

28. Uba, pp. 61–87.

29. M. K. Ho, "Social Work Practice with Asian Americans," in A. Morales and B. W. Sheafor, eds., *Social Work: A Profession of Many Faces,* 8th ed. (Boston: Allyn and Bacon, 1998), pp. 465–483.

30. Lum, Chapter 8.

31. T. V. Tran and R. Wright, Jr., "Social Support and Subjective Well-Being among Vietnamese Refugees," *Social Service Review* 60 (1986): 449–459.

32. J. L. Hodge, D. K. Struckmann, and L. D. Trost, *Cultural Bases of Racism and Group Oppression* (Berkeley, CA: Two Riders Press, 1975).
33. E. Lee, pp. 11–13.
34. B. W. K. Yee, L. N. Huang, and A. Lew, "Families: Life-Span Socialization in a Cultural Context," in L. C. Lee and N. W. S. Zane, eds., *Handbook of Asian American Psychology* (Thousand Oaks, CA: Sage Publications, 1998), pp. 83–135.
35. Lum, Chapter 8.
36. M. Janofsky, "Some Legal Immigrant Benefits May Return," *Sacramento Bee*, January 25, 1999, A4.
37. L. C. Lee, pp. 18, 19.

Social Work Practice with American Indians and Alaskan Natives

E. Daniel Edwards and Margie Egbert Edwards

Prefatory Comment

Drs. E. Daniel Edwards, Professor of Social Work and Director of American Indian Studies, University of Utah, and Margie Egbert Edwards, Professor Emeritus, School of Social Work, University of Utah, present a very thoughtful, sensitive, and careful analysis of the current status of the human condition of American Indians and Alaskan Natives in the United States. These authors' academic efforts are seasoned with practice experience as they recommend that intervention strategies need to be operationalized within the context of numerous cultural beliefs, customs, and values among American Indians and Alaskan Natives. They caution that these techniques may differ depending on the specific tribal group being worked with and the location of that intervention, whether an urban or a rural reservation. Each Native American is unique, as is each of the 562 tribal groups.

The independence and self-contained nature of each tribe was illustrated on the Red Lake Reservation (Minnesota) in 2005 when a 15-year-old student gunned down his grandfather, a girlfriend, a security guard, a teacher, and five classmates—and then committed suicide. In this circumstance the tribe closed ranks, not allowing news coverage to showcase the community's grieving and not allowing nontribal mental health practitioners to provide services as the community began the healing process.

Across the United States, Native American Indians* are reclaiming their heritage. Indian tribes are re-instructing youth and adults in their native languages.

---

*The terms "Native American" and "American Indian/Alaska Native" are used interchangeably to refer to the first native people of this country and their descendants.

Spiritual ceremonies are held to attain and retain a *balance* with nature that is so important to spiritual and temporal well-being. Cultural activities are promoted in social gatherings. Powwows are opportunities to enjoy music, dance, and social traditions, while sobriety powwows celebrate and reinforce the sobriety of Native Americans. Education is available in tribal-owned and -operated schools, as is instruction in tribal arts, their history, and cultural significance. Emphasis on tribal self-determination and self-governance is furthering the unique development of communities and tribal groups. Increased mobility is resulting in larger populations of Native Americans in urban areas. Spiritual ceremonies most often held in reservation settings are becoming more available in urban settings, such as "rites of passage," "sweats," and healing ceremonies. In creative and respectful ways, Native Americans are reinforcing their traditional teachings and positively enhancing their identification with tribal and Native American values, beliefs, and traditions.

Current Demographics

According to the 2000 U.S. Census, the Native American population now numbers 4.1 million people—1.51 percent of the United States population. These figures represent a 110 percent increase from the 2 million population reported in 1990. Of these 4.1 million people, 2,475,956 reported being American Indian and Alaska Native alone, while 1,643,345 reported being American Indian and Alaska Native in combination with one or more other races.[1]

In 2001, there were 562 federally recognized American Indian tribes of which 230 are in Alaska.[2] According to the 2000 U.S. Census, two-thirds (366) of the 562 tribes reported populations of less than 1,000 persons. The ten largest American Indian Tribal Groupings were Cherokee, Navajo, Latin American Indian, Choctaw, Sioux, Chippewa, Apache, Blackfeet, Iroquois, and Pueblo. Eskimos were the largest Alaskan Native tribal group followed by Tlingit-Haida, Alaska Athabascan, and Aleut.[3]

Other data from the Census 2000 reported that 43 percent of American Indians lived in the West. New York and Los Angeles were the cities with the largest populations of American Indians.[4]

It is estimated that approximately two-thirds of American Indians reside in off-reservation areas throughout the United States. Approximately one-third of American Indians reside in tribally governed areas including reservations, trust lands, tribal jurisdiction and tribal designated statistical areas, and Alaskan Native villages.[5]

The impressive increase in population among Native Americans has been influenced by several factors. Significant strides have been made in provision of prenatal and maternal health care to American Indian people. In addition, there are larger numbers of people who are "part" American Indian reporting this information on census surveys. Improved census procedures on reservations have resulted in more accurate population figures. Even with improved reporting procedures, there continue to be concerns that the Native American population may be underrepresented in census surveys.

Socioeconomic Issues

Family is an important unifying concept for American Indian people. "Nuclear" and "extended family" figure prominently in the well-being of Native American people, as do "clan" and "tribal" families. When all these "families" are intact, Native American people maintain a connectedness, individually and collectively, to their tribal heritage and identity. According to 2000 Census data, 35.7 percent of all Native Americans living in the United States had incomes below the poverty level,[6] as compared to a poverty rate of 12.4 percent for the total population.[7] With a median annual family income of $33,144 (compared to $50,046 for the U.S. population),[8] over 600,000—or 30 percent of all American families—lived in poverty[9]. This was the highest reported poverty rate for any racial group classified in the 2000 Census.

Education

Native Americans have well-defined cultural values that encourage attainment of knowledge and wisdom. The judicious use of knowledge has sustained American Indian people in their quest to live harmoniously with nature. Strong cultural values support attainment of education within both non-Indian and Native settings. There is, however, considerable need for exerted efforts to improve American Indian graduation rates from both high school and higher education settings. According to the 1990 U.S. Census, only 65 percent of American Indians, Eskimos, and Aleuts, 25 years of age and older have attained high school graduation or higher in our educational systems. Again, for this group, only 9 percent have attained a bachelor's degree or higher.[10] The American Indian dropout rate is the highest of any minority group. In 1988 the American Indian dropout rate was 35.5 percent, compared with a 1988 United States dropout rate of 28.8 percent.[11] Factors that tend to interfere with educational attainment of American Indian students include: (1) inadequate budgets for Bureau of Indian Affairs (BIA) and tribal-contracted schools; (2) large numbers of young people who repeat at least one grade; (3) low test scores in history, math, reading, and science; (4) inconsistent attendance; (5) higher student expectations that they will not finish high school; (6) lower student expectations that they will attend college; (7) language problems; (8) low income; and (9) siblings who have dropped out of school.[12]

Health and Mental Health Issues

Family issues impact the health and mental health status of Native American people. Culturally, when Indians, individually and collectively, adhere to traditional cultural beliefs, they maintain a "balance" with nature, and achieve wellness—mentally, physically, and spiritually. These beliefs and behaviors promote positive interrelatedness with people, the environment, and all living things. When individuals or systems are "out of balance," ceremonies and "family" actions are necessary to restore this "balance."

The Indian Health Service (IHS) is responsible for providing Federal health services to American Indians and Alaskan Natives. IHS provides a broad range of preventive, corrective, rehabilitative, and environmental services.[13] Some areas in which significant progress has been made on behalf of the health status of American Indian people include a decrease in infant mortality and maternal death rates and an increase in life expectancy rates.

According to IHS publications, the leading causes of death for American Indian people include the following:

Men = diseases of the heart and accidents.
Women = diseases of the heart and malignant neoplasms.
Infants = Sudden Infant Death Syndrome (SIDS) and congenital anomalies.
Children 1 to 14 years of age = accidents.
Young people ages 15 to 24 = accidents, suicide, and homicide.
Adults ages 25 to 44 = accidents, chronic liver disease, cirrhosis, homicide, suicide, diseases of the heart, and malignant neoplasms.[14]

Another area of concern to Native American people is Fetal Alcohol Syndrome, the number one preventable birth defect in our country. This problem is adversely affecting many American Indian children and their families. Aggressive education, outreach, and community prevention programs are recommended to help eradicate the disastrous effects of this crippling birth defect.

Native American Youth

The health of Native American youth has been a cause of concern to American Indian people over the past several years. A recent study of 14,000 American Indian and Alaskan Native adolescents revealed important data.[15] Of concern to Native American people are the following research findings: (1) less than half of these young people lived with two parents; (2) less than half of the youth received preventive health services in the past two years; (3) 65 percent reported being bored; (4) approximately two-thirds of high school seniors reported they have had sexual intercourse; and (5) 29 percent of males and 44 percent of females use no contraceptive devices. Other findings of concern to the researchers included the early experimentation and extent to which youth use alcohol; the extent to which youth worry about economics and domestic abuse; and the extent to which heavy use of substances is linked to every risk behavior described in the report.

Positive findings, however, are also reported from these youth. Approximately 80 percent of the youth reported being happy, not depressed, in good health, and believe that "family" care about them "a great deal."

Several recommendations were offered by the researchers. These included (1) recruiting teenagers and adults to play active roles as peer leaders and supportive role models; (2) strengthening Native American families; and (3) developing community-wide, culturally grounded prevention and intervention programs.[16]

This research was conducted among rural and reservation Native American youth populations. A similar study is needed to address the problems, strengths, and current situations of urban American Indian and Alaskan Native youth. There is also a need for research regarding the "achieving," well-adjusted American Indian and Alaskan Native youth and the factors that contribute to their success.

Ecosystems Framework

Social work practice requires assessment of the interaction between clients and their environments. The social worker will often look to peer and family relationships as important components in an individual's sphere of functioning. Particularly important to Native Americans are the cultural variables that embody all aspects of living. The broader environment also contributes to the individual's adjustment and availability of resources important to personal well-being. Neighborhoods, educational systems, social and health services, employment opportunities, recreational and leisure resources—all may be viewed differently and approached selectively depending on individual preferences, previous experience, and availability of choices. The environmental–structural factors that influence well-being may be quite different for Native Americans living in reservation/rural areas as compared with those in urban/metropolitan areas. The historical experiences of Native Americans are also varied and complex. Many older Native Americans have survived a disparaging and contradictory set of social policies implemented to govern their welfare—with little opportunity for input from American Indian people themselves.

Historical Influences

The "discovery" of the Americas by Columbus subjected American Indians to the control of the dominant groups that settled within their homelands. European settlers enacted governmental systems based on those of their own homelands. Policies were often established for the benefit of their "mother" countries. The emancipation of the Colonies from England began a series of federal legislative actions that have continued today. Initially American Indians were governed by the War Department. Later, the responsibilities were transferred to the Bureau of Indian Affairs (BIA) within the Department of the Interior.

Historically, numerous federal policies have influenced the population, lifestyles, geographical locations, language usage, education, and general well-being of American Indians. Detailed descriptions of American Indian and non-Indian relations in this country are covered in considerable detail in Berry's book, *Race and Ethnic Relations*.[17] Five major governmental policies have been identified by Berry as being most influential. They are (1) extermination; (2) expulsion; (3) exclusion (reservations); (4) assimilation; and (5) self-determination.

Extermination.   Historically, extermination was used as a method of handling conflicts between races. Disease, war, alcohol, and slavery are examples of extermination methods practiced against American Indians. Disease was one of the most effective extermination practices as American Indians were particularly vulnerable to smallpox, measles, and chicken pox. The most prevalent reason for the extermination of American Indians was the unrelenting desire for Indian land and its resources. Because American Indians did not utilize deeds and written agreements, there were no records of ownership, and the land was easily usurped by non-Indians.

Expulsion.   As the nation's westward movements expanded, American Indians were forced to leave their homelands for more remote western areas. Many non-Indians viewed expulsion as a more humane way of resolving the "American Indian problem" and advocated expulsion in lieu of extermination.

Exclusion (Reservations).   Under this policy, American Indians were removed from their larger geographical homelands to smaller, well-defined "reservation" lands. Reservations were strongly resisted by most American Indian tribes. Many negative sanctions and restrictions were imposed on American Indians living on reservations. They were often denied use of their language and participation in religious ceremonies. The reservation system, however, did acknowledge the American Indians' right to live and retain land, and maintain their identity and many components of their culture.

Assimilation.   Assimilation policies were enacted to promote the integration of American Indians within the "American" mainstream. Several laws promoted termination of federal programs and trust relations with American Indian tribal groups, such as the Dawes Act, or Land Allotment Act of 1887. Before the Dawes Act, American Indians owned 188 million acres of land. After the Dawes Act, American Indians were left with 47 million acres. *Relocation* (later Employment Assistance) was another assimilation policy enacted in 1952 by the Bureau of Indian Affairs. Under this program American Indians were recruited for off-reservation employment. Estimates indicate that approximately one-half of the American Indian trainees under this program returned to their reservations. In 1953 Congress passed another resolution declaring termination of Indian reservations to be the official federal policy. In the next five years, the trust status and federal programs of sixty Indian tribes and groups were terminated. This policy was reversed in the early 1960s because of the detrimental consequences that resulted from the termination policy. Many of these "terminated" tribes have once again been restored to trust status.

Self-Determination and Self-Governance.   Present federal policies are promoting self-determination and self-governance of Native American affairs by the Native peoples themselves. These policies are the result of organization and mobilization of American Indian professional groups, such as the National Congress of American Indians (NCAI). This group represents and lobbies for Indian people throughout the country.

Environmental–Structural Factors

Many environmental–structural factors have adversely influenced the lives of Native Americans. Reservation systems were confining for people who had experienced considerable freedom in moving about their vast ancestral lands. Several reservations now accommodate more than one tribe. Some of these reservations include tribes that historically were enemies. American Indian and Alaskan Native children were forced to attend boarding schools located some distance from their families. Many children remained in the boarding school environment throughout the entire year.

Many Native Americans were recruited and enlisted in the Armed Services for World War II and the Korean and Vietnam Conflicts, as well as for the Gulf and Iraq Wars. These experiences and subsequent urban employment training and relocation programs led to the migration of many Native American adults and families to urban areas.

Currently, American Indian people are achieving considerable success through self-governance initiatives. They are addressing "re-burial" issues through legal procedures. Decisions regarding the storage of toxic waste on Indian lands are being debated in Tribal Councils with considerable community input. Tribal economic development projects are actively pursued. Gambling industries continue to be operated on and debated on many Indian lands. Subsistence lifestyles are promoted where important to the survival and economic security of American Indian tribes and Alaskan Native villages. Fishing, hunting, and trapping continue to be debated as they relate to subsistence and treaty rights. The return of Indian land is being pursued through legal avenues and through economic ventures—the revenue from which is being used to purchase Indian land previously sold or awarded to non-Indian people.

Native American Cultural Considerations

The study of Native American culture is a complicated and fascinating educational experience. Each of the 562 Native American tribal groups is unique. Each language is tribal-specific. Customs and beliefs are representative of distinct cultures and daily living practices.

There is considerable interest in and fascination with Native American culture today from non-Indians; people claiming Indian ancestry; Indian people who were adopted as infants and are researching their natural lineage; urban Indians with few ties to their tribal lands; and Native Americans who are strongly identified with their tribes, culture, and heritage.[18]

There is also considerable interest in rediscovering and preserving the cultural teachings of specific tribes. Native American tribal and spiritual leaders are advocating the return to cultural and spiritual teachings. Concepts such as the medicine wheel, the circle, spirituality, sweats, rites of passage, and vision quests are being taught as important to the maintenance of "balance" and "harmony" in individual and group living. One American Indian professional, Larry Brendtro, has conceptualized the "medicine wheel" as a symbol of wellness, with four dimensions: belonging, independence, mastery, and generosity.[19] *Belonging* reinforces the importance of the group. *Independence* recognizes the importance of each individual. *Mastery* denotes respect for the skills and talents of each member. *Generosity* is reflected in the ways in which members share their talents, themselves, and their material goods with others. These four concepts promote "wellness" for the individual and collective good.

While each tribal group maintains considerable uniqueness as demonstrated through their cultural customs, beliefs, and traditions, there are several values that are evidenced in varying degrees among most Native American tribal groups. Some of these values include:

1. Belief in a Supreme Being and the continuity of life.
2. Belief in the importance of achieving balance and living in harmony with nature—showing respect for all living things.
3. Belief in the importance of acquiring and using knowledge judiciously—transforming knowledge into wisdom.
4. Respect for the individuality of all people.
5. Respect for the value of the group and solidarity.
6. Importance of behaving honorably—to avoid shaming one's self, family, clan, or tribe.
7. Belief in honoring and respecting elders as cultural guardians and educators.

Family Considerations

Nuclear, extended, clan, and tribal families play dominant roles in the lives of traditional American Indian people. Traditionally, the rearing of children was a tribal and clan responsibility. It is not unusual, therefore, for families to gather as a group to help resolve problems that, at first glance, appear to be specific to an individual. On occasion, family members may speak "for" the "identified" client. Matriarchal and patriarchal systems continue to rely heavily on the "wisdom" of the designated family matriarch or patriarch. Large numbers of extended family members often participate in healing ceremonies for cousins, aunts, uncles, parents, and grandparents. Cousins may be affectionately referred to as brothers and sisters, and respected aunts and uncles may be addressed as mothers, fathers, and grandparents are. Elders are often referred to as "Grandmother" or "Grandfather" when there are no nuclear ties to these people.

Traditional American Indian families that have relocated to urban areas may often be frustrated by demands of non-Indian systems that require regular school attendance, daily employment performance, and maintenance of strict daily living schedules. When traditional roles are required on behalf of their families on reservations and Indian lands, it is often difficult to meet the demands of both the non-Indian and Indian responsibilities to which Indian people are committed. It is also difficult for some Indian people to explain the conflicts they are experiencing because they have little confidence that either the non-Indian systems or the traditional systems will understand or appreciate the dilemmas they face in fulfilling their traditional and modern-day roles and responsibilities.

Individual Considerations

Just as each of the 562 Native American tribal groups is unique, so, too, is each individual. Some American Indians are traditional people who have learned their Native language as their first language. Others have deep respect for their Native culture and understand their language, but are not fluent in oral Native language expression. Some have been reared in homes with parents from different tribal groups and have experiences with several Native American cultures. Many Indian parents today spent their younger years in boarding schools or foster homes and have had limited year-round exposure to their Indian cultural heritage. Some Indian people were born off-reservation and have returned to their tribal lands for vacations and purposeful visits. All of these factors, and many more, complicate considerably identification and self-esteem issues with which many American Indian people must deal. They also challenge professional social workers who engage with American Indian clients in assessing, understanding, and resolving the psychosocial problems and growth opportunities for which American Indian clientele seek the services of a social worker.

Micro Social Work Practice with American Indians

Given the diversity of American Indian and Alaskan Native tribal groups and individual members, it is important to individualize each client. The following information may be helpful in guiding sensitive social work intervention when considered thoughtfully with each client and assignment.

Casework, group work, marriage/couples counseling, and family therapy are all important social work interventions with Native American people. The treatment of choice is often determined by the presenting problem(s), intervention goals, willingness of the participants, client's previous experiences with professional helping people, and social work practitioner skills.

Relationship Strategies

The development of professional helping relationships requires considerable time with many Native American people. Relationships are complicated by such factors as the therapist's age, sex, race, and professional experience. Native American social workers will be "tested" by clients regarding their knowledge and understanding of Native American culture; their respect for their "brothers and sisters"; their identification with their own tribe and Native Americans generally; their knowledge and experience; and their professional and cultural commitment to Native Americans generally, and their professional roles specifically. In many respects, American Indian social workers are expected to thoroughly know and understand the diversity of Native American culture.

Non-Indian social workers are often tested for longer periods of time than Native American social workers. As a rule, Native people will not expect the same level of cultural understanding from non-Indian social workers as they will from Native professionals, but they will expect that all social workers make efforts to understand and respond in culturally sensitive ways in the provision of their services.

Another area in which professional social workers will be tested relates to professional competency. Clients expect competent services. They expect social workers to follow through on their commitments. Clients often assess professional competence by the extent to which social workers keep their commitments.

Native Americans often approach a beginning relationship with a professional person in a calm, unhurried manner. They observe the friendliness of the professional and assess the atmosphere in the setting. Some clients may greet a professional with a brief handshake (more touching than shaking); while others may acknowledge the person with a nod of the head. It is important to greet traditional Indian people respectfully. Staring and excess eye contact constitute a major breach of etiquette, as does any other action that may be taken as overfamiliar.[20]

In many Native languages, there is no single word to describe systems, programs, or processes important to social work intervention. Many "professional" terms are not easily translated into Native languages. It is often important to explain the details and services of a program, rather than its name.

Each tribal group will have different customs that facilitate relationship building. Newly employed social workers should seek information from more experienced social workers regarding establishing beginning and working relationships, customs and traditions important to the development of professional relationships, and effective termination skills.

Intervention Strategies

Intervention strategies will also be influenced by numerous cultural beliefs, customs, and values. These may differ somewhat depending on the tribal group with which you are working, the client's identification with their culture, and the location of the service delivery system—reservation/rural or urban.

Interventions in reservation/rural areas may be complicated by the fact that tribal members are "related" to large numbers of people and know each other's present and past histories. Group work contracts must be well defined, especially as they relate to issues of confidentiality. Breeches of confidentiality must be addressed quickly and openly to resolve issues and further the attainment of group and individual goals.

Confidentiality in all aspects of the social worker's interventions is extremely important. *Moccasin telegraphs* are active. However, much misinformation circulates freely. Professional people must maintain well-defined boundaries in terms of sharing information.

Indian time is a concept that acknowledges and excuses behavior that results in Indian people being late for appointments. There is considerable difference of opinion regarding the cultural significance of Indian time. Some people maintain that Indian people "live in the present" without much cultural importance attached to promptness in meeting demands for closely monitored schedules. Others insist that Indian people have substantial recent experience with scheduling their time and meeting appointments, and that lateness should not be excused because of past cultural values. Social workers have identified multiple reasons for client failure to keep appointments including: (1) last minute interruptions; (2) unreliable transportation; (3) visits from others to whom it would appear rude to leave; (4) misunderstandings about the appointment time; and (5) apprehensions about the visit. Social workers can encourage maintenance of appointments by: (1) clarifying appointment times; (2) reviewing the schedules and work assignments of the social workers; (3) clarifying procedures to cancel or postpone an appointment; and (4) summarizing the content of the interview, future goals, and the next appointment.

In reservation/rural settings, many social workers find it advantageous to schedule several home visits in the same area on the same day. Many elders and others have limited transportation resources. If family members can provide transportation to a trading post or shopping center, elders will take advantage of that offer, even when they know a social work home visit has been set for that day. Other family, social, and spiritual activities also may take precedence over an appointment with the social worker, and many of these occur spontaneously. If a social worker fails to find one client at home, there are several others with whom appointments have been made to justify the often extensive travel time required on some reservations.

It is important to remember that although clients may miss appointments because of unforeseen difficulties or opportunities, social workers are expected to keep their appointments with clients. When court sessions or crises interfere with a social worker keeping a client appointment, contacts should be made prior to the scheduled appointment to arrange for a later meeting.

Native American clients will likely benefit from services of both professional social workers and Native medicine people. Many tribes use a variety of traditional medical diagnosticians and healers including medicine men, hand tremblers, and Indian doctors.[21] Knowing the different Native medicine specialists in specific tribes, and speaking respectfully about their potential use, will often earn the respect of American Indian clients. While traditional medicine practices are important to many Native American people today, it is often not appropriate to talk in depth about these spiritual beliefs and practices with non-Indians or non-tribal members. Many symbols, totems, and objects have spiritual and healing significance. These may be acknowledged as helpful to a client's recovery, but are seldom discussed with others at any length.

Those Indian people who have a strong belief in the continuity of life view death as a part of nature's plan. This is particularly true with the death of an elder. One Yurok family gathered for the funeral of their patriarch who had lived an active, productive life well into his eighties. At the feast following the funeral, family members recounted stories of their positive experiences with their grandfather, grandmother (also deceased), and extended family members. Many of these stories were humorous in nature. The laughter prompted tears of emotional release, comradery, and closeness as family members validated and celebrated the positive experiences they had enjoyed with their grandparents and other friends and relatives. Deaths of elders are how nature intended life to be. Deaths of children, youth, and young adults, however, are occasions of much sadness and remorse. Given the extent of accidents within American Indian communities, considerable attention should be given to the accumulated losses experienced in many Indian families. Grief groups are being viewed as therapeutic resources for Indian people who are finding support and understanding in releasing accumulated pain and sorrow that has so profoundly impacted their emotional and physical well-being.

Indian people believe that health is nurtured through balance and living in harmony with nature. Professional social workers who understand these concepts can help Indian people restore the spiritual balance that may be affected by personal, family, or extended family problems. All cultural teachings reinforce this principle. Clients can be encouraged to achieve balance in work, leisure, recreation, family, and cultural and spiritual activities.

Casework Intervention

Individual interventions require thoughtful attention to the clients' agenda. Clients may not wish to explore emotional feelings in initial interviews. Some clients will seek help with a tangible problem. When that problem is resolved, they may be willing to discuss problems. Some clients are confused about the roles of social workers. They have known social workers who have been involved in the removal of children for placement in foster homes, boarding schools, or correctional facilities. They have also worked with social workers who were responsible for overseeing the disbursement of their financial resources and those of their children. Developing trusting therapeutic relationships from this memory base is often difficult for clients to achieve. It will take time to develop therapeutic relationships.

A variety of services are now available to American Indians in both reservation/rural and urban settings. Children and youth are receiving casework prevention and treatment services to address issues related to (1) school adjustment and achievement; (2) abuse and neglect; (3) drug and alcohol use/abuse; (4) gang behaviors; (5) development of coping and communication skills; (6) behavioral management skills; (7) teen pregnancy and parenting; (8) emotional crises; (9) suicide prevention; (10) relationship and assertion skills; (11) peer counseling and leadership skills; (12) personal growth development; and (13) future planning.

Adults and elders are utilizing casework prevention and treatment services to address (1) emotional crises, including depression and anxiety; (2) health and wellness concerns; (3) adult and elder protective services; (4) family issues, including violence; (5) employment; (6) alcohol and drugs; (7) AIDS; (8) fetal alcohol syndrome/fetal alcohol effects (FAS/FAE); (9) sexual and physical abuse; (10) poverty and economics; (11) concerns regarding care of children and elders; and (12) development and use of community resources.

Wherever possible, both reservation/rural and urban social workers should assess these issues within the cultural context of the person's American Indian heritage. Regardless of a person's current residence, it is likely that Native American values and beliefs will be important in both the assessment and treatment processes.

Resources from within the Native American community can be helpful in understanding and resolving personal, social, and behavioral problems.

The two case examples below describe social work intervention on behalf of children and their families—one in a reservation/rural setting and the other in an urban setting.

CASE EXAMPLES

Arthur is a bright, active 8-year-old, full-blooded American Indian residing on a reservation with his 10-year-old brother under the care of his maternal grandfather. The social worker was asked to contact the grandfather regarding Arthur's problematic school attendance. The social worker talked with Arthur's school teacher and learned that Arthur's attendance had been irregular throughout the year. He had not attended school during the past two weeks. When Arthur was in school, he was pleasant, completed the assigned work at high levels of competency, and related well with the other children. The grandfather lived alone in a comfortable home near the elementary school. The social worker met with the grandfather and Arthur's aunt who was visiting her father. The grandfather indicated that Arthur left for school each day with his brother, George. The social worker asked if the grandfather and aunt would help her locate Arthur and bring him back to the grandfather's home. Arthur's aunt found Arthur playing nearby at the local park. Arthur willingly went with the social worker to the school where the following plan was developed and agreed to by Arthur, the school teacher, and the social worker: (1) Arthur would attend school each day; (2) the social worker would meet with Arthur sometime during the morning of each day at the school; and (3) Arthur would complete all his school work and bring examples of what he was learning to the social work sessions.

The social worker visited with the grandfather at his home that afternoon. She learned that Arthur and George had lived with the grandfather since their early years, and permanently for the past three years. Their mother and father were divorced, and their natural father was deceased. Their mother had remarried and lived in a neighboring community off-reservation. The mother visited her children regularly, but they had not discussed issues regarding the care of Arthur and George. The social worker asked how the grandfather would feel about the social worker's meeting with the boys' mother to discuss Arthur's current behavior. The grandfather agreed and provided the mother's address and telephone number.

Arthur's mother, Shirley, had remarried and was living with her husband and a new baby in a small community a short distance from the reservation. Her husband was employed full-time, and Shirley was employed, during the school year, as a cook at the local elementary school. Shirley was concerned about her two sons and the burden of care assumed by her father. Shirley was embarrassed by her irresponsible care of Arthur and George. Both she and her husband would like to have Arthur and George live with them, but she was reluctant to discuss this with her father. She didn't know what her father's feelings were regarding his continuing to care for the children. The social worker asked for Shirley's permission to discuss these matters with the grandfather, and Shirley agreed. The grandfather was willing to return the children to their mother. He said he was "too old to take care of such active boys." With his permission, these messages were shared with Shirley, and within two months the children were returned to the care of the mother and their stepfather. To accomplish this goal, the social worker: (1) met daily with Arthur at the school for the first two weeks, then three times a week for two weeks, twice a week for two weeks, and then weekly until the boys were returned to their mother; (2) met with George to discuss his feelings regarding living with his mother and stepfather; (3) set up meetings with the grandfather and Shirley and her husband to discuss the return of the children to their mother and regular visiting schedules with the grandfather; and (4) informed school officials of the social work intervention and reinforced their positive work with Arthur and George.

Cultural Considerations Important to These Interventions.   Many cultural factors were considered in planning social work intervention with this family. Among these were the following:

1. Contacts must be initiated quickly with nuclear and extended family members.
2. The social worker had to act as an intermediary, especially because a family member was ashamed of past behaviors. It is culturally appropriate to have someone speak for you in these situations. Shirley was uncomfortable about asking for the return of her children, especially now that they were getting old enough to be of more help to the grandfather. Traditionally, these roles were strongly reinforced—grandparents cared for grandchildren; and grandchildren, in turn, cared for grandparents in their elder years.
3. A regular visiting schedule was important to support the adjustment and relationships of the children, parents, and grandfather. It was also important to see that the grandfather's needs are met.
4. It was particularly important to keep commitments to the children who were feeling "abandoned" by significant adults in their family systems.
5. It was also important to "check back" with all parties to facilitate any additional adjustment issues and to celebrate goals that have been accomplished.

The following case example details the work that was accomplished with a 14-year-old American Indian boy who was residing in an urban area.

> Robert is a full-blooded American Indian who has lived most of his life in a larger metropolitan area. He was hospitalized in a residential treatment facility for depression, anxiety, weight loss, verbal and social regression, agitated moods, hysterical behaviors, and night terrors. During his hospitalization, his behavior worsened. He would not participate in group therapy and responded poorly to individual casework. Robert lived with his mother and two half-siblings. Robert's mother was recently divorced from his stepfather. Robert's father died six years earlier.
>
> An urban American Indian social worker from Robert's tribe was asked to consult with the hospital staff regarding Robert's deteriorating mental and physical health. The social worker met with the staff and then with Robert. In the initial meeting, Robert and the social worker conversed in their Native language regarding their parents, siblings, clans, home reservation areas, and cultural activities in which they had participated. They then talked about Robert's current situation, the hospitalization, his separation

from his family, and his fears. Robert believed that his father had been hexed and died as a result of evil forces associated with this hex. Robert also believed that these evil forces could be unleashed on him, and that he, too, might die. The social worker talked with Robert about spiritual ceremonies that could be made available to him on his reservation to restore balance and harmony in his life. Robert knew and understood the significance of these healing ceremonies and was willing to participate with the social worker in arranging for a ceremony for him. The social worker also talked with Robert about positive forces from his Native American culture that could provide protection and balance in his life. They discussed the power of the eagle and the protective nature of an eagle feather. The social worker volunteered to give Robert an eagle feather. A healing ceremony was arranged for Robert on his reservation. The Indian medicine people were able to provide information and healing forces to return Robert to a state of balance and wellness. Robert placed the eagle feather under his mattress and from that time on, did not experience any night terrors. Upon Robert's return from the reservation, he was able to participate in group and individual therapy at the residential treatment center and address issues that were interfering with his home and school adjustments in the urban setting.

Culturally significant social work interventions included the following:

1. The Native social worker was able to discuss Robert's situation in his Native language with an understanding of the cultural significance of the problems Robert was experiencing.
2. The Native social worker was able to explain to the non-Indian hospital staff and Robert's mother, Robert's perceptions of his problems and desire to participate in an American Indian healing ceremony.
3. The Native social worker had access to an eagle feather (which is unlawful for non-Indians to possess) and was willing to give the feather to Robert.
4. The gift of an eagle feather demands considerable generosity from the giver and utmost respect for the person to whom the gift is given.
5. It is important to remember that regardless of the current residence or length of time Native people have lived off-reservation, there is substantial likelihood that cultural identification and spiritual connectedness remain strong and highly important to the Native person's health and well-being.
6. Combinations of western and Indian medicine are effective in the treatment of Native peoples and the facilitation of recovery and health promotion.

Social Group Work and Family Interventions

Social group work is often the treatment of choice for interventions with American Indians and Alaskan Natives. Culturally, groups are traditional avenues for recreational, social, community, and planning activities. Feasts, ceremonies, celebrations, and decision making are promoted in Native American group gatherings.

Social workers organize a wide variety of prevention, education, and treatment groups for children, youth, adults, and elders, including the following:

	Prevention/Education Groups	Therapy Groups
Children/Youth Groups	Self-esteem enhancement	Behavioral and anger management
	Cultural skills	Sexual abuse issues
	Drug and alcohol prevention	Residential treatment
	Gang prevention	Learning and Disabled
	4-H, Scouting	School refusal/school achievement
	Peer support and leadership	Alternative education/Stay in School
	Youth/elders mentoring	Alcohol and drug treatment
	Service oriented	Life skills training
	Future planning and goal setting	
Adults/Elders Groups	Relationships/communication	Adults abused as children
	Parent education (cultural focus)	Alcohol, drug gambling treatment
	Cultural education (history and heritage)	Depression, anxiety
	Life and coping skills	Domestic abuse victims
	Foster, adoptive, and single-parent training	Perpetrators of abuse
	Addiction and co-dependency	Posttraumatic stress syndrome
	AIDS prevention	Grief, loss separation
	Diet, nutrition, and weight loss	Stress identification and management
	Native language skill development	Discrimination awareness and resolution
	Grandparenting, mentoring	
	Leadership enhancement	
	"Medicine Men" career training	
Family Groups	Healthy families	Crisis intervention
	Family enhancement	Family separation—grief and loss
	Family cultural skills	Family preservation/reconciliation
Task Groups	Community partnership development	
	Tribal histories	Child protection teams
	Cultural advisory committees	Tribal action plans/alcohol abuse
	Language instruction/revitalization	Community problem resolution
	Community service	

Group Work Examples

Two social group work experiences with Native American clientele are described below.

The University of Utah's Graduate School of Social Work continues to recruit and graduate a significant number of Native Americans with master's degrees in social work. Many of these students are traditional American Indian people, strongly identified with their cultural heritage, and interested in encouraging positive cultural identification of their children with their native heritage. At the request of American Indian graduate social work students, the authors organized a group experience for the daughters of these graduate students—nine girls, 7 to 11 years of age. The purposes of the group were to: (1) increase members' knowledge of Native American culture, generally, and their own tribal groups, specifically; (2) enhance positive identification with Native American culture; and (3) enhance positive feelings of self, talents, and abilities to function within Indian and non-Indian cultures. All of the programming was related to Native American culture. Group sessions were organized according to units related to history, values, beliefs, art, music, dance, games, foods, stories, legends, discrimination, and current events.

During the unit related to music and dance, group members sang songs in the native languages of the group's members, played Native American musical instruments, made their own "shawls" for dancing, and learned a variety of Indian dances. Although interest verbally was high, the responses of the group members to the initial dancing activity were surprising. Only one group member had danced at powwows. She was a talented and accomplished dancer. The taped music was playing as group members entered the meeting room. When members were invited to join the leaders in learning specific dance steps, eight of the nine group members literally dove for cover—under the tables and into the open closetlike shelves. Leaders danced along with the one group member, with no effect on the other group members, who remained hidden. With considerable encouragement, one by one the group members were enticed from their hiding places by opportunities to take turns beating the Indian drums and wearing the "bells" from the group facilitator's fancy dance outfit. *Slowly,* over several weeks' time, the girls became more comfortable in dancing—always with opportunities to take turns drumming and wearing the bells. In the meantime, group members attended monthly powwows, at the Indian Walk-In Center, to observe the dancing of other community members. When the girls had completed their shawls, all of the group members and leaders attended a community powwow, and, finally, group members and leaders made their entrance onto the dance floor. Group members were obviously self-conscious, but with the support of the entire group and the leaders, members circled the dance floor and then broke off from the security of the group, in subgroups of two's and three's and then individually to spend the rest of the evening dancing with other community members.

Cultural Considerations Important to This Group Experience.   Among the cultural considerations important to this dance activity and group experience are the following:

1. It is important to understand that all Native Americans will not have similar interests in or talents for every component of their culture.
2. Native Americans may be reluctant to participate in cultural activities, even in supportive group environments, if they are unsure of their abilities to perform.

3. Embarrassment is to be avoided. Performing poorly not only reflects upon self, but also upon family, clan, and tribe.

4. Removing the focus from an individual to a group may be helpful in encouraging more risk-taking behaviors.

5. If one (or more) group members can perform a cultural skill capably, their expertise may contribute to less willingness on the part of other group members to try to develop these skills.

6. Group leaders must model appropriate risk-taking behaviors for group members.

7. One positive experience may "break the ice," but groups must provide ongoing cultural activity experiences to promote integration of this learning and willingness to take risks in other activities.

8. Support of parents, siblings, and extended family members is crucial to the risk-taking behavior of children in activities in which they perform in front of others.

9. It is important that parents encourage participation of their children in cultural activities.

The second example comes from a group experience with recovering Native American adults enrolled in an American Indian alcoholism counselor training program. One component of each of the one-month, on-campus training sessions required counselors-in-training to participate in group-work laboratories where they processed what they were learning and how it could be applied to their alcoholism-counseling assignments.

In one group session, the members were concerned that one of the recovering alcoholism counselors had left the program—the result of his return to active drinking behaviors. The group members were hurt, disappointed, and saddened. They discussed their friendships with this counselor; their regret that they had not been aware of his struggles; their inability to be of help to him at this time; and their fears that they, too, might "slip" and return to their previous drinking behaviors. After considerable discussion, thoughtful contemplation, and some personal sharing, the session was summarized. At this point, a group member who had been unusually quiet for the entire session asked if the group could help him. He then described a terrifying emotional experience during that day's early morning hours. He had experienced every emotional and physical response he could remember from his prior drinking experiences—but he was certain he had not been drinking—at least he could not remember drinking. The social workers asked if other group members could be of help to him. Almost one-third of the group members admitted to having had a previous "dry drunk" experience, where they, too, suffered similar emotional and physical responses—much like those of their active drinking days. These group members verbalized their experiences while others acknowledged their understanding by quietly nodding their heads. The members shared that dry drunks had happened to them during times of recovery; that the episodes became less frequent and emotionally painful with the passage of time; that members should reassure themselves that they have not been drinking; and that it is often helpful to talk to someone at the time of these reactions, or the next day, as appropriate. At the conclusion of this discussion, the social workers again thanked group members for their sensitive sharing and their help to this group member. The group member also quietly expressed his appreciation to the group and said, "Thank you for helping me. I thought I was going crazy." As group members left, several members shook hands with the group member and the group leaders without any additional verbal expression.

Cultural Considerations Important in This Group Experience. It is important to understand the cultural significance of many of the interactions in this group session. For example:

1. At times of stress, American Indian group members will often respond with nonverbal expressions that may escape the notice of a nonattentive group worker, such as brief nods of the head, short-term eye contact, and active listening behaviors.
2. American Indian people do not often feel a need to express opinions or re-state information that has been adequately conveyed by another group member. (An exception is when elders are asked to advise. Elders often repeat advice or counsel that has already been given by another elder.)
3. The shaking of hands at the end of the group session is an example of sincere respect and appreciation. No verbalization is necessary.
4. It is impolite to interrupt a discussion of significance with an unrelated personal experience. It is not unusual for an American Indian person to wait until a current discussion topic is concluded before beginning a new, different discussion topic of a personal concern. This is not an example of avoidance, or control, or postponing group session termination. It is an example of respect for the discussion and concerns of others.
5. When American Indian people risk sharing an emotional, personal experience, they may be concerned that their respect is diminished in the eyes of other group members. American Indian people are often taught to handle their problems independently. The handshakes and "nods" convey understanding, appreciation, and respect.
6. After sharing an emotional experience of this magnitude, it is likely that the next session may be one of less involvement. It is important to acknowledge the difficult work that was accomplished in the previous session and to allow group member self-determination regarding the depth to which they will discuss problems in the next session.
7. Group workers, too, can discriminately use handshaking after a group session to acknowledge the work and progress of group members.

Macro Social Work Practice with American Indians

Community is an important concept for American Indian people. The most universal symbol in Indian art, the circle, symbolizes cycles of life and tradition. The circle is a metaphor for living in harmony with one another, with the environment, and with the spiritual forces of the Indian universe.[22]

Community organization principles have much to offer in furthering the community concept that is so important to Native American people. Many American Indian communities are implementing programs through activation of all potential resources. An important first step, according to Beauvais and LaBoueff, is to create an awareness that a community problem or need exists.[23] After a thorough assessment of the facts, steps must be taken to actively involve all community members in the planning, implementation, and ongoing evaluation process.[24]

Many reservation and urban communities have implemented these principles in organizing and motivating their communities to achieve problem resolution. Edwards and Egbert-Edwards describe several successful community efforts, including (1) planning and implementation of Tribal Action Plans to combat community alcohol and drug problems; (2) children and youth cultural awareness and cultural arts enhancement programs; (3) establishment of community group homes and residential treatment centers; (4) development of youth community service groups; (5) educational support and achievement programs; and (6) urban and reservation recovery and healing programs.[25]

Examples of Native American community development programs in urban areas include (1) community development/partnership programs to address concerns of urban communities; (2) establishment of American Indian schools for those students who do not adjust to public schools; (3) programs that provide services for children, adults, and elders—at the same time—in consideration of transportation and time issues and developing feelings of community; and (4) task groups that plan and organize powwows, feast days, peer-support groups, holiday celebrations, elders' appreciation days, youth appreciation days, and other cultural and community support activities.

Examples of reservation community development programs include (1) community sobriety activities such as camp-outs, powwows, bowling leagues, traditional dances, rodeos, and holiday celebrations; (2) designation of areas of tribal lands as drug-free "healing" centers to promote recovery, cultural activities, growth activities, and celebrations.

Successful Native American community development programs require strong leadership from community leaders who have long-term, realistic commitments to their programs, goals, and communities. These leaders understand the strengths and developmental needs of their communities. They respond to criticism openly. They welcome suggestions for improving their programs and creatively modify and expand their service delivery systems. They give credit to all factions of the community who are contributing to community development. They support the programs of other agencies. Cultural principles are incorporated into all aspects of their programs. Positive identification with tribal and Indian heritage is enhanced through celebrations that promote and reinforce success.

NATIVE AMERICAN URBAN COMMUNITY CASE STUDY

In several urban areas, Native American communities have recognized the need to involve and support their "elders" by programming community activities that fulfill elders' needs and promote and recognize their contributions to the community.

One American Indian urban community addressed the needs and potential contributions of American Indian elders in their community with the following approach, under the direction of the community Indian Center staff:

1. Surveyed their community and identified American Indian elderly residents;
2. Visited all elderly residents to assess their needs, their interest in contributing to their community, and their suggestions for activities and involvement;
3. Asked each elder to complete a written survey;
4. Provided elders with a "gift of appreciation" for their time and suggestions;
5. With the input of elders formulated a regularly scheduled "American Indian Elders' Group," with appropriate by-laws;
6. Provided agency space and staff consultation to facilitate achievement of Elders' Group goals and purposes;
7. Assisted in fund-raising activities to provide a financial base for the Elder's Group;
8. Requested assistance of elders in various community groups, projects, and activities;
9. Provided access to agency leadership for resolution of questions and problems/issues;
10. Provided opportunities for rotating leadership opportunities for Elders Group members; and
11. Provided assistance with educational, recreational, cultural, and service activities as requested by the Elders Group and the community.

All of these special considerations have assisted in the ongoing development and success of this group experience. Benefits have been derived by the elders attending the group sessions, by the agency sponsoring the group, and by the community members who have benefited from service rendered by Elders group members.

The Future

As indicated throughout this chapter, there continues to be considerable energy and commitment directed by Native American people toward the enhancement of their communities—reservation/rural and urban. Individual and community pride are reinforced through positive program planning and goal achievement. Problems are viewed as challenges to restore balance and promote harmony within individuals and communities. Creativity has been and will continue to be fostered as renewed efforts are directed toward meeting the needs of Native American people.

There is continuing determination to address problems that interfere with the achievement of the potential of individuals and communities. Native Americans are determined to more positively enhance the image of their leaders and expand their leadership base. Leaders are committed to portraying positive leadership roles as culturally appropriate. Backbiting is being addressed and replaced by individual and community partnerships, open communication, and furthered collaboration. Constructive criticism is being directed toward problem resolution and collective development.

Creativity of Indian people is being acknowledged and encouraged in program development and problem resolution. It is likely that the coming years will be eventful and profitable for American Indians and Alaskan Natives and will lead to considerable growth in many areas, including the following:

1. Further attention must be directed toward active participation in political processes.
2. The Indian Child Welfare Act (ICWA) of 1978 was enacted to halt the excessive removal of Indian children from their natural parents and to reestablish tribal rights and responsibilities over the care of their children. Recent research indicates that while progress has been made, compliance under the Act has been uneven.[26] Increased resources and professional staff were recommended to ensure that the intent of the Act was achieved. In 1995–1996, the ICWA was challenged by a Congressional Committee attempting to amend the Act in ways that would diminish tribal responsibility over voluntary adoptions. Subsequent negotiations appear to protect the original intent of the ICWA while promoting more expeditious handling of cases involving American Indian children. Continued vigilance is necessary to ensure that the best interests of Indian children and tribal groups are maintained.
3. Wellness programs must emphasize the "whole" being, including the physical, mental, social, emotional, spiritual, and cultural.
4. Cultural programs could benefit from collaborative efforts of tribal leaders, elders, and Native archaeologists and anthropologists who will instruct all tribal members in the historical and cultural heritage of tribal groups.[27]
5. Culturally oriented therapy groups can continue to expand through use of Native concepts such as *talking circles*.
6. Continuity of care services must be emphasized in planning group homes for children and youth in need of residential treatment for emotional or drug and alcohol problems; halfway houses for those released from residential settings such as correctional facilities, and emotionally disturbed or alcohol and drug treatment programs; and young adult group living homes or apartments for emancipated teenagers and young adults.
7. Family therapy residential homes could be helpful for families who need counseling, parent education, and relationship skill development. Families could maintain residence in a supportive, therapeutic environment, with after care provided when families return to their own homes.
8. Creative, comprehensive drug and alcohol programs must be planned to address individual, family, and community needs, including those related to FAS/FAE and AIDS.
9. Attention should be focused on more training and educational opportunities especially in addressing the new "meth drug activity" on reservations and in urban areas where "meth" is becoming the drug of choice for many American Indian people.
10. Economic development is crucial to the further success of Native American people.

11. Throughout the United States, there is an interest in history and the accurate portrayal of history. Native Americans are championing their cause for the inclusion of historical content into public and higher education systems that more accurately portray the American Indian and Alaskan Native experience. This is not only just, but will result in greater understanding and appreciation of Native Americans, and increased positive identification of Native peoples with their heritage.[28]

Concluding Comment   Social work with American Indians is a challenging and rewarding experience. Native Americans have much to contribute to society—their own tribes, other American Indian and Alaskan Native groups, and the non-Indian world. "Balance" and "harmony" are important concepts, as is the Native American belief in showing respect for all living things. Incorporating these concepts into professional social work practice with Native American people will foster respect, collaboration, and growth. According to Hill, "In the Indian world, culture is not a commodity or a performance, it is the act of living as an Indian. How you live is an art."[29] Professional social work has been defined as an "art." We have much to learn in sharing our art with one another in professional relationships.

KEY WORDS AND CONCEPTS

American Indians   Traditional native medicine
Alaskan Natives   Balance
Indian Child Welfare Act   Talking circles

SUGGESTED INFORMATION SOURCES

Bubar, Roe W., and Vernon, Irene S. *Contempory Native American Issues: Social and Life Issues*. Philadelphia: Chelsea House Publishers, 2006.

Edwards, E. D., and Edwards, M. E. "Family-Centered Social Work Practice," in E. Gonzalez-Santin and T. Perry, eds. *Understanding the Cultural Context: Working with American Indian Children and Families*. Tempe, AZ: ASU, 2003, pp. 27–63.

Edwards, E. D., et al. "A Community Approach for Native American Drug and Alcohol Prevention Programs: A Logic Model Framework," *Alcoholism Treatment Quarterly* 13, no. 2 (1995) pp. 43–62.

Edwards, E. D., and Egbert-Edwards, M. E. "Community Development with American Indians and Alaska Natives," in F. G. Rivera & J. L. Erlich, eds., *Community Organizing in a Diverse Society* 3rd Edition. Needham Heights, MA: Allyn & Bacon, 1998.

Gonzalez-Santin, E., and Perry, P., eds. *Understanding the Cultural Context: Working with American Indian Children and Families*. Tempe, AZ: Arizona State University, 2003.

Moran, J. R. "Prevention Principles for American Indian Communities," *Health Promotion and Substance Abuse Prevention among American Indian and Alaska Native Communities: Issues in Cultural Competence.* Washington, DC: CSAP, 2001, pp. 35–66.

Trimble, J. E., and Beauvais, F. "Prevention of Alcoholism, Drug Abuse, and Health Problems among American Indians and Alaska Natives: An Introduction and Overview," in *Health Promotion and Substance Abuse Prevention among American Indian and Alaska Native Communities: Issues in Cultural Competence.* CSAP Cultural competence series 9, special collaborative edition, pp. 1–34.

Weaver, H. N., and White, B. J. "The Native American Family Circle: Roots of Resiliency," *Cross-Cultural Practice with Couples and Families.* Binghamton, NY: The Haworth Press, 1997, pp. 67–79.

ENDNOTES

1. The American Indian and Alaska Native Population: 2000. Census 2000 Brief. U.S. Census Bureau, U.S. Department of Commerce. Issued February 2002.
2. W. H. Oswalt, *This Land Was Theirs: A Study of Native North Americans.* (NY: Oxford University Press, 2006).
3. The American Indian and Alaska Native Population: 2000. Census 2000 Brief. U.S. Census Bureau, U.S. Department of Commerce. Issued February 2002.
4. Ibid.
5. J. Utter, *American Indians: Answers to Today's Questions* (Norman: University of Oklahoma Press, 2001), p. 40.
6. U.S. Bureau of the Census, "People Below Poverty Level by Race, Sex, and Age," Table 682, http://www.census.gov/statab/www/sa04aian.pdf.
7. Ibid.
8. Ibid. "Money Income of Families—Distribution of Income and Median Income of Families," Table 676.
9. Ibid. "Resident Population by Sex, Race, and Hispanic Origin," Table 13 and Table 682.
10. Bureau of the Census, CPH-L-95, Educational Attainment of American Indian, Eskimo, and Aleut Males and Females, 25 years and over: 1990, No Date Given.
11. H. L. Hodgkinson with J. H. Outtz and A. M. Obarakpor, *The Demographics of American Indians: One Percent of the People; Fifty Percent of the Diversity* (Washington, D.C.: Institute for Educational Leadership, November 1990).
12. Ibid.
13. Indian Health Service: Trends in Indian Health—1991. U.S. Department of Health and Human Services, Public Health Service, Indian Health Service, Office of Planning, Evaluation, and Legislation, Division of Program Statistics.
14. Indian Health Service, *Prevention Resource Guide: American Indians and Native Alaskans* (Washington, D.C.: U.S. Department of Health and Human Services, Office for Substance Abuse Prevention, June 1991), p. 1.
15. *The State of Native American Youth Health* (Minneapolis, MN: University of Minnesota, February 1992).
16. *The State of Native American Youth Health* (Minneapolis, MN: University of Minnesota, February 1992), pp. 54–55.
17. B. Berry, *Race and Ethnic Relations* (Boston: Houghton Mifflin, 1965).

18. D. Johnson, "Census Finds Many Claiming New Identity: Indian," *New York Times* (National) (March 5, 1991).

19. L. K. Brendtro, "Dancing with Wolves: A New Paradigm for Reclaiming Youth at Risk." The Sixth Annual Robert J. O'Leary Memorial Lecture. Ohio State University College of Social Work (February 26, 1991).

20. E. R. Rhoades, "Profile of American Indians and Alaska Natives," in *Minority Aging: Essential Curricula Content for Selected Health and Allied Health Professions*, M. Harper, ed. (Washington, D.C.: U.S.D.H. & H.S., 1990), p. 59.

21. Ibid.

22. R. Hill, Indian Insights into Indian Worlds. *Native Peoples Magazine* 6, no. 1 (Fall 1992): 14.

23. F. Beauvais and S. LaBoueff, "Drug and Alcohol Abuse Intervention in American Indian Communities," *International Journal of the Addictions* 20 (January 1985): 139–171.

24. E. D. Edwards, and M. Egbert-Edwards, "Native American Community Development," in *Community Organizing in a Diverse Society*, F. G. Rivera and J. L. Erlich, eds. (Boston: Allyn and Bacon, 1992).

25. E. D. Edwards, and M. Egbert-Edwards, *Native American Community Development*, 1992.

26. M. C. Plantz, "Indian Child Welfare: A Status Report," *Children Today* 18 (January/February 1989).

27. K. Dongoske, et al., "Understanding the Past Through Hopi Oral Tradition," *Native Peoples Magazine* 6, no. 2 (Winter 1993).

28. I. Thunderhorse, "Democracy: An Indian Legacy," *The Witness* (April 1993).

29. R. Hill, "Indian Insights into Indian Worlds," *Native Peoples Magazine* 6, no. 1 (Fall 1992): 13–14.

Social Work Practice with Mexican Americans

Armando T. Morales and Ramon Salcido

Prefatory Comment

The authors, Dr. Armando T. Morales, Professor of Psychiatry and Biobehavioral Science, Department of Psychiatry, UCLA School of Medicine, and Dr. Ramon Salcido, Associate Professor and Chairman of the Community Organization Planning Concentration, School of Social Work, University of Southern California, maintain that Mexican Americans do have mental health needs and do avail themselves of direct services when they are provided at minimum cost, in their primary language (Spanish), and near their homes. They offer practice suggestions that have implications for macro social work in the barrio, mobilizing various indigenous social support systems such as churches, neighbors, and the family. They also recommend the intervention strategy of advocacy to reduce institutional barriers to services for Mexican Americans. A police brutality case serves to highlight the micro and macro skills required in these delicate cases that are common in the Latino community.

Meeting the ever-increasing social service needs of disadvantaged groups, which are often isolated by class and cultural differences, is a continuing challenge to social work. If the social work profession hopes to be more viable among disadvantaged groups, especially among the Mexican American population, human services institutions must modify their service delivery systems. Moreover, social workers must understand the dynamics of both individual and institutional racism, which have discouraged or prevented Mexican Americans from availing themselves of existing services. At times those services have appeared impersonal and even nonsupportive.

Despite the recent attention focused on the special needs of Mexican Americans, any explanation of their situation is complicated by the difficulty of defining this population as to size and demographic characteristics. More has to be learned about the variations within this group and its immigration pattern.

Demographic Profile

In the 2002 Census data, U.S. Hispanics reported that their ethnic origin was either Mexican, Puerto Rican, Cuban, Central or South American, or of some other *Latino* origin. The terms *Latino* and *Hispanic* are used interchangeably by the Census Bureau and in this chapter. More than one in eight persons in the United States is of Hispanic origin. In 2002, 13.3 percent of the United States population representing 37.4 million people were of Hispanic background. In this group, Mexicans were 66.9 percent; Puerto Ricans, 8.6 percent; Central and South Americans, 14.3 percent; Cubans, 3.7 percent; and "other Hispanics," 6.5 percent. *Latinos* of Mexican background were likely to live in the West and South, 54.6 percent and 33.3 percent, respectively.[1]

According to the 2002 Census, Hispanics are a very young group: 34.4 percent of Hispanics were less than 18 years of age compared to 22.8 percent of non-Hispanic whites. A smaller number of Hispanics were 18 to 64 (60.5 percent) compared to non-Hispanic whites (62.9 percent). In the 45 to 64 age category, Hispanics represented 14.3 percent compared to 25.7 percent of non-Hispanic whites. Mexicans had the highest proportion less than 18 years of age (37.1 percent); those of Cuban origin had the lowest proportion at 19.6 percent.[2]

Fifteen million Hispanics (40.2 percent) in the United States were foreign born in 2002. Of this population, 52.1 percent entered the United States between 1990 and 2002; another 25.6 percent came to the United States in the 1980s; and 22.3 percent entered the United States before 1980. More *Latinos* live in family households with five or more people (26.5 percent) than those of non-*Latino* whites (10.8 percent). Mexican families were most likely to have five or more people (30.8 percent) compared to Central and South Americans (22.3 percent), Puerto Rican (16.8 percent), other Hispanics (19.6 percent), and Cubans, 10.6 percent.[3]

With regard to educational attainment, more than two in five *Latinos* age 25 and older have not graduated from high school. Among Hispanics 25 years of age and older, persons of Mexican descent had a lower percentage of high school graduates (50.6 percent) than Cubans (70.8 percent), Puerto Ricans (66.8 percent), Central and South Americans (70.8 percent), and "other" Hispanics (74.0 percent). Non-Hispanic whites had a much higher graduation rate at 88.7 percent.[4]

Looking at economic characteristics of Hispanics, in March 2002, 8.1 percent of Hispanics in the civilian labor force age 16 and older were unemployed, compared to only 5.1 percent of non-Hispanic whites. Regarding full-time, year-round workers, 26.3 percent of Hispanics and 53.8 percent of non-Hispanic whites earned $35,000 or more. Of all *Latino* groups, those of Mexican descent had the lowest proportion earning $35,000 or more (23.6 percent). The percent of non-Hispanic whites earning $50,000 or more was 31.8 percent compared to 12.4 percent of all and only 10.6 percent of Mexicans. *Latinos* (21.4 percent) are far more likely than non-Hispanic whites (7.8 percent) to live below the poverty level. Puerto Ricans were the most impoverished group among the Hispanics (26.1 percent) closely followed by Mexicans at 22.8 percent. An important issue affecting the future of continued poverty for *Latinos* is the fact that those younger than 18 years of age were about three times more likely than non-Hispanic white children to be living in poverty (28.0 percent compared with 9.5 percent respectively). Whereas *Latino* children represented 17.7 percent of all children in the United States, they constituted 30.4 percent of all children in poverty.[5]

Census data indicate that the percentage of persons speaking Spanish at home in the ten-year period from 1990 to 2000 increased consistently both at the national and state levels. It increased nationally from 7.5 percent to 10.7 percent, with the top three states in 2000 being New Mexico, 28.7 percent; Texas, 27.0 percent; and California, 25.0 percent.[6] Cities reveal an even more dramatic statistic regarding persons age 5 and over who speak a language other than English. The leading four cities were Santa Ana, California, 88.8 percent; Miami, Florida, 80.0 percent; El Paso, Texas, 77.3 percent; and Los Angeles, California, 61.1 percent.[7] These reports did not indicate if those persons speaking Spanish were of Mexican descent, but it can be assumed that Santa Ana, El Paso, and Los Angeles had large numbers of persons of Mexican descent.

Ecosystems Model

The five-level ecosystems model detailed in the introduction to Part Five has been adopted as an assessment tool to analyze the Mexican American. The five levels of analysis include historical, environmental–structural, cultural, family, and individual factors impacting Mexican Americans. The emphasis will be on mental health and psychosocial issues, as social work practice focuses on the interaction between the person and the environment. The term *person* may refer to an individual, a community, or even a larger social structure of society. Social work intervention might be directed at the person, the environment, or both. In each case, the social worker seeks to enhance and restore the social functioning of people and/or to change social conditions that impede the mutually beneficial interaction between people and their environment. This will be seen later in a police brutality case highlighting micro and macro intervention.

The ecosystems orientation involves the application of ecology and general systems theory to professional tasks. It permits social workers to look at psychosocial phenomena, account for complex variables, assess the dynamic interplay of these variables, draw conceptual boundaries around the unit of attention or the specific case, and then generate ideas for intervention. At this point methodology enters in, because in any particular case—meaning a particular individual, couple, family, group, institutional unit, or geographical area—any number of practice interventions might be needed. The ecosystems model can promote social workers' understanding of (1) the psychosocial problems experienced by Mexican Americans; (2) the crippling effects of institutional racism, such as the police brutality detailed in the Part Five introduction; and (3) the oppressive environments in which these people struggle to survive. For the purposes of this chapter, the five levels of analysis will be further subdivided as follows:

1. Historical
   a. History of treating mental illness (international)
   b. Mexico's approach to treating mental illness
2. Environmental–structural
   a. Mental health treatment for Mexican Americans in the United States
   b. The ethnosystem as an adjunctive helping service
3. Cultural
   a. *Barrio* service systems as adjunctive and alternative helping systems
4. The family
   a. Extended family, surrogate family, and support networks
5. The individual
   a. Assessment and treatment of a police brutality victim

Normally, for a deeper and more comprehensive understanding of a client's situation, the ecosystems five levels of assessment should be tied to and relevant to the specific case being assessed as was shown in the case example in the box in Part Five's opener. With the exception of the *individual level,* this was not done in this chapter to allow for greater generalization to other Mexican Americans.

Historical Factors

History of Treating Mental Illness.   Societies throughout the world have developed various approaches for treating persons suffering from psychological problems. Three basic explanations and corresponding intervention strategies pertaining to psychological problems can be traced back to the earliest times: (1) the attempt to explain diseases of the mind in physical terms; that is, the organic approach ("It's in your blood/chemistry"); (2) the attempt to deal with inexplicable events through spiritual or magical approaches ("The devil/spirits made you do it"); and (3) the attempt to find a psychological explanation for psychological problems ("It's all in your mind"). Hippocrates (460–377 B.C.), the father of medicine, pioneered the organic approach, believing that black bile caused depression. Several centuries later, Cicero (106–43 B.C.), the Roman statesman and attorney, objected to the black bile theory, maintaining that depression was the result of psychological difficulties. He proclaimed that people were responsible for their emotional and psychological difficulties—in a psychological sense, they could do something about them. Cicero laid down the theoretical foundations for psychotherapy. The magical/spiritual approach found people treating the afflicted person through appeasement, confession, incantations, magical rituals, or exorcism.[8]

The effectiveness of any treatment approach often depends on the suggestibility of the person on whom the approach is worked, the suggestive power of the influencing practitioner, and the sympathetic connection (relationship) between the practitioner and the person seeking assistance. If a person strongly believes, for example, his or her headache, stomachache, or depression has as its basis a physical or chemical factor and that only a medical person can help, a physician or psychiatrist who prescribes medication may have the greatest likelihood of relieving that person's symptom. If, on the other hand, the person believes he or she is suffering certain symptoms because he or she has sinned and that only a minister or priest can help, the church's representatives may indeed have the greatest impact. And if the person believes his or her symptom has a psychogenic basis and can only be alleviated by talking to someone who can be "objective" in understanding the symptom or problem, the psychiatrist or social worker may offer the best help.

Mexico's Historical Approach to Treating Mental Illness.   Mexican society, like other societies, also developed approaches to help people with psychological problems. The ancestors of Mexican Americans, the Aztecs, numbering 20 million persons in Central Mexico in the fifteenth century, created a wealthy, powerful, and progressive empire. Their culture was highly developed, and in that intellectual atmosphere flourished highly advanced forms of psychiatry and psychotherapy. Translations of Aztec literature reveal that Aztec therapy was provided by competent personnel in institutions of high repute. They had an amazing grasp of psychology and developed concepts about ego formation similar to those advanced by Freud almost 500 years later. Those concepts appear in an Aztec document about dream interpretation. The Aztec psychiatrists knew how to recognize persons who were manic, schizoid, hysterical, depressive, and psychopathic—major mental disorder classifications not unlike the ones used today. Aztec patients were treated by a variety of methods, including an early form of brain surgery, hypnosis, "talking out" bad things in one's mind, and specific herbal potions for specific disorders.[9]

With the colonization of Mexico by Spain in the early sixteenth century came Spanish medicine based on European concepts. Spanish colonial physicians still held primitive ideas about the causes of disease, believing it was a punishment for sins caused by devils who had taken possession of the patient's body and spirit. Because military might was associated with racial superiority, Spanish medicine was also believed by Spaniards to be superior to that of the Aztecs. Had Spanish oppression not occurred, Aztec psychiatry might have made a very significant contribution to the mental health practices of the Western world. In spite of this overt conflict and clash over psychiatric approaches, however, the first hospital for the mentally ill founded in North America was in Mexico City in 1567.[10] The first hospital for the mentally ill in the United States was founded 185 years later, in 1752, in Philadelphia, Pennsylvania.[11] The United States established two additional hospitals for the mentally ill during this period, one in Williamsburg, Virginia, in 1773, and the Bloomingdale Asylum in New York in 1821. In a comparable period, Mexico also established a hospital in Yucatán in 1625, the Manicomio de lä Canoa in Mexico City in 1687, the Hospital Civil in Guadalajara in 1739, a hospital in Belém in 1794, and the Divino Salvado in Mexico City in 1796.

Other mental health milestones found Mexico establishing its first department of psychiatry in 1860 in Jalisco; the United States began its first program in 1906. Mexico began the systematic training of physicians in psychiatry in 1910; the United

States initiated its training program in 1937. Mexico launched its community mental health movement in 1951 by establishing mental health programs in health centers; the United States initiated community programs in 1964 with the passage of the Federal Community Mental Health Act.[12] Today in Mexico the major mental health trends and various theoretical orientations are similar to those in other Western countries. No single therapy orientation prevails, and, as in the United States, psychiatrists are by and large in control of mental health programs, with psychologists, social workers, and psychiatric nurses having lesser roles. From the standpoint of mental health resources, the United States, being a much wealthier country, far overshadows Mexico in terms of mental health resources and manpower. The United States, for example, has 12.4 psychiatrists per 100,000, versus less than one psychiatrist per 100,000 in Mexico.[13]

Environmental–Structural Factors

Mental Health Treatment for Mexican Americans.   In the United States, persons of Mexican descent have found it very difficult to obtain mental health services. The nation's first community mental health program specifically for persons of Mexican descent was established in East Los Angeles in 1967. The staffing pattern included four psychiatrists, four psychiatric social workers, three nurses, a clinical psychologist, a rehabilitation counselor, a community services coordinator, a community worker, and six secretaries. All but one of the staff were bilingual. In applying one measure of utilization (the percentage of Spanish surname population in the area, 76 percent), the program was successful in that 90 percent of the clients seen had a Spanish surname. Clearly here there was maximum utilization of services by Hispanics. The program offered traditional mental health services provided in the clients' primary language and at a fee ranging from 50 cents to $15.[14] There are a few other, rare examples of overutilization of mental health services by Hispanics,[15] but overall the utilization rate by this population rarely exceeds 50 percent. In other words, Hispanic receipt of services is usually one-half or less of their representation in the population.[16]

There are a number of reasons proposed to explain this underutilization. The literature is now making it increasingly clear that the major factors involved are structural in nature and pertain to the availability, accessibility, and acceptability of services to the very heterogeneous bilingual, bicultural characteristics of Hispanics.[17] When Hispanics finally do receive services, they are often of inferior quality, with diagnoses often based on assessment procedures developed for the middle-class Anglo population that have no validity or applicability to these people. Furthermore, Hispanics are more likely to receive somatic and medication treatment and less individual or group therapy. These experiences can and do result in premature treatment termination.[18] Another important factor, accounting for premature termination or resistance to treatment, is whether the Hispanic is a *voluntary client* seeking help for a problem *he* or *she* defines, or an *involuntary client* being referred for treatment regarding a problem of concern to the referring agency.[19] Racist and political policies and economic decisions (raising fees) by mental health agencies to deny services to "undocumented" or poor persons are other growing contributing factors related to the underutilization of services by Hispanics.

The Ethnosystem: An Adjunctive Helping System.   Assuming that social work abandons its constricted methods framework and adopts the ecosystems perspective, then this question must be asked: What other knowledge is needed to understand the psychosocial problems of Mexican Americans that is specific to their ethnic background? Solomon's framework provides one option for integrating Mexican American concerns into a practice framework.[20] She utilizes the ethnosystem and empowerment concepts as major integrative concepts. The *ethnosystem* is defined as a society comprising groups that vary in modes of communication, in degree of control over material resources, and in the structure of their internal relationships or social organization.[21] Moreover, these groups must be in a more or less stable pattern of relationships that have characteristics transcending any single group's field of integration; for example, the ethnosystem's political, educational, or economic subsystems. Solomon defines *empowerment* as a process whereby persons who belong to a stigmatized social category throughout their lives can be assisted to develop and increase skills in the exercise of interpersonal influence and the performance of valued social roles.[22]

Ethnosystems are the natural networks, the primary patterns of interaction, survival, and adjustment indigenous to societies. As used here, the concept of *natural networks* has its origins in several disciplines: social work, sociology, social psychology, and anthropology, as well as in the mental health "community support—significant others" literature.[23] Social workers need to be aware that these natural networks and primary systems exist apart from the usual modes of secondary interactions that Mexican Americans have developed for survival within Anglo-urbanized systems, including those with the social establishment. There is a basic similarity between the ethnosystem with secondary interaction for coping with the Anglo society and the concept of two environments, the immediate or nurturing environment and the wider environment. When, as Norton notes, the larger societal system rejects the minority group's immediate environment or ethnosystem, there is incongruence between the two (Solomon refers to this as negative valuation of a stigmatized collective), and power blocks are directed toward the minority individuals, groups, and communities.[24]

Cultural Factors: Barrio Service Systems

Mexican Americans have been immigrating to *barrios* (Mexican neighborhoods) in U.S. urban areas in large and small waves. The *barrio* is a microcosm of the dominant society as well as an ethnosystem. Although the communities interrelate with external institutional structures such as law enforcement, schools, and the public welfare system, *barrios* also have indigenous service systems that provide mutual aid and psychological support in time of need. Indigenous support systems include churches, neighbors, friends, the family, and alternate services.[25]

Many Mexican Americans, especially the elderly and immigrant groups, have strong religious ties and attend church on a regular basis. The church, whether Roman Catholic or Protestant, is an important spiritual support for many Mexican Americans and, in addition, is a vehicle for disseminating information about *barrio* activities and services, reaching individuals who would be largely inaccessible to public agencies. There is trust in the church. For example, the parish priest or minister often knows of potential adoptive parents who would provide an excellent home for an unwed mother's child.

Concerned neighbors and friends also provide aid and act as a resource. Perceived as confidential sources of advice, these significant persons act as referral agents. Lee's study on the use of the services of a model neighborhood health center by Mexican Americans observed that some groups sought primary groups such as friends and neighbors as their major source of information about health care services.[26]

Family Factors

The family unit clearly plays an important role in providing economic, social, and psychological supports. Families also serve as adoptive parents for family members who are no longer able to care for their children. Especially in the case of older children, grandparents may care for and eventually adopt them. Other relatives, or the child's godparents or *compadres*, may also accept the responsibility of raising the child or children. Infants, of course, may also be adopted in the same manner. However, no matter how effective this network may be, it is the welfare agency, rather than the network itself, that has access at all times to the greatest amount of provision and greatest number of providers in the greatest geographical area; it is the agency that has legal responsibility for bringing services to the community.

As a result of the Chicano movement in the 1960s and 1970s, alternate service systems are being developed within the *barrio* to deal with the special needs of the Mexican American community. Although there are variations in the services offered in each *barrio*, common patterns in both structure and function are observable. Self-help groups, social action organizations, and specialized service agencies staffed exclusively by bicultural and bilingual personnel are considered the most essential aspects of the alternate service system.

Siporin writes that the ecological perspective is an "effort to improve the functioning and competence of the welfare service system of natural self-help mutual aid networks, and to improve the social functioning and coping competence of individuals and their collectivities."[27] This approach calls for the practitioner to broaden his or her view of the client. Intervention involves assessment of the total social, physical, and psychological needs of the client and his or her network system. Intervention also calls for advocacy in the amelioration of identified problems related to barriers created by social welfare systems. Intervention strategies are initiated in anticipation of resolving psychosocial problems. An example of a macrolevel strategy is networking.

Extended Family, Surrogate Family, and Support Networks.   Collins and Pancoast refer to *networks* as consisting of both people and relationships.[28] The social network is relatively invisible, though it is a real structure in which an individual, nuclear family, or group is embedded. The term *support systems,* as used here, parallels Caplan's conceptualization. He states, "Support systems may be of a continuing nature, intermittent or short-term in the event of an acute need or crisis."[29] Both enduring and short-term supports are likely to consist of three elements:[30]

1. the significant others help the individual mobilize his psychological resources and master his emotional burdens;
2. they share his tasks; and
3. they provide him with extra supplies of money, materials, tools, skills, and cognitive guidance to improve the handling of his situation.

Individuals usually belong to several networks at the same time. Networks can be based on kinship, friendship, employment, recreation, education, politics, ethnicity, religion, or whatever interests or elements individuals find in common.

The content of exchanges can also be varied.[31] Although the informal network is important, it cannot provide for all needs. Formal resources (social services agencies, medical services, and other service providers) are likely to be utilized. Social network intervention, therefore, is an approach to service delivery that involves significant individuals in the amelioration of identified psychosocial problems.

Social network intervention takes into consideration both formal and informal systems. Also of significance to Mexican Americans is that this approach incorporates the sociocultural components of the family. The utilization of support systems can be conceptualized into two main divisions: (1) to engage existing networks and enhance their functioning; and (2) to create new networks or "attach" a formerly isolated person or family to a network.[32]

The approach considers both psychological and environmental stresses and incorporates them into the total reality of a family. It focuses on rallying the life-sustaining forces of the individual and family. This viable system of self-help continues to function after the professional helper has been disengaged.

In social network intervention, the goal is to deal with the entire structure by rendering the network visible and viable and by attempting to restore its function. The social network for Mexican American families may include extended kin, *compadres* (co-parents), friends, *curanderos* (folk healers), and other concerned individuals. These subsystems are identified because of their potential to provide emotional strength, support, and other types of assistance to the family. Social network intervention, therefore, emphasizes engagement of the family's network of support systems.

Individual Factors

At the individual level of the ecosystems assessment model, attention is given by the social worker to the biopsychological endowment of the person, which includes personality strengths, level of psychosocial development, mental status, attitudes, values, cultural beliefs, lifestyle, educational attainment, and coping strengths when faced with physical and psychological stresses and problems. In turn, these factors are analyzed, not only within the ecosystems framework, but also in relationship to growth and development life-cycle theories such as those developed by Freud, Erikson, and Bowlby, to name a few.

Armed with the knowledge gained from the ecosystems assessment tool, the social worker is in a better position to plan his or her intervention. The central task for the social worker is to help clients resolve existing or potential problems in psychosocial functioning. This process may involve helping the client resolve problems within themselves or with other people such as a spouse, parent, children, friends, or coworkers. This focus is called direct service, or microlevel social work practice. Intervening on behalf of clients with larger social structures such as neighborhoods, organizations, or the community—in effect all those social work activities that fall outside of the domain of *micro* social work practice—is referred to as indirect service, or macrolevel social work practice. In working with poor people, especially documented or undocumented Mexican immigrants who are often at the mercy of various social, economic, and political forces in society, both levels of intervention, micro and macro, are necessary for optimal helping effectiveness. What follows is a detailed case concerning *micro* intervention by a social worker with a documented Mexican immigrant adult male who was assaulted by the police. Following the *micro* intervention, a discussion will focus on what interventions were made at the *macro* level.

Micro Social Work Practice with Mexican Americans

CASE EXAMPLE

Mr. Sanchez, a Spanish-speaking, married, 35-year-old male of Mexican descent and father of three children, was referred for treatment to the *barrio* community mental health center by his attorney. He came to the center with his wife. He refused to tell the intake worker what his personal problems were that brought him to the center. He was unemployed and did not have money to pay for his treatment. The case was assigned to one of the licensed clinical social workers, Mr. Rubio.

The agency had a policy that in special circumstances when a potential client did not wish to discuss the reason for seeking services, the social worker assigned to the case would discuss this matter with the client. The agency, in addition to having a sliding scale for payment, had a special fund raised through community donations to sponsor clients who did not have the means to pay for services. Mr. Sanchez primarily spoke Spanish, hence a Spanish-speaking worker was assigned to him. In those instances when a bilingual social worker is not available, a trained *translator*, rather than an interpreter, would be used. An interpreter "interprets" (provides his or her interpretation of what is being discussed), but a translator provides a literal word-for-word translation of the communication. To avoid emotional involvement in the translation, it is preferable not to use a family member or friend of the client.

Mr. Sanchez sat down and sighed, looking at Mr. Rubio with one eye as he had a fresh, medical eyepatch bandage over the other.

"Are you in pain?" asked Mr. Rubio.

"Not very much now, but I was in more pain a month ago when this happened," replied Mr. Sanchez.

"Please tell me what happened to you. Take your time, and if there is something I ask that you don't want to answer or find it too difficult to answer, please tell me," instructed Mr. Rubio.

Rather than going through a rigid interview format in this initial meeting in order to obtain a social, family, educational, financial, employment, and health and mental health history, Mr. Rubio decided to begin "where the client is," that is, with what appeared to be an emotional and physical state of discomfort indicated by the sigh, and possibly pain related to an eye injury. By permitting Mr. Sanchez to tell his story at his own pace and allowing him to determine what questions he would answer, the worker was, in effect, "empowering" the client to participate in the interview by having control of the content of the discussion. His wife was quiet and did not say anything. She had a worried, concerned look.

Mr. Sanchez stated that three weeks previously on a Sunday afternoon, he had been playing basketball at the park with a group of friends. The losers of the game purchased the beer. Mr. Sanchez smiled when he said he had been on the winning team and didn't have to pay for the beer. He drank three small cans of beer and was driving home with his brother-in-law seated in the passenger's side of the car. He passed a police car which was going to make a right turn at an intersection. He continued traveling toward his home and noticed the police vehicle in his rearview mirror. Mr. Sanchez then turned right into his neighborhood street and parked his car in his driveway. Then he and his brother-in-law entered Mr. Sanchez's home where their wives were preparing dinner.

Mr. Sanchez entered his bedroom to change out of his gym clothes, which were wet with perspiration. As he was changing his clothes with his back to the bedroom door, the door opened swiftly, and he thought it was his children. He yelled out to close the door as he was changing. He then felt a powerful blow to his eye and did not remember anything after that. Mr. Sanchez bowed his head in silence, nodding "no" in a slow manner. Mr. Rubio joined him in this moment of silence, as if he were resting between rounds in a fight for his life. Mr. Sanchez looked at his wife as if he wanted her to continue with the story. Trying to hold back tears, Mrs. Sanchez stated, "It was the police. They hit him with a "billy club" on his right eye. After they hit him there was complete silence. I was able to peer through the door which was open about three inches, and my husband was lying on the floor, completely unconscious. I saw a lot of blood coming from the area around his eye, and I became very frightened and began screaming. I thought they had killed him." At this point, Mrs. Sanchez became very emotional and sobbed deeply. Mr. Rubio attempted to provide support to Mr. and Mrs. Sanchez by stating, "Few things in life cause so much pain and hardship." Both nodded in agreement. Mrs. Sanchez then continued, "I tried to push the door open but the officers slammed it shut. My children started becoming hysterical and began crying, too. My sister and brother-in-law took my children with them, as they didn't want them to continue seeing their father in his unconscious state. After three or four minutes, the police officers picked up my husband, who was staggering and bleeding even more from his eye, and placed him in the police vehicle. One of the officers stated that they were taking my husband to jail for resisting arrest, assaulting police officers, and drunk driving. I asked the officers *where* they were taking him, and one officer yelled back, "To the station." I asked *"Which* station?" and the officer smiled and said, "Just the station."

At this point in the interview, Mr. Rubio could have stated something like "You must have felt helpless," or "You probably thought you would never again see your husband." But these comments would have elicited even more affect or surfaced fears which might have still have been unconscious, thereby changing the focus and purpose of the interview away from Mr. Sanchez. By coming to the interview and participating, Mrs. Sanchez was in a supportive role to her husband and Mr. Rubio's intent was to help her in that role.

Mr. Rubio stated, "It must have been very difficult for you. You have been very helpful to your husband."

Mrs. Sanchez nodded "yes," as Mr. Sanchez tenderly hugged her. There was a brief silence as both looked at Mr. Rubio to continue the interview. Mr. Rubio then asked, "What was the extent of your eye injury?"

"The doctor said my eye was totally destroyed and it's dying. I can't see anything out of it. In two weeks he'll remove it and then give me a brown leather patch because I can't afford to buy a glass eye." His remaining eye became red and teary as he stared at Mr. Rubio, searching for a solution to his problem.

Resisting the impulse to have a ready, quick answer such as "Everything will turn out all right, you'll see," instead Mr. Rubio went with the feelings Mr. Sanchez's tragic story had invoked in him. Mr. Rubio stated, "I feel stunned and speechless. No one can really know what it is to lose your sight in one eye, other than a person who has experienced it. It must be both physically and psychologically painful."

Mr. Sanchez nodded in agreement, but added; "It is painful, especially at night. I can't sleep well because of the pain. I think I can stand it, and I'll eventually adjust to having only one eye. Maybe that is why God gave us two, in case we lose one." He smiled and then remarked, "But what I find most painful is that I cannot work and support my family and pay the rent. I don't know what I'm going to do. I don't feel like a man anymore."

Now Mr. Rubio had three major interrelated issues to consider in this first interview: (1) to increasingly focus on posttraumatic stress disorder (PTSD) questions to "rule out" PTSD; (2) to shift the focus of questions to determine the existence of and the gravity of depression Mr. Sanchez was experiencing or to rule out major depression; or (3) to focus on the issue of perceived loss of self and role as a man, husband, father, and only "breadwinner" in the family. This is especially catastrophic for those Hispanic males who have internalized a traditional cultural role wherein each family member has a clear, prescribed role. Losing the capacity to fulfill that role expectation for some traditional Latinos is like losing the meaning and purpose in life. For some wives a comparable loss would be never being able to have a child. Cultural expectations are not set in "concrete," hence, people can be helped to modify their position and adapt to a new situation. Mr. Rubio decided to deal with the "I don't feel like a man anymore" response which, if not addressed, would have resulted in increasing depression, perhaps even leading to suicide since Mr. Sanchez was in a very high-risk age level and profile for

Latino male suicide (75 percent of *Latinos* who commit suicide in the United States are married and between 20 to 35 years of age). In Mr. Rubio's clinical judgment, this currently was the most powerful stressor Mr. Sanchez was experiencing. Mr. Rubio had to help Mr. Sanchez view the situation in a less stressful way (cognitive restructuring, reframing).

"You certainly feel like a different person and in some ways you are. I agree with you that eventually you will learn to adapt to using only one eye. You are in a psychological and economic crisis which, in fact, will be only temporary. Once your eye pain lessens, you will be able to resume some type of work and once again support your family." His wife was nodding in agreement and smiling. "I never thought of it that way. I guess you are correct," stated Mr. Sanchez. "But what am I going to do for money now? We need food, and I have to pay the rent."

"I can go to work and you can stay home and take care of the children and send them off to school," commented Mrs. Sanchez enthusiastically. "No, no. That is not right. A man's wife should never have to work. That is an insult," responded Mr. Sanchez, shaking his head from side to side. Mr. Rubio did not comment, creating an atmosphere for dialogue between a man and his wife during a period of crisis. "Why should we have to lose our home and return to Mexico to live with and depend on relatives when we can survive here if I go to work temporarily?" Mrs. Sanchez asked. "I know I can find work as a domestic or in a sewing factory. Besides, the children would really enjoy spending more time with you. They worry about you all of the time."

"*They* worry about me?" responded Mr. Sanchez in a surprised tone. "They really should not! I will be fine!" Mr. Sanchez responded in a firm, confident tone. This gave Mr. Rubio an opportunity to uncover Mr. Sanchez's inner strength and competitive spirit within a *Latino* cultural context.

"You *are* a proud man, good father, and husband. You are loved by your wife and children. You are a real *macho,* a man who provides for and protects his family in the most positive ways. A 'crisis' in Chinese philosophy means 'an opportunity to change.' This crisis has presented you an opportunity to become even more of a man, by providing your children and wife emotional support rather than primarily economic help as the sole breadwinner. You are being challenged to temporarily change in order to continue to help your family."

Mr. Sanchez sat up straighter and smiled again as his wife was nodding affirmatively and holding her husband's hand. "We *can* do it," she said. "I guess we can," replied Mr. Sanchez in a soft tone.

"And I will be here to continue to help you," added Mr. Rubio. "We're just about out of time. Do you want me to schedule an appointment for you three days from now?"

"Is this therapy? Is this all that is going to happen?" inquired Mr. Sanchez.

"This was our first visit, and in this hour we covered many important things," stated Mr. Rubio. "This is just the beginning of therapy, to get information in order to know what to do. Normally, we see people once a week to help them with their concerns. In your case, I want to see you in three days to see how this trauma has affected you. Do you think you feel well enough now so that I can see you in a few days?" Mr. Rubio asked. "Yes, that would be fine," replied Mr. Sanchez.

Mr. Rubio was attempting to assess whether Mr. Sanchez felt sufficiently emotionally and physically capable to return in a few days. It was a subtle way of empowering him to be involved in making important decisions about his welfare. Had he been in significant physical pain, he would have been referred to the center's staff psychiatrist for a medical opinion and treatment referral. Psychologically, Mr. Sanchez seemed intact, possessed good ego strength, and did not appear suicidal. Had Mr. Sanchez replied, "I don't even know where I'll be tomorrow, or if I'll even be alive" or verbal comments to that effect indicating possible suicidal ideation, Mr. Rubio would have extended the interview to assess his suicidality, and, if indicated, treated it by evaluating the need for medication and/or hospitalization with the center's psychiatrist.

Mr. Sanchez returned for his appointment. He appeared less depressed, and his depression was "reactive" in nature; that is, it was in response to his two major losses—loss of an eye and loss of employment. In addition, Mr. Rubio confirmed his clinical opinion that Mr. Sanchez qualified for a diagnosis of PTSD, and he was placed on the appropriate antianxiety medication by the center psychiatrist. Subsequent treatment sessions involved conjoint sessions with Mr. Sanchez and his wife, who was now working, to help *them* adapt to their changing roles in the family, and evaluation sessions with the three children. They had all observed their bleeding father taken away in the police car. One of the children was found to also be suffering from PTSD, and the other two children had adjustment disorder symptoms. The children were treated by another social worker. After ten visits, Mr. Sanchez's symptoms diminished significantly with the exception of being very fearful of uniformed police and "black and white" police vehicles. After three months of treatment, Mrs. Sanchez phoned to state that her husband had been convicted of misdemeanor drunk driving and had been sentenced to ninety days of jail. She added that her husband wanted her to communicate his appreciation for the help extended to him and his family and that he felt stronger and confident that he could handle this new crisis. Mrs. Sanchez stated that Mr. Sanchez's mother was coming up from Mexico to take care of the children to give her the opportunity to keep working.

 ## Macro Social Work Practice with Mexican Americans

Mr. Rubio knew quite well that excessive force from police was not an uncommon experience in the *barrio*, occurring on the average of three to four times per day, and usually the victims were African Americans or *Latinos*. Mr. Rubio was also aware of volunteer "alternative community resources" in the *barrio* such as the "Police Misconduct Lawyer Referral Service." This service has a board of directors comprised of community people, attorneys, and social workers and has a panel of private attorneys for representation in those cases where the conduct of the police was improper and caused injury or damages. Prior to his assault, Mr. Sanchez was working as a plumber's assistant earning $9 per hour. He did not have medical or unemployment insurance, as he was working for a relative who was a licensed, freelance plumber. Mr. Sanchez was also going to night school to learn English and more about plumbing to prepare for his plumbing certificate. Mr. Rubio referred Mr. Sanchez to the police misconduct referral service.

This service was codirected by Cindy Torres, a licensed master's level social worker, and Roland Goya, an attorney. Both volunteered a few evenings per week to the program. They were assisted by a few social work and law students who handled most of the incoming calls and initial in-person interviews. Based on the legal merits of the cases, some were referred to the panel of volunteer attorneys who did "pro bono" (free service) work for the *barrio*. A panel of licensed and prelicense clinical MSWs belonging to *Trabajadores de La Raza*, a *Latino* social work organization, likewise provided free clinical services for victims of police misconduct who could not afford to pay a modest fee for services.

In addition to clinical and administrative skills, Cindy Torres also had macro community organization skills and was attempting to mobilize several "key" community players, both elected and appointed leaders, and "grass-roots" *barrio* residents, to help reduce police malpractice and improve *barrio*–police relations. Law enforcement representatives were also invited to meetings, including the Chief of Police. Rather than emphasizing the negative by simply organizing groups to protest and be critical of the police, hence alienating them even further, Ms. Torres appealed instead to the positive forces, both in the police department and the *barrio,* who wanted to work on the problem of *barrio*–police conflict.

Ms. Torres prepared for the first meeting and had a good response from various members of the community, including the Chief of Police who was going to send his Deputy Chief and local Precinct Captain as his representatives to the first meeting. At the meeting, which was the first of several meetings, Ms. Torres used a "force-field analysis" procedure developed for use with community groups in problem identification and problem solving. The basic concept in force-field analysis is to identify forces that are potential supports for, or barriers to, the achievement of a specific goal.[33] A group must already have a clear idea of the problem and have a desired goal. *Barrio* residents wanted the police to stop beating them and treat them with more respect. The police wanted more respect and cooperation from the community in reducing crime.

Figure 23.1 illustrates the force-field chart written on the blackboard by Ms. Torres during the meeting as she obtained the input from the thirty-two participants.

As can be seen in Figure 23.1, after the major goal had been established, and the competing forces (driving vs. restraining forces) list was created to show the status quo, Ms. Torres guided the group in determining how powerful each force was and then drew an arrow (thin, medium, or thick depending on the estimated power of the force) in the direction of the force (toward or away from the goal). For example, the thicker the arrow, the stronger the driving or restraining force. This would indicate that more effort would be required to improve the situation in the identified problem area, especially when a thick arrow indicating a driving force encountered a thick arrow representing a *restraining force*. Such was the case in *barrio* anger toward the police (driving forces) being met with police resistance to change (restraining forces).

Thereafter, Ms. Torres helped the group establish small committees to mobilize the driving forces to work on the problem and other small committees to reduce the impact of the restraining forces. Applying her knowledge of group dynamics, she

Figure 23.1

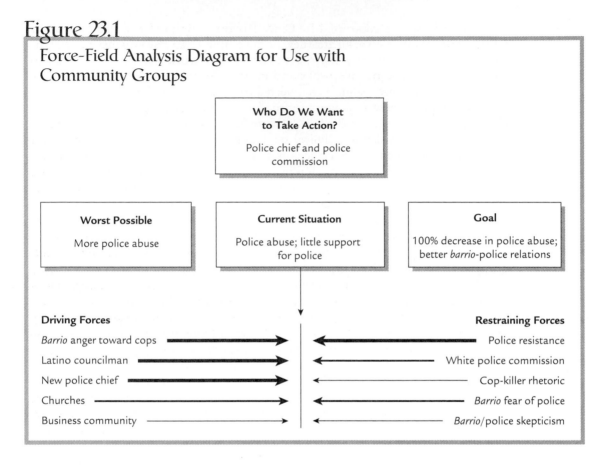

Force-Field Analysis Diagram for Use with
Community Groups

Who Do We Want to Take Action?
Police chief and police commission

Worst Possible
More police abuse

Current Situation
Police abuse; little support for police

Goal
100% decrease in police abuse; better *barrio*-police relations

Driving Forces

Barrio anger toward cops

Latino councilman

New police chief

Churches

Business community

Restraining Forces

Police resistance

White police commission

Cop-killer rhetoric

Barrio fear of police

Barrio/police skepticism

asked the group to establish mixed, balanced committees reflecting persons with law enforcement, *barrio,* political leader, church, "militant," and business community perspectives. Through such group composition, the committees were able to work out their differences in the small groups and develop cohesion before they approached other groups and bodies of resistance, such as the police commission.

The large group continued to meet on a monthly basis over a period of fifteen months, with the small committees meeting more regularly. An unexpected outcome was that the group, in working toward its goals, also planned and conducted a *Barrio*–Police Relations Conference a year later, which featured as speakers the District Attorney, the *Latino* Councilman, the Chief of Police, and a police brutality victim. The latter was Mr. Sanchez!

Following Mr. Sanchez's three months in jail for his drunk-driving conviction, his attorney filed a civil suit in his behalf against the police department and the city for pain, injury, permanent blindness in one eye, and suffering. The jury ruled that the police did not have a right to enter his home without a bench warrant because Mr. Sanchez had not committed a felony offense, only a misdemeanor drunk-driving violation. Mr. Sanchez was awarded $250,000. He donated $5,000 to the Police

Misconduct Referral Service and $5,000 to the *barrio* mental health center where he had been treated by Mr. Rubio. He told Mr. Rubio that he would prefer to have his eye back rather than the money he had received. Mr. Sanchez planned to return to Guadalajara, Mexico, because he found Southern California to be too violent.

Concluding Comment

Mexican Americans are one of this country's most diverse ethnic groups. Because they were an indigenous population, in their own land, prior to the Anglo-American conquest of Mexico in 1848, they, like Native Americans, are one of the oldest minorities. On the other hand, continuing immigration from Mexico also makes them one of the newest and largest immigrant groups. They are a very heterogeneous Hispanic group, responding to all categories of any language and cultural scale. Mexican Americans primarily reside in urban areas in the Southwest, generally occupy a low socioeconomic status, and have large families, a high unemployment rate, and low educational attainments—all symptoms of working class exploitation, sexism, and racism. Mexican Americans have a small elderly population (4 percent), almost one-third the proportion of elderly whites, and a very large youth population. Because their age profile is the opposite of that of whites, their human services needs are different from those of whites, who are currently preoccupied with the needs of the elderly. As is the case with African Americans, Hispanics are increasingly being caught up in the juvenile justice system, a field of practice in which social work has not expressed much interest.

Mexican Americans *do* have mental health needs, and many do avail themselves of direct services when they are provided at modest cost, in their primary language, and near their homes. A rich psychiatric history, originating almost 700 years ago with the Aztecs, provides Mexican Americans with a foundation to build on, as both consumers and providers of mental health services. However, the current regressive trend in the United States, with its accompanying stresses, is creating new racism and poverty casualties among the poor and minorities. As needs for services increase, there is a corresponding increased effort to "economize" by "phasing out" or denying services to the poor. Mexican Americans are particularly affected by these trends, especially new Mexican immigrants and the "undocumented."

Practice suggestions were offered that may have implications for macro social work in the *barrio*. The *barrio* as an ethnosystem is comprised of indigenous social support systems such as churches, neighbors, friends, alternative services (self-help groups), and the family. Applying the concept of social network intervention to Mexican Americans signifies the inclusion of extended family members, *compadres* (co-parents), friends, coworkers, and other concerned persons in their support systems. These subsystems have the potential to provide emotional strength, support, and other types of assistance to the family.

This chapter highlighted micro and macro social work practice intervention in a police brutality case. Police brutality has been an NASW practice priority since April 1992. These tragic incidents committed by a few irresponsible law enforcement officials under the "color of law" (in uniform, on official duty) number some 10,000 to 15,000 episodes per year. Police brutality impacts

60,000 to 90,000 persons—mostly poor and racial/ethnic minorities—when emotionally affected family members are included. This is definitely a human rights and quality-of-life issue for the profession. The values and ethics of the profession demand social work practice involvement and inclusion in the curriculum of schools of social work.

KEY WORDS AND CONCEPTS

Mexican Americans

Curanderismo

Chicano

Mexicans

Aztec psychiatry

Barrio

Compadres

Treaty of Guadalupe–Hidalgo

Barrio service system

Positive *machismo*

SUGGESTED INFORMATION SOURCES

Burnette, Denise, "Custodial Grandparents in Latino Families: Patterns of Service Use and Predictors of Unmet Needs," *Social Work* (January 1999): 22–34.

Casas, J. M., and Vasquez, M. J. T. "Counseling the Hispanic Client: A Guiding Framework for a Diverse Population," in P. Pedersen, J. Draguns, W. Lonner, and J. Trimble, eds., *Counseling Across Cultures*, 4th Edition. Honolulu: University of Hawaii Press, 1996, pp. 146–176.

Ruiz, Pedro, "Challenges in Providing Psychiatric Services to Hispanic Americans," *Psychline*, Vol. 2, No. 4, 1998, pp. 6–10.

Skolnick, Jerome H., and Fyfe, James J. *Above the Law: Police and the Excessive Use of Force* (New York: The Free Press, 1993).

Vargas, Luis A., and Koss-Chioino, Joan D., eds., *Working with Culture: Psychotherapeutic Interventions with Ethnic Minority Children and Adolescent*. San Francisco: Jossey-Bass Publishers, 1992.

Vega, William A., Kolody, Bohdan, Aguilar-Gaxiola, Sergio, Catalano, Ralph, "Gaps in Service Utilization by Mexican Americans with Mental Health Problems," *American Journal of Psychiatry* 156 (June 1999): 928–934.

Vega, William A., Kolody, Bohdan, Aguilar-Gaxiola, Sergio, Alderete, Ethel, Catalano, Ralph, Caraveo-Anduaga, Jorge, "Lifetime Prevalence of DSM III-R Psychiatric Disorders among Urban and Rural Mexican Americans in California," *Archives of General Psychiatry* 55 (September 1998): 771–781.

ENDNOTES

1. Roberto R. Ramirez, and G. Patricia de la Cruz, *The Hispanic Population in the United States: March 2002*, Current Population Reports, P20–545, (U.S. Census Bureau, Washington, D.C., 2002), pp. 1–2.
2. Ramirez, p. 3.
3. Ramirez, p. 4.
4. Ramirez, p. 5.
5. Ramirez, p. 6.

6. Sylvia A. Marotta, and Jorge G. Garcia, "*Latinos* in the United States in 2000," *Hispanic Journal of Behavioral Sciences* 25, no. 1. (February 2003), pp. 21–22.

7. U.S. Census Bureau, American Community Survey Office, August 10, 2004, pp. 1–3.

8. Franz G. Alexander and Sheldon V. Selesnick, *The History of Psychiatry* (New York: Harper & Row, 1966), pp. 7–14.

9. Guido Belsasso, "The History of Psychiatry in Mexico," *Hospital and Community Psychiatry* 20 (November 1969): 342–344.

10. Ibid.

11. Alexander and Selesnick, p. 120.

12. Belsasso.

13. Ramon Parres, "Mexico," *World Studies in Psychiatry* 2, no. 3 (Medical Communications, Inc., 1979).

14. Marvin Karno and Armando Morales, "A Community Mental Health Service for Mexican Americans in a Metropolis," *Comprehensive Psychiatry* 12 (March 1971): 116–121.

15. Morales, "Institutional Racism in Mental Health and Crinimal Justice," pp. 394, 395.

16. *Report to the President's Commission on Mental Health*, "Special Populations Sub-Task Task Panel on Mental Health of Hispanic Americans" (Washington, D.C.: U.S. Government Printing Office, 1978), p. 3.

17. Ibid.

18. Joe Yamamoto, Quinston James, and Norman Palley, "Cultural Problems in Psychiatric Therapy," *Archives of General Psychiatry* 19 (1968): 45–49.

19. Armando Morales, "Social Work with Third-World People," *Social Work* 26 (January 1981): 49.

20. Barbara Bryant Solomon, *Black Empowerment: Social Work in Oppressed Communities* (New York: Columbia University Press, 1976), p. 6.

21. Dolores G. Norton, *The Dual Perspective: Inclusion of Ethnic Minority Content on the Social Work Curriculum* (New York: Council of Social Work Education, 1978).

22. Solomon.

23. Ramon Valle, "Ethnic Minority Curriculum in Mental Health: Latino/Hispano Perspectives" (Paper presented at Mental Health Curriculum Development Conference sponsored by Howard University School of Social Work, November 16–18, 1979, Chicago.)

24. Norton.

25. Valle, p. 7.

26. E. P. Tsiaiah Lee, "The Pattern of Medical Care Use: Mexican American Patients at a Model Neighborhood Health Center in Los Angeles" (Doctoral thesis, University of California at Los Angeles, 1975).

27. Max Siporin, *Introduction to Social Work Practice* (New York: Macmillan, 1975).

28. Alice H. Collins and Diane L. Pancoast, *Natural Helping Networks: A Strategy for Intervention* (Washington, D.C.: National Association of Social Workers, 1976).

29. Gerald Caplan, *Support Systems and Community Mental Health* (New York: Behavioral Publications, 1974).

30. Ibid.

31. Collins and Pancoast.

32. Carol Swenson, "Social Networks, Mutual Aid, and the Life Model of Practice," in Carel B. Germain, ed., *Social Work Practice: People and Environment and Ecological Perspective* (New York: Columbia University Press, 1979), pp. 213–238.

33. Mark A. Mattaini, *More Than a Thousand Words: Graphics for Clinical Practice* (Washington, D.C.: National Association of Social Workers, 1993), pp. 135–37.

Social Work Practice with African Americans

Malcolm E. Scott and Jeffrey K. Shears

Prefatory
Comment

"Social Work Practice with African Americans" is an original, commissioned chapter written for this textbook by Malcolm E. Scott and Jeffrey K. Shears, Assistant Professors in the School of Social Work at Colorado State University. This chapter replaces Barbara Bryant Solomon's distinguished African American chapter, which was a valued companion to this textbook for several editions.

Dr. Scott and Dr. Shears bring a new perspective to the psychosocial needs of African Americans and provide us with the most current census demographics pertaining to African Americans. They remind us that even though African Americans represent only 12 percent of the U.S. population, they sadly comprise 22 percent of persons falling below the poverty level, which is nearly three times that of non-Hispanic whites. They describe African Americans as a diverse and resilient people in spite of a historical subjugation to whites, and having been bought and sold as property, subjected to slavery on southern plantations, and victims of the brutality suffered through the civil unrest of the 1960s.

They resist the notion advanced by some scholars who describe African Americans as having a pathological culture, or a culture of poverty. Rather, these authors document how African American culture should be viewed as being "adaptive-vital," that is, that it has survived and adapted to the traumas of slavery and institutionalized racism. "Institutional racism" is a condition that our society wishes to believe no longer exists. Perhaps that is one of the foremost lessons in this new well-documented chapter—that institutional racism, although much more subtle today, is nevertheless still very "alive and kicking."

At the core of the profession of social work is serving people in need and creating or enhancing societal conditions that increase social functioning—especially for the most vulnerable members of society. Consequently, it is essential that services be client focused and that practitioners aggressively seek to dismantle barriers that may prevent clients from receiving assistance. In implementing such admirable professional goals, it is important that social work practice skills and competencies are relevant to the populations being served and are culturally sensitive to those persons most apt to seek the multitude of programs and services social workers offer. Understanding the dynamic interrelation among individual, family, culture, and environment, as well as the various historical factors that have influenced each population group, helps to establish the foundation for holistic change, rather than depending on "band-aid" approaches that too often mitigate against people feeling empowered to problem-solve.

In a national study conducted by Teare and Sheafor, 7,000 BSW (Bachelor of Social Work) and MSW (Master of Social Work) practitioners were asked to identify as many as three racial or ethnic groups they regularly served in their practice. Ninety-one percent of BSW practitioners and 86 percent of the MSW practitioners indicated they worked with white clients regularly. In addition, 42 percent of the BSWs and 45 percent of the MSWs indicated that they regularly worked with African American clients. Interestingly, only 11 percent of MSW practitioners reported working with Chicano/Mexican Americans regularly and even fewer BSW practitioners, 10 percent, report working with this population.[1] Although regional differences in the distribution of the several racial/ethnic population groups will affect the make-up of their clientele, it is clear that throughout most of the United States social workers must be sensitive to African American culture if they are to be prepared to serve a substantial part of their clients.

In order for social workers and other professionals to keep pace with the ever-changing populations in America, if they are to provide comprehensive and culturally sensitive practice, it is vital that they study the various groups to understand their demographic characteristics and cultural uniqueness. One of the groups most vulnerable to social problems in America is clearly the African American population. Lagging well behind whites and other minority groups in social, economic, and health indicators, the African American community deserves and requires the most competent services social workers can offer. Efforts to revive a sense of community, build a sound infrastructure among the African American people, and secure needed community resources require social work practitioners who are professionally and culturally competent.

Issues once thought to be isolated incidences relegated to culturally and morally deficient inner-city minority neighborhoods, such as male youth violence, teenage pregnancy, and illicit drug use, can no longer be rationalized as "their" community's problems. As middle-class urban and suburban communities frantically search for solutions to recent school shootings, it becomes "our" problem. Thus, all practitioners must be prepared to provide services to counter a number of different issues. Attaining the competence to provide this wide range of services is a sizable undertaking for social work, but one that most other professions are unprepared and ill-equipped to take on.

Current Demographics

African Americans are a significant minority in the United States. The 2004 U.S. Census reports 35.1 million African Americans residing in the United States, which represents a little over 12 percent of the U.S. population. Over 55 percent of African Americans reside in the southeastern United States, with other significant numbers located primarily in metropolitan areas in the Northeast (19 percent), Midwest (18 percent), and the West (8 percent).[2] Demographic, social, and economic isolation have, over time, created gross disparities between African Americans and whites, as well as with other ethnic groups whose history in America does not include enslavement.

African Americans, though only representing 12.2 percent of the U.S. population, make up 24.7 percent of individuals living below the poverty level, which is nearly three times that of whites who experience poverty at a 8.6 percent rate (see Table 24.1). Although this number has decreased steadily since the 1970s (then 33.5 percent; 1980, 32.5 percent; and 1990, 31.9 percent), the disparity continues.[3] The median household income in 2004 for black families was $30,100, while the household income for whites of non-Hispanic origin was substantially higher at $48,900.[4] The differences are even more pronounced for single-female-headed households. Of black female-headed households 42.7 percent are below the poverty

Table 24.1

Percent of Individuals Below Poverty Level by Race, Age, and Female Head of Household

	2003–04	2000
Total Population	12.2	11.3
African American/Black	24.7	22.0
Total Population under age 18	17.8	16.1
African Americans under age 18	34.1	30.6
Total Population 65 and older	9.8	10.2
African Americans 65 and older	23.7	22.4
Total Population of female-headed households	35.0	27.9
African American female-headed households (no husband present)	42.7	38.6

Sources: U.S. Census Bureau, http://factfinder.census.gov/servlet/ACSSAFFFacts

U.S. Bureau, Current Population Survey, Annual Social and Economic Supplement, 2003

U.S. Census Bureau, http://www.census.gov/hhes/poverty/histpov/hstpov4.html

U.S. Census Bureau, http://www.census.gov/hhes/poverty/histpov/hstpov3.html

level, compared with 31.8 percent for their white counterparts. In addition, 23.7 percent of older African Americans are below the poverty level, compared with 8.8 percent for older whites.[5] These numbers represent, at least in part, the reality that many socioeconomic differences are clearly related to one's race and gender. They speak, however directly or indirectly, to the institutionalized racism, sexism, and ageism, as well as the related discriminatory practices that marginalize and disenfranchise ethnic populations in America—particularly African Americans.

These trends shed light on differences among population groups that too often go unnoticed. In addition, examination of America's dominant social issues also reflects a consistent pattern of disparity that is as great, if not greater than, the differences related to any one issue. As reported throughout other sections of this book, the disparities that exist among these population groups are clearly reflected in such critical social indicators as, infant mortality rates, access to health care, access to health insurance, unemployment rates, rates of incarceration, and the elevated number of African Americans on death row. These discrepancies should be unacceptable in a democratic society and are reason for social workers to advocate for massive restructuring of local, state, and national welfare policies and practices.

African Americans: A Diverse and Resilient People

History records the struggles, adversities, and successes of both cultural groups and the larger society. Relative to African Americans in the United States, history paints a controversial, yet colorful, portrait. The discriminatory practices toward African Americans have, throughout history, been a factual reality. However, in spite of being subjugated to whites, bought and sold as property, subjected to the harsh fields of southern plantations, and victims of the brutality suffered through the civil unrest of the 1960s, African Americans, with great resolve, became a resilient people.

Despite a popular perception that the first Africans arrived in North America as slaves, there is evidence that Africans were in North America long before they were forced over on slave ships.[6] In fact, the first African Americans arriving in the colonies were not slaves, but indentured servants like many others who came to the Americas during that time. Later the time spent in servitude grew longer, until African Americans and their offspring became lifelong servants of Anglo settlers. The initial rationale for the enslavement of Africans was due, in part, to economic practicality, the population's previous agricultural experience, their immunity to certain diseases, and their ability to be easily identified—which made escape difficult. Although the primary reason for enslaving Africans was economic, its continuance was based on a white supremacist ideology, which was supported by academics and Christian theologians alike. These ideologies, which made the enslavement of Africans legal and widely accepted by the society, assuredly impacted the psychological development of both whites and blacks, and established the foundation for the superiority/inferiority perceptions of these populations that continue to exist in academic, religious, and society today.

The Civil War marked the official end of slavery for African Americans in the United States. Though emancipated, blacks were not publicly accepted as citizens with the same rights and privileges given to members of the white population. This inequality continues today, even though the discrimination is not as overtly recognizable as was the case in the not too distant past.

At the turn of the twenty-first century, despite the many limitations placed on them, African Americans had made great individual, social, and economic strides. There were large-scale migrations from the South to northern cities and midwestern communities, with cities in the North becoming centers of African American artistic expression, as well as places offering greater opportunities to achieve self-sufficiency and experience life in thriving communities. It was during this time that many African Americans were able to pursue educational advancement by taking advantage of the opportunities provided by black schools and colleges. It was only later that the white schools were opened to African American students and greater educational equity was achieved. Other important events were the desegregation of the military in 1948 and the Civil Rights and Voting Rights Bills passed by the federal government in the 1960s. Understanding this history and the experiences of African Americans is essential if the social worker is to appreciate the cultural characteristics and practices of the black population in the United States today.

Key Social Issues and Elements of African American Culture

Recognizing the historical experiences of African Americans in the United States helps to explain some of the present-day cultural values within this community. Although many scholars[7] have attempted to describe African Americans as having a pathological culture or, at best, a culture of poverty, these conclusions are usually derived by comparing African Americans' cultural values to those of whites, that is, to the dominant cultural values. African American culture should, however, be viewed as being adaptive–vital in that it has survived and adapted to the traumas of slavery and institutional racism and is a vital influence in the success of many members of the black community.[8] Another explanation of the uniqueness in African American culture is that it is unlike other ethnic groups that immigrated to the United States because, as former slaves, African Americans have had a difficult time wholeheartedly adopting the culture and values of their oppressors. Given this reluctance, African Americans have a unique culture that is fundamentally an African culture that has been adapted to survive in America. This adaptive–vital culture has profound underlying ramifications for the present demographic and cultural characteristics of African Americans.

Examination of four social issues related to the African American experience reveals their status in the United States today. These issues—poverty, family structure, educational attainment, and experience with the justice system—are not exhaustive of the relevant social issues experienced by the black population, but rather serve as useful examples of areas social workers should examine.

The Poverty Predicament

Given the history of African Americans in the United States, it is not surprising that there is economic disparity between African Americans and whites. Governmental promises of opportunity and economic support have not eliminated the disproportionately high poverty rate among African Americans that remains a modern-day reality for many (see Figure 24.1). Even during the economic boom of the mid 1990s, the child poverty rate for black children was nearly 40 percent. The inability of many blacks to secure full-time employment and the resulting high rate of part-time low-wage service jobs they occupy, along with pervasive joblessness, are some of the many factors that have helped to create the current socioeconomic disparity that exists between African Americans and their Caucasian counterparts.

The institutional obstacles that continue to oppress and disenfranchise many in this population often overshadow the resiliency mentioned earlier. For example, the role of the black church in the black community has been historically, and is still today, one of support, spiritual uplift, and a means of community engagement and activism. However, Savage (2000) concluded in her study that increased research in the area of the church's role in political struggles is required.[9] That is not to say that strides have not been made to enhance opportunities for African Americans through governmental progress and services. Indeed, American society has moved, however slowly, forward in its treatment of African American people. One additional change that is needed is for more adequate social

Figure 24.1

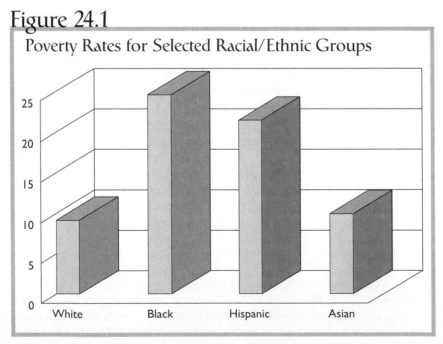

Poverty Rates for Selected Racial/Ethnic Groups

Source: U.S. Census Bureau. http://www.census.gov/prod/2005pubs/p60-229

programs directed at curing poverty, which has been and continues to be a topic of much social and political debate.

The current conservative political trend regarding social welfare has attempted to decrease societal responsibility for the welfare of vulnerable people and to place the burden/blame on the individual. The Welfare and Reconciliation Act of 1996, passed during the first term of President Bill Clinton, reflects the reluctance of the welfare state in America—even under a supposedly liberal democratic administration. In an effort to further decrease spending on social programs that were originally conceived and designed to move people from poverty, the current George W. Bush administration clearly reflects a movement even further to the "right" on social welfare issues. Though America is not commonly viewed as a society divided into social classes, such distinctions are evident. Take as an example the natural disaster of Hurricane Katrina that devastated the gulf region of the United States in August 2005. This incident reflects, in part at least, how in the face of an impending threat of potentially catastrophic proportions, a major metropolitan American city failed to evacuate the most vulnerable of its citizens to safety. The human suffering and death that resulted still seems unreal and senseless.

Consider the impact of poverty in this disaster. New Orleans and much of the Gulf Coast had a majority African American population in 2005 and, as is estimated above, the black population has a poverty rate twice as high as the white population. When the New Orleans mayor gave a warning for people to evacuate it was virtually impossible for the poor (black and white) to leave. Most didn't have their own vehicles for transportation; they didn't have credit cards to reserve rooms further north if they did find transportation; and those who remained to weather the storm didn't have food stockpiled to help them survive until the crisis passed or they were rescued. Literally hundreds of vulnerable low income, largely African American, people died in the flooding because they were poor. However bleak this social reality, it serves to remind us that whether knowingly or unknowingly our society tends to neglect and often abandons the poor, the frail, and the elderly.

Limited social mobility is especially a problem for African Americans who continue to struggle in poor inner-city neighborhoods, abandoned by public support, and void of any significant economic resources to stimulate their local economy. They continue to survive in a society that demands them to be economically self-sufficient, yet is reluctant to provide adequate employment opportunities and training/educational programs to make that a reality. Marked by low-paying service jobs (underemployment) or no jobs at all (unemployment), many African Americans find themselves trapped in a never-ending cycle of poverty and deprivation, with no means of escape.

Family Structure

The family has perhaps been the most studied institution in the African American community, and the dynamics of the African American family have often been compared to a traditional white family model.

This comparison can potentially be problematic as traditional American social and families values hardly "fit" with traditional African American social and family values. Van Wormer identifies seven value dimensions of Anglo culture—work, mobility, status, independence, individualism, moralism, and ascription. Kerenga offers seven principles of the African/African American social community;[10,11] these include unity, self-determination, collective work and responsibility, collective economics, purpose, creativity, and faith. Understanding such cultural differentiation in values may provide some explanation for the resistance on the part of African Americans to adopt wholeheartedly the values of a culture that was so brutally oppressive and exclusive in the not too distant past. A strength often observed by researchers is the perception of the African American family consisting of the extended members of one's collective circle of blood relatives and non-relatives. It is generally believed that this extended family is a strong cohesive unit, with individual members being more concerned with the collective unit than with self. It is common in African American families to refer to those with whom they have had long-term relationships as family even though they may not be biologically related to such as cousins, aunts, or uncles. Generally, when African Americans speak of their family they are referring to extended family and friends and not just to its nuclear members. Unlike some other family models, the oldest member is usually the head of the family clan, and this may well be the oldest female family member. One explanation for this phenomenon is that it is reflective of the slave era, when particularly on smaller plantations the father of the family may have lived on a neighboring farm and was allowed to visit his family only sporadically.[12] This required the woman of the house to take the leadership role in the family. Another reason for the high incidence of female-headed households is the high mortality rate for young African American males. Whatever the circumstances, the elder member of the African Americans family is, many times, an African American woman.

Early sociological studies identified African American families as dysfunctional and highlighted the characteristics of their family structure that the researchers considered unhealthy. These researchers interpreted as problematic the fact that African American families were matriarchal and asserted that men did not have a substantive role within those families. Factors within the African American family were thought to contribute to the higher levels of poverty and violence and the poor parental relationships that existed in the African American community.[13] These conclusions have been viewed as suspect, as they were conducted by researchers who failed to account for the effects of institutional racism and discrimination.[14] These findings at least have some usefulness, however, for explaining how the structure of African Americans families and communities tends to differ from other ethnic populations.

Recent census data support some of the conclusions of this research in that African American families today are largely headed by single parents, usually females. Specifically, the 2000 U.S. Census found that 62 percent of African Americans families have only one adult living in the home.[15] As indicated in Figure 24.2, single-parent-headed households are significantly more common in the African American community than among other populations. This family structure has a profound effect on the quality of life for many African American children, as many grow up in poverty without the advantage of two-parent incomes.

Figure 24.2

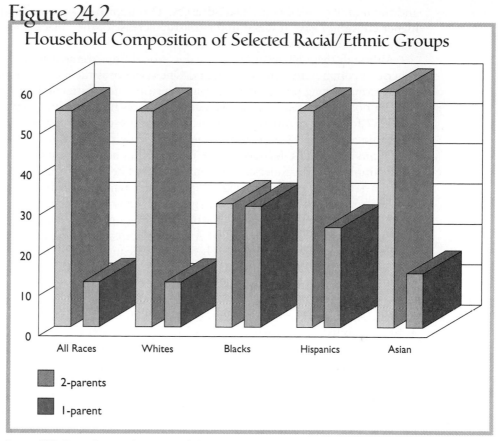

Household Composition of Selected Racial/Ethnic Groups

Legend:
- 2-parents
- 1-parent

Source: U.S. Census Bureau, Current Population Survey, Annual Social and Economic Supplement, 2003.

Education

Because of the association between education and economic level, obtaining equal educational opportunities has been a historical focal point of the African American community. One of the major results of the Civil Rights Movement of the 1950s and 1960s was increasing the accessibility of quality education for all Americans. A highly applauded Supreme Court decision that impacted the African American community was *Brown v. Board of Education* in 1959 that declared it unconstitutional for "separate but equal" schools to receive federal funding. Before this Supreme Court decision, African Americans were typically educated separately, which for years resulted in their lagging behind in such educational success indicators as enrollment and college completion rates. Nearly fifty years after the *Brown v. Board of Education* decision, we are now seeing improvements among African Americans in higher education based on indicators such as an increase in the rate of high school students taking standardized entrance exams to qualify for college, undergraduate graduation rates, and the number pursuing graduate degrees. This improved access to and pursuit of higher education have resulted in the drastic increase of the "black middle class," a fairly new phenomenon in America.

Although there has been notable educational improvement within the African American community, concerns remain. One concern is the standardized test score gap existing among school-age African American and white children. In 2002, the College Board reported that the average SAT scores for white youths was 1060 and only 857 for African American youths, which represents the lowest SAT scores for all ethnic and racial groups.[16] Another concern is the disparity between African Americans and whites in college enrollment, grades achieved, and graduation rates. For example, African American students are less likely to graduate from college in five years and have higher dropout rates than white students.[17] Concern also remains regarding the relatively low graduate school enrollment and completion rates of African American males. Further, although graduate enrollment and completion have drastically increased for African American women, overall educational indicators have improved only slightly for the African American population over the past ten years.[18]

Another concern that remains in the African American community relates to the educational experiences of school-age children. It should be noted that many African American youth enter kindergarten behind their white counterparts in academic skills. This disparity in educational readiness in the African American community can be attributed to lower educational levels of parents, more authoritarian parenting styles, and the lack of educational exposure experienced by many African American children. Given sufficient educational exposure, however, African American children generally improve and are typically operating at grade level by the time they reach the third and fourth grades. Unfortunately, at these grade levels many African American males show a decreased interest in school that is evidenced by an increase in discipline problems, receiving lower grades, and poor attendance records.[19] Interventions that may address these issues include having a positive relationship with a male role model and involvement in sports, music, and other extracurricular school activities in which these young men can find success.[20]

Experience with the Justice System

Although African Americans constitute approximately 12 percent of the United States' population, they make up over 44.8 percent of those arrested for violent crimes and 50 percent of those who are incarcerated.[21] In fact, African American males have an inordinate likelihood of spending time in prison. As Figure 24.3 indicates, the chance of an African American male spending some time in prison is nearly twice that of Hispanic males and three times the rate of white males.

A factor associated with the disproportionate rate of incarceration among African American males is the type of crimes that they commit. Although the U.S. Constitution does not indicate that certain types of criminal activity should be punished more severely than others, the types of crimes African American males commit tend to receive stiffer penalties. Further, these crimes are most likely to be perpetrated

Figure 24.3

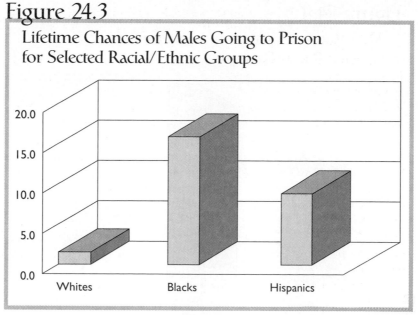

Lifetime Chances of Males Going to Prison
for Selected Racial/Ethnic Groups

Source: Bureau of Justice Statistics, http://www.ojp.usdoj.gov/bjs/abstract/11gsfp.htm

on other African Americans, and thus African Americans are also the most likely to become victims of violent crimes (see Figure 24.4). Illustrative of this fact is a report from the U.S. Department of Justice indicating that the leading cause of death for African American males under the age of 30 is homicide.[22]

Why such a high number of African Americans males are in the criminal justice system is unclear. Perhaps this points to a justice system that may be flawed and more punitive to African American males than to the general population. Some scholars have also attributed this to the poverty and hopelessness encountered by many African American males residing in the inner cities while others suggest that this violence is caused by a pathological culture. It should be noted that few studies have examined how the history of African Americans may have had an impact on the level of violence presently in this community. One could readily hypothesize that many of these negative factors in the African American community could be a direct cause of its recent history of being victimized by the larger society.

Like those in New Orleans who felt abandoned by elected officials, and the government these officials represent, it is not difficult to consider why distrust, anger, and conflict sometimes occur. Such distrust and experiences of deprivation and poverty potentially sabotage the helping relationship when the practice situation requires us to serve clients from varied backgrounds and settings. We must seek to serve all of our clients, regardless of ethnicity, race, or socioeconomic status, as competently and effectively as possible. For many in the social work profession, that may require additional training in working in cross-cultural, multicultural, and diverse settings.

Figure 24.4

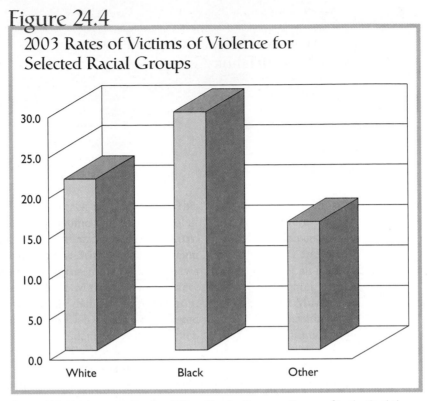

2003 Rates of Victims of Violence for Selected Racial Groups

Source: U.S. Department of Justice, Office of Justice Programs, Bureau of Justice Statistics, http://www.ojp.usdoj.gov/bjs/glance/race.htm

The Ecosystems Model and African Americans

In order to help conceptualize the multiple levels of interactions between person and the environment, and the various interventions possible, the ecosystems framework is used in conjunction with a case example for additional clarity. Using this multidimensional framework, it is possible to address the historical implications that impact black identity development, the environmental and structural factors that aid and sometimes hinder progress for African Americans, the cultural stereotypes that are often projected toward the African American population, the influences and adaptation of family structures, and the biopsychosocial (biological, psychological, and social) characteristics the individual social worker faces in troubleshooting/problem-solving with this population.

For social workers, it is essential that problems and their solutions be focused on the individual client but that they also take into account the very dynamic relationships among individual, family, culture, environment, and historical implications.

Success, regardless of the approach and the use of interventions, hinges on the ability of the social worker to establish a genuine relationship and his or her understanding of the various individual and cultural factors that must be considered, which become more evident when considering the ecosystems model. Using the case example below as a practical illustration, one can see with greater clarity the purposes and value of using such an approach in social work practice.

INDIVIDUAL FACTORS

Marquise Blacksmith, a second-semester freshman at a local junior college, has just completed a meeting with his advisor, which he had requested after several of his teachers suggested that he seek additional help with his course work. Marquise has had tremendous difficulty adjusting to college life and fitting in with his peers on campus. Late-night parties, drinking, and experimentation with marijuana are starting to have an effect on his ability to be attentive in his classes, and this has resulted in the suggestion by several teachers, as well as by his faculty advisor, that he seek assistance from the school's counseling center.

Marquise had been the only African American in his rural high school until his senior year, when another black student transferred from a neighboring county. Marquise was a very successful student-athlete, participating in both football and track, and had become very popular with his peers and coaches. His experiences in high school had been, for the most part, positive even though on occasion rival athletes would make racially derogatory comments during intense competition. Racial tension at Marquise's high school was primarily between white and Hispanic students, who were the two dominant groups. Being a student-athlete helped Marquise resist the temptation to choose sides, and he stayed neutral because his team members were both white and Hispanic.

Marquise had hoped to attend a four-year college or university, but advice from the school counselor and the guidance from his white adoptive parents had resulted in his taking few college prep courses. The reality that he was academically ill-prepared for a four-year university had left Marquise disillusioned and angry and cast a deep wedge between him and his parents. That he would have to attend a junior college rather than a four-year school when he had always been an exceptional student and athlete was unacceptable to Marquise, but the outcome was unavoidable. However well-intentioned his parents, when he left for the junior college the relationship between Marquise and Mr. and Mrs. Blacksmith could be categorized as tumultuous at best.

Addressing the issues at the micro level or biopsychosocial level of functioning is vitally important. Marquise is in a new environment where he is experiencing difficulties establishing new relationships and adjusting to college life. His attempts to cope by drinking and experimentation with marijuana exacerbate the adjustment challenges Marquise faces. His poor academic performance has made him ineligible to participate in football or track at the school, both of which have been areas of safety and opportunity for positive interpersonal relationships. To compound these issues, Marquise has only spoken with his parents twice since he moved on campus, which was a family decision because of the turbulent interactions between them. Now, Marquise wonders if he will ever fulfill his dream of becoming an athlete at a major university and ultimately playing professional football.

Family Characteristics

Mr. and Mrs. Blacksmith, unable to have their own biological children, had adopted Marquise after having been foster parents for nearly eight years. Mr. Blacksmith and his wife ran a successful farm and had done so their entire adult lives. Even when poor weather had destroyed crops, the family always seemed to do well enough to get through difficult times. The two (parents) had discussed adoption, but could never get a child who fell into the appropriate age range, that is, under 1 year old. The Blacksmiths had been foster parents for over 30 different children of varying ethnic backgrounds in their years as an active foster family, but they earnestly desired to become adoptive parents in order to have a child of their own. Even though Mr. and Mrs. Blacksmith had not considered adopting a black child, when the foster care agency temporarily placed Marquise with them, and when Marquise subsequently was freed for adoption after the termination of his mother's parental rights, 10-month-old Marquise had found his way into their hearts. The family welcomed this opportunity to have a child of their own and concluded their role as foster parents.

Both the father and mother had good relationships with Marquise throughout his infant, toddler, and early adolescent years. Although some racial issues arose in the early years during school open houses, school plays, and other social and community gatherings, the Blacksmiths had always sought to explain why their family was different in terms young Marquise could understand. Mrs. Blacksmith, remembering the conversations with the adoption caseworker, had tried to help Marquise understand his ethnic origin and heritage. Mr. Blacksmith also understood the importance of Marquise having balance in his life and supported his interest in sports as a way to stimulate his interpersonal development, while at the same time teaching him the inner working of the family business.

Having not completed college themselves, Mr. and Mrs. Blacksmith felt that the college prep class schedule might be a little difficult for Marquise to manage and decided that a less rigorous academic alternative would be best. In addition, the family had hoped that Marquise would choose to stay in the rural town and one day take over the family farm. Now that Marquise was away at college, however, they questioned everything, and their relationship with him was so stressful for everyone that they had seldom had much communication during his entire senior year in high school because of the anger over the inevitability of attending a junior college.

Cultural Issues

Marquise feels isolated and ill-prepared to relate with other black students in his new environment. In spite of his mother's efforts to expose him to literature on African American culture, Marquise continues to struggle to make black friends and fit in. Unable to participate in sports, Marquise is facing an identity crisis. In the past he has always been able to easily manage his social relationships, which resulted from his participation in school athletics. With this avenue for social interaction closed, Marquise has found his way to the college party crowd in the town's bars and pubs.

A young African American male, Marquise finds himself in a serious predicament. Drinking regularly and occasionally smoking pot to fit in, he is frantically searching for some semblance of his former social status, but to no avail. Although black students make up about 25 percent of the college's student body, Marquise feels in many ways disconnected from these students, because his personal experiences do not include much interaction with them. His interactions with black students have been, at best, suspect and lacking in depth and genuineness, as he feels he has little in common with them. Although these black students are mostly from urban and inner-city neighborhoods, and their experiences are far removed from Marquise's rural upbringing, he desires to learn more about black culture and black identity.

Culturally, Marquise is in a double-bind. On the one hand, he has the physical features of a young black male but lacks the cultural depth to feel a part of this population. On the other hand, Marquise knows he is on the road to failing in school and eliminating his future participation in college or professional sports, which has always provided him with balance in his life. The current situation offers little relief because he is unable, as a result of his grades, to interact with other student-athletes. With mounting frustration, Marquise is becoming increasingly aware of the possibility that he could very well flunk out of school and have to return as a failure to the rural community and his parents' home, if changes are not made soon.

Environmental–Structural Factors

Marquise is fortunate because the school he attends recently adopted and implemented procedures that provide him with personal counseling through the new Getright Campus Counseling Center. The assistant director of the center, Brian, has a master's in social work and has a particular interest in student support services and enjoys the diversity of services the center provides for struggling students. Several years earlier the college also adopted a memorandum of understanding with a four-year university that is predominantly African American. This historically black college has three campuses and is the largest of its kind in the country. It prides itself on transforming and increasing opportunities for those students who have low scores on college entrance exams and, consequently, are being admitted into other four-year universities.

Through these counseling services, many students have been able to seek assistance with family problems and substance abuse issues, and are able to receive academic assistance in the form of tutoring and academic advising. Since its conception and implementation, the Center has assisted many young students in successfully completing their junior college preparation and making the transition to four-year institutions of higher learning.

Historical Issues

Although historical issues of discrimination and oppression do not directly apply to this particular case example, many questions surface for consideration that would warrant interventions at the macro level of social work practice. For example, why was it not possible to place Marquise with a black adoptive family? Could adoption policies, internal agency practices, or practitioner bias have played an integral role in Marquise being placed with a white family rather than a black family? Did understanding the need for expedited permanency placement plans for young children in order to offset the negative consequences of languishing in the foster care system have an impact on where Marquise was placed and on how soon he was placed after the termination of his biological parents' parental rights? Is it possible that recruitment initiatives designed to increase the number of potential black adoptive homes are underdeveloped? Is Marquise's inability to connect with his African American peers a consequence of his being reared by a rural white family and in a community absent of other black children and a sizable black community? These questions are just a few that could be considered as having some significance, especially in light of many of the historical approaches of dealing with black children in the foster care system. It is noteworthy that the National Association of Black Social Workers (NABSW) does not support adoption of black children by white families.

MULTILEVEL INTERVENTIONS

As fate would have it, Marquise, on the advice of his advisor, did seek assistance at the school's counseling center, and Brian, a social worker on the Centers Staff, became his primary counselor. Brian, after becoming very familiar with the details of Marquise's situation, and understanding the services offered by the center and those also available in the community, together with Marquise, embarked on a journey in search of solutions.

After several counseling sessions, Brian began to map out an action plan with Marquise resulting from understanding gained from their sessions. First, Marquise truly wanted to establish more positive social relationships on campus and terminate his associations with the party crowd. Second, he was also experiencing feelings of guilt from the rapidly diminishing relationship between him and his adoptive parents. In addition to these goals, Marquise longed to play football, but his deplorable grades—not to mention his recent use of alcohol and marijuana as a primary means of coping with his issues—prevented him from doing so.

Brian, equipped with this information, referred Marquise to the junior college's Academic Center. The Academic Center is a division of Student Support Services that offers free individual and group tutoring, as well as individual academic assistance to qualified students. The Center provides these services to first-generation, low-income, and disabled students attending the college through federally funded grant resources. Marquise qualified for assistance, being a first-generation college student, and could receive the academic help he needs for successful performance in his classes.

Next, Brian would move toward the mezzo level of practice and recommend that Marquise attend a substance abuse group composed of college students that meets twice a week. Brian knew that this group was ethnically diverse and could serve as a catalyst for the development of more positive social relationships for Marquise while addressing his drinking and drug use.

Regarding sports, Brian knew that the school's intramural sports program was very good, and this could potentially be yet another avenue for developing social relationships and friendships. Brian, at the request of Marquise, contacted the director of the program and set up an appointment to meet and discuss next fall's flag football activities. This made Marquise extremely happy, because he could stay active and maintain his youthful agility and conditioning.

Brian also knew that the Center's upcoming "Alternative Spring Break" would take several students to visit the black college with which the school had the memorandum of understanding and which could potentially be a great four-year university for Marquise. The university had a well-known athletic program that excelled in both football and track. As well, the social environment of a black university would assist Marquise in furthering his identity development as a young African American, because of the school's African American professors, Afro-centric pedagogy, and rich heritage.

Finally, Brian wanted to work on restoring the family relationship that had been a source of stress and tension for the entire family since Marquise's junior year in high school, yet had been the source of love and nurturance before the more recent turbulent times. This would be a little more difficult because much had been said, and done, that both his parents and Marquise would have to move beyond before the healing process could begin. Brian agreed to work with Marquise to rectify the floundering relationship with his parents and would help him when he was ready to make the initial telephone call.

Competent Social Work Practice with African American Clients

For the modern-day social worker, cultural competency is necessary to the helping relationship because approaches to service provision that fail to recognize the significance and value of culturally sensitive practice are becoming more problematic. If social workers are to follow the well-established social work practice principle of "beginning where the client is," they must adapt their practice to the personal and cultural characteristics of each client. Yet, they must also consider information about characteristics that may be more prevalent in each special population group.

Indeed, some cultural realities may hold true for many African Americans. The distrust of whites is one example. Stemming from more than a hundred years of slavery, broken promises, and institutional racism, it is not difficult to find cause for this apparent distrust. Social workers who are not of African American background should be aware of this possible distrust of them and their work when they begin the process of attempting to establish a professional relationship.

Other realities that may affect helping relationships exist because social workers of majority background often are socialized to the images of African Americans that characterize the dominant society's misperceptions of this population. Even in the helping professions, African Americans continue to be stigmatized as being less intellectual, less motivated, more prone to violence, and less apt to be open to change. Such overgeneralizations about African Americans and their culture help to perpetuate the distrust and tensions many feel on both sides. It is imperative that social workers seriously address the validity of these societal stereotypes and examine their own belief systems to minimize the influence of such generalizations in their practice.

In social work practice, it is difficult to attribute cultural incompetence solely to white workers. In fact, such one-way stereotyping would be a fallacy. All social work professionals must guard against cultural incompetence, even when working with persons of similar ethnic origin. As Ryan proposes in his book, *Blaming the Victim,* we are likely to cast blame on those in need of help if we are not careful.[23] Deeply rooted in each of us are cultural biases and prejudices that cause us to act and react in certain ways to diversity and value differences. These values and biases shape our perceptions of the world and our socialized worldviews. Such perceptions potentially limit our ability to think objectively regarding situations that call into question these values.

Emerging Considerations for Work with African Americans

Traditional approaches and models of thinking about groups of people often assume that homogeneity exists among group members. This assumption postulates that members share most characteristics regarding their ecosystem, that is, family form, socioeconomic status, values, and so on. However, it is important to note that group members often exhibit variations within groups that can be as extensive as those between groups.[24]

With this understanding, there are several considerations that could serve practitioners in becoming more culturally competent for work with African Americans. Traditional theories often fall short in giving sufficient consideration to such factors as geographical location, socioeconomic status, sociopolitical issues, and countless other environmental and institutional influences that could make work with this population more successful. Following are topics social workers might consider studying in more depth as they add to their cultural competence:[25]

▶ African American history, culture, values, and traditions
▶ Help-seeking behaviors of African Americans
▶ Theories of black identity development
▶ Alternative perspectives on intelligences
▶ Oppression theory
▶ Ecological systems theory
▶ Ethnicity, biculturalism, and bicultural socialization
▶ Levels of acculturation and their impact on the helping process
▶ Theories of ethnicity, culture, and social class
▶ African American family functioning and family forms
▶ Racial identity development across the life span
▶ African American male development
▶ Community building/community renewal
▶ Strengths-based perspectives
▶ The digital divide
▶ People- and place-based strategies
▶ Economic perspectives on community

Concluding Comment

This chapter sought to address some of the emerging practice implications for work with African Americans. Understanding these implications is important to every social worker if he or she is to engage in culturally competent practice that, for many social workers, equates to competent practice. Failing to become a culturally sensitive and competent practitioner could result in the continuation and persistence of poor access to services for the most vulnerable populations and further widening of the socioeconomic gap between the "haves" and the "have-nots." Truly the cultural, racial, and ethnic differences that are so often used to divide us pale in comparison to the vast similarities which, if tapped, can unlock the rich human potential that too often lies mostly dormant. Frantz Fannon, a black West Indian revolutionary psychiatrist who had much to say in his theories on oppression, died in 1925 at the age of 36. During his short life, however, Fannon made great contributions to our understanding of the challenge and necessity to expand our knowledge and appreciation of human diversity. In his writing he characterized our challenge this way: "The human condition, plans for mankind, and collaboration between men in those tasks which increase the sum total of humanity are new problems, which demand true invention."[26]

Therefore, in making the world a better place for African American people, and all people, in spite of religious, economic, and cultural differences, we must move ever closer to a more inclusive, mutually beneficial coexistence and celebration of difference. Lum proposes that we engage in a continuous process of enlightenment and discovery regarding the constantly changing nature of multicultural individual, family, and community dynamics.[27]

The profession of social work today and throughout its history has been motivated and resolute in seeking multilevel systems change, both domestically and abroad, which increases the social well-being of the society's most challenged members. In keeping with this tradition, practitioners must seek new and inventive ways to overcome obstacles and barriers to better serve clients and create those societal conditions that make social functioning better for all people.

KEY WORDS AND CONCEPTS

Adaptive–vital culture
African Americans
Black culture
Black family structure

Black identity development
Blacks in the criminal justice system
Matriarchal
Oppression theory

SUGGESTED INFORMATION SOURCES

Alexander, R., Jr. *Racism, African Americans, and Social Justice*. Lanham, MD: Rowman and Littlefield, 2005.

Carlton-LaNey, Iris B. *African American Leadership: An Empowerment Tradition in Social Welfare History*. Washington, DC: NASW Press, 2001.

Davis, King, and Bent-Goodley, Tricia. *The Color of Social Policy*. Alexandria, VA: Council on Social Work Education, 2004.

Lum, Doman. *Culturally Competent Practice: A Framework for Understanding Diverse Groups and Justice Issues*, 2nd Edition. Pacific Grove, CA: Brooks/Cole, 2003.

Sholnick, Jerome, and Currie, Elliott. *Crisis in American Institutions*, 12th Edition. Boston: Pearson Education, Inc., 2004.

The Center for African American Research and Policy. "Answering One Question at a Time," http://www.caarpweb.org/

ENDNOTES

1. Robert Teare and Bradford W. Sheafor, *Practice-Sensitive Social Work Education: An Empirical Analysis of Social Work Practice and Practitioners* (Alexandria, VA: Council on Social Work Education, 1995), pp. 37 and 63.

2. U.S. Census Bureau. Current Population Reports, P60-229. Income, Poverty, and Health Insurance Coverage in the United States: 2004, http://www.census.gov/prod/2005pubs/p60-229pdf

3. U.S. Census Bureau. Table 3. People and Families in Poverty by Selected Characteristics: 2003 and 2004, http://www.census.gov/prod/2005pubs/p60-229pdf

4. U.S. Census Bureau. Table 1. Income and Earnings Summary Measures by Selected Characteristics: 2003 and 2004, http://www.census.gov/prod/2005pubs /p60-229pdf

5. U.S. Census Bureau. Historical Poverty Tables: Table 3. Poverty Status of People, by Age, Race, and Hispanic Origin: 1959–2003. http://www.census.gov/hhes/poverty/histpov/hstpov3/html

6. Ivan Van Sertima, *African Presence in Early America* (New Brunswick, NJ: Transaction Publishers, 1992).

7. Dinesh D' Souza, *The End of Racism: Principles for a Multicultural Society* (New York: Free Press, 1995).

8. Maulana Kerenga, *Introduction to Black Studies*, 2nd edition (Los Angles, CA: University of Sankore Press, 1993).

9. Barbara D. Savage, W.E.B. Du Bois and "The Negro Church" *Annals of the American Academy of Political and Social Science*, (2000), pp. 235–249.

10. Katherine Van Wormer, *Social Welfare: A World View* (Chicago: Nelson Hall Publishers, 1997).

11. Maulana Kerenga, *Introduction to Black Studies*, 3rd edition (Los Angles, CA: University of Sankore Press, 2002).

12. Marie J. Schwartz, *Born in Bondage: Growing Up Enslaved in the Antebellum South* (Cambridge, MA: Harvard University Press, 2000).

13. Daniel Moynihan, *The Negro Family* (Washington, D.C.: Office of Planning and Research, U.S. Department of Labor, 1965).

14. Kerenga, *Introduction to Black Studies*.

15. U.S. Census Bureau, 2000. Family Data.

16. The College Board College-Bound Seniors Tables and Related Items. http://www.collegeboard.com/prod_downloads/about/news_info/cbsenior/yr2002/pdf/gra

17. U.S. Census Bureau, "Educational Attainment by Race, Hispanic Origin, and Sex: 1960 to 1999," *Current Population Reports* P20-528 (Washington D.C.: U.S. Department of Commerce, 2000).

18. Ibid.

19. National Center for Educational Statistics. http://nces.edu.gov/nationsreportcard/geography/results/natachieve-re-g4.asp

20. Jeffrey Shears, *Interpersonal Racial Relationships and Delinquency Across Racial and Ethnic Samples* (Denver, CO: University of Denver, School of Social Work, Dissertation, 2001).

21. Michael Tonry, *Malign Neglect: Race, Crime, and Punishment* (New York; Oxford University Press, 1995), p. 49.

22. Bureau of Justice Statistics, *Violent Victim and Race, 1993–1998,* NCJ-176354 (Washington, D.C.: Department of Justice, 2001).

23. William Ryan, *Blaming the Victim* (New York: Pantheon Books, 1971).

24. Lawrence Shulman, *The Skills of Helping Individuals, Families and Groups,* 3rd Edition (Itasca, IL: Peacock Publishers, 1992), p. 35.

25. Joe M. Schriver, *Human Behavior and the Social Environment: Shifting Paradigms in Essential Knowledge for Social Work Practice*, 3rd Edition (Boston, MA: Allyn and Bacon, 2001), and Ruth G. McRoy, "Cultural Competence with African Americans," in Doman Lum, *Culturally Competent Practice: A Framework for Understanding Diverse Groups and Justice Issues,* 2nd Edition (Pacific Grove, CA: Brooks/Cole, 2003).

26. Neil Badmington, *Posthumanism* (New York: Palgrave, 2000, p. 24).

27. Lum, *Culturally Competent Practice.*

chapter 25

Social Work Practice with Puerto Ricans

Gloria Bonilla-Santiago

Prefatory Comment

Dr. Gloria Bonilla-Santiago, Board of Governors Distinguished Service Professor of Public Policy and Administration, Rutgers University, New Jersey, is one of the nation's premier scholars on social work policy research and the Puerto Rican population on the mainland. Puerto Ricans are the nation's second largest Hispanic group, having nearly 4 million persons living on the mainland. They are perhaps the most heterogeneous of all Hispanic subgroups and one of the poorest. Dr. Bonilla-Santiago reports that Puerto Ricans come in many forms, structures, and colors, reflecting extended families whose appearances range from black skin, dark hair, and dark eyes, to blond hair, blue eyes, and white, freckled skin.

Among Hispanic groups, tragically, they remain among the poorest and as a community struggle with a myriad of issues that include: extreme multigenerational poverty, high alcoholism and drug addiction rates, undereducation, poor housing, limited job skills, and lack of access to adequate health care. Puerto Ricans in the United States are truly the only "colonized" population group. While they do not face the problems associated with illegal immigration, they remain marginalized and trapped in cycles of poverty and social dysfunction.

Understanding the diversity of the Hispanic family requires a fundamental understanding of the different Hispanic subgroups in the United States. The total Hispanic population in 2004 was 40.4 million—a 14 percent population increase since 2000[1]. Each group has a particular history with the United States that has shaped the manner in which the family and its supportive institutions have emerged. Only one group, Mexican Americans/Chicanos, originates in the area that is now the continental United States, but the bulk of the Hispanic population, like Puerto Ricans, Cubans, Dominicans, and Central/South Americans, immigrated into this country. Hispanics are not a homogenous population group, and have different countries of origin. This fact becomes one of the most important differentiators between Hispanic population subgroups. The diversity in birth places influences many of the attitudes and experiences of Hispanics on the mainland. Puerto Ricans are U.S. citizens and move freely between the island of Puerto Rico and the mainland. The adaptation of the Puerto Rican population in both urban and rural settings stems from the socioeconomic and historical relations between their home country and the United States. Migration in their case continues to be based primarily on labor needs, and, to varying degrees, a continued relationship with home regions.

 ## Current Demographics

Population

Mainland Puerto Ricans are the second largest Hispanic subgroup in the United States. There are approximately 3.8 million Puerto Ricans living in the United States, and over 3 million live in the Commonwealth of Puerto Rico. They constitute 10 percent of the U.S. Latino population and are relatively youthful, highly urbanized, and primarily concentrated in a few states in the Northeast, although their numbers are increasing in Midwestern, Western, and Southeastern states. The states with the largest Puerto Rican populations in 2000 were New York, Florida, New Jersey, Pennsylvania, and Massachusetts. During the last 30 years, there has also been significant population growth in Connecticut, Illinois, California, Ohio, Texas, and areas in the Midwest, thus expanding the national resence of Puerto Ricans.[2]

Puerto Ricans became citizens of the United States with the passage of the Jones Act in 1917. They began a northward migration in the late 1940s and 1950s as part of "Operation Bootstrap," a plan to establish a yearly migration of thousands of Puerto Ricans to the agricultural farmland of the Northeast corridor. As a result of this plan, an Economic Development Administration that brought industrial incentives designed to develop and diversify the economy was created in Puerto Rico. That plan is responsible for what today is a relatively stable, growing middle class of Puerto Ricans on the island, and a growing underclass of Puerto Ricans on the island and mainland experiencing the most serious socioeconomic problems of any minority group, including Native Americans. Of important significance are the socioeconomic changes on the Island of Puerto Rico, resulting from the discontinuation of tax incentives essential to job creation and the changing federal policy contributing to the growing erosion of education, health, and welfare systems on the island. The resulting socioeconomic outlook for Puerto Rican families is concerning and challenging, and translates into a community that is increasingly economically polarized. Puerto Ricans continue to have the highest poverty rate in comparison with other Hispanic subgroups. Growing poverty on the island coupled with circular migration patterns makes Puerto Rico a major exporter of poverty to the mainland.[3] For example, as of 2000, 26 percent of Puerto Rican families lived below the poverty level. A significant number of these families were headed by single women. Forty-four percent of the single-female-headed households on the mainland are poor and 91 percent on the island.[4] Zavala-Martinez attributes this to four social and historical processes that have a direct impact on the reality of Puerto Rican women: (1) the political and economic relationship between Puerto Rico and the United States shaped by "colonialism"; (2) the development of capitalism in Puerto Rico and the economic transformation from an agricultural to an industrial society; (3) the role and social status of women in Puerto Rico and in the class society; and (4) the emerging forms of consciousness and struggle among Puerto Ricans, given the political relationship with the United States.[5]

Education

Although Puerto Ricans have made gains in educational attainment over the past ten years, nationally only 67 percent of Puerto Ricans and 57 percent of Hispanics over the age of 25 hold at least a high school degree, as compared with 89 percent of non-Hispanic whites. Only 14 percent of Puerto Ricans under age 25 have earned a BA or more.[6] A number of risk factors contribute to this disproportional educational outlook. The majority of Hispanic and Puerto Rican students attend underperforming schools that do not prepare them for postsecondary education. A survey conducted by the Pew Hispanic Center documents that only 1 in 4 Latino students were qualified for the postsecondary world.[7] Other risk factors include parents without a high school degree; low-family income; multigenerational history of school dropout; lack of achievement in the early grades that leads to grade retention; high mobility rates among families; teen pregnancy; and lack of aspirations. Those students who enter postsecondary education tend to begin their studies in a community college, thus reducing their chances for completing a four-year degree. These numbers grow slimmer when looking at Master's and doctoral degrees. Cabrera and La Nasa argue that students who have been historically underrepresented at the postsecondary level—those who are poor, of color, and first generation—are less likely to prepare for, apply for, enroll in, and persist through postsecondary education.[8] The long-term effects of the undereducation of Puerto Ricans and other Hispanics is a factor in the persisting low socioeconomic conditions of these communities.

Characteristics of Poverty

During the mid-1980s when most families experienced economic recovery, Puerto Rican families continued to experience extremely high poverty rates. The 1990s began with the Puerto Rican poverty rate at the same level at which it peaked in the 1980s. The pattern of poverty and despair remained constant in the early 2000s. Child poverty is one of the most pressing challenges Puerto Ricans face and is an important factor in the development of intervention strategies and policy initiatives. Puerto Rican children represent the poorest population group in the United States.[9] In 2001, over 33 percent of Puerto Rican children lived in poverty, as compared with 28 percent of Latinos and 9.5 percent of non-Latino white children. In addition, more than half (58.4 percent) of the child population in Puerto Rico lives below the poverty level.[10] Children in families with high poverty rates are less likely to report being in good health than children in higher income households. Poverty also has a negative impact on child nutrition, what neighborhood a family can afford to live in, and the quality of schools. These conditions can give rise to cyclical patterns as poor families have greater difficulties rising out of poverty.

A disproportionate number of Puerto Rican families remain trapped in the welfare system, without options or hopes for adequate long-term employment. Factors such as low educational attainment, inadequate job skills, language barriers, lack of access to transportation, and poor employment opportunities in their communities contribute to this overreliance on the welfare system. As a result of the "work first" nature of the welfare system, many welfare recipients do not receive the training they need to obtain jobs that pay a livable wage. Even when a family is able to leave the system, it often remains underemployed and poor.

Housing and healthy neighborhoods are also factors that contribute to the development and growth of families and their communities. Home ownerships and greater access to financial resources are critical requirements for a healthier lifestyle and for better family outcomes. Puerto Ricans and Hispanics face low rates of homeownership and tend to live in substandard housing. Though overall homeownership rates have increased on a national level to 68 percent, the Latino homeownership rate is still 20 points below that, at 48 percent, and nearly 30 percent below the non-Hispanic white homeownership rate of 75 percent. Low wages and lack of a good credit history hinder their access to decent housing. As a result many Puerto Rican families are forced to live in overcrowded and/or substandard homes, and pay a higher percentage of their income for rental housing. Other factors such as discrimination, predatory lending practices, language barriers, and lack of trust in financial institutions make it difficult for Latinos to achieve the dream of homeownership.[11]

Among some factors associated with Puerto Rican poverty are low educational attainment, concentration in low-wage work, growth in single-mother families, immigration, and discrimination, but these factors only partially explain the persistence of high Puerto Rican poverty. According to research, six principal factors underlie and help to explain the persistent poverty of Puerto Ricans. These include industrial and economic changes; changes in skill requirements; gaps in educational attainment between Puerto Ricans and non-Hispanics; growth in women-maintained households; unstable participation in the labor force; and geographical location and concentration.

Industrial Economic Changes.   Industrial and economic changes in the economy during the 1960s and 1970s greatly affected the Puerto Rican community. Specifically, U.S. cities lost thousands of low-skilled, well-paid manufacturing jobs when the shift from a manufacturing to a service economy began. The "deindustrialization" of cities, especially in the Northeast where Puerto Ricans were heavily concentrated at that time, eliminated jobs filled by Puerto Ricans with limited levels of education.

Changes in Skill Requirements.   The demands of the growing service sector economy increased the labor market demand for higher literacy and numeric skills, displacing low-skilled segments of the population. Since 1979, almost nine out of every ten new jobs created have been in industries like business and health services that require high levels of education and for which many Puerto Ricans are not qualified.

Gaps in Educational Attainment between Puerto Ricans and Non-Hispanics. Over the past two decades, Puerto Ricans have made gains in their educational attainment, as measured by median years of school completed. However, examination of high school dropout rates and high school and college completion data show that there are still wide educational disparities between Puerto Ricans and non-Hispanics that put Puerto Ricans at a disadvantage when competing for jobs.

Growth in Women-Maintained Households.   The proportion of Puerto Rican female-headed households increased during the 1980s but has been decreasing since 1989. Such families experience higher rates of family and child poverty than do two-parent families; Puerto Rican single mothers tend to have limited work experience and to rely heavily on public assistance.

Unstable Participation in the Labor Force.   The labor force status of Puerto Ricans has changed dramatically since the major migration of Puerto Ricans to the United States during the early 1950s. Upon their arrival, Puerto Ricans, including women, were more likely to be working or looking for work than their non-Hispanic counterparts. For economic reasons highlighted in this chapter, forty years later both Puerto Rican men and women lag behind non-Hispanics in labor force participation and they experience higher unemployment rates than whites, other Hispanics, and, in some cases, African Americans.

Geographical Location and Concentration.   Recent research has begun to examine the labor market experiences of mainland Puerto Ricans based in the area of the country in which they reside—primarily the Northeast and Midwest, which have been especially affected by economic changes and which offer Puerto Rican workers poor employment opportunities.

Health and Mental Health Risk Factors

The 1980s had seen significant growth in the mental health literature addressing cultural, socioeconomic, clinical, and developmental issues of Puerto Ricans in the United States.[12] In addition there was more cross-cultural therapy and counseling literature concerning Puerto Ricans.[13] However, a gap seemed to exist between the valuable information being published and the application of that knowledge. The "pathologization" of Puerto Ricans and other minority groups in the United States continues to be a problem of significant proportion, as are the blaming, judgmental, and moralistic attitudes of many service providers. Furthermore, some authors still offer heavily stereotyped descriptions of Puerto Ricans, presenting a static rather than an evolutionary, dynamic, transactional view of the culture.[14]

Cultural awareness in therapy must include awareness of class differences, an awareness often absent in family therapy literature and practice. Socially disempowered families or individuals cannot be assessed separately from the position they occupy in the power structure of the society in which they live. Behaviors labeled as "mental illness" or "dysfunction" may actually be survival strategies in response to poverty, racism, sexism, or other types of oppression. In such instances, the victims end up being blamed.

Even when therapist and client share the same ethnic background, if issues related to poverty and migration are not considered, therapy is not likely to be successful. Values and belief systems usually differ significantly across classes, and ideology is usually linked to one's position in the social hierarchy. Having a common national origin or language does not mean that significant class differences will disappear inside the therapy room; in fact, they may be exacerbated.[15]

The scarcity of bilingual professionals available to offer mental health services to Puerto Ricans increases the difficulties in therapy. Although recruitment of Puerto Ricans by U.S. agencies is becoming common, it seldom includes basic orientation and training sessions about the characteristics and socioeconomic environment of the population these professionals are to serve. It is often incorrectly assumed that a common national origin will automatically increase the quality of services.

In mental health clinics, newly arrived clinicians from middle-class backgrounds often feel overwhelmed, frustrated, and impotent when they face the types of problems that migrant Puerto Rican clients present. Clients may far outnumber available bilingual practitioners; thus, clinicians may be assigned large case loads with no backup support system provided by the clinic. During their years of study, these practitioners may have never dealt with mental health issues related to poverty and migration.[16]

It is imperative that orientation and training be provided to practitioners and that they engage in clinical practice with Puerto Ricans. Comas-Diaz states that cross-cultural mental health training is not only useful where racial and ethnic differences exist between patient and clinician, but is also needed when the clinician and the patient are racially and ethnically similar but have different socioeconomic backgrounds and/or different value systems.[17] This is seen in the following cases.[18]

CASE ONE

The G family comprised both parents Pedro (49 years old) and Teresa (41), plus seven children. Carmen, the oldest, was 23, and Papo, the youngest, was 10. Pedro, Jr., Jaime, Fernando, Margarita, and Flor ranged in ages from 14 to 21 years. An eighth child had died five years previously at age 4. The circumstances of her death are described below.

The request for mental health and medical services was initiated by the father, who for six years had been the "identified patient." He attended the first therapy session with his older daughter, Carmen. He arrived tearful, head hung low, and depressed. Carmen did most of the talking during the initial stage. She reported that her father's symptoms included depression, crying spells, social withdrawal, insomnia, irritability, lack of appetite, excessive cigarette smoking (two packs a day), and continuous coffee drinking.

To get Pedro to talk, I asked him questions about the history of his present emotional state. Highlights of his report are as follows:

Six years previously, he had suffered an accident while working in Puerto Rico. The accident occurred while Pedro was driving a trailer. The fellow worker who was with him died instantly. Pedro spent three months hospitalized with head and back injuries, the first three weeks of which he was unconscious.

Upon discharge he went back to work, still experiencing visual and memory problems in addition to back pain. A year later he had a second accident while driving. The company laid him off with a total compensation of less than $2,000. (He had worked for the company for more than twenty years.) Pedro requested help from the Legal Services Corporation (a U.S. federal agency with offices in Puerto Rico), but in his opinion the services offered were not adequate and an appeal of the company's decision never reached the court.

Pedro began experiencing mood swings from severe depression to rage. This created crisis situations for the entire family, who, according to their report, had a fairly normal life up until then. During this time Pedro underwent eye surgery for lesions caused by the accidents.

Shortly after his layoff, his 4-year-old daughter was hospitalized with a high fever of unknown origin. She died of a generalized infection caused by an infected intravenous tube administered at the public hospital. His daughter's death increased Pedro's depression, sense of despair, and feeling of powerlessness. Moreover, his wife Teresa also experienced severe depression as a result of their child's death.

Three years ago the family started to break up. The oldest daughter, Carmen, moved to the East Coast of the United States, followed gradually by her older siblings. Two years later Pedro's wife, Teresa, left him and also migrated to the United States with the two younger children. According to Pedro, she could no longer deal with his mood swings and outbursts of anger. Pedro reported that he often became very irritable, could not tolerate noise, and screamed and threw things when he got very upset. He stated that he had never become physically violent with his family.

Pedro remained in Puerto Rico, living alone in the family's house. Shortly after Teresa left, Carmen was contacted by an uncle who requested that she visit her father because his depression was getting worse and he was becoming physically ill. Carmen complied. She went to see her father and decided to bring him back to the United States with her.

When I started working with the Gs, Pedro and Teresa did not speak to each other and lived in separate apartments. Pedro was living with Carmen and her husband. Margarita, who had already been "adopted" by her older sister, also lived with them. Teresa lived with Papo and Flor in an apartment next to one of the older sons.

Jaime and his wife, who was pregnant, were estranged from the rest of the family. Carmen explained that she thought they avoided the family because her brother's wife, although Puerto Rican, did not speak Spanish and didn't feel comfortable with the family because of the language barrier. (This was a vague response, but I respected their apparent wish to maintain areas of privacy at that point.)

Fernando lived with friends and was also in conflict with his parents. Pedro explained that Fernando had a tendency to get himself in trouble (for example, borrowing more money than he could possibly repay) and then rush to his father requesting help. These requests, Pedro said, made him feel even worse because it made it more obvious that he could no longer "support or even help his family economically."

Pedro had "given up." The changes in the family structure from how they lived and functioned in Puerto Rico to their circumstances in the United States were too much for him to handle. Having lost his role as the family provider, he declared himself "terminally disabled" and allowed Carmen to "mother" him by taking care of all his needs except for personal hygiene. His depression continued, and the crying spells occurred more frequently. However, his outbursts of anger, which appeared to have been the only expression of power he had left, disappeared. Carmen even became his "voice" as a result of the language barrier.

The living arrangements gave Teresa a "break" from dealing with Pedro's depression as well as space to let her own depression be expressed. Teresa described herself as being "sick of her nerves" since her daughter died. The younger children, all of whom described Pedro as having been a "very strict father," found themselves liberated from his "law and order," as well as from his anger, while still maintaining physical closeness to both parents.

The family was experiencing turmoil when they started therapy: the sudden separation and lack of communication of the parents after more than twenty years of marriage; the migration of all family members to the United States, with the consequent difficulties of adaptation to a new land (the parents did not speak English); the organization of the family in the United States; the older daughter as the focus of support for the entire family system; the humiliation of having to request welfare support from local agencies (expressed by both parents in tears in one of the sessions); and the two teenage daughters having to work as waitresses for the first time due to economic difficulties.

The family's expressed goal in therapy was to get the parents back together: "If father could get his nerves cured!" I interpreted their request for therapy as a sign of readiness to assume control of their lives again. They needed me to facilitate the process by "legitimizing" their emotional reactions to the tragedies they had experienced and by helping them obtain financial aid from the disability, welfare, and rent-subsidy programs. Pedro was ill with a kidney infection; as a result of his accident, he still had visual problems and severe back pains. Teresa had never worked outside the home. In addition, their lack of skills in English reduced their job opportunities. Nonetheless, Pedro wanted to be recognized as the family provider, even at the cost of being declared "officially disabled."

Part of the work during therapy was to reframe their sense of shame at having to ask for help from Puerto Rican immigrants already established in the community while they reestablished themselves as a new immigrant family. A series of family rituals, such as collective dinners and presenting the history of their family through photographs and role playing, were incorporated into the treatment process.

In addition, throughout the process I shared with them my interpretations of their situation and development stages while requesting their feedback. I made it clear that therapy required teamwork and that their input and expertise about themselves were of utmost importance. I have found emphasizing teamwork to be very effective for empowering families: they are the experts, and I am the facilitator.

Family therapy lasted five months, at the end of which Pedro and Teresa were back together, had been granted the diverse financial aids for which they had applied, and had a support system in the community to help them deal with ongoing challenges.

CASE TWO

In the late 1970s, at age 16, Javier migrated to the United States from a slum in metro-politan San Juan. He had dropped out of school prior to completing the seventh grade because he felt he "wasn't learning anything, and it was a waste of time." He learned auto mechanics while helping a friend who had a garage. His father had left home when Javier was 10 years old, and they seldom saw each other. His mother had migrated to the United States the previous year with two younger children. Javier joined them with the intention of getting a job quickly as a mechanic and moving into his own apartment. He acquired basic English language skills within several months.

After a year of searching unsuccessfully for a job, he started to drink and get into fights. In one fight, he mortally stabbed another Puerto Rican. While in prison, he was diagnosed as "schizophrenic" by the consulting psychiatrist, apparently due to his continuous expression of anger, and was transferred to a psychiatric prison. After four years, during which he was medicated with antipsychotic drugs, he was released on pro-bation. He returned to his mother's apartment and resumed his search for a job. Four months later he got a job at a gas station working for minimum wage. He lasted three weeks at this job. Someone informed the owner that Javier had been in a psychiatric prison, and he was fired. Once again, he turned to drinking to work out his frustrations.

Javier was 23 when I first saw him in therapy. He was seeking to be declared "disabled" so that he could get financial assistance. He was willing, he said, to "act crazy if that was necessary—he was already carrying the label anyway." Therapy lasted six months and consisted of several components: individual work with Javier on rebuilding self-esteem; and family work, which meant including his mother in some of the sessions in an effort to establish additional support and to plan strategies that could help Javier deal with the stigma of "madness." Together, they decided that moving to another community would help them in obtaining a fresh start.

During therapy, we contacted various agencies until we located one that was willing to train and certify Javier as an auto mechanic. With the certification in hand, Javier started his own business of fixing cars in front of his apartment (not uncommon in Puerto Rican *barrios*). He soon earned a solid reputation; staff from the clinic and other related agencies began going to him with their cars.

Discussion of Cases

These two cases are typical of the low-income migrant Puerto Rican situation in the United States. In both cases, disability was regarded as the solution to economic dif-ficulties that the identified patients were facing.

Understanding these phenomena requires knowledge of the impact of socioeco-nomic conditions on people's lives. Without such knowledge, it is difficult, if not impossible, to understand how illness, either physical or mental, may become an asset. Low income and poor families confront the therapist with issues of economic survival, compared to the more existential or other clinical issues commonly addressed in graduate training programs.

The loss of jobs or absence of jobs poses a severe problem for male and female heads of households. Moreover, a significant number of employed Puerto Rican migrants continue to work at low-paying jobs. The fact that women receive even lower salaries than do men complicates the economic survival of the Puerto Rican family.

Clinicians need to be aware of these environmental circumstances and be sensitive to the particular situations of the family. Making generalizations about the unwillingness of a people to work helps no one. The quality of the clinician's interaction with the clients is essential to how the family reality is constructed, interpreted, and dealt with. It is important when working with families who are disempowered within societal structures that an ecosystemic assessment be conducted for the family.

General Data on Health Care and Puerto Ricans

The data concerning Puerto Ricans' national health status provide several overall findings. In general, the major national killers—heart disease, stroke, and cancer—are also the major causes of death among Puerto Ricans. Rates may be distorted, however, by the population's relative youthfulness. Among Puerto Rican families, the leading cause of death is heart disease; the second leading cause of death is AIDS; and the third leading cause is violence, including accidents, suicides, and homicides. Health status is significantly affected by lifestyle and behaviors. For example, improper diet, smoking, and excessive alcohol consumption are known to increase the risks for developing significant health problems such as diabetes, cardiovascular disease, and cancer.

Data from the National Health Interview Survey suggest that the overall rate of smoking among Puerto Ricans is 54 percent higher than that of other groups, largely because of its low incidence among females in general. Prevalence of smoking also was highest for Puerto Rican men and women (35 percent) compared to any other Hispanic subgroup.[19]

Puerto Rican families are under considerable stress as they adapt to a different culture and way of life, as they cope with low income and poor housing, and as they experience exploitation and mistreatment from both individuals and institutions. For some people, such stressors increase the risk for somatic and functional illness, depression, organic disease, and interpersonal tensions.[20] Indeed, Puerto Ricans have been identified as a high-risk group for mental health problems, particularly depression, anxiety, and substance abuse.[21] Health professionals and social work providers working with Puerto Rican populations need to be aware that many Puerto Ricans believe in the interaction between mental health and physical health—that the physical affects the mental and vice versa.[22] Thus, it is important to understand mental health issues prevalent among Puerto Ricans in order to better address their specific needs and to design relevant preventive modalities.

Migration and subsequent culture shock are thought to engender anxiety and depression.[23] People in transition often experience feelings of irritability, anxiety, helplessness, and despair. They must mourn the loss of family, friends, language, and culturally determined values and attitudes. Some Puerto Ricans respond to migration with a "hangover depression" that may include suicide attempts.[24] Puerto Rican women are particularly vulnerable to depression. Severe psychiatric disorders are sometimes diagnosed incorrectly when practitioners are not aware of prevalent cultural beliefs and practices. This is further exacerbated by the use of psychological tests that have not been standardized for bilingual populations.

In general, babies born with low birth weights are at highest risk for neonatal illness and death. Teenage mothers tend to have less prenatal care and to bear a larger percentage of low-birth-weight babies than do mothers in their twenties. Puerto Ricans bear children at about the same rate as African Americans, and their incidence of low-birth-weight infants (9–10 percent) falls between that of non-Hispanic whites and African Americans.[25] Puerto Rican women also tend to have the lowest levels of early prenatal care (55 percent) and the highest levels of delayed or no care (17 percent).[26]

Beliefs and Practices That Influence Puerto Ricans' Health

Factors such as economic status, level of education, and length of time in this country (recent arrivals, first or second generation, etc.) may influence individuals' health behavior more than cultural factors. Thus, among Puerto Ricans in the United States, there is not one predictable "Puerto Rican response." For example, the traditional Puerto Rican diet is high in fiber, relying heavily on beans and grains, rather than on meats, for protection. However, Puerto Rican diets reflect many current dietary recommendations and also play a key role in some illnesses.

Healthy practices can be encouraged through use of traditional cultural sayings. The "health beliefs model" postulates that, in order for people to make changes in their lifestyle, they must believe that they are susceptible to a disease, that the disease is serious, and that prevention can be helpful. Some commonly known Puerto Rican sayings suggest that events in one's life result from luck, fate, or other powers beyond an individual's control: *Que sera* (What will be will be); *Que sea lo que Dios quiera* (It's in God's hand); *Esta enfermedad es una prueba de Dios* (This illness is a test of God); and *De algo se tiene que morir uno* (You have to die of something). Indeed, persons with acute or chronic illness may regard themselves, and often are regarded by others, as innocent victims of malevolent forces. In such cases family and friends expect support throughout the healing process. Similarly, when receiving traditional health services, Puerto Ricans may become passive, expecting the provider to "take charge" of them—a stance that doesn't fit with the active participation required to prevent or heal much disease.

Balance and harmony also are considered important to health. A person's sense of *bienestar* (well being) is thought to depend on balance in emotional, physical, and social arenas. Imbalance may produce disease or illness. For example, some Puerto Ricans attribute physical illness to *los nervios* (nerves), believing that illness results from having experienced a strong emotional state. Thus, they try to prevent illness by avoiding intense rage, sadness, and other emotions.

In the absence of adequate access to health care, some Puerto Rican families seek the services of folk healers instead of, or simultaneously with, mainstream health care. However, Puerto Ricans' reliance on folk medicine is minimal—fewer than 4 percent of any group consult a folk healer over a twelve-month period.[27] Belief in folk healers assumes that one can have contact with God and the supernatural without intervention of the traditional church; indeed, the traditional church and folk healing coexist. The following briefly describes the folk healing systems used by Puerto Ricans: *Santeria* combines the African Yoruban deities with Catholic saints; *Santeros/santeras* are both priests/priestesses and healers.

Among Puerto Ricans, a belief in *espiritismo* holds that the world is populated with spirits, including religious figures, who intervene in the lives of individuals. These *espiritistas* can communicate with the spirits and have the power of healing. These persons may know about different types of home remedies, herbs, and so on, and have skills in treating certain physical conditions (such as joint deviation) or have other special powers.

The extent of Puerto Ricans' reliance on folk healers is a subject of some controversy in research. Perhaps, because the belief systems and practice are so interesting, many people have studied and reported on them. Their prevalence in the literature, however, does not reflect its very modest use among Puerto Ricans.

In other Hispanic groups, one observer found the use of folk healers to be common though ancillary to a health care system among Mexicans in southern California. Apparently, they used them when they were pressured by family or friends, when they disagreed with a physician's diagnosis, or when they were disappointed with the quality of care provided by a physician.[28]

Folk healers and some home remedies cause no harm and may well be helpful, but such remedies or practices may be harmful when they are used as substitutes for needed medical care. In such instances, social workers and other social service providers must carefully consider what approach to take so that clients are not "driven underground." It usually does not help to ask people if they use folk healers or folk medicine. People don't think of what they do in those terms. It does help to ask routinely, "Which prescription medications, over-the-counter medicines, or herbs are you taking now?" If you want to know something specific, ask a specific question. For example, pediatric health providers in certain areas routinely ask, "What do you do when your child has *empacho* (lack of appetite, stomachache, diarrhea, and vomiting)?

Respecting and affirming your patients' efforts to stay or become healthy will enhance your ability to influence them through positive education. Opportunities abound to educate through one-to-one interaction, culturally sensitive program posters, pamphlets, and other displays in your waiting room, and so on.

 ## Ecosystems Perspective

The practice of social work focuses on the interaction between the person and the environment. The goal of social work practice is to enhance and restore the psychosocial functioning of persons or to change oppressive or destructive social conditions that negatively affect the mutually beneficial interaction between persons and their environment. In assessing Puerto Ricans' needs for services, the social worker should seek to understand the clients' feelings and attitudes about those oppressive and destructive factors and to ascertain their negative impacts.

The ecosystems model of practice developed by Morales and Sheafor[29] is adopted for analysis of psychological factors impacting Puerto Ricans. The ecosystem consists of five interconnected levels: (1) historical; (2) environmental–structural; (3) cultural; (4) family; and (5) individual. An analysis of each level as it affects the lives and social conditions of Puerto Ricans follows.

Historical Influences

Puerto Ricans, the second-largest Hispanic group in the United States, have been migrating to the mainland United States since the turn of the twentieth century. In 1917, the Jones Act granted all Puerto Ricans born on the island U.S. citizenship. This is a striking difference from all other Latino immigrants to the country, as Puerto Ricans can move freely between their country of origin without the legal restrictions and entanglements of U.S. immigration law.

Migration to the continental United States became a viable alternative to living in the deteriorating economic and social situation on the island. Economic changes on the island, brought about by foreign control of land for sugar and coffee plantations and tobacco, created high unemployment and a steady stream of emigrants to the United States that has continued to the present. One of the first casualties of this economic change was the incremental decline of family patterns based on subsistence. High unemployment coupled with gradual industrialization caused both increased unemployment and dependence on outside commodities. This imbalance created surplus labor at a time when jobs in New York City and elsewhere on the mainland needed to be filled. Puerto Ricans began migrating to the United States and, in particular, to New York City.

The decades before 1945 are considered the period of the "Great Migration" and pioneer migration. Many of the people emigrating from Puerto Rico were contract laborers who came to work in industry and agriculture. These individuals were the basis for many of the Puerto Rican communities that currently exist outside of New York City. By 1940, there were a total of almost 70,000 Puerto Ricans in the United States; more than 87 percent, or almost 61,000, were living in New York City.

By 1960, a total of 887,662 Puerto Ricans had migrated to the mainland; 69 percent of these people, or about 612,000, resided in New York City. Like other Hispanic immigrants, Puerto Ricans did not travel together in family groups at the beginning of the migration. Usually, young men immigrated to find work and then began sending for spouses and families. But the social conditions in the United States, especially in New York where new communities were established, set parameters that changed family patterns and continued the adaptation of Puerto Ricans to the city.

Poverty became a significant factor in the lives of families in both Puerto Rico and the United States. It is impossible to discuss the Puerto Rican family in the United States without discussing the extreme conditions that have pervaded the Puerto Rican community here. From a historical perspective, Puerto Ricans have never recovered from the early colonial period when U.S. capital interest took over the ownership of the majority of land on the island and created a labor force that was dependent on cash crops. Puerto Rico had one of the highest infant mortality rates in the world and one of the lowest rates of average income per worker during the early years of U.S. jurisdiction over the island. Consider, for example, that in 1899 Puerto Ricans maintained ownership of 93 percent of all farms, but by 1930 foreign (U.S.) interest controlled 60 percent of sugar cultivation, 80 percent of tobacco lands, 60 percent of all banks, and 100 percent of maritime lines that controlled commodities entering and leaving the island.[30]

Although migration between Puerto Rico and mainland United States has been described as a primary reason for the poor socioeconomic status of Puerto Ricans in the United States, migration as a contributor to Puerto Rican poverty is difficult to confirm because Puerto Rican migration data are not regularly, or scientifically, collected. Moreover, little research exists on the demographic characteristics of migrants and the effects of migration on the socioeconomic status of mainland Puerto Ricans. The limited research that has been done has examined the number of Puerto Ricans migrating and the reasons behind their migration.

Significant Puerto Rican migration to the United States continued into the late 1940s and the early 1950s. As economic opportunities on the mainland increased during the post–World War II economic boom, low airfares between New York and Puerto Rico were introduced, thereby facilitating migration between Puerto Rico, where there was a surplus of low-skilled labor, and the mainland. According to the Bureau of Applied Research on the Puerto Rican Population in New York City, Puerto Rican migrants in the early 1950s included both men and women of all ages. The data showed that about four in ten were men between the ages of 15 and 45; the Bureau noted that Puerto Rican migration, compared to foreign immigration, was characterized by family, as opposed to individual, movement.

At the end of the 1960s and into the early 1970s, what has become known as "revolving door" migration began. This is a back-and-forth stream of people moving between the United States and the island. It is no longer focused in New York, although a majority of Puerto Ricans continue to migrate and settle in the Northeast.

Since those early dates of migration to the mainland, the economies of both the United States and Puerto Rico have undergone serious changes. Instead of leaving the island because of economic opportunities in the United States, many Puerto Ricans are now leaving the island because of the lack of economic opportunity in Puerto Rico. Therefore, in addition to the promise of jobs, a wider range of employment options, and higher salaries on the U.S. mainland, the lack of economic opportunity in Puerto Rico also influences migration. Shifts and trends in the mainland economy also have consequences for the Puerto Rican economy, causing some islanders to migrate when they cannot find employment.[31] Migration to and from Puerto Rico between 1982 and 1988 showed that over 151,000 more Puerto Ricans left the island than moved to it.

Environmental–Structural Factors

Puerto Ricans have had a history of being victims of exploitation and racism in the United States. Unlike mainstream culture, which is predominantly Western European, the ancestral roots of the Puerto Ricans are Indian (indigenous to Puerto Rico), African, and Spanish. In the past a number of publicly accepted practices excluded people of color, and in particular Puerto Ricans, from many institutions and positions of influence. Jobs were advertised in separate categories (male or female, white or "colored"), allowing organizations to exclude people who were viewed as undesirable. Puerto Ricans were largely confined to low-paying jobs and perceived as being inferior in intellect, training, and motivation to white men, women, and African Americans in the workplace.

When affirmative action legislation started to take hold, it did little to address the underlying assumptions and stereotypes that plagued nontraditional managers and created the barriers to advancement that persist today in views about Puerto Ricans. When the law forced them to hire and promote nontraditional employees, some responded with "malicious compliance" by deliberately appointing nontraditional candidates who were weak or ill suited to the jobs available so that they would have little chance of succeeding.

Barriers to Advancement for Puerto Ricans.   The most significant barriers today are the policies and practices that systematically restrict the opportunities and rewards available to Puerto Ricans and other Hispanics. This is a fundamental finding in Bonilla-Santiago's[32] study wherein managers agreed that prejudice is still a serious problem and the number one employment barrier.

Prejudice is defined here as the tendency to view people who are different from some reference group in terms of sex, ethnic background, or racial characteristics, such as skin color, as being deficient. For example, prejudice is the assumption (without evidence) that nontraditional individuals are less competent or less suitable than white males.

Ethnic and sex differences are sometimes used, consciously or not, to define "inferior" groups in a caste system. For example, Puerto Ricans were labeled as "unassertive people"—they "sit back" in meetings while others hurl and debate ideas. Some whites consider Puerto Ricans and Latinos "too polite" (and, consequently, as lacking in conviction), perhaps because of their concern for showing respect or maintaining cooperative teamwork.[33] There is also a trust barrier. Puerto Ricans and Latinos are perceived as dishonest and corrupt by individuals from the dominant culture. The prevailing stereotypes of African Americans are that they are lazy, uneducated, and incompetent. Women are often assumed to be indecisive and unable to be analytical. A survey by the University of Chicago's National Opinion Research Center, along with other research findings, shows that these stereotypes are still prevalent. This survey revealed that whites believe that people of other ethnic backgrounds are less intelligent, less hard working, less likely to be self-supporting, more violence prone, and less patriotic than whites.[34]

Restrictions against Puerto Ricans consist of additional discrimination in housing, employment, educational opportunities, and access to social services. Such structural, social, and psychological barriers are prevalent in the Puerto Rican culture today.

Puerto Rican Culture

Social workers need to focus on understanding the cultural values, belief systems, and societal norms of U.S. culture as Puerto Rican culture. In an attempt to understand the Puerto Rican client and to work effectively with this population, the following describes several important cultural values operating among Puerto Ricans: importance of the family; familism versus individualism; and the values of *respeto* and *personalismo,* styles of communicating that will continually affect your interaction with the client. To the extent that you can appreciate and respond to the client's values and language needs, you will be more effective. A further look at these cultural values follows:

1. Importance of the Family: Traditionally, Puerto Ricans include many relatives as "family," not only parents and siblings but grandparents, aunts, uncles, cousins, close family friends (who are often considered honorary uncles or aunts), and *padrinos* (godparents). All may be involved in an individual's health. During illness, people frequently consult other family members and often ask them to come along on medical visits.

2. Familism versus Individualism: Familism emphasizes interdependence, affiliation over confrontation, and cooperation over competitions.[35] Within familism, important decisions are made by the family, not by the individual alone. Thus, family members expect to be involved in treatment plans that require a shift in lifestyle; for example, a change in diet, if the family network is involved in providing and preparing food. Migration and geographic mobility may put stress on Puerto Ricans' values of familism. For example, a young family that has recently moved into your area may have left behind its extended family support system. Similarly, teenagers who are quickly adopting the manners of their peers in the U.S. culture may be in marked conflict with their parents who maintain traditional values and customs.

3. *Respeto* Requires Deference: The way Puerto Ricans show respect to one another, establish rapport, express caring, treat each other as males and females, and communicate nonverbally to one another is different from that of the dominant culture. *Respeto* dictates appropriate deferential behavior toward others on the basis of age, sex, social position, economic status, and position of authority. Elders expect to receive respect from younger individuals, adults from children, men from women, teachers from students, employers from employees, and so on. Social work providers, by virtue of their treating functions, education, and training, are seen as authority figures and as such are awarded *respeto.*

Respeto Establishes Rapport: *Respeto* further implies that relationships are based on a common humanity, wherein one is required to establish—not simply assume—rapport, decency, and respect.[36]

As like the general population, positive interactions between social workers and the Puerto Rican client require providing information about the examination, diagnosis, and treatment; listening to the client's concerns and taking individual needs into consideration in planning treatment; and treating the client in a respectful manner. For example, Puerto Rican clients can be shown *respeto,* even by providers with limited Spanish, by always using the formal *"usted"* (Sir) for "you" until the patient explicitly offers the use of the informal *"tu"* (you). Address Puerto Ricans formally as *Señor* (Mr.) or *Don* (Sir), *Señora* (Mrs.) or *Doña* (Madam); and greet clients in Spanish with *buenos dias* (good morning) or *buenas tardes* (good afternoon).

4. *Personalismo*—Warm, Friendly, Personal Relationships: Younger social workers, even though they will be awarded *respeto* as authority figures, are expected to be especially formal in their interactions with older Puerto Rican clients. Formality as a sign of respect, however, should not be confused with distance. Puerto Ricans tend to stress the importance of *personalismo*—personal rather than impersonal or institutional relationships. Thus, many Puerto Ricans expect social work providers to be warm, friendly, and personal, and to take an active role in the client's life. For example, a social worker might greet a client, *"Buenos dias, Señora* Santiago. How are you today? How is your family feeling after the accident?" or "How are the children doing at school?" Such a greeting acknowledges *personalismo,* conveying to the client that the provider is interested in her as a human being. *Personalismo* also stipulates that the client's relationship is with the individual provider, not with the institution. When asked where they receive medical care, Puerto Ricans often respond with the name of the provider: "I am seeing Doctor (nurse)" rather than with the name of the institution.

5. Communication Styles Guided by *Respeto* and *Personalismo:* Verbal communication among Puerto Ricans tends to be structured, guided by the cultural values of *respeto* and *personalismo.* When interacting with social work providers, many Puerto Rican clients tend to avoid confrontation and conflict by not disagreeing, not expressing doubts about the treatment, and, often, by not asking questions. Many would rather not admit that they are confused about their instructions or treatment.

Communication Style Includes Nonverbal Communication and Expressiveness: Many Puerto Ricans communicate intense emotion and may appear quite animated in conversations—behavior that is sometimes misperceived by non-Puerto Ricans as being "out of control."

Physical Touching: Puerto Ricans tend to physically touch others. Many expect the provider to shake hands when greeting; males often hug family members and friends to express their affection, and they may express their gratitude to providers and other health care personnel by kissing or giving gifts.

Expression of Pain: Similarly, Puerto Ricans may express pain more openly than is expected among other cultural groups. For example, some Puerto Rican patients moan when in pain.

Eye Contact: Traditionally, Puerto Ricans have been taught to avoid eye contact with authority figures (such as health or mental health providers) as a sign of *respeto;* such behavior should not be misinterpreted as disinterest in the communication. Conversely, the provider is expected to look directly at the client, even when communicating through an interpreter.

Closeness versus Distance: When interacting with others, Puerto Ricans typically prefer being closer to each other in space. Overall, Puerto Ricans tend to be highly attuned to others' nonverbal messages. Non-Spanish-speaking providers must be particularly sensitive to this tendency when establishing relationships with patients who speak only Spanish.

6. *Fatalismo* (Fatalism): Fatalism and Puerto Rican values need to be examined in the context of Catholicism and colonialism. The notion of a "colonialist personality" is found throughout a good part of the literature. A few may see life's events as inevitable (*"Lo que Dios manda"*—What God wills). They feel themselves at the mercy of supernatural forces

and are resigned to their fate. This fatalistic attitude of some Puerto Ricans has partly contributed to their unwillingness to seek outside professional help.

Family Structure

The Puerto Rican family is not monolithic. The traditional Puerto Rican family is no longer the norm. Although the family continues to be central in Puerto Rican lives, it has taken on a variety of forms to meet changing personal and social conditions. The high unemployment of the 1980s and the change in the American economy from one based on manufacturing to one based on information and services has had staggering consequences on the Puerto Rican family. In fact, the Puerto Rican family is changing as the world around them changes. Family size, geographical distribution, and other characteristics in U.S. society have had obvious effects on the Puerto Rican family. Still, the Puerto Rican family tends to be family-oriented with strong kin networks, and fertility rates are about 50 percent higher than in the rest of the U.S. population. These relatively high rates result from a combination of traditional Catholic beliefs and relatively low family income and individual educational attainment. Because of profound psychological stressors caused by poverty and white racism, Puerto Rican families are also more likely to divorce or separate than Anglos.

Puerto Rican families come in many forms, structures, and colors. Extended families may have members whose appearances range from black skin, dark hair, and dark eyes to blonde hair, blue eyes, and freckled white skin. Within one family, all or some may speak Spanish, all or some may speak English, all may be bilingual, and in some families members may speak three or more languages. They also vary in social class. Many are poor and uneducated, and others are middle class in income and education; however, Puerto Ricans are the poorest of any Hispanic subgroup. Puerto Ricans tend to be mostly urban. They usually cluster together in communities where they can preserve their language, customs, and tastes. Generally, there are three types of Puerto Rican families: recently arrived families, return migration families, and second-generation descendant families.

Intervention Strategies

Social workers who provide direct service, or microlevel social work intervention, and indirect service, or macrolevel societal intervention, with Puerto Ricans need to have firsthand knowledge of how this unique ethnic minority group has traditionally responded to mental health and social services.

Puerto Rican families for the most part retain values, attitudes, and behaviors that can be used constructively in the context of mental health services. Such strengths include the affective bonds among extended family members, the value placed on the community in providing diverse types of support to its members, and *personalismo* as a commonly shared character trait. The willingness of the Puerto Rican family to be warm and sharing in relationships allows the social worker to approach and intervene. Open discussion among family members can resolve many problems, some of which may be related to conflicts caused by the closed bonds of the extended system. Knowledge of the family's specific cultural, socioeconomic, and religious background, together with sound intuitive skills, help clinicians use the strengths of Puerto Rican families.

Concluding Comment

When working with Puerto Rican families, social workers need to possess personal qualities that reflect genuineness, empathy, nonpossessive warmth, and the capacity to respond flexibly to a range of possible solutions. It is important that an acceptance of and openness to differences among people be respected. Willingness to learn to work with clients that are ethnically different is also important.

The social workers' articulation and clarification of their personal values, stereotypes, and biases about their ethnicity and social class, as well as those of others, and ways they may accommodate or conflict with the needs of the Puerto Rican client are essential in any process of intervention. Understanding the culture (history, traditions, values, family systems, and artistic expressions) of Puerto Rican clients is very important. It is important that the impact of ethnicity on therapists' and clients' behavior, attitudes, and values is understood.

When helping Puerto Rican families, the social worker must always consider cross-cultural issues and account for multiple components beyond those that pertain specifically to "culture." Issues related to socioeconomic class are particularly important to consider, as affluent Puerto Ricans have, for example, far more resources than impoverished Puerto Ricans, whose poverty becomes an additional psychosocial stressor. Social workers must always be clear about their professional practice role and intervention methods, being careful not to promote conformity and dependence in their clients. A cross-cultural micro and macro practice will achieve the best results.

KEY WORDS AND CONCEPTS

Puerto Ricans
Colonialism
Espiritismo
Mainland Puerto Ricans

Jones Act
Island Puerto Ricans
Independence
Puerto Rican culture

SUGGESTED INFORMATION SOURCES

Bonilla-Santiago, G. *Breaking Ground and Barriers: Hispanic Women Developing Effective Leadership*. San Diego, CA: Marin Publications, 1993.

Comas-Diaz, L., and Griffith, E. H., eds. *Clinical Guidelines in Cross-Cultural Mental Health*. New York: John Wiley & Sons, 1988.

Facundo, America. "Sensitive Mental Health Services for Low-Income Puerto Rican Families," in Marta Sotomayor, ed., *Empowering Hispanic Families: A Critical Issue for the 90s*. Milwaukee: Family Service America, 1991.

Garcia-Coll, C. C., and Mattei, M. L., eds. *The Psychosocial Development of Puerto Rican Women*. New York: Praeger, 1989.

Mizio, Emelicia. "The Impact of Macro Systems on Puerto Rican Families," in Armando T. Morales and Bradford W. Sheafor, *Social Work: A Profession of Many Faces,* 6th Edition. Boston: Allyn and Bacon, 1992.

Zavala-Martinez, Iris. "En La Lucha: The Economic and Socioemotional Struggles of Puerto Rican Women," in Lenora Fulani, ed., *The Politics of Race and Gender in Therapy*. New York: Haworth Press, 1987.

ENDNOTES

1. *Hispanic Trends 2005*, Pew Research Center (Washington, D.C., 2005). http://www.pewhispanic.org.

2. "Latinos in the United States and Puerto Rico," *March 2002 Current Population Survey,* no. 1. (Puerto Rican Legal Defense and Education Fund: Latino Data Center. May, 2004). http://www.prldef.org/policy.htm

3. Ibid.

4. Ibid.

5. Iris Zavala-Martinez, "En La Lucha: The Economic and Socioemotional Struggles of Puerto Rican Women," in Lenora Fulani, ed., *The Politics of Race and Gender in Therapy* (New York: Haworth Press, 1987).

6. *Latino Youth Finishing College: The Role of Selective Pathways* Pew Hispanic Center (June 2004). http://www.pewhispanic.org.

7. Ibid.

8. A. F. Cabrera and S. M. La Nasa, "Understanding the College Choice of Disadvantaged Students," *New Directions for Institutional Research* (San Francisco: Jossey-Bass, 2000).

9. "Hispanic Poverty Fact Sheet." National Council of La Raza, Census Information Center, November 2000. http://www.nclr.org

10. "Latinos in the United States."

11. "Public Policy Agenda." Washington, D.C.: National Puerto Rican Coalition. (February 2005). http://www.bateylink.org/publications.htm

12. C. C. Garcia-Coll and M. L. Mattei, eds., *The Psychosocial Development of Puerto Rican Women* (New York: Praeger, 1989); L. Comas-Diaz and E. Griffith, eds., *Clinical Guidelines in Cross-Cultural Mental Health* (New York: John Wiley, 1988); C. Falicov, ed., *Cultural Perspectives in Family Therapy* (Rockville, MD: Aspen Press, 1983); M. McGoldrick, J. K. Pearce, and J. Giordano, eds., *Ethnicity and Family Therapy* (New York: Guilford Press, 1982); I. Canino and G. Canino, "Impact of Stress on the Puerto Rican Family," *American Journal of Orthopsychiatry* 50 (1980).

13. P. B. Pedersen, "Ten Frequent Assumptions of Cultural Bias in Counseling," *Journal of Multicultural Counseling and Development* 15 (1987); I. Ibrahhim and P. M. Arrendondo, "Ethical Standards for Cross-Cultural Counseling: Counselor Preparation, Practice, Assessment and Research," *Journal of Counseling and Development* 64 (1986); C. Falikov, ed., *Cultural Perspectives in Family Therapy* (Rockville, MD: Aspen Press, 1983); D. Sue, *Counseling the Culturally Different* (New York: John Wiley, 1981).

14. J. M. Dillard, *Multicultural Counseling: Toward Ethnic and Cultural Relevance in Human Encounters* (Chicago: Nelsen-Hall, 1983).

15. America Facundo, "Sensitive Mental Health Services for Low-Income Puerto Rican Families," in Marta Sotomayor, ed., *Empowering Hispanic Families: A Critical Issue for the 90s* (Milwaukee: Family Service America, 1991), p. 124.

16. G. Bernal and I. Flores-Ortiz, "Latino Families in Therapy: Engagement and Evaluation," *Journal of Marital and Family Therapy* 8 (1982): 357–365.

17. L. Comas-Diaz and E. Griffith, eds., *Clinical Guidelines in Cross-Cultural Mental Health.*

18. These cases are reprinted from America Facundo, *Empowering Hispanic Families: A Critical Issue for the '90s,* Marta Sotomayor, ed., pp. 126–130. © 1991, Family Service America. Used with permission.

19. S. Haynes, B. Cohen, C. Harvey, and M. McMillan, "Cigarette Smoking Patterns Among Mexicans and Puerto Ricans" (paper presented at the 113th Annual Meeting of the American Public Health Association, Washington, D.C., November 19, 1985).

20. W. A. Vega and M. R. Miranda, "Stress and Hispanic Mental Health: Relating Research to Service Delivery" (Rockville, MD: U.S. Department of Health and Human Services, National Institute of Mental Health, Public Health Service, 1985).

21. L. Comas-Diaz and E. Griffith, *Clinical Guidelines.*

22. A. Padilla and R. Ruiz, *Latino Mental Health: A Review of the Literature* (Rockville, MD: National Institute of Mental Health, 1973).

23. A. C. Garza-Guerrero, "Culture Shock: Its Mourning and Vicissitudes of Identity," *Journal of the American Psychoanalytic Association* 22 (1974): 408–429.

24. E. Trauatman, "Suicidal Attempts of Puerto Rican Immigrants," *Psychiatric Quarterly* 35 (1961): 544–554.

25. S. J. Ventura, "Births of Hispanic Parentage, 1983 and 1984," National Center for Health Statistics, Monthly Vital Statistics Report, 36 (4) Supplement (PHS), 87–1120 (Public Health Service, National Center Statistics, 1987).

26. Ibid.

27. N. Garcia-Preto, "Puerto Rican Families," in M. McGoldrick, J. K. Pierce, and J. Giordano, eds., *Ethnicity and Family Therapy* (New York: Guildford Press, 1982), pp. 164–186.

28. S. E. Keefe, "Acculturation and the Extended Family," in A. Padilla, ed., *Acculturation* (Boulder, CO: Westview Press, 1980).

29. Armando Morales and Bradford W. Sheafor, *Social Work: A Profession of Many Faces,* 10th Edition (Boston: Allyn and Bacon, 2004), pp. 230–235.

30. J. Jennings and Monte Rivera, *Puerto Rican Politics in Urban America* (Westport, CT: Greenwood Press, 1984).

31. I. Perez-Johnson, "Industrial Change and Puerto Rican Migration to the United States, 1982–1988" (Paper presented at conference on Puerto Rican Poverty and Migration, New School for Social Research, New York, May 1, 1992).

32. G. Bonilla-Santiago, *Breaking Ground and Barriers: Hispanic Women Developing Effective Leadership* (San Diego, CA: Marin Publications, 1993).

33. Bonilla-Santiago, 1993.

34. T. W. Smith, "Ethnic Images," National Opinion Research Center, GSS Topical Report No. 19 (Chicago: University of Chicago, December 1990).

35. Falicov, 1983.

36. R. Maduro, "Curanderismo and Latino Views of Disease and Curing," *Western Journal of Medicine* 139 (1983): 868–874.

part six

Social Workers in Action

Every three years, as each new edition of this volume is prepared, some national or global catastrophic event victimizing humans occurs. For example, when the 9th edition was being prepared in 1999, foremost in the news was the Trench Coat Mafia gang massacre at Columbine High School in Littleton, Colorado, on April 20. This massacre resulted in the deaths of 13 students and one teacher, followed by the immediate suicide of the two adolescent perpetrators, Eric Harris and Dylan Klebold, who attended that school.[1] Several school homicides, most involving one to three victims, continued to occur around the country over the following years. Then, as the 11th edition of this book was in the works, another Columbine-type firearm mass killing took place at the Indian Red Lake Reservation in Minnesota on March 21, 2005, when 15-year-old Jeffrey Weise killed his grandfather, his girlfriend, a security guard, a teacher, and five Red Lake High classmates, followed by his suicide.[2]

When the 10th edition of this book was being conceptualized, the greatest American catastropic event in terms of deaths in one day occurred on September 11, 2001, as terrorist acts in New York, Washington, D.C, and Pennsylvania killed 3,200 people, at least 1,000 more American deaths than in the attack on Pearl Harbor in 1941. The 9/11 terrorist acts aroused even more emotion and anger than

Pearl Harbor because they happened on U.S. soil and were witnessed by millions of Americans in person and on television. Adding to the trauma and frustration was the fact that there was not an identified country responsible for the slaughter, rather a band or "gang" of international Muslim terrorists called al-Qaeda led by Osama bin Laden, who for over four years has continued to remain at large.[3]

On December 26, 2004, a disaster of even greater magnitude than America's painful 9/11 tragedy, in terms of human casualties, occurred as Asia's 12-country coastlines were hit by massive tsunamis, which caused an estimated 226,566 deaths.[4] Hardest hit by the tsunami was Indonesia with 166,320 deaths. The hundreds of thousands of tsunami survivors literally lost everything—families, homes, and businesses.

Whether "natural," like the tsunami, or "manmade," like the terrorist acts of 9/11, disasters make life even more difficult for those who are often already vulnerable and are struggling economically and emotionally. Yet, people seem to become more philosophical and more understanding when reflecting on natural disasters, believing that "nature" follows its plan of action as it has for millions of years, totally ignoring humans in its destructive path. How can one get angry at nature's motive or specific intention for causing natural disasters? Natural disasters can all be scientifically explained, or attributed to God, who is omniscient and had a reason. As 4-year-old

Amy Tyre Vigil was being laid to rest during funeral services following the 1994 Los Angeles earthquake in which her home collapsed around her, her father commented, "Nature gave her to us, and nature took her away."[5]

Man-made disasters elicit many of the same feelings as natural disasters, such as posttraumatic stress disorder (PTSD), depression, and grief. In addition, however, they also invoke a significant amount of anger because of the specific *intention* by the perpetrator or perpetrators to cause harm to fellow humans, as was the U.S. reaction to 9/11. The hurricane named Katrina, born on August 25, 2005, in the Bahamas, may be teaching us a new lesson: that what starts as a natural disaster can become a man-made disaster as well.

Hurricane Katrina hit New Orleans and the surrounding Gulf region as a maximum, category 5 storm. Shortly after midnight on August 29, a main levee protecting New Orleans from the adjacent Lake Pontchartrain broke, leaving 80 percent of the city immediately submerged. At least 100,000 people, mostly poor, African Americans, were trapped, drowning and abandoned, without medical treatment, food, or water for several days. Looting for food and water occurred, but there was also looting by some for personal gain. Unofficial estimates are that at least 1053 people died. Although Hurricane Katrina was initially a major natural disaster, the government's bungling response at all levels, including President Bush's lack of leadership, additionally converted it into a man-made disaster with its associated rage. Much finger-pointing followed, with part of the blame being placed on the Department of Homeland Security, which, under the new disaster preparedness reorganization, subsumed the demoted and subsequently under-funded previously potent Federal Emergency Management Agency (FEMA).[6] In contrast to the initial lack of response within the country, the international response to Hurricane Katrina was overwhelming, as 55 nations around the world volunteered to help the United States, including Sri Lanka, one of the nations hardest hit by the tsunami.

How did social workers respond to these natural and man-made disasters? Did they follow in the path of good neighbors and Samaritans, or, armed with their professional knowledge and macro and micro intervention skills, did they really make a difference? The final chapter in the text, "Social Workers in Action: School Homicide and the Death Penalty" gives some answers to these types of questions. This chapter examines a high school homicide incident, one of hundreds across the nation, showing how one social worker responded to this crisis, which resulted in the death penalty for the female adolescent offender. The intervention model presented is very applicable to other school homicides occurring in the country. Under the leadership of a social work faculty member, BSW students developed a concept paper concerning the controversial issue of capital punishment.

ENDNOTES

1. http://en.wikipedia.org/wiki/EricHarris-DylanKlebold, p. 1.
2. P. J. Huffstutter and Stephanie Simon, "10 Dead After School Shooting," *Los Angeles Times*, Part I, (March 22, 2005), p. 1.
3. "Today's 9/11 News Headlines and Archives of the September 11, 2001 Attack on America," on-line at http://www.september11news.com.
4. http://www.msnbc.msn.com/id/6758619.
5. "Earthquake: The Long Road Back," *Los Angeles Times*, Valley Section (January 22, 1994), p. 1.
6. Amanda Ripley, "An American Tragedy: How Did This Happen?," *Time* (September 12, 2005), pp. 52–59. Also see several related articles, pp. 27–85.

chapter 26

Social Workers in Action: School Homicide and the Death Penalty*

Prefatory Comment

"Social Workers in Action" is an original chapter written especially for this volume for the purposes of showing how the profession and the schools of social work can be more relevant to the nation's great need for knowledge and practice intervention as it involves ever-increasing violence and homicide among youths. The country is threatened and intimidated by this rising tide of random violence occurring at shopping malls, fast-food restaurants, schools, and other public places.

Knowledge about violence and who is predisposed to violence, and even homicidal behavior, can be gained either through a scientific deductive process, that is, by drawing conclusions from a large number of cases obtained through a random sample, or through an inductive process, that is, drawing conclusions from a scientific, in-depth analysis of one case and then generalizing to many cases. The latter, in-depth approach was adopted for this chapter; it concerns a school homicide. It has applicability to Columbine High types of school homicide, such as the recent Red Lake High School massacre (ten dead) in Minnesota in March 2005.

The chapter is based on a court case composite, re-created to convey important concepts, underlying theories of violent and homicidal behavior, and details the multiple micro and macro roles of an advanced social work practitioner in addressing this problem. Under the supervision of a social work professor, BSW students developed a position paper concerning capital punishment and the execution of women.

---

*Chapter written by Armando T. Morales

Background to the Case

Bob Pla, MSW, was making his usual fifteen-minute morning drive to work on a sunny, yet windy, clear day. Bob was singing along with his favorite "Oldies but Goodies" radio station. He was happy and felt very fortunate to be living in Olas,* California, a moderately sized, predominantly middle-class beach community of nearly 200,000 people. It had a small minority population of mostly working class people, which included 5 percent African Americans, 7 percent Asian Americans, and 12 percent Latinos. Bob thought it was a good place to raise a family because of the community's outstanding schools and very low crime rate, ranked fourth in the nation as to the least ratio of crime per population. Although there were a few gangs in the community, Bob knew from prior street gang group work in violent, crime-ridden Los Angeles that they were not the violent type. They were more like "wanabes" (want-to-be), trying to impress their peers in school. Bob smiled as he reflected that Olas was a relatively safe, crime-free community.

Homicides Are in Every Community

Actually, there had been four to five homicides each year in Olas, but Bob had blocked them out of his mind. Bob was seduced by the media into believing that violence and homicide were predominantly a poor "black and brown inner-city" common event. Olas did have about thirty, mostly minority-group, gangs, and, even though they had committed some burglaries and minor and serious assaults, they had not committed any homicides in the past ten years.

Bob also reminded himself, from providing forensic court testimony in violent crimes cases in Los Angeles, that nationally, out of nearly 25,000 annual homicides, two-thirds to 70 percent involved a family member killing another; spousal homicides, a parent, usually a mother, killing her child under four years of age;[1] a homicide resulting from conflicted hetero- or homosexual relationships; or killings of friends or close acquaintances. These are called *criminal homicides*, where the primary intent is to kill another human being.

Criminal versus Felony Homicides

The majority of public media attention, however, focuses on *felony homicides*, which involve the killing of another person during the commission of a felony crime such as a robbery, burglary, or "carjacking." "We're in greater danger from being killed by someone we know well rather than by a complete stranger," concluded Bob, recalling the love-triangle killing in San Diego, adjacent to Olas. This multiple murder, a criminal homicide, involved three Navy officers. George P. Smith, a nuclear submarine engineer, shot and killed his perceived rival, Alton Grizzard, a former star quarterback from the

---

*In Spanish, *olas* means ocean waves.

Naval Academy, and his ex-girlfriend, Kerryn O'Neill, a former track star at the Naval Academy. Immediately thereafter, Lt. Smith committed suicide with the same gun.[2] Emotions and passions can humble even the most upstanding, moral citizens. Desperate women sometimes kill when they are trying to get away from a bad relationship, and some possessive men kill to keep "their" woman from getting away from them.

The Olas Family Services Center

Bob continued on his way to work, and he began to collect his thoughts in preparation for the Monday morning staff meeting. He had been Executive Director of the Olas Family Services Center for nearly four years. He enjoyed his job and believed he had a very competent staff, comprised of ten MSW-licensed clinical social workers, four BSW-level social workers, a quarter-time psychiatrist, and five administrative and clerical staff. The music on his radio was suddenly interrupted. Danny Jones, the popular Olas DJ, stated:

> Sorry folks. We have to take a time out. I just received a bulletin. There was a possible homicide at Olas High School. Details are not yet confirmed, but police report that a 12-year-old girl was shot several times by an unknown assailant, in what appears to be a gang "drive-by" shooting. Three ambulances are on the scene, but so far only one person is confirmed injured. Hundreds of students entering the campus on their way to their first class witnessed the tragic event. Many are hysterical.

Bob resisted the impulse to drive to the school to see if he could help. He wondered if some of his staff had had the same thought and had already gone to the school. Using his cellular telephone, he called his office from his car and asked his secretary to notify all staff to remain at the office for a staff meeting. The agency had to coordinate an appropriate response to this crisis at Olas High. Danny Jones again interrupted the music on the radio, and said:

> I have just been handed some current information concerning that shooting at Olas High. The 12-year-old white female victim died at the scene. She has been identified, but this information will remain confidential until her parents have been notified.

A School Homicide Shocks Any Community

Bob turned off his radio. He was shocked and saddened and did not wish to hear any more music. He arrived at the Olas Family Services Agency promptly at 9 A.M. and quickly went into the conference room where most of the staff were congregating. They appeared to be upset and angry and wanted to go immediately to the school to help. Two staff members were arguing with each other. One member stated that Olas was a fine, safe community until Mexican immigrants and L.A. African Americans moved into town. The other staff member, a Hispanic female social worker, argued that, had it not been for the racism in Olas, there would not be any problems in the community. Two social workers demanded that Bob cancel the staff meeting so that they all could go to the school to help the distraught students.

Others were numb with shock and did not say anything. Mrs. Scott, a social worker, asked for permission to take time off and go to the school to look after her two children who were students there. She was the only staff person with children at Olas High. Her request was granted as she now was functioning as a parent and not as a representative of the agency. Bob also knew that her anxiety and emotional state of mind would interfere with her attempts to help others at the school. Several thoughts ran through Bob's mind. His professional staff was in chaos given the current high school crisis. Anxiety, guilt, anger, and feelings of helplessness were quite prevalent. He wondered how his staff could go out and help others given their current states of mind. He had to assume leadership for the staff and to develop an overall strategy to address the problem and its various manifestations.

Social Work Psychosocial Intervention

Bob Pla knew that, with input from his staff, he had to develop several levels of intervention for them in order to be most effective. He organized the tasks into three levels of intervention, going from a micro to a macro level perspective:

First-Level Tasks (Micro Practice)

1. Encourage sharing and venting of feelings among agency staff prior to contacting the school.
2. Attend to the emotional needs of the agency's most vulnerable clients.
3. Obtain agency board permission for overtime and weekend work to deal with the crisis.
4. Develop a team strategy for providing assistance to the school and obtain authorization to work with the school and their counselors.
5. Contact and coordinate resources with other mental health agencies and professionals in the community in providing mental health services to the school, especially those students most affected by the school homicide.

Second-Level Tasks (Micro Practice)

1. Provide clinical assistance for deceased victim's family.
2. Provide clinical and mental health consultation to students as needed.
3. Provide clinical and mental health consultation to school faculty and administrators as indicated.
4. Provide clinical and mental health consultation to paramedics and law enforcement personnel as needed.

Third-Level Tasks (Macro Practice with a Prevention Goal)

1. Meet with the media to encourage calm, brief reporting to avoid provoking fear, anger, anxiety, and hysteria in the community by dramatic, sensationalistic reporting.

2. Provide mental health consultation to the Mayor and Board of Supervisors Chair to call for calm in the community and discourage minority-group scapegoating and vigilantism.
3. Provide mental health consultation to the informal leaders of the minority communities, appealing to "cool heads" during this crisis period.
4. Spearhead the creation of a multidisciplinary, multiethnic task force to investigate the causes of the campus violence and develop recommendations for the prevention of such incidents.

Mobilizing the Agency and Staff for Action

The First-Level Tasks 3 and 4 had to be dealt with immediately. Bob had his secretary phone the president of the board. He gave Bob permission for staff overtime and weekend pay. Bob personally called the school principal, who was familiar with the agency's work because the school often referred students with behavioral problems. The principal appreciated the agency's offer to provide assistance because his two school counselors were trained in psychometrics and educational counseling rather than treating emotional crises. In addressing task 2, Bob asked the staff to assess the ego strengths of their clients and to anticipate how they would respond to the current crisis. Special consideration would be given to those clients who themselves had been victims of violence as the campus homicide may cause a relapse among some clients.

Crises Breed Mixed Emotions

Before Bob could continue on the remaining first-level tasks pertaining to the community, he had to give the staff the opportunity to vent their feelings (First-Level Task 1). The staff responses to the tragedy were not predictable. Some minority staff believed they had worked very hard to advance themselves and their families to get out of the *barrio* and ghetto, and now their safety was being threatened. They wanted to see schools built in the poor minority communities so that these children would not have to travel into the affluent areas. Some staff members strongly objected, stating that this thinking was racist and would take them back to segregated schools such as they had prior to the 1950s. Mrs. Smith, one of the senior social workers, wanted to see metal detectors installed in all schools and police stationed on campuses. Others argued against this, pointing out that the perpetrator of the homicide was in a vehicle and not on campus when the incident occurred. Miss Garcia asserted that the availability of guns was the main "culprit." Many agreed, but Mr. Karls, an NRA member and hunter, strongly disagreed, stating that "people, not guns, kill people!"

Building Staff Cohesion

Bob seemed very surprised by the varied responses and the divisiveness among his staff. He had been under the impression that he had a cohesive staff. "Social workers are no different from the general public," he reflected, "and represent

the many faces not only of social work, but of the society at large." He decided
to try to unify them around a common goal. He assumed control of the meeting
by stating:

> I can see that we have several conflicting viewpoints, reflecting the general views of society.
> There is not one single answer or cause of this problem. The causes are many as are the
> solutions. We have to agree on a common strategy and intervention as social workers. We
> have to do our best for our clients—the students, their families, and the general community,
> which includes the minority communities. We really do not have a lot of facts concerning
> this homicide, other than that "someone" fired a weapon from a vehicle into a crowd of
> students on campus, resulting in the death of a white, twelve-year-old female student.
> Things are still rather sketchy, and we really do not know whether the perpetrator was a
> minority-group person or even whether the crime was gang-related. These incidents are not
> uncommon in the inner cities of Los Angeles, New York, Chicago, or Detroit, but the
> general public in Olas does not become too alarmed because many believe in their minds:
> "Thank God it doesn't happen here." But it did happen here, in our "nice" community,
> and this time the victim was a white girl from an affluent family. We feel rage and guilt, and
> we project blame onto many people and factors. But we all carry a lot of fear because, on
> some level, we do not feel safe—it's just like living in the poor, minority community. We're
> feeling powerless, just like the poor. As professionals, we need to go to our strength and
> look at the total psychosocial situation. Let us bring our micro and macro skills to the tasks
> that must be accomplished in order to reduce the anger, guilt, anxiety, frustration, and fear
> in our clients. Our clients are the students, their families, the high school faculty and
> administrators, the minority communities, the police, and the general community. We are
> all in a crisis. We must be challenged by that crisis and respond with the best that social
> workers have to offer. We must work together toward that goal and not lose sight of that
> goal. This campus homicide was a "wake-up call" for all of us.

Social Workers Respond to the Challenge

There was initial silence in the group. Then Mrs. Smith remarked that she felt proud
to be a social worker and that they all had a professional role to play. Another social
worker responded that this was like a natural disaster and that usually people
respond accordingly and pitch in to help. Yet another social worker commented,
"I feel overwhelmed. What are we supposed to do?"

Bob took this opportunity to explain in detail the three levels of micro and
macro tasks previously outlined. Knowing that people do their best in activities
suited to their skills, he asked the staff to volunteer for their choice of activities
within these three levels of tasks. The staff began to show some enthusiasm and
believed they could accomplish their goals now that the tasks were outlined.

Applying Crisis Theory to the Tasks at Hand

Bob asked the group to review the literature related to crises. He reminded them that
a crisis can occur at any point in a person's life and that some people react to a greater
degree than others to the emotional hazards inherent in certain events. The *crisis* is the

emotional state, the reaction of the individual, family, or community to the hazardous situation, not the hazardous situation per se. A hazardous event calls for a solution new to the individual, group, family, or community in relation to that life experience.[3]

There are three broad types of crisis situations that may enrich or endanger people's functioning: (1) those that are "biologically tinged," such as adolescence or menopause, and therefore may be anticipated by all people as part of the life cycle; (2) those that are "environmentally tinged," such as a change of job or retirement, and hence are somewhat less inevitable but are usually anticipated; and (3) those that are "adventitious," such as disasters, floods, and fire, which are attributable to chance and cannot be anticipated.[4]

Natural versus Man-Made Disasters

Floods, fires, and earthquakes are *natural disasters*. Wars, mass killings, and public homicides such as the Olas High student killing are *man-made disasters*. Victims of the latter often have more difficulty getting over their symptoms because they were intentionally caused by another human being, who, if not apprehended, could strike again. People feel especially vulnerable. Bob Pla had learned that during the crisis period an individual is in a state of acute anxiety. Feelings of helplessness and hopelessness are evident.

In this situation, ego patterns are more likely to be open to influence and change. Because defenses are lowered during this temporary period of disequilibrium, the client is usually more accessible to therapeutic influence than prior to the crisis or following establishment of a new equilibrium with its accompanying defense patterns.[5] During this period of upset, there are emotional symptoms such as tension, anxiety, shame, guilt, and even hostility. Past conflicts that may or may not have been satisfactorily resolved may be reactivated because the stresses of a crisis may be viewed as a threat, either to "instinctual" needs or to one's sense of integrity; as a loss of either a person or something else causing a feeling of acute deprivation; or as a challenge.[6]

The Unique, Subjective Perception and Response to a Crisis

Each of these states is usually accompanied by a typical emotional effect. If the crisis situation is primarily experienced as a threat, it will be accompanied by a great deal of anxiety. If the crisis is experienced primarily as a loss, it will involve depression and mourning. If viewed as a challenge, it will be accompanied by some anxiety or drive for problem solving.[7] In many respects, a crisis presents a new opportunity for change that might result in a higher level of psychosocial functioning.

Biopsychosocial Considerations in Responses to Crises

Crisis intervention strategies should also take into consideration the biopsychosocial development stages of the persons being helped. For example, Olas High included grades seven through twelve, hence, these youths ranged in age from 12 to 18 years. The deceased victim, Tammy Rowan, was 12; therefore it would be anticipated that those students most affected would be her peers, particularly those who might have witnessed the shooting. Twelve-year-olds are usually growing out of the latter developmental stages of latency and the security of childhood experienced in the family and grammar school. They are now entering a period of greater independence coupled with increased anxieties spurred on by physical development and hormonal changes. In addition, they are in the less secure social and physical environment of a high school that has significantly more students than the previous elementary school. In this respect, then, the random killing of a peer can traumatize seventh graders who are already psychologically vulnerable.

Mobilizing Related Mental Health Disciplines

In working to fulfill First-Level Task 5—coordinating mental health resources to help the school—Bob Pla called the local NASW Chapter, the Olas Community Mental Health Center, the Olas Psychological Association, and the Olas Psychiatric Association. As an executive, he knew the directors of these professional bodies when they pooled their resources three years previously in response to a severe wind and rain storm. This storm, called "Super Olas" (Super Waves), left more than one hundred families homeless when their beach-front homes were completely destroyed by the constant battering of massive waves. Bob volunteered to coordinate the helping effort of these professional groups, and their first meeting was held the first evening at the Olas Community Mental Health Center, which was closest to the school.

Developing a School-Based Intervention Strategy

The twenty-member mental health group called itself the "Olas High Crisis Team" and appointed Bob Pla Chairperson. The majority of assistance would be provided at the school. They agreed to divide their consultation services based on the targeted population (Second-Level Tasks 1, 2, 3, and 4). The highest priority would go to those students who actually witnessed the killing, irrespective of age or grade level.

Second in priority would be all of the seventh graders, followed by eighth and ninth graders. A crisis team member would visit each classroom for one period. With the tenth-, eleventh- and twelfth-grade students, the approach would involve inviting them, via the public address system, to meet with the crisis team in the auditorium after school. Still another identified high-risk group would be those students who were too frightened or "stressed out" to attend school. With this latter group, it is possible that the traumatic event reactivated preexisting, unresolved conflicts or severely impacted a fragile, vulnerable individual. A special outreach effort would have to be made in their behalfs.

Reaching Out to Related High-Risk Groups

Another targeted group would be the school parents and their other children who were not students of Olas High. Evening and weekend meetings would be provided for them. Consultation services would also be available for administrators and teachers, either individually or in groups. Similar offers were made to law enforcement agencies and paramedics involved in handling the case.

Developing an Appropriate Clinical Intervention

To minimize the traumatic effects of the school homicide on all affected parties described above and reduce any long-term psychiatric consequences related to the event such as posttraumatic stress disorder (PTSD) and adjustment disorder symptoms, the Olas High Crisis Team developed the following psychosocial intervention model. The goal of the model is to help people return to their previous level of functioning:

1. The team makes assessments of symptom responses, being particularly sensitive to *physical* changes such as eating, sleeping, headaches, and other somatic symptoms, and *psychological* changes such as anger, irritability, anxiety, frustration, poor concentration, preoccupation, depression, and increased family dependence or withdrawal.
2. The crisis team attempts to diffuse and neutralize some of these feelings through group and individual counseling. Calm listening, venting, and assisting the consultees to "problem solve," make decisions, and refocus has been found to be helpful in these crisis situations.
3. The crisis team will teach persons to use their inner strengths and to develop techniques for managing stress.
4. The crisis team is prepared to make referrals in those cases that are found to require more intensive, in-depth treatment. They will develop a list of licensed clinical social workers and psychologists in private practice who will be able to see clients on a reduced fee, or no-fee (pro bono) basis. The parents and siblings of Tammy Rowan were already being seen by a social worker in private practice (fulfilled Second-Level Task 1).

 ## Dealing with the Media

The first of the Third-Level tasks concerned dealing with the media. The Chief Executive Officers (CEOs) representing the various mental health disciplines decided to meet with representatives of the media. The CEOs, however, felt that it was important to also involve the Chief of Police and the County Sheriff in order to present a united front. A press conference was called the third day after the homicide, and by this time rumors were rampant. Some media were reporting that L.A. gangs were fighting for the "turf" around Olas High in order to sell drugs. Others were saying that the killing was an "initiation rite" by "Crips" (African American gang members). Other media reports were that local Olas minority group gangs were attempting to establish a reputation so that big city gangs would respect them. These media reports, all unfounded but fed by the typical bravado of nongang- and gang-member adolescents, caused the white community to begin patrolling their neighborhoods in the evening hours. There were also rumors that some of these residents were armed and were planning to go into the minority communities to "teach them a lesson" to stay on their side of town.

Confronting Rumors

The Chief of Police and the County Sheriff opened the meeting stating that they had the license number of the vehicle involved and were very close to apprehending the suspects, who were local adolescents. They did not know whether they were gang members but asked the media not to print the speculative stories because this might cause retaliation and conflict between gangs. Representatives of the press replied that they had a First Amendment right of freedom of speech to report the news (including speculation) as they saw fit.

Fears Immobilize Schoolchildren

Bob Pla joined in the discussion, identified himself as representing the Olas High School mental health crisis team, and commented that the speculative reporting was causing a significant amount of unnecessary fear and anxiety in the community and that even small children were reluctant to attend school. Some parents were also prohibiting their children from going to school. Mr. Pla pleaded for more restrained reporting to keep the incident in perspective. He reminded the news reporters that this was the first homicide at a school in Olas since the founding of the town in 1888—a little more than one hundred years ago. The reporters had not done their homework, hence, did not know how to respond. One of the reporters asked Reverend Hudson, who was 87 years of age and born in Olas, if Mr. Pla's statement was true. The Reverend confirmed Bob's statement.

Presenting Accurate Facts

Bob Pla also pointed out that, even if the killing had been gang-related, Olas gangs had not committed one homicide in the past ten years. "There is your story," replied Bob. "We have a fine community that really is very safe. The killing of Tammy Rowan was an aberration—an extremely rare occurrence! The odds of this happening in Olas are forty million to one." Some members of the press thought that people really did not want to hear about statistics, rather, they feared that their community was "going down the tubes," and many wanted to move out of Olas.

Sensing that what the media really wanted was a "story," the law enforcement representatives again called for restrained, factual reporting, promising that, if they would pursue a policy of discretion in reporting, the media in Olas would be the first to know who the suspects were once they were apprehended. Representatives of the media were very responsive to this suggestion and agreed to cooperate.

Involving the Elected Officials

Bob Pla, representing the crisis team, contacted the Mayor and the Board of Supervisors Chair (Third-Level Task 2) to apprise them of the importance of their exercising their formal influence as elected officials of the community to call for calm, rational thinking and to ask the public to wait for actual facts evolving from the ongoing law enforcement investigation to avoid prejudging or jumping to conclusions. Both elected representatives thought it was a helpful suggestion. The Mayor, however, decided to reach the public through a prepared five-minute television announcement, to be aired several times a day. The Board of Supervisors Chair decided to call a press conference and to have his staff prepare a brief article for the local newspapers.

Contacting the Minority Communities

Mr. Pla asked his BSW minority-community liaison staff to contact the informal leaders in the African American, Latino, and Asian American communities to assess their current thoughts regarding the school homicide (Third-Level Task 3). The Asian Americans, especially those of Japanese descent, believed that Americans were too violent as a people and very trigger-happy, calling the United States a land of "sick shooters." They recalled the slaying of 16-year-old Yoshihiro Hatori on his way to a 1992 Halloween party in Baton Rouge who made the mistake of knocking on the door of the wrong house and was killed by the homeowner who thought the youth was an intruder. The perpetrator was acquitted of manslaughter, which generated 1.6 million petition signatures in Japan urging the removal of guns from U.S. homes.[8] (In Japan, in one year, handguns claimed forty-six lives, compared with the United States, where handgun homicides numbered 8,092.)[9] The Asian community representatives did not want any involvement in the current crisis and just wanted to be left alone to manage their own community, which they felt was the safest in Olas.

Reacting to the vigilante threats emanating from the Olas white community, the African American and Latino communities promised retaliation if any minorities were attacked in the white community. Latinos were particularly worried about a resurgence of anti-immigrant sentiment among whites and an escalation of U.S. Immigration and Naturalization Services "raids" into their *barrio*. These two minority communities also threatened violent retaliation if armed white vigilantes invaded their communities. This was primarily the position of the veteran gang members.

Bob hoped that all of this posturing was simply rhetoric to frighten off the white community. Nevertheless, he presented this information to law enforcement intelligence officials, urging them to be especially alert to armed or unarmed whites entering the minority communities. He also asked law enforcement to be particularly careful in making any arrests in the minority communities during this tense climate, because even a routine arrest could trigger a riot, as had been the experience in other communities that rioted in the 1960s and 1970s.

Cooperation by the Media Is Rewarded

A week later, as promised, law enforcement representatives and the District Attorney contacted the Olas media for a special press conference. The suspects had been identified. At the press conference, the District Attorney announced that he had in custody an 18-year-old female adolescent, Rita Gomez, who admitted to the police that she had been in the moving vehicle and had fired the shots that struck Tammy Rowan. Police did not believe the incident was gang-related, because Ms. Gomez was not a gang member. She was a resident of Olas, living in *Barrio Town,* the poor, Latino section of Olas. She did not know the victim. After waiving her rights to an attorney, she confessed to the police that she had fired the semiautomatic weapon at the students merely to "scare them." She was not intending to injure anyone.

One Suspect Eludes Arrest

The co-defendant, who was driving the vehicle, was 33-year-old Michael Webster, a native of Olas and an unemployed school dropout and laborer. He was residing with his parents in the white, affluent section of Olas at the time of the murder. He had a long history of substance abuse and heroin and cocaine addiction, both as a juvenile and as an adult. He had just completed a five-year prison sentence for selling drugs and was on parole. According to Ms. Gomez, he left the state the same day of the shooting. A warrant for his arrest was issued. First-degree murder charges with "special circumstances" were filed against Ms. Gomez; if convicted Ms. Gomez could receive the death penalty.

 ## A Town Tries to Heal

After the announcement by the media of the primary suspect's being in custody and confessing that she had fired the weapon that had killed Tammy Rowan, the community appeared quite relieved and more secure. The mental health crisis team consultation groups and services continued for a few more weeks, with most of the groups disbanding by the eighth week. Several of the students who actually witnessed the slaying continued in individual treatment, as many of their PTSD symptoms were still in the acute stage. A few needed psychiatric medication to calm symptoms such as insomnia and nightmares, as the memories of violence were interfering with their school functioning.

A Right to a Speedy Trial

Daily television and newspaper interviews of Olas residents kept asking the same question: "Why did Rita Gomez kill Tammy Rowan?" Even the police did not understand the motive. Rita Gomez was relatively unknown in Olas. She did not attend high school, and some rumored that she had dropped out of school in the seventh grade. The court appointed an attorney on her behalf, Eddie Falls, a new resident of Olas, who, like Bob Pla, had left Los Angeles to enjoy a healthier and safer environment for his family. Mr. Falls wanted to change Ms. Gomez' plea to "not guilty," but Ms. Gomez insisted on pleading "guilty" because she wanted to "get it over as soon as possible."

The defense attorney attempted to plea bargain with the District Attorney to have the charge reduced to manslaughter or even second-degree homicide with a guilty plea, but to no avail. The community was angry and wanted "the book thrown at her." "Nothing less than first-degree murder and the death penalty," argued the District Attorney representing the people of California. Attorney Falls finally was able to persuade Ms. Gomez to enter a "not guilty" plea, hoping to have the jury reduce the charge to second-degree murder or manslaughter to avoid the death penalty. The determining factor for Ms. Gomez was that she wanted to avoid being executed because she wanted to be able to see her two children, aged two and four, grow up.

During the following weeks a jury was impaneled. It comprised six middle-class non-Hispanic white women and six non-Hispanic white men. All were from the Olas community. In a ten-week period, the jury completed its work and went into deliberation. In one day, they returned a unanimous "guilty" verdict of first-degree homicide with "special circumstances." (All thirty-seven states with death penalty statutes have special circumstances criteria, such as the killing of a police officer or a judge, which, if found present in a homicide, could warrant the death penalty.)[10] In California, Penal Code Section 190.2 specifies nineteen special circumstances, of which only one of those that have been charged needs to be found to be true.[11] In Ms. Gomez's case, the jury found the following two special circumstances to be true:

#14. The murder was especially heinous, atrocious, or cruel, manifesting exceptional depravity. As utilized in this section, the phrase *especially heinous, atrocious, or cruel manifesting exceptional depravity* means a conscienceless or pitiless crime which is unnecessarily torturous to the victim.

#16. The victim was intentionally killed because of his or her race, color, religion, nationality, or country of origin.

The jury determined that eight 9-millimeter bullets struck and killed an innocent, unsuspecting, 12-year-old child in the upper chest, heart, neck, and head, and that this was a heinous and atrocious violent act manifesting exceptional depravity on the part of the perpetrator. Second, because the victim was a white Anglo-American and the perpetrator a person of a different nationality (Mexican descent), the jury concluded that the homicide had a racial and nationality motive.

The Death Penalty Phase of the Trial

Following the guilty verdict with special circumstances, the jury now had to deliberate the death penalty phase of the case to decide whether there were any mitigating factors (for or against) that might justify life imprisonment without the possibility of parole rather than execution by the state. While in his office reading the newspaper concerning the Rita Gomez Case, Bob Pla received a telephone call from attorney Eddie Falls. The attorney asked Bob whether he would be willing to participate in the death penalty phase of the Gomez case by evaluating Ms. Gomez, writing a report with accompanying recommendations, and thereafter testifying in court.

Bob's evaluation would have to address two central questions before the jury and the court: (1) Are there any mitigating factors in the case justifying life imprisonment without the possibility of parole rather than execution? and (2) Of what value is Ms. Gomez' life to society that she should not be executed? Initially Bob felt overwhelmed by the proposed assignment, stating that he had not been trained to play God. The attorney stated that he had read about Bob's testimony in a legal newspaper concerning a few homicide cases in Los Angeles in which he had evaluated defendants prior to sentencing.

Bob admitted he had done this and had established expertise in testifying in assault, suicide, riot, gang violence, police brutality, and homicide cases, but never in a death penalty case. The attorney argued that, because of these experiences, he would be in the most advantageous position to "educate" the judge and jury about what factors would lead a teenaged girl to commit such a heinous crime. "How can Olas learn from this experience? How can we prevent this from happening again?" demanded the attorney.

Bob decided to do it. "You've just convinced me. You are correct! How else are we going to learn? And you used the magic word—*prevention!* There might be dozens or even hundreds of persons like Rita Gomez out there. As social workers, we are trained to look at the interface of the person and the environment and the transactions occurring between the person and the environment. What are the biopsychosocial factors relevant to this case? What went wrong?" Bob agreed to take the case contingent on receiving authorization from his agency board.

He was later granted permission by the board because they saw this as an opportunity for the agency to make a contribution to the community in reducing tension and learning more about factors that contribute to violence. The board felt honored that one of its employees was being asked to participate in a very high-profile case that was in the news daily. Bob felt proud that, as a representative of the social work profession, he was being asked to use his micro and macro knowledge and skills in the comprehensive assessment of a case extremely important to the welfare of the community and to the 18-year-old Hispanic female whose life was at stake.

Preparing for the Case.   The attorney submitted a written request to Superior Court Judge William Banks who was presiding in the Rita Gomez case, asking him to appoint Bob Pla, MSW, as an expert defense witness. The Judge approved and signed the order, defining Bob Pla's role as an expert in violence and homicide. Bob was given a copy of the order, which permitted him to visit Ms. Gomez in the Olas County Jail. The attorney also gave Bob several boxes of case materials that included the police investigation reports, the medical autopsy report, all school, health, and employment records, a record of the defendant's prior contacts with law enforcement, her psychiatric and psychological evaluations, numerous witness accounts, videotapes showing a four-hour taped confession with an accompanying typed copy of the confession, and selected court transcripts of the murder trial including testimony by various forensic, medical, and law enforcement experts.

Planning a Case Strategy.   A "strategy conference" was also held with the defense team led by Attorney Falls, his assistant attorney, and the chief investigator. At this conference, Attorney Falls set forth his theories related to causation, which would form the foundation of mitigating factors that, if accepted by the jury, would warrant life imprisonment without the possibility of parole rather than death. The attorney believed that the strongest mitigating factor was that Ms. Gomez was a drug addict and, while under the influence of drugs, her judgment had been impaired, leading to the killing of Tammy Rowan. Bob agreed to this approach, stating that he would look carefully into the drug problem as well as the possibility of other mitigating factors presently unknown. The attorney believed that any additional mitigating factors could "score points" with the jury.

The Jail Visit.   Visiting someone in jail is a sobering experience, even for Bob Pla, who has worked with jail and prison populations for many years. The suspicious, skeptical looks from jail personnel that one receives even after presenting the appropriate documents, authorization, and identification, is something one never gets used to. This discomfort was further exacerbated by having to go through a metal detector and having one's briefcase searched for hidden weapons or contraband such as drugs. "Don't personalize it," Bob thought to himself. "It's just a part of their job for security reasons." Then the female Sheriff's Deputy cautioned Bob that he was entering the women's jail at his own risk and that the Sheriff had a policy of not recognizing or responding to demands if he were to be taken hostage by the inmates. "Thanks a bunch," responded Bob in a somewhat sarcastic tone. "I'm only doing my job," responded the Deputy in a defensive manner. "Now I'm going to pay for it," Bob reflected. "They're really going to make me wait a long time."

Interviewing a "Killer."   Bob was sitting in the empty attorney's room, which was filled with about thirty stalls. "I guess attorneys do not work on Sundays like social workers," mumbled Bob. After waiting only thirty minutes rather than the usual hour to an hour-and-a-half, Bob was pleasantly surprised when Rita Gomez was led into the interview room by a deputy. She did not look mean or hard and actually was quite cooperative, friendly, and soft-spoken. She was an attractive, slim, 18-year-old Mexican American Catholic female, born and raised in Olas. Bob already had a psychosocial framework in mind as to the information he was seeking that related to her early childhood, family, marital, educational, and social history, and health, drug, and delinquency history.

He did not want to delve into the specific offense during the first interview. He preferred to wait until a subsequent interview when she would have more trust in him. He explained to her that this would be the first of three interviews, and that, with her permission, he was also planning on interviewing her parents, grandparents, aunts and uncles, husband, and children. Bob also explained the reasons why it was important to interview all these family members. She approved of this plan. She warned Bob that he was going to hear a lot of bad things about her and that she had worn out the welcome mat with her immediate family as well as with other close relatives. "What did you do?" asked Bob.

Rita rolled her eyes, smiled, and stated, "What didn't I do?" She went on to say that she was a "junkie" and had stolen from the family to support her habit and had lied to everybody, including her husband, to get money for drugs. "I even was turning tricks for money to buy drugs," she confessed. She became emotional and began to cry, stating that, most of all, she missed her children, aged four and two. "And that poor little girl who I killed. I can imagine the pain her mother is in. I didn't mean to shoot her. I've never physically hurt nobody. I'm an alcoholic and an addict, but not a violent person," she cried. She seemed very remorseful, and Bob recalled that in the videotapes she was crying nonstop for nearly four hours. Bob decided to change his plan of not going into the specific offense because Rita seemed comfortable with him and was herself leading the interview into this painful area.

"Why do you think you killed her?" inquired Bob. "I did not know her and was not planning on hurting anyone," replied Rita. "Mike (Michael Webster, second suspect, at large) and me were slamming several times that morning (injecting heroin and cocaine), and then Mike said 'Let's go cruising in my car.' We got in his car and then he showed me a gun. It was real heavy. I don't know what kind it was. I've never held a gun in my life. Then Mike said 'Let's go by the school and scare the squares. I'll drive by, and you just wave the gun at them and watch them run and drop.' Mike was laughing and I thought it was funny, too. We drove by the school once and I waved the gun out of the window and some of the students saw us and started running, yelling 'Drive-by, drive-by!!!' That was a real trip. Then we went around the block a second time and I waved the gun again and we were laughing real hard. Then Mike said 'Pull the trigger, pull the trigger!' I did and the gun went off a lot of times, like a machine gun. I was so loaded that I could hardly aim the gun. I aimed above their heads and didn't think I hit anyone. Then we sped away. We were still laughing. Then later we heard on the radio that someone had been shot at the school. I got real scared. Mike dropped me off at home and then took off. I haven't seen him since. A few days later I was arrested at home after someone at school ID'd me."

The Report: A Psychosocial Evaluation

Bob Pla followed through with his plan of interviewing Rita's family members, spouse, children, and significant relatives who could provide an insight into Rita's personality and behavior. There was one area of common agreement; during periods of complete abstention from drugs and alcohol, that is, in a state of remission, she was a sensitive, responsible, loving, and caring daughter, mother, wife, and person. But when using drugs and alcohol, she became a completely different person, doing anything short of violence to get money or things of value to use to purchase her drugs. Sometimes she would exchange sex for drugs. In addition to the interviews described above, Bob relied on various reports and documents to arrive at his conclusions and recommendations. He then prepared a report for the attorney, who in turn, would present it to the judge and prosecutor for their consideration. The report initially highlights Bob Pla's area of expertise, because, as in most cases, the prosecutor will challenge and oppose the appointment of Bob Pla because the prosecutor, who represents the people of the State of California, wants to see Rita Gomez executed. By law, the jury comprises only persons who support the death penalty. All opponents of the death penalty are excluded as jurors. The following is Bob Pla's evaluation.

Olas Family Services Agency
2301 N. Pacific Coast Highway
Olas, California 92133

December 1, 2005

Eddie Falls
Attorney at Law
321 South Oak Street
Olas, California 92134

Re: Rita Gomez, Case #C-93187

Dear Mr. Falls,

On November 7, Superior Court Judge William Banks signed an order appointing me as a violence, homicide, and psychosocial evaluation expert for the Defense in the case of Rita Gomez, case #C-93187. The information in this report should assist the jury in resolving the issue of the appropriateness of life without the possibility of parole *versus* execution by the state.

By way of professional credentials, I received my master's degree in social work from the University of Southern California and thereafter had twenty years of professional experience in probation, parole, community mental health, and, later, as a faculty member at the UCLA Department of Psychiatry, establishing the first psychiatric clinic in the University of California system specializing in the assessment and treatment of Spanish-speaking patients.

For the last four years, I have been directing the Olas Family Services Agency where I supervise a staff of fifteen persons and where I continue to treat clients. I have given numerous presentations at professional conferences concerning the assessment and treatment of suicidal and homicidal patients and homicide perpetrators. Additionally, I have had over twenty years' experience in working with juvenile and adult male and female criminal offenders, including many who abused drugs and alcohol. For the last ten years I have been providing mental health consolation to parole officers concerning the management of parolees.

PSYCHOSOCIAL EVALUATION

What follows is my psychosocial evaluation of Ms. Gomez, which is based on three interviews with her in the Olas County Jail, totaling five hours, and fourteen hours of interviews with her parents, maternal grandparents, four aunts and uncles, and her husband and two children. In addition, I analyzed numerous reports and documents related to her medical, psychological, psychiatric, and juvenile history, and her law enforcement investigation, including a lengthy videotaped confession. This psychosocial evaluation has two major functions:

1. to provide the court with a comprehensive analysis to understand what factors contributed to making a Hispanic adolescent female (18.2 years of age at the time of the offense) commit such a violent crime, and
2. to assess whether this youthful lady has any value to society as a human being that might warrant a life sentence rather than execution by the state as the result of her conviction for first-degree murder with special circumstances.

This report will not be prepared in a traditional psychiatric or psychological report format primarily emphasizing the individual. Rather, this social work–oriented psychosocial evaluation will focus not only on the individual, but also on the interface of Ms. Gomez with her total environment, which includes her family, relatives, and other groups in the community. This psychosocial evaluation will have two major sections: Part one will concern six "predisposing factors" within a relevant topic framework, followed by an analysis. Part Two will focus on Ms. Gomez' value to society.

PART ONE: DATA AND DIAGNOSIS

1. IDENTIFYING DATA

Rita Gomez is a slim, attractive, dark-haired, eighteen-year-old, bilingual, bicultural Hispanic female of Mexican descent born at the Olas County General Hospital. She is the mother of two male children, aged two and four. She married the father of her children, Pedro Gomez, age twenty-two, when she was fourteen years of age. He works six days a week at a gas station during the days and as a parking lot attendant during the evenings. The marital relationship has always been conflictual due to his wanting to know her whereabouts during his long working hours. Having one child by age sixteen, let alone *two* children by that age, and being uneducated and unemployed, places a young adolescent female at even higher risk for additional problems.

2. PERTINENT GENETIC-BIOLOGICAL FAMILY HISTORY

There is a strong genetic factor for alcoholism that is seen to run in families. Children of alcoholics become alcoholic four times more often than children of nonalcoholics. Studies report higher rates for alcoholism among twins than among nontwin siblings.[12] Ms. Gomez is an alcoholic in remission, as well as a drug addict, also in remission. She continues to be addicted to the nicotine in cigarettes and has been a chronic smoker of one to two packs per day since she was twelve years old.

Rita Gomez comes from a traditional, male-dominated, hard-working, religious, Catholic Mexican family originally from Puebla, Mexico. Her great-grandfather on her maternal grandfather's side was a ranch-hand and died at age eighty due to cirrhosis of the liver. He was an alcoholic. His wife had died two years previously due to heart disease. She had been a chronic smoker. Ms. Gomez' great-grandmother on her maternal grandmother's side was also a nicotine addict who smoked three to four packs of cigarettes per day. She died of lung cancer at age seventy, and her husband, a general construction worker, was an alcoholic, and died of cirrhosis of the liver at age forty. Ms. Gomez' biological father is also an alcoholic, as is his mother. Both of her parents are chronic smokers.

Ms. Gomez' maternal grandparents, ages sixty and sixty-two, report good health, with the exception of the grandmother who suffers occasional anxiety attacks related to stresses brought on by her granddaughter's murder case. The grandparents, as well as Ms. Gomez' mother, are employed at the local Sears Department Store, where the mother is head of the shoe department and the grandparents are in the janitorial department. Combining their modest incomes, they purchased and reside in their home located just inside the lower-middle-class area of Olas. They moved here because the area had better schools. This area, which is near *Barrio Town*, is 90 percent non-Hispanic white.

With the exception of Ms. Gomez, no member of the family dating back to the great-grandparents, has received psychiatric treatment, been hospitalized for mental illness, or been arrested for any violent or criminal acts. Ms. Gomez' maternal grandparents had eight children, currently ranging in age from twenty-three to forty-two, with her mother being the second oldest of these children. In turn, her mother had four children with Ms. Gomez being the second oldest child. Her older brother graduated from college and is a high school teacher in a neighboring community. The other two siblings are attending high school. Ms. Gomez has two male children of her own, aged two and four, who reportedly are in good health. According to her mother, Ms. Gomez was drug-free during her pregnancies, with only occasional light alcohol consumption.

3. EARLY CHILDHOOD DEVELOPMENTAL FACTORS

Ms. Gomez was a seven-pound, four-ounce natural-birth baby who was bottle-fed by family members because the mother had to work to support the family. She always had a healthy appetite but was always thin. She was quite active as an infant and began walking rather early, at ten months of age. Ms. Gomez slept well, had a calm demeanor, and did not present behavioral problems as a child. She was a very affectionate, trusting child and bonded well with her mother and other family members residing in the home, especially her maternal grandmother. Her first and primary language was Spanish, but this did not handicap her in kindergarten, or first and second grade at Olas Tree Elementary School located in *Barrio Town,* which had 85 percent Latino students. As they improved their economic circumstances, the family moved to a more affluent area where they currently reside. She transferred to Cherry Lane Elementary, which had only 3 percent Latino students, and the rest were non-Hispanic white students.

At this school she began to experience stress, as students mimicked and made fun of her Spanish accent and her very slim appearance, calling her "toothpick," "ostrich legs," and "dirty Mexican." Quite often she would cry at home because she did not want to go to school. She developed various somatic complaints and on occasion would vomit, causing her mother to keep her home from school, thinking her ill. The mother often complained to school officials but "nothing was done about it," and the insults continued. In spite of frequent absences and the prejudice and scapegoating she was suffering, she still was able to maintain above average grades, such as a few As, a few Bs, and the rest Cs. She began to resent school because it had become a very negative experience. She felt not only rejected, but also that she did not fit in. Her academic performance suffered and was reflected in poorer grades in the fourth, fifth, and sixth grades. Rejection during these important, formative years can lead to a child's low self-esteem at a critical time in his or her life, when the psychosocial developmental task is learning to become industrious in an atmosphere of validation by the school and peers.

4. FAMILY EMOTIONAL ENVIRONMENT

A warm, secure, loving, home environment is extremely important for a child to develop healthy emotions, emotional security, confidence, and self-esteem. According to the parents and grandparents, this happened for Ms. Gomez during her first five years of life in spite of the negative experiences she was having in school. The loving validation provided by her warm, very traditional Hispanic family helped her feel that, at least somewhere in her life, she was valued. This was reflected in her being a loving child who reached out to and established close relationships with her siblings, immediate relatives, and playmates. This emotional foundation and empathic capacity still exist, according to all of her relatives, except when she is under the influence of drugs and/or alcohol, when she becomes a totally different person who is emotionally distant and cold and exploits people for her own benefit.

During these initial developmental years, her hard-working father was a light-to-moderate drinker of alcohol. However, as she approached seven years of age, his drinking escalated because he had been laid off from a few low-skilled jobs. His arguments with her mother evolved into physical battering in the presence of little Ms. Gomez, which caused her a significant amount of anxiety. Sometimes she was afraid of leaving her mother at home and would not go to school.

5. CHILDHOOD PSYCHOLOGICAL TRAUMA

It is very traumatic for children to observe their parents in violent confrontation, especially when it occurs frequently. On one occasion when Ms. Gomez was nine years old, she attempted to protect her mother from the father's abuse by stepping in between them, but this was met with physical retaliation against her. Thereafter, these physical beatings that the father thought was his right as a husband and a father also began to include Ms. Gomez. The beatings lasted for a few years until the father left home when she was almost twelve years old. Ms. Gomez cannot recall these beatings even though she had a few scars on her arms that her mother stated had been caused by them. This "blocking out" of painful trauma is not uncommon for post-traumatic stress disorder (PTSD) victims, especially children.

Ms. Gomez did recall one painful episode when she was ten years old and "glue-sniffing" with friends in a neighbor's garage. She was raped by two fifteen-year-old boys. Fearing that she would be blamed for this incident, she did not tell anyone. Such a traumatic event could also cause PTSD.

In my assessment of Ms. Gomez, she clearly had several psychiatric symptoms that met the criteria for a PTSD diagnosis. These symptoms of acute anxiety, hypervigilance, fear, and depression were never treated. In such situations, some people, especially when they are poor and do not have the resources to obtain professional treatment, have been known to "treat" themselves. No doubt this motivated her to seek her own self-prescribed medication with chemical substances such as paint, gasoline, "glue-sniffing," marijuana, PCP, heroin, cocaine, and alcohol. These substances help numb the person from psychological pain and, while in the intoxicated state, help suppress painful memories at least temporarily until the next "high." A psychological and physical dependence upon this "solution" reinforces its repetition.

6. SEARCHING FOR A SUBSTITUTE FAMILY

When children are rejected by the school and their families as they approach early adolescence (which is a developmental period of wanting to be part of a social group), they begin to gravitate to and are attracted to other youths having similar experiences and needs. These are the seeds that give growth to gangs. As Ms. Gomez was approaching age thirteen, she began to absorb some of the nonviolent aspects of adolescent female gang culture. She avoided school even more to be with her new friends. Michael Webster, the "at-large" co-suspect in this case, introduced her to heroin at age thirteen when he was twenty-eight years of age.

She quickly developed a psychological and physical dependence on this drug and had a new group of friends that she called "street junkies." In her frequent association with this group, she began to incorporate the subculture and lifestyle of the lower-class female street addict. She was now in a "retreatist gang" (a group in society that "retreats" into drugs and alcohol consumption). To support her drug habit, she stole from her family and friends, lied, and manipulated people in her pursuit of drugs. She was nicknamed "Bandit" by her group, and she had this name tattooed on her left arm when she was fourteen. Female street addicts rarely, if ever, are violent. Instead, they prey on potential victims whom they might be able to exploit for drugs, particularly recently paroled ex-convicts who are potential sources for drugs with their "gate money" (prison release money). In the street drug culture, they are labeled "Black Widows" for this behavior.

Ms. Gomez has no formal criminal history other than the current homicide offense. Her record indicates only one petty theft arrest as a juvenile when she stole cosmetic items at a Thrifty Drug Store. She did not have to appear in court because no petition was filed. She simply was counseled and released by the police.

7. PSYCHOSOCIAL ANALYSIS AND DIAGNOSIS

In analyzing the above six predisposition factors, any one of these factors could place a child, adolescent, or adult at a high risk for emotional, behavioral, criminal, or substance abuse and dependence problems. In the case of Ms. Gomez, her primary strength was the foundation of her relatively normal early childhood up until the age of five. The six factors were: (1) beginning motherhood before the age of 16, being unemployed, having only a seventh grade education, and being in a conflicted marriage; (2) having inherited four generations of a biological vulnerability to alcoholism addiction, which also made her biologically vulnerable to other addictions such as drugs and nicotine; (3) language and cultural difficulties in elementary school, further complicated by discriminatory rejection by non-Hispanic white students; (4) being raised in an unstable family after age five, which progressively deteriorated due to her father's alcoholism and physical abuse of her mother; (5) the traumatization of Ms. Gomez' rape at age ten by two fifteen-year-old males while all were glue-sniffing, compounded by beatings by her father until age twelve; and (6) her increased involvement with a "surrogate family" (the street addict subculture), which met her needs for companionship, affection, and drugs.

Throughout her young life from age five to eighteen, the dynamics of these six interacting, predisposing factors negatively impacted her psychosocial development and functioning, thereby contributing to her offense, which occurred while she was under the influence of heroin, cocaine, and alcohol. In this intoxicated state, her judgment was impaired and, being with an older, more experienced ex-convict and drug addict—who often enjoy respect and status among the younger, less experienced "junkies"—she was more vulnerable and prone to influence.

Being the victim of sexual and physical assaults as a child severely traumatized this adolescent. To this day, these emotional scars remain untreated. These symptoms demanded calming and, through self-medication beginning at the tender age of ten when most little girls are still playing with dolls, she began to ingest mood-altering chemicals (sniffing paint, gasoline, and glue). Four generations of a dormant, chemical genetic vulnerability toward addiction surfaced. In a relatively brief time after graduating to heroin and cocaine use, she became an addict and joined the street addict culture.

Ms. Gomez' career as a female street drug addict did not follow the usual pattern of most female drug addicts, that is, continued use with the possibility of death due to AIDS resulting from prostitution and/or using infected needles, suicide evolving from major depression, or "burning out" as an aging addict and then becoming an alcoholic. A few are able to leave drugs and assume a normal life. In the case of Ms. Gomez, however, she did not have the maturity nor the physical and emotional strength to alter her 8-year-old street drug addict pattern, which culminated in the death of a 12-year-old child, and which now may even result in her own death.

DIAGNOSIS

In my interviews with Ms. Gomez, it is my diagnostic impression that she definitely is depressed. Following arrest she was suicidal but did not make any attempts. A year ago when her husband was threatening to leave her and take her children, she made a suicide attempt by slashing her wrists with a broken bottle. It was a serious attempt while intoxicated and required emergency room treatment and seventy-two hours of hospitalization. She did not receive treatment following release due to lack of insurance and financial resources. Such attempts are not uncommon among very depressed female adolescents. Her depression, in part, is also *reactive,* that is, it is an emotional reaction to being separated from her children, husband, family, and friends. Her depression may also be a long-term *dysthymic* (chronic low to moderate) depression arising from untreated PTSD symptoms since age ten. In addition to four generations of genetic factors predisposing toward alcoholism in the family history, there might also be an underlying *endogenous* (biological) depression having a genetic origin. With regard to the latter, a careful, extensive psychiatric evaluation would have to be made of the defendant and selected family members. The following is my diagnostic impression of the defendant:

> DSM IV-TR, 312.82. Adolescent Conduct Disorder (stealing, lying, running away), severe, present since age twelve to date arrested in present offense.
> DSM IV-TR, 309.81. Post Traumatic Stress Disorder, chronic type, present since age 10.
> DSM IV-TR, 303.90. Alcohol Dependence, in full remission since arrested in present offense.
> DSM IV-TR, 304.80. Polysubstance Dependence, in full remission since arrested in present offense.

PART TWO: THE DEFENDANT'S VALUE TO SOCIETY

1. In complying with the social work profession's ethical responsibility to promote the general welfare of society and to respond to this nation's great need for new and current knowledge to advance its understanding of violence and homicide, it becomes imperative that Ms. Gomez be permitted to live in order to assist social and psychiatric scientists toward that end. This tragic case presents a unique opportunity to advance our current state of knowledge concerning the nature versus nurture debate and the relationship between American and Mexican culture. The Gomez case represents five generations of genetic vulnerability to addiction in one family,

from the great-grandparents to and including Ms. Gomez' two children. Where this genetic vulnerability to alcohol and drug addiction coexists with too-easy access to firearms in the context of a violent Anglo-American culture, many young women with similar characteristics are being transformed into agents of violence and homicide. Ms. Gomez may simply be a female "pioneer" in this regard.

2. From this case we can also learn about the specific points of the process of early adolescent decision making, which lead a troubled youngster to choose a gang or a street addict group, to become a "loner," a criminal offender, a homeless, runaway youth, or some other alternative. All this information is valuable to society in the identification of genuine high-risk youths and their families in order to prevent these excessively violent crimes, by either young females or young males.

3. There is sufficient research information that documents the severe emotional impact upon immediate family members when there is a suicide in the family. This impact places each of them at very high risk for suicide, because, in periods of major depression, they tend to identify with the "solution" adopted by the dead family member.[13]

   In those cases in which a family member was a victim of a homicide, similar emotional vulnerabilities occur. Furthermore, it is a fact that *any* child who has lost a parent "by any means before the age of thirteen," has a higher risk for affective disorders and suicide than does a child who has not experienced such a loss.[14] In the defendant's case, the execution of Ms. Gomez by the state would place both of her children at a very high risk for possible homicidal and/or suicidal behavior in later years, because they would have to live with the emotions and the label of having been given birth by a mother who was so "evil" she had to be executed by the state. The defendant is a classic case of a victim of childhood sexual and physical abuse who later becomes a perpetrator of violence. Her execution would perpetuate this cycle of violence in her children.

4. Ms. Gomez would become the first woman and mother with minor children to be executed in the United States and in the world. Granting her a life sentence without the possibility of parole will spare her children this overwhelming, high-risk burden. When sober, Ms. Gomez can be an affectionate, nurturing mother, and she can continue her mothering responsibilities with her children through weekly and even once-a-month, weekend prison visits available to mothers with minor children.

5. She is quite remorseful and accepts full responsibility for all her actions in the homicide. All her statements to me have been corroborated by her family and other secondary sources. Her attitude was very positive, and this was quite evident in reading unsolicited letters shown to me by her relatives. Over the last few months, she has written letters to several of her younger cousins, nieces, and nephews, advising them to do well in school and listen to their parents. Her misfortune can be of a continuing educational benefit to other youths. Her death would end that important communication link.

Sincerely,

Bob Pla, MSW
Executive Director

The Report Is Challenged by the People

After the report was read by the judge and the District Attorney representing the people of the State of California, the District Attorney exercised his option to call for a "402 Hearing" without a jury being present. This special disclosure hearing permits the District Attorney to challenge Mr. Pla's credentials as an "expert" in a specific area and, secondly, to challenge parts, or even all, of Mr. Pla's report if the District Attorney is of the opinion that it might undermine his efforts in obtaining a death penalty verdict. The District Attorney challenged Bob Pla's MSW degree, stating that a social worker's training did not qualify him to be an expert on violent and homicidal behavior. The defendant's attorney, Eddie Falls, granted that Mr. Pla's graduate training and education did not in itself qualify him as a violence expert, but that, following graduation, one of Mr. Pla's specialty areas had become the assessment and treatment of violent offenders as well as murderers who had been released on parole. Attorney Falls added that Mr. Pla had testified in juvenile and superior court on at least fourteen occasions and had been accepted as an expert witness in these violence-related cases. The judge ruled that he was satisfied that there was sufficient evidence to show that Mr. Pla had earned expert witness status in previous trials.

Social Workers Can't Diagnose

The District Attorney also challenged Mr. Pla's "psychosocial evaluation" report and diagnosis, stating that only a licensed physician, psychiatrist, or psychologist, was qualified to render a diagnosis, *not* a social worker. "Therefore," shouted the District Attorney dramatically, "this report is worthless!" Rita Gomez seemed stunned. Attorney Falls calmly showed a current copy of Mr. Pla's LCSW, his professional license, which originally had been granted twenty-six years previously, and stated to the Judge that Division 2, Chapter 14, of the California Business and Professions Code, authorized licensed clinical social workers not only to diagnose a patient or client but also to provide that person psychotherapy of a nonmedical nature. The judge ruled that the Business and Professions Code permitted Mr. Pla to diagnose patients, and that section of the report would be admissible evidence for the trier of fact (the jury). Rita Gomez smiled at Mr. Pla and her attorney.

The District Attorney Scores Major Rulings

Being cognizant of the fact that a four-generation genetic vulnerability for alcoholism in the defendant's family could be construed as a favorable mitigating factor and a foundation for a life sentence rather than the death penalty, the District Attorney attempted to strike out factor 2 in the report. He argued that the family history was based on "hearsay," there were no medical records to prove the existence of alcoholism, and that the great-grandparents were deceased, hence, could not testify as to their addictions. Attorney Falls argued that the grandparents could testify as to their parents' addictions if permitted. The judge inquired of Mr. Pla whether the genetic alcoholism studies pertained to males or females. Mr. Pla responded that so far, all of the studies concerned males, but that in 1971 China had discovered the same genetic link from mothers to daughters and fathers to daughters. The judge ruled that scientific knowledge on this point had to be restricted only to research in the United States, and because there was no evidence to show the specific genetic link to daughters, the mitigating factor of genetic inheritance of alcoholism could not be heard by the jury. This was a major setback for Ms. Gomez in fighting for her life.

Reported History versus Corroboration

The District Attorney accepted predisposition factors 3 (early childhood developmental) and 4 (family emotional environment) in the report. However, in factor 5 (childhood psychological trauma), the District Attorney accepted the physical abuse history because this had been corroborated by the defendant's mother under oath on the witness stand. The District Attorney, however, did not accept the rape experience at age ten, because Ms. Gomez had not reported the incident to anyone, including the police. The judge supported the District Attorney in this request to keep the jury from hearing this information.

Clinical High-Risk versus Courtroom High-Risk Perception

The District Attorney mounted his strongest challenge to Mr. Pla's assertion that the execution of Ms. Gomez would place both of her children at very high risk for subsequent suicidal or homicidal behavior in later years. Mr. Pla quoted from the most recent research that concluded that the death of a parent increased suicide risk twenty-fold for a child 13 years of age and under, and that violent and homicidal behavior in family members placed youth at very high risk for modeling that violent behavior. The judge calculated that, since the suicide rate was on the average twelve per 100,000 according to Mr. Pla's figures, increasing the rate twenty-fold would result in a figure of "only" 240 per 100,000. The judge concluded that the fact that 99,760 persons would *not* commit suicide following the death of a parent was statistically a stronger argument.

The judge further inquired of Mr. Pla whether there was any research to indicate that the execution of a mother resulted in suicide and/or homicidal behavior on the part of her children. Mr. Pla replied that, although there were many women on "death row" in the nation, there had not been any specific research to address that question. Mr. Pla restated the documented argument, however, that the death of the parent for *any* reason—including execution by the state—placed a child 13 years of age and under at very high risk for suicide. The judge ruled that the jury would not be permitted to hear the argument that Ms. Gomez' execution would place her children at risk for either suicide or homicidal behavior. Ms. Gomez' mouth dropped open as she nodded her head from side to side in disbelief. Her attorney protested but was firmly silenced by the judge.

The Defendant's Value to Society?

The District Attorney argued that he did not want to see Ms. Gomez kept alive for the benefit of social and psychiatric scientific curiosity at the expense of taxpayers. He stated that the taxpayers and voters of California wanted to see the prompt execution of criminals committing heinous crimes, especially the killing of a child on her way to school. The judge ruled that the jury would not be able to hear Mr. Pla's testimony concerning Ms. Gomez' value to social science. The arguments presented by Mr. Pla of Ms. Gomez' value to her own children if kept alive for mothering–nurturing purposes and her value to young, extended family members and other potential youths she might be able to impact in a positive way because of her tragic story, were accepted by the judge over the opposition of the District Attorney.

The Competition

Bob Pla testified for two days before the jury under a barrage of challenging, often cynical questions advanced by the People's legal representative. Attorney Falls made a valiant effort in his *direct* (initial testimony) examination of Mr. Pla, which was followed by a lengthy *cross* (challenging the initial testimony) examination of Mr. Pla by the DA. The factual premise of each of Mr. Pla's statements in his report (minus all of the sections withheld from the jury as the result of the "402 Hearing") was challenged by the District Attorney as to its source, research methodology, and conclusions. Bob Pla was well prepared and defended each position with confidence and a presence of authority, hoping to impress the jury. This competitive interaction reminded him of his one-on-one boxing ring experience or perhaps preparing for and taking his LCSW oral examinations. Attorney Falls fought to retrieve any "points" scored by the District Attorney during his *redirect* (further clarification of initial testimony provided during the direct examination) examination of Mr. Pla.

Finally, following two days of the direct, cross, and redirect testimony of Mr. Pla, the defense rested its case. The attorneys were given two days to prepare their closing arguments for the jury.

The Verdict

As dictated by law, the prosecution was first to present its closing argument on behalf of the people of the state of California, followed by the closing argument of the defense. The District Attorney's tough law and order delivery calling for the death penalty was followed by the closing statement of the defense. Attorney Falls pleaded to the jury that, because Ms. Gomez was an adolescent and a mother with no prior criminal convictions whose judgment was gravely impaired because she was under the influence of alcohol and drugs at the time of the commission of the crime, these mitigating factors should warrant a sentence of life imprisonment without the possibility of parole, rather than execution.

The prosecution then was permitted to rebut the defense's closing arguments. The District Attorney argued that, in California, an 18-year-old is legally an adult, not an adolescent, and the fact that she is a mother had matured her far beyond her age. The prosecutor granted that Ms. Gomez was an alcoholic and a heroin and cocaine addict, but that there was no factual evidence to prove that she was intoxicated at the specific moment that she fired the gun at the victim. The District Attorney further advised the jury that, even though there were no criminal convictions in her history, by her own statements she had admitted stealing items from home to sell in order to purchase her drugs. The closing arguments ended after two days.

The all-white jury that consisted of six women and six men who had already convicted Ms. Gomez of first-degree murder with special circumstances deliberated the death penalty phase of the trial for two days. The jury was called back into the courtroom because they had reached a verdict. The courtroom was filled to capacity, and media cameras were running. The judge asked the jury whether it had reached a decision. The jury foreman stood up and replied, "Yes we have, your honor." The verdict, which was written on a piece of paper, was given to the judge by the bailiff to be read. The bailiff then returned it to the foreman who read the verdict in a rather businesslike voice, stating:

> Based upon the court instructions given to us, we the jury can find no mitigating factors or circumstances which would warrant life imprisonment without the possibility of parole for the defendant. We are unanimous in our opinion that her criminal actions involved in the taking of a child's life, warrant the death penalty.

After the first sentence had been read, the victim's family and supporters were crying and cheering, drowning out the second sentence. Ms. Gomez held her head down, crying, and loudly stated to the victim's family, "I'm sorry! I'm sorry!" Her attorney, who also had tears in his eyes, attempted to comfort his client by patting her on the shoulder.

A Social Worker's Work Is Never Finished

It had been a little over a week since Bob Pla had testified in the Rita Gomez case. It was the noon hour, and Bob was driving to the local In & Out Burger for his favorite double-burger and fries. He was again tuned in to Danny Jones and his "Oldies but Goodies" program. He pulled up to the speaker and placed his order and was waiting in the long line of cars. It was 12:05 and, in the middle of "Misty," Danny Jones cut in stating:

> Well folks. The verdict that you've all been waiting for has just come in. It looks like one of our Olas residents is going to fry! I guess what goes around, comes around. It's too bad that we'll be losing two beautiful young ladies. Catch you later . . . .

Bob was immobilized until the car in back of him honked its horn, waking him out of his preoccupied trance. He pulled up and paid for his order and received his lunch. As he drove away he could not recall whether he was given change—or even whether he had change coming. By habit he reached for the hot fries, but they seemed tasteless. "Maybe they forgot to put salt on them," he thought. For some reason, he had lost his appetite. He could not believe the verdict. He felt that he had done his very best given the unfair circumstances of having to spar with two, rather than one, opponents, the District Attorney *and* the judge. He thought that Eddie Falls was a good attorney who had also given his best. Danny Jones' words "what goes around, comes around," kept interfering with his thoughts about the case. "That's it! That is what all of this is about. What goes around, comes around. Rita was abused, and in turn, she abused!" Bob reasoned. She was subjected to physical punishment, and she had easy access to weapons; she killed, and now the state is going to kill her. "As social workers out to improve the human condition," Bob reflected, "we need to stop physical punishment, reduce easy access to firearms, and end capital punishment."

Regenerating Interest after a Crisis Is Over

Bob recalled that, in the original micro and macro psychosocial intervention strategy he had developed, all tasks had been addressed and completed except for the last task, no. 4. This final task was a macro Third-Level Task with a prevention goal. It involved the creation of a multidisciplinary and multiethnic task force to investigate the causes of the campus violence and develop recommendations for the prevention of such incidents. After making at least two dozen phone calls to social workers and other professionals, school representatives, and minority community people to work on this project, he found very little interest. Most believed that the case was closed and that everyone should move beyond it and "heal."

Others felt that Olas was still a safe community and the Gomez case was just an aberration and would never happen again. "I guess communities are just like people," thought Bob. "As soon as the crisis is over, everything cools off, and denial once again darkens our path so we don't have to see how dangerous it really is—and then we're more likely to get injured." Some minorities advised Bob, "Let sleeping dogs lie, man. Don't wake up the white monster (racism in Olas). Don't you remember how they wanted to come into our neighborhoods and shoot us?" Bob was becoming a little discouraged and had to remind himself that, just because he had been so intimately involved in practically all aspects of the case and understood clearly its wide-ranging implications to Olas and other communities, others did not seem to share his concerns. He also knew, however, that one can always find others who share one's concerns.

Bob decided to begin "at home," that is, with other social workers. He asked to be placed on the agenda for the following month's Olas NASW chapter meeting. At the meeting he explained his concerns regarding the growing youth violence problem, not only in Olas but throughout the nation, stating that the Gomez case was *not* an abnormality, rather that there were literally hundreds of persons in Olas with similar predispositional factors and dynamics, just waiting to explode. Many of the social workers agreed, because they had also observed these factors in the caseloads of the county Department of Children's Services.

Early childhood experiences of physical and sexual abuse were not uncommon in many families. "They should outlaw corporal punishment of children by parents as they did in the schools," exclaimed one of the social workers, with others quickly joining in and nodding agreement. "Corporal punishment starting with children is just at the beginning of a continuum of punishment," commented Ms. O'Leary, "that ends with the ultimate punishment—death!" "Maybe we need to get rid of the death penalty too," remarked still another social worker. Others thought that more social welfare services were needed for the poor as a violence prevention measure, rather than building more prisons.

One of the recent MSW graduates set forth what she believed was a progressive thesis, stating: "Perhaps we can look at the death sentence of Rita Gomez as 'progress for women,' as they are now really being treated as equal to men who commit horrendous crimes. I for one favor the death penalty and believe that women should also be executed for the same behaviors for which men are executed." Initially, the group of twenty-five social workers stared at one another in silence, some having surprised expressions.

Ms. O'Leary then spoke and agreed with the philosophical premise of equality in her colleague's statement. "It reminds me of the positions we used to take in the sixties and seventies as young student feminists and, that is that in our political protests and demonstrations, we did not wish to be protected and treated in any special way because we were women. We strongly believed that if we were demanding equal pay and treatment, we also had to be ready to assume the consequences of our new assertiveness, including being jailed like the male protestors. We fought against special treatment, better food, and far less crowded housing accommodations provided for women in prisons and jails. Our black and brown brothers and sisters 'doing time' brought it to our attention that, unlike young white feminists, they were quite overrepresented in correctional institutions, and that, if we really wanted to help, we should advocate 'up' rather than 'down.' They believed that the quality of living standards in institutions should rise to a higher standard of decency as women's were, rather than going down to the almost barbaric level found in many overcrowded men's prisons and jails. So, perhaps we shouldn't be executing a Rita Gomez, nor a mother, nor a married or single woman, nor *any* woman *or* man." "Amen to that and I second the emotion, sister," responded Bill Kennon from the Black Social Workers' Union, "and let's not forget guns. Everybody seems to have a gun, and a lot of people are using them."

Bob was sensing a certain enthusiasm in the group, often generated when people got together to discuss a particular issue. No longer were they feeling isolated or powerless. Indeed, social workers like to work together. People can be good medicine for one another. The group wanted to develop strategies related to violence prevention, agreeing that what was most needed was the massive social welfare needs of people with very few resources in society. NASW, through its national committees, commissions, and local chapters, was already working on these social welfare issues. The group did not see any reason to involve itself in that area, nor in the discussion of capital punishment since NASW already had a policy statement favoring its abolition.

"Even though NASW has officially taken a position against the death penalty," interrupted group member Rocco Vincent, "do we really know much about which women are being sentenced to death and for what capital crimes?" The group pondered the inquiry and had to admit that they did not know much about who was on death row and for what capital offenses. Rocco Vincent was a professor of social work at a local college and was teaching in the BSW program. "I would like to raise this issue with my students and see if I can interest a few of them to take this on as an assignment for extra credit," added Professor Vincent. The group seemed very interested in the professor's idea, which quickly resulted in a consensus for action.

Professor Vincent presented this information to his upper division BSW students the following week. "I assume that many of you have been following the newspapers concerning the Rita Gomez teenager case. And you probably know that she received the death penalty as punishment for her involvement in the high school homicide," Professor Vincent reminded the class. He then led a discussion of the class attitudes for and against the death penalty as it concerned women. The class seemed to mirror society's attitudes, as nearly 70 percent of the students favored the death penalty. When Professor Vincent inquired about their attitudes concerning the state execution of women, however, the percent favoring this outcome dramatically dropped to about twenty percent.

"I notice that about 90 percent of the class is comprised of women," Professor Vincent pointed out, "and I wonder if there might be an element of sexism or gender bias in your attitudes as you seem to favor the death penalty significantly more for men than women." This caught the class by surprise and some began to become defensive regarding the accusation of sexism. Some students began to argue that it was a "fact" that men were just naturally more violent than women. Some argued that men were just biologically different "and carried all that testosterone in their balls." The class laughed heartily at the comment. Even Professor Vincent, who was caught by surprise, laughed at the student's statement.

"Yes indeed, there can be biological factors contributing to violence and aggression and even murder. Can you think of anything else?" the Professor asked, challenging the group. One of the male students, who was still red-faced by the "balls" comment, stated that culture could also be a contributing factor as males beginning as early as childhood, were acculturated to be more aggressive and violent as compared to females. The class nodded in agreement. "But let us get back to why women end up on death row and the crimes they committed leading to this bleak outcome," Professor Vincent said, trying to re-focus the discussion. "Everyone knows why some women end up on death row. It's because they killed their mate who had been subjecting them to spousal abuse over a period of years and the women just got tired of it," pointed out one of the students receiving support from other female students. "But aren't we just guessing and playing with 'facts' that we grab out of the thin air and which just might be layman notions? As social work students, should you not be able to prepare yourself with documented data as it concerns human behavior?" asked Professor Vincent. The class was quiet as many nodded in agreement with this assessment.

"I have been meeting regularly for several months with a crisis mental health committee since the high school homicide tragedy. Following the death penalty sentence for Rita Gomez, the committee became interested in the issue of the death penalty, specifically which women received this harsh sentence, and for what capital crime. Are there any students who would be willing to research this issue for the class and the crisis committee in lieu of the required term paper?" Three students, one a combined BSW MSW student, and two BSW students volunteered for this assignment. A month later the three volunteers were ready to give their report, which Professor Vincent reproduced for the class. The students were anxious to report their findings concerning women on death row. They were surprised by the volume of information available and were able to identify the major Internet resources for this data, specifically the Death Penalty Information Center, Amnesty International, the American Civil Liberties Union, and law professor Victor Streib at Ohio Northern University. Professor Streib had by far the most comprehensive information available, as he had been the only person in the United States specializing on death penalty research for female offenders for many years. The following represents the concept paper they developed.

Alternatives to Capital Punishment for Women in the United States

The death penalty dates as far back as the eighteenth century, B.C. under the rule of the King of Babylon, with a significant influence of modern thinking being based on the Bible, specifically the phrase in Exodus 21:23–25, which states "you are to take life for life, eye for eye, tooth for tooth, hand for hand, foot for foot, burn for burn, wound for wound, bruise for bruise." In addition to religious perspectives, U.S. history reveals that there indeed was a racism factor, as 2,954 African Americans were executed by lynch mobs between 1889 and 1932. Some of these lynch-mob executions involved law enforcement either as participants or spectators or both. Racism continues to be a factor in modern times: in 90 percent of the cases in the 38 states with capital punishment (12 states and the District of Columbia do not have capital punishment), there was evidence of disparities in relation to the race of the victim, that is, under similar circumstances, a defendant was more likely to receive a death sentence if the victim was white than if the victim was black. More specifically, 12 non-Hispanic whites were executed for killing African Americans, while 192 African Americans were executed for killing non-Hispanic white victims.[15]

There appears to be a strong connection between conservative, oppressive governments and their use of the death penalty in attempting to intimidate or control the masses. Following a "regime change" by the public however, capital punishment is one of the first practices to be eliminated. For example, following the death of Spain's 83-year old dictator General Francisco Franco in 1975, the death penalty was abolished with the introduction of a new constitution in 1978. Nelson Mandela, who was the democratically elected President of South Africa in 1994, abolished capital punishment in spite of the fact that 93 percent of the white public was in favor of it. Following major political reform in Russia, in 1999 President Boris Yelstin commuted over 700 death sentences to life, thus ending the death penalty. Part of the motive was the changing public opinion about capital punishment but perhaps the primary reason was political and economic advantages as abolition paved the way for Russia's admission to the Council of Europe.[16]

In April 1999, the United Nations Commission on Human Rights voted overwhelmingly on a moratorium on the death penalty. The resolution was introduced by the European Union. The only nations opposing the resolution were China, Rwanda, Sudan, and the United States. Of 33 nations executing 1,625 prisoners in 1998, China had the most executions, with 1,067; followed by Congo (Democratic Republic) with 100 executions; and the United States in third place with 68 executions.[17] The international human rights community has seen the United States as among the worst violator of human rights because of its stated commitment to the same ideals that have resulted in other countries questioning the death penalty. The international human rights community has identified the following issues warranting U.S. reform:[18]

▶ The execution of juvenile offenders (under 18 when capital crime committed).
▶ The execution of those with mental retardation or severe mental illness.
▶ The execution of foreign nationals not informed of their rights under the Vienna Convention on Consular Relations (VCCR).
▶ The application of the death penalty and related problems of racial and economic bias.
▶ The length of time the condemned spend in extreme isolation and deprivation between sentencing and execution.

Finding itself increasingly isolated as a nation especially after the lack of European support in the preemptive Iraq War, the United States is beginning to make some positive changes in three of the five death penalty policies listed above. On June 20, 2002, the U.S. Supreme Court issued a ruling ending the execution of mentally retarded prisoners, stating that it was a violation of the Eighth Amendment of the U.S. Constitution, i.e., cruel and unusual punishment. However, there are countless cases of persons being executed who were mentally ill. In following the law, juries often find that a psychotic defendant knew right from wrong when God or the Devil told them to kill someone.

Even though the United States signed Article 36 of the Vienna Convention on Consular Relations in 1969, for nearly thirty years the United States has ignored the requirement to inform foreign national of their right to have their consulate notified of their detention and death sentence. Complying with Article 36 would require the foreign national to be returned to his non–death penalty country under a life without parole sentence. The same legal right gave protection to U.S. citizens traveling abroad who were convicted of a capital crime. From 1976 to 2005, the United States has executed 21 foreign nationals, with 119 remaining on death row representing 31 nations.[19] In March 2004, Mexico brought a suit against the United States in the International Court of Justice concerning the U.S. failure to inform 54 Mexicans on death row of their right to talk to their consular officials prior to sentencing. The International Court of Justice ruled in favor of Mexico and ordered the United States to have a judicial review of these capital convictions.[20] On March 9, 2005, President Bush, bowing to international law, issued a Presidential Order that the 49 Mexican nationals on death row in several states who were not notified of their right to contact Mexican officials about their death sentence will be granted a new hearing to determine if they were harmed by this error.[21]

Another landmark five-to-four Supreme Court decision occurred on March 2, 2005, when the Court ruled that the Constitution forbids the execution of homicide perpetrators on death row who were under 18 years of age when they committed a capital crime.[22] The United States was the only nation in the world following the practice of executing juveniles. The continuing execution of poor minorities, mostly African American and *Latinos,* and housing death row inmates for 30 to 40 years, however, continues to keep the United States lagging behind the rest of the world as it concerns capital punishment reform. One hundred and ten persons age 60 and over were on death rows in the United States by the end of 2003, with 89 year-old LeRoy Nash on Arizona's death row being the oldest.[23]

Reacting to mounting international human rights criticism, the U.S. policy response is that it believes it reserves the right within U.S. Constitutional constraints to impose capital punishment on any person (other than a pregnant woman) duly convicted under existing laws permitting the imposition of capital punishment.[24] While only sparing the execution of pregnant women on death row for up to nine months, should not the international human rights community also recommend to the United States the abolition of the death penalty for all women, since it is the only country in the world—with an occasional rare exception—following this practice?

As of January 1, 2005, there were 3,455 inmates on death row, including 50 women.[25] Women represent 10 percent of all homicide arrests in the United States, yet only 2 percent (1 in 50) of persons receiving the death penalty following conviction. This appears to reflect an ambivalent and less punitive attitude at all levels of the criminal justice system toward the execution of women. From 1632 to 2004, a period of 372 years in the United States, 566 women out of 20,000 males were executed, representing about 3 percent (2.8 percent). Women account for 1.4 percent (1 in 71) of persons currently on death row, and 1.1 percent (1 in 92) of persons actually executed in modern times. The reluctance to execute women escalated from 1900 through September 2004: only 0.6 percent (49) of 8,264 of all executions were females. However, since 1998, 9 (1.8 percent) of 496 total executions were women, showing a significant increase.[26]

Whereas nearly 90 percent of males on death row were convicted of a capital offense involving a *felony homicide* (the killing of one or more persons during the commission of a felony offense), for women it is significantly less, 40 percent, or 20 out of 50 cases. The majority of women, 28 out of 50 (56 percent) are on death row for having killed a loved one. More specifically, 15 killed a spouse or boyfriend, and in most of these cases a "hit man" was hired for insurance benefits or other economic gain. Eleven mothers (22 percent) committed *filicide* (killing of their children between 2 years and 14 years of age). Two women were convicted for *familicide* (killing their spouse and children). One woman was convicted for having killed a police officer, and one woman on death row intentionally killed six pedestrians with her vehicle.[27]

With regard to race and ethnicity, 26 of 50 are non-Hispanic white, 15 African American, 7 Hispanic, and 1 American Indian. In analyzing felony homicide, 9 inmates were non-Hispanic white, and 9 were African American, followed by 1 Hispanic and 1 American Indian. Twelve non-Hispanic white women, 2 African American, and 1 Hispanic female are on death row for having killed their spouse or boyfriend. Five Hispanic mothers, 4 non-Hispanic white mothers, and 2 African American mothers committed filicide. One African American and 1 non-Hispanic white spouse/mother committed familicide. One African American killed a police officer, and 1 non-Hispanic white woman killed six pedestrians with her automobile.[28] Minority women who number nearly 50 percent on death row are greatly over-represented, as they do not represent this ratio in the general population.

From November 1984 to October 2002, 10 women (9 non-Hispanic white and 1 African American) have been executed, with Oklahoma, Texas, and Florida leading, respectively.[29] Although there are many factors to consider, might this represent a discriminatory issue related to non-Hispanic white women or perhaps reluctance on the part of the criminal justice system to execute minority women for fear of being labeled racist? Among the 10 women who were executed, 3 in particular drew national and/or global media and public attention. One was a non-Hispanic white, Christina Riggs, a licensed registered nurse who committed filicide in 1997 by medicating and smothering her 5-year old son and 2 year-old daughter; she was convicted in Arkansas. She was suffering from major depression and PTSD as the result of her clinical work during the Oklahoma City bombing. During her lethal act, she attempted suicide using antidepressant medication. She was actively seeking the death penalty to join her deceased children and therefore "used" the criminal justice system as a vehicle to achieve her ultimate wish, i.e., "suicide by capital punishment." She was executed on May 2, 2000.[30]

Karla Fay Tucker, an attractive, 39-year old, non-Hispanic white, was executed by Texas on February 3, 1998, for her double murder felony crime, committed in 1983 at the age of 24 with her boyfriend. The case received world attention and protests as there was a belief that (1) a woman should not be executed, and (2) that Karla Fay Tucker had transformed herself into a born-again Christian; hence, she was a different person than the one who committed the heinous crime.[31] The powerful American ambivalence and interest concerning the execution of women is evident in the Florida execution of Aileen Wuornos, a non-Hispanic white female, on October 9, 2002. She was the only female serial killer (confessing to six murders of men) on women's death row. This public interest resulted in a 2003 movie called *Monster* about her life and death. It starred Charlize Theron who was awarded an Oscar for best actress.[32]

In conclusion, there are indications that capital punishment reform is beginning to surface in the United States as seen in recent major policy actions taken by state governors, the President of the United States, and the U.S. Supreme Court.

On January 11, 2003, Republican Governor George Ryan of Illinois, previously a supporter of the death penalty, commuted the death sentences of all 156 inmates on death row. In defending his actions, he stated: "Because the Illinois death penalty system is arbitrary and capricious and therefore immoral, I no longer shall tinker with the machinery of death." He had halted executions 3 years previously after discovering that 13 death row inmates had been wrongfully convicted.[33]

The other death penalty reforms in the United States include: (1) the prohibition of executing the "mentally retarded" or those with severe mental illness (U.S. Supreme Court); (2) the prohibition of executing those who committed a capital-crime when they were less than 18 years of age (U.S. Supreme Court); and (3) the suspension of the death penalty for foreign nationals (President George W. Bush). In light of these reforms, it is now timely to seek strategies to end capital punishment for women in the United States.

Recommendations:

1. Since the United States is the only nation in the world that, with very rare exceptions, still executes women, it is recommended that this human rights violation be terminated.
2. It is recommended that the local NASW chapter of Olas adopt our recommendations and forward them to the main body of the 153,000 member NASW for adoption and distribution to the local chapters in the 38 death penalty states.
3. It is further recommended that the local NASW chapters, in turn, contact their elected state officials for adoption and recommendation to the state governor for a prohibition of the death penalty for women, and a commutation (changing the death sentence to life without parole) of the death penalty of women currently on death row.

Concluding Comment

The profession of social work is indeed a profession of many faces as seen in the high school homicide case. The "social workers in action" in the Olas tragedy possesses a repertoire of micro and macro level intervention skills based on a foundation of biological, psychological, social, and community social work-related knowledge obtained through graduate school education, training, and subsequent experience.

Whereas psychiatrists rely primarily on the strengths of their biological training in medicating and treating individuals, and psychologists rely heavily on their psychological testing instruments in assessing their patients, social workers are trained to have the potential for macro as well as micro level intervention.

In the high school homicide case, Bob Pla, MSW, was an advanced professional practitioner involved in various direct service (micro) tasks and competencies, such as assessment and treatment of individuals, couples, families, and nonfamily groups. His in-depth, comprehensive assessment skills were evident in the Gomez case where he uncovered a generational alcoholism genetic link and identified other predispositional factors related to Ms. Gomez becoming a homicide perpetrator. Additionally, he was the chief administrator and director of a social work family services agency and was part of a team in identifying and organizing resources in the community to deal with the Olas crisis to help hundreds of residents in need.

Bob Pla also undertook various indirect service (macro) tasks and competencies utilizing prevention theories to help create conditions that would result in a safer community. During a period of heightened community tension and anger, he deployed staff members into the minority communities to help them vent their frustrations in response to being scapegoated by the dominant white community. Simultaneously, he was working with law enforcement and community groups in the majority community to discourage any vigilante-type retaliation.

Another indirect service prevention task to create a safer community directly evolving from the Rita Gomez case concerned the increasingly easy access to guns by youths and the dependence on corporal and capital punishment to "solve" problems of violence in the United States. The nation's obsession with firearms and its long-term continued commitment to corporal and capital punishment with its powerful "modeling" impact for the country were prevention issues and tasks that Bob Pla and his colleagues could have undertaken, but there were simply not enough hours in a day—even for social workers—to tackle all three issues. Therefore, with BSW student resources provided by Professor Rocco Vincent, the timely issue of abolishing the capital punishment of women, brought on by new death penalty reforms, became the focus of attention. In their review of the literature, the students uncovered unique, interesting information resulting in a concept paper with accompanying recommendations concerning the execution of women in the United States. Utilizing the vehicle of NASW and its local chapters, they developed state and national strategy recommendations for its commutation and abolition.

It may be that one social worker *can* make a difference, as was seen in the Gomez case, and that a social work committee and a faculty member with the assistance of social work students, can make even *more* of a difference.

KEY WORDS AND CONCEPTS

Homicide	Dysthymia
Natural disasters	Felony homicide
Pro bono	DSM IV-TR, 312.82
Man-made disasters	Endogenous depression
Criminal homicide	Capital punishment

SUGGESTED INFORMATION SOURCES

Meyer, Cheryl L., and Oberman, Michelle. *Mothers Who Kill Their Children* New York: New York University Press, 2001.

Morales, Armando. "Homicide," in Richard L. Edwards, ed., *Encyclopedia of Social Work*, 19th Edition, Washington, D.C.: NASW Press, 1995, pp. 1347–1358.

O'Shea, Kathleen A. *Women and the Death Penalty in the United States, 1900–1998* (Westport, Conn.: Praeger Publishers, 1999).

Scheck, Barry, Neufeld, Peter, and Dwyer, Jim. *Actual Innocence* (New York: Doubleday: 2000).

Streib, Victor L. "Death Penalty for Female Offenders, January 1, 1973, through September 30, 2004," pp. 1–21, on line at http://www.law.onu.edu/faculty/streib.

ENDNOTES

1. Homicides of children 4 and younger number about 2.5 per 100,000 in the United States. Mothers are the most frequent perpetrators, followed by fathers, mother's boyfriends, and caretakers. See "Children's Safety Network," in *A Data Book of Child and Adolescent Injury* (Washington, D.C.: National Center for Education in Maternal and Child Health, 1991).

2. In the Supreme Court of the United States, October Term, 1997, No. 98–194, Bonnie A. O'Neill, et al., Petitioners, *v.* United States of America, September, 1998, p. 3.

3. Lola G. Selby, "Social Work and Crisis Theory," *Social Work Papers* 10 (1963): 3.

4. See John Cummings and Elaine Cummings, *Ego and Milieu* (New York: Atherton Press, 1962), as cited in Howard J. Parad, "Crisis Intervention," in Robert Morris, ed., *Encyclopedia of Social Work* 1, no. 16 (New York: National Association of Social Workers, 1971), pp. 196–202.

5. See Gerald Caplan, *Principles of Preventive Psychiatry* (New York: Basic Books, 1964); Erich Lindemann, "The Meaning of Crisis in Individuals and Family Living," *Teachers College Record* 57 (February 1963), as cited in Howard J. Parad, "Crisis Intervention," pp. 198–199.

6. Lydia Rapoport, "Crisis-Oriented Short-Term Casework," *Social Service Review* 41 (March 1967): 35.

7. Ibid., p. 37.

8. "They Think We're a Land of Sick Shooters," *U.S. News and World Report,* June 7, 1993, p. 9.

9. L. A. Fingerhut and J. C. Kleinman, "International and Interstate Comparison of Homicide Among Young Males," *Journal of the American Medical Association* 263, No. 24, June 27, 1990.

10. Arlene Bowers Andrews, "Social Work Expert Testimony Regarding Mitigation in Capital Sentencing Proceedings," *Social Work* 36 (May 1991): 440.

11. "1992 Penal Code," Abridged California Edition (San Clemente, CA: Qwik-Code Publications), pp. 44–46.

12. Harold I. Kaplan and Benjamin J. Sadock, *Synopsis of Psychiatry,* 5th Edition (Baltimore, MD: Williams and Wilkins, 1988), p. 222.

13. Kaplan and Sadock, p. 456.

14. Ibid., p. 456.

15. M. Robinson, "International perspectives on Death Penalty: A Costly Isolation for the U.S.," Death Penalty Information Center, Washington, D.C., p. 18, on-line at http://www.deathpenaltyinfo.org. The states and districts without the death penalty include Alaska, Hawaii, Iowa, Maine, Massachusetts, Michigan, Minnesota, North Dakota, Rhode Island, Vermont, West Virginia, Wisconsin, and the District of Columbia.

16. Robinson, p. 5.

17. Robinson, p. 4.

18. Robinson, p. 7.
19. M. Warren, "Foreign Nationals and the Death Penalty in the United States," Part II, Death Penalty Information Center, Washington, D.C., p. 1–2, on-line at http://www.deathpenaltyinfo.org.
20. "U.S. Violated Rights of Mexicans on Death Row," Human Rights Watch, March 31, 2004, on-line at http://hrw.org.
21. D. Savage, *Los Angeles Times* Wednesday, March 9, 2005, p. 1.
22. D. Savage, *Los Angeles Times* Wednesday, March 2, 2005, p. 1.
23. "Growing Elderly Population on Death Row," Death Penalty Information Center, p. 2, on-line at http://www.deathpenaltyinfo.org.
24. Robinson, p. 40.
25. "Facts about the Death Penalty," Death Penalty Information Center, February 23, 2005, on-line at http://www.deathpenaltyinfo.org.
26. V. L. Streib, "Death Penalty for Female Offenders, January 1, 1973, through September 30, 2004," pp. 1–21, on-line at http://www.law.onu.edu/faculty/streib.
27. V. L. Streib, p. 3.
28. V. L. Streib, pp. 4–6.
29. Streib, p. 6.
30. http://www.clarkprosecutor.org/html/death/US/riggs629.htm.
31. http://www.geocities.com/RainForest/canopy/2525/karlamain.html.
32. http://www.ccadp.org/aileenwuornos.htm.
33. http://www.ccadp.org/news-ryan2003.htm.

Photo Credits

Name Index

Subject Index